Hans Christian Andersen
in Russia

Hans Christian Andersen in Russia

Edited by
Mads Sohl Jessen,
Marina Balina,
Ben Hellman,
and Johs. Nørregaard Frandsen

University Press of Southern Denmark 2020

Publications from the Hans Christian Andersen Center
Volume 8: Hans Christian Andersen in Russia
University of Southern Denmark Studies in Scandinavian Languages and Literatures, vol. 144
© The authors and University Press of Southern Denmark
Printed by Narayana Press
Cover design by Narayana Press
Cover illustration: Watercolor by Oskar Klever. Published with
permission from the Hans Christian Andersen Museum

This publication was made possible through the generous support of
The Carlsberg Foundation,
The Augustinus Foundation,
The N. M. Knudsen Foundation, and
The Hans Christian Andersen Foundation

ISBN 978-87-408-3194-8

University Press of Southern Denmark
Campusvej 55
DK-5230 Odense M
www.universitypress.dk

Distribution in the United States and Canada:
Independent Publishers Group
814 N. Franklin Street
Chicago, IL 60610
USA
www.ipgbook.com

Distribution in the United Kingdom:
Gazelle Book Services Ltd.
White Cross Mills, Hightown,
Lancaster, Lancashire
LA1 4XS
UK
www.gazellebookservices.co.uk

Contents

Acknowledgements   9

Hans Christian Andersen in Russia   11
Introduction
*Mads Sohl Jessen, Marina Balina, Ben Hellman,
and Johs. Nørregaard Frandsen*

Part I: Andersen and Russia in His Time

Russia under Hans Christian Andersen's Western Eyes, Part   21
1, 1830-47:
The Fairy Tale Writer as a Young Liberal Poet
Mads Sohl Jessen

Russia under Hans Christian Andersen's Western Eyes, Part   43
2, 1847-95:
From Integration into Europe to the Hansen Translation
Mads Sohl Jessen

A Time of Fairy Tales: 61
Hans Christian Andersen, a Danish Princess,
and the Telegraph Business
Johs. Nørregaard Frandsen

Part II: Andersen in Russia's Cultural Contexts

*A) Andersen's Place in Prerevolutionary Russian
Literature and Criticism*

Hans Christian Andersen as a Children's Writer, as Reflected   77
in Russian Criticism from the Latter Half of the Nineteenth
Century to 1917
Inna Sergienko

Hans Christian Andersen's Legacy in the Works of 115
Dostoevsky, Tolstoy, and Vagner:
Negotiating Aesthetics and Meaning
Ben Hellman

B) Creative Affinities: Andersen in Silver Age Poetry and Prose

Hans Christian Andersen and the Acmeists: 137
Notes toward a Theme
Oleg Lekmanov

"The Fairy Tale is Simple": 159
Marina Tsvetaeva and Hans Christian Andersen
Karin Grelz

Strelnikov and Kay: 195
"The Snow Queen" in *Doctor Zhivago*
Peter Alberg Jensen

C) Andersen's Transformational Legacy in the Soviet Union

Hans Christian Andersen and Russian Classical Music: 229
Igor Stravinsky and Sergei Prokofiev
Vladimir Orlov

The Double and Its Theater: 243
Evgenii Schwartz's Andersen Plays
Boris Wolfson

Konstantin Paustovsky and the Making of Hans Christian 259
Andersen, Paragon of the Soviet Thaw
Marina Balina

Hans Christian Andersen and the Soviet Biedermeier 279
Ilya Kukulin

Part III: Visualizing Andersen in Russian Illustration, Film, and the Digital Sphere

The Danish Little Mermaid vs. the Russian *Rusalka*: Screen Choices *Helena Goscilo*	319
Tales and Holes: Illustrating Andersen the Russian Way *Yuri Leving*	341
Hans Christian Andersen and Russian Film: The Case of "The Snow Queen" *Andrei Rogatchevski*	367
Yearning for a Soul: "The Little Mermaid" in Graphics *Helena Goscilo*	389
Hans Christian Andersen in Contemporary Russian Popular Culture *Elena Gurova, Elena Krasnova, and Boris Zharov*	429

Appendix

Anderseniana in Soviet and Post-Soviet Russia: An Overview *Inna Sergienko*	453
Contributors	471
Index of Names	476

Acknowledgements

This volume has received generous financial support from The Carlsberg Foundation, which funded the initial Hans Christian Andersen in Russia workshop in May 2016 and subsequently a very large part of the publication of this book. We would like to express our heartfelt gratitude to The Carlsberg Foundation, as well as The Augustinus Foundation, The N. M. Knudsen Foundation, and The Hans Christian Andersen Foundation: this project would not have come to fruition without their assistance.

The editors also wish to express their deep appreciation to Avram Brown, who translated several of the articles from Russian to English, and from whose editorial and research assistance the volume benefited greatly; and to Olga Kaufmann, an extremely valuable partner in the difficult process of obtaining copyright permissions for the illustrations.

We would also like to thank the research associates of the Hans Christian Andersen Center as well as the Hans Christian Andersen Museum in Odense for their support and critical engagement. Our gratitude goes also to the University Press of Southern Denmark, which afforded us an ideal working relationship in the publication of this volume.

Last but not least, we would like to thank our contributors for their patience and continued enthusiasm for this project. We are grateful for their years of support, confidence, and understanding.

Mads Sohl Jessen, Marina Balina,
Ben Hellman, Johs. Nørregaard Frandsen

Hans Christian Andersen in Russia

Introduction

Mads Sohl Jessen, Marina Balina, Ben Hellman, and Johs. Nørregaard Frandsen

For his Russian readers, Hans Christian Andersen's longstanding canonical status is owed specifically to his fairy tales. The works of Andersen as poet, playwright, and prose writer existed for many years as not just a "grownup" but primarily an academic interest, the bailiwick of specialists in Scandinavian literature; but his fairytale oeuvre had a magical ability to create admirers regardless of age or professional category. Children and adults alike fell in love with Andersen's plots, and carried memories of the fairy tales they had read for the rest of their lives. Among creative people—writers, poets, musicians, and artists—this memory often took the particular form of communication with their favorite author. The lines they had read became works of music or illustrations to these beloved tales; and their own poems and prose were full of allusions to the Andersen texts they had become acquainted with as children. As Maria Tatar observes in her book on the "power of stories in childhood": "[W]e can recall moments in which something burst right out from the story, seizing us with unprecedented emotional force, to the point where words seemed to register on our flesh. But it is not always easy to recall these exact moments, and often we need to do so with the aide-memoire of the original book."[1] These artists' communication with Andersen's tales thus represented a very complex form, and should be considered in the terms of Iurii Lotman's "semiosphere"—simultaneously, that is, in the contexts of different artistic traditions, different social discourses, and, most importantly, personal experience.[2]

There existed in Russia, then, a never-broken connection with Andersen, which became—at times involuntarily, but most often consciously—a special form of creative dialogue with the storyteller, in which a beloved fairy tale, or particular image remembered from it, turned out to be a sort of answer-key to the most varied but always existentially crucial questions of modernity. For the nearly two centuries of their presence

---
1 Tatar, *Enchanted Hunters: The Power of Stories in Childhood*, 28.
2 See Lotman, *Semiosfera*, 159-65.

in Russian culture, Andersen's fairy tales have become an organic part of the cultural memory of generations of readers, his texts constituting a particular cultural code that is actualized in various artistic fields.[3] The studies in this collection are devoted to analyzing how Andersen's texts function in Russian cultural memory.

The perception of Andersen's legacy as a cultural code is not solely a Russian phenomenon. In the volume *Hans Christian Andersen in China* (ed. Johs. Nørregaard Frandsen, Sun Jian, and Torben Grøngaard Jeppesen, Odense: University Press of Southern Denmark, 2014), the authors analyze the legacy of Andersen in the national cultural space of China. The "Hans Christian Andersen in Russia" project, which commenced in 2016 at the Hans Christian Andersen Center of the University of Southern Denmark in Odense, has been undertaken with the same approach. Russian Anderseniana is extremely extensive: critics and educators, translators and literary scholars from the prerevolutionary period to the present have addressed themselves to analysis of Andersen's texts. The Andersen heritage, moreover, has been constantly enriched with new texts and themes. For instance, the classic translations of Andersen's works by Peter and Anna Hansen have been supplemented by new translations of previously little-known fairy tales made by Liudmila Braude and Irina Streblova for a 1995 edition.[4] The bicentennial of Andersen's birth, moreover, stimulated a great number of new publications and translations of his works.[5] In 2013, the Molodaia gvardiia (Young Guard) publishing house issued, as part of its *Lives of Remarkable People* series, a new biography of Andersen, written by the translator and specialist in Scandinavian literature Boris Erkhov.[6] All these works have greatly expanded readers' understanding of both Andersen as a person, and the diversity of his artistic legacy.

The scholars involved in the "Andersen in Russia" project—specialists in Russian literature—were motivated by a somewhat different goal. First and foremost, they aimed to analyze the cultural code of Russian Anderseniana (the legacy, specifically, of Andersen's fairy tales), which has influenced the most diverse spheres of Russian culture: literature

---

3   On cultural code as an analogue of cultural memory, see Knabe, *Semiotika kul'tury*, 64.
4   Andersen, *Skazki. Istorii. Novye skazki i istorii*.
5   For instance, such editions as Andersen, *Sobranie sochinenii v chetyrekh tomakh* (a collected works prepared in conjunction with the "Hans Christian Andersen 2005" Jubilee Committee); and Vishevskaia, Korovin, and Saprykina, *Po nebesnoi raduge za predely mira*. This period has also seen the publication of landmark works on Andersen's Russian illustrators: Zvonareva and Kudriavtseva, *H. C. Andersen i russkie illiustratory* (2005) and the expanded version of this edition: *Andersen i ego russkie illiustratory za poltora veka* (2012).
6   The first Andersen biography published in this series was Murav'eva, *Andersen* (1959).

and literary criticism, music, various media forms, and the art of illustration. And while traditional, text-based analysis in the articles here that deal with Russian literature reveals the particular "quotability" of Andersen's fairy tales for several generations of Russian writers and poets, the transplantation, as traced by other contributors, of Andersenian plots into newer media realms (animation and live-action film; computer games and Internet/digital spaces) attests unequivocally to the ongoing relevance of Andersen's stories. The demand for Andersen's fairy tales at the most varied cultural levels goes to confirm Kornei Chukovsky's statement that "the goal of storytellers is ... to cultivate humanness in a human being—that wondrous ability of a person to be moved by other people's misfortunes, to take joy in someone else's joy, to experience someone else's destiny as one's own."[7]

The collection is divided into three parts, the first of which, "Andersen and Russia in His Time," focuses on how Russia was conceptualized by Andersen and by Danish culture at large. In his double article, **Mads Sohl Jessen** demonstrates how the Danish writer's view of Russia changed from an initially negative one—based mainly on Andersen's youthful hero worship of Napoleon as well as the liberal ideas of his time—to a more positive attitude, not only acknowledging Russian literature and culture as increasingly worthy of attention, but also actively communicating with a number of Russian acquaintances made during his European travels. In particular, **Jessen** emphasizes the overlooked fact that Andersen carefully omitted politically charged passages (pertaining among other things to Russia's suppression of the Polish Uprising in 1831) from the first German collected edition of his works (1847-51), in effect committing self-censorship in an effort to promote himself to an international public. In the article that follows, **Johs. Nørregaard Frandsen** emphasizes the crucial role played by Denmark's Princess Dagmar in forging stronger Danish-Russian cultural bonds. On 9 November 1866, she married the future Emperor Alexander III. As **Frandsen** shows, her marriage benefitted the Russian fortunes of Andersen's art to a surprising extent.

In the second and third parts of this volume, the reader is guided through an overarching chronological framework from the earliest Russian references to Andersen in the 1840s to his pervasive presence in the Russian digital sphere of our time.

Part two of the volume has three subdivisions: the first, "Andersen's Place in Prerevolutionary Russian Literature and Criticism," begins with **Inna Sergienko's** discussion of the initial Russian responses to Ander-

---

7   Chukovskii, *Ot dvukh do piati*.

sen's works. She demonstrates how early critics (1860s) took a largely dim view of Andersen, with the evaluation gradually growing ever more positive (even panegyric) from the 1880s on. Influential components in the debate included the increasing availability of suitable translations, and changing attitudes toward the fairy tale as a genre, and in particular toward fantastic elements in children's literature, among Russian literati of this period.

Then follows **Ben Hellman's** investigation of the relationship between three major Russian writers of the nineteenth century and Andersen. **Hellman** convincingly argues that Dostoevsky and Andersen appear to have had the same German source of inspiration, Friedrich Rückert, for their respective stories about a child freezing to death at Christmastime. While Dostoevsky does not seem to have read Andersen, Lev Tolstoy, for his part, clearly did so quite closely. In particular, the tale "The Emperor's New Clothes" was of profound interest to Tolstoy in his complex thinking on the nature of politics and art. The third author considered by **Hellman,** Nikolai Vagner, actively sought to become "the Russian Andersen" by using some of Andersen's most famous fairy tales as templates for his own.

In the second section of part two, "Creative Affinities: Andersen in Silver Age Poetry and Prose," the extraordinarily important role Andersen played for a number of major Russian Silver Age poets is addressed. **Oleg Lekmanov** subtly shows how three of the main acmeists (Anna Akhmatova, Osip Mandelshtam, and Nikolai Gumilev) engaged with the fairy tales. While the symbolists treated the Danish storyteller as, first and foremost, a mystic and a visionary of childhood purity, the acmeists were primarily interested in the material world of Andersen's stories of animated toy figures. Analyzing the allusive connections between these poets' works, **Lekmanov** reveals how these figures were all preoccupied with deeply imaginative readings of Andersen.

Karin Grelz offers the reader a compelling narrative of how Marina Tsvetaeva modelled aspects of her life and the imaginative landscape of her poetry after Andersen. **Grelz** shows how, till the very end of her life, Tsvetaeva conceptualized her predicament according to stories and images from Andersen's fairytale universe. The sense of creative affinity Tsvetaeva felt for Andersen is movingly seen as one of crucial importance by **Grelz**.

Peter Alberg Jensen comprehensively traces the presence of Andersen's "The Snow Queen" in Boris Pasternak's *Doctor Zhivago*. Discussing how the fairy tale contributed both a paradigmatic figure and a symbolic key to the novel, **Jensen** shows the unexpectedly intricate way in which Andersen's story of Gerda, Kay, and the Snow Queen inspired Pasternak's canonical work.

The third section of part two, "Andersen's Transformational Legacy in the Soviet Union," begins with **Vladimir Orlov**'s interpretation of Igor Stravinsky's and Sergei Prokofiev's use of Andersen's fairy tales to map their own original musical agenda. **Orlov** pays special attention to how the two composers "privatized" and "internalized" Andersen, employing his fairy tales to express certain highly intimate traits of their own aesthetic vision and personalities.

Evgenii Schwartz plays a crucial role in Andersen's meaning for the Soviet stage, as he authored three influential Andersen-based plays—*The Naked King* (1934-37), *The Snow Queen* (1938), and *The Shadow* (1940)—and was hugely successful as a dramatist for children. In "The Double and Its Theater: Evgenii Schwartz's Andersen Plays," **Boris Wolfson** highlights Schwartz's radically innovative dramatic departure from the original Andersen works and his uncanny sense of the performative power of the theatrical vis-a-vis Stalinist repression and persecution. **Wolfson** clearly registers Schwartz's artistic independence and individuality.

In her study "Konstantin Paustovsky and Hans Christian Andersen in the Soviet Culture of the Thaw," **Marina Balina** begins by addressing the complexities of the "Thaw" in Soviet cultural life and highlighting the author Konstantin Paustovsky's role as one of the major moral authorities of this period. In two texts from 1955, one an autobiographical piece dealing with Andersen, the other a fictionalized account with the Danish author as its protagonist, Paustovsky, as **Balina** shows, construes Andersen as an improvisatore and an emblem of imaginative freedom. As **Balina** concludes, Paustovsky's own Thaw thus began with his hero Andersen.

Ilya Kukulin, in his study of late-Soviet culture in "Hans Christian Andersen and the Soviet Biedermeier," provides an engaging discussion of the numerous artists and writers who in the 1950s, '60s, and '70s employed Andersen as a kind of "safety valve" for the conformist pressures of this period, and as a foundation for formulating new artistic visions. In **Kukulin's** original conceptual approach, Andersen is centered as a key figure, to whom artists looked for support in expressing liberating ideas, but who also helped legitimize the escapist tendencies of the time.

In the last part of the collection, "Visualizing Andersen in Russian Illustrations, Film, and the Digital Sphere," **Helena Goscilo** begins her comparative study "The Danish Little Mermaid vs. the Russian *Rusalka*: Screen Choices" by contrasting the native Russian rusalka, erotically alluring and dangerously heathen, with Andersen's mermaid heroine, who represents the transition to Christianity. Using this distinction as an analytical tool, **Goscilo** discusses the remarkable aesthetics of the numerous *rusalka*/mermaid adaptations in twentieth-century Russian film and highlights the complex gender representations this tradition has produced.

Yuri Leving in "Tales and Holes: Illustrating Andersen the Russian Way" invites his readers on a fascinating tour through twentieth-century Russian traditions of illustrating Andersen's tales, in search, in particular, of imagery that would speak specifically to a Russian audience; and with an eye to the realities of the relationship between Soviet politics and art. Throughout his study, **Leving** pays special attention to how the artists under discussion sought to mark a difference from official Soviet socialist-realist doctrine. Andersen's importance to Russian illustrators, in **Leving's** view, lies in the liberating vision his tales afforded their art form.

In "The Case of 'The Snow Queen': Andersen and Russian Film," **Andrei Rogatchevski** studies the various animated and live-action film adaptions of "The Snow Queen," from Lev Atamanov's famous version of 1957 to today's attempts at a Russian blockbuster, arguing that this particular tale's focalization of Russian attention is due at least in part to its mirroring of Russia's self-identification with the North. "The Snow Queen" is central to the Russian quest for a national identity and for the Russian conceptualization of womanhood. **Rogatchevski** cogently argues that Andersen's tale has thus played an important role in Russian identity formation.

In her second contribution to the volume, "Yearning for a Soul: 'The Little Mermaid' in Graphics," **Helena Goscilo** dives into the wonderful trove of Soviet and post-Soviet Russian graphic art inspired by Andersen's story of the little mermaid in search of human love and the prospect of eternal life. From Ivan Bilibin's masterpieces of the 1930s to works produced by gifted contemporary artists like Gennadi Spirin and Natalya Akimova, **Goscilo** provides an in-depth evaluation of the aesthetic achievements of certain major modern Russian illustrators.

In their collaborative article "Hans Christian Andersen in Contemporary Russian Popular Culture," **Elena Krasnova**, **Elena Gurova**, and **Boris Zharov** analyze how Andersen's fairy tales and the image of their author permeate, to an almost bewildering degree, the commercial, digital, and primary-educational culture of present-day Russia. The scholars attend to the many nuances and developments of Andersen's breakthrough as a major avatar of the post-Soviet era.

The scholars involved in this project have attempted to offer a diverse picture of Andersen's cultural legacy, which traverses all boundaries of time and genre in Russia. The editors of this volume hope to have demonstrated both the unusualness and the diversity of the cultural patterns brought to life by the Danish writer's literary style and his personality. To be sure, the work done so far represents only an initial stage of research into the manifold cultural influence of Russian Anderseniana; it is to be hoped that this work will continue in the future, as Andersen and his legacy remains a constant component in the ever-expanding and changing space of Russian cultural memory.[8]

Works Cited

Andersen, Kh. K. *Skazki. Istorii. Novye skazki i istorii*. Seriia "Literaturnye pamiatniki." Moscow: Ladomir, 1995.

—. *Sobranie sochinenii v chetyrekh tomakh*. Edited by A. Chekanskii, A. Sergeev, and O. Rozhdestvenskii; commentary by A. Sergeev. Moscow: Vagrius, 2005.

Chukovskii, Kornei. *Ot dvukh do piati*. Available electronically: http://www.chukfamily.ru/kornei/prosa/knigi/onetofive/glava-tretya

Knabe, Georgii. *Semiotika kul'tury*. Moscow: RGGU, 2005.

Lotman, Iurii. *Semiosfera*. St. Petersburg: Iskusstvo-SPB, 2000.

Murav'eva, Irina. *Andersen*. Moscow: Molodaia gvardiia, 1959.

Tatar, Maria. *Enchanted Hunters: The Power of Stories in Childhood*. New York: W. W. Norton & Co., 2009.

Vishevskaia, N. A., A. V. Korovin, and E. Iu. Saprykina. *"Po nebesnoi raduge za predely mira." K 200-letnemy iubileiu Kh. K. Andersena*. Moscow: Nauka, 2008.

Zvonareva, L., and L. Kudriavtseva. *H. C. Andersen i russkie illiustratory. Al'bom-entsiklopediia. Illiustratory Kh. K. Andersena v Rossii i russkom Zarubezh'e za poltora veka – 1868-2005*. Moscow: Arbor, 2005.

—. *Khans Kristian Andersen i ego russkie illiustratory za poltora veka*. Moscow: Moskovskie uchebniki, 2012.

---

[8] All quotations from Hans Christian Andersen's fairy tales in the following articles are from Jean Hersholt's translation published by the Hans Christian Andersen Center at https://andersen.sdu.dk/vaerk/hersholt/. Note that this version has no pagination.

Part I

Andersen and Russia in His Time

Russia under Hans Christian Andersen's Western Eyes, Part 1, 1830-47:

The Fairy Tale Writer as a Young Liberal Poet[1]

Mads Sohl Jessen

From the moment his German autobiography was published in early 1847 and onwards to today, Hans Christian Andersen's life-trajectory has been conceptualized, for most international readers, as beginning as a poor boy in Odense, then quickly moving up the social ladder to become a well-established figure in European literature and high society. In his autobiography, Andersen presents himself as a writer largely disinterested in politics and a person of conservative and Christian views of life. The most common view of Andersen's political and religious stance can be said to derive from his autobiographical writings. For example, when Jack Zipes writes that "Andersen was much more conservative and conventional than most Andersen scholars admit," and "a God-fearing, superstitious, and anxious writer,"[2] he seems to base this judgment on the autobiographies Andersen wrote in his later life—and, moreover, on a reading of the fairy tales seemingly filtered through those autobiographical writings.

The later Andersen could certainly be characterized as a religious man of conservative leanings, but in his early years, Andersen was a liberal who especially admired such progressive writers as Heinrich Heine, Victor Hugo, and Lord Byron. The standard international biographies by Jens Andersen and Jackie Wullschlager pay little if any attention to Andersen's political engagement in his early years.[3] This is surely connected to the fact that it is his lyric poetry—in which the general reading public remains largely uninterested—that most clearly features Andersen's political outlook. In the early 1830s, for instance, the young

---

1   I would like to thank Johs. Nørregaard Frandsen for envisioning a large "Andersen in Russia" study, which has resulted in this anthology. I wish to also thank Marina Balina, Ben Hellman, and Avram Brown for their important comments on my two articles. I am also grateful to Ole Westermann for transcribing all the letters (holdings of the Royal Library) I analyze here, and to Solveig Brunholm and Ejnar Stig Askgaard of the Andersen Museum in Odense for introducing me to Andersen's picture books.
2   Zipes, *Hans Christian Andersen*, xv, 146.
3   Andersen, *Hans Christian Andersen*; Wullschlager, *Hans Christian Andersen*.

Danish poet lionized Napoleon as a heroic figure who embodied the great revolutionary ideals of liberty, equality, and fraternity. This was not common among his fellow Danish poets, the most influential of whom in this period, like Adam Oehlenschläger (1779-1850) and B. S. Ingemann (1789-1862), were, rather, national romanticists, drawing their motifs from Nordic mythology or medieval times. Indeed, in taking an interest in contemporary European history on a grand scale, Andersen broke new ground across different literary genres. In his early years, he was an engaged poet, just like his politically progressive models.

For the Andersen of the early 1830s, Russia's victory over Napoleon in 1812 symbolized the end of a period that had harbored the possibility of profound change to the aristocratic and royalist power structures in Europe. Later, in 1846, as he was writing his first autobiography, he chose to make his early liberal engagement invisible to his German and international readers, as I will describe below. As such, his first official autobiography marked a point of no return for Andersen: henceforth would his life story be that of a Danish Aladdin who was happily ignorant of politics, but blessed by God with a gift for storytelling that would be celebrated throughout the world, not least in Russia.

Two periods in Andersen's attitude toward Russia should be distinguished. The first, from around 1830 to 1840, is defined by antipathy toward the repressive, reactionary reign of Nicholas I—a stance common among liberals throughout Europe (and in Russia itself). In the second period, from the mid-1840s to the end of his life, Andersen sees Russia in more positive terms, as a powerful empire that is a rightful constituent of the European identity. In both periods, we find evidence of Andersen's interest in Russian literature and culture. In the two parts of my study, then, I will seek to discuss and interpret Andersen's evolution from the liberal poet of his younger years to the later, more conservative fairy tale writer who eschewed the writing of politically minded literature.

Andersen's Sense of Triumph in 1845-46

In his 1940 dissertation on Andersen's autobiographical writings, the Danish Andersen scholar Helge Topsøe-Jensen describes the storyteller's visit to Germany in the winter of 1845-46 as "the first of Hans Christian Andersen's European triumphal journeys."[4] One aspect of this triumph was the flurry of flattering offers from German publishers hoping to

---

4 Topsøe-Jensen, *Mit eget Eventyr*, 13. My translation; unless otherwise indicated, all translations from Danish-language sources are mine.

be the one to issue his collected works. In a letter (30 January 1846) to Jonas Collin, his fatherly advisor, Andersen sounds a note of supreme satisfaction:

> I almost think that these days are the culmination of my happiness. Here in the world I have, it seems to me, achieved everything. Everywhere I go I find a home, leading personalities heartily consort with me, and my writings are esteemed beyond their worth. I am recognized in a way that my fatherland does not know about! The clever bookseller Simion in Berlin and the well-known Brockhaus are vying for the rights to publish a complete edition of my writings, which I am to revise myself.[5]

In the end, neither Simion nor Brockhaus acquired the coveted rights for a German translation of Andersen's collected works. During a February stay in Leipzig, "the center of German book production,"[6] Andersen met with fellow Dane Carl Berendt Lorck (1814-1905), who had started his own eponymous publishing house in that city in 1845. In a matter of days, Andersen had decided to sign a contract with his countryman.

Andersen now undertook to write the collected edition's envisioned first volume, an autobiography. Immediately after his stay in Leipzig, Andersen embarked on a European trip that would take him (from March to October 1846) through Austria, Italy, southern France, and Switzerland, and back to Denmark through Germany. His main preoccupation during these travels was the writing of this first autobiography, to be entitled *The Fairy Tale of My Life without Poetry: A Sketch by Hans Christian Andersen*.[7] Having finalized the contract with Lorck on 19 February, Andersen sent him this autobiography's last pages on 18 August. Lorck had the Danish manuscript translated into German, and it was published in early 1847 as the first volume.

Andersen's Self-Construction as Apolitical in *The Fairy Tale of My Life without Poetry*

In the autobiography's ninth chapter, covering the period from 1841-44, Andersen begins by reflecting on the state of politics in Denmark, declaring his attitude toward this topic unequivocally thus: "Politics are no affair of mine. God has imparted to me another mission: That I felt,

---

5 Topsøe-Jensen, *H. C. Andersens Brevveksling med Jonas Collin*, 1: 285.
6 Topsøe-Jensen, *H. C. Andersens Breve til Carl B. Lorck*, 8.
7 In German: *Das Märchen meines Lebens ohne Dichtung. Eine Skizze von H.C. Andersen.*

and that I feel still. I met in the so-called first families of the country a number of friendly, kind-hearted men, who valued the good that was in me."[8] Andersen had indeed begun to live a life among these "first families," the Danish and European aristocracy, in the 1840s. Topsøe-Jensen argues that the first sentence just cited—what he calls Andersen's "declaration of [political] neutrality"—was based on the premonition of political troubles ahead: "The struggle of 1848 was dawning."[9] This seems to be the case; but equally important, I believe, is the retrospective significance of Andersen's apolitical stance.

Andersen's Self-Censorship in His German Collected Works

Andersen's 1847 claim to have never felt the call of politics ignored certain politically charged passages from his writings of the 1830s; and indeed, as if to "corroborate" his statement, he opted to omit these from the new German collected works. This does not go unnoticed by Topsøe-Jensen; in his edition of Andersen's letters to Lorck, the scholar remarks that in them, Andersen had performed a "radical revision" of his first travel writings, *Shadow Pictures from a Journey to the Harz Mountains, Saxon Switzerland, etc. etc., in the Summer of 1831* (1831), as well as a "cut-up" of his poetry collection *The Twelve Months of the Year, Drawn with Ink and Pen* (1833).[10] In his postscript to the 1968 edition of *Shadow Pictures*, Topsøe-Jensen categorizes the different forms of deletions Andersen made, noting that "it is characteristic that the political parts are now absent";[11] but Topsøe-Jensen does not elaborate on this important insight.

In his first travelogue *Shadow Pictures* (1831), Andersen muses on the relationship between the dream of an individual and that of a whole people: "The heart—the poet's dreaming heart—with its yearning and agony. What is this compared to how an entire people feels in a determined last, powerful struggle for life?"—but think of the "heroic hearts of poor Poland!"[12] During his German travels in the summer of 1831, Andersen was not far from battles between Russian and Polish forces.

The uprising staged in November 1830 by Polish officers in Warsaw against Russian rule escalated into all-out hostilities, which Russia man-

---

8 Andersen, *The True Story of My Life*, 159-60. (This is the title Mary Howitt chose for her English translation, which came out the same year as the German original.)
9 Topsøe-Jensen, *Mit eget Eventyr*, 98.
10 Topsøe-Jensen, *H. C. Andersens Breve til Carl B. Lorck*, 13.
11 Topsøe-Jensen, "Efterskrift," 213.
12 Andersen, *Shadow Pictures*, 76.

aged to suppress by September 1831.[13] The liberal public in Western and Northern Europe considered the Russians to be the oppressors. Andersen, too, was clearly on the side of Poland.[14]

The quotation just cited from *Shadow Pictures* did not become part of the German collected edition, but this was not the publisher's decision, but rather Andersen's own. In a letter of 15 January 1847, Andersen writes to Lorck: "The Harzen travel I have cut, so that all that remains is the poetic flower."[15] This means, one gathers from a letter Andersen sent Lorck a month later, that he made pen deletions in the first German translation of *Shadow Pictures*[16] from 1836—which included the passage on "the heroic hearts of poor Poland"—and sent this marked book to Lorck to indicate which text portions were to be omitted. Lorck, moreover, decided to produce a new translation, regarding which, Andersen states in this letter: "You now write that Kannegieser [Lorck's new translator] will translate the Danish *Shadow Pictures*, but I ask you most firmly, I insist, I beg and demand of you that my markings regarding the desired omissions be accurately followed. I will give my permission to publish it only with these changes; but, given these changes, I very much look forward to seeing it published."[17] From so emphatic a statement, it is clear that something important was at stake for Andersen when deleting certain passages.

Another example of Andersen's self-censorship can be found in his correspondence with Lorck on what to exclude from his poetry collection *The Twelve Months of the Year*. It is in this work that we find the most explicit expression of Andersen's hero-worship of Napoleon in the early 1830s. In this collection, the reader is introduced to different viewpoints, voiced, as the title suggests, by the successive months. In January, "the old year," that is the year 1831, decries "Russia's death-baptized [*Døds-indviede*] armies"[18]—again Andersen refers to the Russo-Polish war of that year. A little later, in March, the reader is confronted with a speaker called "human life," who implores his contemporaries to recall the greatness of Napoleon:

---

13 For a description of these events, see Davis, *God's Playground*, 2: 232-45.
14 In February 1832, Andersen also published an elegy titled "The Two Graves (after Klopstock)," in which he mourns the Poles who rebelled against Russia in vain. This poem has not been translated into English. See Andersen, *Andersen. H. C. Andersens samlede værker*, 7: 340. (In the following notes, the title of this standard Danish collected edition will be abbreviated as *SV*.)
15 Topsøe-Jensen, *H. C. Andersens Breve til Carl B. Lorck*, 75.
16 Anderson [sic], *Umrisse einer Reise von Copenhagen nach dem Harze*. The standard work on the early German reception of Andersen is Möller-Christensen, *Den gyldne trekant*.
17 Topsøe-Jensen, *H. C. Andersens Breve til Carl B. Lorck*, 81-82.
18 Andersen, *SV*, 7: 373.

You, the present, saw Prometheus,
He is well known even among the lowly!
The spirit rose heavenward,
Jauntily he forced the forms into obedience;
The dwarves of the day collapsed
By way of Napoleon the Great![19]

In his contemporary review, the influential Danish critic Christian Molbech rebuked Andersen's glorification of the deceased French emperor, his failure to see that Napoleon's goal had been, in reality, to "chain the whole European world to the footstool of his imperial throne."[20] At the time, Andersen's implicit viewpoint was the opposite: Napoleon had served the peoples of Europe in their uprisings against their oppressors. The American historian David P. Jordan describes the contemporary view of Napoleon as "the Revolution on horseback," the embodiment of liberatory dreams: "The will of the people would replace God's will. Those who were last would become first, centuries of social hierarchy marked and rewarded with privileges would disappear."[21] For many during the Napoleonic wars and the decades to follow, Napoleon was he who would, through the waging of justified warfare, spread the French revolutionary ideals of liberty, equality, and brotherhood throughout Europe. This was also the early Andersen's stance, and his father's; but this point of view is irreconcilable with Andersen's portrayal of himself in his first published autobiography as apolitical. He thus chose to delete the passages critical of Russian militarism, as well as his apotheosis of Napoleon, instructing Lorck "that January should be left by the wayside," and the passage entitled "Human Life" omitted.[22]

In my judgment, Andersen's self-censorship is primarily related to the fact that during the 1840s, he had come to be on friendly terms with a German-Russian political elite reminiscent of *l'ancien régime*—that is, representatives of the aristocratic and court milieu, persons whose privilege and wealth derived from their bloodline. Andersen well understood that in these circles, his youthful veneration of the memory of Napoleon, and his liberal, denunciatory stance vis-à-vis Russia and particularly its suppression of the 1830-31 uprising, would be (to say the least) a major *faux pas*.

---

19   Ibid., 387.
20   Molbech, "Om den nyeste danske Poesie," 875.
21   Jordan, *Napoleon and the Revolution*, 1.
22   Topsøe-Jensen, *H. C. Andersens Breve til Carl B. Lorck*, 123-24.

Andersen and Mariia Pavlovna's Meeting in 1846

One example of Andersen's mingling with figures of exalted rank would be the peculiarly informal conversation he had in Weimar in January 1846 with Grand Duchess Mariia Pavlovna (1786-1859), wife of Grand Duke Carl Friedrich of Sachsen-Weimar-Eisenach (1783-1853). As a daughter of Emperor Paul I (1754-1801), and sister of the Emperor Alexander I (1777-1825) who in the winter of 1812 had defeated Napoleon, the grand duchess was a prominent member of the Romanov dynasty, and influential at the court of Weimar. Andersen mentions a particular detail of their conversation of 30 January in his diary, as well as in the above-cited letter to Jonas Collin. Here is how this talk is described in the diary:

> The Grand Duchess asked me if, as a child, I had ever preferred one profession to another. She told me that as a little girl, she had wished to be a chimney sweep: "When in Petersburg I looked out the castle window," she said, "and I saw a chimney sweeper walking across the square, and imagined how he would soon go up into a chimney, I thought, he must be happy, because he would have such a great view!" I was struck by this thought from the daughter of the Russian emperor.[23]

Andersen's narration to Collin of the grand duchess's comment concludes similarly: "There is something strange about hearing such a childlike thought from the daughter of the tsar of the great Russian Empire."[24] Andersen then asks Collin not to relay this anecdote to anyone in Copenhagen, and also mentions the stock response he gives while traveling whenever anyone asks him about politics: "You sense that I have grown cautious! Yes, here in Germany and in our troubled times, one has to think terribly about everything. I get many questions about home [Denmark], which I studiously avoid, or I say: I am not familiar with these things, I do not understand anything about politics!"[25]

Andersen thus admits to Collin that his feigning of ignorance regarding Danish and European politics is a matter of strategy; but this strategy would actually structure his entire self-presentation in his first published autobiography. Andersen hoped to go on being accepted as a peer and friend by what he probably saw in 1847 as his most important

---
23 Andersen, *H. C. Andersens Dagbøger*, 3: 53-54. This entry is not included in the English-language *Diaries of Hans Christian Andersen*.
24 Topsøe-Jensen, *H. C. Andersens Brevveksling med Jonas Collin*, 1: 286.
25 Ibid.

readership: the (conservative) German-Russian political elite and their network in Europe. In censoring his youthful writings for his first collected German edition in 1847, Andersen sought to protect his way of life as an extremely successful writer who was welcome and admired among aristocrats, even royals, wherever he went.

In his 1847 German autobiography, Andersen does not discuss his hero-worship of Napoleon in the 1830s. In his 1855 Danish autobiography, wherein he brings the previous narrative up to the time of writing, he does include some wording on his affinity for the first French emperor, but solely as it pertains to fond memories of his upbringing: "Napoleon was the hero of my childhood and my father's hero. I looked up to him as the Catholic believer does to his saint."[26] Thus does he trivialize, for his Danish as well as international audience, his earlier Napoleonic engagement and his former identity as a young liberal-minded poet. These revisions of the past had their effect: most readers of Andersen's autobiographies have taken his *strategic* self-description as an apolitical poet at face value. However, Andersen's acts of self-censorship in 1847 attest to his keenness to protect his standing as the premiere Danish figure in European literature.

Andersen's Poems and Prose on Napoleon and Russia in the 1830s

In the early 1830s, Andersen was most of all preoccupied with developing his reputation as a lyric poet. He published many of his first poems in the journal *Kjøbenhavns flyvende Post* (1827-28, 1830, 1834-37), which was modeled after the French *Le Globe* (1824-32). Johan Ludvig Heiberg (1791-1860), the journal's editor, was at the time Denmark's most influential critic and dramatist. In 1827—the journal's first year of existence—Heiberg wrote an overview of contemporary French literature, highlighting, among other figures, Pierre-Jean de Béranger (1780-1857). In the 1820s and 1830s, Béranger's songs ("chansons") were immensely popular in France for their national-republican sentiments and hymning of Napoleon's glorious deeds. Béranger formed, with Victor Hugo and Casimir Delavigne, the literary triumvirate most responsible for the development of the hero-worship of Napoleon in France after the former emperor's death in 1821. Heiberg writes: "Béranger is truly a poet of the people who in his songs has shown a knack for perceiving and expressing the general liberal ideas of

---

26 Andersen, *SV*, 17: 113.

the times."²⁷ One of Béranger's most influential songs, from *Chansons* (1821), was "Le cinq Mai"–the day of Napoleon's death. For his part, Andersen in January 1833 published a Danish translation of this poem that mourns the passing of the man who "destroyed / the thrones of proud kings wherever he looked!"²⁸

Andersen's first original contribution to the European tradition of memorializing Napoleon in lyric was "The Sentry" (dated 12 May 1830). The poem is narrated by an elderly Parisian working as a guard at the residential estate of one of the Restauration period's *nouveau riche*. The sentry reminisces nostalgically about his career as a loyal soldier under Napoleon's direct command, making his contribution to the victories of the 1790s and to France's military zenith in the first decade of the nineteenth century. He also took part in the invasion of Russia, which would lead to Napoleon's downfall:

> He was Europe's hero–Europe was his kingdom,
> His star only knew to sink, or rise,
> "To *Moscow–Moscow*!" he proclaimed aloud,
> But it proudly made itself go up in flames.
> Our lungs inhaled only fire and ashes,
> The red tongues of fire swelled into mountains,
> Everything was ablaze, even the corpse in its grave,
> And the star of fortune disappeared in the sea of flames.
> –Every day *Russia's* soil burst forth armies,
> We would have won, though!
> It was the winter and not the Cossacks' lance,
> That robed *France* of its best wreaths.²⁹

Andersen here pays indirect homage to two of the best-known contemporary Napoleonic poems. Just as in Victor Hugo's poem "Lui" (*Les Orientales* [1829]), Andersen refers to Napoleon repeatedly as "he" so as to aggrandize his charisma. And just as in Heinrich Heine's poem "Die Grenadiere" (*Buch der Lieder* [1827]), the reader hears of France's invasion of Russia from the viewpoint of a rank-and-file soldier under Napoleon's command. The sentry's military pride is evident: *Le Grande Armée* could not have been defeated by Russia's army–only its winter. The fire of Moscow, which began on 14 September 1812 and destroyed

---

27 Heiberg, "Om den nye Retning," 112.
28 Andersen, *SV*, 7: 442.
29 Ibid., 231. I have maintained Andersen's use of italics, but not his end-rhymes.

most of the city, is interpreted by the sentry as a symbol of the beginning of Napoleon's demise rather than a Russian catastrophe. Andersen's sentry is clearly (re-)imagining Russia from a decidedly Western European perspective.

Another poem, "Winter Piece, Drawn with Ink and Pen" (April 1831), likewise reflects Andersen's interest in the Napoleonic soldier's perspective during the invasion of Russia. The poem paints a brutal picture of the tsar's Cossack troops waiting at the foot of a tree so as to kill the fleeing (presumably Napoleonic) soldier who has taken refuge in it. Though harking back nearly two decades, the poem bore a clear contemporary resonance, representing Andersen's contribution to the anti-Russian sentiment among Danish liberals stemming from the November Uprising and the military battles between Russian and Polish forces in the spring of 1831:

> It thunders beneath the horse's hoof
> Since the snow is solid on the ground in the dark wood;
> Look, the full moon shines from the scene of the sky
> Between the naked branches.
>
> We see a bunch of Cossacks on horseback,
> They camp on the white snow,
> The horses, perspiring strongly, are tied together
> Next to the trunk of the beech.
>
> Now a fire is lit next to the big beech.
> Look at the red fire with the dark smoke,
> And the men who are sitting in the snow
> Gathered round the flame.
>
> The chin is brown-yellow, dark every look,
> They are drinking the clear strong beverage,
> But above them, up high in the green branches,
> A refugee sits alone.
>
> He dares not breathe; fixedly he gazes
> But his thought flies to his faraway home,
> Such a long way off, on the other side of the waves of the Rhine.
> Where sleeps his betrothed—

She dreams of embracing him;
She does not hear the hungry raven,
Screeching "Dobbra" many times
Toward the sorrowing prisoner.[30]

Andersen, who knew Byron's romantic depiction of the eponymous Cossack hero in *Mazeppa* (1819), does not romanticize the Cossacks, but rather represents them as merciless. As Iver Neumann has remarked, "European representations of Russia show a marked proclivity for treating Russians as what can be called the liminal case of European identity"[31] – an observation confirmed once more by Andersen's portrayal of the Cossacks as anonymous and "Oriental" killers. The poem is structured by two clear-cut poles between Eastern and Western Europe, with France, the soldier's home country, representing the realm of love, and Russia the opposite. Any hope the reader might have for the fleeing soldier's survival is dispelled with the raven's "dobbra," by which Andersen presumably meant to render the Russian *dobro*, that is, "good."

The raven is undoubtedly awaiting the death of the soldier – the "good" outcome – so it can eat his corpse. Andersen's gothic use of the raven derives from his drama *The Bride of Lammermoor*, based on Walter Scott's 1812 novel. Andersen completed his work on the drama in February 1831. In his preface, he elaborates on his use of Scottish songs not found in the novel; he borrowed the song "Two Ravens Sit in the Tree Yonder,"[32] which opens the fourth and last act, from Scott's song collection *Minstrelsy of the Scottish Border* (1802-3), where its title is "The Twa Corbies." Andersen's raven follows those of Scott in craving human flesh.

In a footnote to the drama's preface, in which Andersen refers to Scott's "The Twa Corbies," he mentions Aleksandr Pushkin, whom German literary circles in the early 1830s were beginning to recognize as a major poet. Andersen writes: "In *Blätter für literarische Unterhaltung* 1830, no. 59, the survey of new Russian poetry mentions the poet A. Puschin, of whom a poem is singled out and translated into German; but this poem is not a Russian original, but rather a version of the same one as mine."[33] At this point, Andersen clearly knows little if anything about Pushkin, whose name he spells incorrectly, as Nielsen has noted;[34]

---

30 Ibid., 291.
31 Neumann, *The Uses of the Other*, 67.
32 Andersen, *SV*, 10: 225.
33 Ibid., 161.
34 Nielsen, *Fra Neva til Øresund*, 49.

but he is right in observing that the article's anonymous writer fails to mention that Pushkin's poem, in German "Die beiden Raben," is based on "The Twa Corbies."[35]

The Leipzig-based daily *Blätter* communicated literary news to German readers from all corners of Europe. Compared to the Scottish original, Pushkin's poem "Raven flies to raven" ("Voron k voronu letit," 1828) represented a considerably condensed version. The Russian poet, moreover, emphasizes the guilt of the bride in her husband's murder, which in the Scottish ballad is only implied in her eager awaiting of the killer's return.[36] Unlike Pushkin's and Scott's versions, Andersen's poem takes place in a historically defined context. Furthermore, the soldier's betrothed has no part (indirect or otherwise) in his demise; rather, she is unaware of his cruel destiny. It may be that his reading of Pushkin's poem prompted Andersen to transpose the gothic raven from the Scottish highland to a Russian landscape. In the winter of 1812, tens of thousands of Western European soldiers retreated under extreme conditions, while some were being attacked by Cossacks. The young Andersen wanted his readers to empathize with the terrified soldier as he is about to die on Russian soil, far from his home west of the Rhine.

In one stanza of the poem "Background to the Vignettes" (December 1831), Andersen again envisions a Russian winter landscape:

Siberia with fog, ice, and snow,
Covers him who strode for the flags of freedom;
Alone in infinite suffering,
His life withers away among dark pines,
His dream of freedom—the animals of the desert are free—
Is poetry![37]

The "him" of the poem is probably an unknown Polish rebel whose participation in the November Uprising earned him deportation to Siberia—a so-called *sibiriak*. For Pushkin, the November Uprising and Russia's subsequent crushing of Polish aspirations for independence represented a strictly intra-Slavic affair. The Western powers should not interfere,

---

35 All volumes of the journal from 1826-98 can be found here: http://digital.slub-dresden.de/werkansicht/dlf/89826/1/. The article "Neueste russiche Gedichte" to which Andersen refers is found in the 1830 volume (235-36); its author begins by emphasizing the great and rapid progress of contemporary Russian literature. "Die beiden Raben" is on p. 235.

36 Interestingly, the prominent Swedish-Finnish poet J. L. Runeberg produced a translation (via German) of Pushkin's poem in 1841; see Hellman, "Himmelske Hälsninger," 27-33.

37 Andersen, *SV*, 7: 336.

as he asserts in his poem "To the Slanderers of Russia" ("Klevetnikam Rossii," 1831). From Andersen's perspective, the exiled Polish soldiers' hope of national sovereignty was now not a possibility, but rather a theme for heroic poetry.

In Andersen's third novel, *Only a Fiddler* (1837), the protagonist Christian's father is characterized as a peculiar man, and ardent admirer of Napoleon, who dreams of traveling abroad—a figure quite similar to Andersen's own father. In the following passage from the novel, Andersen refers to the battle at Bornhøved in Holstein in December 1813, where Danish and French troops were pitted against Prussian and Swedish forces backed by Russian Cossacks. Andersen is quite precise in his understanding of Denmark's shrinking role in European power relations at this point in history:

> On the Danish frontiers lay hostile bands. The son of the Steppes, the Asiatic from the Marshes of the Don, wild and fleet captains, with their lances couched, hunted over the corn fields of Denmark. The god of battle, (the Age termed him Napoleon) fought alone, against the knights from all lands. It was a great Tournament,—the last time of the last display of chivalry; and for that reason he fought singly. Little Denmark was his squire, a true and courageous heart; but his force was unequal to his will.[38]

Siding with France in the Napoleonic period, Denmark had ultimately bet on the wrong horse. "The Asiatic" is a euphemism for Russian Cossacks who fought under Prussian leadership. The seemingly exotic presence of Cossacks on Danish soil in December 1813 and January 1814 led the period to be dubbed, in Danish lore, the "Cossack winter."[39] In Andersen's fiction, Christian's father is taken as a prisoner of war by the Cossacks and brought to Siberia. (Such a fate did not in fact befall any Danish soldiers.) The father explains what happened in the aftermath of the tumultuous battle:

> My countrymen had not spared the foe: they spared me as life is concerned. The Cossacks had made some prisoners,—I was added to the number. These savages bound us by the thumbs together, and drove us like oxen to the slaughter-house. My fancy was always for the south, but I was now sent

---

38 Andersen, *Only a Fiddler*, 1: 88.
39 For a description of these events, see Henningsen, "Kosakvinteren." The Cossack military presence in Denmark (December 1813 – January 1814) involved no actual hostilities after Bornhøved and came to an end with the treaty of Kiel on 14 January 1814.

another way, and had to suffer the winter's cold on the Russian fields of snow; a cold of which we in Denmark can form no conception.[40]

This translation—that of Mary Howitt, published 1845—reveals a bias. Andersen does not call the Cossacks "savages" in the Danish original, but simply "they" [de]. Napoleon's invasion had left tens of thousands of Europeans as prisoners of war in Russia.[41] Andersen makes his fictional Danish character part of this great historical drama; subjecting Christian's father to Siberian captivity of course lends the narrative a certain melodrama, and a particular historical intensity to its main character's life-trajectory. Notably, in making this move, Andersen stereotypically associates Russia with extreme weather and grim living conditions.

Andersen's view of Russia as a political entity was negative in the 1830s, but in this period he was in fact critical of the European imperial powers as such. This is evident in one of his most explicitly political poems, "Mene, mene, tekel upharsin"[42] (written in February 1838; published posthumously, in 1878). The title is taken from the famous "writing on the wall" (God's prophecy) in Aramaic in the book of Daniel (5: 27): "Thou art weighed in the balances, and art found wanting." The poem was intended to be read aloud at the Royal Danish Theater before a play, but the board of directors disapproved, and so it was never publicly performed. The poem has a peculiarly apocalyptic tone, associated with certain recent conflagrations: on 17 December 1837, the Winter Palace in St. Petersburg caught fire; on 10 January 1838, the Royal Exchange in London burned down; and on 13 January 1838, the Favart theater in Paris was also destroyed by fire. In the poem, Andersen's prophetic lyrical voice suggests that these fires harbor a secret meaning. They have been incurred by the hubris of each of these nations, and their idolatry: the British worship mammon; the French, entertainment; the Russians, their tsar. Thus have the most representative buildings of these three great powers caught fire. Andersen evidently associates Russia with authoritarianism: "See the mighty Empire of the East / There, where peoples rise / When the ruler bids them to do so, ... / The tsar is an earthly god."[43]

Referring to Edward Said's classic study *Orientalism* (1978), Lawrence Wolff has suggested that Western European scientists and thinkers' Enlightenment-era attempts to describe and map Eastern Europe may

---

40 Andersen, *Only a Fiddler*, 1: 203.
41 See Mikaberidze, "Napoleon's Lost Legions."
42 Dreyer, *H. C. Andersens Brevveksling med Signe Læssøe*, 1: 185-87.
43 Ibid., 186.

be thought of as "an intellectual project of 'demi-Orientalization.'"[44] During the reign of Nicholas I (1825-55), the Orientalization of the Russian state and its people became a common interpretive frame in the liberal sphere in Western and Northern Europe.[45] Andersen's sardonic allusion to "the mighty Empire of the East" thus places him squarely in the liberal camp. Moreover, in the context of this "fiery" poem, his reference to the tsar as an "earthly god" may be seen as drawing on the "apocalyptic" interpretation of imperial polities encoded in Revelation itself (which casts the Roman Empire as the antichrist). In Andersen's time, the most illustrious "apocalyptic" treatment of the Russian Empire would have been that of Adam Mickiewicz in the poem (in *Forefathers' Eve*) "Oleszkiewicz: The Day before the St. Petersburg Flood of 1824," in which a Polish artist sojourning in the Russian capital prophesies the Lord's judgement of this "Assyrian throne" and "city of Babylon."[46] (The most notable Russian response to Mickiewicz's "Satanization" of St. Petersburg would come in Pushkin's *The Bronze Horseman*.[47]) Thus we have a remarkable instance—for a writer of generally so conservative a reputation—of Hans Christian Andersen, contributor to the European tradition of "prophetic" anti-imperial literature.

Literary Russia and the Romantic North

Andersen's avid appreciation of Russian literature dates from the early 1830s. In August 1832, he published a suite of six poems titled *Poetic Bagatelles*. The heading of the second poem is in capitals: AFTER THE RUSSIAN. Andersen does not inform the reader what this title refers to. The poem is about a lover mourning the death of his beloved:

> So white is she, my beloved,
> You cannot find anything more white.
> I love her!—it will not happen
> That I can love her anymore;
>
> Now she is dead, my beloved,
> More whitely than before does she now smile.

---

44 Wolff, *Inventing Eastern Europe*, 7.
45 See for example the chapter "Russia as Oriental Despotism: 1815-1855" in Malia, *Russia under Western Eyes*, 85-159.
46 Cited from Weintraub, *The Poetry of Adam Mickiewicz*, 189.
47 As described in Blagoi, "Mitskevich i Pushkin."

Now she is dead! Oh my heart is pained!
And even more do I love her now.[48]

I was able to discover Andersen's source for this poem by going through volumes of the above-mentioned Leipzig journal *Blätter* and examining the articles that dealt with Russian and Slavic culture. An article titled "Ruthenian Ballads" ("Russinische Volkslieder"), which ran on 11 April 1832, contains the ballad, in German, that Andersen made a direct translation of.[49] In his Danish version, Andersen changed the genre from ballad to bagatelle and designates it as "after the Russian," when it should read "after the Ruthenian [or Rusyn]." (The Rusyns are an ethnic group nowadays living mainly in the borderland region of Slovakia, Poland, and Ukraine.)

It may seem odd that Andersen did not bother to differentiate between a large nation (Russia) and a much smaller one (the Rusyns). For that matter, what was Andersen's intention in producing this poem? One can only guess, but it seems safe to conclude that Andersen did peruse the articles on Russian literature in *Blätter* with interest. By showing the Danish reading public in 1832 that he was inspired by Russian literature, he may have wished to underscore that he, an aspirant to the title of prominent lyricist, was well aware of contemporary Russian poetry's rising star.

In 1839, the Danish critic Peder Ludvig Møller (1814-65) wrote an article on Pushkin that marked the first full-length Danish piece of criticism devoted solely to Russian literature.[50] Møller presents Pushkin as embodying the great literary breakthrough in Russian literature whose advent was inevitable: "It could have been foreseen that here [in Russia] something great and characteristic would be born in the world of poetry, at the point when this Greek and Oriental spirit, young and fresh in terms of culture, was touched by the spirit of a Northern romanticism."[51] Møller thus includes Pushkin and, by extension, Russia at large, within the broad conception of a Northern European romanticism that had become common at this time.

This conception is also evident in a letter Andersen wrote to his

---

48 Andersen, *SV*, 7: 359.
49 "Weiß bist du mein Mädchen / Weißer wirst du nicht / Heiß wie ich dich liebe / Heißer werd' ich es nie! / Ach da sie gestorben, / Ward sie weißer noch, / Und ich Armer lieb' sie / Heißer als zuvor." *Blätter für literarische Unterhaltung* 1 (1832): 436.
50 The early reception of Russian literature in Denmark has been closely studied by Jørgen Erik Nielsen, who devotes a whole section of *Fra Neva til Øresund* (62-69) to Møller's article.
51 Møller, "Digterskildringer," 239.

friend Henriette Hanck on 20 September 1837. Here Andersen mentions a French critic, Xavier Marmier (1808-92), a specialist in Scandinavian literature who had produced a biographical article on him: "Regarding Marmier: he has written biographies of Oehlenschläger, Pushkin, and Tegnér, and one of me, which will soon be published in one of Paris's most-read journals."[52] Adam Oehlenschläger and Esaias Tegnér (1782-1846) were at the time widely regarded as the most important poets of Denmark and Sweden respectively. Andersen now clearly sees himself as belonging to the pantheon of contemporary Northern writers, which included Pushkin (of whom Andersen apparently now had some knowledge). Just as proudly does he write in the same letter to Hanck: "I gather that I have been beautifully spoken of in a Russian journal. Little by little my name begins to shine. This is… the only thing I live for."[53] As Karin Sanders has emphasized, Andersen was determined, from the very beginning of his literary career, to make a name for himself beyond Denmark.[54] His joy in hearing news of his success in Russia is thus certainly authentic.

In a journal entry of 30 May 1838, Andersen makes a note of having read the Norwegian geologist Baltazar Mathias Keilhau's travelogue *Travels in East and West Finnmark and Bear Island and Spitsbergen in 1827 and 1828* (1828). In the fairy tale "The Garden of Paradise" (1838), Andersen recycles almost verbatim Keilhau's description of the skeletons of walruses and polar bears seen on the coast of Bear Island. In Andersen's tale, the four winds tell their mother of what they have seen on their travels. The north wind describes his visit to Bear Island: "The surface of the island is all half-melted snow, little patches of moss, and outcropping rocks. Scattered about are the bones of whales and polar bears, colored a moldy green, and looking like the arms and legs of some giant."[55] Andersen thus paints a grotesque and humorous picture of the high North.

Bear Island had been used for walrus hunting by the Dutch, British, Norwegians, and Russians for centuries. Andersen opts to situate the anthropomorphized north wind aboard a Russian ship: "The North Wind now talked of whence he had come, and where he had traveled for almost a month. 'I come from the Arctic Sea,' he told them. 'I have been on Bear Island with the Russian walrus hunters. I lay beside the helm, and slept as they sailed from the North Cape.'" In his 2015 study

---

52 Larsen, *H. C. Andersens Brevveksling med Henriette Hanck*, 199.
53 Ibid. Researchers have been unable to determine which journal Andersen is referring to.
54 See Sanders, "A Man of the World."
55 For Keilhau's description, see *Reise i Øst- og Vest-Finmarken*, 113.

The Dream of the North. A Cultural History to 1920, Peter Fjågesund refers to the period of 1830-80 as the "Northern heyday"; this was when the North, which included Russia, was conceptualized as a locus of the greatest fascination—a realm of mystery, danger, and sublime experiences. In "The Snow Queen," Andersen would choose the Finn woman and the Lapp woman as his representative natives of the high North, but here in "The Garden of Paradise," the first of his tales to include the Arctic as a setting, the people he envisions as living and working in that region are specifically Russians—presumably because he knew from Keilhau that Russians had long hunted walruses there.

Andersen's Waning Liberal Engagement in the Early 1840s

In his most extensive travel writing, *A Poet's Bazaar* (1842), Andersen avoids any comment on contemporary politics. In the early 1840s, Europe was rife with tensions between liberals who wanted change and conservatives, and especially conservative powers, opposing it; but Andersen represents the countries his travels take him through—Germany, Italy, Greece and the Ottoman Empire, and Austria-Hungary—not as political structures, but rather as touristic hotspots; places of interest, and even magic, for a writer to comment on. With this work's prospective translation into various European languages and its international marketing in mind, Andersen evinces potentially thorny anti-imperial attitudes only in the most veiled form.

In the section entitled "A Steppe-Journey between the Black Sea and Donau"—his route from the Ottoman Empire to Austria-Hungary—Andersen describes encountering a singing Wallachian nomad, whom he empowers via the loan of an invented voice:

> Thou green willow, with the hanging boughs! Where the Cossack leans on his lance in the Czar's land; where the sun glitters on the Austrian sabre and on Mohammed's minaret; where two rivers separate three emperors' lands, there stood my father's hanging wooden house amongst the rushes; close by grew the green willows! I watched the herd; I drove it into Bessarabia's steppes, solitary and alone! But the night has stars, the heart has thoughts! Thou green willow with the hanging boughs![56]

Andersen remains suffused with a romantic sympathy for the nomad dwelling in the Wallachian borderlands, over which the Russian,

---

56 Andersen, *A Poet's Bazaar*, 274.

Habsburg, and Ottoman empires had long vied for control; but whatever complaints he might have lodged against these great powers are kept to himself. Thus does Andersen also allow this and similar passages to be included in his collected edition published by Lorck. Who could take offense at these romantic, decontextualized elegies for the downtrodden? His success as a writer, and his new, elite life in European society in the 1840s, induced Andersen more and more to refrain from literary-political pronouncements. As such, his liberal engagement wanes in the early 1840s, and after the publication of his German autobiography in 1847, it disappears from his published works entirely.

Andersen's views of Russian politics in the 1830s were not formed as independent judgments but shaped by the liberal political context in Europe and Denmark, which made of Nicholas I's reign a byword of oppression. European liberals could laud Russia's military assistance to Greece in its wars of independence from the Ottoman Empire in the latter half of the 1820s, but the suppression of the Polish Uprising in 1831 quickly caused whatever goodwill Russia had accrued to evaporate. While it is well known that Andersen was supported by certain wealthy families of the Copenhagen bourgeoisie in the 1830s, it is less widely acknowledged that he sympathized with the liberal cause in Denmark and Europe. As a lyric poet, Andersen had also produced political verse, modeled on Béranger's popular Napoleonic mode. These contexts explain Andersen's early negative views of Russia. When Andersen begins to depart from his earlier liberal engagement, for example in the highly apolitical *Poet's Bazaar*, it did not go unnoticed. In a May 1842 review in the anti-royalist Danish journal *Corsaren*, Andersen is criticized for not commenting on the material privations he must have witnessed in his European travels: "We would have expected from Hans Christian Andersen, who has come from the people, who has fought the harsh fight of poor against rich, who has seen the subjugation and subjection eye to eye, a sensitivity toward the common people, their poverty and their subjection."[57] Andersen would thus have been reminded of his early liberal engagement; but as his self-censorship in 1847 makes clear, he was increasingly determined to mute his former political outlook so as not to risk causing offense among his conservative elite readership. After his autobiography of 1847, and the European upheavals of 1848, Andersen would present himself in public discourse as apolitical and/or a royalist. This does not mean that Andersen did not sympathize with

---

57 "Review of *A Poet's Bazaar*" (anonymous), published in *Corsaren* (1842); cited from the photographic reprint *Corsaren 1840-1846*, 2: 175.

the plight of the poor or their struggles; in fact, he did, but he kept his views to himself. The focus of part two of this study will be Andersen's increasingly positive view of Russia, as well as his enhanced knowledge of Russian literature.

Works Cited

Andersen, Hans Christian. *Andersen. H. C. Andersens samlede værker* 1-18. Copenhagen: Gyldendal, 2005.

—. *The Diaries of Hans Christian Andersen.* Selected and translated by Patricia L. Conroy and Sven H. Rossel. University of Washington Press: Seattle & London, 1990.

—. *H. C. Andersens Dagbøger* I-XII. Copenhagen: Gads Forlag, 1971-76.

—. *Only a Fiddler and O. T. or Life in Denmark.* Translated by Mary Howitt. London: Richard Bentley, 1845.

—. *A Poet's Bazaar: Pictures of Travel in Germany, Italy, Greece, and the Orient.* New York: Hurd and Houghton, 1871.

—. *Shadow Pictures from a Journey to the Harz Mountains, Saxon Switzerland, etc. etc., in the Summer of 1831.* Translated by Anna Halager. Edited by Sven Hakon Rossel and Monica Wenusch. Vienna: Praesens Verlag, 2011.

—. *The True Story of My Life: A Sketch.* Translated by Mary Howitt. London: Longman, Brown, Green and Longmans, 1847.

—. *Umrisse einer Reise von Copenhagen nach dem Harze, der Sächsischen Schweiz und über Berlin zurück.* Aus dem Dänischen übers. vom Verf. der See-Anemonen etc. (i.e., Wilhelm Volk). Hrsg. Von Friedrich Wilhelm Genthe. Breslau: Richter, 1836.

Andersen, Jens. *Hans Christian Andersen.* Translated from the Danish by Tiina Nunnally. Overlook Duckworth: New York, 2005.

Blagoi, D. "Mitskevich i Pushkin." In *Ot Kantemira do nashikh dnei* by D. Blagoi, 1: 289-319. Moscow: Sovetskii pisatel', 1972.

Corsaren 1840-46. M. A. Goldschmidts årgange genudgivet ved Uffe Andreasen. Copenhagen: C. A. Reitzel, 1997.

Davis, Norman. *God's Playground: A History of Poland.* Oxford: Oxford University Press, 2005.

Dreyer, Kirsten (ed.). *H. C. Andersens brevveksling med Signe Læssøe og hendes kreds.* Copenhagen: Museum Tusculanums Forlag, 2005.

Heiberg, Johan Ludvig. "Om den nye Retning i den franske Literatur" (nr. 22-28, 30-31). *Københavns Flyvende Post*, 1: 97-136. Photographic reprint. C. A. Reitzel: Copenhagen, 1980.

Hellman, Ben. "Himmelska hälsningar från Pusjkin till Runeberg. Den svenska Pusjkinreceptionen i Finland." In *Historiska og litteraturhistoriska studier*, edited by Pia Forssell and John Strömberg, 17-54. Helsingfors: Ekenäs, 2001.

Henningsen, Lars. "Kosakvinteren 1813-1814–den halvhjertede krig." *Sønderjyske årbøger* (2012): 7-30.

Jordan, David P. *Napoleon and the Revolution*. London: Palgrave Macmillan, 2012.

Keilhau, Baltazar Mathias. *Reise i Øst- og Vest-Finmarken samt til Beeren-Eiland og Spitsbergen, i Aarene 1827 og 1828*. Oslo: Johan Krohn, 1828.

Larsen, Svend. *H. C. Andersens Brevveksling med Henriette Hanck. 1830-1846*. Copenhagen: Munksgaard, 1941-46.

Malia, Martin. *Russia Under Western Eyes*. Cambridge, MA: Harvard University Press 1999.

Mikaberidze, Alexander. "Napoleon's Lost Legions. The Grande Armée Prisoner of War in Russia." *Napoleonica. La Revue* 21, no. 3 (2014): 35-44.

Molbech, Christian [anonymous]. "Om den nyeste danske Poesie." *Maanedsskrift for Litteratur* 10 (1833): 867-82.

Møller, Peder Ludvig. "Digterskildringer." *Brage og Idun* 1, no. 1 (1839): 231-58.

Möller-Christensen, Ivy York. *Den gyldne trekant. H. C. Andersens gennembrud i Tyskland 1831-1850 med tilhørende bibliografi*. Odense: Odense Universitetsforlag, 1992.

Neumann, Iver B. *The Uses of the Other: "The East" in European Identity Formation*. University of Minnesota Press 1998.

Nielsen, Jørgen Erik. *Fra Neva til Øresund. Den danske modtagelse af russisk litteratur 1800-1856*. Copenhagen: Museum Tusculanum Press, 1998.

Sanders, Karin. "A Man of the World: Hans Christian Andersen." In *Danish Literature As World Literature*, edited by Mads Rosendahl Thomsen and Dan Ringgaard, 91-114. New York/London: Bloomsbury Academic & Professional, 2017.

Topsøe-Jensen, Helge. "Efterskrift." In *Skyggebilleder af en Reise til Harzen, det sachsiske Schweitz etc. etc., i Sommeren 1831* by Hans Christian Andersen, 185-213. Copenhagen: Nordlundes Bogtrykkeri, 1968.

—. ed. *H. C. Andersens Breve til Carl B. Lorck*. Fynske Studier VIII. Odense Bys Museer, 1969.

—. *H. C. Andersens Brevveksling med Jonas Collin den Ældre og andre Medlemmer af det Collinske Hus* I-III. Copenhagen: E. Munksgaard, 1945-48.

—. *Mit eget Eventyr uden Digtning. En Studie over H. C. Andersen som Selvbiograf*. Copenhagen: Gyldendal, 1940.

Weintraub, Wiktor. *The Poetry of Adam Mickiewicz*. The Hague: Mouton, 1954.

Wolff, Larry. *Inventing Eastern Europe: The Map of Civilization on the Mind of the Enlightenment*, Stanford: Stanford University Press, 1994.

Wullschlager, Jackie. *Hans Christian Andersen: The Life of a Storyteller*. Alfred A. Knopf. New York, 2001.

Zipes, Jack. *Hans Christian Andersen: The Misunderstood Storyteller*. New York: Routledge 2005.

Russia under Hans Christian Andersen's Western Eyes, Part 2, 1847-95:

From Integration into Europe to the Hansen Translation

Mads Sohl Jessen

In 1937, the Danish poet and critic Otto Gelsted (1888-1968) published a book consisting of an article on Pushkin (commemorating the hundredth anniversary of the poet's death) and an essay on Danish-Russian literary relations entitled "Literary Interaction between Denmark and Russia through the Ages." In the latter, Gelsted mentions that "the only nineteenth-century Danish poet to have broken through in Russia, as everywhere else, is Hans Christian Andersen."[1] Gelsted also argues that the Denmark of Andersen's time, the romantic period, was "indifferent... to Russian culture."[2] This is largely correct. (Although the lack of interest was not mutual: there had existed a Russian romantic/nationalist avidity for medieval history and Old Norse literature.)[3] As a communist who had been in the Soviet Union in 1928, Gelsted was part of the broader pro-Soviet trend among the Danish left-wing intelligentsia in the 1930s, together with such prominent figures as the critic Harald Rue (1895-1957) and the novelist Martin Andersen Nexø (1869-1954), who actively sought cooperation with Soviet artists and writers. By stark contrast, in the first half of the nineteenth century, there were no real bonds to speak of between Danish and Russian writers.

On the other hand, Gelsted's treatment of Danish romanticism is superficial, entirely omitting, for example, the first important Danish translator of Russian literature. Jørgen Erik Nielsen, in his fine study of the romantic-era reception of Russian literature in Denmark (1800-56), notes that while interest in the century's first decades was modest, "[i]t was in the 1840s that we first find a Dane, E. M. Thorson, who really got to know the Russian language and literature."[4] P. L. Møller's 1839 essay

---

1 Gelsted, "Litterært Samspil," 55. My translation; unless otherwise indicated, all translations from Danish-language sources are mine.
2 Ibid., 57.
3 See Blom, "Rasmus Rask in St. Petersburg 1818-1819."
4 Nielsen, *Fra Neva til Øresund*, 12.

on Pushkin attests (as discussed in part one) to an authentic focus on this particular poet in Denmark; but it is only with Thorson (1816-89) and his efforts as a translator that Danish literary culture begins to evince a broader and deeper interest in Russian literature.

Thorson's first translation directly from the Russian (1842) is that of Pushkin's story "The Undertaker" ("Grobovshchik," 1831). Then, in 1843, Thorson publishes a gothic tale by Karamzin of special interest to Danish readers, "The Island of Bornholm" ("Ostrov Borngol'm," 1794),[5] set in part on that Danish island situated in the Baltic Sea. In the 1850s, Thorson's efforts culminate in a string of translations of Russian literature, including new renderings of Pushkin, as well as of Mikhail Zagoskin, Kazak Lugansky (pseudonym of Vladimir Dal), Aleksandr Bestuzhev, Gogol, and Lermontov.[6] Thus while Gelsted is correct that Danish literary culture showed only scant interest in Russian literature in the first three decades of the nineteenth century, the situation did change thereafter. The 1850s and 1860s, moreover, saw an increasingly positive image of Russia begin to emerge in the writings of Hans Christian Andersen.

Reimagining the Kremlin and Moscow

In the period of the 1840s–60s, Andersen produced, for his friends' children, a total of thirteen books of images from magazines and newspapers pasted next to Andersen's papercuts and short poems.[7] One girl, Agnethe Lind (1849-1915), daughter of Andersen's friend and correspondent Louise Collin (1813-98), was particularly lucky, receiving a full five such books. One of these picture books was entitled *Agnete* [sic] *Goes to See a Comedy* (1856).[8] It is structured as a fictive narrative in which Agnethe is accompanied by Andersen down Copenhagen's fashionable Amaliegade—the street her family resided on, which leads directly to the Royal Theater—on their way to see a show. As they walk, they notice odd and humorous occurrences in the city; for example, down one alleyway, an elderly woman happens to be teaching her grandson about the Kremlin. Over an image of that famous structure (captioned "The Kremlin in the country of the Russians"), and continuing down aside the purported grandmother and child, Andersen inscribed the following verse:

---

5   For a study of this story, see Offord, "Karamzin's Gothic Tale."
6   Nielsen, *Fra Neva til Øresund*, 97-116.
7   The best recent analysis of Andersen's picture books may be found in Müller-Wille, *Sezierte Bücher*, 314-22.
8   As this never-published picture book was stolen from the Hans Christian Andersen Museum in Odense in 1992, only a photocopy remains (hence the low quality of reproduction here).

In the back yard is a grandmother with her daughter's son.
Agnete does not see them,
but now she shall hear about them:
A castle with towers
highborn
long alleyways
Dark and long
Snakes Buh

Fig. 1. Collage by Andersen. Agnete Lind Picture Book 1855. Hans Christian Andersen Museum.

Uh!
You little troll,
Sit quiet
And listen to the story
The Ugly Duckling
Will he hear
Or I will tear
His little ear
and shake him
Will he remember
Creepy crawly
Old castle
He knows very well
Its name is "Kremlin."[9]

Andersen's primary intention with his picture books of this sort was to entertain the recipient in a clever and aesthetically pleasing way. In this case, it may have amused Agnethe to see Andersen construct a weird scene just for her by linking two unrelated pictures with a poem. The picture of the old woman imparting instruction seems to have been taken from a religious illustration; except in this context, the grandmother is informing the infant of the Kremlin at which she points, and also scaring the child with gothic allusions to the fortress's interior, and mentioning, at the same time, one of Andersen's most famous fairy tales.[10]

Humorously, the picture book ends with Agnethe and Andersen discovering that the play they had hoped to attend has been cancelled. Indeed, Agnethe (as reader) may realize that the true theatrical magic is what she has experienced (as a fictive character) during her walk with Andersen on the street leading to the Royal Theater. The adult artist's play with meanings invites her to pause and reflect. Andersen's visual technique is collage, but his poem also constitutes a verbal collage of self-referential, geographic, and didactic meanings. Andersen seems to poke fun at the harsh instructional methods of the older generation so as to provide a bit of fun for a representative of the younger generation. Just as Andersen's literary art is addressed to readers of all ages capable of understanding complex layers of meaning, so too in his picture books

---

9   I have not tried to retain Andersen's end rhymes.
10 I have been unable to determine the source of the picture of the grandmother and grandson. The image of the Kremlin is a reproduction of a drawing captioned "Vue generale du Kremlin" from the French painter Auguste Cadolle's collection *Vues de Moscou, dessinées d'après nature et lithographiées* (1825).

does he joyfully challenge young readers' potential for appreciating humor, irony, and the absurd.

Andersen may have found the picture of the Kremlin in a magazine from around 1855, as it was at this time that the media was covering the death of Nicholas I and the impending coronation of the new tsar, Alexander II. In the story "The Porter's Son" (1866), Andersen has particular reason to mention the site of dynastic ceremonies in Russia. The main character Georg, who later in life becomes a successful professor, draws pictures of the Kremlin, which he sends to his beloved Emilie, who has fallen ill:

> He drew the Czar's palace, the ancient Kremlin in Moscow, exactly as it was, with turrets and cupolas; in George's drawing they looked like big green and gilt cucumbers. Little Emilie was so pleased that during the week George sent her several more pictures, all of buildings, because that would give her plenty to think about, wondering what went on inside the doors and windows.

Here, as in his picture book poem on the Kremlin, Andersen addresses children's curiosity, upon seeing drawings of buildings, as to what they look like from the inside. According to the story, moreover, the city of Moscow is a frequent topic of conversation among Danes: "There was talk of Russia and Moscow, and so, of course, this brought one right to the Kremlin, of which little George had made that drawing for little Miss Emilie. How many pictures he used to draw!" The story was published in December 1866, shortly after one of the most significant royal weddings in Danish history—most likely the particular subject of the "talk of Russia and Moscow" mentioned by Andersen's narrator.

Princess Dagmar of Denmark (1847-1928) had already in 1864 been betrothed to Grand Duke Nikolai Aleksandrovich, the Russian Empire's heir apparent, who died in 1865. On 9 November 1866, she was married in St. Petersburg's Winter Palace to her deceased fiancé's younger brother, the new crown prince, who would rule as Emperor Alexander III from 1881-94.[11] Upon her conversion to Russian Orthodoxy and marriage, she was known as Grand Duchess (later Empress) Mariia Fedorovna of Russia. From then on until the Russian Revolution, the Danish and Russian royal families were intimately connected. Andersen's friend the journalist Robert Watt (1837-1894) traveled to Russia to cover the wedding, which he would describe in his *Letters from Russia* (1867). At one point in this book, Watt states that "Russia is undoubtedly a

---

11 For an in-depth biography, see Ulstrup, "Kejserinde Dagmar/Marija Fjodorovna."

mighty country"[12] – a reference to its great geographical vastness, but at the same time also an acknowledgement of its stature as a European imperial power.

In Andersen's picture book, the Kremlin may be a castle replete with mystique and uncanniness, but is nevertheless a landmark for children to learn about in geography lessons. A similarly "integrative" tendency is seen in "The Porter's Son": no longer does Andersen associate Moscow with Napoleon's invasion in 1812 and the great conflagration; it is now a European city among others. This new positive attitude toward Russia among the Danish public and in Andersen's writings may well have been formed mainly by the circumstance of the royal wedding, but it was also part of a larger European trend. Martin Malia has called the period from 1855-1914 the time of "Russia as Europe regained." Increasingly, he writes, Russia "appeared not as an alien entity but as one national culture within a common European civilization."[13] This is also how Andersen seems to view Russia in the later decades of his life.

Andersen and his Russian Acquaintances and Publishers

In Montreux, Switzerland in August 1862, Andersen made the acquaintance of a Russian family, one of whose members, Elisabeth von Manderstjerna (1821-1904), would write him three years later that she had got hold of a Pushkin manuscript fragment.[14] Andersen had expressed the wish to obtain something by Pushkin for an album he was keeping – a collection of handwritten documents by contemporary European artists and writers.[15] Manderstjerna's discovery – a sheet containing two poems – had been the very first page (with the first two elegies) of Pushkin's fair copy (1825) for the publication of his debut collection of poetry, *Poems by A. Pushkin* (*Stikhotvoreniia A. Pushkina*, 1826). This so-called Kapnist manuscript has been lost, and so Manderstjerna's gift to Andersen, now in the Royal Library in Copenhagen, is today the only remnant of it.[16]

In his reply, written in German, Andersen thanks his correspondent

---

12 Watt, *Breve fra Rusland*, 91.
13 Malia, *Under Western Eyes*, 163.
14 The letter, which is written in German, can be found in the digital collection of Andersen's letters: andersen.sdu.dk/brevbase/brev.html?bid=18602. For a (Danish-language) description of this correspondence, see Vliet, "H. C. Andersens Puschkinautograf."
15 For a copy of the Pushkin manuscript, as well as of Manderstjerna's letter, see the 1980 reproduction of this album: Andersen, *H. C. Andersens Album I-V*, 2: 232-34.
16 On the loss of the "Kapnist manuscript," and the folklorist P. G. Bogatyrev's 1939 discovery in Copenhagen of the two poems sent to Andersen, see Braude, "Avtograf Pushkina v arkhive G. K. Andersena."

thus: "The manuscript by the world-famous Pushkin is a treasure to me. Please accept my sincerest gratitude."[17] In this letter, Andersen also makes reference to the sudden death of Grand Duke Nikolai Aleksandrovich and the close relations between the Danish and Russian royal families:

> How sad that the young heir to the throne has died! The poor princess Dagmar! She is beautiful, lovely, and kind, and now God has already given her such a difficult test. Her brother, our crown prince, has recently been to Petersburg and was received lovingly, like a son, by the emperor's family. This gives me great joy, because I hold him most dear.[18]

Albeit technically a "personal letter," this text reflects the public stance of Andersen in the period after the 1847 publication of his German autobiography—as a royalist with close connections to the Danish court and as a faithful Christian.

In the 1860s, Andersen engaged in direct communication with Russian publishers, in particular, Nadezhda Stasova (1822-95) and Mariia Trubnikova (1835-97). These two had established (St. Petersburg, 1863) the Women's Publishing Cooperative (*Zhenskaia izdatel'skaia artel'*), which had a special focus on literary translation.[19] As their first publication, they chose new translations of Andersen and produced this collection already in the first year of the cooperative's existence, 1863. This collection of fairy tales was reissued in 1867, and the following year, further translations were made, and illustrated by Mikhail Klodt.[20] Trubnikova and Stasova enclosed a letter (in Danish) to Andersen with their gift to him (May 1868) of the new translation; here they write: "The Russian reading public loves these stories and fairy tales, and their author is counted among the greatest poets of the present day."[21] Here the two publishers also inform Andersen that it was specifically female employees who had performed every step of the book's production, from translation to typesetting to binding and marketing.[22]

---

17 See http://andersen.sdu.dk/brevbase/brev.html?bid=18636.
18 Ibid.
19 On the history of this cooperative, see Noonan and Nechemias, *Encyclopedia of Russian Women's Movements*, 118-19; for biographical portraits of its two founders, see de Haan, Daskalova, and Loutfi, *Biographical Dictionary of Women's Movements and Feminisms*, 526-29, 584-87.
20 On Klodt, see Zvonareva and Kudriavtseva, "Realisticheskoe prochtenie skazok Andersena pervym illiustratorom M. P. Klodtom."
21 See http://andersen.sdu.dk/brevbase/brev.html?bid=18908.
22 Liudmila Braude remarks that this letter "shows how highly Russian progressive circles of the time rated [Andersen's] work" ("Hans Christian Andersen and Russia," 3).

In his reply of 28 August 1868, Andersen begins by calling their book, and Klodt's illustrations, "beautiful." It is gratifying, he continues, to see his work recognized in Russia: "It makes me glad to know that my writings are read in the great and mighty Russia. I know a few of the writers of Russia's flowering literature, from Karamzin to Pushkin into our days."[23] As had his friend Watt in *Letters from Russia*, Andersen now refers to that country as "mighty," and emphasizes his awareness that its contemporary literature is a flourishing one.

It is impossible to say exactly which translations of Karamzin and Pushkin Andersen was familiar with, but the most likely candidates would have been the above-mentioned by Thorson from the 1840s–50s. As described in part one of this article, Andersen also read about Pushkin and Russian literature in German journals. He may have known the very early (1801) Danish translation of Karamzin.[24] It is likewise possible that Andersen had read the 1856 Danish translation of four of Turgenev's stories from *Notes of a Hunter* (*Zapiski okhotnika*, 1852).[25] What we do know for sure, however, is that late in his life, Andersen did read Turgenev.

Turgenev's impact on Scandinavian literature in the 1870s and the decades that followed was profound.[26] The 1870s saw the publication in this region of most of his novels and stories, albeit generally retranslated from German translations. In an April 1874 diary entry, we see Andersen commenting on the quality of various stories of Turgenev as translated into Danish from German in 1873: "Yesterday evening and today I read some of the Russian writer Ivan Turgenev's stories: 'The Diary of a Superfluous Man' ["Dnevnik lishnego cheloveka"]—very exciting, not to be read by nervous people; 'Phantoms' ["Prizraki"], a fever-fantasy, completely bloodless; 'The Execution of Tropmann' ["Kazn' Tropmana"]—extremely uncanny! 'Mumu' ["Mumu"], on the other hand, is a characteristic little story."[27] A little less than a month later, on 5 May, he makes a note of having finished reading Turgenev's *Rudin* (*Rudin*, 1856) in the 1872 Danish translation; he compares this work to

---

23 http://andersen.sdu.dk/brevbase/brev.html?bid=13295.
24 See Nielsen, *Fra Neva til Øresund*, 15-16. The collection consisted of four stories: "Poor Liza" ("Bednaia Liza," 1792), "Frol Silin" ("Frol Silin," 1802), "Natalya the Boyar's Daughter" ("Natal'ia, boiarskaia doch'," 1792), and "Iuliia" ("Iuliia," 1796).
25 See Nielsen, *Fra Neva til Øresund*, 109-10. The four stories are "The Bailiff" ("Burmistr"), "Death" ("Smert'"), "The Meeting" ("Svidanie"), and "My Neighbor Radilov" ("Moi sosed Radilov").
26 The main study of the Danish context is Fjord Jensen, *Turgenjev i dansk åndsliv*.
27 Andersen, *Dagbøger*, 10: 245.

the Danish writer and theater director F. L. Høedt (1820-85)[28]—hardly a great endorsement, as Høedt was no favorite of Andersen. These are the only mentions in Andersen's writings of his reading of particular works of Russian literature. His comments are impressionistic and do not exhibit a profound understanding of Turgenev's art; rather, they attest to Andersen's lifelong desire to be familiar with what was in vogue in the contemporary literary field: Turgenev had taken center stage in Danish literature in the 1870s, just as had Heine, Byron, and Hugo when Andersen set out on his career as a professional writer in the 1830s.

Andersen's travels in Europe often involved making acquaintances among poets and writers. During a stay in Dresden in April 1872, he met the Russian poet and translator Karolina Pavlova (1807-93), who had been living in that city since 1857.[29] Andersen notes in his diary that he heard her "reciting one of her German translations."[30] She may well have been reading from one of her renderings of Aleksei Tolstoy (1817-75), because the following day Andersen remarks that she has left a "translation of the Russian poet Tolstoy's tragedy *Tsar Fedor Ioannovich* [*Tsar' Fedor Ioannovich*]" as a gift for him.[31] Andersen's library also contains Pavlova's German translations of Aleksei Tolstoy's drama *The Death of Ivan the Terrible* (*Smert' Ioanna Groznogo*, 1866) and of a collection of his poetry (1868); these may thus have been presents from her as well.[32] Andersen probably read Pavlova's three translations through, although he left no comments on them. Turgenev and Aleksei Tolstoy were apparently the last Russian writers Andersen read in his life.

Peter Emanuel and Anna Hansen's Russian Translation of Andersen

In the 1860s, Russia was beginning to be integrated into Western European capitalism. The Danish Great Northern Telegraph Company was contracted by the Russian government in 1869 to help build and maintain telegraph cables across the country. Another key consequence of this business endeavor was that it brought Peter Emanuel Hansen (1846-1930) to Russia, where he would become half of the husband-and-

---

28 Ibid., 248.
29 On Karolina Pavlova's work as a poet and translator in Dresden, see Göpfert, "The German Period in the Life and Work of Karolina Pavlova."
30 Andersen, *Dagbøger*, 9: 263.
31 Ibid.
32 See entry "632," "632a," and "633" in *Auktion efter H.C. Andersen*. Copenhagen 1876, 16-17.

wife team that would be the modernist period's most important source of Russian translations of Scandinavian literature. His and his second wife Anna Hansen's translation of Andersen's fairy tales and selected other writings (1894-95) became the canonical Russian translation of the Danish storyteller in the twentieth century, through the Soviet period and beyond. (Notably, the Hansens' translations of Andersen's poetry would invariably omit the political verses discussed in part one—whose inclusion would have been a marketing misstep in tsarist Russia.) In his thorough studies of the Hansens, Kenneth H. Ober justly situates the couple at the center of the Russian reading public's greatly enhanced interest in Scandinavian literature in the period from Andersen's death in 1875 to the Russian Revolution.[33]

In 1871, Hansen was employed by the Great Northern Telegraph Company as a telegraphist in Siberia. His first work as a translator was Goncharov's *A Common Story* (*Obyknovennaia istoriia*, 1847); this Danish rendering was published in 1877. This work also brought him into contact with Grand Duchess Mariia Fedorovna, who sent him a letter and a ring in thanks for the effort. In 1881, Hansen moved to St. Petersburg, now employed by the Russian state in the Municipal Telegraph Administration. The following year, he began teaching English at the school of St. Petersburg's Main (later, Central) Telegraph Station, and would soon be appointed director of this school. He would subsequently (1886-1906) teach English and telegraphy at the Alexander III Electrotechnical Institute, becoming a Russian subject in 1887.[34] (The Electrotechnical Institute adopted Hansen's Morse transmitter training methodology; he thus stands as what one commentator calls a "pioneer of telegraphy instruction in Russia."[35]) In the mid-1880s, he translated several of Lev Tolstoy's essays and autobiographical texts into Danish, but from the early 1890s on, he and his wife devoted themselves solely to translating Scandinavian literature into Russian.[36]

In 1881, Hansen married Mariia Aleksandrovna Engelfeldt, who died of tuberculosis in 1888.[37] He then married Anna Vasilyeva (1869-1942), who would learn Danish and the other Scandinavian languages, and be his co-translator until the Russian revolution. In their collaboration,

---

33 See his excellent dissertation "Peter Emanuel Hansen and the Popularization of Scandinavian Literature in Russia, 1888-1917." For a shorter study, see Ober, "A Literary Missionary."
34 Partala, "Petr Gotfridovich Ganzen—prepodavatel' Elektrotekhnicheskogo instituta," 142-44.
35 Ibid., 141.
36 This overview of Hansen's career draws on Ober, "Peter Emanuel Hansen," 1-36, where sources of these facts may be found. On Hansen's fascinating visit to Lev Tolstoy at Iasnaia Poliana, see Hellman, *Hemma hos Tolstoj*, 37-65.
37 On Hansen's first wife, see Ober, "Peter Emanuel Hansen," 22, 27.

Peter, the team's native speaker of Danish, would ensure the translation's semantic correctness, while Anna, the native speaker of Russian, would polish the finished product. Ober cites an interesting comment by Hansen on the couple's resulting combined advantage: in a letter to the Norwegian writer Bjørnstjerne Bjørnson on the success of their translation (1891) of Henrik Ibsen's *Hedda Gabler* (1890) in Russia, Hansen notes that "from the standpoint of language, it is being called a masterpiece, which I am comfortable mentioning since this is mainly to the credit of my wife, whereas I may take pride only in the translation's faithfulness to the original."[38] In the period from 1890 to 1917, the Hansens would be the driving force in making available to Russian readers prominent Scandinavian authors such as, among others, Bjørnstjerne Bjørnson, Georg Brandes, Henrik Ibsen, Jens Peter Jacobsen, Johannes V. Jensen, Knut Hamsun, Selma Lagerlöf, August Strindberg, and Sigrid Undset.[39]

Hansen began work on the Andersen translation around 1891-92. On 13 April 1892, he wrote a letter to the Copenhagen publishing house of C. A. Reitzel, which Andersen had worked with throughout his life, and which had acquired the copyright for Andersen's complete works in 1877:

> I have translated half a dozen of the most characteristic tales ("The Darning Needle," "The Shirt Collar," "It's Quite True!," "The Jumpers," "The Butterfly," "The Snow Man," "Thumbelina," "The Steadfast Tin Soldier," "The Snail and the Rosebush," "The Elf Mound," and "The Happy Family"), wherein the difference between the Russian translation from German and mine from the original is especially evident. It is clear overall that the tone, which makes the music, has been completely lost in these second-hand translations. So, now that I have gained a good name as the only Russian translator from Danish, the new translation has every chance of making a quick breakthrough.[40]

Hansen's manner of thinking is of course understandable. Andersen was the only Nordic writer to have achieved a large readership in Russia, and an excellent new translation directly from the Danish must have seemed a most promising venture to the couple undertaking it.

---

38 The Bjørnson-Hansen correspondence is housed in the Bjørnson collection of the University Library in Oslo. Ober discusses this letter in "Peter Emanuel Hansen," 38.
39 Ober has published a complete bibliography of all the couple's translations: "A Hansen (Ganzen) Bibliography."
40 Manuscript collection (NKS 2937, 4°) of the Royal Library in Copenhagen. As Ober explains in connection with this letter, Hansen's translations of the Norwegian writer Bjørnstjerne Bjørnson in 1891 had brought him a "good name" as the rare (or unique) translator directly from Scandinavian languages ("Peter Emanuel Hansen," 42).

In a May 1893 letter to the famous Danish critic Georg Brandes (1842-1927), Hansen again emphasizes the superior quality of the translation then in progress, but also laments the lack of attention to the couple's Andersen project among potential Danish benefactors.[41] As Ober comments: "He here expressed a complaint which he was to repeat to various correspondents in Denmark—he was unable to interest anyone in Denmark in offering him support."[42] In his reply (15 July 1893), Brandes does not mention Andersen at all, but instead offers a general recommendation that Hansen translate contemporary Danish writers, rather than Norwegian ones like Bjørnson: "If I were to address a patriotic wish to you, it is this: Let Bjørnson and the Norwegians be and use all your force on poor Denmark."[43] In 1883, Brandes had published *The Men of the Modern Breakthrough*, which included portraits of seven writers—two Norwegian (Bjørnson and Ibsen) and five Danish.[44] Brandes here is thus trying to persuade Hansen to join his campaign in promoting these same Danish authors. While Hansen is certainly respectful, even deferential, to Brandes in their correspondence, he would decidedly not follow this "patriotic" advice, as witness his and his wife's many translations of Norwegian and Swedish writers in the years to come.

The following year (September 1894), Hansen replies to Brandes and explains why, in his view, the promotion and further translation of Andersen was likely to make a big impact on behalf of Danish literature:

> For over thirty years here [in Russia], only the fairy tales have been known, and in spite of the poor translations of them from German, they have achieved such circulation that there have been twelve translations, some of which have gone through as many as nine editions. This circulation, though, has been, all in all, restricted to the world of children: the poor translations have not been able to satisfy adults, who have restricted themselves merely to buying the books for their children without themselves reading them. While the fairy tales have thus served only as reading material for children, now our translation has opened up adults' eyes to their true significance. Both verbally and in written form, we have received comments on "the great service

---

41 The Hansen-Brandes correspondence is housed in the Brandes Archive at the Royal Library in Copenhagen. Ober provides a close analysis of the letters in "Peter Emanuel Hansen," 31-51.
42 Ober, "Peter Emanuel Hansen," 49-50.
43 See ibid., 50f.
44 These were J. P. Jacobsen, Holger Drachmann, Edvard Brandes, Sophus Schandorf, and Erik Skram.

we have hereby rendered to Russian literature, insofar as these masterpieces have hitherto been hardly known."[45]

Hansen's insistence on Andersen's art as wide-ranging in its tonality ("music") and appropriate for adult readers as well as children may in part explain the success the couple's translations would enjoy with generations of Russian readers. In fact, Hansen's view was very much in line with Andersen's own conception of his authorship. From the outset of his career as a fairy tale writer, Andersen regarded the deeper strata of his art to be mainly recognizable to older readers. In the preface to his 1837 collection, Andersen suggests that "The Little Mermaid" contains "a deeper meaning only the mature will understand."[46] While Andersen's literary art is aimed at readers of all ages capable of understanding complexity, its allegorical and ironic dimensions are difficult to grasp for children.[47] As Andersen put it in an 1875 diary entry: "The naïve is only part of my fairy tales; humor is the real salt in them."[48] The concept of humor meant, for Andersen and his contemporaries, an integration of irony and wit that involves reflection and artistic distance.

In the postscript to the complete edition, Hansen likewise insists on what critics today refer to as Andersen's "double articulation"—the fairy tales' simultaneous address to children and adults alike.[49] The prominent Soviet Andersen scholar Liudmila Braude commended the translators for trying to "dispel the popular conception of [Andersen] as a purely children's writer."[50] She cites from the postscript in which Hansen, in line with his statement to Brandes, emphasizes that the fairy tales are also for adult readers:

> It is quite mistaken to regard the fairy-tales and stories as written exclusively for children. What makes them so remarkable is precisely that they nourish

---

45 Ober does not discuss this passage.
46 Andersen, *SV*, 3: 364.
47 This aspect of Andersen's art was famously "missed" by one of his country's most illustrious critics. In Brande's above–mentioned first study of Andersen, an 1869 article published in three parts in the journal *Illustrerede Tidende*, the critic analyzed Andersen's writing solely in terms of the concepts of the naïve and the childlike. Unlike Hansen (and Andersen himself), Brandes gives no consideration to any deeper meanings graspable in particular by adult readers. Brandes has been (justly) blamed for offering too simplistic an account of Andersen's fairy tales—a reading that has unfortunately proved quite tenacious; on this aspect of the history of Andersen's Danish reception, see Müller-Wille, *Sezierte Bücher*, 99f.
48 Andersen, *Dagbøger*, 10: 458-59.
49 Several authors, in particular, Gorm Larsen and Per Krogh Hansen, discuss this concept in an anthology dedicated to a narratological approach to Andersen; see Krogh Hansen and Lundholt, *When We Get to the End*.
50 Braude, "Hans Christian Andersen and Russia," 7.

the minds, hearts and imaginations of readers of all ages. Children, of course, will be attracted chiefly by the plot itself, whilst grown-ups will understand and appreciate the depths of theme; for the majority of Andersen's fairy-tales and stories—outwardly innocent, narrated at times in a playful and witty style, at times in a childlike, naïve tone, and always in an extremely poetic and at the same time unusually simple language close to colloquial speech—are brilliant satires, in which Andersen ironically and pointedly pokes fun at various human foibles.[51]

As a reading strategy as well as a statement on Andersen's style and rhetoric, this is an excellent recommendation. The Hansens succeeded with their translation of Andersen because they appreciated the challenge of the task, and were capable of transposing Andersen's ironic and allegorical richness into idiomatic Russian.

Hansen's Russian Polyglot Edition

Amid work on the couple's voluminous Andersen translation, Hansen also made a polyglot edition of Andersen's "The Story of a Mother" (1847) available to the Russian book market. Having sent the finished work to Brandes, Hansen in October 1894 received this expression of the critic's gratitude: "Thank you for your great kindness in sending me the interesting polyglot edition of Andersen's story, and rest assured that you have my sympathy in your pursuit of disseminating the knowledge and love of Danish cultural life in Russia."[52] When Andersen had turned seventy (2 April 1875; he would live only four months longer), the Danish journalist Jean Pio (1833-84) and linguist Vilhelm Thomsen (1842-1927) had prepared him a special birthday present: a polyglot edition of his "Story of a Mother" in fifteen European languages.[53] In 1894, Hansen asked Thomsen for permission to reuse some of the texts from the original edition, but Hansen also added more languages.

As the title in French made clear, Hansen's edition featured twenty-two languages: *Une Mère. Contes d'Hans Christian Andersen en vingt-deux langues* (1895). The Russian translation of "The Story of a Mother" was of course the Hansens' own. Seven new renditions were added, in a range of languages generally showing a Slavic and/or "eastward" orientation: Belarusian, Slovak, Serbian, Italian, Armenian, Tatar, and Hebrew. In the

---

51 Ibid; for Hansen's Russian wording, see Ganzen, "K chitateliam," 497 (footnote).
52 Letter dated 26 October 1894 (Brandes Archive, Royal Library in Copenhagen).
53 In the following order: Danish, Swedish, Icelandic, German, Low German, Dutch, English, French, Spanish, Modern Greek, Russian, Polish, Czech, Hungarian, and Finnish.

French preface, Hansen writes that his intention is to make Andersen's name known among "all nationalities of [the] vast" Russian Empire.[54] Hansen's primary intention with the polyglot edition may indeed have been to pay homage to the tsar and his (Danish-born) wife. In a March 1894 letter to Vilhelm Thomsen, Hansen explains that he had contacted the empress, who had immediately offered him the financial support that would make it possible to complete the Andersen project.[55] The Hansens' translation is also dedicated to her. In the mid-1890s, this husband-and-wife translating team must surely have looked upon the Russian royal family as the greatest potential benefactors for their grand plan to introduce the best of Scandinavian literature to Russian readers in the following decades.[56]

Emblematic of Andersen's practice of (from the 1840s on) mingling with Danish aristocrats and royals was his June 1867 visit to the royal family. As he noted in his diary, Princess Dagmar / Grand Duchess Mariia Fedorovna, who was in Denmark on holiday at the time, informed him that she had "learned Russian by reading a Russian edition of my fairy tales."[57] No doubt, Andersen would have been delighted to learn that thirty years later, she would provide crucial support for the Hansens' translation of his works. Andersen, moreover, personally made the acquaintance of Peter Emanuel Hansen in the mid-1860s, taking an interest in this young man who might have become the next lead actor at the Royal Theater.[58] They visited one another and met at social gatherings. Andersen also provided Hansen with a letter of recommendation (dated 17 May 1871) when the latter traveled to London.[59] Andersen's final reference to Hansen in his diary (in the entry of 30 May 1873) mentions having received a letter from "Emanuel Hansen in Siberia."[60] Unfortunately the letter itself has not survived. Andersen, of course, could hardly have suspected that the young man would become one of the most important promoters of his writing in Russia. As Kenneth

---

54 "[N]ous espérons qu'elle aidera à propager le nom et les oeuvres d'Andersen parmi célles dés nationalités de ce vaste Empire, auxquelles notre ecrivain est encore à peu près ou entièrement inconnu" (vi).
55 The letter is housed in NKS 4291, 4°, Royal Library in Copenhagen.
56 In 1917, the Russian Revolution brought their joint venture to a halt, as Peter Hansen remained in Denmark and ceased translating, while Anna Hansen continued to live in Russia working as a translator and teacher; for a brief discussion of her post-1917 translations, see Ober, "Peter Emanuel Hansen," 178-79.
57 Andersen, *Dagbøger*, 7: 306.
58 See the twenty entries under "Hansen, Emanuel" in Andersen, *Dagbøger*, 11: 285. On Hansen's failed early career as an actor, see Ober, "Peter Emanuel Hansen," 3-7.
59 http://www.andersen.sdu.dk/brevbase/brev.html?bid=14397
60 Andersen, *Dagbøger*, 9: 94.

Ober puts it, "the signature 'A. and P. Ganzen' was to become a warranty of excellence in translation" in Russia from the 1890s on.[61] The Hansens' translation of Andersen laid the groundwork for the couple's outstanding reputation in the Soviet period, and beyond it to this day. Andersen's correspondence with Russian acquaintances and publishers was part of his grand strategy to tirelessly market his work to a world audience, but it was the Hansen couple's vibrant translation, as this anthology attests, that would truly fuel the rich Russian literary and artistic response to his fairy tales.

Works Cited

Andersen, Hans Christian. *Andersen. H. C. Andersens samlede værker 1-18*. Copenhagen: Gyldendal, 2005.

—. *H. C. Andersens Album I-V*. Edited by Kåre Olsen, Helga Vang Lauridsen, and Kirsten Weber. Copenhagen: Lademann, 1980.

—. *H. C. Andersens Dagbøger 1825-1875*. Edited by Kåre Olsen and H. Topsøe-Jensen. Copenhagen: Society of Danish Language and Literature, 1971-76.

Blom, Alderik. "Rasmus Rask in St. Petersburg 1818-1819: Russian-Scandinavian Scholarly Networks and the Old Norse Sources of Medieval Russia." *Journal for the Study of Romanticisms* 6 (2017): 15-31.

Braude, Liudmila. "Avtograf Pushkina v arkhive G. K. Andersena." *Pushkin. Issledovaniia i materialy*, 357-62. Moscow/Leningrad: AN SSSR, Institut russkoi literatury, 1956.

—. "Hans Christian Andersen and Russia." *Scandinavica. An International Journal of Scandinavian Studies* 14, no. 1 (1975): 1-15.

—. "H. C. Andersen i Rusland." *Anderseniana* 4, no. 4 (1987): 5-24.

de Haan, Francisca, Krasimira Daskalova, and Anna Loutfi, eds. *Biographical Dictionary of Women's Movements and Feminisms: Central, Eastern, and South Eastern Europe, 19th and 20th Centuries*. Budapest/New York: Central European University Press, 2005.

Fjord Jensen, Johan. *Turgenjev i dansk åndsliv: studier i dansk romankunst 1870-1900*, Copenhagen: Gyldendal, 1961.

Ganzen, P. "K chitateliam." In *Sobranie sochinenii Andersena* by Kh. K. Andersen, 4: 496-510. St. Petersburg: S.M. Nikolaev, 1894.

Gelsted, Otto. "Litterært Samspil mellem Danmark og Rusland gennem Tiderne." In *Danmark-Rusland i Litteraturen* by Otto Gelsted, 45-74. Copenhagen: Mondes Forlag, 1937.

Göpfert, Frank. "The German Period in the Life and Work of Karolina Pavlova." In *Essays on Karolina Pavlova*, edited by Susanne Fusso and Alexander Lehrmann, 240-50. Evanston: Northwestern University Press, 2001.

Hansen, Peter Emanuel, ed. *Une Mère. Contes d'Hans Christian Andersen en vingt-deux langues*. St. Petersburg: Lithographie S. M. Nicolaieff, 1894.

---

61 Ober, "Peter Emanuel Hansen," 27.

Hellman, Ben. *Hemma hos Tolstoj. Nordiska möten i liv och dikt*. Stockholm: Appell Förlag, 2017.

Krogh Hansen, Per & Marianne Wolff Lundholt, eds. *When We Get to the End...Towards a Narratology of the Fairy Tales of Hans Christian Andersen*. Odense: University Press of Southern Denmark, 2005.

Malia, Martin. *Russia Under Western Eyes*. Cambridge, MA: Harvard University Press, 1999.

Müller-Wille, Klaus. *Sezierte Bücher. Hans Christian Andersens Materialästhetik*. Paderborn: Wilhelm Fink, 2017.

Nielsen, Jørgen Erik. *Fra Neva til Øresund. Den danske modtagelse af russisk litteratur 1800-1856*. Copenhagen: Museum Tusculanum Press, 1998.

Noonan, Norma Corigliano, and Carol Nechemias, eds. *Encyclopedia of Russian Women's Movements*. Westport, CT/London: Greenwood Press, 2001.

Ober, Kenneth H. "A. Hansen (Ganzen) Bibliography of Translations, Books, and Articles in Russian 1885-1917." *Svantevit* 3, no. 2 (1977): 89-100.

—. "P. E. Hansen and P. Ganzen: A Danish Literary Missionary in Russia." *Svantevit* 2, no. 2 (1977), 5-17.

—. "Peter Emanuel Hansen and the Popularization of Scandinavian Literature in Russia, 1888-1917." PhD Dissertation, University of Illinois, 1974.

Offord, Derek. "Karamzin's Gothic Tale: *The Island of Bornholm*." In *The Gothic-Fantastic in Nineteenth-Century Russian Literature*, edited by Neil Cornwell, 37-59. Amsterdam-Atlanta: Rodopi, 1999.

Partala, M. A. "Petr Gotfridovich Ganzen—prepodavatel' Elektrotekhnicheskogo instituta." *Izvestiia SPbGETU "LETI"* 10 (2012): 141-46. Available electronically: http://www.eltech.ru/assets/files/university/izdatelstvo/izvestiya-spbgetu-leti/2012-10.pdf

Ulstrup, Preben. "Kejserinde Dagmar/Marija Fjodorovna." In *Danmark og zarernes Rusland 1600-1900 / Danija i Rossijskaja imperija 1600-1900*, edited by Thomas Lyngby, 197-269. Hillerød: Det Nationalhistoriske Museum, Frederiksborg Slot, 2013.

Watt, Robert. *Breve fra Rusland, skrevne i September og October 1866*. Copenhagen: Vilhelm Trydes og Kristian Vissings Forlag, 1866.

Vliet, W. van der. "H. C. Andersens Puschkinautograf. Søstrene Manderstjerna." *Anderseniana* 8 (1940): 75-78.

Zvonareva, Lola, and Lidiia Kudriavtseva. "Realisticheskoe prochtenie skazok Andersena pervym illiustratorom M. P. Klodtom." In *Skazki Andersena i chetyre russkikh khudozhnika-illiustratora* by L. Zvonareva and L. Kudriavtseva, 47-59. Moscow: Vishera, 2010.

A Time of Fairy Tales:

Hans Christian Andersen, a Danish Princess, and the Telegraph Business

Johs. Nørregaard Frandsen

Hans Christian Andersen was not only a writer and artist who contributed to world literature with the invention of new literary genres and narrative forms. Andersen was also masterful at creating real-life networks and connections with prominent contemporary figures. It is surely his art, the fairy tales in particular, that have made him an enduring and unavoidable icon in Russian literature and culture. However, Andersen's esteem as a writer was also enhanced by the important connections he maintained and developed. These associations helped plant his fairy tales in Russian literary and cultural contexts. Some of these connections involved royals; others, members of the technological and commercial sphere of Danish society. It is well known that Andersen in his later life cared a great deal for the Danish royal family, which he often frequented. He admired and was also acquainted with Princess Dagmar, who became Grand Duchess and then Empress Mariia Fedorovna of Russia at a decisive moment in Russian history. Likewise, Andersen was on friendly terms with the most powerful Danish industrialist of the latter half of the nineteenth century, Carl Frederik Tietgen (1829-1901), who forged another highly important connection between Denmark and Russia when his Great Northern Telegraph Company won the concession to build telegraph lines across Russia from St. Petersburg to Vladivostok, with extensions to China and Japan.[1]

Hans Christian Andersen should not simply be regarded as an eyewitness to history. He actively sought to affect the world with his literary art. As such, his impact on Russian culture for the last one hundred and fifty years renders his oeuvre a bridge between Denmark and Russia, between Danish and Russian culture.

Andersen lived in a time of great cultural, political, and technological upheaval. In his writings, he constantly visualizes and reflects on these

---

[1] For a comprehensive history of the Danish-Russian telegraph enterprise and Tietgen's role in it, see Lange, *Finansmænd, stråmænd og mandariner* and *Partnere og rivaler*. The best recent English-language study of the global nineteenth-century telegraphy project is Müller, *Wiring the World*.

changes, which were invariably fraught with ever more far-reaching developments. For example, Andersen was equally fascinated and disconcerted by steam power and electromagnetism, both of which became central conditions for industrialization and the shaping of the modern world in the latter half of the nineteenth century. In his later life, Andersen avoided publicly discussing politics, but an examination of not just his art, but also his diaries and his correspondence with persons in his own country and Europe at large, yields a panorama of the transformational political and cultural developments of his epoch. Andersen was keen to describe, observe, and reflect on these changes. At the same time, he frequented many figures central to key events in Europe.

A Time of Fairy Tales

As a person and a poet, Hans Christian Andersen was fully aware that the times were changing, and that he stood amid the creation of a new world while the old one went under. "Our time is indeed a time of fairy tales." This sentence is placed by Andersen near the beginning of the tale "The Dryad" (1868). The dryad in this case is a little tree spirit or fairy who lives in a chestnut tree in the countryside near Paris. From her tree, she can catch a glimpse of the light rising from the metropolis, of which she longs to be a part, just for once. Her wish having been granted, she comes to Paris and experiences its light and bustling modern urban life. The dryad's dream becomes reality, but also costs her her life. She cannot live for more than a day away from her tree. At the end of the story we are told: "All this has happened and been experienced. We ourselves have seen it, at the Paris Exposition in 1867, in our time, the great and wonderful time of fairy tales."

To Andersen, the term "fairy tale" not only referred to a literary genre, but also served to describe his own contradictory epoch. He entitled his best-known autobiography *The Fairy Tale of My Life* (1855), which begins with the famous statement: "My life is a beautiful fairy tale [*eventyr*], so rich and happy!"[2] On the last page Andersen explicitly affirms that he completed the writing of this autobiography in Copenhagen on 2 April 1855, which happened to be his fiftieth birthday. His autobiography was thus also a symbolic gesture. The Danish genre designation Andersen uses here, *eventyr*, derives from the Latin *adventura*, which originally meant an occurrence, or something that arrived or "came into sight." This etymological background was known to Andersen, who thought

---

2   My rendering; in English translations, Andersen's *eventyr* is given (imprecisely) as "story."

of his authorship, and his fairy tales (*eventyr*) in particular, as a way to understand his own experiences, and even, in the broadest sense, as a way of life. Many, perhaps even most of his tales represent transformations or metamorphoses, most famously, for example, when a mermaid is changed into the form of a beautiful young woman; but more often than not the changes end in unsettling pain and tragedy. Even in the case of a technically "happy ending," as with the becoming of a beautiful swan in "The Ugly Duckling," the character in question is forced to undergo a disturbing amount of pain on his way to recognition.

Andersen was interested in technological breakthroughs and the natural sciences. In 1744, the Scottish inventor James Watt (1736-1819) produced the first workable steam engine. This machine laid the groundwork for new revolutionary forms of transportation, especially the steamship and locomotive. Andersen, experiencing such inventions, wrote enthusiastically about these "wonders." In his travelogue *A Poet's Bazaar* (1842), he celebrated the great potential of the steam locomotive, and the dizzying sense of speed and power it afforded, as a sort of modern fairy tale. He writes:

> And what a tremendous effect this invention has on the spirit! One feels so powerful, just like a magician of olden days. We harness the magic horse to our carriage and space disappears. We fly like clouds before the storm, as birds of passage fly. Our wild horse sniffs and snorts, black steam rising from his nostrils. Mephistopheles could not fly more quickly with Faust in his cloak. By natural means we are, in our day, as powerful as in the Middle Ages man thought only the devil could be. With our wisdom we have drawn alongside him—and before he knows it, we have passed him by.
>
> I remember but few times in my life when I have felt myself so affected as here, as though with all my mind and being I was face to face with God.[3]

In another story, "Thousands of Years from Now" (1853), Andersen envisions a future time when "men will fly on wings of steam through the air, across the ocean." In 1820, the Danish physicist Hans Christian Ørsted, who happened to be a friend of Andersen's for many years, discovered electromagnetism, touching off a technological revolution that led eventually to the invention of the electric motor and also the telegraph, the first truly global means of communication. During the 1860s and 1870s, cable connections were made between Europe and China and Europe and North America. Andersen's attitude toward these

---

3 Andersen, *A Poet's Bazaar. A Journey to Greece, Turkey & Up the Danube*, 11.

technical advances vacillated: at times he would hail and celebrate them; at others, he expressed a distinct unease at the changes they would lead to. In the story "The New Century's Goddess" (1861) and in the above-mentioned "The Dryad," Andersen refers to the steam engine as "Master Bloodless," implying that the machinery, for all its power, lacked a soul, and would ultimately not serve mankind well.[4]

The Telegraph and Carl Frederik Tietgen

Carl Frederik Tietgen, who was born in Odense in 1829 and died in Copenhagen in 1901, was the greatest Danish businessman of his time. He founded and directed several successful companies in the fields of manufacture, transport, and infrastructure. As a young man, Tietgen had worked for a Danish company in Manchester in England for five years and was inspired by this European powerhouse of industrial commerce. In 1868 Tietgen took the crucial step of founding a Danish-Norwegian-English telegraph company and a Danish-Russian telegraph company. The following year he merged these two with a British-Norwegian firm, and thus did the Great Northern Telegraph Company, one of the world's largest, come into being. Tietgen's international outlook from his young days and his passion for technology and infrastructure now formed a coherent whole.

In his memoirs, published posthumously in 1904, Tietgen mentions his relationship with Hans Christian Andersen. The industrialist had read Andersen and admired his work, but also saw the poet as suffering from "an indomitable vanity,"[5] which Tietgen illustrates with an anecdote. The two men had met by chance in 1857 on a boat crossing from Calais to Dover. The weather was bad, and Andersen became queasy: "In between his bouts of seasickness [Andersen] managed to relate that he had been invited by Charles Dickens to come and visit him and that *The Two Baronesses* had been published at the same time in Denmark and London."[6] Tietgen goes on to report how the two later met at dinners in Copenhagen, where Andersen would often read fairy tales that the business tycoon always enjoyed. It was at a gathering in 1862 at the Melchior family estate "Rolighed" in the northern outskirts

---

4 For a discussion of modernity as interpreted in Andersen's fairy tales, see Frandsen, "The Insoluble Conflict and Transformation."
5 Tietgen, *Erindringer og Optegnelser*, 84; all translations from Danish-language sources are mine unless otherwise indicated.
6 Ibid., 85.

of Copenhagen, declares Tietgen, that Andersen "won over my whole heart." He explains:

> Hans Christian Andersen proposed a toast to me, saying that, on his way walking out here to "Rolighed," he could sense a strange sound coming from the telegraph cables overhead. He pondered for quite some time what could occasion this phenomenon, when he suddenly realized that it was a regards from the big Hans Christian (Ørsted), which the little Hans Christian (Andersen) wished to convey as a note of thanks from heaven because I, by constructing the Telegraph [Company], had brought [Ørsted's] discovery out to the whole world. The toast was proposed to me in the most flattering and appreciative manner, and then I was conquered.[7]

From this account, it becomes unclear which of the two, Andersen or Tietgen, was the more vain. In any event, after this particular encounter, Tietgen and Andersen had a solid relationship, with the former preoccupied in particular with supporting the latter's art.

Tietgen's company was not the only enterprise involved in constructing the world's longest telegraph line—from Europe through Russia and Siberia to Vladivostok, with later extensions to China and Nagasaki in Japan—but the Great Northern Telegraph Company was the central player in the gigantic undertaking, which forged important bonds between Denmark and Russia. In his memoirs, Tietgen describes how his company managed to win this prize contract from the Russian government: "The Grand Duchess Dagmar was also interested in us, and we most likely owe it to her that the concession was given to the Danish."[8] This is presumably an understatement. Grand Duchess Mariia Fedorovna undoubtedly played a key role as a "lobbyist" for her home country's then-largest company and was crucial in enabling it to secure a deal for this enormous (and enormously profitable) project. Of particular interest in this context is that this great Danish-Russian telegraph joint venture, and the further efforts of Princess Dagmar herself, would also impact the transmission of Andersen's fairy tales into Russia in a profound way.

Princess Dagmar Becomes Mariia Fedorovna

Throughout his life, Hans Christian Andersen was captivated by the Danish royal family and its members. It was perhaps Princess Dagmar—

---

7 Ibid.
8 Ibid., 88.

full name: Maria Sophie Frederikke Dagmar, the fourth child of King Christian IX (who reigned 1863-1906) and his wife Queen Louise—who held a special place in the poet's heart. Andersen met her several times and read his fairy tales to her along with other members of the royal family. In Andersen's eyes, it may be supposed, what was most salient about Dagmar was that here was a pretty young princess who (gratifyingly to him) enjoyed and even praised his tales. In the summer of 1864, when she was only seventeen, Grand Duke Nikolai Aleksandrovich, the Russian Empire's heir apparent, who at that time together with the rest of the tsar's family was visiting Denmark, proposed to her at Bernstorff castle (north of Copenhagen). The engagement having been settled, the tsarevich departed for an already-planned journey to southern Europe, while Dagmar began preparing herself for her coming life in the Russian royal family by studying the Russian language, culture, history, and religion under the tutelage of the Russian priest Ioann Ianyshev.[9] When the tsarevich died of tuberculosis in Nice in early 1865, the young couple's fathers, Alexander II and Christian IX, decided to arrange the engagement of Dagmar and Nikolai's younger brother, the new heir apparent Aleksandr Aleksandrovich.[10]

The royal connection between imperial Russia and the smaller kingdom of Denmark was naturally also an important brick in the edifice of European power politics. Denmark had just suffered defeat in a costly conflict with Prussia and Austria (the so-called Second Schleswig War), losing about one third of its territory when the duchies of Holstein, Schleswig, and Saxe-Lauenburg were annexed to Prussia. For his part, the Russian emperor may not have been particularly concerned with these duchies per se, but he was certainly keen to prevent the emboldened Prussia from controlling the waters around Denmark, and to see that country remain a sovereign state. Some prominent Danes hoped that one day, perhaps with the aid of this powerful Russian ally, Denmark might regain its lost territories. It is thus difficult, in considering the arrangement of this marriage, to disentangle the political from the amatory.

In any case, on 22 September 1866, Princess Dagmar sailed from Denmark aboard the royal ship Slesvig, and on 9 November, she was

---

9   A professor of theology, Ianyshev would from 1877 on serve as confessor to the Russian royal couple Alexander III and Dagmar / Mariia Fedorovna, and as religious instructor to their children; see Ulstrup, "Kejserinde Dagmar/Marija Fjodorovna," 204. A recent Russian source on the empress's life is a 2009 entry in the *Lives of Remarkable People* (*Zhizn' zamechatel'nykh liudei*) series: Kudrina, *Mariia Fedorovna*.
10 See ibid., 215f.

married in St. Petersburg's Winter Palace to Aleksandr Aleksandrovich. Upon his father Alexander II's assassination by members of the People's Will (Narodnaia volia) organization in 1881, the tsarevich ascended to the throne and would rule as Emperor Alexander III until his death in 1894. Leaving aside, however, further discussion of the troubled history of the Romanov family in the twentieth century, let us go back in time to focus on the close relations between Hans Christian Andersen and Dagmar/Mariia Fedorovna.

In his autobiography, which he continued until 1869, Andersen writes in a tone of great affection about a wonderful day spent in the company of the Danish royal family in November 1866 at Fredensborg Castle outside Copenhagen in the northern part of Zealand:

> The pleasantest picture which my memory holds of this time is a short and charming visit at Fredensborg. The King was so gracious as to receive me. Two apartments in the castle were given me, and I found, as always, the most cordial, if I dare use the expression, most friendly reception. The King's family wished to hear me read my last written stories. I have seen all the King's children grow up, and always from their childhood they have given me the hands of friends. To know this family is to be drawn to them.... All the King's children have heard me read my Wonder Stories—the Crown Prince Frederick and his brother, now King of Greece, the princesses Alexandra and Dagmar. Now there sat here the two youngest children, Princess Thyra and little Valdemar, who had this evening got a promise that he should stay up half an hour longer so that he could hear a part of the reading.[11]

In the latter half of his life, Andersen was anchored in his love for the royal family, and this love was mutual. As mentioned, it was on 22 September 1866 that Dagmar left Copenhagen; in a diary entry from the previous day, Andersen notes that his farewell poem to Dagmar has been received by the newspaper *Dagbladet*, and on the day of her departure, he writes:

> Headache and didn't feel well. Changing weather with sunshine and rain. Went to the city, and for the first time I wore my Knight's Order [the *Ridderkorset*, a royal order conferred on Andersen in 1847], to say goodbye to Dagmar at the wharf. I met many acquaintances. Duchess Friis came and offered me her hand. It was raining, but all of a sudden the sun broke through

---

11 Andersen, *The Story of My Life*, 513.

when the royals arrived. When Dagmar passed, she stopped and shook my hand. I was tearful.[12]

Andersen used this dairy entry to dramatize his depiction of the scene in his autobiography:

> As she left, I stood in the crowd of men on the wharf where she, with her royal parents, went on board. She saw me, stepped up to me and shook my hand warmly. Tears started from my eyes: they were in my heart for our young princess. Everything promises for her happiness; an excellent family like that she left, is that she has entered. A fortunate pair are she and her noble husband.[13]

In his Danish autobiography, Andersen also quotes his farewell poem to Dagmar, which was published in the aforementioned Danish newspaper (omitted from Horace E. Scudder's edition):

> Goodbye, Princess Dagmar! You are on your way to Glory and Esteem;
> An emperor's crown grows from your bridal wreath;
> May God shed the light of sunshine on you and your new home;
> Then shall the tears, which separation now calls forth, turn to pearls.[14]

There can be no doubt that Andersen cared deeply for the young princess. He was also evidently moved by the emotional state of the people present at Dagmar's departure bidding her adieu and good luck on her journey to the mighty tsarist empire.

Dagmar/Mariia Fedorovna and Andersen met again in 1867, the year King Christian IX and Queen Louise celebrated their silver wedding anniversary. On 26 May of the same year, Andersen was conferred the rank of councilor, which meant that the Danish court would invite him to occasional celebrations and dinners. Andersen narrates his visit to the royal family to thank the king for the appointment thus:

> The royal family was at Fredensborg. Princess Dagmar, now Grand Princess of Russia, was here on a visit to her royal parents. I went out there; it was not an audience day, but I was nevertheless received, and that with great warmth and kindness. The King asked me to stay to dinner, where I met

---

12 Andersen, *H. C. Andersens Dagbøger 1825-1875*, 7: 190.
13 Andersen, *The Story of My Life*, 542.
14 Andersen, *Andersen. H. C. Andersens samlede værker 1-18*, 18: 321.

and talked with the amiable, noble Princess Dagmar. She told me that she had read a Russian edition of my stories, which she knew so well before in Danish, and so I had spent another delightful day with the King's family.[15]

Andersen was evidently proud to discover from Dagmar that she was learning Russian by way of reading and studying his fairy tales in Russian translations. As a girl, she had heard and learned the stories by heart in Danish and thereby improved her understanding of the art of narrative. Later, as empress dowager, Dagmar's life turned turbulent: during the Russian Revolution, she managed to flee, first to Kiev, then to Crimea, from where she was transported out of Russia on an English warship. In the infamous events at the Ipatiev House in Ekaterinburg (summer 1918), her closest family members were murdered, which she long refused to believe. After a brief stay in England, she returned to Denmark where she remained at Hvidøre castle until her death in 1928. However, it is important to realize how much she and her presence in Russia had meant. She had worked tirelessly to forge stronger connections between Denmark and Russia, and it pleased Andersen to convey to his friend Louise Melchior in 1872 a Russian official's statement that Dagmar was "extremely well-liked in Russia."[16]

In the context of the subject of this book, one of Dagmar's most remarkable achievements was the support she offered for the soon-to-be canonical Russian translations of Andersen's works by Peter and Anna Hansen. In his contribution to this anthology, Mads Sohl Jessen discusses the importance of Peter Hansen's employment (beginning in 1871) with the Great Northern Telegraph Company in Russia; had Hansen not opted to find work abroad, his and his future wife's remarkable translation of 1894-95 would never have been undertaken. In his article, Jessen also highlights Kenneth H. Ober's excellent (but unpublished) study on Hansen, which, indeed, emphasizes the crucial role played by Mariia Fedorovna in the project of that famous husband-and-wife translation of Andersen.

Assessing Dagmar's overall influence on the Hansens' literary venture, Ober states that she was of "great assistance to Hansen in his activity as translator by granting him financial aid and by insulating him to a great extent from the more senseless whims of the tsarist censors."[17] In two letters of particular note to the Danish philologist Karl Verner,

---

15 Andersen, *The Story of My Life*, 549-50.
16 http://andersen.sdu.dk/brevbase/brev.html?bid=14682
17 Ober, "Peter Emanuel Hansen," 11.

Hansen emphasizes just how important Dagmar's intercession was to his enterprise. In the first, dated 8 April 1893, Hansen complains that he has been unable to obtain any financial assistance from Denmark for his Andersen translation, adding, however, that he has written a "petition to the Empress, who from the very beginning has showed my endeavor the greatest recognition."[18] Then, in a letter of 15 October 1893, he remarks to Verner that his petition has been successful: "Immediately after the letter had been submitted to her Majesty the Empress, I was offered 1000 Rubles in support of the edition of Andersen."[19] In another letter, to the prominent Danish scholar Vilhelm Thomsen[20] on 19 March 1894, Hansen stresses that this grant has made it possible for him "to begin the edition of Andersen's selected writings."[21] Anna and Peter Hansen, moreover, acknowledged the empress's role when they decided to dedicate the translation to her (the dedication can be found in volume four). In this curious way, the Danish protagonists of this study are all connected. Had it not been for Tietgen's ambitious transnational telegraph empire, Peter Emanuel Hansen would never have found employment in Russia, and were it not for Dagmar's marriage, he would most likely never have been able to begin his translation.

To conclude this study, let us discuss a letter from Dagmar/Mariia Fedorovna that has never been published or discussed in scholarship (not even by Ober). This is her only surviving letter to Andersen. At Christmastime 1874, she wrote Andersen, who was ill at the time, the following words of consolation:

> From my earliest childhood, one of my greatest pleasures has been to read your lovely fairy tales. As each year goes by, I have learned to understand them even better and have also come to feel an ever-growing admiration for the spirit who created them. Often I have felt a desire and need to thank you for all the joyful and happy hours that you have thus given me. Allow me now during this Christmas celebration to give voice, in these lines, to my thoughts. With sincere sorrow and compassion, I have heard that you have fallen ill, and now it is my profound joy to hear that you are feeling better.

---

18 Cited ibid., 53. The original letter is housed in the collection of the Danish Royal Library.
19 Ibid., 54.
20 At the time, the linguist and historian of languages Vilhelm Thomsen was particularly well known in European scholarship for having deciphered the so-called Orkhon inscriptions (in Old Turkic) in 1893. He had also made a noteworthy contribution to Slavic-Scandinavian studies with his English-language monograph *The Relations Between Ancient Russia and Scandinavia, and the Origin of the Russian State* (1877), a key text in debates around the "Norman theory" of Russian statehood.
21 Ober, "Peter Emanuel Hansen," 54.

God willing, everything will move in the right direction and you will be fully recovered, and you will have many more years to live, happily for you, and joyously for all who hold you in the highest esteem and admiration. That the Christmas celebration will bring you comfort despite your remaining ill in bed, I am assured. Nevertheless, I offer you my deepest-felt thanks for all the beauty, profoundness, and truthfulness that you have been able to fit into brief fairy tales, not least in your last Christmas present to us.

  Yours gratefully,
  Dagmar[22]

This letter, which is undated and not written in Dagmar's handwriting, was most likely dictated to someone capable of writing Danish. In any event, we can be sure that Andersen did receive it in December 1874, insofar as, early in the new year, which would be Andersen's last, he presented an edition of his illustrated fairy tales from 1873 to the Danish crown prince, who was soon to travel to Russia and visit Dagmar. In his dedication, Andersen alludes to her letter and her mention of her childhood reading: "Your royal Highness Grand Duchess Mariia Feodorovna. Please receive, most graciously, these pieces of poetry from your childhood home, which are given you in faithful gratitude and the deepest reverence."[23] While Andersen did not mention her letter in his diary, we may be certain that it indeed brought him consolation.

Conclusion

Thus were Hans Christian Andersen's writings and fairy tales nurtured and cared for in Russia by a princess who admired their author, and whose marriage to the heir apparent to the Russian throne was part of grand European power politics. Princess Dagmar became Empress Mariia Fedorovna but never forgot Denmark or Hans Christian Andersen and his fairy tales. Quite the contrary: she became a crucial agent in the dissemination of Andersen's writings in Russia, not least with her financial and moral support of the Hansens' translation, which ensured that the Russian reception of Andersen after 1894-95 would be built on an excellent foundation. As mentioned, Andersen refrained from making political statements in his later life, but he was extremely adept at forging connections between himself, his writings, and influential per-

---

22 The letter is housed at the Danish Royal Library (NKS 2315, 4º). My thanks to Mads Sohl Jessen for alerting me to its existence and Ole Westermann for transcribing it for me.
23 The dedication may be examined online: http://andersen.sdu.dk/brevbase/brev.html?bid=22830.

sons of his time. This was a considerable advantage to his art, and also meant a great deal for the reputation of Denmark abroad. There can be no doubt that Carl Frederik Tietgen and the Great Northern Telegraph Company's enterprise in Russia benefitted greatly from the empress's influence on her husband and his government. That such close ties should connect a Danish princess who became a Russian tsarina, Hans Christian Andersen as a biographical person and a writer of fairy tales, and the founder and an employee of the Danish company that would build the telegraph line across that vast empire, is something wondrous. It was indeed a time of fairy tales.

Works Cited

Andersen, Hans Christian. *Andersen. H. C. Andersens samlede værker 1-18*. Copenhagen: Gyldendal, 2005.

—. *H. C. Andersens Dagbøger 1825-1875*. Edited by Kåre Olsen and H. Topsøe-Jensen. Copenhagen: Society of Danish Language and Literature, 1971-76.

—. *A Poet's Bazaar: A Journey to Greece, Turkey & Up the Danube*. Translated by Grace Thornton. New York: Michael Kesend Publishing, 1988.

—. *The Story of My Life*. Translated by Mary Howitt. Edited and additional authorial material translated by Horace E. Scudder. Boston: Houghton, Mifflin, and Co., 1871.

Frandsen, Johs. Nørregaard. "The Insoluble Conflict and Transformation: The Modern Aspect of Hans Christian Andersen's "Galoshes of Fortune.'" *Forum for World Literature Studies* 4, no. 1 (2012): 78-86.

Kudrina, Iu. N. *Mariia Fedorovna*. Moscow: Molodaia gvardiia, 2009.

Lange, Ole. *Finansmænd, stråmænd og mandariner. C.F. Tietgen, Privatbanken og Store Nordiske. Etablering 1868-76*. Copenhagen: Gyldendal, 1978.

—. *Partnere og rivaler. C.F. Tietgen, Eastern Extension og Store Nordiske. Ekspansion i Kina 1880-86*. Copenhagen: Gyldendal, 1978.

Müller, Simone M. *Wiring the World. The Social and Cultural Creation of Global Telegraph Networks*. New York: Columbia University Press, 2016.

Ober, Kenneth H. "Peter Emanuel Hansen and the Popularization of Scandinavian Literature in Russia, 1888-1917." PhD Dissertation, University of Illinois, 1974.

Tietgen, C. F. *Erindringer og Optegnelser*. Published by O. C. Molbech. Copenhagen: Gyldendal 1904.

Ulstrup, Preben. "Kejserinde Dagmar/Marija Fjodorovna." In *Danmark og zarernes Rusland 1600-1900 / Danija i Rossijskaja imperija 1600-1900*, edited by Thomas Lyngby, 197-269. Hillerød: Det Nationalhistoriske Museum, Frederiksborg Slot, 2013.

Part II

Andersen in Russia's Cultural Contexts

A)
Andersen's Place in Prerevolutionary Russian Literature and Criticism

Hans Christian Andersen as a Children's Writer, as Reflected in Russian Criticism from the Latter Half of the Nineteenth Century to 1917

Inna Sergienko

In Russian culture, Hans Christian Andersen enjoys the status of a universally recognized classic children's author. His books are essential reading for children of virtually every sociocultural stratum, which, however, does not keep modern readers from also attributing to him the tales of Charles Perrault, the brothers Grimm, E. T. A. Hoffmann, Wilhelm Hauff, and Selma Lagerlöf, and vice versa. Andersen could be said to stand, in the mass consciousness, as a universal figure, as *the* Storyteller, the author of virtually every European literary fairy tale, while Charles Perrault or the brothers Grimm, whose tales are also extremely popular in Russia, do not enjoy such a reputation. The names of Perrault and the brothers Grimm to some extent represent the French and German folkloric and literary tale, whereas Andersen, despite the vivid national flavor of his fairy tales, is perceived by the general Russian reader as the author of the Western European fairy tale overall—which undoubtedly attests to a certain mythologization of his image.

Having appeared in Russia in the 1850s,[1] by the late nineteenth century Andersen's tales had come to be perceived (thanks in large part to the translations of Peter and Anna Hansen) as children's classics, and have since been regularly reprinted. The publication of the tales did not cease even amid the devastation wrought by the revolution and civil war (1917-22), nor during the economic crisis of the 1990s—that is, periods when the publishing of children's books in Russia was reduced to a minimum. As corroboration of this phenomenon, we might recall the widely known edition of Andersen's tales that was published in 1943 in Leningrad during the Nazis' horrific siege of that city (fig. 1).

The first Russian critical responses to Andersen's writings appeared in the 1840s; today, critical and scholarly articles on Andersen and his

---

[1] First to become part of the typical reading of children and adults were such French-language editions as *Contes d'Andersen, traduits du danois par D. Soldi*. Paris: Hachette, 1856.

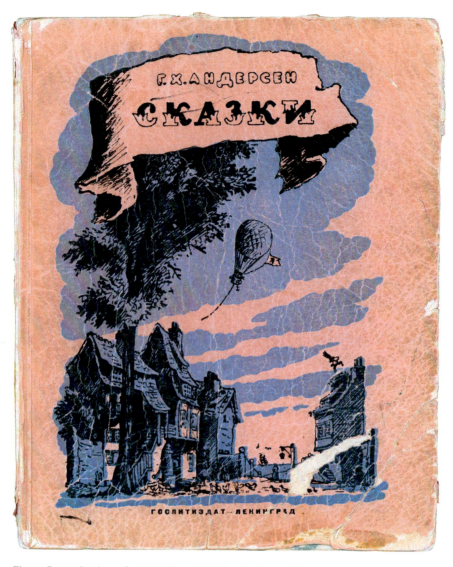

Fig. 1. Cover. Leningrad, 1943. Hans Christian Andersen Museum.

oeuvre number in the hundreds. An exhaustive bibliography of Russian studies of the author has not yet been compiled, but certain stages in Andersen's critical reception in Russia have already been analyzed in detail by Danish and Russian researchers and covered in their scholarly publications.[2]

---

2   Dane, "H. C. Andersen-receptionen i Rusland og Sovjetunionen"; Braude, "Andersen v russ-koi i sovetskoi kritike"; Pereslegina, *Khans-Kristian Andersen: bibliograficheskii ukazatel'*; Braude, "Khans-Kristian Andersen v Rossii"; Orlova, *Kh.-K. Andersen v russkoi literature kontsa XIX–nachala XX veka*.

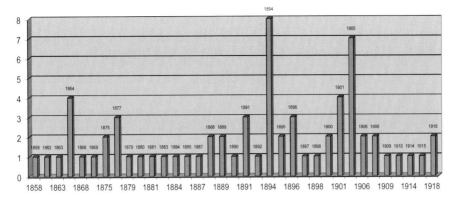

Fig. 2. Critical pieces on Andersen published in the Russian press, 1845-1918. Inna Sergienko.

This study examines articles on Andersen published in the latter half of the nineteenth century and the early years of the twentieth (often referred to in the Russian tradition as the "prerevolutionary period"). The primary focus will be on the process by which Andersen gained the status of a classic writer of children's literature in the eyes of nineteenth- and early twentieth-century Russian critics. It should be noted that the question of dividing Andersen's works into "children's" and "adult" (given the conventionality of these categories) is not entirely obvious. Neither is it always possible to clearly state whether a given critic discusses Andersen's work as something addressed to the universal reader, or exclusively to children. In this regard, the only works not considered in this study are those few that deal exclusively with Andersen's writings for adults.[3]

This study is based on the corpus of critical articles from the period of 1845-1918 that deal with the Andersen works now considered essential children's reading, and that describe Andersen himself as a children's writer. Analyzed here are such forms of critical literature, included in various bibliographic indexes and lists on children's literature, as reviews, literary-critical and pedagogical articles, Andersen biographies (including fictionalized ones), and instructional texts (so-called *razbory* or analyses). Not considered, except in a few isolated cases, were the prefaces to various editions of Andersen's works for children, although these too are of great interest.

The graph in figure 2 shows the trend in the publications of works on Andersen's writings in the prerevolutionary period, with interest peaking

---

3   For example: Anon., "Retsenziia na: *Improvizator ili Molodost' i mechty ital'ianskogo poeta.* SPb, 1844," *Finskii vestnik* 2, otd. 5 (1845): 17; Berg, "Neskol'ko slov o novoi datskoi poezii."

in 1894 (in connection with the publication that year of the four-volume collected works translated by the Hansens) and in 1905 (in connection with the centenary of the author's birth). This interest then subsides, to reemerge with new vigor in the Soviet and post-Soviet periods.

Andersen's books first appeared in Russia in the years 1840-50, a period that saw the emergence of the revolutionary-democratic movement's first wave. Most of this movement's ideologists—Vissarion Belinsky (1811-48), Aleksandr Herzen (1812-70), Nikolai Chernyshevsky (1828-89), Aleksandr Dobroliubov (1836-61), and others—were active literary critics, setting in this capacity a certain tone. The representatives of the revolutionary-democratic trend believed that the primary goal of literature and art in general was to reflect the "truth of life." They welcomed the active expression of a civic position and encouraged authors to focus on depicting modern society's social evils, including class inequality, as the main source of social and spiritual troubles. Among artistic methods, they hailed realism, were sympathetic to naturalism, and looked upon romanticism as hopelessly outdated. On the whole, their views were conditioned by the same ideas and sentiments permeating European literature of this period, in which the social novels of Stendhal, Balzac, Dickens, Flaubert, and others had come to the fore.

It was in this period that Russian critics began to take an interest in children's literature, for the first time treating it as a topic for analysis and reflection. Representatives of the revolutionary-democratic trend demanded, first and foremost, that children's literature attend to social problems and depict reality realistically; they vociferously condemned "empty fantasies," and had no particular fondness for the genre of fairy tales. However, even against this background, Andersen's works earned, along with criticism, also appreciation.

The first publication to address the issue of whether Andersen's works should be recommended for children's reading is thought to be a review by Vissarion Belinsky, the well-known literary critic who, among other things, helped to establish children's literary criticism in Russia. In 1845, he published a review of Andersen's novel *The Improvisatore* (1835), in which he remarked on the protagonist's childishness and the farfetchedness of the plot, which relegate the novel, according to Belinsky, to the rubric of "adolescent reading." "However," writes Belinsky, "this innocent romance may be read with pleasure and benefit by young girls and boys in their free time outside class," perspicaciously adding that "this novel may not, perhaps, be Andersen's finest work."[4]

---

4   Belinskii, "Retsenziia na: *Improvizator ili Molodost' i mechty ital'ianskogo poeta*. SPb, 1844," 4.

In 1857, one of the first works on Andersen's biography appeared, presaging the later veritable torrent of publications on this subject. (Andersen biographies, both documentary and fictionalized, would constitute a significant part of Russian Anderseniana.) The book *The Tales of Andersen* (*Povesti Andersena*) included, as an afterword, an essay ("Something about Andersen") by the book's translator, Iuliia-Sharlotta von Ikskiul (?–1863), who indicated that in writing it, she had relied on material found in the autobiographical *The Fairy Tale of My Life without Poetry*, published in German in 1847. The essay recounts the main episodes of *The Fairy Tale of My Life*, but Ikskiul also offers her own treatment of the writer's personality, an interpretation that would subsequently prove integral to the "Andersen myth" in Russia.

One of Ikskiul's starting points is a metaphor Andersen uses repeatedly in *The Fairy Tale of My Life*, that of the author as a "wild bird that has flown into an environment alien to it" (in Andersen's narrative of his confirmation), a "frightened forest bird, languishing in a cage" (describing his time at the grammar school in Slagelse), etc. Iuliia Ikskiul thus became one of the first in the Russian critical tradition to portray Andersen as a "child of nature," emphasizing the opposition between his natural "simplicity and childlike tenderness" and, on the other hand, genteel society: "The most famous poets of Denmark ... extended him a brotherly hand, and the beautiful ladies bestowed smiles of favor on this innocent young man who guilelessly sang tender elegies and idylls full of freshness."[5] Along with the image of the poet who was "not of this world," Iuliia Ikskiul's essay also includes the image, which would become "textbook" in Russian treatments of the author, of Andersen the fighter: "Born of low rank, Andersen was animated from quite a young age by a premonition of his higher calling and fought courageously, inexorably, tirelessly against the poverty oppressing him, against the obstacles blocking his path.... [H]e made for himself a name that shall always be celebrated in the history of ingenious people and the misfortunes that befall them."[6]

It is characteristic that, despite the didactic nature of her essay, the translator analyzes Andersen's "adult" works—the novels *The Improvisatore*, *O. T.*, *Only a Fiddler*, the play *The Mulatto*, poems, etc.—and makes no mention of the fairy tales. The composition of the collection, which included "The Steadfast Tin Soldier" (later consistently categorized by publishers, critics, and educators as a tale for children), as well as more

---

5   Ikskiul', "Nechto ob Andersene," 113.
6   Ibid., 117.

adult-oriented works like "The Darning Needle," "The Buckwheat," "The Fir Tree," "The Naughty Boy," "The Story of a Mother," and "Scenes from Children's Life" (fragments from the series "A Picture-Book without Pictures"), may likewise attest that the readerly address of Andersen's prose was not yet fully clear.

One of the first works to deal specifically with Andersen's tales for children was an article by the critic Aleksandr Dobroliubov published in 1858.[7] Reviewing a collection of Andersen's fairy tales published in French, Dobroliubov gives a positive evaluation of his talent as a children's writer. Being one of the most radical representatives of the revolutionary-democratic movement, the critic warmly welcomes the social relevance and satirical thrust of Andersen's tales. In particular, he singles out "The Emperor's New Clothes," "The Little Match Girl," "The Princess on the Pea," and "The Traveling Companion." Somewhat unusual for the discourse of revolutionary-democratic commentary here is that Dobroliubov approves of the inclusion of elements of the fantastic in children's reading. Commenting on the tales "The Steadfast Tin Soldier," "Little Ida's Flowers," and "The Flax" Dobroliubov is the first critic to draw attention to one of Andersen's primary techniques: "Realistic representations take on, in a highly poetic way, a fantastic character.... Andersen animates ordinary inanimate objects and makes them act," he writes.[8] This stylistic feature would go on to be remarked on by most critics (to the present day), who refer to it as the "Andersen tradition."

From this point on, Russian criticism treated Andersen primarily as a children's writer. At the same time, the border between "Andersen for children" and "Andersen for adults" was not easy to draw, insofar as the readerly address of the works included in the collections *Fairy Tales Told to Children* (1835-42) and *New Fairy Tales* (1844-48) was and remains controversial in and of itself, as critics everywhere have discussed heatedly and at length.

In the late 1860s, Andersen's tales appeared in Russia in the Russian language, and the number of editions and translations continued to increase. Responding to this phenomenon were literary critics (in pieces addressed to adult readers) as well as pedagogical critics, who addressed their statements on Andersen to teachers, parents, and other persons concerned with the question of children's reading. As Gaiane Orlova has observed in her research,[9] it was generally in the former,

---

7   Dobroliubov, "Frantsuzskie knigi. Retsenziia na: *Contes d'Andersen traduits du danois par Soldi.* Paris, 1856," 370.
8   Ibid., 370.
9   Orlova, *Kh.-K. Andersen v russkoi literature kontsa XIX–nachala XX veka.*

the literary as opposed to pedagogical criticism, that Andersen's tales were spoken of approvingly as reading matter for children. This was in part because educators in this period were generally oriented toward realism, usefulness (*pol'za*), and educational significance as the main criteria of children's literature. They harbored a considerable antipathy for the fairy tale genre, and for the whole aesthetic of the fantastic (and also romantic) in general.

The author of the first Russian bibliography of children's literature (*Our Children's Literature* [*Nasha detskaia literatura*], 1862), the well-known educator Feliks Toll (1823-67), says of Andersen's tales: "Andersen's stories are not without great and vivid merit, but they aim solely to moralize, and they thus serve to blunt the child's memory and deprive him of precious minutes of exercise, and distract him from more useful reading."[10] By "useful reading," Toll means, primarily, popular science literature. We might note that, given Feliks Toll's status as one of the staunchest adherents of revolutionary-democratic ideals (for which he even spent some time in penal servitude), his evaluation of Andersen's fairy tales appears quite natural and, on the whole, is in keeping with typical revolutionary-democratic views on children's literature.

Such commentators' consistent antipathy toward the genre of magic tale led, at times, to curious statements. Thus, for instance, the educator Evgenii Kemnits (1832-71), a colleague and fellow-thinker of Feliks Toll, penned one of the most devastating reviews of Andersen's tales ever to appear in the whole Russian critical Anderseniana—published, characteristically, in the journal *Teacher* (*Uchitel'*) in 1864.

Kemnits fiercely opposes the fairy tale genre on principle: "[I]n adults, the inclination toward the fantastic is a sign of an abnormal state of mind!"[11] He sees the Russian people's penchant for fairy tales and fables as causative of the "people's moral apathy" and considers it dangerous to give fairy tales to Russians as reading material. The critic is similarly merciless to the tales of Andersen: "Without denying Andersen's wit and talent, we find that his works are too redolent of the ravings of a frustrated imagination ('The Bell,' 'The Rose Elf,' 'The Story of a Mother,' 'The Shepherdess and the Chimney-Sweep,' etc.).... 'The Galoshes of Fortune' and 'The Shadow'—these 'stories' have nothing to offer but bad puns."[12]

As for the idea of including Andersen's fairy tales in children's reading, Kemnits writes:

---

10 Toll', *Nasha detskaia literatura*, 177.
11 Kemnits, "Retsenziia na: *Polnoe sobranie skazok Andersena v perevode M. V. Trubnikovoi i N. V. Stasovoi.* SPb, 1863," 537.
12 Ibid., 539.

> With the exception of two or three, which can be selected with some difficulty, the tales must not be given to children! Andersen has not written his fairy tales for children at all! Some of them are too sentimental, others are mystical, and still others are too affected and elaborate. Some of the tales contain indecent hints that are in no wise compatible with childhood ("The Naughty Boy"), and neither children nor adults would want to read such rubbish as "The Flying Trunk"![13]

Kemnits especially disapproves of Andersen's tales based on folkloric plots: "'The Tinder Box' and 'The Swineherd'—how long can we keep having plots like this, in which some honest pauper, some simpleton, after certain tribulations, invariably marries a princess?"[14] Consciously or otherwise, the critic here is distorting the plot of "The Swineherd," insofar as the tale's main character could hardly be called a "pauper" or "simpleton," and, as the reader might well recall, he does not marry the princess at all.

(We might note that throughout the prerevolutionary period, Russian educators considered "The Tinder Box" and "Little Claus and Big Claus" to be Andersen's crudest and most indecent tales. These were published in separate editions in comparatively minimal quantities.)

At the same time, critics oriented toward adult readers appreciated Andersen's works and recommended them for children: "Anyone wishing to give fairy tales to children could do no better than the books of Grimm and Andersen";[15] "Fantastic imagery full of poetry; a childlike, naive tone; such an inimitably charming presentation, such originality and ease of form.... Even as they are children's tales, they are entertaining for adults as well; Andersen's fantasy is strong in its content!"[16]

However, pedagogical criticism in the late 1860s remained quite conservative and concomitantly skeptical as to the Danish storyteller's edificatory worth: "In terms of educational value, most of Andersen's tales can be dismissed," writes the author of an anonymous review published in the journal *People's School* (*Narodnaia shkola*) in 1869. "Many of them arouse interest only by the unexpectedness and extreme unnaturalness of their events, like folktales: 'Little Claus and Big Claus,' 'The Tinder

---

13 Ibid., 540.
14 Ibid., 539.
15 Anon., "Retsenziia na: *Polnoe sobranie skazok v perevode M. V. Trubnikovoi i N. V. Stasovoi.* SPb, 1863," *Russkoe slovo*, no. 11-12 (1863): 43.
16 Anon., "Retsenziia na: *Polnoe sobranie skazok v perevode M. V. Trubnikovoi i N. V. Stasovoi.* SPb, 1863," *Sovremennik* 9, no. 1 (1864): 96, 100.

Box,' 'The Traveling Companion,' 'The Flying Trunk,' 'Little Ida's Flowers,' 'The Darning Needle,' 'Little Tuck,' 'The Old House'... 'The Princess on the Pea' is an utterly vacuous tale. To put such books in the hands of children would be perverse!"[17]

On the other hand, the critic remarks that some of Andersen's stories would serve as "an excellent developmental tool," should children read them under the guidance of their parents. The tales "The Fir Tree," "Thumbelina," "The Daisy," "Flax," "The Little Mermaid," "The Ugly Duckling," and "The Snow Queen," says the anonymous critic, are permeated with an "extraordinary warmth of feeling," contain "poetic and comforting descriptions of nature," and may be included in children's reading material, so long as parents make an effort to forestall "the indiscriminate excitation of fantasy" in their children.[18]

Thus, in the 1850s–60s, publications on Andersen represented (with a single exception)[19] reviews of the translations of Andersen's books published during this time: *The Tales of Andersen* as translated by Iuliia Ikskiul; *The Complete Fairy Tales*, translated by Mariia Trubnikova and Nadezhda Stasova;[20] and *The Complete Fairy Tales*, translated by Petr Veinberg and Marko Vovchok.[21] It is important to emphasize that all these translations were made not from the original Danish but from German translations. Evaluating Andersen as a children's writer, critics vacillate between the aesthetic and the pedagogical mode: "While we share the views ... regarding the artistic value of Andersen's fairy tales, as recognized [throughout Europe], we cannot recognize all the tales as being educationally effective," writes the anonymous *People's School* critic in 1869.[22] One and the same translation receives a positive evaluation, if the critic writes for a journal covering "literature for adults"–"The choice of translators is a successful one.... The Russian public will for the first time get to know the works of a remarkable, one-of-a-kind storyteller, whose fairy tales are fresh and poetic"[23]–and negative, when it comes to children's reading; in the latter case, it is said that the translators would have been better advised "to separate

---

17 Anon., "Retsenziia na: *Polnoe sobranie skazok G. Kh. Andersena v perevode Petra Veinberga so 120 kartinkami i biograficheskim ocherkom*," *Narodnaia shkola*, no. 2 (1869): 34.
18 Ibid., 35.
19 Anon., "Sutki v Kopengagene," *Biblioteka dlia chteniia*, no. 6 (1864).
20 Andersen, *Polnoe sobranie skazok v perevode M. V. Trubnikovoi i N. V. Stasovoi*.
21 Andersen, *Polnoe sobranie skazok v 3-kh tomakh. V perevode P. Veinberga, Marko Vovchka, S. Maikovoi*.
22 Anon., "Retsenziia na: *Polnoe sobranie skazok G. Kh. Andersena v perevode Petra Veinberga so 120 kartinkami i biograficheskim ocherkom*," *Narodnaia shkola*, no. 2 (1869): 34.
23 Anon., "Retsenziia na: *Polnoe sobranie skazok v perevode M. V. Trubnikovoi i N. V. Stasovoi*. SPb, 1863," *Sovremennik* 9, no. 1 (1864): 100.

the stories that are suitable for children from those that are not; and to remove, from those that are suitable, anything that does not meet the requirements of healthy pedagogy."[24] As we can see, Andersen is still far from gaining the status of classic and luminary of children's literature, but in the next two decades this road will have been traversed.

The 1870s saw an increase, albeit not a significant one, in critical interest in Andersen's work. In part this critical reticence was due to the fact that there were no significant new translations. *The Last Tales of Andersen* (*Poslednie skazki Andersena*) translated by the children's writer Ekaterina Sysoeva, came out in 1876; but despite the fact that the collection came with an essay on the history of the writing of tales, and reminiscences by Andersen's friends on his last days, this edition received only a few reviews. And even upon the writer's seventieth jubilee and death in 1875, the press response was surprisingly meager. The magazine *Field* (*Niva*)[25] ran a lead article (accompanied by a striking page-one portrait of the anniversary celebrant), which spoke mainly of the "Danish poet's" warm love for children; and one of the literary journals published a biographical sketch[26]—but this is the sum total of the 1875 publications it has been possible to find.

Critics did, however, continue to discuss whether Andersen's books should be included in children's reading material: "[I]t is unclear how Andersen's tales came to be considered reading material for children. The ideas behind many of his older tales are either inaccessible to children, or are so vaguely expressed, for a child's comprehension, that the

---

24 Anon., "Retsenziia na: *Novye skazki Andersena v perevode M. V. Trubnikovoi i N. V. Stasovoi*. SPb, 1868," *Delo*, no. 6 (1868): 37. By "healthy pedagogy," the anonymous critic refers to the new currents in educational ideas and techniques that came to Russia in the mid-nineteenth century and were associated with changes in the historical and cultural situation in Russian society as a whole: the process by which the conservative-protective paradigm from the reign of Nicholas I (1825-55) was being replaced by a more liberal one since the accession of Alexander II (1855-81), which led to a revival of public life. In pedagogy, these tendencies were reflected in a changeover from the system of unquestioning obedience to a greater recognition of the child's independence. Representatives of the democratic trend in pedagogy believed that the child was capable of understanding social problems, and called for the child's leisure to be organized such that this time be spent in an exclusively "useful" manner (*s pol'zoi*). They frowned on the reading of fiction and were skeptical of fairy tales, fantasy, and "reveries," which they saw as incompatible with the primary aim of education—the inculcation of civic-mindedness and morality. Teachers of both the old and new "schools" did not approve of the topic of love in works for children, and would not tolerate any erotic motifs or motifs that struck them as erotic.
25 One of Russia's most popular mass illustrated magazines of the late nineteenth and early twentieth centuries; a weekly, it was considered a magazine for family reading.
26 Anon., "Gans-Khristian Andersen: biografiia i kharakteristika," *Niva*, no. 16 (1875): 1-2; Anon., "Gans-Khristian Andersen," *Vsemirnaia illiustratsiia*, no. 344 (1875): 106-7; no. 345 (1875): 121-22.

only thing children will get out of them is the plot."[27] The "excitation of fantasy," crudeness and impropriety—this is what representatives of pedagogical criticism of the 1860s–70s feared most. Some publications of this period proposed that Andersen's *Tales and Stories* be adapted for children in accordance with these ideas: for example, in 1879 the educator and future censor Nikolai Treskin (1828-94) published an article titled "On Adapting Andersen's Fairy Tales for Children" ("O pererabotke skazok Andersena dlia detskogo chteniia").

Here Treskin states directly: "Andersen's famous fairy tales are not suitable to be read by children without adaptation!" And so he undertakes to explain how this task should be carried out. To begin with, the critic advises that "thirty-four of the forty-seven tales should be discarded," without explaining his choice, although some of the "discarded" tales are accompanied by brief remarks: "The story 'Under the Willow Tree' tells of the bitterness of an unhappy love—not for children, is it?"; "'The Nightcap of the 'Pebersvend'' depicts all the bleakness of bachelorhood—it's no good"; "The moral of 'The Money Pig' is alien to a child";[28] and so on. It is proposed that the thirteen tales selected for adaptation ("She was Good For Nothing," "The Girl Who Trod on the Loaf," "The Ice Maiden," "Psyche," "What the Old Man Does is Always Right," "The Old Oak Tree's Last Dream," "The Old Tombstone," "Five Peas from a Pod," "Something," "The Bottle Neck," "The Bell," "There Is a Difference," and "The Metal Pig") be abridged, and that "all details of love and mention of drunkenness be removed." In this regard, the selection of the story "Psyche" for this purpose seems mysterious, insofar as its entire plot hinges on the unrequited passion of a brilliant sculptor for a proud aristocratic woman, upon whose rejection of him, he seeks oblivion in a binge—even, at one point, in the company of "Bacchantes." But the critic is determined to act decisively: "The whole story needs to be adapted to another plot, so as to remove the amatory foundation on which it is based."[29] The critic proposes doing the same with the story "The Bottle Neck."

Treskin's recommendations were never literally implemented, but the idea of "correcting" Andersen's fairy tales in editions for children was carried out frequently, both in the prerevolutionary and Soviet periods, and this is still done today. Tales have been abridged or amended; and "indecent," ideologically unacceptable, obscure, or "crude" episodes have

---

27 Anon., "Retsenziia na: *Poslednie skazki Andersena v perevode E. Sysoevoi*. SPb, 1876," *Vospitanie i obuchenie*, no. 2 (1877): 73.
28 Treskin, "O pererabotke skazok Andersena dlia detskogo chteniia," 129.
29 Ibid., 130.

been cut. Thus for example, in the translation of O. I. Rogova, which she herself calls a retelling (*pereskaz*), many of the storylines and details of well-known fairy tales are left out: in "The Wild Swans," the episode of Elisa's bathing, during which her stepmother sends toads to torment her, is omitted; the description of Elisa's walk in the graveyard is abridged (in particular, a fragment mentioning the vampires there has been cut), etc.[30] In an anonymous translation of "The Ice Maiden" published in 1918,[31] the sentimental episode about the "cretin," Saperli, "a poor imbecile," is omitted; in the 1924 collection translated by S. G. Zaimovskii,[32] the tale "Little Claus and Big Claus" is run without the description of the death of Little Claus's grandmother and the various tricks played with her corpse; the finale of "The Little Mermaid" is abridged, so that the story concludes with the death of the little mermaid; etc. The most frequent victim of abridgment-minded translators was "The Snow Queen." Most editions omitted the stories told by the flowers (the chapter "The Flower Garden of the Woman Skilled in Magic"), and the psalm that Kai and Gerda sing upon returning home (in the chapter "What Happened in the Snow Queen's Palace and What Came of It").

In the 1880s, certain changes took place in Russian public life that would influence the particular manner in which Andersen's tales were incorporated both in children's reading and in Russian culture generally. This period saw a decline in the revolutionary-democratic movement, and was marked by public disenchantment with political struggle and by spiritual and political reaction. Readers' interests now shifted from politics and social issues to the sphere of private life, psychological experience, contemplation, and even mysticism.[33] Leaving civic activism behind, many among the educated classes turned to literature and theater, and sought support in art. Thus despite the increased censorship and political crackdown, the 1880s constituted a new stage in the flourishing of Russian culture.

It was in this period, for instance, that the first currents of modernism came to Russia, which led to the rehabilitation of the fantasy genre and of the aesthetic of the fantastic in general, and to a new surge of interest

---

30 Andersen, *Izbrannye skazki v pereskaze O. I. Rogovoi*.
31 Andersen, *Skazki. Ledianitsa*.
32 Andersen, *Ognivo*.
33 In 1881, Tsar Alexander II was killed by a member of the People's Will terrorist organization, which led to the onset of political reaction in the country and the curtailing of public rights and initiatives. Society was gripped with the fear of political persecution, bureaucratization intensified, and art was dominated by censorship. The prominent early twentieth-century literary critic Arkadii Gorenfeld described the 1880s thus: "All was quiet, sedate, and genteel in that period of deathly lifelessness" ("O khudozhestvennoi chestnosti," 69).

in folklore. At the same time, the Russian reading public was for the first time swept up in a wave of enthusiasm for Scandinavian literature, due mainly to the plays of Henrik Ibsen. Readers likewise took an interest in the Scandinavian literary fairy tale; now published in Russian, along with books by Andersen, were the tales of Svend Grundtvig, Peter Christen Asbjørnsen, Zachris Topelius, and others.[34] As Nikolai Chekhov, Russia's first historian of children's literature, would say of this period in 1915: "Scandinavian literature, which made a triumphant march through Europe in the late nineteenth century, continues to live and develop. Its sincerity, the peculiar beauty of its images, the depth of its thoughts—all this is reflected in the children's branch of this literature."[35]

As the book market expanded, so did the range of children's books: not only did publishers issue (every year!) collections of Andersen's fairy tales, but also certain of the tales as standalone books, including some that would number among the most beloved children's publications of the twentieth and twenty-first centuries: *The Ugly Duckling*, *Thumbelina*, *The Steadfast Tin Soldier*, and *The Tinder Box*. In 1887, the legendary Moscow publishing house of Ivan Sytin (1851-1934), which specialized in the production of low-cost and colorful mass literature, published the first Russian popular print (*lubok*) editions of Andersen's fairy tales: *The Mermaid Princess* (*Tsarevna-rusalochka*) and *The Twelve Swan Brothers and the Star-Princess* (*Dvenadtsat' brat'ev lebedei i Tsarevna-Zvezda*).

The 1880s also saw a growing interest in the figure of Andersen himself. It was not only his literary legacy, available to an ever-broadening readership, that helped make Andersen a cult writer of this period; it was also the writer's colorful and eccentric personality, his amazing biography. In 1880, the journal *Russian Speech* (*Russkaia rech'*) published an extensive essay by the writer Max Nordau (1849-1923) titled "A Visit to Andersen," in which the author discusses his meeting with Andersen in 1874. Nordau reverently describes details from the everyday existence of the dying Andersen and calls him "a genius."[36] The number of biographical materials on Andersen now grew; most significantly, works by the critic Georg Brandes provoked a lively polemic among Russian readers. Biographical sources of varying quality—from the sensationalistic to the painstakingly researched—continued to fuel the "Andersen myth," that of the sensitive and impressionable eccentric, the "eternal

---

34 Grundtvig, *Datskie narodnye skazki*; Topelius, *Skazki Z. Topeliusa, professora Aleksandrovskogo universiteta v Gel'singforse*; Asb'ernsen, *Norvezhskie skazki Petera Asb'ernsena*.
35 Chekhov, *Vvedenie v izuchenie detskoi literatury*, 54.
36 Nordau, "Poseshchenie Andersena."

child" and intuitive genius, "the son of a shoemaker" who made a dizzying social ascent.

The biographical trend in Russian Anderseniana was matched by a literary-critical one. In the 1880s it became increasingly common to see positive, even panegyric evaluations of Andersen's oeuvre, including in pedagogical criticism. One of the more ecstatic articles to speak of the significance of Andersen's fairy tales for children's reading was published in 1881. Its author, the educator and commentator Ivan Feoktistov (1845-?), includes autobiographical elements in his article:

> My goodness! How I devoured these tales as a child! Downtrodden and despised, I withdrew into myself, but my head labored much. Nowhere did I find succor; the future was dark, and nowhere did I hear a warm word. Then, suddenly, I got hold of Andersen's *Tales*, and it was like a breath of fresh air, a burst of warm concern; and hope smiled upon me. I put myself in the position of the ugly duckling; I recited: "Gilding fades fast; but pigskin will last!"
>
> And to this day, I associate the name of Andersen with something fragrant, something lofty, noble, and pure....
>
> These tales are especially dear to unusual, talented, ingenious, sensitive, and nervous natures. These natures do not fit the general standard; they do not know how to lay eggs like a chicken, or curve their back prettily like a cat! For these natures, Andersen's tales are their childhood pals.[37]

In the early 1880s, antipathy to Andersen could still be heard in some corners, especially among still-active representatives of the revolutionary-democratic movement of the sixties. Thus, one of the first Russian feminists, the writer Mariia Tsebrikova (1835-1917), critiqued Andersen's works as bereft of a social conscience and excessively sentimental, writing: "Andersen did not see social relations in life, and this is why his women are not women, and his men are not men, but beings either loving and meek, or hateful and rude—and that's it! His writing has the whiff of coldness, boredom, a feeling of pique!" (1883).[38] But already by the end of the decade, the tone is set by critics who see Andersen as one of the best children's writers, one whose works need no recommendation, and whose positive influence on the child-reader is beyond doubt. One review of the late 1880s begins with a sort of apophatic turn: "It would be utterly superfluous to expatiate on the artistic merits of Andersen's

---

37 Feoktistov, "Andersen i Vagner kak detskie pisateli," 201.
38 Tsebrikova, "Datskaia literatura," 124.

stories. To whom might these charming tales be unknown?"[39]—a rhetorical device that would become somewhat of a cliché.

Against this background, the attitude toward the pedagogical censorship of Andersen's texts changed as well. Readers and critics now began to resent, not only cases in which educators sought to thoroughly remake his tales, but *any* interference in the text. Such was the reaction, for example, that met the collection *Selected Tales* (1889), as retold by the children's writer Olga Rogova (1851-?).[40]

It would seem that in retelling Andersen's texts, Rogova was taking her cue from the truculent pedagogues of the 1860s–70s, who had been eager to "rewrite everything." The changes Rogova made to the fairy tales are significant: she removes not just particular details, like the mention of the sadness in the little robber girl's dark eyes ("The Snow Queen"), or the phrase in the finale of "The Steadfast Tin Soldier" to the effect that the heat melting him may have been that of "his love"; but also whole episodes and plot lines—for example, the final fragment of "The Little Mermaid," which tells of the "daughters of the air"; an episode from the tale "Ole Lukoie" that mentions insomnia and the pangs of conscience (the chapter "Friday"); the stories of the flowers and the psalm about roses in "The Snow Queen"; etc. Rogova boldly reworks Andersen's texts, retelling them in her own words and abridging them mercilessly. Where in the original we see a paragraph of ten or fifteen sentences, the translator gets by with two or three. (Most substantially reworked is the "Little Robber Girl" chapter from "The Snow Queen.") Sometimes the urge to "improve on Andersen" results in something that not only outrages critics, but is also comically absurd: for example, in the fairy tale "The Snow Queen," the crow's wife is for some unknown reason referred to as his *kuma* (mother of one's godchild[41]), etc. In the devastating review of Rogova's work by the pedagogical journal *Education and Learning* (*Vospitanie i obuchenie*), the very idea of censoring Andersen's texts is called into question: "The title of the book itself, *Andersen's Tales Retold* [*v pereskaze*], is really something! Who could have any need of retellings of Andersen, and why?"[42] The translator's changes are interpreted quite dramatically by the critic: "We have before us a scrubbed and neutered

---

39 Anon., "Retsenziia na: *Skazki, perevedennye s nemetskogo, pod redaktsiei P. Veinberga.* SPb, 1889," *Vospitanie i obuchenie*, no. 5 (1889): 214.
40 Andersen, *Izbrannye skazki v pereskaze O. I. Rogovoi*.
41 The old-timey words *kum* and *kuma* signify the father and mother of one's godchild. In Russian folklore, the *kum* and *kuma* are primarily comic characters, frequently associated with ribaldry.
42 Anon., "Retsenziia na: G. Kh. Andersen. *Izbrannye skazki v pereskaze O. I. Rogovoi.* SPb, 1889," *Vospitanie i obuchenie*, no. 5-6 (1890): 233-34.

Andersen!" Rogova's educational qualifications are likewise called into question: "Mme. Rogova, as we know, gives lectures on the history of children's literature at the Froebel courses[43].... But what can she teach, what principles can she inspire her students with, if she herself is sowing all manner of lies and untruths in children's hearts and minds?"[44]

Of particular significance here is that, among other things, the reviewer remarks that "we are surprised at Mme. Rogova! She ought to be ashamed of herself for mangling *classic works* [emphasis mine—IS]!"[45] This detail is quite important: by this time—1890—Andersen had become, in Russia, a universally recognized classic. From this point on, the subsequent critical tradition, both in the prerevolutionary and Soviet periods, would develop and reinforce precisely this assessment. Even during the radical campaigns of the 1920s, when the party's literary authorities denounced the fairy tale genre as "ideologically harmful and alien" to Soviet children, private publishers still brought out editions of Andersen's tales, despite the sharp official criticism this earned them. In the 1930s, Soviet culture rehabilitated and appropriated Andersen's writings and persona, interpreting him as a fighter in the war on social injustice and a son of the exploited class—indeed, practically a harbinger of the Russian Revolution.[46] Thus was Andersen restored to the pantheon of literary classics, revered in Soviet Russia by readers and the authorities alike.[47]

In the 1890s–1900s, and right up to the revolution of 1917, the image of Andersen-the-classic rapidly took hold in Russian criticism; the first books on his biography were published,[48] and Andersen's tales became the subject not only of a pedagogical-advisory approach,

---

43 The Froebel courses were tuition-based educational institutions that existed in Russia from 1872 to 1917. Their distinctive feature was that their students were mainly women.
44 Anon., "Retsenziia na: G. Kh. Andersen. *Izbrannye skazki v pereskaze O. I. Rogovoi*. SPb, 1889," *Vospitanie i obuchenie*, no. 5-6 (1890): 233.
45 Ibid., 234.
46 See, for instance, the critic Aleksandr Deich's comment in an article on Andersen: "Now that children's literature is successfully developing under the Stalinist slogan of socialist realism, we draw abundantly from the treasury of world literature all the best and noblest works that promote the victory of socialism, and we restore Hans Christian Andersen's legacy to its proper place" ("Skazki Andersena," 13).
47 One fascinating aspect of Russian Anderseniana is that the first publication to sound skeptical notes about Andersen's tales appeared—after a nearly hundred-year hiatus—in 1980, as Soviet authoritarianism was on the wane; and it would be only in 1995, that is, after the collapse of the USSR, that the Russian reading public would see an article openly criticizing the idea of Andersen's tales as children's classics.
48 Beketova, *Gans-Khristian Andersen*; Sysoeva, *Bessmertnyi tvorets skazok*; Anon., *Gans Khristian Andersen (biograficheskii ocherk)* (Moscow: Obshchestvo rasprostraneniia poleznykh knig, 1901); etc.

but also of literary analysis.[49] Now appeared such generically original critical works as, for instance, a little-known study by the historian Iurii Shcherbachev (1851-1917), who served from 1893 to 1897 at the Russian embassy in Copenhagen. In his article "Another Tale by Andersen" ("Eshche odna skazka Andersena"), Shcherbachev gives a detailed historical commentary on "Godfather's Picture Book"—not among Andersen's best-known stories in Russia—and performs his analysis with great enthusiasm. Admiring its poeticism, precision, and meaningfulness, the critic quite categorically asserts that "this is the fairy tale Danish kids love the most."[50] It might be noted that, unlike in the modern period, the genre of so-called *real'nyi kommentarii* ("real commentary"[51]) is virtually absent from the prerevolutionary criticism of children's literature.

In 1894 Russian Anderseniana received a powerful new impetus: the publication of the first translation of Andersen's tales to be made from the original Danish, by the husband-and-wife team of the Hansens. This event, whose importance cannot be overstated, caused a flurry of reviews (see fig. 1), in which, in the process of discussing the merits and shortcomings of the translation, critics adopted certain formulas in praise of Andersen's oeuvre that would become standard, alluding, for instance, to "Andersen's ability to animate and spiritualize everything around him";[52] his "poetry, wealth of fantasy, humor... lyricism, the manifestation of personal psychic life in allegorical imagery";[53] "the elegance, poetry, and truthful simplicity of his works";[54] etc.

As such critical clichés took shape, the myth of Andersen himself developed apace. This process was stoked in part by the publications and oral accounts of Georg Brandes, who visited Russia in 1887. Reaching out to youthful literary circles of St. Petersburg, Brandes regaled his listeners with various stories characterizing Andersen in the most unflattering terms (as, for example, the famous story of the poisoned jam, etc.). In Brandes's telling (as described, for example, in the memoirs of

---

49 Krasnov, "Datskii skazochnik"; Alferov, "Skazki Andersena"; Kruglov, *Literatura "malen'kago naroda"*; etc.
50 Shcherbachev, "Eshche odna skazka Andersena," 143.
51 *Real'nyi kommentarii* is a genre of scholarly commentary that seeks to provide a detailed description of the historical events mentioned in a text, to explain the historical realities: antiquated customs, rituals, topics, turns of phrase, etc.
52 Krasnov, "Datskii skazochnik," 182.
53 Anon., "Retsenziia na: Andersen, *Sobranie sochinenii v perevode A. i P. Ganzen*. SPb, 1894," *Mir Bozhii*, no. 6 (1894): 198.
54 Balobanova, "Retsenziia na: *Sobranie sochinenii Andersena v 4-kh tomakh*," 160.

Sergei Makovsky[55]), Andersen came across as a hypochondriac, morbidly self-involved, infantile, vain, narrow-minded, petty, and selfish.

Coming to the defense of their favorite writer were translators, teachers, and literary critics, who sought in their publications to ascribe the negative view of Andersen to the machinations of the jealous; caught up in these polemics were not just Brandes, but also members of the Collin family,[56] and even the translators, the Hansens, who were said to "get so carried away in defending Andersen that they do not always remain completely impartial."[57] As the well-known public figure, journalist, and literary critic Pavel Gaideburov (1841-93) commented in his article "A Story with Andersen on Russian Soil" ("Istoriia s Andersenom na russkoi pochve"): "Great talents always find people ready to denigrate them";[58] on the basis of a letter that Jonas Collin took the occasion to send to St. Petersburg, Gaideburov in this piece refutes the "anecdotes" of Brandes—the story of Andersen giving hungry poor people champagne with nothing to eat it with; the story of him supposedly giving poisoned jam to the children of Collin himself (!); the story of how Andersen, fearing being caught in a fire, carried a rope ladder around on his person; etc.—in effect, repeating these stories once more, and acquainting Russian readers with them.

Despite the "Brandes anecdotes," Andersen's image in Russian criticism in this period becomes more and more idealized, as befits a writer generally recognized as a classic. And in biographies of Andersen aimed at children, he is ultimately ascribed the features of a classic and a demigod; assisting in this process were, among other things, the many publications that came out in connection with the Andersen centenary.[59] One of the most indicative in this regard is the lengthy article (1906) by the elementary school teacher Iakov Aleksandrov, who describes Andersen as "a mighty elder," "the grandfather of all Danish children," and "a wise man and seer to whom are vouchsafed the intentions of the Lord God."[60]

---

55 "It was old Andersen who caught it the most from him. Brandes had anecdote upon anecdote about his famous countryman's self-centeredness" (Makovskii, *Portrety sovremennikov*, 135).
56 Krasnov, "Datskii skazochnik," 189.
57 Anon., "Retsenziia na: *Sobranie sochinenii Andersena, perevod s datskogo podlinnika A. i P. Ganzen*," *Russkaia mysl'*, no. 7 (1895): 319.
58 Gaideburov, "Istoriia s Andersenom na russkoi pochve," 274.
59 Press, "Gans-Khristian Andersen: po povodu stoletiia"; Anon., "Stoletie so dnia rozhdeniia Andersena," *Vskhody*, no. 5 (1905): 379-80; Abramovich, "Gans Khristian Andersen (K 100-letiiu so dnia rozhdeniia)"; Fedorov-Davydov, "Gans-Khristian Andersen"; Leont'eva, "O detskom chtenii (iz nabliudenii uchitel'nitsy)"; etc.
60 Aleksandrov, "Velikii skazochnik," 71-72.

Alluding to the story (published in the newspaper *News* [*Novosti*] in 1887) of the famous Russian traveler Vladimir Mainov, Aleksandrov unfolds for his readers certain rather unnatural pictures "from the life of Andersen," in which real facts are closely intertwined with fiction. Here he describes, for example, a scene of Andersen being feted by "the children of Denmark" in his native Odense, which, however, has no parallel in *The Fairy Tale of My Life*, even as that text contains scrupulous descriptions of celebrations:

> Having left the town... Mr. Mainov saw many schoolchildren... holding banners aloft and climbing uphill. Amid this boisterous, cheerful throng, you could see a broad-brimmed feather hat, under which there fluttered the hair, white like silver, of a certain small man in a gray jacket. The children sang, and the man shouted something and waved his hat. When he started to lag behind this crowd and fell in with the next, the ones in front shouted back to him: "Our dear *gubbe* (grandpa) has fallen behind again! Better we should wait for you, than give our *gubbe* to others!" These others started to clamor with the first ones.... Clutching the hands of the standard-bearers of both groups, the old man clambered with them up the hill.... This old man was Andersen. He knew almost all the schoolchildren by name, and had already managed to note which of them was healthy, and which was ill; who had lost weight, and who had recovered.... The evening rang with a choir of two thousand children's voices. Standing on a table, Andersen read the story of "The Steadfast Tin Soldier," and in the face of the noble elder, everyone understood that he too had in his youth experienced the torments of the little soldier, with the only difference being that he himself was made not of tin, but of blood and nerves.[61]

At this point, things become even more implausible. Aleksandrov writes that, the evening of that same day, "Mr. Mainov and his acquaintance Professor V. listened in on the poet's conversation with a thirteen-year-old peasant girl,"[62] and cites a grotesque dialogue between the writer and the girl in which these interlocutors speak of eternal love, heavenly bliss, the souls of the departed winking to their loved ones from nearby little stars, etc. "So that's how Andersen gathered plots for his immortal tales!"[63]—concludes the critic, clearly unaware of how comical such a conclusion sounds.

---

61 Ibid., 77.
62 Ibid., 78.
63 Ibid.

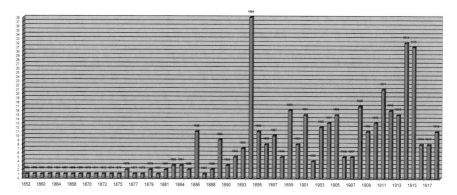

Fig. 3. Russian translations of Andersen's tales published from 1845-1918. Inna Sergienko.

Iakov Aleksandrov's article is marked by a combination of detailed literary analysis of Andersen's fairy tales—not devoid, in places, of depth and insight—and (on the other hand), the broadcast of sensational inventions about Andersen the person. These extensive quotations from Aleksandrov, an ardent and sincere admirer of Andersen, are given here in order to show how Andersen's image begins, in this genre of belletristic biography, to acquire fairytale and even kitschy or *lubok*-like features. This trend will continue, and at times even intensify, both in Soviet and post-Soviet literary and pedagogical criticism.

One common device critics now adopted was to compare (or at times even identify) Andersen with his characters: the ugly duckling, the steadfast tin soldier (Aleksandrov), Ole Lukoie, the swineherd, the gardener (from "The Gardener and the Noble Family"), and even Thumbelina (A. Altaev[64])—which may be connected with the reading public's increasing familiarity with Andersen's autobiography *The Fairy Tale of My Life*, as well as with the Andersen biographies by Russian authors.

Something of an ebb can be observed in critics' and educators' interest in Andersen's works after 1905-6 (even as publishers retained this interest entirely, and editions of Andersen's fairy tales continued to proliferate—see fig. 3). During this period, Andersen's tales are more typically mentioned in reading lists and indexes compiled by those preoccupied mainly with the age-appropriateness of particular tales—and coming, at times, to opposite conclusions.[65]

One of the last pre-Soviet articles on Andersen, published in the January 1918 issue of the magazine *Game* (*Igra*), is devoted to recommenda-

---

64 Altaev, *Velikii skazochnik*.
65 Korol'kov, *Chto chitat' detiam*; Lemke, *Chto chitat' detiam do piatnadtsati let*; etc.

tions on organizing a theatrical children's festival in honor of Andersen. It begins with the question: "How to arrange an Andersen festival, now that children's festivals have come into fashion?" And continues with the statement that "the Andersen day should by all means be a day of fairy tales and flowers"[66] (and proposes, in particular, the staging of "The Girl Who Trod on the Loaf" and "The Old Tombstone"). It is recommended that the festival conclude with a recitation of the latter tale's final words: "The good and the beautiful perish never; they live eternally in story and song!" Considering the historical context, this article may be seen as not so much treating the subject of "Andersen on Russian soil" as bearing witness, rather, to the moment when prerevolutionary Russia was about to become the irrevocable past: at the very same moment when the educator and bibliographer Nikolai Bakhtin (1866-1940), who would go on to be a prominent figure in Soviet children's theater, was writing this article, Russia's political system, and the country's whole ideological paradigm, were changing. Amid the civil war,[67] interventions, famine, and the devastation that followed the revolutionary overthrow in 1917, the issue of "children's festivals" was long relegated to the realm of vanished prerevolutionary life. It would be seventy-odd years before Russian critics would return to the view of Andersen predominant in prerevolutionary pedagogical and literary criticism—that of a Christian and humanist writer. (Bakhtin's article develops this interpretation using the image of Andersen as the "kindly gardener"[68]).

To sum up, views of Andersen's work in Russian criticism may be presented as follows:

In the period from the late 1850s through the 1870s, Russian critics were generally unenthusiastic about Andersen's works for children, or outright rejected them—a view connected with such factors as a lack of quality translations, a general negativity toward fairy tales and the fantastic in children's literature, etc. Some critics appreciated Andersen's works for featuring social issues (Dobroliubov, Treskin, anonymous authors), while others would have preferred that the social element be sharper-edged and more profound (Toll, Kemnits, Tsebrikova, anonymous authors). From the 1880s on, the dominant trend was to hail Andersen's works for children enthusiastically, even panegyrically. Critics empha-

---

66 Bakhtin, "Kak ustroit' andersenovskii prazdnik," 12.
67 The Russian Civil War (1918-22) represented a series of battles between various political, ethnic, and social groups in the territory of the former Russian Empire after the Bolsheviks came to power in the October Revolution of 1917. A large-scale and bloody struggle, it was marked by great casualties, from eight to thirteen million people.
68 Bakhtin, "Kak ustroit' andersenovskii prazdnik," 13.

sized the humanistic nature of Andersen's creativity, remarking on his artistic talent and the edifying influence his tales had on child-readers (Feoktistov, Krasnov, Kruglov, Leontieva, Aleksandrov, etc.). It was in this period that the main elements of the "Andersen myth" took shape; subjecting the writer's persona to a notable idealization, critics developed ideas and rhetorical clichés about Andersen that would return to Soviet criticism in the 1950s, and remain in Russia to this day.

Works Cited

Abramovich, N. A. "Gans Khristian Andersen (K 100-letiiu so dnia rozhdeniia)." *Detskoe chtenie*, no. 6 (1905): 835-39.

Aleksandrov, Ia. "Velikii skazochnik: neskol'ko slov o zhizni Andersena, ego istoriko-literaturnom znachenii, ob otnoshenii poeta k detiam i pedagogicheskikh dostoinstvakh ego skazok." *Nachal'noe obuchenie*, no. 2 (1906): 71-80.

Alferov, A. "Skazki Andersena." *Chitatel'*, no. 38 (1896): 386-87.

Altaev, A. *Velikii skazochnik*. Moscow: Redaktsiia zhurnala 'Iunaia Rossiia,' 1915.

Andersen, [G. Kh.]. *Izbrannye skazki v pereskaze O. I. Rogovoi*. St. Petersburg: Tipografiia A. F. Devriena, 1889.

—. *Ognivo*. Moscow: Novaia Moskva, 1924.

—. *Polnoe sobranie skazok v perevode M. V. Trubnikovoi i N. V. Stasovoi*. St. Petersburg, 1863.

—. *Polnoe sobranie skazok v 3-kh tomakh. V perevode P. Veinberga, Marko Vovchka, S. Maikovoi*. St. Petersburg, 1868-85.

—. *Poslednie skazki Andersena*. Translated from the German by E. Sysoeva. St. Petersburg: Tipografiia R. Golike, 1876.

—. *Skazki. Ledianitsa*. Moscow: Izdatel'stvo Knebelia, 1918.

Asb'ernsen, Peter. *Norvezhskie skazki Petera Asb'ernsena*. St. Petersburg/Moscow: Tovarishchestvo M. Vol'fa, 1885.

Bakhtin, N. "Kak ustroit' andersenovskii prazdnik." *Igra*, no. 1 (1918): 12-19.

Balobanova, E. "Retsenziia na: *Sobranie sochinenii Andersena v 4-kh tomakh. Illiustrirovannye skazki Andersena. V perevode A. i P. Ganzen*. SPb, 1894." *Vospitane i obuchenie*, no. 3 (1894): 159-63.

Beketova, M. *Gans-Khristian Andersen: ego zhizn' i literaturnaia deiatel'nost*. St. Petersburg: Tipografiia S. N. Khudekova, 1892.

Berg, F. "Neskol'ko slov o novoi datskoi poezii." In *Poety vsekh vremen i vsekh narodov* by V. D. Kostomarov and F. N. Berg, 157-66. Moscow, 1862.

Belinskii, V. G. "Retsenziia na: *Improvizator ili Molodost' i mechty ital'ianskogo poeta*. SPb, 1844." *Otechestvennye zapiski* 38, no. 1 (1845): 3-4.

Braude, L. Iu. "Andersen v russkoi i sovetskoi kritike." In *Istoricheskie sviazi Skandinavii i Rossii IX-XX vekov*, edited by N. E. Nosov and I. P. Shaskol'skii, 313-22. Leningrad: Nauka, 1970.

—. "Khans-Kristian Andersen v Rossii." In *Skazki, rasskazannye detiam* by Kh.-K. Andersen, 321-38. Moscow: Nauka, 1983.

Chekhov, N. V. *Vvedenie v izuchenie detskoi literatury.* Moscow: Izd-vo Sytina, 1915.

Dane, B. "H. C. Andersen-receptionen i Rusland og Sovjetunionen." MA thesis, University of Copenhagen, 1994.

Deich, A. "Skazki Andersena." *Detskaia literatura,* no. 12 (1935): 13-14.

Dobroliubov, A. N. "Frantsuzskie knigi. Retsenziia na: *'Contes d'Andersen' traduits du danois par D. Soldi.* Paris, 1856." *Zhurnal dlia vospitaniia* 4, kn. 12 (1858): 377-78.

Fedorov-Davydov, A. "Gans-Khristian Andersen." *Putevye ogni,* nos. 7, 8, 9, 10 (1905): 216-18; 241-42; 273-75; 298-300.

Feoktistov, I. "Andersen i Vagner kak detskie pisateli." *Pedagogicheskii listok,* no. 3-4 (1881): 195-218.

Gaideburov, P. "Istoriia s Andersenom na russkoi pochve." *Knizhki 'Nedeli,'* no. 4 (1896): 274-76.

Gorenfel'd, A. "O khudozhestvennoi chestnosti." In *Kritika nachala XX veka,* edited by I. Ivanova, 66-76. Moscow: Olimp, 2002.

Grundtvig, Sven. *Datskie narodnye skazki.* St. Petersburg: Tip. Likhacheva i Suvorina, 1878.

Ikskiul', Iu. "Nechto ob Andersene." In *Povesti Andersena v perevode s nemetskogo baronessy Iulii fon Ikskiul'* by Kh.-K. Andersen, 96-113. St. Petersburg: Tipografiia I. Glazunova, 1857.

Kemnits, E. K. "Retsenziia na: *Polnoe sobranie skazok Andersena v perevode M. V. Trubnikovoi i N. V. Stasovoi.* SPb, 1863." *Uchitel',* no. 13-14 (1864): 536-40.

Korol'kov, A. E. *Chto chitat' detiam.* Moscow: Tipografiia I. I. Pashkova, 1906.

Krasnov, P. "Datskii skazochnik." *Knizhki 'Nedeli,'* no. 9 (1895): 182-89.

Kruglov, A. V. *Literatura "malen'kago naroda": kritiko-pedagogicheskie besedy po voprosam detskoi literatury.* Moscow: Lito-tip. O. Iu. Sheibel', 1897.

Lemke, M. *Chto chitat' detiam do piatnadtsati let.* St. Petersburg: Tipografiia M. M. Stasiulevicha, 1910.

Leont'eva, N. "O detskom chtenii (iz nabliudenii uchitel'nitsy)." *Obrazovanie,* no. 11-12 (1905): 111-41.

Makovskii, S. *Portrety sovremennikov.* New York: Chekhov Publishing House, 1955.

Nordau, M. "Poseshchenie Andersena." *Russkaia rech',* no. 3 (1880): 356-63.

Orlova, G. K. *Kh.-K. Andersen v russkoi literature kontsa XIX–nachala XX veka: vospriiatie, perevody, vliianie.* Moscow: Izdatel'stvo MGU, 2003.

Pereslegina, E. V. *Khans-Kristian Andersen: bibliograficheskii ukazatel'.* Moscow: Kniga, 1979.

Press, A. "Gans-Khristian Andersen: po povodu stoletiia." *Priroda i liudi,* no. 4 (1905): 86-90.

Shcherbachev, Iu. N. "Eshche odna skazka Andersena." *Russkoe obozrenie,* no. 5 (1891): 143-180.

Sysoeva, E. *Bessmertnyi tvorets skazok: Kartinki iz zhizni Andersena.* St. Petersburg: Tipografiia N. Moreva, 1898.

Toll', F. *Nasha detskaia literatura: Opyt bibliografii sovremennoi detskoi literatury, preimushchestvenno v vospitatel'nom otnoshenii.* St. Petersburg: Tipografiia E. Veimara, 1862.

Topelius, Z. *Skazki Z. Topeliusa, professora Aleksandrovskogo universiteta v Gel'singforse.* Translated from the Swedish by M. Granstrem and A. Gur'eva. Moscow: Tip. Stasiulevicha, 1882.

Treskin, N. "O pererabotke skazok Andersena dlia detskogo chteniia." *Narodnaia detskaia biblioteka*, no. 5 (1879): 129-32.

Tsebrikova, M. K. "Datskaia literatura." *Delo*, no. 10 (1883): 104-26.

Appendix

This appendix represents an addendum to the article "Hans Christian Andersen as a Children's Writer, as Reflected in Russian Criticism from the Latter Half of the Nineteenth Century to 1917." It is based on materials from the collections of the Russian National Library, the Library of the Academy of Sciences, and the National Electronic Children's Library.

The appendix includes articles and reviews by critics and educators, excerpts from recommendatory manuals, and a few prefaces; in all, there are 100 sources. The appendix does not claim to be exhaustive, but it does reflect the main body of pieces published during this period on the figure and oeuvre of Hans Christian Andersen. The brief annotations focus especially on the opinion of the given work's author as to the readerly address of Andersen's tales, insofar as this question was hotly debated throughout the period under consideration. Most of the annotations also indicate which particular works the given critic analyzes and mentions, which can go to show which tales and stories were most popular with Russian readers, and which remained in the shadows.

The author of this appendix hopes that these materials will be of help in tracing Hans Christian Andersen's path in the Russian pantheon of classics of children's literature.

Belinskii 1845: A detailed review of the novel *The Improvisatore* (published in the journal *Sovremennik* in 1844). Here Belinsky is one of the first to write that Andersen's works make appropriate reading for children and adolescents.

Ikskiul' 1857: One of the first biographical pieces about Andersen, based on the German-language original of Andersen's first biography, *Das Märchen meines Lebens ohne Dichtung* (1847).

Dobroliubov 1858: One of the first Russian-language reviews of Andersen's tales (as published in Russia in French translation). Dobroliubov gives high marks to tales and stories such as "The Emperor's New Clothes," "The Princess on the Pea," "The Little Match Girl," and "The Traveling Companion," and offers a description of Andersen's artistic method.

Toll' 1862: The first review of Andersen's fairy tales by a Russian educator; included in a collection of essays on children's books.

Toll' 1863: A brief positive review; the author writes that "Andersen's naive humor is inimitable, and his fairy tales are as rich in content as they are in wit." The reviewer does note that the fairy tales are more suitable for adult reading: "Only adults will understand their content."

Lavrent'ev 1864: A piece about a personal meeting with Andersen; among other things, the writer's appearance is described.

Kemnits 1864: A harshly negative review, in which the tales included in the collection are called "fantastic ravings." The author of the review was an educator, bibliographer, and translator. The review mentions the tales "The Rose Elf," "The Bell," "The Story of a Mother," "The Shepherdess and the Chimney-Sweep," "The Galoshes of Fortune," "The Shadow," "The Tinder Box," "The Darning Needle," and "The Flying Trunk."

Anonymous 1864: A detailed positive review of the collection. The reviewer notes the "inimitable charm of [Andersen's] manner of presentation," "the originality of his form," his "profound artistic thought," etc. "The Steadfast Tin Soldier" is analyzed in detail.

Anonymous 1868: A brief review in which Veinberg's translation is given high marks.

P.T. 1868: An extensive review of the collection, focused mainly on the pedagogical aspects of the tales and stories. The reviewer deems some of the works unsuitable for children ("The Psyche," "The New Century's Goddess," "Under the Willow Tree," "The Thorny Road of Honor," and "A Rose from Homer's Grave"), and in others ("Five Peas from a Pod," "What the Old Man Does is Always Right") sees "harmful thoughts." The author urges translators to use greater caution in selecting Andersen's works for editions for children, and teachers and parents, to provide guidance for children in reading Andersen's tales.

Anonymous 1869: A negative review of the collection. The author criticizes the tales "Little Claus and Big Claus," "The Tinder Box," "The Traveling Companion," "The Flying Trunk," "The Darning Needle," "Little Ida's Flowers," "The Old House," "The Shadow," "The Shirt Collar," "The Naughty Boy," and "The Princess on the Pea" as incapable of exerting a positive educational influence on the child reader.

Anonymous 1872: This piece includes discussion regarding the accusation that Marko Vovchok, who translated this edition's second volume, borrowed from renderings of the first volume's translator Petr Veinberg.

Anonymous 1875: A jubilee piece of a biographical and sensational nature, based on a retelling of *The Fairy Tale of My Life*. Discussed in detail in the piece is the creation of the poem "The Dying Child"; also mentioned are the novels *The Improvisatore*, *O. T.*, and *Only a Fiddler*, the tale "The Red Shoes," travel notes, etc.

Anonymous 1875: A biographical sketch based on *The Fairy Tale of My Life* and an article by Georg Brandes. The author of the article asserts that Andersen was very fond of children and that the "character of Ole Lukoie was a self-portrait." Comments the reviewer: "Beneath the light, fairytale form there lies serious content; important issues are raised."

E. C. 1877: A brief negative review. The author finds fault with the translator's "unfortunate selection" of Andersen's works for children's reading and considers that children will find tales such as "Godfather's Picture Book," "Vänö and Glänö," "What Old Johanne Told," and "The Gate Key" incomprehensible and uninteresting, while the tale "The Cripple" teaches submissiveness. "As for Andersen's reputation," says the reviewer, "his translators' excessive zeal is only hurting him in our country."

Anonymous 1877: A brief review in which Andersen's writings are generally accorded high praise. The reviewer notes that Andersen's tales cannot be categorized exclusively as children's reading. The reviewer considers the tales "Godfather's Picture Book" and "The Gate Key" unsuitable for children, which makes it possible that this review and the one listed just above (E. C. 1875) were written by the same person.

Anonymous 1877: A brief review in which it is observed that Andersen's works represent the most successful example of the genre of the literary fairy tale.

Treskin 1879: Here the educator and future censor Nikolai Treskin proposes that Andersen's tales be reworked to be made suitable for children. The article's author finds the themes of drunkenness and "love stories" particularly undesirable. Analyzed in the article are the tales "She Was Good for Nothing," "The Girl Who Trod on the Loaf," "The Ice Maiden," "The Psyche," "What the Old Man Does is Always Right," "The Old Oak Tree's Last Dream," "The Old Tombstone," "Five Peas from a Pod," "Something," "The Bottle Neck," "The Bell," "There Is a Difference," and "The Metal Pig."

Anonymous 1880: A biographical sketch, supplemented by a description of the Andersen monument in Copenhagen. An enthusiastic evaluation is given of Andersen's oeuvre; it is said that "his wondrous, incomparable tales have had the greatest success!"

Nordau 1880: A piece by the German-Jewish writer and public figure Max Nordau about visiting Andersen in his home.

Feoktistov 1881: A detailed article by the educator Ivan Feoktistov in which the tales of Andersen are compared to the works of the Russian writer Nikolai Vagner. The author gives Andersen's work high marks, and examines features of his artistic method; the article also touches on episodes from Andersen's biography. The tales mentioned include "The Ugly Duckling," "The Nightingale," "The Daisy," "The Emperor's New Clothes," "The Shadow," "The Galoshes of Fortune," "The Jumpers," "The Little Match Girl," "The Bell," "The Drop of Water," "The Shirt Collar," "The Tinder Box," "The Traveling Companion," "Little Claus and Big Claus," and "The Old House."

N. P-ia 1883: This piece constitutes a review of a low-cost edition of fairy tales by Andersen published for distribution to peasants and workers. The reviewer approves of the idea of reworking Andersen's tales for "the people," insofar as these works "develop literary taste, and contain honest, wholesome, and noble morals." Concludes the reviewer: "Andersen's tales are highly beneficial, both for children and for the people."

Tsebrikova 1883: In this article, the public figure and feminist Mariia Tsebrikova examines Andersen's work in the context of developments in Western European literature. Giving Andersen's literary talent its due, she reproaches him for lacking a social temperament, characterizing his worldview as "immature and idealistic."

Chto chitat' narodu? (*What Should the People Read?*) 1884: This is a recommended-reading list for students of Sunday and public schools, including adults. Andersen's tales are evaluated here from the standpoint of their comprehensibility to "the child and the commoner [*prostoliudin*]," and that of pedagogical "usefulness." The index cites responses by peasant children to Andersen's tales (in particular, "The Ugly Duckling"), and gives retellings by them; and reflects on and attempts to interpret this readerly reception.

Feoktistov 1885: A detailed article by the educator Ivan Feoktistov that examines Andersen's tales in the context of the genre of the literary fairy tale. The author analyzes the features of Andersen's artistic style, and touches on biographical episodes. The author gives high marks to Andersen's work, calling his tales the "swan song of the fairy tale." The article analyzes translations of Andersen, including that of Ekaterina Sysoeva, and observes that Andersen's later tales are not as good as the earlier ones: they are "dry allegories, lacking artistic merit."

Anonymous 1885: A brief review, in which Andersen's tales are called "a welcome guest in our children's literature." However, the reviewer remarks that not all the latest tales "are worthy." The translation is evaluated positively.

Feoktistov 1886: This extensive article is devoted to the controversial issue of the folkloric vs. literary fairy tale in children's reading. Andersen's tales are considered in this context and given the highest marks. The critic calls Andersen's tales the "people's book of Denmark" and asserts that they deserve their "enormous worldwide success." Andersen's oeuvre is compared with that of the Russian authors Nikolai Vagner and Vsevolod Garshin, who wrote literary fairy tales.

Anonymous 1886: A short review of "The Ugly Duckling," in which it is said that "this story's details are so gracefully rendered, and conveyed by the author with so subtle a mind, that your tenth reading of the tale gives you no less pleasure."

Anonymous 1887: This review was written in connection with the issuing of Andersen's tales in low-cost editions for "the people" (the so-called *lubok* [popular-print] editions, i.e., with pictures and captions). The reviewer notes that the texts have been reworked; they are not only abridged but in some cases added to (e.g., an introduction has been added to "The Wild Swans"), and their titles have been changed to match the *lubok* tradition. The reviewer approves of an Andersen edition for "the people," but is indignant at the alteration of the texts. "The details of Andersen's tales have to be handled with care!" In the reviewer's opinion, "The Galoshes of Fortune" is too complex and incomprehensible, "The Tinder Box" is crude, and "The Girl Who Trod on the Loaf" should be read only under the guidance of one's teacher.

T. A. 1888: This is a brief preface to a publication by Georg Brandes. It repeats the cliché that likens Andersen to a capricious woman, and cites stories about how Andersen was "furious" to discover that a sculptor wanted to sculpt him surrounded by children, and how Andersen supposedly gave poisoned jam to an acquaintance. The author of the preface remarks that in the published article, "the critic independently and impartially gives an accurate view of the writer."

Anonymous 1888: A brief piece containing biographical information about Andersen. Describing his oeuvre, the reviewer comments that Andersen's tales are the only Danish works to make it into the ranks of world literature. The monument to Andersen is compared with the monument to the famed Russian writer I. A. Krylov in St. Petersburg.

Brandes 1888: An extensive article on Andersen's life and works.

Alchevskaia 1889: The editors of this volume approve of such tales as "The Nightingale," "Thumbelina," and "The Girl Who Trod on the Loaf" for peasant children's reading. Tales they believe "children will not understand" include "The Steadfast Tin Soldier," "The Darning Needle," "The Shepherdess and the Chimney-Sweep," and "The Ugly Duckling." They discuss their experience with reading "A Traveling Companion" and "The Girl Who Trod on the Loaf" with "children at different levels of development."

Anonymous 1889: The reviewer gives high marks to Andersen's tales and warmly recommends their inclusion in the category of reading material for children. The reviewer remarks on the great educational potential of tales such as "The Story of a Mother," "The Snow Queen," "The Wild Swans," "The Little Mermaid," "The Elder-Tree Mother," "Holger Danske," "Little Ida's Flowers," and "Ole Lukoie." The reviewer considers the tales "The Bell," "The Galoshes of Fortune," and "The Shadow" to be "beyond children's understanding," and that "Little Claus and Big Claus" should not be included in children's reading material, on the grounds that it is "too crude."

Rogova 1889: A highly tendentious consideration of the appropriateness of Andersen's tales as reading material for children. Rogova believes that irony and allegory are incomprehensible to children and that Andersen has an excessive predilection for stories and plots about love. "What makes these tales so harmful to the young soul is that the imagery in them is so bright, vital, and bold, and that they describe the feeling of love in all its details." She mentions the tales "The Butterfly," "Thumbelina," "Under the Willow Tree," "She Was Good for Nothing," "The Nightcap of the 'Pebersvend,'" "The Ice Maiden," "The Gardener and the Noble Family," "Beautiful," "Aunty Toothache," "The Racers," etc.

Feoktistov 1889: A detailed article in which the educator and literary critic Ivan Feoktistov polemicizes with pedagogical evaluations of Andersen's tales that categorize them "by age." He protests against the idea that tales such as "The Shirt Collar," "The Naughty Boy," "The Steadfast Tin Soldier," "The Galoshes of Fortune," and "The Shadow" should be excluded from the category of children's reading. "How lucky we were that we lived when Andersen's tales had not yet been put into pedagogical categories!"

Anonymous 1890: A negative review of Olga Rogova's retellings of Andersen's tales. The reviewer expresses indignation at the very idea of reworking the tales, and analyzes the abridgments and distortions of tales such as "The Snow Queen," "The Steadfast Tin Soldier," "The Flying Trunk," and "Little Ida's Flowers."

A. B. 1890: A review of four editions of Andersen. The reviewer praises Nadezhda Stasova's translation and, from among these editions, deems the best selection of tales to be found in that published by Vladimir Marakuev (which includes "The Steadfast Tin Soldier," "The Darning Needle," "The Tinder Box," "The Girl Who Trod on the Loaf," "Thumbelina," "The Flying Trunk," "What the Old Man Does is Always Right," "The Daisy," "The Bottle Neck," "The Little Mermaid," "The Galoshes of Fortune," "She Was Good for Nothing," and "The Wild Swans"). The reviewer notes that the existence of Andersen publications in different price categories—from the cheap to the luxurious "gift" editions (like "The Snow Queen" as published by Mavrikii Volf)—attests to the Russian reader's love for Andersen's oeuvre.

N. P-ia 1890: A brief review of the collection. Rogova's retelling is criticized; the reviewers question why she felt the need to "pluck and chop up a famous text."

Dr. A. B. 1890: The reviewer categorizes this book as belonging to the genre of "charming poems in prose" and remarks that it would be "premature" to give this book to children.

Anonymous 1891: A brief note about Andersen's parents, the circumstances of his birth, and the first years of his life.

Shcherbachev 1891: A brief article about Andersen's tale "Godfather's Picture Book," written in the genre of historical commentary. Iurii Shcherbachev, a historian and diplomat, writes about events from Danish history reflected in the tale, and calls for an edition of this text for children accompanied by commentary of this sort.

Pozniakov 1892: "At last we have a collection of Andersen's tales successfully selected for children's reading," writes the educator, commentator, and children's author Nikolai Pozniakov. "What is chosen here is suitable for children." Appropriate for children, in the reviewer's opinion, are such tales as "The Snow Queen," "The Flax," "The Nightingale," "She Was Good for Nothing," "Thumbelina," "The Old House," "The Shadow," "What the Old Man Does is Always Right," "The Girl Who Trod on the Loaf," "The Wild Swans," "The Ugly Duckling," "The Old Tombstone," "The Darning Needle," "The Galoshes of Fortune," "The Angel," "The Fir Tree," "The Flying Trunk," "The Daisy," "The Traveling Companion," "The Story of a Mother," "The Metal Pig," "The Little Mermaid," "The Shepherdess and the Chimney-Sweep," "The Tinder Box," and "The Steadfast Tin Soldier."

Beketova 1892: The first Andersen biography to be published in Russia as a separate book. The author goes into detail about the life and oeuvre of Andersen, relying on *The Fairy Tale of My Life* and his collected letters.

Pozniakov 1894: A brief review that discusses the project of the publisher Florentii Pavlenkov, who had conceived the idea of an illustrated multivolume (thirty in all) edition of the fairy tales "of all the peoples of the world," including a selection of Andersen works, the translation of which, by Berta Porozovskaia, is praised by the reviewer.

Anonymous 1894: A brief advertising annotation, in which the book is called "an adornment for any desk or coffee table."

M. A. Ch. 1894: The author of this article examines the role of fairy tales in children's reading and education. The fairy tale is said to be integral to children's reading, insofar as, according to the author, it helps to develop the imagination and sense of fantasy. The author attempts to distinguish between "useful" and "harmful" fairy tales, with the former category including the tales of the brothers Grimm, Wilhelm Hauff, and Andersen.

Anonymous 1894: In this brief piece, the reviewer analyzes features of the translation of the Hansens, noting that this was the first Russian translation to be made from the original Danish.

Anonymous 1894: A brief review of the collection that among other things emphasizes the controversy surrounding the readerly address of *Tales and Stories*. The reviewer believes that to a great extent, Andersen wrote for adults.

Anonymous 1894: This brief review gives biographical information, and emphasizes the importance of fairy tales in Andersen's oeuvre and the significance of their having been translated in this case from the original language. The reviewer comments that not all the tales "are suitable for children, and Andersen is hardly a children's writer." "A careful and prudent selection is called for" when compiling collections for children's reading.

Anonymous 1894: This brief review compares translations, with B. Porozovskaia's rendering from a German translation earning praise along with the Hansens' translation. The reviewer discusses the principles behind the publishers' selection of which Andersen tales were to be translated.

Balobanova 1894: This review compares translations; also discussed is the Russian translators' growing interest in Scandinavian ("northern") literature generally. The reviewer writes that "no one can compare with Andersen, with the elegance, poetry, and truthful simplicity of his works." Mentioned here are the tales "The Tinder Box," "The Galoshes of Fortune," "The Wild Swans," "The Princess on the Pea," and "Little Claus and Big Claus."

Anonymous 1894: This is a lengthy review of vols. I, II, and III of the *Collected Works*. The Hansens' translation is given high marks. The reviewer offers recommendations on how to incorporate Andersen's tales into children's reading. Noting that some of the tales "may even be read to a four-year-old child," the reviewer remarks that, "given a prudent and reasonable apportioning of one's reading of these works, they will serve as excellent learning material for all ages." Mentioned here are "The Ice Maiden," "The Metal Pig," "She Was Good for Nothing," "The Story of a Mother," "The Dying Child," *The Improvisatore*, and *Lucky Peer*.

W. 1894: A detailed review of the collected works that examines Andersen's oeuvre in the context of the development of Scandinavian literature. The reviewer remarks that Andersen has created a "new genre" of literature, emphasizing the dual address of his tales, which are aimed at both the adult and child reader. The reviewer admires the tales' artistic style, but criticizes Andersen's penchant for "cheap and sentimental finales." The tales mentioned include "The Nightingale," "The Little Mermaid," "The Wild Swans," "The Ugly Duckling," and "The Emperor's New Clothes."

Krasnov 1895: Platon Krasnov evaluates Andersen's oeuvre positively, and expands on certain features of his personality and biography, denouncing the Danish storyteller's "slanderers," among whom he includes Georg Brandes and some members of the Collin family. Discussed in the article are "The Little Mermaid," "The Ugly Duckling," "The Shepherdess and the Chimney-Sweep," "The Nightingale," "The Girl Who Trod on the Loaf," "The Story of a Mother," "The Little Match Girl," *The Improvisatore*, *Lucky Peer*, and *The Fairy Tale of My Life*.

Anonymous 1895: This brief review gives information on Andersen's biography, evaluates the translation and makeup of the *Collected Works*, and touches on the polemic surrounding Andersen's reputation.

Gaideburov 1896: In this article, the writer Pavel Gaideburov, publisher of the liberal journal the *Week* (*Nedelia*), responds to an interview with Georg Brandes that had been published in the newspaper *New Times* (*Novoe vremia*). The author seeks to defend "the famous Danish storyteller" from the attacks of Brandes, refuting stories about Andersen's alleged eccentricities and unseemly acts.

Khir'iakov 1896: A short essay on the genre of the literary fairy tale in children's reading. Andersen's tales are considered a classic example of this genre, and are recommended to be read to children. "The Little Mermaid" is mentioned.

Kruglov 1897: A collection of essays on children's literature and children's reading. The well-known educator and commentator Aleksandr Kruglov, generally skeptical as to the fairytale genre, recognizes the great artistic and educational value of Andersen's tales. "Andersen's *Tales* is a book that can scarcely be rivaled in this area."

Sysoeva 1898: A biographical sketch prefacing the publication ("for the people and children") of the tales "The Fir Tree," "Thumbelina," "The Ugly Duckling," "The Nightingale," "The Story of a Mother," "The Daisy," and "The Little Match Girl."

Klausen and Umanskii 1899: A brief essay about the publication of Andersen's works (mostly tales) in Denmark and Russia.

Hansen and Hansen 1899: In this article, the husband and wife team of the Hansens discuss the principles informing their translation, and the dual address of Andersen's stories and tales: "Children will be engaged by the plot itself; adults will appreciate the depth of the content."

A. B. 1900: A brief review. "There is no need to speak of the incomparable charm of Andersen's tales; they are too familiar to young and old alike," writes the reviewer. Tegner's illustrations are given high marks.

A-v S. 1900: A survey article that discusses Andersen's works for children and the artistic merit of his tales. The article includes some biographical information. The tales "The Shadow," "The Elder-Tree Mother," "The Swineherd," "The Princess on the Pea," "The Jumpers," and "The Shirt Collar" are briefly discussed.

Anonymous 1901: A brief piece depicting Andersen as a combination of a genius and an oddball. Certain episodes from his biography are cited: meeting compatriots in Italy, etc. Andersen is called "a meek, mild person full of inexhaustible humor." Of particular note is the description of him as "a poor, defenseless child of the people."

Koltonovskaia 1901: An essay by the writer Elena Koltonovskaia prefacing a publication of Andersen's tales. Along with biographical fragments, the piece discusses the issue of the tales' readerly address and analyzes Andersen's artistic techniques. "The Emperor's New Clothes," "The Shirt Collar," and "The Ugly Duckling" are mentioned. The description of Andersen's personality emphasizes his piety and humble origins.

Leont'eva 1905: This article is devoted to schoolchildren's reading material and readerly reception. Andersen's tales are discussed in this context and evaluated quite highly by the author, a schoolteacher. The author remarks that, according to her observations, the tales most beloved by children are "The Little Mermaid," "The Snow Queen," and "The Ice Maiden." She states that works of "a fantastic nature" are a necessary part of the reading material of children and adolescents.

Anonymous 1905: This jubilee piece gives biographical information about Andersen and an ecstatic evaluation of his oeuvre. In particular, the author claims that "Andersen pioneered a new species of literature—the children's artistic fairy tale." Remarking on the humanism of Andersen's works, the author calls him "the great storyteller for the children of all the peoples of the earth."

Anonymous 1905: A biographical sketch on the occasion of the Andersen jubilee, this essay also gives a brief description of his oeuvre, with the highest marks going to the stories and tales. "You can't read your fill of them—so much poetry, humor, and wit do they contain." "The Emperor's New Clothes," "The Swineherd," "The Shadow," and "The Story of a Mother" are mentioned. "The Ugly Duckling" is said to be autobiographical.

Anonymous 1905: A jubilee piece on Andersen, including a biography and a brief survey of his work as a whole. It is remarked that it is specifically the fairy tales that represent "the culmination of his talent."

Alchevskaia 1906: The authors recommend the Andersen collections translated by the Hansens, Petr Veinberg, and Sofiia Maikova for reading in public schools, and remark on standalone publications of "The Ugly Duckling" and "The Wild Swans." A detailed review of the tale "The Cripple" is given; Andersen's tales are said to be meant for "serious children—children who are already contemplating life and its difficult conditions."

A. Ia. 1906: One of the most voluminous and significant articles in all Russian Anderseniana. Based on articles by Georg Brandes and biographical materials on Andersen, the teacher Iakov Aleksandrov offers his own interpretation of Andersen's work and gives methodological recommendations for using Andersen's texts in the classroom. Mentioned in the article are "The Ugly Duckling," "The Snow Queen," *The Fairy Tale of My Life*, the travelogue *A Poet's Bazaar*, and other works. Andersen's image is subjected to a substantial mythologization.

Anonymous 1907: A brief advertising note that emphasizes that "the selection of fairy tales is canonical."

Press 1908: An essay by the writer and bibliographer Arkadii Press written in the form of a dialogue. The central theme is the personality of Andersen as an author of fairy tales and stories.

Anonymous 1908: An endorsement of the tales of Andersen. The tales are given high marks, with the authors of the index recommending them "for every library." Suggested for younger children are "The Nightingale," "The Emperor's New Clothes," and "The Ugly Duckling"; for teenagers, "The Snow Queen" and "The Little Mermaid"; and for the adult reader, "The Naughty Boy," "The Shadow," "Anne Lisbeth," "The Psyche," and "The Goblin and the Woman." "The Swineherd," "The Tinder Box," and "Little Claus and Big Claus" are said to be "crude" and not suitable for children.

Chekhov 1909: Andersen's tales are analyzed in the context of the history of children's literature, and a quick description of his creative manner is given. Also discussed is the issue of the readerly address of *Fairy Tales and Stories*.

Galanin 1910: An article on the subject of reading material for schoolchildren. Andersen's tales are considered in this context. Cited in the article are children's responses to tales they had read by Andersen.

Liapina 1912: This biographical sketch of Andersen, based on already well-known biographies and *The Fairy Tale of My Life*, is aimed at the child reader and is marked by a moralizing message; the biography emphasizes that Andersen studied diligently and a lot, that he traveled "for educational purposes," etc.

Altaev 1915: A fictionalized biography of Andersen based on the biography by Mariia Beketova. It is addressed to the child reader, and conveys a mythologized and legendary image of Andersen. A parallel is drawn between the image of the writer and his characters: the ugly duckling, Thumbelina, and others.

Bakhtin 1918: One of the last publications about Andersen to be written before the October Revolution. Along with methodological recommendations for theatrical performances based on the tales, Andersen's personality is described; in particular, he is likened to a "kindly gardener." Recommended for staging are "The Girl Who Trod on the Loaf" and "The Old Tombstone."

П-я Н.	Рецензия на: О чем рассказывает месяц, СПб, 1890	Женское образование	1890	6-7	648-649
анонимно	Рождение Андерсена	Нива	1891	23	518
Щербачев Ю.Н.	Еще одна сказка Андерсена	Русское обозрение	1891	5	143-180
Позняков Н.И.	Рецензия на: Избранные сказки Андерсена. Москва. Издание В.Н.Маракуева, 1892	Образование	1892	12	448
Бекетова М.А.	Ганс-Христиан Андерсен: его жизнь и литературная деятельность, СПб.		1892		
анонимно	Рецензия на: Собрание сочинений Андерсена в 4-х томах. В переводе А. и П.Ганзен. СПб., 1894	Север	1894	6	325
Позняков Н.И.	Рецензия на: Сказочная иллюстрированная библиотека. Издание Ф.Павленкова, СПб, 1894	Образование	1894	9	241
анонимно	Рецензия на: "Мать" - сказка Андерсена на 22-х языках. в переводе П.Ганзена, СПб, 1894	Литературное приложение к журналу "Нива"	1894	6	360
анонимно	Рецензия на: "Мать" - сказка Андерсена на 22-х языках. в переводе П.Ганзена, СПб, 1894	Русский вестник	1894	6	298
М.А.Ч.	Воспитательное значение сказки	Воспитание и обучение	1894	1	45-50
анонимно	Рецензия на: I том Собрания сочинений Андерсена в переводе А. и П. Ганзен. СПб., 1894	Русский вестник	1894	2	292-294
анонимно	Рецензия на: Иллюстрированные сказки. Полное собрание сказок Андерсена в 6 томах в пер. В.Д.Порозовской. СПб, 1894	Неделя	1894	5	155
Анонимно	Рецензия на: "Мать" - сказка Андерсена на 22-х языках. в переводе П.Ганзена, СПб, 1894	Неделя	1894	26	834
анонимно	Рецензия на: Собрание сочинений Андерсена в 4-х томах. В переводе А. и П.Ганзен. СПб., 1894	Русская мысль	1894	2	60-61

анонимно	Рецензия на: Иллюстрированные сказки Андерсена в переводе Б.Д.Порозовской. Издание Павленкова, 1894 и Собрание сочинений Андерсена в 4-х томах в переводе А. и П. Ганзен. СПб., 1894.	Северный вестник	1894	2	62-63
Балобанова Е.	Рецензия на: Иллюстрированные сказки Андресена в переводе Б.Д.Порозовской. Издание Павленкова, 1894 и Собрание сочинений Андерсена в 4-х томах в переводе А. и П. Ганзен. СПб., 1894.	Воспитание и обучение	1894	3	159-163
Краснов Пл.	Рецензия на: Собрание сочинений Андерсен в переводе А.и П.Ганзен. СПб., 1894	Всемирная иллюстрация	1894	51	302
анонимно	Рецензия на: Собрание сочинений Андерсена в 4-х томах. В переводе А. и П.Ганзен. Спб., 1894	Русская мысль	1894	12	584-88
W.	Рецензия на: Андерсен Собрание сочинений в переводе А.и П.Ганзен. СПб., 1894	Мир Божий	1894	6	198-200
анонимно	Рецензия на: "Мать" - сказка Андерсена на 22-х языках. в переводе П.Ганзена, Спб, 1894	Русская мысль	1894	6	290
анонимно	Рецензия на: Собрание сочинений Андерсена в 4-х томах. В переводе А. и П.Ганзен. СПб., 1894	Новости печати	1895	4	25
анонимно	Рецензия на: Собрание сочинений Андерсена в 4-х томах. В переводе А. и П.Ганзен. СПб., 1894	Литературное приложение к журналу "Нива"	1895	12	803
Краснов Пл.	Датский сказочник	Книжки "Недели"	1895	9	132-134
анонимно	Рецензия на: Собрание сочинений Андерсена, перевод с датского подлинника А. и П.Ганзен. СПб.,1985	Русская мысль	1895	7	318-321

Острогорский, В.	Еще об идеализме в детской литературе	Педагогический листок	1895	2	20-29
Гайдебуров В.П.	История с Андерсеном на русской почве	Книжки "Недели"	1896	4	274-276
Алферов А.	Сказки Андерсена	Читатель	1896	38	86-87
Хирьяков А	Сказки, собранные братьями Гримм: Рец. на издание "Иллюстрированная сказочная библиотека", Спб, 1894	Образование	1896	2	107-109
Круглов А.В.	Литература маленького народа: Критико-педагогические беседы по вопросам детской литературы. Выпуск 2.		1897		84-86
Сысоева Е.	Бессмертный творец сказок: Картинки из жизни Андерсена	Читальня народной школы	1898	7-8	3-46
Клаусен Н., Уманский А.М.	Библиографические сведения	Собрание сочинений Г.-Х. Андресена в 4-х тома. Перевод А.и П.Ганзен. Том. 4	1899		493-495
Ганзен А. Ганзен П.	К читателям	Собрание сочинений Г.-Х. Андресена в 4-х тома. Перевод А.и П.Ганзен. Том. 4	1899		496-500
А.Б.	Рецензия на: Сказки Андерсена с иллюстрациями Тегнера в переводе А. И П.Ганзен, Спб.,1899	Мир Божий	1900	2	84
Б.А.	Рецензия на: Сказки Андерсена с иллюстрациями Тегнера в переводе А. И П.Ганзен, Спб.,1899	Русская мысль	1900	1	20-21
А-в С.	Гений сказки	Семья	1900	31	6-7
анонимно	Ганс Андерсен как человек	Новый журнал иностранной литературы	1901	12	491-492

анонимно	Ганс Христиан Андерсен: биографический очерк датского поэта с приложением его стихотворений, М. Издание Общества старающегося о распространении полезных книг.		1901		
Колтоновская Е.	Ганс Христиан Андерсен (биографический очерк)	Юный читатель	1901	16	49-68
анонимно	Ганс-Христиан Андерсен (1806-1875): биографический очерк. М. Издание Общества старющегося о распространении полезных книг.		1904		
Леонтьева Н.	О детском чтении (из наблюдений учительницы)	Образование	1905	11-12	111-141
анонимно	Столетие со дня рождения Андерсена	Всходы	1905	5	379-380
Федоров-Давыдов А.	Ганс-Христиан Андресен	Путеводный огонёк	1905	7,8,9	
Абрамович Н.А.	Ганс Христиан Андерсен (К 100-летию со дня рождения)	Детское чтение	1905	6	835-839
Пресс А.	Ганс-Христиан Андерсен: по поводу столетия	Природа и люди	1905	4	86-90
анонимно	Г.Х.Андресен	Нива	1905	13	259
анонимно	Ганс Христиан Андерсен (К столетию со дня рождения)	Живописное обозрение	1905	14	340-342
Алчевская Х.Д.	Что читать народу? Критический указатель книг для народного и детского чтения. Составлен учительницами Харьковской частной женской воскресной школы. / Алчевская Х.Д. - Т.III; СПб.		1906		68; 102
А. Я.	Великий сказочник: несколько слов о жизни Андерсена, его историко-литературном значении, об отношении поэта к детям и педагогических достоинствах его сказок	Начальное обучение	1906	1, 2	23-31; 71-80
анонимно	Рецензия на: Избранные сказки Андерсена в переводе А.и.П.Ганзен, М., 1906	Всходы	1907	5	без нумерации страниц

Пресс А.	Ганс Христиан Андерсен:Литературная беседа	Пресс А. В царстве книг. Очерки и портреты. СПб.	1908	т.I	
	О детских книгах: критико-библиографический указатель книг, вышедших до 1 января 1907 года, рекомендуемый для чтения детям в возрасте от 7 до 16 лет. М.: Изд-во книжного магазина С.Скирмунта "Труд".		1908		38-39
Чехов Н.В.	Переводная литература для детей	Детская литература, М.	1909		179; 190-191
Лемке М.	Что читать детям до пятнадцати лет: Указатель более 600 лучших детских книг. СПб.		1910		
Галанин Д.	Детское чтение	Педагогический листок	1910	3; 5	172-193; 315-326
Лялина М.	Ганс-Христиан Андерсен: биографический очерк	Андерсен Г.-Х. Избранные сказки в переводе М.А.Лялиной. Петроград. Издание В.И. Губинского	1912		3-8
Елачич Е.	Сказка как материал для детского чтения	Сборник статей по вопросам детского чтения	1914		67-115
Алтаев А.	Великий сказочник:Биографический рассказ		1915		
П.М.	Детство Андерсена	Игра	1918	2	35-40
Бахтин Н.И.	Как устроить андерсеновский праздник	Игра	1918	1	12-19

Hans Christian Andersen's Legacy in the Works of Dostoevsky, Tolstoy, and Vagner:

Negotiating Aesthetics and Meaning

Ben Hellman

Hans Christian Andersen opened up the genre of fairy tale to new, inherent possibilities. Instead of the traditional folktale type, with its clear-cut battle between good and evil, praise of cunningness and bravery, and standard set of characters, he introduced extraordinary protagonists, individual symbols, and radical forms of personification. Scenes of everyday life featuring the colloquial language thereof alternated with poetic fantasies; conventional morality, especially the happy-ending reward of virtue, was questioned; and allegorical depths, more often than not understandable only to adult readers, were added.

Not only Russian readers, young and old, but writers, too, took an interest in Andersen and his particular brand of tales. Fedor Dostoevsky, while not necessarily even having read the Danish writer, worked in the same tradition as him, transposing the story of a child freezing to death during Christmas to a Russian milieu. Lev Tolstoy made his adaptation of "The Emperor's New Clothes" part of a political and philosophical discourse; and Nikolai Vagner, the popular children's writer, openly appropriated some of Andersen's most famous fairy tales, trying to build up a career on models provided by his illustrious Danish predecessor.

Fedor Dostoevsky: The Death of a Child during Christmas

In January 1876, Fedor Dostoevsky published a short story, "A Boy at Christ's Christmas Party" ("Mal'chik u Khrista na elke"), in his monthly magazine *A Writer's Diary* (*Dnevnik pisatelia*). This tells of a little boy's tragic fate at Christmas time. The death of his mother makes him leave the cellar they share with other outcasts. He goes out into the big city; hungry and cold he wanders the streets. Through the windows, he can see well-off families dining and happy children playing around beautifully decorated Christmas trees; toyshops display amazing dolls, moving as if alive. Everyone treats the boy harshly and, frightened, he seeks refuge behind a stack of wood in a dark courtyard, where he falls asleep. In his sleep, a mild voice invites him to a Christmas party together with other ill-fated children. They all rejoice at the festivity that Christ arranges specially for them. Their mothers, too, are present, crying with happiness at the sight of their children, now become angels. The next morning the porter finds the dead body of the boy. The fate of his mother is also now revealed.

Behind this fictional sketch was Dostoevsky's decision to devote a whole issue of *A Writer's Diary* to the children of contemporary Russia. At Christmas 1875, a beggar boy, hardly more than six years old, had caught his attention. Shortly afterwards, Dostoevsky's visit to a penal colony for juvenile delinquents formed a provocative contrast to a Christmas ball for children that the author had attended in the company of his daughter.[1] Readers had to be made aware of the plight of the many unfortunate children in the big cities, and one result of this impetus was "A Boy at Christ's Christmas Party."

There was, however, also a literary impulse for Dostoevsky's short story. In his notebook he wrote: "A Christmas tree/party,[2] Rückert's boy, Christ, ask Vladimir Rafailovich Zotov."[3] "Rückert's boy" has been deciphered as a reference to "The Orphaned Child's Christmas" ("Des fremden Kindes heiliger Christ"), a poem by Friedrich Rückert (1788-1866) from 1816. As this had never been translated into Russian, Dostoevsky must have read it in the original German or perhaps heard it recited at some Christmas festivity, either in St. Petersburg or in Germany.[4] The wish to depict the tragic life-situation of a child brought Rückert's poem to the Russian writer's mind, and now he apparently hoped to locate a copy of it with the help of the writer and journalist Vladimir Zotov.

The event described in Rückert's "The Orphaned Child's Christmas" takes place on Christmas Eve. A lonely child runs around a town, looking through windows as other, more fortunate children celebrate Christmas around gorgeous Christmas trees. Christmas is a family celebration, and for the outsider, the freezing child, all doors are closed; nowhere is he invited to enjoy the bliss of the moment. He is an orphan with no help to expect from his fellow-beings. In a beam of light, Christ suddenly appears in the form of a child, dressed in white clothes. He promises the child a Christmas more splendid than anyone has ever seen. As in

---

1   Fridlender, *Realizm Dostoevskogo*, 292-94.
2   The Russian word *elka* can be translated as either "Christmas tree" or "Christmas party."
3   Dostoevskii, *Polnoe sobranie sochinenii*, 24: 102.
4   Frank, *Dostoevsky*, 747.

a dream, a fir tree appears in the starry heavens. Angels lift the child up to their holy feast, as he now returns to his rightful home, where all earthly hardship can be forgotten.

The parallels between "A Boy at Christ's Christmas Party" and "The Orphaned Child's Christmas" are obvious. Russian commentators, however, from leading Dostoevsky scholar Georgii Fridlender on, have been reluctant to admit Dostoevsky's debt to a minor German poet, stressing instead the differences found.[5] The fact that Dostoevsky fills his sketch with Russian realia and creates the image of a genuine street child is nevertheless but a natural outcome of the different genres (poetry versus prose) and the different literary periods (romanticism versus realism) of the two writers. More important are the striking similarities: the titles; the compassionate theme; the main character—a lonely, "outsider" orphan (Dostoevsky takes Rückert's child to be a boy); the setting—a big, "alien" city; the one-day plot ending with the death of the child; the grandiose religious denouement, with the lofty figure of Christ intervening as the child's friend and savior. In addition, certain motifs—e.g., freezing hands; viewing other people's happiness through windows; beautifully decorated Christmas trees; and the binary oppositions of poor/rich, dark/light, and cold/warm—appear in both texts.[6]

Hans Christian Andersen's "The Little Match Girl" (1845) is mentioned in passing by Fridlender as constituting a Christmas tale tradition together with Charles Dickens's "A Christmas Carol" (1843).[7] However, no comparison is made, nor are any conclusions drawn. The link was instead picked up and forcefully stressed in two articles by later literary scholars, Alina Denisova and Olga Dekhanova. The importance of Rückert and his poem is here rejected in favor of a clearly more prestigious bond. The fact that Dostoevsky nowhere mentions the Danish writer's name, let alone "The Little Match Girl," is not seen as a problem. Instead, it is asserted that Dostoevsky *must* have come across the name of his popular contemporary, on the grounds that Andersen was initially published in Dostoevsky's "own" magazine of the forties, the *Contemporary*

---

5   Fridlender (*Realizm Dostoevskogo*, 304) dismisses Rückert's poem as nothing more than "a ready-made frame," a canvas to be filled with personal choices, adding that "A Boy at Christ's Christmas Party," in its "style, tone, and coloring," is a quite different work. According to O. A. Dekhanova ("F. M. Dostoevskii i G. Kh. Andersen," 77-78), Rückert and Dostoevsky here share only a motif; otherwise there are no common structural or stylistic features. A. V. Denisova ("Andersenovskii kontekst," 34), for her part, stresses the utmost simplicity of the plot in Rückert's poem. It is not only Russians who defend Dostoevsky's originality: Frank (*Dostoevsky*, 747-48), too, stresses the differences more than the parallels.

6   The opposition of coldness/warmth in four Christmas tales by writers such as Rückert and Andersen is the subject of an article by S. A. Gorbunova ("Motivy tepla i kholoda," 2011).

7   Fridlender, *Realizm Dostoevskogo*, 306.

(*Sovremennik*); that translators of Andersen's tales, and reviewers of the Russian Andersen anthologies, included friends and acquaintances of Dostoevsky; and that magazines containing translations of Andersen's works can be found in his library (but not books by Andersen). The library also includes an issue of the magazine *Field* (*Niva*) (April 1875) with an article noting Andersen's seventieth jubilee (with no mention, however, of "The Little Match Girl").[8] Dekhanova goes so far as to claim that Dostoevsky *knew* Andersen's tale and, what's more, that it is likely the two writers met on the narrow streets of Copenhagen, or sat next to each other in the Royal Opera, when Dostoevsky visited the city in October 1865.[9]

All this is, needless to say, speculation, hardly proving that Dostoevsky knew "The Little Match Girl." The tale had first been published in Russian in the important Andersen anthology of 1863, but after that, never again during Dostoevsky's lifetime. Naturally, he could have read "The Little Match Girl" in a German translation, but again, this possibility is not documented.

Any link between Dostoevsky's "A Boy at Christ's Christmas Party" and Andersen's "The Little Match Girl" must thus be based on the existence of significant internal literary motifs and devices having no parallel in Rückert's poem. Dekhanova sees repetitions and the importance of the number three as unifying traits—a suggestion that does not seem convincing. The same goes for the claim that Andersen's and Dostoevsky's religiosity and Christ imagery are different from those of Rückert.[10] The strongest argument for a conscious bond between the two works would be the shared manner in which their finales add information not found in the German poem. While Rückert's child disappears into a spiritual world, both Dostoevsky and Andersen let the ecstatic vision of a blessed afterlife be followed by a sober rendering of how the child's dead body is found the next day. The happy ending is thus undermined. Furthermore, in both tales, there appears the figure of an alternative model of a child: a nasty boy who engages in either thievery or violence. His opposite is the grandma (Andersen) and the mother (Dostoevsky), the memory of whom gives comfort in times of trouble. The two writers also share a sporadic deployment of *erlebte Rede*, the use of the voice and inner thoughts of their characters.

---

8 "Gans Khristian Andersen," *Niva* 16 (1875): 241-42.
9 Dekhanova, "F. M. Dostoevskii i G. Kh. Andersen," 79, 83. Both Andersen and Dostoevsky arrived in Copenhagen on 13 October, but there is no evidence of them visiting the opera during the following week.
10 Ibid., 78, 86-87; Denisova, "Andersenovskii kontekst," 36.

At the same time, we should not lose sight of the conspicuous differences between the two works. That Andersen's main character is a girl, and that the time of the event here is not Christmas Eve but New Year's Eve, is not important. More salient is the detail that Andersen's girl has been sent out into the street by her mean-spirited father to earn money by selling matchsticks. Every match she burns gives her a short-lived, escapist feeling of happiness, while simultaneously making a return home to the feared father more and more impossible. This is a central conflict, which has no equivalent in Dostoevsky's short story. The same goes for Andersen's absurd humor, with the malevolent boy claiming that he will use the stolen clog as a cradle for his future children, and the goose that "waddle[s]" toward the girl "with a knife and fork in its breast," ready to quell her hunger.

The question of whether Dostoevsky knew "The Little Match Girl" and actually used it, consciously or unconsciously, in addition to Rückert's poem, as a model for his own short story must thus be answered with a "it is possible, but not likely." By contrast, it does seem likely that Andersen knew "The Orphaned Child's Christmas." He mentions Rückert in *The Fairy Tale of My Life* as a skillful poet, a master of his native tongue;[11] and he even devoted a poem to the German writer, "Rückert's 'Gedichte'" (1844).[12] This can be interpreted as a reference either to Rückert's *Gedichte* from 1841 or to the three *Gedichte* volumes from 1843,[13] both of which included Rückert's Christmas poem.

The decisive impetus in Andersen's composition of "The Little Match Girl" was an 1843 woodcut by the Danish graphic artist Johan Thomas Lundbye. The image of a ragged little girl clutching a handful of matches has its equivalent in Dostoevsky's beggar boy. But both writers also needed a strong story line, and such a legend they could find in Friedrich Rückert's poem "The Orphaned Child's Christmas": a lonely child freezing to death in late December in a big, alien city while experiencing a mystical moment of bliss as Christ appears as its friend and savior.

Lev Tolstoy: The Tsar is Naked

Hans Christian Andersen was first translated into Russian in 1838, but his Russian breakthrough occurred only in the early 1860s, when a three-volume set of his fairy tales was published in St. Petersburg. However,

---

11 Andersen, *Samlede værker*, 16: 251; 18: 292.
12 Ibid., 8: 83.
13 Ibid., 563.

Lev Tolstoy, like many other educated Russians, was not dependent on Russian translations. In his Iasnaia Poliana library, a few volumes of Andersen's *Gesammelte Werke* (1847-54) have been preserved. Presumably, it was from the German that in 1857 Tolstoy produced a translation of what he called "a little fairy tale by Andersen."[14] "Andersen is splendid," he wrote in his diary.[15] The tale has been identified as "The Emperor's New Clothes" (1837), an Andersen work to which Tolstoy was to return over and over again. Its theme—the revelation of a fraud—appealed to him, and gave him a model of thought useful in quite diverse connections.

The translation from 1857 was neither published nor preserved. But fifteen years later, as Tolstoy in the early 1870s worked on his *Primer* (*Azbuka*, 1872), he returned to Andersen's "The Emperor's New Clothes." The result was a shortened version, a simplified adaptation, suitable for beginning readers, but also in tune with his new stylistic ideals. The choice of title was a precarious moment. The alternatives for Tolstoy to choose from were three: *korol'* ("king"), *imperator* ("emperor"), or *tsar'* ("tsar"), all of which had been used in existing Russian translations of Andersen's fairy tale. Tolstoy selected the latter—"Tsarskoe novoe plat'e," a rather provocative solution, as it made the fairy tale part of the political discourse in Russia. The Russian censors had already kept their eye on the fairy tale, as it seemed to satirize "the manners of high society and partly ridicule the halo of the royal dignity."[16] Another notable adjustment is that Tolstoy changed the child, the revealer of the fraud, to a *durachok*, that is, a fool. In the Russian context, this evokes the image of a holy fool, a *iurodivyi*, who without fear tells the ruler difficult truths. The final scene from Andersen's fairy tale is in this case a parallel to what we have in Pushkin's *Boris Godunov* (*Boris Godunov*), where the holy fool accuses the tsar of murder.

In 1907, Tolstoy made a new, again fairly substantial adaptation of "The Emperor's New Clothes" for a planned but never realized children's reader to be called "Children's Reading Circle" ("Detskii krug chteniia").[17] He added a few details and changed the fool to "a little child" and the innocent onlooker's exclamation from "Look, the tsar walks in the streets without any clothes on!" to the more natural and forceful "He is naked!"

---

14 Tolstoi, *Polnoe sobranie sochinenii*, 47: 108 (diary entry of 1 January 1857).
15 Ibid., 141 (diary entry of 27 June / 9 July 1857).
16 See Braude and Shillegodskii, "Skazki G. Kh. Andersena v Rossii," 280; and Blium, "'Novoe plat'e korolia' i tsarskaia tsenzura," 61.
17 The translation was first published in Gudzii and Gusev, *Lev Tolstoi: Neizdannye teksty* (1933); it is available in Tolstoi, *Polnoe sobranie sochinenii*, 40: 403.

First and foremost, "The Emperor's New Clothes" presented Tolstoy with a model of thought. The fairy tale contained an allegorical meaning applicable in many different circumstances. In 1857, Tolstoy used it to refer to art in general and his own writing in particular: "Andersen's fairy tale about the clothes. The task of literature and the written word is to make things clear to everyone, so that the child will be believed [*vtolkovat' vsem tak, chtob' rebenku poverili*]."[18] The writer must present the theme, the main idea of a literary work in a convincing way, easy for everyone to grasp; and not get bogged down in extravagant stylistic embroidery and imagery.

This reading corresponds to Tolstoy's interpretation of another fairy tale by Andersen, "The Old House." In discussing Maksim Gorky's play *The Lower Depths* (*Na dne*), Tolstoy found an appropriate quotation in "The Old House": "Gilding fades fast, but pigskin will last." This is the old house's motto, spoken by its leather-covered walls as a comment on the new, finer houses on the same street.[19] According to Tolstoy, Andersen's saying had its counterpart in the wise words of the Russian peasant: "Everything passes, only the truth remains."[20] Tolstoy's advice to Gorky was thus to simplify his style and avoid modern devices, that is, create not for the moment, but the centuries to come. That Tolstoy and Andersen were on a similar wavelength in this respect was confirmed by the literary critic Aleksandr Izmailov. When Tolstoy confessed his antipathy for the word *kotoryi* ("who/which"), which he found cumbersome, Izmailov could tell him that Andersen, too, tried to avoid subordinate clauses.[21] Simplify—that was the golden rule.

In *The Kingdom of God is Within You* (*Tsarstvo Bozhie vnutri vas*, 1893), Andersen's fairy tale has the function of a revolutionary appeal. Tolstoy predicts that there will come a time when everyone will see (as he does) that society is based on violence. Here Tolstoy takes up the role of the child-like (or holy fool-like) unmasker, in this case to expose the true nature of the army and police as incompatible with the teaching of Christ.[22] Although seen and understood by everyone, this truth has been covered up by the state and church.

Eleven years later, Tolstoy would develop this view further, stripping

---

18 Tolstoi, *Polnoe sobranie sochinenii*, 47: 202 (note 16, dated 28 February 1857).
19 On other Russian treatments of this motto, apparently popularized in the Russian context by Tolstoy, see the contributions to this volume by Karin Grelz and Inna Sergienko.
20 Gor'kii, "Lev Tolstoi," 478.
21 Lakshin, *Interv'iu i besedy s L'vom Tolstym*, 258-59.
22 Tolstoi, *Polnoe sobranie sochinenii*, 28: 218.

the so-called "great men" of society of their importance. "I must make a note of this," he writes.

> People invent signs of greatness for themselves: emperors, army commanders, poets. However, it is all lies. Everyone sees straight through it, understands that there is nothing there, that the tsar has no clothes. What about all the wise men, the prophets, then? They may appear to be more useful than others, but they are insignificant, not in the least greater than other people. All their wisdom, holiness, predictions are nothing compared to true wisdom and holiness. Moreover, they are no greater than anyone else. There is no greatness among men, only a fulfilment, more or less complete, or a failure to fulfill what one must do. That is good. It is better this way. Don't look for greatness, just duties.[23]

Tolstoy here appears in two roles: one, the world-famous writer and thinker, "Russia's second tsar," facing the risk of himself being unmasked; the other, the little child, or the simple holy fool, who strips the great man of all semblance of importance. The same thought is expressed still more starkly in a letter to the writer Leonid Semyonov in 1908. Tolstoy finds Semyonov's opinion of him too lofty. He himself is fully aware of his own pitiful insignificance in the face of his high ideals and the people he deals with: "I am just waiting for it to happen to me like it happened to the naked tsar walking down the street—for a child to come up and say: he has no clothes—and everyone will immediately realize that they have seen in me something that is not there, while they haven't seen the bad things *que crève les yeux*."[24] Tolstoy repeated this self-criticism the following year, calling himself a bad, insignificant person on the verge of being exposed: "When will *ein kleines Kind* come up to me and exclaim: *Er hat nichts an*."[25]

The Revolution of 1905, too, led Tolstoy to recall Andersen's fairy tale. The process of Russian society's radicalization, he considered, had begun in the early 1870s, when the student populists "went to the people." Like the child of the tale, they deprived the tsar of his false greatness, and caused the people to lose their belief in the chosenness and inviolability of the ruler.[26] In 1910, Tolstoy developed his thought:

---

23 Ibid., 55: 75-76 (diary entry of 15 August 1904).
24 Ibid., 78: 137 (letter dated 10 May 1908). "Que crève les yeux" = "which are obvious."
25 Makovitskii, *U Tolstogo*, 3: 105 (diary entry of 17 November 1909).
26 Ibid., 2: 318 (diary entry of 3 December 1906).

> The revolution made our Russian people suddenly realize the unfairness of its situation. This is the fairy tale about the tsar's new clothes. The child who frankly said that the tsar had no clothes was the revolution. Among the people there awoke an awareness of the lies in which they had been living, and the people reacted to this untruth in different ways (the majority, sadly enough, with hatred); but the people at large has already understood the situation. To remove this insight is already impossible. However, what our government does when it tries to stifle the irrepressible knowledge of the prevailing untruth is to strengthen this untruth, something that only leads to even greater aggressions toward this untruth.[27]

When Tolstoy in 1909 was working on a speech for the planned international peace conference in Stockholm, it was "The Emperor's New Clothes" that most clearly expressed his standpoint on the peace issue:

> When the tsar in Andersen's fairy tale paraded along the streets and all the people admired his beautiful new clothes, then a single word from a child changed everything—a child who said what everyone knew but no one spoke. He said: "He has nothing on at all," and the suggestion evaporated, the tsar felt ashamed, and everyone who had told themselves that they had seen the tsar dressed in fine new clothes now saw that he was naked. We, too, must say the same thing, say what everyone knows but does not want to say, say that whatever you call a murder, the murder is always a murder—a criminal, shameful deed. And all that is needed, and what we here today can do, is to speak up, loud and clear, so that the people will stop seeing what they think they see, and see what they really see. They will stop seeing "serving one's native country," "the heroic deeds of war," "the honors of war," and see what there really is: a naked, criminal act of killing. And if people see this, then it will be like in the fairy tale: those who committed these shameful acts will be ashamed, and those who told themselves that they did not see anything criminal in murder will see it and stop being murderers.[28]

In his famous article "Lev Tolstoy as a Mirror of the Russian Revolution" ("Lev Tolstoi kak zerkalo russkoi revoliutsii," 1908), Lenin called Tolstoy a would-be holy fool, "tearing off every and all kinds of masks."[29] Inspired by Andersen's fairy tale, Tolstoy indeed repeatedly took up the role of the pseudo-naïve fool who does not uncritically accept common

---

27 Tolstoi, *Polnoe sobranie sochinenii*, 58: 24 (diary entry of 11 March 1910).
28 Ibid., 38: 124.
29 Lenin, "Lev Tolstoi kak zerkalo russkoi revoliutsii."

truths, but boldly states what his common sense tells him. It was an act of simplifying, undressing, revealing the falseness of the politics, religion, science, and culture of modern society. In *What I Believe* (*V chem moia vera*, 1884), Tolstoy stated that he was not out to interpret the Gospel, but, on the contrary, to forget all existing interpretations and commentaries, and read the words of Christ as such, accept them as such. This too was an act very much in the spirit of "The Emperor's New Clothes," the Andersen tale that molded the Tolstoyan strategy.

Tolstoy's use of the artistic technique of defamiliarization (*ostranenie*), with examples like Levin at the opera (*Anna Karenina*) or Nekhliudov participating in an Orthodox service (*Resurrection* [*Voskresenie*]), is well known. Like the child in Andersen's fairy tale, these heroes of Tolstoy's novels stand free from all conventions and are thus able to see the world unadulterated, just as it is in reality. And when Napoleon is deprived all greatness in *War and Peace* (*Voina i mir*), he, too, is a "an emperor without clothes," painfully exposed by the Russian writer Lev Tolstoy.

In the summer of 1857, the same year as his first translation of "The Emperor's New Clothes," Tolstoy made a tour of Europe. His travel reading also included Andersen's Italian-set novel *The Improvisatore* (1835). The novel already existed in two Russian translations (1844 and 1848-49), but there is good cause to believe Tolstoy read it in German.[30] "Andersen is excellent," he wrote in his diary,[31] and, indeed, in *The Improvisatore* there was much that must have appealed to him. There was a kinship with his own childhood trilogy, likewise a *Bildungsroman* told in the first person by a teller inclined to introspection. The Danish author's thoughts on religion and art (music, painting, poetry) must have felt stimulating; and his brilliant description of the setting may well have played a part in influencing Tolstoy to choose Italy as the destination of his second journey abroad four years later.

Primarily, however, Tolstoy admired Andersen's fairy tales. Besides "The Emperor's New Clothes," two other tales are mentioned in his diary or notebook. One is the above-mentioned "The Old House," the other, "Five Peas from a Pod." In his diary, Tolstoy writes: "Andersen's fine fairy tale about the peas who thought the whole world was green so long as the pod was green, but then the world turned yellow and then ... something was torn apart and the world ended. But one pea fell out and started to grow."[32] What attracted Tolstoy was the parallel with human

---

30 Ibid., 47: 475.
31 Ibid., 60: 257 (diary entry of 7 January 1858).
32 Ibid., 55: 481 (diary entry of 15 September 1904).

life: people look at life from their own restricted point of view, believing that this is the final truth, the only possible, but then their protective shield is removed and they have to face the genuine truth.[33] There is a definite connection with "The Emperor's New Clothes" to be seen here.

In 1894-95, the Dane Peter Hansen and his Russian wife Anna published a Russian translation of Andersen's *Collected Works*. This was the first time the tales were translated into Russian directly from Danish rather than from German translations. Hansen, a longtime friend of Tolstoy, sent the first volume to Iasnaia Poliana together with a letter to Tolstoy's wife:

> When I stayed at Iasnaia Poliana, Lev Nikolaevich told me among other things that he "had once thought very highly of Andersen." I hope this love, if it for some reason has died, will awaken again when he reads our translations. Earlier translations—no offence—gave a completely wrong picture of Andersen; if the tone creates the music in the works of some writers, this is very much the case for Andersen, and when translating from translations, it is natural that this is completely lost.[34]

We know that Tolstoy had found previous translations, especially those made by Marko Vovchok (pseudonym of Mariia Vilinskaia), utterly weak. Was he pleased with the Hansens' translations? He never commented on them. The four volumes are not to be found in his library—perhaps a sign that they were read and cherished not only by Tolstoy, but also by his children and grandchildren.

Nikolai Vagner: "The Russian Andersen"

Nikolai Vagner (1829-1907) was already in his forties when he turned to children's literature. A scientist and professor of zoology at the University of Kazan, he had almost no previous experience of writing fiction, let alone children's literature. Still, his collection *The Tales of the Cat Murlyka* (*Skazki Kota-Murlyki*), published in 1872, became a bestseller, with nine editions before the revolutions of 1917.

Vagner made no secret of where the impulse to write fairy tales came from. In his autobiographical sketch "How Did I Become a Writer? Something of a Confession" ("Kak ia sdelalsia pisatelem? Nechto vrode ispovedi," 1892), he remarks that in 1868, he read "positive and even

---

33 Makovitskii, *U Tolstogo*, 2: 541 (diary entry of 22 November 1907).
34 Iukhansen and Mioller, "Perepiska S. A. Tolstoi," 60.

enthusiastic reviews" of the first Russian volume of tales by Andersen. His curiosity piqued, he went out to buy the book. While he liked many of the tales, he found others weak. A challenging thought arose: "Surely I can write something like this, or even better?"[35] In the next three years, Vagner wrote the fifteen tales that make up the first edition of his *Tales of the Cat Murlyka*.[36]

At the same time, Vagner sought to downplay his indebtedness to the Danish writer. Asked which book had made the greatest impression on him and most contributed to his writerly talent, he would have said "none." "Living people, living language influenced me much more than any book. Andersen's fairy tales found a ready ground, which had been laid already in my childhood. It had been fostered by my nanny [*nian'ka*], my elder sister."[37] Still, Vagner needed literary models to give his thoughts and ideas form and structure. The fairy tales he had read prior to Andersen were Russian folk tales, Petr Ershov's *The Little Humpbacked Horse* (*Konek-gorbunok*) and, undoubtedly, although not mentioned, Pushkin's fairy tales in verse, the Grimm brothers' tales, and E. T. A. Hoffmann's "The Nutcracker and the Mouse-King." Even so, within this literary context, Andersen's tales stand out as the most obvious source of influence and inspiration. Vagner became "the Russian Andersen," with parallels to this famous predecessor noted already during his lifetime.

Vagner claimed that it was positive reviews of Andersen that had sparked his interest in that writer. The truth is, however, that the praise given the Danish storyteller by Russian critics was seldom unqualified.[38] His artistic brilliance was acknowledged, but in reviews from the period 1863-69, other recurring opinions were voiced as well. Thus, it was said that there is usually a serious thought at the core of Andersen's tales, but the moral is sometimes unclear or even dubious, and that quite a few of his tales are unsuitable for children, being too complicated, sentimental, or mystical. When we speak of Andersen's great popularity in

---

35 Vagner, "Kak ia sdelalsia pisatelem," 37.
36 Vagner's canonical fairy tales are "A Fairy Tale" ("Skazka"), "The Wondrous Boy" ("Chudnyi mal'chik"), "The Two Ivans" ("Dva Ivana"), "Pimperle" ("Pimperle"), "Gulli" ("Gulli"), "Max and the Spinning Top" ("Maks i volchok"), "The New Year" ("Novyi god"), "Uncle Pood" ("Diadia-Pud"), "Kurilka" ("Kurilka"), "Song of the Earth" ("Pesenka zemli"), "Kotia" ("Kotia"), "The Major and the Cricket" ("Maior i sverchok"), "Mila and Nolli" ("Mila i Nolli"), "Happiness" ("Shchast'e"), and "The Birch Tree" ("Bereza"). Most of these were published in Vagner's first anthology.
37 Vagner, "Kak ia sdelalsia pisatelem," 38.
38 See A. F. Golovachev, "Bibliograficheskii listok," *Russkoe slovo* 11/12 (1863): 43; *Sovremennik* 100, no. 2 (1864), 96-91; *Uchitel'* 4, nos. 13-14 (1864): 536-537; *Novoe vremia* 38 (1868): 3; *Narodnaia shkola* 2 (1869): 33-34, 34-35; *Delo* 6 (1869): 34-37.

Russia, this is, especially prior to the modernist period, more a matter of readerly than critical reception (on which, see the contributions to this volume by Inna Sergienko). Even before reading Andersen, Vagner could, however, have already drawn two important conclusions on what might be called "the modern fairy tale." Firstly, it could and even should not just entertain, but have a serious theme and purpose. Consequently, "the philosophical fairy tale" has been called Vagner's most important genre.[39] Secondly, fairy tales need not be adjusted to the level of the child-reader, but could boldly address a dual audience. And indeed, already in Vagner's first volume of fairy tales, the fictive author, the cat Murlyka, anticipates and answers the question: "Why do you tell fairy tales not suitable for children in a childlike way?"[40]

In a Russian bookshop in 1868, Vagner could choose between two volumes of Andersen's tales, both called *Complete Collected Fairy Tales* (*Polnoe sobranie skazok*). One was the second edition of the three-volume set published by Stasova and Trubnikova (1867), the other the first volume of a new set of three volumes, published by K. Plotnikov (1868). It hardly matters which one Vagner chose, as both books include the tales on which Andersen's fame rests, and which are seen as having influenced Vagner as he decided to try his hand at children's literature. In the forewords of both volumes, moreover, Vagner could find unreserved praise of Andersen's talent. In the 1867 publication, it is said that Andersen occupies "a brilliant place among the greatest writers of the nineteenth century. One can boldly say that no one stands higher than he when it comes to fantasy, fresh images, and fascinating stories,"[41] and the volume from 1868 states that "Andersen is among the most popular Danish writers and, what's more, has a prominent place in the history of European literature."[42] These texts could well have been what Vagner had in mind when referring to "enthusiastic" reviews. Undoubtedly, they also offered a challenge to the Russian writer *in spe*.

There is a general agreement that three pairs of tales most clearly attest to the Andersenian influence on Vagner.[43] Andersen's "The Fir Tree," "The Shirt Collar," and "Ole Lukoie" have their counterpart in Vagner's

---

39 Mil'don, "Vagner Nikolai Petrovich," 385.
40 Vagner, *Skazki Kota-Murlyki*, 1: 45.
41 Andersen, *Polnoe sobranie skazok Kh. K. Andersena* (1867), iii.
42 Andersen, *Polnoe sobranie skazok Kh. K. Andersena* (1868), 1: i.
43 Feoktistov ("Vagner i Andersen," 202) was the first to point out the similarities in these cases.

"The Birch Tree," "Kurilka,"[44] and "Pimperle"[45] respectively. Parallels have also been drawn between Andersen's "The Little Match Girl" and Vagner's "Fanni" ("Fanni"), "The Snow Queen" and "Mila and Nolli," and "The Story of a Mother" and "The Song of the Earth."[46]

In the first four cases, there are parallels between the main characters, their life situation, and the plot. Both Andersen's fir tree and Vagner's birch have a longing for something other than their present situation. Their inability to be satisfied with what they have leads them to perdition. The shirt collar and Kurilka, that is, the burning wood chip, are self-assured braggarts, doomed by their blindness to reality. As for Ole Lukoie and Pimperle, they are both a child's best friend, creating pleasant fantasies and assuaging the fear of death. And finally, the fate of Andersen's nameless match girl and Vagner's Fanni is to die a lonely death from cold, hunger, and/or disease. In these cases, Vagner's readers were sure to associate his fairy tales with those of Andersen.

Naturally, there are also differences. Andersen's fir tree has its moment of happiness and pride, while Vagner's birch is doomed to fight a hopeless battle for existence. The shirt collar is a self-centered Lovelace, while Kurilka is more of a Gogolian Khlestakov, never able to refrain from bragging and making up stories.[47] Ole Lukoie is mainly a creator of dreams, while Pimperle's central function is to amuse and support.

However, the similarities are not restricted to the level of plot and the main protagonists. Andersen's "trademark," so to speak, is the literary device he employs in a marked, radical manner—the personification and animation of the material world. No longer is this process reserved, as in folk tales and fables, for animals. Already in E. T. A. Hoffmann's "The Nutcracker and the Mouse-King" (1816), a model for both Andersen and Vagner, dolls come to life at night, and we find the same image of a secret nocturnal life, created in dreams or in a state of delirium, in Andersen's "Ole Lukoie" and Vagner's "Fanni." Hjalmar in Andersen's

---

44 *Kurilka* is a burning wood chip, which in the game is passed from hand to hand. The child in whose hands it is when it goes out has lost the game. Similar games were known also in England ("Jack's Alive") and France ("Petit bonhomme") (Tylor, *Primitive Culture*, 76).
45 "Pimperle" comes from the "Kommando Pimperle" game, the German equivalent of the English "Simon says." Vagner's Pimperle is, however, more like the Sandman, or the Swedish John Blund.
46 For his part, Dmitrii Kobozev ("Kot-Murlyka," 24) adds a few more pairs: "Two Small Bottles" ("Dve sklianki") and "Pen and Inkstand," "The Song of the Earth" and "The Story of the Year," "The Two Ivans" and "Little Claus and Big Claus," "Abu Hassan" ("Abu-Gassan") and "A Story," and "Two Evenings" ("Dva vechera") and "On the Last Day." Andersen's "The Daisy," "Little Ida's Flowers," "The Darning Needle," and "The Sweethearts" are included in Kobozev's discussion as well.
47 Bakhtin, "Etiudy po detskoi literature," 50.

fairy tale is introduced to a world where furniture sings, and droopy letters in a copybook straighten themselves out under threat of being given medicine, while Vagner's heroine has a conversation with a thimble and watches a needle dancing with a pin cushion. Not only do letters dance at this ball, but even the parts of speech join in.

In Andersen's tales, for example "The Daisy," "Little Ida's Flowers," and "Five Peas from a Pod," trees, flowers, and vegetables are thinking beings with a rich inner life. The author goes still further in "The Sweethearts," where the relationship between a top and a ball is pictured as one between two human beings. The tale "Darning Needles" depicts a conversation between a needle and the fingers holding it. Likewise, "The Silver Shilling" is a thinking object, capable of feeling joy and fear. In many cases, Andersen uses personification to describe not only friendship or jealousy, but also erotic feelings. The shirt collar is determined to find a bride, be it a garter, flatiron, or comb, just because the time is ripe. The scene of a mouse wedding in Vagner's "Fanni" can be seen as a fulfilment of the shirt collar's stubborn proposals.

Vagner, in this respect, followed in the footsteps of Andersen, giving life to dolls, gingerbread biscuits, wood chips, and needles. In "The Birch Tree," the storm and the wind communicate with the tree (cf. the activity of the sunbeams and the air in Andersen's "The Fir Tree"). Vagner is at his most animating in "Kurilka," where the chip has a serious conversation with a flagstone, and in "The Birch Tree," where stones and moss are given voices and human traits and emotions. Surely, all these objects would have been mute and lifeless, had it not been for Andersen.

Unlike conventional folk tales, neither Andersen nor Vagner shied from tragic endings. Andersen's "The Story of a Mother" and Vagner's "The Song of the Earth" tell of a child's and a young girl's death. The fir tree, the birch tree, the shirt collar, and Kurilka are all annihilated. The flowers in Andersen's "The Daisy" and "Little Ida's Flowers" mercilessly fade, while the ball in "The Sweethearts" loses all its colors and charm. The little match girl and Vagner's dressmaker Fanni die of hunger and cold at the end of their stories. And Pimperle, the very source of joy among humans, cannot save little Theodor from dying.

Still, death is not the end, and its tragicness can be questioned, a thought more pronounced in Vagner's fairy tales than in Andersen's. Vagner was later to become prominent in Russia's spiritualism movement, always ready to debate nonbelievers; but already in the fairy tales of the early 1870s, there is the comforting certainty of a life beyond the grave. The happiness that Fanni could not experience in life, she will find in heaven. In "The Birch Tree," the moss comes to the realization that there are no beginnings and no ends. Used as firewood, the birch tree heats the pan with porridge for hungry children, and its ashes give new life to nature, just like the remains of Kurilka. In "Pimperle," Vagner paints a rosy picture of an existence beyond earthly life, where the key word is "eternal." The promise of "a land of eternal happiness and eternal joy," open to all who are united by "eternal love," makes Theodor (and presumably also the reader) forget all fear and even long for Death—here a personified being who on "wings of eternity" takes the child away from a life of sickness and sorrow.[48]

For Andersen's fir tree, there is no promise of a new existence after it has been burned to ashes, and the question is left open as to whether its brief moment of triumph in the role of Christmas tree was worth sacrificing its life. The shirt collar, on the other hand, lives on in the form of paper. The little match girl is given a conventional Christian heaven where God receives her. Like Vagner's Theodor, she dies with a smile on her lips. Interestingly, Ole Lukoie anticipates Vagner's Pimperle in the sense that he has a sympathetic brother, Death, who takes children for a ride in his horse-drawn wagon if they have been good.

Vagner often lets a ruthless Darwinism reign in his works. The critic Nikolai Bakhtin, the brother of Mikhail Bakhtin, went so far as to say that Vagner learned fairytale form from Andersen, while the Gospels and Darwin gave him the content.[49] The weak and the sick have to give way; their function—both in nature and in human society—is to serve as "manure" for a stronger life. The small birch tree must perish and make way for its supplanters. The reader is not invited to feel pity for the tree; what might seem like heartless cruelty is, for the author, just a fact.

The act of storytelling with an explicit narratorial voice is more prominent in Andersen's tales than in those of Vagner. When Andersen employs the traditional opening line "Once upon a time" (*Der var engang*), as for example in "The Shirt Collar," this is not just an homage to the folkloric and fairytale tradition, but also a way of stressing the role of narrator. Ole Lukoie is first and foremost a storyteller; he sees his job as entertaining children with tales. Andersen's reader is often reminded that what he or she has heard is a story. Vagner does achieve the same effect in "Kurilka," which he opens with a "Once upon a time" (*Zhili-byli*) and ends with a "That's all" (*Vot i vse*), but this is more of an exception. In general, he only sparingly uses fairytale

---

48 Vagner, *Skazki Kota-Murlyki*, 1: 151-52.
49 Bakhtin, "Etiudy po detskoi literature," 50.

markers, inclining instead toward the prevailing Russian realism—a move reminiscent of Andersen's development from a writer of *eventyr* to that of *historier*.

The fictive creator of Vagner's fairy tales is the cat Murlyka. She appears only in the foreword, giving her view of fairy tales and modern life. The device has its roots in the Russian romantic tradition, as exemplified by Pushkin's *Tales of Belkin* (*Povesti Belkina*) and Gogol's *Evenings on a Farm near Dikanka* ("Vechera na khutore bliz Dikan'ki"). But whence, specifically, this cat? The book's motto may lead us astray: the cat is definitely not the cunning and cruel Siberian cat Fedot Murlyka from Vasilii Zhukovsky's poem "The War between the Mice and the Frogs" ("Voina myshei i liagushek," 1832). A more likely Russian source is Pushkin's "learned cat" from *Ruslan and Liudmila* (*Ruslan i Liudmila*, 1818), who endlessly produces songs and fairy tales. Another important prototype is E. T. A. Hoffmann's *Kater Murr* (1819-21), likewise a learned cat with literary ambitions. From Andersen, Vagner had nothing to learn in this respect.

Vagner wanted not only to write something similar to what Andersen did, but also to surpass him. Did he succeed? In a review of 1881, the critic Ivan Feoktistov answered in the affirmative. Skeptical about the value and importance of fairy tales in general, Feoktistov put the Russian above his Danish counterpart, not so much in terms of literary merit, but thanks to a sharper social awareness and analysis of modern life.[50] To him, Vagner represented the next inevitable step in the development of fairy tales, a move toward realism. Other critics have pointed out that some of Vagner's fairy tales, like "Max and the Spinning Top" and "Basil Granzho (The Wheel of Life)" ("Bazil' Granzho [Koleso zhizni]") were used in populist propaganda, spurring revolutionary youth.[51] And, finally, Nikolai Bakhtin stressed that Vagner's Fanni has a real profession and social status, unlike Andersen's nameless little girl, who freezes to death in an unspecified town.[52]

In 1922, the same Bakhtin anticipated a renaissance for Vagner, but what actually happened, after one last edition of Murlyka's fairy tales published in 1923, was a total ban lasting nearly seventy years. While Andersen enjoyed a steady popularity at home and abroad, Vagner became a nonperson in his homeland. When called back to life in 1991, the author was totally bereft of his prerevolutionary popularity. Vagner's

---

50 Feoktistov, "Vagner i Andersen," 202 ff.
51 Kobozev, "Kot Murlyka," 29.
52 Bakhtin, "Etiudy po detskoi literature," 54.

(or rather, the cat Murlyka's) fairy tales are now published again, but so far without any great success. The 2015 two-volume collection of fifty-six fairy tales and short stories represents the most serious attempt so far to reintroduce Vagner into children's reading. Undoubtedly, there are fewer masterpieces among Vagner's fairy tales than in Andersen's much larger oeuvre, and, unlike Andersen, Vagner was hardly ever, if at all, translated into other languages. Still, he represents an interesting phenomenon: a Russian writer of fairy tales, provoked by Andersen's popularity to create something similar, or, if possible, even better.

***

Adaptation and appropriation were only two ways of relating to Hans Christian Andersen. While Vagner and Tolstoy openly cited fairy tales by him as the starting point for certain of their creative works and thoughts, the case of Dostoevsky discussed here is an example of a shared influence, with a third writer being the source of inspiration. Taken together, the three examples give a sense of the myriad ways in which the Danish writer influenced nineteenth-century Russian literature.

Works Cited

Andersen, Hans Christian. *H. C. Andersens samlede værker* 1-18. Copenhagen: Gyldendal 2003-2007.
Andersen, Kh. K. *Polnoe sobranie skazok Andersena*. Second ed. St. Petersburg: Izdanie Trubnikovoi i Stasovoi, 1867.
—. *Polnoe sobranie skazok Kh. K. Andersena*. St. Petersburg: Izdanie K. Plotnikova, 1868.
Bakhtin, N. M. "Etiudy po detskoi literature." *Pedagogicheskaia mysl'* 1-2 (1922): 29-63.
Blium, A. V. "'Novoe plat'e korolia' i tsarskaia tsenzura." *Detskaia literatura* 2 (1971): 60-62.
Braude, L. Iu., and S. P. Shillegodskii. "Skazki G. Kh. Andersena v Rossii." In *Uchenye zapiski Len. gos. ped. instituta im. A. I. Gertsena* 198 (1959): 271-96.
Dekhanova, O. A. "F. M. Dostoevskii i G. Kh. Andersen: Fantazii i real'nost'." *Vestnik Cheliabinskogo universiteta. Seriia 2. Filologiia* (1999): 77-88. Available electronically: http://www.lib.csu.ru/vch/2/1999_02/007.pdf.
Denisova, A. V. "Andersenovskii kontekst 'Mal'chika u Khrista na elke' F. M. Dostoevskogo." In *Letnie chteniia v Darovom: Materialy mezhdunarodnoi nauchnoi konferentsii 27-29 avgusta 2006 g.* Kolomna: KGPI, 2006: 34-37. Available electronically: http://darovoe.ru/wp-content/uploads/2012/03/denisova_andersenovsky.pdf.

Dostoevskii, F. D. *Polnoe sobranie sochinenii v 30 tomakh*. Leningrad: Nauka, 1972-90.

Feoktistov, I. "Vagner i Andersen kak avtory skazok dlia detei: Po povodu vtorogo izdaniia 'Skazok Kota-Murlyki'." *Pedagogicheskii listok dlia roditelei i vospitatelei* 3-4 (1881): 195-218.

Frank, Joseph. *Dostoevsky: A Writer in His Time*. Princeton University Press, 2010.

Fridlender, G. M. *Realizm Dostoevskogo*. Moscow-Leningrad: Nauka, 1964.

Gorbunova, S. A. "Motivy tepla i kholoda v rozhdestvenskikh rasskazakh evropeiskikh pisatelei (F. Riukkert, G. Kh. Andersen, S. Lageliof, Ch. Dikkens)." In *Zarubezhnaia literatura: Kontekstual'nye i intertekstual'nye sviazi*. Ekaterinburg: Ural'nyi federal'nyi universitet, 2011: 98-101.

Gor'kii, A. M. "Lev Tolstoi." In *L. N. Tolstoi v vospominaniiakh sovremennikov*, edited by N. M. Fortunatov, 2: 68-508. Moscow: Khudozhestvennaia literatura, 1978.

Gudzii, N. K., and N. N. Gusev, eds. *Lev Tolstoi: Neizdannye teksty*. Moscow: Academia-GIKhL, 1933.

Iukhansen, D. S., and P. U. Mioller. "Perepiska S. A. Tolstoi s P. G. Ganzenom." *Scando-Slavica* 24 (1978): 49-62.

Kobozev, Dmitrii. "Kot-Murlyka: Literator i uchenyi." In *Skazki Kota Murlyki* by Nikolai Vagner, 1: 5-32. Moscow: Knizhnyi Klub Knigovek, 2015.

Lakshin, V. Ia., ed. *Interv'iu i besedy s L'vom Tolstym*. Moscow: Sovremennik, 1987.

Lenin, V. I. "Lev Tolstoi kak zerkalo russkoi revoliutsii." Available electronically: https://royallib.com/book/lenin_vladimir/lev_tolstoy_kak_zerkalo_russkoy_revolyutsii_i_drugie_raboti_vi_lenina_o_ln_tolstom.html

Makovitskii. D. P. *U Tolstogo. 1904-1910: Iasnopolianskie zapiski*. Kn. II-III. *Literaturnoe nasledstvo*. Vol. 90. Moscow: Nauka, 1979.

Mil'don, V. I. "Vagner Nikolai Petrovich." In *Russkie pisateli 1800-1917*, edited by K. M. Chernyi, 1: 385-86. Moscow: Sovetskaia entsiklopediia, 1989.

Tylor, Edward B. *Primitive Culture*. Vol. 1. Sixth ed. London: John Murray, 1920.

Tolstoi, L. N. *Polnoe sobranie sochinenii v 90 tomakh*. Moscow: Khudozhestvennaia literatura, 1928-1958.

Vagner, N. P. "Kak ia sdelalsia pisatelem? Nechto v rode ispovedi." *Russkaia shkola* 1 (1892): 26-39.

—. *Skazki Kota-Murlyki*. Moscow: Knigovek, 2015.

B)
Creative Affinities:
Andersen in Silver Age Poetry and Prose

Hans Christian Andersen and the Acmeists:

Notes toward a Theme[1]

Oleg Lekmanov

Let us begin with a brief comparison of two quotations—the first, a recollection by Konstantin Balmont from 1910:

> The multicolored thread of my friendship/enmity with Valerii Briusov kept dragging on and getting more tangled; the two of us trod along our souls as one might tread through a night- and morning-garden in moments of happiness; and as Andersen's little mermaid trod along shards of glass.[2]

The second, a statement by Anna Akhmatova from 1940:

> My feet are swollen again, this time both of them. Yesterday I was barely able to trudge to the House of Writers, and while I was there I realized that I wouldn't be able to make it home.... I trod the streets like Andersen's mermaid.[3]

Neither the symbolist Balmont nor the acmeist Akhmatova had any trouble pulling a fitting Hans Christian Andersen image from the baggage of their memory when they needed one; and no wonder—for both the elder and younger generations of Russian modernists, Andersen's tales had been required childhood reading. In this case, however, the distinctions are more revealing and important than the resemblance. Balmont situates his Andersen quotation in a luxurious and flowery context; Akhmatova, in a minimalist one. In Balmont, it is a matter of a romantic "night- and morning-garden"; in Akhmatova, the Soviet House of Writers. Balmont has the neutral *khodili*, "we trod" or "walked";

---

[1] This article makes use of conclusions from the "European Literature in a Comparative Light: Method and Interpretation" project, implemented under the aegis of the Fundamental Research Program of the Higher School of Economics (HSE) National Research University in 2016.
[2] Bal'mont, *Morskoe svechenie*, 197.
[3] See Chukovskaia, *Zapiski ob Anne Akhmatovoi*, 1: 158.

Akhmatova, the lower-register *doplelas'*, "trudged." In Balmont, the foot pain is metaphorical; in Akhmatova, it is entirely real.

And while the specific life-situations described by Balmont and Akhmatova obviously differ, this is far more a matter of the fundamentally distinct worldviews of the symbolist and the acmeist, and consequently their distinct methods of reading, interpreting, and employing their predecessors' imagery for their own purposes. The group of Russian poets who in 1912 declared themselves acmeists (Anna Akhmatova, Sergei Gorodetsky, Nikolai Gumilev, Mikhail Zenkevich, Osip Mandelshtam, and Vladimir Narbut) quite consciously and consistently trained themselves to combat the ideology and poetics of Symbolism.[4] However, the acmeists' primary polemical charge was aimed not at the older symbolists (Konstantin Balmont and Valerii Briusov) but rather the younger ones (Aleksandr Blok, Andrei Bely, and Viacheslav Ivanov).

The younger symbolists were captivated, first and foremost, by how the deceptive simplicity of Andersen's tales masked the mystical, almost ineffable Mystery of childhood and childlike purity. Accordingly, they saw Andersen as a preacher-writer whose fairytale motifs nearly always turn out religious. This is why, for instance, it is precisely Andersen that Blok invokes in the final lines of an exalted, enigma-laden letter he sent to Andrei Bely in 1904:

> "Forget" You—what does that mean? That would never happen. My Bible is lost somewhere among my numerous dusty bookshelves, or else I'd copy out for You: "Woe unto him who has abandoned his first love..." I mean as pertains to You and me—but that cannot be. I existed, reading Your Book. And nothing has happened, has it? The year 1904 = 1902... The snow is falling today just as softly. I am the same young and rosy boy today as... even in 1888. It's just that now I have a terribly ridiculous silver thread in my beard. But the pictures in Andersen's fairy tales for children still mean the same thing.[5]

The acmeists, by contrast, were interested in Andersen as first and foremost the describer and in part the creator of a cozy miniature world whose little *riddles* could easily be contrasted with the metaphysical *Mysteries* hymned by Russian Symbolism, "afflicted" as it was by the

---

4 The focus below will be an analysis of works by three acmeists—Akhmatova, Mandelshtam, and Gumilev.
5 Belyi and Blok, *Perepiska*, 184-85. On Andersen's influence on Andrei Bely, see Lavrov, *Andrei Belyi v 1910-e gody*, 23, 30, 60.

"dropsy of grand themes" (*vodianka bol'shikh tem*) (to borrow Mandelshtam's acerbic definition).[6]

> To read only children's books,
> To cherish only children's thoughts,
> To disperse far everything large,
> To rise out of profound sadness.[7]

> Только детские книги читать,
> Только детские думы лелеять,
> Все большое далёко развеять,
> Из глубокой печали восстать.[8]

With these lines did the same Mandelshtam begin a 1908 poem.

2.

The acmeists (or at least, two of them—Mandelshtam and Akhmatova), then, kept an intent eye on the material world of Andersen's tales, a world consisting primarily of fragile toy-objects.[9] Their heightened attention to these, like their almost demonstrative lack of interest in the Danish storyteller's religious motifs, was a legacy of the acmeists' poetic teacher Innokentii Annensky, the author of a poem quite important for this subject, "Lilac Mist" ("Sirenevaia mgla"):

> Our street lies blanketed in snow,
> Along the snows runs a lilac mist.
>
> In passing it peeped through the window,
> And I realized that I had long since loved it.
>
> I begged of it, that lilac mist,
> "Come visit with me for a while in my corner,
>
> Instead of trying to disperse my age-old melancholy,
> Share with me, O beloved, your own!"

---

6 Mandel'shtam, *Sobranie sochinenii v 4-kh tomakh*, 2: 290.
7 Mandelstam, *Poems from Mandelstam*, 59.
8 Mandel'shtam, *Sobranie sochinenii v 4-kh tomakh*, 1: 3.
9 One of the first to note Akhmatova and Mandelshtam's fondness for "toy" motifs was Omry Ronen; see *An Approach to Mandelstam*, xv.

But all I heard in response, from a distance, was:
"If you love me, then you'll track me down on your own.

Where the maelstrom is overlain with thin blue ice,
There shall I visit for a bit, when I have finished my flight,

But no one saw us by the stove...
Only those who are free and bold are mine."[10]

Наша улица снегами залегла,
По снегам бежит сиреневая мгла.

Мимоходом только глянула в окно,
И я понял, что люблю ее давно.

Я молил ее, сиреневую мглу:
"Погости-побудь со мной в моем углу,

Не мою тоску ты давнюю развей,
Поделись со мной, желанная, своей!"

Но лишь издали услышал я в ответ:
"Если любишь, так и сам отыщешь след.

Где над омутом синеет тонкий лед,
Там часочек погощу я, кончив лёт,

А у печки-то никто нас не видал ...
Только те мои, кто волен да удал".[11]

There is much in this poem to remind a reader of Andersen's tale "The Snow Queen" (1845). In Annensky and Andersen alike, the action unfolds against a wintry backdrop. And in both, signs of winter (a "lilac haze" and a snowflake) are personified into women (*mgla*, "haze," is grammati-

---

10 As a prominent figure in pedagogy, Annensky would of course have been well-read in works both by and about Andersen. In particular, in 1904 he wrote a review of V. Chernyshev's *Collection of Articles for Written and Oral Exposition* (*Sbornik statei dlia pis'mennogo i ustnogo izlozheniia*), which among other texts included tales by Andersen. See Annenskii, *Uchebno-komitetskie retsenzii 1904-1906 godov*, 72.

11 Annenskii, *Stikhotvoreniia i tragedii*, 85.

cally feminine) who "in passing," in flight, peek through the window and induce the male characters to join them in a perilous, fraught journey.

In Andersen, as we recall, this is done like this:

> [Kay] climbed on the chair by the window and looked out through the little peephole. A few snowflakes were falling, and the largest flake of all ... grew bigger and bigger, until at last it turned into a woman.... She was beautiful and she was graceful, but she was ice-shining, glittering ice. She was alive, for all that.... She nodded toward the window and beckoned with her hand.

Of course, in the very first description of the Snow Queen's appearance, Andersen is quick to mention that "there was neither rest nor peace" in her eyes. The whole tale is permeated with the opposition between warmth and cold, beginning with its prologue: "A few people even got a glass splinter in their hearts, and that was a terrible thing, for it turned their hearts into lumps of ice."[12] And all the way to its finale: "Gerda shed hot tears, and when they fell upon [Kay] they went straight to his heart. They melted the lump of ice and burned away the splinter of glass in it."

The opposition of warmth versus cold is presented with particular expressiveness in the following episode from "The Snow Queen":

> The windows often frosted over completely [in the winter]. But [the children] would heat copper pennies on the stove and press these hot coins against the frost-coated glass. Then they had the finest of peepholes.

The Russian translation by Anna and Peter Hansen renders this last phrase as a "wondrous" or "miraculous little round opening" (*chudesnoe kruglen'koe otverstie*[13]), which is quite apt. The point is that all that is warm in "The Snow Queen" bears directly on the theme of the Christian miracle, whereas all that is cold pertains, by contrast, to the theme of devilish temptation:

> It was so cold that, as little Gerda said the Lord's Prayer, she could see her breath freezing in front of her mouth, like a cloud of smoke. It grew thicker and thicker, and took the shape of little angels that grew bigger and bigger the moment they touched the ground. All of them had helmets on their heads and they carried shields and lances in their hands. Rank upon rank, they

---

12 These wicked mirror-splinters from "The Snow Queen" would also become a key motif in Valerii Briusov's late poem "The Magic Mirror" ("Volshebnoe zerkalo," 1922).
13 Andersen, *Skazki. Istorii*, 169.

increased, and when Gerda had finished her prayer she was surrounded by a legion of angels. They struck the dread snowflakes with their lances and shivered them into a thousand pieces. Little Gerda walked on, unmolested and cheerful. The angels rubbed her hands and feet to make them warmer, and she trotted briskly along to the Snow Queen's palace.

Devilish cold contrasts with the primary Christian motif in still another episode of "The Snow Queen": as Kay "trembles from the cold" flying behind the Snow Queen's sleigh, he "tried to say his prayers, but all he could remember was his multiplication tables." Whereas, in the tale's opening, Kay threatens his future sovereign: "I would put her on the hot stove and melt her."

"Lilac Haze" concludes with lines about a stove. But unlike his predecessor, Annensky is hardly inclined to contrast positively coded warmth with negatively coded cold. He consciously refrains also from the religious symbolism so significant to "The Snow Queen." Obeying the paradoxical laws by which his volume *The Cypress Chest* (*Kiparisovyi larets*) is constructed, the poet is disposed to prefer cold to warmth, much as, in the final poem of the "Twilight Trefoil" ("Trilistnik sumerechnyi") cycle (which opens with "Lilac Haze"), darkness is unexpectedly preferred to light:

Does it not seem to you sometimes,
When the twilight makes its way about the house,
That suddenly right there beside you, there exists another environ
Where we live completely differently?

Shadow merges there so softly with shadow,
Such moments occur there,
That it's almost as if we recede
Into each other with invisible eye-rays.

Не мерещится ль вам иногда,
Когда сумерки ходят по дому,
Тут же возле иная среда,
Где живем мы совсем по-другому?
С тенью тень там так мягко слилась,
Там бывает такая минута,
Что лучами незримыми глаз
Мы уходим друг в друга как будто.[14]

---

14 Annenskii, *Stikhotvoreniia i tragedii*, 86.

In Andersen, the combination of the motifs of cold and water harbor potential danger. When Kay has gone missing from the city, "[p]eople said that he was dead—that he must have been drowned in the river not far from town. Ah, how gloomy those long winter days were!" This could also be compared with the description of the hall in the Snow Queen's palace:

> In the middle of the vast, empty hall of snow was a frozen lake. It was cracked into a thousand pieces, but each piece was shaped so exactly like the others that it seemed a work of wonderful craftsmanship. The Snow Queen sat in the exact center of it when she was at home, and she spoke of this as sitting on her "Mirror of Reason." She said this mirror was the only one of its kind, and the best thing in all the world.

In Annensky, ice-covered water is likewise perilous, but the danger holds an ineffable attraction. "Where the maelstrom is overlain with thin blue ice, / There shall I visit for a bit, when I have finished my flight." Cf., in "The Snow Queen": "They flew over forests and lakes." Thin, fragile, doomed to melt, and at the same time, beautiful—ice fits ideally among the multitude of fragile but beautiful objects populating Annensky's poetry (balloons, butterflies, dandelions, lilacs, clouds...). No wonder that in the poem "Palm Week" ("Verbnaia nedelia"), Annensky sings a dirge for the "final," "ruined snow-field" (*pogiblaia snezhnaia l'dina*).[15]

The author of "Lilac Haze" has acted out his own deeply original drama against the backdrop of Andersen's "The Snow Queen." As Mandelshtam wrote of him: "Innokentii Annensky set the example of how an organic poet should be: the whole ship is hammered together from other people's planks, but it has a character all its own."[16]

Still another elder poet who influenced the acmeists should be mentioned here—Mikhail Kuzmin. His views on the Danish storyteller's writings would seem to have predetermined much in how the tales were perceived both by the early Akhmatova and early Mandelshtam. In one of his later newspaper pieces, dated 1919, Kuzmin employs a series of formulas to describe Andersen's tales: "the poetry of indoor life," "the coziness of nurseries," "domestic fantasy (without too much of the fantastic)," "a touching and kindly humor."[17] It seems apparent

---

15 Ibid., 91.
16 Mandel'shtam, *Sobranie sochinenii v 4-kh tomakh*, 2: 239.
17 Kuzmin, "Andersenovskii Dobuzhinskii," 1.

that all these definitions describe not only, and perhaps not so much, the world of Andersen's works, as a fairly large group of poems by Kuzmin himself.

Little wonder, then, that the poet should on several occasions have turned directly to the tales of Andersen. In 1918, Kuzmin fashioned a verse prologue to "The Shepherdess and the Chimney-Sweep." Here the work's main characters are somewhat unexpectedly inscribed into the setting of the fairy tale "The Nutcracker and the Mouse King" by Kuzmin's beloved Hoffmann.

In Kuzmin and Hoffmann alike we find the motifs of "fir candles," the sounding of horns "trumpeted" by toy hunters, toy generals, and most of all, twice, the insistent screeching of mice: "The mice quietly begin to scratch," and "There is the scratching of thin little paws / Of mice against the nursemaid's bed."[18]

In April 1919, Kuzmin helped organize an Andersen evening at the Comedians' Rest Stop (*Prival komediantov*) cabaret-theater.[19] This involved the performance of three short plays based on tales by Andersen ("Little Ida's Flowers," "The Comet," and "The Swineherd") staged by K. K. Tverskoi, with sets and costumes by the prominent designer Mstislav Dobuzhinsky. The princess was played by Kuzmin's beloved Olga Glebova-Sudeikina;[20] in his review of the Andersen event, Kuzmin called her performance "one of the best" in her stage repertoire.[21]

In 1922, Kuzmin wrote a play based on the tale "The Nightingale." And in a journal entry of 1934, he uses imagery from the prologue to "The Snow Queen" to describe his mental state:

> The sun comes out after the rain, the bushes all sparkle like diamonds and crystal, and some Hoffmannesque wizardry seems to breathe under a light breeze. It's strange that all this goes on so long as I look without my glasses. I put on my glasses, and all the drops vanish somewhere, every leaf sticks out separately, there's no chest, no breathing, no sprites—as if the devil from Andersen's tale has stuck a mirror-splinter in my eye.[22]

---

18 Kuzmin, *Stikhotvoreniia*, 399-401.
19 For more on this, see Malmstad and Bogomolov, *Mikhail Kuzmin: A Life in Art*, 78.
20 On relations between Glebova-Sudeikina and Kuzmin, see for instance the quite interesting book on the former: Mok-Biker, *Kolombina desiatikh godov*, 85-92.
21 Kuzmin, "Andersenovskii Dobuzhinskii," 1.
22 Kuzmin, *Dnevnik 1934 goda*, 37.

3.

Motifs from "The Snow Queen" are interpreted also in at least two poems from Osip Mandelshtam's debut collection *Stone* (*Kamen'*, 1913).[23]

The book opens with the first of these, "Breathing" ("Dykhanie," 1909):[24]

This body given to me—what shall I do
with it, this thing so single, so much mine?

For the quiet joy of breathing and of living,
tell me, to whom have I to give my thanks?

I am the gardener, I am the flower too,
Not lonely in the prison of the world.

My warmth, my breathing, has already lain
upon the glass panes of eternity.

On it will be imprinted a design
unrecognizable in recent times.

Let the moment's lees come flowing down—
the gracious pattern cannot be struck out.[25]

Дано мне тело—что мне делать с ним,
Таким единым и таким моим?

За радость тихую дышать и жить
Кого, скажите, мне благодарить?

Я и садовник, я же и цветок,
В темнице мира я не одинок.

---

[23] "The Snow Queen" was relevant to Akhmatova as well; see, for instance, the self-commentary to her *Poem without a Hero* (*Poema bez geroia*): "A New Year's, almost Andersenian blizzard" (*Zapisnye knizhki Anny Akhmatovoi*, 94). Cf. also the whimsical contamination from "The Snow Queen," "Snow White," and Pushkin's "Tale of the Dead Princess" ("Skazka o mertvoi tsarevne") in the futurist Elena Guro's poem "The Stern, Wicked Queen Lets Down Her Raven Hair" ("Strogaia zlaia Koroleva raspuskaet voron'i volosy," 1913): "Nora, my Snow White, / Nora, my snow-flower, / My lamb-cloud. / Ah, you snow queen" (Guro, *Nebesnye verbliuzhata*, 115).

[24] On this lyric, which is known by this title and also by its first line (depending on the edition cited), see also Karin Grelz's contribution to this volume.

[25] Mandelstam, *Poems from Mandelstam*, 61.

На стекла вечности уже легло
Мое дыхание, мое тепло.

Запечатлеется на нем узор,
Неузнаваемый с недавних пор.

Пускай мгновения стекает муть—
Узора милого не зачеркнуть.[26]

The second of Mandelshtam's "Andersenian" poems, written in 1910, is fourth in the *Stone* collection (1913):

More sluggish is the snowy hive,
more limpid is the window's crystal,
and on the chair a turquoise veil
lies where it has been carelessly thrown.

The fabric, heady with itself,
and pampered by the light's caress,
feels it's experiencing summer,
as if it were not touched by winter;

and if, enclosed in icy diamonds,
there streams the frost of endless time [or "eternity," *vechnosti*–trans.],
here is the palpitation of
ephemeral, blue-eyed dragon-flies.[27]

Медлительнее снежный улей,
Прозрачнее окна хрусталь,
И бирюзовая вуаль
Небрежно брошена на стуле.

Ткань, опьяненная собой,
Изнеженная лаской света,
Она испытывает лето,
Как бы не тронута зимой;

---

26 Mandel'shtam, *Sobranie sochinenii v 4-kh tomakh*, 1: 6.
27 Mandelstam, *Poems from Mandelstam*, 63.

И, если в ледяных алмазах
Струится вечности мороз,
Здесь—трепетание стрекоз
Быстроживущих, синеглазых.[28]

Using mathematical language and with mathematical precision, the opening of "Breathing" formulates the terms of the problem to be solved by the lyric hero not only of this poem, but of the whole book. Given: a body; what is to be done with it?[29] Before deciding what to do with the given body, however, the identity of its giver must be determined: "For the quiet joy of breathing and of living, / tell me, to whom have I to give my thanks?"

The very next line of "Breathing" would seem to contain an unambiguous answer: oneself. "I am the gardener, I am the flower too." Let us compare this with lines from a Mandelshtam poem from that same year of 1909 that was not included in *Stone*: "An indecisive hand / portrayed these clouds, / and a sad gaze meets / their design covered with fog. / Dissatisfied and silent I stand—/ I, the creator of my worlds, / where skies are artificial / and crystal dew sleeps."[30]

But such an identification of creature and creator, taken as an answer, contradicts the poem's opening: "This body given to me—what shall I do with it?" *Given*—thus does the self merely cultivate its life from an already-given seed. Compare, in the Book of Genesis: "And God said, Behold, I have given you every herb bearing seed" (1: 29).

Here we might note that in Mandelshtam's original, the pronoun *Kogo* (*whom* am I to thank?) comes in the line-initial position, which makes it possible to capitalize it unobtrusively.

In general, the first poem in *Stone* is likewise absolutely bereft of the affectation and "loud" words so characteristic of the poetics of Symbolism. It would be interesting to compare it from this standpoint with Fedor Sologub's 1896 poem "An Aching Heart is Wont" ("Bol'nomu serdtsu liubo") with its lines: "Who gave me this body / And with it, so little strength?" The lines cited from "Breathing" undoubtedly constitute a form of push-back on Mandelshtam's part; if Sologub, in full accord with the daring of decadence, is ready to curse the Creator for the life given him—

---

28 Mandel'shtam, *Sobranie sochinenii v 4-kh tomakh*, 1: 8.
29 Cf. V. N. Toporov's observation that "at the center of the early texts stands a poem about the body that begins almost like a theorem" ("O 'psikho-fiziologicheskom' komponente poezii Mandel'shtama," 12).
30 Mandelstam, *Poems from Mandelstam*, 90.

Who gave me the earth and water,
Fire and the heavens,
And did not give me freedom,
And took away miracles?
On the cooled ashes
Of former existence,
I pine crazily
For freedom and the body.

Кто дал мне землю, воды,
Огонь и небеса,
И не дал мне свободы,
И отнял чудеса.
На прахе охладелом
Былого бытия
Свободою и телом
Томлюсь безумно я.[31]

—Mandelshtam experiences entirely different feelings: "For the quiet joy of breathing and of living, / tell me, to whom have I to give my thanks?"[32]

As was first noted by Grigorii Freidin, the theme of "Breathing" becomes clearer in the light of subtexts from "The Snow Queen."[33] Mandelshtam's image of the "glass panes of eternity" almost certainly harks back to the motif, key to Andersen's tale, of the pieces of ice from which the Snow Queen bids Kay form the word "eternity." "If you can puzzle that out, you shall be your own master, and I'll give you the whole world and a new pair of skates." But the following lines would seem to be particularly significant in identifying the function of Andersenian

---

31 Sologub, *Taina zhizni*, 98.
32 Cf. D. M. Segal's comment that "'This body given to me' means that the creator gave it to me—someone endowed me with a body, not I myself; even as, later in the poem, it says 'I am the gardener, I am the flower too'" ("Istoriia i poetika u Mandel'shtama," 479). As Ronen notes: "These verses represented the highpoint of that abstract, somewhat decadent idealism that in Russian poetry was associated with the names of Ivan Konevskoi and Fedor Sologub" ("Osip Mandel'shtam," 514). The topic of "Mandelshtam and Sologub" has been touched on by several researchers; here we might cite just two works: Toddes, "Zametki o rannei poezii Mandel'shtama"; and Broitman, "Rannii O. Mandel'shtam i F. Sologub."
33 Freidin, *A Coat of Many Colors*, 36-37. See also the considerations (albeit perhaps not too convincing) on subtexts in this poem from Andersen's tale "The Story of a Mother": Faustov, "Ia i sadovnik, ia zhe i tsvetok," 120-22. Certain Andersenian reminiscences (including from "The Snow Queen") in Mandelshtam are pinpointed in Soshkin, *Gipogrammatika*, 52-53, 113-14, 321-22, 337, 418.

reminiscences in "Breathing": "I am the gardener, I am the flower too, / Not lonely in the prison of the world."

Garden and flower motifs are crucial to "The Snow Queen." At the very outset of the tale, we are told that Gerda and Kay have "a garden... a little bigger than a flowerpot"; and later Gerda winds up in the "flower garden" of an old sorceress whose little house has flowerlike windows with "red, blue, and yellow panes." This old lady manages to keep Gerda for a time in a sort of unaccentuated captivity; but then the little girl leaves the house with the flowery windowpanes and sets out once more to rescue Kay, who is being held in turn, like a prisoner, in the palace of the Snow Queen. Cf. in "Breathing": [I am] "Not lonely in the prison of the world."

Key to understanding the image of the flower and garden in "The Snow Queen," meanwhile, are the lines (repeated three times, and at very important parts of the tale) of the "rose psalm." The first instance comes at the very beginning of the tale, when we are told that "the little girl had learned a hymn in which there was a line about roses that reminded her of their own flowers. She sang it to the little boy, and he sang it with her: 'Where roses bloom so sweetly in the vale, / There shall you find the Christ Child, without fail.'"

The second instance comes toward the end of the tale, as Gerda cries while embracing Kay: "Gerda shed hot tears, and when they fell upon him they went straight to his heart. They melted the lump of ice and burned away the splinter of glass in it. He looked up at her, and she sang: 'Where roses bloom so sweetly in the vale, / There shall you find the Christ Child, without fail.'"

The third time comes at the very end of the tale: "Kay and Gerda looked into each other's eyes, and at last they understood the meaning of their old hymn: 'Where roses bloom so sweetly in the vale, / There shall you find the Christ Child, without fail.' And they sat there, grown-up, but children still—children at heart. And it was summer, warm, glorious summer." Just before this, we are told that Gerda's grandmother had been sitting in "sunshine, reading to them from her Bible: 'Except ye become as little children, ye shall not enter into the Kingdom of Heaven.'"

The flower-motif in "The Snow Queen" is thus closely connected with the theme of the knowledge of God. For the Mandelshtam who authored "Breathing," this was likely crucial.

In the fourth poem of Mandelshtam's *Stone* collection—"More sluggish is the snowy hive" ("Medlitel'nee snezhnyi ulei")—the connection with "The Snow Queen" is signaled still more explicitly. Here the "frost of eternity" [*vechnosti moroz*] "streams... enclosed in icy diamonds" (in precise accordance with the tale); and warmth here is directly contrasted to cold (summer to winter): "feels it's experiencing summer, / as if it were not touched by winter." Cf. the tale's final sentence, just cited: "And it was summer, warm, glorious summer." And even the very image of the "snowy hive" in Mandelshtam's first line harks back to the following passage from "The Snow Queen":

> Outside the snow was whirling.
> "See the white bees swarming," the old grandmother said.
> "Do they have a queen bee, too?" the little boy asked, for he knew that real bees have one.
> "Yes, indeed they do," the grandmother said. "She flies in the thick of the swarm. She is the biggest bee of all, and can never stay quietly on the earth, but goes back again to the dark clouds."

For the poem "More Sluggish is the Snowy Hive," however, the religious meanings of Andersen's imagery do not seem relevant; it may thus be said to be more of a foreshadowing than the poem "Breathing" of the poetic orientation of Mandelshtam as acmeist.[34]

4.

Anna Akhmatova's first definite reference to Andersen comes in a 1912 poem addressed to Nikolai Gumilev that describes their adolescence together at secondary scool, which the poem's opening line represents via kindly objects that evoke nostalgia for the pair's lost childhood ("book-strap," "pencil-case," schoolbooks):

> *N. G.*
> I was returning home from school,
> With books and a pencil-case in my book-strap.
> Those lindens have certainly not forgotten
> Our meeting, my cheerful boy.
>
> But the grey cygnet changed
> When he became a haughty swan,

---

[34] Cf. Mandelshtam's line about Gumilev recorded in 1935 by Sergei Rudakov: "I told him—touch on God less in your poetry (and that goes for A[khmatova] too: 'Lord'—and then a Chinese garden gazebo)." "O. E. Mandel'shtam v pis'makh S. B. Rudakova k zhene (1935-1936)," 59.

And across my life fell a ray
Of eternal sorrow, and my voice is muted.[35]

В ремешках пенал и книги были,
Возвращалась я домой из школы.
Эти липы, верно, не забыли
Нашей встречи, мальчик мой веселый.

Только, ставши лебедем надменным,
Изменился серый лебеденок.
А на жизнь мою лучом нетленным
Грусть легла, и голос мой незвонок.[36]

Lurking in the situation reproduced from Andersen's "The Ugly Duckling" (1843) at the end of this poem is a hint quite important both to addresser and addressee. Akhmatova knew that the first book Gumilev read as a boy was the tales of Andersen, and subsequently told Pavel Luknitsky "how Gumilev zealously guarded this book and loved to reread it even when he was a famous poet."[37] The poetic persona thus gently reminds her male counterpart of the time when he was a "cheerful boy" and used to engross himself in reading the tales of Andersen.[38]

No wonder, then, that this reference to "The Ugly Duckling" was highly meaningful to Gumilev; and, somewhat like an experienced tennis player, he lobbed Akhmatova's reproachful hint back at her. In his review of her second poetry collection *Rosary* (*Chetki*), which includes the poem just cited, Gumilev himself employs the image of the ugly duckling that turns into a swan. Unlike Akhmatova, he references Andersen directly;

---

35 Trans. cited from Sampson, *Nikolay Gumilev*, 18.
36 Akhmatova, *Stikhotvoreniia i poemy*, 74. On certain somewhat less distinct Andersenian subtexts in Akhmatova, see Goncharova, "Akhmatova i Andersen."
37 Luknitskaia, *Nikolai Gumilev*, 18.
38 Here we might note that Andersen's tale later gave cause for reflection to still another post-symbolist poet, Aleksandr Tiniakov, in his poem "The Ugly Duckling (on a Motif from the Tale by Andersen)" ("Gadkii utenok [na motiv skazki Andersena]," 1921). Cf. also, the ironic poem "The Swan" ("Lebed'," 1915) by Valentin Goriansky, whose works were published in the journal *Satyricon* (*Satirikon*): "But all around, I was considered a fool! / You, they said, are a person like no other! / Alas, it's been that way throughout the ages / With people endowed with the divine spark… / I must confess, I myself stopped believing in myself… / Like all poets, I'm as naïve as a child; / I remember how at some point in my childhood I read / Andersen's tale 'The Ugly Duckling,' / Which, it turns out, was a swan, the jewel of the lake, / It's just in the chicken yard that he was considered ugly. / And the city I live in—isn't it that same duck yard, / And aren't I a swan in my splendid solitude?…" And still another *Satyricon* contributor, Sasha Chernyi, begins one of his 1913 poems with a reference to Andersen: "Hello, bronze boar,— / Do you recall the fairy tale by Andersen?"

and most importantly, he reinstates the original, positive meaning of the "duckling's" fairytale transformation, which in Akhmatova's poem is lost due to her use of the pejorative epithet "haughty." If in Akhmatova, the poem's lyric hero (read Gumilev) is essentially spoiled by his transformation into a swan, in Gumilev such a change is portrayed as the natural result of any poet's development, including that of Akhmatova herself:

> I think everyone has had occasion to be surprised at how great was the ability and desire, in youth, to suffer. The laws and objects of the real world suddenly replace their former counterparts, which had been permeated with a dream in whose fulfillment one had believed: the poet cannot help seeing that these things have a beauty that suffices unto itself and cannot conceive of himself among them, cannot reconcile the rhythm of his spirit with their rhythm. But the force of life and love in him is so strong that he begins to love his orphanhood itself, comes to comprehend the beauty of pain and death. Later, when his spirit, tired of always being in the same position, begins to be visited by an "accidental joy," he will feel that a person can joyously perceive all aspects of the world, and he will turn, from the ugly duckling he has hitherto been in his own eyes, into a swan, as in Andersen's tale.[39]

Even in his acmeist period, unlike Akhmatova and Mandelshtam, Gumilev himself was never enchanted by coziness, whether of the fairytale or domestic variety. His lyric persona invariably strived rather to leave hearth and home and go out into the big, wide world. The author of *The Quiver* (*Kolchan*) could, however, express warm sympathy for the fragile characters of Andersen's tales, as he does for instance in the poem "Happiness" ("Schastie," 1915), in which an explicit use of motifs from "The Princess and the Pea" (1835) seems to go hand-in-hand with a hidden quotation from "The Snow Queen" (the image of those same "roses" alongside mention of "fairy tales of poverty"):

> The sick believe in May roses,
> And tender are the fairy tales of poverty;
> Awakening in prison, you shall probably see
> Visions of paradise.
> But there's nothing more alarming and godforsaken
> Than sorrow among silks,
> And I am ready to give over all my blood
> To the princess on the pea.

---

39 Gumilev, *Sochineniia v 3-kh tomakh*, 3: 139.

Больные верят в розы майские,
И нежны сказки нищеты,
Заснув в тюрьме, виденья райские
Наверняка увидишь ты.
Но нет тревожней и заброшенней—
Печали посреди шелков,
И я принцессе на горошине
Всю кровь мою отдать готов.[40]

Far more typically does Gumilev seek and find in Andersen such tales as feature toy-characters striving to break out of their tiny little worlds. Exemplifying this would be the reminiscence of the Danish storyteller contained in the final stanza of Gumilev's 1913 (?) manifesto-poem:

I am polite to modern life,
But there's a barrier between us,
Everything that makes it laugh in its haughtiness
Is my sole joy.

Conquest, glory, the exploit—pale
Words now mislaid,
Thunder in the soul like thunderclaps of bronze,
Like the voice of the Lord in the wilderness.

Tranquility has always entered my home
Unneeded and unbidden:
I vowed to be an arrow
Hurled by the hand of Nimrod or Achilles.

But no, I am no tragic hero,
I am more ironic, drier;
I rage like a metal idol
Among porcelain dolls.

He remembers the curly heads
Bowed toward his pedestal,
The sublime prayers of sacrificers,
The thunder in forests seized by trembling.

---

40 Ibid., 1: 195.

And grievously mocking, he sees
An ever-stationary swing
Where a shepherd plays a panpipe
To a lady with a prominent bust.

Я вежлив с жизнью современною,
Но между нами есть преграда,
Все, что смешит ее, надменную,
Моя единая отрада.

Победа, слава, подвиг—бледные
Слова, затерянные ныне,
Гремят в душе, как громы медные,
Как голос Господа в пустыне.

Всегда ненужно и непрошено
В мой дом спокойствие входило:
Я клялся быть стрелою, брошенной
Рукой Немврода иль Ахилла.

Но нет, я не герой трагический,
Я ироничнее и суше,
Я злюсь, как идол металлический
Среди фарфоровых игрушек.

Он помнит головы курчавые,
Склоненные к его подножью,
Жрецов молитвы величавые,
Грозу в лесах, объятых дрожью.

И видит, горестно-смеющийся,
Всегда недвижные качели,
Где даме с грудью выдающейся
Пастух играет на свирели.[41]

This poem's two concluding lines apparently refer not only to the suggestive tradition of French rococo ("a lady with a prominent bust"),

---

[41] Ibid, 193-94. As early as 1923, in a review of Gumilev's book of prose *Palm Shade* (*Ten' ot pal'my*), Vsevolod Rozhdestvensky noted Andersen's influence on the story "The Last Court Poet" ("Poslednii pridvornyi poet"); see *Kniga i revoliutsiia*, no. 23-24 (1923): 63.

but also to Andersen's tale "The Shepherdess and the Chimney-Sweep" (1845), in which two porcelain dolls try to escape from the "table top under the mirror... [out] into the big, wide world." In making this allusion, Gumilev returns in the finale of his poem to the imagery of its fourth stanza, in which the poet himself is depicted as "a metal idol / among porcelain dolls." A huge, ponderous "metal idol" seems absurd among the light and miniature "porcelain dolls" of Andersen's tale, in which the chimney-sweep hardly differs from an "ornamental" prince:

> Close by [the shepherdess] stood a little chimney-sweep, as black as coal, but made of porcelain too. He was as clean and tidy as anyone can be, because you see he was only an ornamental chimney-sweep. If the china-makers had wanted to, they could just as easily have turned him out as a prince, for he had a jaunty way of holding his ladder, and his cheeks were as pink as a girl's. That was a mistake, don't you think? He should have been dabbed with a pinch or two of soot.

The saccharine little world of "porcelain dolls" ironically described in Andersen's tale is contrasted in the Gumilev poem cited here to the grim and heroic world of myth—that of the Old Testament and classical antiquity (the second and third stanzas) and/or of the primordial variety (the fifth stanza). In this world, the "metal idol" seems absolutely organic, entirely other than it appears in the "table top under the mirror."

Here we might advance the cautious hypothesis that Akhmatova may have taken Gumilev's lines about "porcelain dolls" personally, insofar as she had in 1911 composed a poem about a shepherdess with a reed-pipe ("Above the Water" ["Nad vodoi"]) and had, in a poem of that same year of 1911 ("The Little Horses Are Led along the Avenue" ["Po allee provodiat loshadok"]) stated, not without a certain flirtatiousness: "But now I have become toy-like [*igrushechnoi*[42]], / Like my pink friend the cockatoo."[43]

In any case, in 1914 Akhmatova wrote a poem from the standpoint of a man (Gumilev?).[44] Its first stanza features an image of a wily woman (the poet herself?) whose portrait is constructed using two key and contrapuntal words from the Gumilev poem under discussion:

---

42 This word has the same root as Gumilev's *farforovye igrushki*, "porcelain dolls" (lit. "porcelain toys")—trans.
43 Trans. cited from Sandler, *Commemorating Pushkin*, 183.
44 On the few such poems by Akhmatova, see e.g. Kormilov, "Akhmatovskii vzgliad izvne."

She approached. I did not give away my agitation,
Gazing indifferently out the window.
She sat down, like a *porcelain idol*,
In a pose she had chosen long ago.

Подошла. Я волненья не выдал,
Равнодушно глядя в окно.
Села, словно *фарфоровый идол*,
В позе, выбранной ею давно.[45]

In their poetry, then, the three "main" acmeists, like their symbolist predecessors, used imagery from works by Hans Christian Andersen that they had assimilated already in childhood. Their recourse to quotations from the Danish storyteller is most frequent when they depict a miniature toy-world sympathetically (Mandelshtam, Akhmatova) or with antipathy (Gumilev).

Works Cited

Akhmatova, Anna. *Stikhotvoreniia i poemy*. Leningrad: Sovetskii pisatel', 1977.
—. *Zapisnye knizhki Anny Akhmatovoi*. Moscow: Torino, 1996.
Andersen, Khans Kristian. *Skazki. Istorii*. Moscow: Izd. Khudozhestvennaia literatura, 1973.
Annenskii, Innokentii. *Stikhotvoreniia i tragedii*. Leningrad: Sovetskii pisatel', 1990.
—. *Uchebno-komitetskie retsenzii 1904-1906 godov*. Ivanovo: Izdatel'skii tsentr "Iunona," 2001.
Belyi, Andrei, and Aleksandr Blok. *Perepiska. 1903-1919*. Moscow: Progress-Pleiada, 2001.
Bal'mont, K. *Morskoe svechenie*. Moscow, St. Petersburg: Izdatel'stvo T-va M. O. Vol'f, 1910.
Broitman, S. N. "Rannii O. Mandel'shtam i F. Sologub." *Izvestiia RAN. Seriia liter. i iazyka* 55, no. 2 (1996): 27-35.
Chukovskaia, L. *Zapiski ob Anne Akhmatovoi*. Moscow: Soglasie, 1997.
Faustov, A. A. "'Ia i sadovnik, ia zhe i tsvetok...' Ob odnoi sub"etknoi konstruktsii v tvorchestve Mandel'shtama." In *Uslyshat' os' zemnuiu. Festschrift for Thomas Langerak*, edited by Ben Dhooge and Michel De Dobbeleer. Amsterdam: Pegasus, 2016.
Freidin, G. *A Coat of Many Colors: Osip Mandelstam and His Mythologies of Self-Presentation*. Berkeley: University of California Press, 1987.
Goncharova, N. G. "Akhmatova i Andersen." *Literaturnaia ucheba*, no. 2 (2004): 133-54.

---

45 Akhmatova, *Stikhotvoreniia i poemy*, 99; emphasis mine—OL.

Gumilev, N. *Sochineniia v 3-kh tomakh*. Moscow: Khudozhestvennaia literatura, 1991.

Guro, Elena. *Nebesnye verbliuzhata. Izbrannoe*. St. Petersburg: Limbus-Press, 2001.

Kormilov, S. "Akhmatovskii vzgliad izvne: Stikhotvoreniia Anny Akhmatovoi, napisannye ot litsa muzhchiny." *Izvestiia Iuzhnogo federal'nogo universiteta. Filologicheskie nauki*, no. 3 (2013): 8-27.

Kuzmin, M. "Andersenovskii Dobuzhinskii." *Zhizn' iskusstva*, no. 123 (29 April 1919).

—. *Dnevnik 1934 goda*. St. Petersburg: Izd. Ivana Limbakha, 2007.

—. *Stikhotvoreniia*. St. Petersburg: Akademicheskii proekt, 1996.

Lavrov, A. *Andrei Belyi v 1910-e gody. Zhizn' i literaturnaia deiatel'nost'*. Moscow: Novoe literaturnoe obozrenie, 1995.

Luknitskaia, V. *Nikolai Gumilev. Zhizn' poeta po materialiam domashnego arkhiva sem'i Luknitskikh*. Leningrad: Lenizdat, 1990.

Malmstad, John E., and N. Bogomolov. *Mikhail Kuzmin: A Life in Art*. Cambridge, MA: Harvard University Press, 1999.

Mandelstam, Osip. *Poems from Mandelstam*. Translated by R. H. Morrison. London: Associated University Presses, 1990.

Mandel'shtam, O. *Sobranie sochinenii v 4-kh tomakh*. Moscow: Art-Biznes-Tsentr, 1993.

Mok-Biker, E. *Kolombina desiatYkh godov*. St. Petersburg: AO "Ardis," 1993.

Ronen, Omry. *An Approach to Mandelstam*. Jerusalem: The Magnus Press, The Hebrew University, 1983.

—. "Osip Mandel'shtam." In *Stikhotvoreniia* by O. E. Mandel'shtam, 496-538. Moscow, 1992.

Rudakov, S. B. "O. E. Mandel'shtam v pis'makh S. B. Rudakova k zhene (1935-1936)." In *Ezhegodnik rukopisnogo otdela Pushkinskogo doma na 1993 god. Materialy ob O. E. Mandel'shtama*, edited by L. N. Ivanova and A. G. Mets, 12-22. St. Petersburg: Akademicheskii proekt, 1997.

Sampson, Earl D. *Nikolay Gumilev*. Boston: Twayne, 1979.

Sandler, Stephanie. *Commemorating Pushkin: Russia's Myth of a National Poet*. Stanford: Stanford University Press, 2004.

Segal, D. M. "Istoriia i poetika u Mandel'shtama. A. Stanovlenie poeticheskogo mira." *Cahiers du Monde russe et sovietique* 33, no. 4 (October-December 1992): 447-95.

Sologub, Fedor. *Taina zhizni*. Moscow: NeksMedia, 2013.

Soshkin, Evgenii. *Gipogrammatika. Kniga o Mandel'shtame*. Moscow: Novoe literaturnoe obozrenie, 2015.

Toddes, E. A. "Zametki o rannei poezii Mandel'shtama." In *Themes and Variations: In Honor of Lazar Fleishman*, edited by Konstantin Polivanov, Irina Shevelenko, and Andrey Ustinov, 283-92. Stanford: Stanford University Press, 1994.

Toporov, V. N. "O 'psikho-fiziologicheskom' komponente poezii Mandel'shtama." In *Osip Mandel'shtam. Poetika i tekstologiia. Materialy nauchnoi konferentsii, 27-29 dekabria, 1991*, edited by Iu. L. Freidin, 7-27. Moscow: Akademiia nauk, 1991.

"The Fairy Tale is Simple":

Marina Tsvetaeva and Hans Christian Andersen

Karin Grelz

Introduction

Marina Tsvetaeva (1892-1941) integrated Hans Christian Andersen's fairy tales into her imaginative thinking to an extent unparalleled among the literati of her generation. Like her peers, she had been brought up on his stories and read them to her own children. She often interpreted her life-situations, moreover, according to his tales, and she also modeled her poetic persona and imaginative landscape after his.

Hitherto the only systematic analysis of the influence of Andersen's fairytale world on Tsvetaeva's oeuvre appears in an account by Tartu scholar Roman Voitekhovich.[1] Sofiia Poliakova's book *Those Fading Days: Tsvetaeva and Parnok* (*Zakatnye oni dni: Tsvetaeva i Parnok*, 1983) contains some trailblazing observations on references to Andersen in Tsvetaeva's cycle "Girlfriend" ("Podruga," 1914-16), and Tsvetaeva's Andersen references have also been analyzed from the standpoint of the childhood theme in general.[2] Developing these observations further, this study aims at providing a conceptualization of the Andersen theme as it bears on Tsvetaeva's work as a whole. In order to highlight the coherence of Tsvetaeva's creative myth, by contrasting it to her more diversified associations as a private person, texts that were printed or intended for publication will be treated separately from other genres. The first part will thus be devoted to Andersen in diaries, notebooks, and letters, while the second looks at references in her poetry and prose. In the conclusion, however, an attempt will be made to combine the observations on the different kinds of material.[3]

---

[1] Voitekhovich, "M. Ts. i Andersen."
[2] Poliakova, *Zakatnye oni dni*, 83-85; Grelz, *Beyond the Noise of Time*, 35-36.
[3] Tsvetaeva's notebooks and letters make direct reference to "The Old House" (1847), "The Little Mermaid" (1837), "The Snow Queen" (1844), "The Story of a Mother" (1847), "The Garden of Eden" (1839), and "Kept Secret but not Forgotten" (1866). In her poetry and prose, she refers to "Ole Lukoie" (1841), "The Snow Queen," "The Little Mermaid," "The Garden of Eden," and "Little Ida's Flowers" (1835). Moreover, Tsvetaeva's daughter Ariadna Efron (1912-75) recalls in her autobiography a conversation with her mother about "The Girl who Trod on the Loaf" (1859). Voitekhovich also suggests ("M. Ts. i Andersen") that Tsvetaeva

Tsvetaeva read Andersen throughout her life. As a child she most likely listened to and read his tales in Russian and German translation. Little is known as to which sources she had access to during her adult years in Moscow, but in emigration she evidently read his novel *Only a Fiddler* (1837) in German, as well as his autobiography *The Fairy Tale of My Life* (1847).[4] In a 1935 letter to Czech writer and translator Anna Tesková, she also announced that she had been given a copy of Andersen's fairy tales in German published by Reclam Verlag.[5]

1. Andersen in Notebooks and Letters

Pigskin Will Last
As a young poet in prerevolutionary Russia, Tsvetaeva used Andersen as a given cultural reference. In a letter to her colleague and mentor Maksimilian Voloshin (1877-1932), she cites Andersen's "The Old House" without naming her source. In Andersen's story about a little boy who befriends a lonely man in an old house with walls covered with pigskin the young Tsvetaeva apparently recognized an artistic manifesto of sorts:

> There remains a sense of utter solitude for which there is no cure. The body of another person is a wall, it prevents me from seeing his soul. Oh, how I hate this wall! But I do not want a paradise where everything is blissful and airy—I so much love faces, gestures, the everyday life. My eyes and hands seem to involuntarily rip the covers—so shining!—off everything.
> Gilding fades fast;
> But pigskin will last![6]

Tsvetaeva used Andersen's tales in the upbringing of her children as well and was careful to note their responses. She read both "The Little Mermaid" and "The Snow Queen" to Ariadna, her eldest, and proudly reported that her daughter included "grandpa Andersen" in her evening

---

might owe her tendency to anthropomorphize trees and groves to Andersen's "The Fir Tree" (1844) and "The Elder-Tree Mother" (1844). The latter, indeed, comes up in a letter from the poet Nikolai Gronsky: "I read about us in Andersen—'she kissed the boy and became the same age as he.' I've never noticed this before, although I read this story often" (Tsvetaeva and Gronskii, *Neskol'ko udarov serdtsa*, 78). Translations by A. S. Brown unless otherwise indicated.

4 Tsvetaeva, *Spasibo za dolguiu pamiat' liubvi*, 262, 273.
5 Ibid., 279.
6 Tsvetaeva, *Neizdannoe. Sem'ia*, 96. Trans. (except the final sentence in prose, and the couplet) cited from Karlinsky, *Marina Tsvetaeva*, 36.

prayer.[7] Even as a teenager, Ariadna shared her mother's enthusiasm for "The Snow Queen," and in 1928 in Paris she produced a booklet with illustrations to this tale.[8]

In emigration, Tsvetaeva read "The Little Mermaid" also to her six-year-old son Georgii (1925-44), nicknamed Mur after E. T. A. Hoffmann's *Lebensansichten des Katers Murr*. Apparently curious as to the boy's response, she especially noted his sensitivity to the gender aspect:

> Today the 24th I read Andersen's Mermaid to him in three sittings. Afterwards:—What did you like most of all in the tale?—The city with the fires.—But what about the mermaid, her love, how kind she was... In reply not *yes*, but hm-hm, dryly. As if he wanted neither to admit, nor to concede what he admits to. [It's like that] every time—as soon as the subject of kindness or love comes up—in a female image [*v zhenskom obraze*]. The tale as a whole he understood perfectly.[9]

Unlike Ariadna, with her enthusiasm for the mermaid, Mur is described as reluctant to recognize kindness and love as linked specifically to a female character—a tendency Tsvetaeva seems to have found, in a little boy, entirely natural. Tsvetaeva's curiosity as to her son's reaction may have reflected more than just a mother's interest. It could have been triggered also by some specific questions raised by her literary forerunners in Russian Symbolism in connection with the image of femininity in Andersen.

The Fairy Tale of My Life
Judging from the notebooks, Tsvetaeva herself turned to Andersen at especially difficult stages of her life and sought to conceptualize her situation through his tales. In 1919, when in the aftermath of war and revolution the family experienced poverty for the first time, she described this condition as a virtuous one associated directly with Andersen: "My love for poverty. (Poverty—Andersen.) For the hominess of poverty, for garrets under mansard-roofs, for folksy outings."[10]

When in 1920, during the last winter of the Russian Civil War, three-year-old Irina died of malnutrition in an orphanage, Tsvetaeva again

---

7 Tsvetaeva, *Neizdannoe. Zapisnye knizhki*, 1: 186. "Grandpa Andersen" is also mentioned in the introductory sentence of the autobiographical essay "The House at Old Pimen" ("Dom u starogo Pimena," 1933).
8 Tsvetaeva, *Spasibo za dolguiu pamiat' liubvi*, 113, 127.
9 Tsvetaeva, *Neizdannoe. Svodnye tetradi*, 470.
10 Tsvetaeva, *Neizdannoe. Zapisnye knizhki*, 2: 43.

turned to Andersen. In this situation, she recognized in "The Story of a Mother" an image of her own fruitless attempts to negotiate with death for the salvation of her child:

> Andersen's tale "A Mother." "Give me back my boots," I will say. "Give me back my earrings," I will say. "Give me back my wrists... eyes–teeth–hair."
> The fairy tale is about me.
> Only–
> Only, when I give things back, no one says anything, because I don't ask for anything when I give things away. The whole story is meaningless.
> I am totally meaningless.
> It turns out there was just a silly woman who threw her shoes into the river, her hair into the fire, her eyes into the apron of a beggar-woman (or the hat of a pauper) who had no need of them, and so on.
> Oh![11]

In a letter from the orphanage, Ariadna retold the entire story of "The Snow Queen" to her mother.[12] When during this winter Tsvetaeva sought to contact her husband Sergei Efron (1893-1941), from whom she had been separated since the political turbulence after 1917, she also found a fitting image for their situation in "The Snow Queen." Quoting in her notebook a message from Efron about how their reunion was to be arranged, her thoughts turned to Andersen: "Oh, my Serezhenka!–Gerda will find Kay."[13] Having been left alone with the children in Moscow, she apparently identified with Gerda and her search for Kay during his captivity by the Snow Queen, convinced that eventually she would see him once more. This aspect of the fairy tale reoccurred in a 1927 letter to Boris Pasternak–another person with whom she yearned to reconnect after years of separation. Now she compared Andersen's tale to the medieval story of Tristan and Isolde, as "[a] tale that in no way differs from the story of Kay and Gerda, who love, lose... and come together again."[14]

Andersen in general, and "The Snow Queen" in particular, continued to be topical for Tsvetaeva in the final two years she spent in Moscow before emigrating. In May 1920 she compared herself to Kay: "I am as enchanted as little Kay–but in the opposite direction."[15] She was to re-

---

11 Ibid., 190.
12 Ibid., 28.
13 Ibid., 83.
14 Tsvetaeva and Pasternak, *Dushi nachinaiut videt'*, 360.
15 Tsvetaeva, *Neizdannoe. Zapisnye knizhki*, 2: 141.

turn to this particular directionality of Kay in a cryptic 1933 passage in a notebook she kept in Paris: "Found[ation] (Mur). / Kay—in reverse."[16]

These sparse notations leave considerable room for interpretation, but, understood spatially, the image of "Kay in reverse" suggests a journey or apprenticeship with reversed signs. Falling in love with the Snow Queen, Andersen's Kay "falls" out of the paradisiacal state of childhood innocence and naïve faith and makes a journey into the world of knowledge and adult reason, with his heart frozen to ice. After this odyssey, he returns home a more experienced person but still "a child at heart," having been freed from the Snow Queen's spell by Gerda's innocent tears. Tsvetaeva may have conceived of herself in the spring of 1920 as temporarily enchanted *away* from the world of reason, politics, and adult relations, into a more naïve dimension—bewitched, that is, "in the opposite direction."

Supporting such an interpretation is a reference to "The Snow Queen" Tsvetaeva made the following year in a letter to Prince Sergei Volkonsky (1860-1937). Inspired by contemporary discoveries in physics, Volkonsky in his book *Artistic Responses* (*Khudozhestvennye otkliki*, 1912) had written about how in music, the spatial dimension is substituted, and made superfluous, by time.[17] Volkonsky's reflections on time, space, and movement prompted Tsvetaeva to describe the extent to which, for her, language was something perceived spatially, as if words created a separate space or otherworld into which she was enchanted when reading. In order to make her point clear, she drew a comparison with Kay's journey in the kingdom of the Snow Queen:

Two impressions, one audible and one visual.

When reading, a querying voice is heard—through the ears—live—in the room. Somebody is posing a question, not to you, but in your presence, to him- or herself. A query that gradually (one word after another!) transforms into an exclamation: a vocal way out [or "vocal output, conclusion," *golosovoi vyvod*].

The second impression (imprint) is visual. Dear S. M., if you have the book at hand, grab it and take a look at the bottom of p[age] 134...

It is no delusion, it is a visual authenticity—seen with one's own eyes. Words in themselves are immense spaces (like those over which the Snow Queen led Kay)... the very appearance [or "shape," "sight"; *vid*] of words. (Width and length.) Here the appearance of words equals their meaning.[18]

---

16 "Осн<ова> (Мур) / Кай–наоборот." Tsvetaeva, *Neizdannoe. Zapisnye knizhki*, 2: 417.
17 Volkonskii, *Khudozhestvennye otkliki*, 131-32.
18 Tsvetaeva, *Neizdannoe. Svodnye tetradi*, 15.

When reading Tsvetaeva thus seems to have imagined herself as being under the spell of language, moving within a linguistic-semantic otherworld, like Kay in the thrall of the Snow Queen. She later copied the above entry into one of her notebooks of the 1930s, apparently valuing it as a reflection worth remembering and developing further.

After emigration in 1922, Tsvetaeva's life slowly became materially easier, with the Czech government supporting Russian émigrés in Prague. In hindsight, positive memories from the Bohemian capital led Tsvetaeva to conceive of her life in fairytale terms, with reference to Andersen's autobiography: "What little I saw of Prague—living so far away—has, for me, forever become a part of *Das Märchen meines Lebens*, as Andersen called his life. And the Prague knight is forever *mine*."[19] On the first page of his book, Andersen envisions his life as a journey from poverty and outcasthood to prosperity and inclusion. As such he presents it as a story with a happy ending, by which some sort of eternal justice had finally been administered. Tsvetaeva would hardly have looked upon her own journey as anything of the sort—rather the opposite. But with the Bruncvík knight on Prague's Charles Bridge as her guardian angel—"a symbol of loyalty (to one's own self, not to others)"[20]—she seems still to have found moral support in Andersen. His biography exemplified how painful experience could be conceptualized via the projection of an imaginative world of fairy tales on an unbearable or threatening reality.

If God Created Andersen...
With fascism advancing in Europe and Stalinist terror on the rise in the Soviet Union, the situation of Russian émigrés worsened. In Paris, where the Tsvetaeva-Efron family had settled in 1925, Russian émigré circles became radicalized, partly due to pressure from Soviet intelligence operatives. In the fall of 1937, Efron was suspected of organizing the assassination of a defected Soviet agent. In order to avoid interrogation by the French police, it was arranged for him to return to the Soviet Union. After Efron's abrupt flight, Tsvetaeva spent two more years among the Russian émigrés in Paris—who now regarded her with great suspicion—before she finally left France on a boat from Le Havre to Leningrad.

Tsvetaeva's notebook entry of 16 June 1939, from the combined cargo- and passenger-ship Mariia Ulianova, is a singular, typically Tsvetaevan combination of factual detail and personal mythmaking. As

---
19 Letter to Anna Tesková, 1935. Tsvetaeva, *Sobranie sochinenii*, 6: 428.
20 Ibid., 341.

the boat passes through the Öresund, she waves to Andersen's home country of Denmark and sends her heartfelt greetings to the author who sailed the same waters. She observes the roofs of the houses hidden in the green on the Danish side, interpreting the sight through Andersen's story "Kept Secret but not Forgotten," as if finding in the landscape a mirror of the state of mind she now had to get used to: "Denmark—first impression: deep and dark [*dremuchaia*]. A grayish fairytale forest with old rooftops sticking out. An enormous windmill. Churches. Denmark equals a fairy tale by Andersen, everything is within, everything is hidden ('hidden but not forgotten') ... A forest grew and houses emerged."[21] Leaving France for the Soviet Union definitely meant keeping certain things hidden, although not forgotten, and Tsvetaeva apparently had no illusions about the regime of the country to which she was sailing on a boat full of refugees from the Spanish Civil War. Already in 1919 in Moscow, she had made a pronouncement about Soviet power, declaring Andersen to be its antithesis: "The Revolution and Andersen.—It makes no sense. And the conclusion is: if God created Andersen, then the Revolution was created—there's no alternative—by the Devil."[22] Her 1939 notebook ends with the recognition that she would not long survive her return: "When I woke up this morning, it occurred to me that my years are numbered (then it will be months)."[23]

This fear was entirely justified. A year later, both her daughter and husband were imprisoned, accused of counterrevolutionary activity, while Tsvetaeva had taken her son and fled the Moscow suburb of repatriated agents to which they arrived. As destitute and politically suspect former émigrés, they had to move around while trying to arrange for Georgii's schooling and to find somewhere to store their belongings, mainly books.

Andersen in Heavy, Eternal Bindings
The decision to return to the Soviet Union was not an easy one to take for an émigré writer in 1939. As a former émigré Tsvetaeva was not accepted as a writer and struggled to make a living. With her husband and daughter imprisoned, she was shunned by landlords and employers as potentially dangerous. She turned to the Writer's Union and Writer's Fund for financial and practical assistance, and even wrote a letter to Stalin in which she asserted her and her family's right to fair treat-

---

21 Tsvetaeva, *Neizdannoe. Zapisnye knizhki*, 2: 442-45.
22 Ibid., 31.
23 Ibid., 450.

ment—but with no result.[24] In an August 1940 letter to her sister-in-law, Elizaveta Efron, she described the situation:

> I don't live anymore. I don't write and don't read. All the time I want to do something, but I don't know what. I just made a list of books to sell, but they are ancient, for the book-lover—will the store take them?
>
> If not, I am going to put a box out on the street, or *would*—if I could move it: these are the heftiest Miserables, Buffons, Napoleons, Christopher Columbuses, Dickenses, Dumases, Andersens—and all in heavy, *eternal* bindings.... And this is only the *fifth* box!...
>
> The fairy tale is simple: there was a house, there was a life, there was a large hallway *of one's own*, which accommodated *everything*, and now there is NOTHING—and EVERYTHING turns out to be superfluous.[25]

Directly after these comments about the "simple" "fairy tale" of her life and her weighty, now "superfluous" books (including by Andersen) in their "eternal bindings" (cf. "the pigskin" from Andersen's tale), Tsvetaeva refers to an incident that may be seen as a poet's recognition of life's symbolic qualities. A tale by Andersen, that is—namely, "The Little Match Girl" (1845)—is hintingly invoked as a lens through which her life at this specific moment could be interpreted:

> I have stopped cleaning my room and *barely* wash the dishes: I am sick—of everything and of *this*!—and, moreover, a whole box of matches flared up in my hand—all the heads were burnt—my hand has a sore, and my chin is burnt. (The chin does not matter, I am just mentioning it [*no ia–k slovu*].)[26]

Did Tsvetaeva actually identify with the poor girl locked out in the cold and burning her final matches in the snowdrifts on New Year's Eve? Had Andersen's fairytale world become so integral to her imagination that she intuitively thus recorded an occurrence befitting it? Or was this perhaps her way of telling her sister-in-law in coded, Aesopian language, that her days were now numbered? We cannot know. The beginning of the letter is lost, and with it the exact date and other clues to the author's intention, but Elizaveta Efron would have well understood the symbolic weightiness of Andersen's collected works and seen the reference to his "Little Match Girl" in the letter cited above. Andersen's name was

---

24 Kudrova, *The Death of a Poet*, 215-22.
25 Tsvetaeva, *Neizdannoe. Zapisnye knizhki*, 2: 398; emphasis in original.
26 Ibid.

directly associated with the authorial aspirations that her brother and Tsvetaeva had shared as young adults. As newlyweds, they had organized a private publishing house in Moscow named after Andersen's fairy tale "Ole Lukoie."

If this was indeed a message of impending doom, Tsvetaeva would seem to have had good reason to communicate it to her sister-in law. On 31 August 1940, around the time the above letter is thought to have been written, she was summoned to a meeting at the party Central Committee, the upshot of which may have driven home to her that she was definitively locked out in the cold. But writing about this openly would have put her addressee in danger. In less than a year—after the German invasion on 22 June 1941—she left Moscow for Elabuga, an evacuation village on the Kama River, where she took her own life, having possibly been pressured by the local secret service to either inform on family and colleagues or commit suicide.[27]

2. Andersen in Tsvetaeva's Poetry and Prose

The Evening Album
In her book *The Same Solitude: Boris Pasternak and Marina Tsvetaeva* (2006), Catherine Ciepiela describes how Tsvetaeva as a child of Symbolism took up the male symbolist poets' mythologizing and life-creating strategies, but from another perspective and with a different attitude toward both femininity and sexuality.[28] Playing the role of a "girl muse," she appeared in her first books of poetry as an independent poetic agency and a literary voice of the next generation, evaluating and taking charge of this new position.[29]

References to Andersen appear to be central to this dialogue with the symbolists in general, and with Aleksandr Blok and his conception of Andersen in particular. In a creative and sometimes ironical dialogue with the symbolist's cult of the Beautiful Lady and the principle of the eternal feminine, Tsvetaeva's *The Evening Album* (*Vechernii al'bom*, 1910) presents a number of fairytale-like female personages—the Christmas Lady, Snow White, the Lady in Blue, etc. The lyrical *I* both addresses and identifies with these women, and Tsvetaeva is thus accommodating

---

27 Kudrova, *The Death of a Poet*, 169.
28 Ciepiela, *The Same Solitude*, 10-42.
29 In a 2005 article, Samson Broitman gives a detailed analysis of Tsvetaeva's variations on Blok's image of the Beautiful Lady in her first two volumes of poetry, which support Ciepiela's observations (Broitman, "M. Tsvetaeva i A. Blok," 222-51).

an alternative poetic persona, as well as the imagery of same-sex love, and often with references to Andersen.[30] This is manifest especially in the poem "To Nina" ("Nine"), in which she paraphrases Pushkin's love poems and casts herself in the role of Kay, hypnotized by an aloof and beautiful woman:

> I loved you like a sister
> More tenderly and deeper, perhaps!
>
> Like a sister, now at a distance,
> Like a queen from Andersen's dreams...
>
> Я любила тебя как сестру
> И нежнее, и глубже, быть может!
>
> Как сестру, а теперь вдалеке,
> Как царевну из грез Андерсена...[31]

Some critics dismissed the poems in Tsvetaeva's first collection as naïve and sentimental trifles. What they failed to see was that in *The Evening Album* Tsvetaeva developed a markedly symbolist conception of the poet-child with a virginal and playful creative mind, able to transform herself and transcend the world. As such, the mannered naiveté echoed the French as well as Russian symbolists' romanticism of childhood,[32] and also Nietzsche's idea of eternal innocence or innocence on a higher level ("Unschuld des Werdens"), with the child representing the new beginning as formulated in *Thus Spake Zarathustra* (1883-91).[33]

The Evening Album evokes a childlike fairytale world and the child's ambivalent feelings before impending adolescence, but as seen from an outside perspective. The poem "Little World" ("Mirok") features allusions to popular children's tales like Pushkin's "Tale of Tsar Saltan" ("Skazka o Tsare Saltane") and Andersen's "The Little Mermaid," but it also includes a hint at Nietzsche's *Gay Science* (1882)—a source frequently referred to by the elder generation:

---

30 See on this Broitman, "M. Tsvetaeva i A. Blok."
31 Tsvetaeva, *Sobranie sochinenii*, 1: 26-27.
32 On the former, see Lawler, *The Language of French Symbolism*, 21-70.
33 This book was, for Russian symbolists, of course a major text; Tsvetaeva read it at the age of fifteen. On Tsvetaeva and Nietzsche, see Shevelenko, *Literaturnyi put' Tsvetaevoi*, 76, 78, 82-83.

Little World

Children are the gazes of fearful little eyes,
The patter of mischievous little feet on a parquet floor,
Children are the sun amid gloomy strains,
A whole world of hypotheses of joyous sciences.

An eternal jumble in the gold of ringlets,
The whisper of tender little words, half-asleep,
The placid little pictures of birdies and little lambs
That slumber on the wall of a cozy nursery.

Children are an evening, an evening on the couch.
Out the window, in the fog, streetlamps glimmer,
The measured voice of the tale about Tsar Saltan,
About mermaid-sisters in fairytale seas.

Children are a rest, a brief moment's respite,
A tremulous vow to God by the side of a little bed.
Children are the world's tender riddles,
And the answer lies in the riddles themselves!

Мирок

Дети—это взгляды глазок боязливых,
Ножек шаловливых по паркету стук,
Дети—это солнце в пасмурных мотивах,
Целый мир гипотез радостных наук.

Вечный беспорядок в золоте колечек,
Ласковых словечек шепот в полусне,
Мирные картинки птичек и овечек,
Что в уютной детской дремлют на стене.

Дети—это вечер, вечер на диване,
Сквозь окно, в тумане, блестки фонарей,
Мерный голос сказки о царе Салтане,
О русалках-сестрах сказочных морей.

> Дети—это отдых, миг покоя краткий,
> Богу у кроватки трепетный обет,
> Дети—это мира нежные загадки,
> И в самих загадках кроется ответ![34]

This poem's lyrical *I* is not a child, but a poet who identifies with children and ironically mimics the diminutives used by adults. With the children's "little world" (*mirok*) emphasized in the title, the poem demonstratively evokes the symbolists' cult of the adolescent child and Charles Baudelaire's (1821-67) famous poem "The Voyage" in *Flowers of Evil* (1857), which begins with a description of the child's journey out of the nursery—a world seen in hindsight as tiny, although it once appeared immense.[35]

In one of the more programmatic poems of *The Evening Album*, "The First Voyage" ("Pervoe puteshestvie"), Tsvetaeva launches children on a similar journey. With a "kindly sorcerer" at the rudder and Andersen as their inspiration, they sail away on a magic couch. The "lakes of sleep," and the "umbrella of wonders" in the shadow of which the girls visit exotic places during this journey, serve as obvious references to both "Ole Lukoie" and "The Little Mermaid." But, as Voitekhovich observes, there is an ironic, somewhat absurd dimension to this poem's exaggerated fairytale scenes.[36] With the children escorting their Cinderella-like storyteller home when the bell tolls, the roles of children and adults seem, in the end, inverted:

The First Voyage

—"Set sail," quoth the Spring.
The earth disappeared, foam glittered,
And over lakes of sleep, the couch-ship
Carried us into a fairy tale by Andersen.

A kindly Sorcerer
Guided it out of the sleepy waters
To a country of giant orchids,
Sorrowful eyes, and lemon groves.

---

[34] Tsvetaeva, *Sobranie sochinenii*, 1: 13.
[35] Tsvetaeva was to translate this poem in Moscow in 1940; cf. Smith, "Toward the Poetics of Exile."
[36] http://www.tsvetayeva.com/poems/pervoe_puteshestvie

We sailed past shores
Where stands the green World Palm,
And palaces of serene pearl,
And towers of sapphire.

Winter's last snow had vanished;
A fragrant snow of magnolias blossomed for us.
Where were we flying? We did not know!
And for what purpose? What difference does it make!

The supple flowers stretched
Like enchanted serpents.
From an illumined darkness
Blinked crafty pygmies…

The last ray has long since faded,
Melting in the realms of the last clouds.
A little Pegasus-cloud flit past,
And a school of air-fish hid,

And between stalks of grass, the moon
Was glimpsed in the water, like a circle of enamel…
It was so close, but, alas—
We couldn't catch it in our net!

Under a multicolored umbrella of wonders,
Full of cherished dreamings
We lay, and our fear vanished
Under the gaze of someone's green eyes.

On the shore, wine streamed
Into crystal carafes.
We were served by two-legged
Whales and portly dolphins.

And suddenly, a chiming! He's here! There is no mercy!
That's the chime, drawn out and resonant, of the clock!
What, is this papa's study?
The couch? Our familiar side street?

Morning is already dawning! My goodness!
Half-asleep and half-wakeful
Through damp streets
We escorted the Sorcerer home.

Первое путешествие

–"Плывите!" молвила Весна.
Ушла земля, сверкнула пена,
Диван-корабль в озерах сна
Помчал нас к сказке Андерсена.

Какой-то добрый Чародей
Его из вод направил сонных
В страну гигантских орхидей,
Печальных глаз и рощ лимонных.

Мы плыли мимо берегов,
Где зеленеет Пальма Мира,
Где из спокойных жемчугов
Дворцы, а башни из сапфира.

Исчез последний снег зимы,
Нам цвел душистый снег магнолий.
Куда летим? Не знали мы!
Да и к чему? Не все равно ли?

Тянулись гибкие цветы,
Как зачарованные змеи,
Из просветленной темноты
Мигали хитрые пигмеи…

Последний луч давно погас,
В краях последних тучек тая,
Мелькнуло облачко-Пегас,
И рыб воздушных скрылась стая,

И месяц меж стеблей травы
Мелькнул в воде, как круг эмали…
Он был так близок, но, увы–
Его мы в сети не поймали!

Под пестрым зонтиком чудес,
Полны мечтаний затаенных,
Лежали мы и страх исчез
Под взором чьих-то глаз зеленых.

Лилось ручьем на берегах
Вино в хрустальные графины,
Служили нам на двух ногах
Киты и грузные дельфины...

Вдруг—звон! Он здесь! Пощады нет!
То звон часов протяжно-гулок!
Как, это папин кабинет?
Диван? Знакомый переулок?

Уж утро брезжит! Боже мой!
Полу во сне и полу-бдея
По мокрым улицам домой
Мы провожали Чародея.[37]

The biographical background of Tsvetaeva's "The First Voyage" is well known. The sorcerer conjuring up Andersen's fairytale world was the symbolist poet Lev Kobylinsky (1874-1947), or Ellis, translator (not incidentally) of Baudelaire's *Flowers of Evil*.[38] A frequent visitor to the Tsvetaev household in the spring of 1909, he appeared before Marina and her sister as a poet, mentor, and potential lover, sharing his knowledge of current literary life during the period when he conceived his book on the symbolist movement and its crisis, *The Russian Symbolists* (*Russkie simvolisty*, 1910).

"The First Voyage" also features another key subtext in the symbolist connection. Taking place as it does on a couch (*divan-korabl'*, *divan*), and in the company of a tale-weaving sorcerer, Tsvetaeva's poem recalls Aleksandr Blok's "In the Corner of the Couch" ("V uglu divana") from *The Snow Mask* (*Snezhnaia maska*). In this 1907 poem, Blok had seated his reader-listener in the eponymous location and presented himself as a hypnotizing conjurer:

---

37 Tsvetaeva, *Sobranie sochinenii*, 1: 21.
38 Sharl Bodler, *Tsvety zla*. Moscow: Zaratustra, 1908.

In the Corner of the Couch

But in the hearth,
The embers finished their chiming.

Outside the window,
The lights died down.

And on the blizzardly sea,
Ships sink.

And over the southern sea,
Cranes howl.

Believe only me, heart of the night,
I am a poet!

Any tale you like,
I'll tell you,

And any mask you like,
I'll bring.

And the fire will cast whatever sort
of shadows,

The outlines of strange apparitions
On the wall.

And anyone shall bend his knee
Before you...

And anyone shall drop
A blue flower...

В углу дивана

Но в камине дозвенели
Угольки.

За окошком догорели
Огоньки.

И на вьюжном море тонут
Корабли.

И над южным морем стонут
Журавли.

Верь лишь мне, ночное сердце,
Я—поэт!

Я какие хочешь сказки
Расскажу

И какие хочешь маски
Приведу.

И пройдут любые тени
При огне,

Странных очерки видений
На стене.

И любой колени склонит
Пред тобой...

И любой цветок уронит
Голубой...[39]

Against the backdrop of Blok's poem, the situation described in Tsvetaeva's "The First Voyage" appears to match the methodology of symbolist life-creation, with *The Snow Mask* as the literary reference modeling the biographical material. This time, however, the point of view is that of the poet-child, seated on the couch. In a later poem dedicated to Tsvetaeva, "To Paradise" ("V rai," 1914), Ellis also repeated the image of the couch ("the children are settled on the couch"), while Tsvetaeva in her answering piece, "The Sorcerer" ("Charodei," 1914), continued to cast Ellis as a magician, albeit now as one who fails in his magic intentions.

---

39 Blok, *Sobranie sochinenii*, 2: 174.

In *The Snow Mask*, Blok had borrowed and explored central motifs from Andersen's "The Snow Queen," as well as his lesser-known "The Ice Maiden." As Irene Masing-Delic has shown,[40] the lyrical *I* gives in to an elementary force with a female face, embraces the knowledge of evil, and is left with a heart turned to ice by this encounter, just like Andersen's Kay; he is likewise taken to a snow castle and forgets his past amid swirling blizzards. Unlike Kay, however, Blok's poet is not miraculously saved, and becomes instead a victim of the Mask. Like Rudi in "The Ice Maiden," he remains in the icy otherworld, freely giving himself over to the captivating snow-dream offered by the Mask.

The poet and critic Georgii Chulkov pinpointed Andersen as an inspirational source for Blok's *The Snow Mask* as early as 1908, when his article "A Snow Maiden" ("Snezhnaia deva") was published in the symbolist journal *The Golden Fleece* (*Zolotoe runo*). It seems highly likely that Tsvetaeva read or at least discussed Chulkov's article with Ellis, who had recently been involved in Blok's private life, appearing as a second in the poet's duel with Andrei Bely.[41] According to E. F. Knipovich, Blok spoke of Andersen often, interpreting his tales on a private, biographical level. In particular, he found the happy ending of "The Snow Queen" less convincing than the story of "The Ice Maiden," in which the eponymous conjurer lures her victims into glacial crevasses, and the male protagonist perishes in an ice-cold lake.[42]

The Magic Lantern

The references to Andersen in Tsvetaeva's first volume appear to be metaquotations of sorts—variations on, first and foremost, Blok's creative adaption of Andersenian imagery. This also adds a polemical dimension to Tsvetaeva's choice of name of the private publishing-house established by her and Efron: Ole Lukoie.[43] Under this label, Tsvetaeva published her second book of poems, *The Magic Lantern* (*Volshebnyi fonar'*, 1912), and Efron a collection of semi-autobiographical short stories called *Childhood* (*Detstvo*, 1912). Both volumes were highly mannered, stylized celebrations of the Golden Age of childhood. The cover of Efron's book featured two naively drawn children—an autobiographical intimation likely inspired by the story of Kay and Gerda in "The Snow Queen."

---

40 Masing-Delic, *A. Blok's 'The Snow Mask'*, 91-92.
41 On Ellis's relations with Blok, see Lavrov, "Pis'ma Ellisa k Bloku (1907)."
42 Knipovich, "Ob Aleksandre Bloke," 22.
43 Tsvetaeva herself never explained this choice of name, but Irina Shevelenko sees it as a conscious display of ironic disregard for the conventions of "serious" literature and its marketing. (Shevelenko, *Literaturnyi put' Tsvetaevoi*, 17, n. 1.)

Fig. 1. Cover of Sergei Efron's *Childhood* (*Detstvo*), Ole Lukoie 1912.

In *The Magic Lantern*, Tsvetaeva continued to develop the legacy of the previous generation, with "The Snow Queen" as a given frame of symbolic reference. Whereas the lyrical *I* of Blok's *The Snow Mask* had his heart turned to ice just like Kay ("The pride of my new baptism / Has turned my heart to ice"),[44] Tsvetaeva in *The Magic Lantern* seems to have chosen Gerda as a female mask for an otherwise prototypically male Orphic quest. In an apostrophe to the French poet Marceline Desbordes-Valmore—lauded by Baudelaire as representing the eternal feminine—she demonstratively employs the image of tears melting a frozen heart. Here she describes how in literary reception, poet and reader become indistinguishable from one another, and the melting of Kay's heart by Gerda's tears in Andersen is hinted at to analogize the compassionate reader's ability to bring the poet back to life:

In the Mirror of M. D.-V.'s Book

This heart is mine! These lines are mine!
You live, you are in me, Marceline!
Your frightened verse is no longer silent in oblivion,
And the ice has melted in tears.

---

44 Blok, *Sobranie sochinenii*, 2: 145.

We gave ourselves together, we suffered together,
We, loving, fell in love to our torment!
The same grief pierced us and with the same lance,
And on my exhausted scorching brow
I feel a cool hand.

I, asking for kisses, received a lance!
I, like you, did not find my master!...
These lines are mine! This heart is mine!
Who is Marceline—you, or I?[45]

В зеркале книги М. Д. В.

Это сердце—мое! Эти строки—мои!
Ты живешь, ты во мне, Марселина!
Уж испуганный стих не молчит в забытьи,
И слезами растаяла льдина.

Мы вдвоем отдались, мы страдали вдвоем,
Мы, любя, полюбили на муку!
Та же скорбь нас пронзила и тем же копьем,
И на лбу утомленно-горячем своем
Я прохладную чувствую руку.

Я, лобзанья прося, получила копье!
Я, как ты, не нашла властелина!...
Эти строки—мои! Это сердце—мое!
Кто же, ты или я—Марселина[46]

In the next to last poem of *The Magic Lantern*, "Out of a Fairy Tale—into a Fairy Tale" ("Iz skazki–v skazku"), Tsvetaeva likewise makes reference—subtle, yet recognizable by contemporary readers—to "The Snow Queen." The poem is set on a winter's evening. The lyrical *I* rejects reason and asks for a future with her beloved, where he would remain as a young boy, and she, astounded, like a little girl, although his wife. This echoes how Kay and Gerda, after their respective journeys, and released from the fetters of reason, are said by Andersen to be "grown-up, but children still":

---

45 Cited from Ciepiela, *The Same Solitude*, 26.
46 Tsvetaeva, *Sobranie sochinenii*, 1: 99.

Out of a Fairy Tale—into a Fairy Tale
Everything is yours: the yearning for a miracle,
All the yearning of April days,
Everything that was so drawn toward heaven,—
But don't ask for reason.
Till death I will remain
A little girl, although yours.

My dear, on this winter evening
Be like a small boy with me.
Don't disturb my marveling,
Keep, like a little boy, a scary secret
And help me remain a little girl
Even as a wife.[47]

Из сказки—в сказку

Все твое: тоска по чуду,
Вся тоска апрельских дней,
Все, что так тянулось к небу,—
Но разумности не требуй.
Я до смерти буду
Девочкой, хотя твоей.

Милый, в этот вечер зимний
Будь, как маленький, со мной.
Удивляться не мешай мне,
Будь, как мальчик, в страшной тайне
И остаться помоги мне
Девочкой, хотя женой.[48]

The title "Out of a Fairy Tale—into a Fairy Tale" indicates an intertextual dimension: the symbolist adaptation of the fairy tale is transposed into her own creative paradigm, with the magical powers of Gerda matching or defying those of the Snow Queen. As if to make her point clearer, Tsvetaeva published a third volume, *From Two Books* (*Iz dvukh knig*, 1913), as a compilation of the first two, and also under the label of Ole Lukoie. This book concluded on the same Andersenian note as

---

47 Trans. of the second stanza cited from Ciepiela, *The Same Solitude*, 27-28.
48 Tsvetaeva, *Sobranie sochinenii*, 1: 174.

The Magic Lantern, with the poem "Out of a Fairy Tale—into a Fairy Tale," and added only one new piece: "To V. Briusov" ("V. Briusovu").[49] Tsvetaeva formulated this latter as a poetic challenge to Valerii Briusov (1873-1924), one of the most influential literary figures of her time, ascribing to her illustrious elder the heart of a "night-light" (*nochnik*).[50] Though technically appearing in a negative comparison ("not a star—but a night-light"), the light source in question could nevertheless be interpreted positively, as a reference to a night-lamp in a nursery, which the child takes for a star. With Briusov thus telling bedtime stories to the "naughty children" of Tsvetaeva's generation, an Ole Lukoie of sorts, her own magic lantern, or *camera obscura*, would then be the poet-child's suggestive counterpart.

"Girlfriend"

Tsvetaeva soon extended her creative application of Andersen's fairytale world to a full and gender-transgressing identification with the persona of the male symbolist poet, with the image of Kay and his enchantment by the Snow Queen at its center. In the fifth poem of the poetic cycle "Girlfriend," the lyrical *I* sees a sleigh rush by outside the window, just as Blok in *The Snow Mask* and Annensky in his "Lilac Mist" ("Sirenevaia mgla," 1910) had described the poet's first glimpse of the beautiful ice-lady.[51]

In its first version, "Girlfriend" was titled "The Mistake" ("Oshibka"), and meant to be included in Tsvetaeva's fourth volume, *Poems of Youth* (*Iunosheskie stikhi*, 1913-15).[52] It was catalyzed by Tsvetaeva's affair in 1914 with the older poet Sofiia Parnok (1885-1933) and conceived as a lyrical diary, inspired by Bettina von Arnim's (1785-1859) fictionalized correspondence with Karoline von Günderrode (1780-1806).[53] This was Tsvetaeva's first attempt to compose a longer poetic cycle, and, as an experiment in form, it examined Parnok's practice as poet and critic, as well as Blok's longer poems; it also developed Andersenian imagery further.[54]

---

49 On Tsvetaeva's conception of youth in this poem, see Grelz, "Ungdomens musa," 94-98.
50 In a critical review Briusov wrote: "[Tsvetaeva] is a poetess with a certain gift. But there is something unpleasantly treacly in her descriptions of a semi-childish world, in her tender emotion before all that comes to hand…. Perhaps two or three such poems would be pleasant. But a whole book in a nice velvet cover, and in a cardboard protective sheath, and published by 'Ole Luk-Oie'—no." Cited from Field, "A Poetic Epitaph," 57.
51 See Ciepiela, *The Same Solitude*, 259, n. 69; and Oleg Lekmanov's contribution to the present volume.
52 The volume was not published in Tsvetaeva's lifetime.
53 *Die Günderode* (1840).
54 Poliakova, *Zakatnye oni dni*, 83, 119; Borovikova, *Poetika Mariny Tsvetaevoi*, 61, 67.

At first glance, the scene by the window in Tsvetaeva's poem would seem to be given from the point of view of a Gerda watching her Kay depart on his long journey. But the notion of "another" having taken the protagonist's place beside the beloved, and the concluding apostrophe to the Snow Queen, change the picture. The lyrical *I* is now identifying not with Gerda but Kay, safely returned, his would-be seat in the sleigh taken by the *next* partner:

> About eight this evening, a sleigh
> rushed past me, recklessly,
> along Bolshaya Lubyanka
> like a bullet or a snowball.
>
> I heard your tinkling laugh
> in the distance and froze,
> staring: your fawn-coloured fur,
> the tall figure at your side...
>
> You are enjoying the pleasures
> of a sleigh with someone else,
> a chosen lover, already more
> desired than I was!
>
> *'Oh, je n'en plus, j'etouffe!'*
> you screamed at me today.
> And now, boldly, you cover her
> with the furs inside the sleigh.
>
> The rest of the world is happy.
> The evening glamorous.
> Gifts and muffs... and you both rushing
> into the blizzards—fur to fur.
>
> Then a brutal surge of snow
> turns everything white.
> I could only follow the two of you
> for a matter of seconds.

I stroke the long hair on my
coat and feel no anger...
Your little Kay has frozen to death [or "was cold," *zamerz*–KG]
O great Snow Queen.

26 October 1914[55]

Сегодня, часу в восьмом,
Стремглав по Большой Лубянке,
Как пуля, как снежный ком,
Куда-то промчались санки.

Уже прозвеневший смех...
Я так и застыла взглядом:
Волос рыжеватый мех,
И кто-то высокий—рядом!

Вы были уже с другой,
С ней путь открывали санный,
С желанной и дорогой,—
Сильнее, чем я—желанной.

—Oh, je n'en puis plus, j'étouffe!—
Вы крикнули во весь голос,
Размашисто запахнув
На ней меховую полость.

Мир—весел и вечер лих!
Из муфты летят покупки...
Так мчались Вы в снежный вихрь,
Взор к взору и шубка к шубке.

И был жесточайший бунт,
И снег осыпался бело.
Я около двух секунд—
Не более—вслед глядела.

---

55 Tsvetaeva, *Bride of Ice*, 34.

И гладила длинный ворс
На шубке своей—без гнева.
Ваш маленький Кай замёрз,
О, Снежная Королева.

26 октября 1914[56]

Caressing the fur of her coat, which she wears as some kind of ennobling sign, this "Kay" seems to have been released from the Snow Queen's spell. Assuring her interlocutor that she cast only a brief glance after the sleigh, she seems content to have recovered from the freeze. Whereas the lyrical I experiences, in the cycle's third poem, the sensation of "some kind of great feeling / [having] melted in the soul today," the addressee is described as a tragic lady, unsaved by anyone, and indeed beyond rescue.[57]

The Swansong of the Poet

In the spring of 1916, during a period of intense poetic dialogue with Osip Mandelshtam, Tsvetaeva touched on still another aspect of "The Snow Queen," indirectly referring in her poem "It Is Shattered in Silver Smithereens" ("Razletelos' v serebrianye drebezgi") to the story of the troll's broken mirror, slivers of which freeze Kay's heart and pervert his sight.

This aspect of Andersen's tale had been creatively interpreted by Blok in his famous speech on the death of the actress Vera Kommisarzhevskaia in 1910.[58] According to Blok, Kommisarzhevskaia possessed a unique combination of adult intellect and childlike gaze. Retaining the magical insight of the child, she was capable of looking deeper into the truths of life, and as such Blok compared her to Kay with the magic splinter in his eye.

In "It Is Shattered," Tsvetaeva turns the curse of Kay's vision into a heavenly gift, just as Blok had done in his Kommisarzhevskaia speech. Upon evoking the shattered mirror and the theme of distorted vision in the first two lines, she goes on in the third and fourth to identify with the sister of the eleven swans in "The Wild Swans," another Andersen tale featuring a rescuing female agency. Like Andersen's Elisa, who frees

---

56 Tsvetaeva, *Sobranie sochinenii*, 1: 219.
57 As Poliakova notes (*Zakatnye oni dni*, 119), Tsvetaeva tries on still another mask in this cycle, alternative to that of the Snow Queen, when in the sixth poem she imagines herself as the little robber girl from Andersen's story, pouring lavish gifts over her "Gerda."
58 Blok, *Sobranie sochinenii*, 5: 418.

her swan-brothers from the bewitchment cast by their stepmother-queen, Tsvetaeva's persona looks for the swans in the sky and prays for them in secret. Instead of a mirror-shard in her eye, she receives a feather-pen on her chest, rhyming on the "small silver" that in her dream she scatters over the world:

It is shattered in silver smithereens—
The mirror and—all it says.
The swans, my swans, my little ones,
Are flying back home today!

From cloudy heights came fluttering
A quill—straight onto my breast.
I dreamed today I was scattering
Small silver to right and left.

The silvery call is—sonorous.
In silvery tones I'm—to sing.
My little swan, raised as one of us!
Is it fine to be on the wing?

I'll go and I'll tell no one—
Nor mother, nor near relatives.
I'll go and I'll stand in church,
And call down the saints' blessings
On my little swan fledgling.
1 March 1916[59]

Разлетелось в серебряные дребезги
Зеркало, и в нем—взгляд.
Лебеди мои, лебеди
Сегодня домой летят!

Из облачной выси выпало
Мне прямо на грудь—перо.
Я сегодня во сне рассыпала
Мелкое серебро.

---

59 Tsvetaeva, *Milestones*, 16-17.

Серебряный клич–звонок.
Серебряно мне–петь!
Мой выкормыш! Лебеденок!
Хорошо ли тебе лететь?

Пойду и не скажусь
Ни матери, ни сродникам.
Пойду и встану в церкви,
И помолюсь угодникам
О лебеде молоденьком.
1 марта 1916[60]

If the mirror pieces in Andersen's tale distort the sight and freeze the heart of those they afflict, the feather-pen in Tsvetaeva's version has an inspirational function and encourages her song. By extension, the poetic image of the young swan could be interpreted as a reference to the youngest brother in Andersen's tale. With a swan's wing instead of an arm, he remains partly under the spell—as good an image as any for a fellow poet-brother like Mandelshtam or Blok.

The image of the swan and the idea of the poet's swansong, and its infectious power, is developed further in Tsvetaeva's poems to Blok of 1916, which she later included in the cycle "Poems to Blok" ("Stikhi k Bloku," 1921). In "Gentle Phantom" ("Nezhnyi prizrak"), she portrays him as a swan beyond rescue, dying at her feet. Dressed in a coat of snow, the blue-eyed poet bewitches her with a song that sounds like a jingling outside the window:

Behold, the snow-clad
Blue-eyed poet
Has cast his spell upon me.

The snowy swan scatters
Its plumes before me.
The plumes flutter
And fall slowly into the snow.

So, plumes before me,
I make for the doorway,
Beyond which is—death.

---

60 Tsvetaeva, *Sobranie sochinenii*, 1: 255.

He sings to me
Beyond deep blue windows.
He sings to me
With sleigh bells in the distance.

With a long-drawn sigh,
With a swanlike cry—
He calls.

Dearest phantom!
I know this is all dream fancy.
Do me this favor:
Amen, amen, fade now!
Amen.
1 May 1916[61]

Голубоглазый
Меня сглазил
Снеговой певец.

Снежный лебедь
Мне под ноги перья стелет.
Перья реют
И медленно никнут в снег.

Так по перьям,
Иду к двери,
За которой—смерть.

Он поет мне
За синими окнами,
Он поет мне
Бубенцами далекими,

Длинным криком,
Лебединым кликом—
Зовет.

---

[61] Tsvetaeva, *Milestones*, 102-5.

Милый призрак!
Я знаю, что все мне снится.
Сделай милость:
Аминь, аминь, рассыпься!
Аминь.
1 мая 1916[62]

This poem echoes the atmosphere of Blok's *The Snow Mask*.[63] Tsvetaeva moreover co-opts Blok as her muse, thus once again effecting a reversal of gender and genre expectations.[64] This model of reversal can be extended also to the fairytale references. With his swansong sounding like sleigh bells, the snow-clad elder poet appears in a role equivalent to that of the Snow Queen in the sleigh outside Kay's window, challenging the younger poet to follow him into an icy otherworld.

However, Tsvetaeva in 1916 also tried on the role of the Snow Queen herself, when in the final line of her poem "Muse of Lament" ("Muza placha," June 1916), dedicated to Anna Akhmatova, she paraphrased the Snow Queen's promise to reward Kay, if he could solve the ice-puzzle.[65] This identification with the Snow Queen's position is developed further in a poem of autumn the same year. The lyrical I now moves as a forgetful wanderer over a frosty landscape, holding a child by the hand:

Down the roads the frost sets crisply ringing,
With a silver child of royal lineage,
I proceed. All's—snow, all's—death, all's—dream.

Skies in rosy, frosty, smoky raiment.
Once upon a time I had—a name and
—Body too, but is not all that—smoke?

Once there was a voice, a flame, deep throated...
Everybody says the ermine-coated
Blue-eyed child beside me is—my own.

---

62 Tsvetaeva, *Sobranie sochinenii*, 1: 289.
63 "The snowy and elemental atmosphere of [Blok's] poetry (particularly *The Snow Mask*) is reproduced within this cycle." Broitman, "M. Tsvetaeva i A. Blok," 229.
64 Dinega, *A Russian Psyche*, 42.
65 Voitekhovich, "Pol'skaia gordynia i tatarskoe igo," 440.

And yet no one sees, along the wayside,
That long, long ago now, from the grave I
Watched from end to end my mighty dream.
15 November 1916[66]

По дорогам, от мороза звонким,
С царственным серебряным ребенком
Прохожу. Всё–снег, всё–смерть, всё–сон.

Небо в розовом морозном дыме.
Было у меня когда-то–имя,
Было–тело, но не всё ли–дым?

Голос был, горячий и глубокий…
Говорят, что тот голубоокий
Горностаевый ребенок–мой.

И никто не видит по дороге,
Что давным-давно уж я во гробе
Досмотрела свой огромный сон.
15 ноября 1916[67]

In the double guise of Kay and the Snow Queen, and in words (*imia, telo*) conveying associations with Mandelshtam's "Dano mne telo" ("This Body Given to Me"), the lyrical I now appears to be trapped in the same icy otherworld as Blok's in *The Snow Mask*.[68]

Focusing on the dynamics of love, loss, and recovery in "The Snow Queen," Tsvetaeva in 1916 developed Andersen's tale into an Orphic drama set in an icy landscape, in which her own poetic persona ultimately proves captured. From this position, she appears able to capture others, just like Blok's Snow Mask and Andersen's Ice Maiden. As Ciepiela notes, the reference to "The Ice Maiden" is rather obvious in "The Chasm" ("Rasshchelina"), addressed to Pasternak in 1923: "You sleep inside me like you're in / A crystal coffin–inside me like you're in // A deep wound–the ice chasm is narrow!"[69]

---

66 Tsvetaeva, *Milestones*, 195.
67 Tsvetaeva, *Sobranie sochinenii*, 1: 326.
68 This poem (also known as "Breathing" ["Dykhanie"]), is discussed in Oleg Lekmanov's contribution to this volume.
69 Ciepiela, *The Same Solitude*, 118, 272, n. 83.

After "The Chasm" references to Andersen become more rare. Still, Tsvetaeva's poetic dialogue with Blok and Parnok appears to be an important background for understanding her reaction to the miraculous retrieval of the crew of the Soviet steamship SS Cheliuskin in 1934. In her poem "The Cheliuskinites" ("Cheliuskintsy") of the same year, she labels their marvelous return after several months in the Arctic icefields "a dream for the younger age" (*mechta / dlia mladshego vozrasta*).[70] This line can be read as a belated comment on her earlier emphasis on Gerda's youthful mission, interpreting a historical incident as affirming the basic message of a possible rescue in Andersen's "The Snow Queen."

"The Story of Sonechka"
In dialogue with her predecessors, Tsvetaeva treats "The Snow Queen" as a tale about an otherworldly call that summons in both directions: into death as well as life. She seems to have recognized in Boris Pasternak's poetry her own youthful belief in the possibility of a reversal, a return to a form of innocence on a higher level. In her 1933 essay "Poets With History and Poets Without History" ("Poety s istoriei i poety bez istorii"), she uses Andersen's story "The Garden of Eden" to describe Pasternak as a poet constantly returning to a pristine dimension:

> The first step of the young Pasternak was a step *back*—into paradise, into the *depth*. Into that very paradise that, according to Andersen, is none other than the garden of Eden, which has departed entirely, just as it was and with everything it had contained, underground, where it flourishes to this day, and will flourish forever more.[71]

To this creative myth of eternal innocence Tsvetaeva returns in her final and longest autobiographical work, "The Story of Sonechka" ("Povest' o Sonechke," 1939), on the actress Sofya (or Sonechka) Gollidei and other members of Evgenii Vakhtangov's Third Theater Studio in Moscow. This was her last and lengthiest prose piece, and she began writing it in 1937 after receiving word of Gollidei's passing from cancer. As such, the tale may be read as the last in a line of texts on representatives of Russian culture (mainly symbolists), works that also serve as epitaphs. As a text about a homoerotic liaison that followed upon Tsvetaeva's break with Parnok, it has been interpreted also as a belated revenge upon the latter. In 1917, Parnok had actually written a libretto for "The

---
70 Tsvetaeva, *Sobranie sochinenii*, 2: 321.
71 Tsvetaeva, *Sobranie sochinenii*, 5: 423.

Little Mermaid"[72]—a fact that adds an intriguing background to the images of the Snow Queen and the little mermaid as two different models of love and creativity.

The actors' world is described as one of gender transgression, innocent desire, and pure communication, while the narrator sits like a Snow Queen of sorts, isolated with her companion Volodia in a house of ice with snowdrifts piling up outside the window. With Sonechka dreaming of starring in Pavel Antokolsky's (1896-1978) play *Infanta's Doll* (*Kukla Infanty*, 1916), the theater studio is presented as a world of innocent children: "But these were children—and actors, that is, doubly children [*dvoinye deti*]."[73] This creative otherworld is conveyed via consistent hints to Andersen's "The Little Mermaid."

Like the mermaid, Sonechka dreams of an unattainable man from another world, loves pearls and coral, and is ashamed of her blunt feet. She also compares her muteness to the little mermaid's and is even said to look at Marina as if from underwater. Moreover, "The Little Mermaid" is said to be Sonechka's favorite tale, about her favorite kind of love. As such, Tsvetaeva's story of Sonechka can be read as a story of love—and art—as a lost cause.

As a counterpart, or answer, to her male symbolist colleague's obsession with the *first* encounter with the Beautiful Lady—symbolized by the Snow Queen passing Kay's window in her sleigh—Tsvetaeva in this text focuses instead on the power of the *last*. The last scene, the last minute, the last exit, the last blush—examples abound in the text of such final occurrences. Taken together, these last moments render the substantiality or evident manifestations of the final encounter a far more intrinsic part of the relationship than the metaphysics of the first. This focus on the final encounter resonates well with Andersen's tale of the little mermaid. At her final encounter with, or rather glance at, the unattainable prince sleeping in the arms of another, Andersen's little mermaid remains loyal to her love and refuses to kill him, leaving him free to love another, although this means she cannot return to her underwater world. As a result she disintegrates into foam, but is also rewarded with the possibility of gaining an immortal soul. In a similar way Tsvetaeva says she left her Sonechka to be loved by others, without trying to punish, captivate, or make a captive of her.

"The Story of Sonechka" ends with Tsvetaeva quoting a friend's report about the actress's death: "When was this? In the summer, yes, in the

---

72 Poliakova in: Parnok, *Sobranie stikhotvorenii*, 20.
73 Tsvetaeva, *Sobranie sochinenii*, 4: 355.

summer. When the Cheliuskinites arrived."[74] Tsvetaeva clings to this detail and says it sounds like a natural phenomenon—like, *when the swallows come*—which leads her thoughts to springtime. Springtime, she concludes, was the season of her first encounter with Sonechka. This was in 1919, during a reading of her play *The Snowstorm* (*Metel'*), in which Sonechka starred as the Lady in the Cloak.

Summing up her "Story of Sonechka," Tsvetaeva thus seems to come full circle and connect the final moment with the first encounter and the image of the Beautiful Lady/Snow Queen with that of the little mermaid. Conceived both as a fairy tale and as an epitaph, the text comments explicitly on Tsvetaeva's Orphic undertaking. As a witness and chronicler, she considers it her duty to restore this lost world to life by abolishing the barrier between the living and the dead:

> The more I return you to life, the more I die myself, die away for life [*otmiraiu dlia zhizni*]—die to you, into you. The more you are here, the more I am there. As if the barrier between the living and the dead were removed, and both the former and the latter walked freely in time and space—and in their opposites. My death is a payment for your life. In order to revive the shades of Hades, they had to be given living blood to drink. But I have gone further than Odysseus, I give you—my own.[75]

Tsvetaeva's descent into Sonechka's underwater otherworld, together with her explicit wish to reverse the signs of life and death, can actually be understood as an application of her concept of "Kay in reverse." This would then be Tsvetaeva's formula for art as an act of salvage rather than sacrifice: the roles of the rescuer and the rescued are forever interchangeable, depending on how the signs of life and death are placed.

Conclusion: The Andersenian Dimension

Over the course of her life, Marina Tsvetaeva identified with and referred to several of Andersen's protagonists and tales. As such, her personal myth changed and appeared differently at different stages of her life. Her creative myth, by contrast, remained more or less the same, primarily based on "The Snow Queen" and "The Little Mermaid." The images of the fatal Snow Queen and the rescuing Gerda prove integral to the romantic and Nietzschean concept of creative innocence evinced

---
74 Ibid., 414.
75 Tsvetaeva, *Sobranie sochinenii*, 4: 409.

throughout Tsvetaeva's work, retaining the basic tension of the symbolist creational myth. Her elaboration of the image of Sofya Gollidei as the little mermaid—a counterpart to Blok's tribute to Kommisarzhevskaia-Kay—on the other hand, takes the discussion a step further.

The Andersenian layer, or dimension, reveals a polemical intention in the young Tsvetaeva vis-à-vis her immediate predecessors that proves to have gone gravely underappreciated. Her eventual suicide has perhaps made it easy to overlook her decisive protest against the programmatic death-wish in Blok's poetry. "To captivate or to become a captive"—this was the central question of Russian Symbolism. Through Andersenian imagery, it was rearticulated by Tsvetaeva in the form of the Orphic question "to rescue or to be rescued."

In Tsvetaeva, Andersen's fairytale world constitutes a sort of supplemental mythology. To the traditional myths of classical antiquity and Christianity, it adds a Nietzschean and gender-bending vision of the poet-child as a female Orpheus, which lends additional support to the main thesis of Olga Hasty's *Tsvetaeva's Orphic Journeys in the Worlds of the Word*. The most intriguing part to follow, from this perspective, is how the spatiality of her proto-symbolist creativity-myth—the concept of a semantic or linguistic *dimension* from within which the labels of life and death can be relativized—was formed under the influence of Andersen's imagery.[76]

After her return to Russia, when she found herself in the dead-end of Stalinist repression, this creativity myth seems to have been superimposed upon that of her life journey. In a Soviet world entranced by politicized historicism, where seemingly no one had any use for her poetry, Tsvetaeva may have conceptualized her situation through the image of the child freezing in the snowdrifts in "The Little Match Girl"—as analogous to Kay's captivity by the Snow Queen. From Tsvetaeva's own youthful perspective, however, burning her last matches would still mean to move into life, rather than death—into a dimension, that is, where literature begins, and where the signposts of life and death could be changed.

---

[76] On spatiality in Tsvetaeva in general, see Burghart, *Raum-Kompositionen*.

Works Cited

Berdnikov, G. P., ed. *Literaturnoe nasledstvo. Aleksandr Blok. Novye materialy i issledovaniia. Kniga pervaia*. Moscow: Nauka, 1980.

Blok, A. A. *Sobranie sochinenii v vos'mi tomakh*. Moscow: Khudozhestvennaia literatura, 1960.

Borovikova, Mariia. *Poetika Mariny Tsvetaevoi (lirika kontsa 1900-x–1920-x godov)*. Dissertationes Philologiae Slavicae Universitatis Taruensis 28. Tartu: Tartu ülikool, 2011.

Boym, Svetlana. *Death in Quotation Marks: Cultural Myths of the Modern Poet*. Cambridge, MA: Harvard University Press, 1991.

Broitman, S. N. "M. Tsvetaeva i A. Blok." *Novyi filologicheskii vestnik*, 1 (2005): 7-37.

Burghart, Anja. *Raum-Kompositionen. Verortung, Raum und lyrische Welt in der Gedichten Marina Cvetaevas*. Frankfurt am Main: Peter Lang, 2013.

Ciepiela, Catherine. *The Same Solitude: Boris Pasternak and Marina Tsvetaeva*. New York: Cornell University Press, 2006.

Dinega, Alyssa W. *A Russian Psyche: The Poetic Mind of Marina Tsvetaeva*. London: The University of Wisconsin Press, 2001.

Field, Andrew. "A Poetic Epitaph: Marina Tsvetaeva's Poems to Blok." *Tri-Quarterly*, Spring (1965): 57-64.

Grelz, Karin. *Beyond the Noise of Time*. Stockholm: Almqvist & Wiksell International, 2004.

—. "Ungdomens musa. Ännu en gång om Marina Cvetaeva och Valerij Brjusov." In *Literature as a World View*, edited by Irina Karlsohn, Morgan Nilsson, and Nadezjda Zorikhina Nilsson, 89-99. Göteborg: University of Gothenburg, 2009.

Hasty, Olga. *Tsvetaeva's Orphic Journeys in the Worlds of the Word*. Evanston: Northwestern University Press, 1996.

Karlinsky, Simon. *Marina Tsvetaeva: The Woman, Her World and Her Poetry*. Cambridge: Cambridge University Press, 1985.

Knipovich, E. F. "Ob Aleksandre Bloke." In *Literaturnoe nasledstvo. Aleksandr Blok, novye materialy i issledovaniia. Kniga pervaia*, edited by G. P. Berdnikov, 16-44. Moscow: Nauka, 1980.

Kudrova, Irma. *The Death of a Poet: The Last Days of Marina Tsvetaeva*. Translated from the Russian by Mary Ann Szporluk. New York: Overlook Press, 2004.

Lavrov, A. "Pis'ma Ellisa k Bloku (1907)." In *Literaturnoe nasledstvo. Aleksandr Blok. Novye materialy i issledovaniia. Kniga pervaia*, edited by G. P. Berdnikov, 273-91. Moscow: Nauka, 1980.

Lawler, James R. *The Language of French Symbolism*. Princeton: Princeton University Press, 1969.

Masing-Delic, Irene. *A. Blok's 'The Snow Mask': An Interpretation*. Stockholm Slavic Studies 4. Stockholm: Almqvist & Wiksell, 1970.

Parnok, Sofiia. *Sobranie stichotvorenij*. Ann Arbor: Ardis, 1979.

Poliakova, S. V. *Zakatnye oni dni: Tsvetaeva i Parnok*. Ann Arbor: Ardis, 1983.

Shevelenko, Irina. *Literaturnyi put' Tsvetaevoi*. Moscow: Novoe Literaturnoe Obozrenie 2002.

Smith, Alexandra. "Toward the Poetics of Exile: Tsvetaeva's Translation of Baudelaire's *Le Voyage*." *Ars Interpres* 2 (2004): 179-98.

Tsvetaeva, Marina. *Bride of Ice: New Selected Poems*. Translated by Elaine Feinstein. Carcanet Press, 2009.

—. *Milestones*. A Bilingual Edition. Translated and with an introduction and notes by Robin Kemball. Evanston: Northwestern University Press, 2003.

—. *Neizdannoe. Sem'ia. Istoriia v pis'makh*. Moscow: Ellis Lak, 2012.

—. *Neizdannoe. Svodnye tetradi*. Moscow: Ellis Lak, 1997.

—. *Neizdannoe. Zapisnye knizhki*. Moscow: Ellis Lak, 2000.

—. *New Year's, an Elegy for Rilke*. Translated by Mary Jane White. United States: Adastra Press 2008.

—. *Sobranie sochinenii*. Moscow: Ellis Lak, 1994.

—. *Spasibo za dolguiu pamiat' liubvi. Pis'ma k Anne Teskovoi*. Moscow: Russkii put', 2009.

Tsvetaeva, Marina, and Boris Pasternak. *Dushi nachinaiut videt'. Pis'ma 1922-1936*. Moscow: Vagrius, 2004.

Tsvetaeva, Marina, and Nikolai Gronskii. *Neskol'ko udarov serdtsa*. Moscow: Vagrius, 2004.

Voitekhovich, R. S. "M. Ts. i Andersen." Available electronically: http://tsvetaeva.livejournal.com/23951.html

—. "Pol'skaia gordynia i tatarskoe igo v stikhakh Tsvetaevoi i Akhmatovoi." *Studia Russica Helsingiensia et Tartuensia* XII (2011): 427-50.

Volkonskii, S. M. *Khudozhestvennye otkliki*. St. Petersburg: Apollon, 1912.

Strelnikov and Kay:

"The Snow Queen" in *Doctor Zhivago*[1]

Peter Alberg Jensen

> And meanwhile in my "oddnesses" I am always subject to some forgotten examples or something transmitted that I myself am not conscious of.
>
> Boris Pasternak[2]

Hans Christian Andersen's "The Snow Queen" is a fairy tale unusually rich in content. It unites in itself a mythologem of the Fall (Kay tastes the fruit of the Tree of Knowledge and leaves a state of paradisiacal innocence) and redemption (his guilt is expiated by the innocent Gerda) with the Faustian (becoming a pupil of the Hobgoblin and the Snow Queen, Kay surrenders his heart and soul for the sake of knowledge) and Orphic myths (through her love and the singing of a hymn Gerda rescues him from the realm of the dead).

At the wellspring of the fairy tale lie the universal conceptual oppositions of the divine and the demonic, love and rationality, female and male, remembrance and forgetting, synthesis and analysis, etc. The tale is founded on archetypical motifs, like abduction, disappearance, imprisonment and liberation from imprisonment, and in their turn these motifs unfold via a range of fairytale motifs—both folkloric and literary. Given its richness of meaning "The Snow Queen" has a claim to be both a "mega-" and "meta-fairy tale" of European culture. Its special suggestiveness, however, is also due to the original theme of snow and cold.

Inasmuch as this potency is embedded in Andersen's incomparable manner, it is no surprise that "The Snow Queen" held out a strong appeal to the representatives of the "mythopoetic" Russian Symbolism. It formed the basis of Aleksandr Blok's collection of poetry "The Snow

---

[1] This article is a revised version of my article "Strel'nikov i Kaj..." I am extremely grateful to John Kendal for the translation from Russian. I also thank Susanna Witt, Roman Leibov and Mikhail Lotman for their valuable comments on the topic and text of the original article.

[2] From Pasternak's draft notes for the novel, *Sobranie sochinenii*, 3, 624.

Mask"[3] and found its way into Andrej Bely's "Goblet of Blizzards". Andersen and "The Snow Queen" played a special role in the writings of Marina Tsvetaeva, and echoes of the fairy tale are to be found in Osip Mandelshtam's early verse.[4]

The peak of interest in "The Snow Queen" coincided with the years when Boris Pasternak was being formed as an artist, and the significance of the fairy tale was not lost on him. However, the question of the importance for Pasternak's art of this tale and of Andersen in general has not as yet been addressed by scholars. It is this question that I shall be considering in the present article.

My purpose is to uncover the role of "The Snow Queen" in the novel *Doctor Zhivago* (1957). This may appear to involve an unwarranted leap in time – from the poet's youth to the years of his maturity. However, I am convinced that *Doctor Zhivago* came into being thanks partly to a reverse movement by the author, that is a return to the sources of his creative work.[5] Instead of a leap forward, I propose a step backwards: to the reading of Pasternak's youth we shall add the reading (and theme) of childhood.

My article argues that Andersen's fairy tale entered into *Doctor Zhivago*, both in the structure of the novel and in the world depicted in it.[6] The connection can be seen at the level of the characters, first and foremost in Iurii Zhivago's "antipode" Antipov-Strelnikov, but also at a symbolic level – in reoccurring key details from the tale such as the *little round hole in the ice* on the window through which the children could peep, and *the rowan tree*. As in the tale, so in the novel, the given components are organically linked. The main part of my article sets out to demonstrate this; in the conclusions I shall try to interpret what we have seen.

The article does not aim to study the genesis of *Doctor Zhivago* in a comparative sense, nor to examine its intertextuality. Rather I shall try to uncover elements of a certain aesthetic archi-text in which the author inscribed his novel. Among these elements an important role is

---

3   See Masing, *A. Blok's "The Snow Mask"*, 91-92.
4   On Andersen in Tsvetaeva and Mandel'shtam, see the contributions to the present volume by Karin Grelz and Oleg Lekmanov respectively.
5   On this, cf. my article "Nil's Ljune i Jurii Zhivago" about the role of the novel *Niels Lyhne* by Jens Peter Jacobsen in *Doctor Zhivago*.
6   I do not know whether Pasternak turned to the text of the tale while writing the novel. His son Evgeny Pasternak has reported that Pasternak read Andersen, but knew specifically only about his reading the memoir *The Fairy Tale of My Life* (as stated by Konstantin Polivanov in a letter to me of 11 July 1995).

played by literary *biographemes*, i.e. formants of the life paths of literary characters.[7]

With my observations in the following I do not intend to replace other interpretations of Antipov-Strelnikov, nor of other components of *Doctor Zhivago* considered here. Rather, my proposed reading is meant to add to the growing understanding of the special complexity of this novel.

1. Antipov-Strelnikov: Kay Caught up in the Revolution

Antipov-Strelnikov reproduces basic characteristics and modes of behaviour of the boy Kay and in many ways shares a fate parallel with that of Andersen's young protagonist.

The gift of imitation
Key features of Pavel Antipov's and Kay's character and behaviour are identical; what is more, they appear in parallel situations.

As soon as the splinter from the magic mirror enters Kay's eye, he begins to notice the defects in everything around him: "Ugh! that rose is all worm-eaten. And look, this one is crooked!" We shall return to this aspect, but first let us look at the second consequence of what has happened:

> (1) Afterwards, when she brought out her picture book, he said it was fit only for babes in the cradle. And whenever Grandmother told stories, he always broke in with a "but –." If he could manage it he would steal behind her, perch a pair of spectacles on his nose, and *imitate her. He did this so cleverly that it made everybody laugh, and before long he could mimic the walk and the talk of everyone who lived on that street. Everything that was odd or ugly about them,* Kay could mimic so well that people said, "That boy has surely got a good head on him!" But it was the glass in his eye and the glass in his heart that made him tease even little Gerda, who loved him with all her soul.[8] (Emphasis here and in all quotations below are mine. P. A. J.)

---

7   Roland Barthes introduced the concept 'biographeme' in his *Camera Lucida* as a designation for significant and fascinating details in a writer's life. My use of the term is more specific. By biographeme I understand the constitutive unit of a literary biographical narrative, i.e. a narrative about a life embedded in historical time. The biographeme enables us to make sense of a particular moment by virtue of its correlation with other moments outside the given situation; such a correlation is a "claim" to continuity (in the Kierkegaardian sense), which in turn constitutes the meaning of a life sought by biography.
8   "The Snow Queen" is quoted here and below from the translation by Jean Hersholt published by the Hans Christian Andersen Centre, at http://www.andersen.sdu.dk/vaerk/hersholt/

The direct consequence of the accident and the first trait of Kay's to be mentioned by the author is a special gift of imitation. Let us look at the description of Pavel Antipov in Pasternak's novel:

> (2) He was a neat boy with regular features and dark blond hair parted in the middle. *He kept smoothing it with a brush and kept straightening his jacket* and his belt with its school buckle. Patulya could laugh to the point of tears and was very observant. *He imitated everything he saw and heard with great likeness and comicality.*[9]

In the first place, the boy assiduously corrects any deficiencies in his outward appearance, and, secondly, he possesses a gift of imitation. When Pavel appears on the scene of the novel, the first thing he does is to demonstrate his art; the grandmother's place in the fairy tale is here occupied by Marfa Tiverzina – the boy is temporarily living with the Tiverzins – who has taken Pasha with her to a political demonstration. During their walk he has all the while been "amusing her with a *highly skillful imitation* of the last orator", (33) and a little later Marfa Gavrilovna asks the boy to do the speaker once again:

> (3) And that speechifier, how about him, Pashenka? Show me, dear, show me. Oh, I'll die, I'll die! It's perfect, it's him to a tee! (34)

When we compare this with Andersen's *He did this so cleverly that it made everybody laugh*, it is as if we have before us a Kay who has become entangled in the start of the Russian Revolution.

Fifteen years later the boy Pasha's imitative talent is also to be found in the adult Antipov-Strelnikov, and once again immediately – this is the first thing we are told about him. When Doctor Zhivago is brought before Antipov to be interrogated and observes him in the railway coach, he makes the following conclusion:

> (4) This man must possess *some gift*, not necessarily an original one. The gift that showed in all his movements might be *the gift of imitation*. (221R)

TheSnowQueene. html This version has no pagination. Pasternak presumably read the tale in the classical four-volume edition of Andersen translated by Anna and Peter Hansen – *Sobranie sochinenii Andersena v 4-kh tomakh* (S.-Peterburg 1894, 1899) – which, according to Evgeny Pasternak, was present in the family's library.

9   Pasternak, *Doctor Zhivago*, 31. Henceforth page numbers referring to this edition will be given in brackets after the quotation. My analysis is based on the Russian original of the novel; in a few instances where I needed a more literal translation, I have allowed myself to revise the wording of the quotation; these instances are marked with a capital R.

This gift of imitation remains Antipov-Strelnikov's leitmotif to the end of his life. On the eve of his suicide, in the last conversation with Zhivago about Lara, his wife and Zhivago's great love, in the deserted house in Varykino, Strelnikov reproduces with precision the behaviour of his beloved, guessing how she would shake a carpet together with Zhivago:

> (5) – You held opposite ends of the rug, and she threw herself back, waving her arms high, as on a swing, and turned away from the flying dust, squinting and laughing. Right? [...] And then you started walking towards each other, folding the heavy rug first in two, then in four, and she joked and pulled all sorts of antics while you did it. Right? Right? (413)

Strelnikov not only reproduces his wife's behaviour, but also mimics her way of speaking with the frequent insertion of a question tag "right?".

At the end of the novel it turns out that Antipov's gift of imitation has been inherited by his and Lara's daughter Katia, as we see from Lara's characterisation of her:

> (6) Katyusha has shown extraordinary abilities, partly dramatic, but also musical, *imitates everybody wonderfully* and acts out whole scenes of her own invention, but, besides, she also sings whole parts of operas by ear – *an astonishing child, right?* (443)

Here once more we hear an echo of Andersen's *That boy has surely got a good head on him!*

The glass splinter in the eye
With the splinter in his eye Kay sees only defects around him, and this determines his fate, – from this comes his fascination with abstract perfection at the expense of reality, making him a pupil of the Snow Queen. In Pasternak's novel we can see an analogous development in Antipov-Strelnikov.

After the arrival of the young Antipovs in Iuriatin the husband is less favourably impressed than the wife – he is irritated by the locals, whom he considers to be "wild and ignorant". There soon follows a concrete example of his dissatisfaction with them:

> (7) The Antipovs had guests – several teachers, Pavel Pavlovich's colleagues [...]. *From Pavel Pavlovich's point of view, every man and woman of them*

was an utter fool. He was amazed at Lara, who was amiable with them all, and did not believe that she could sincerely like anyone there. (95)[10]

From then on Antipov sees only defects in the way the world is constituted, which it is his duty to remedy before settling down to family life; to accomplish this he leaves for the front and joins the Revolution.

In a conversation with Zhivago Lara, reflecting on how Pavel Antipov has turned into Strelnikov, makes use of a comparison that, as it were, plays on the entry of the glass splinter into the eye of the hero:

> (8) [...] I saw him once from a distance [...]. I found him almost unchanged. [...] And yet I noticed one change, and it alarmed me. It was *as if something abstract had entered into that look and discolored it.* A living human face had turned into the *embodiment, the principle, the portrayal of an idea.* (359-60)[11]

Lara's words correspond to the impression of Galiullin, Antipov's childhood friend, when after many years he met him at the front (and witnessed his presumed death). It also seemed to Galiullin that something alien had entered Antipov's appearance; and here it is associated with a fairy tale:

> (9) When Pavel Pavlovich left Yuriatin and landed in their regiment, Galiullin *was struck by the change* that had come over his old friend. The bashful, laughter-prone, prissy prankster, who looked like a girl, had turned into a nervous, all-knowing, scornful hypochondriac. He was intelligent, very brave, taciturn, and sarcastic. At times, looking at him, Galiullin was ready to swear that *he could see in Antipov's heavy gaze, as in the depths of a window, some second person,* a thought firmly embedded in him, a longing for his daughter or the face of his wife. *Antipov seemed bewitched, as in a fairy tale.* (102)

This can be read as the key to the enigma of Antipov; the significance of a *window* in connection with him will soon become apparent, and we guess which *second person* could be seen in its *depth*. However, the link with Kay is not limited to this, since the given phrase about Antipov contains a cluster of features that can be related with the

---

10 In an early version of the novel this characteristic was even more pronounced, cp. Pasternak, *Sobranie sochinenii*, 3: 565-67.

11 Antipov's *discolored look* corresponds to Kay's "icing"; and that his face had turned into an *embodiment* or even a *portrayal* is also noteworthy, since Antipov may be seen as precisely that – a portrayal of Kay.

splinter of glass (and the importance of which will be made evident below): window glass – mirror reflection – duplication. Finally, in our context, the cliché *bewitched as in a fairy tale* is "declichéfied" – it resembles the truth.

Pupil and teacher. Exact sciences
As was the case with Kay, Antipov's tendency to see only defects goes hand in hand with a theoretical education. In "The Snow Queen" the theme of pupillage is presented in the introductory story about the magic mirror:

> (10) All those who went to the hobgoblin's school – for he had a school of his own – told everyone that a miracle had come to pass. Now, they asserted, for the very first time you could see how the world and its people really looked.

Correspondingly, after the change that has taken place in him, Kay reveals that he possesses great knowledge and boasts about it to the Snow Queen:

> (11) He told her how he could do mental arithmetic even with fractions, and that he knew the size and population of all the countries.

But Kay immediately feels that his knowledge is insufficient:

> (12) [...] and he began to be afraid that he did not know as much as he thought he did. He looked up at the great big space overhead, as she flew with him high up on the black clouds [...]

We shall be returning to this *moment of decision*. Shortly before, mathematics and calculations have already become the emblem of theoretical knowledge with which Kay's mind is filled; when the Snow Queen's sled carried the boy's toboggan away, he was frightened by the swiftness of their flight, and wanted to pray to God, but only mathematics came out:

> (13) He tried to say his prayers, but all he could remember was his multiplication tables.

And Gerda also says of Kay: "He was so clever that he could do mental arithmetic even with fractions."

An analogous theme of pupillage is of primary importance in *Doctor Zhivago*, and the biography of Antipov-Strelnikov is in part founded on it. I have already quoted excerpts from the characterisation of Antipov in Iuriatin; let's go back to it:

(14) Now in retrospect it became clear that *he had an extraordinary ability to acquire and retain* knowledge drawn from cursory reading. Even before, partly with Lara's help, he had read a great deal. During these years of provincial solitude, he read so much that now *even Lara seemed insufficiently informed to him.* (95)

(Cf. [1], in which Kay deems Gerda's picture book *fit only for babes in the cradle*). Soon Antipov's passion for mathematics is emphasized:

(15) Pavel Pavlovich had graduated in classics. He taught Latin and ancient history in the high school. But *suddenly* the almost extinguished *passion for mathematics, physics, and the exact sciences* awakened in him, the former progressive school student. By self-education he acquired a command of all these disciplines at a university level. (95)[12]

In the course of the already mentioned meeting between Zhivago and Antipov in the railway coach the latter's knowledge, especially of mathematics, is underlined once again: "He had, by his own efforts, supplemented his historico-philological education with a mathematical one" (223), and later, when Zhivago questions Lara about her husband, she also emphasizes his knowledge, especially of mathematics:

(16) And think what abilities he has! [...] he achieved [...] the summit of contemporary university knowledge in two fields, mathematics and the humanities. (360)

Magnifying glasses
The urge towards the exact sciences of both our main characters is set off with the help of a specific detail, which has been transposed from Kay's accessories to Antipov's. Kay's new rationality comes out in his amusing himself with a magnifying glass:

(16) Now his games were very different from what they used to be. They became more sensible. When the snow was flying about one wintry day, he brought *a large magnifying glass* out of doors and spread the

---

[12] The enumeration of the sciences Antipov had studied brings to mind the beginning of Goethe's *Faust*: "I have, alas! Philosophy, / Medicine, Jurisprudence too, / And to my cost Theology, / With ardent labour, studied through. / And here I stand, with all my lore, / Poor fool, no wiser than before" (Goethe).

tail of his blue coat to let the snowflakes fall on it. "Now look through the glass," he told Gerda. [...] It was marvellous to look at. "Look, how artistic!" said Kay. "They are much more interesting to look at than real flowers, for they are absolutely perfect. There isn't a flaw in them, until they start melting."

Later Gerda, approaching the palace of the Snow Queen, remembers how large and strange the snowflakes had appeared "when she looked at them under the magnifying glass".

In *Doctor Zhivago* the theme of magnifying glasses is not introduced by Antipov himself, but it is related to him. When Iurii Zhivago arrives in Varykino together with his father-in-law Aleksandr Gromeko, they meet the Mikulitsyns there, the estate manager and his wife. At tea the hostess Elena Proklovna disconcerts the unexpected visitors with no less "unexpected" questions (in themselves reminiscent of Kay's boasting of his knowledge before the Snow Queen in [11]). Her first question goes "what was the year of Griboedov's death?" (248), and the third question is a regular examination:

> (17) Now here's what interests me. List for me, please, *the kinds of magnifying glasses* and what images they produce in each case: actual, inverted, direct or imaginary. (248)

The visitors do not answer and instead one of them asks where the questioner had acquired such knowledge of physics. It turns out that she had been taught by a special person:

> (18) We had an excellent mathematician here in Yuriatin. He taught in two schools, the boys' and ours. How he explained things [...]! Like a god! He'd chew it all and put in your mouth. Antipov. (248)

Kay taught Gerda to look through a magnifying glass in order to see the ideal beauty of snow crystals; Elena Proklovna reveals that lenses played an important role in Pavel Antipov's teaching.[13]

---

[13] In Pasternak's draft jottings for the novel we find the following note: "Alternate with reading of Lenin the articles on Optics in the Encyclopaedia and of Ural folklore" (*Sobranie sochinenii*, 3, 635); the note apparently refers to Zhivago's disagreement with Antipov at the end of the novel. In the house at Varykino there is also a *stereoscope* made by the son of the house Liberius, the future partisan leader; it is noteworthy that like Strelnikov (cf. "Blinded versus seeing" below), this revolutionary activist is also characterised as having *double* sight: "These are views of the Urals, *double*, stereoscopic, and taken by a camera he made himself." (247); I agree with Smirnov ("Antiutopiia i teoditseia", 162), who sees in these pictures the work of a Utopian. Given the significance of *optics* for the figure of Antipov,

2. Two Symbols:
The Peephole in the Ice and the Rowan

So far I have examined the similarities between Antipov and Kay's mindsets, and below I shall continue the analysis of the parallels between the two on the level of plot. But first I wish to show that two very important symbols in *Doctor Zhivago* have exact correspondences in "The Snow Queen".

The peephole in the ice
In summer the children in Andersen's tale visit each other along flower boxes placed like a little bridge between the houses.

> (19) Winter, of course, put an end to this pleasure. The windows often frosted over completely. But they would heat copper pennies on the stove and press these hot coins against the frost-coated glass. *Then they had the finest of peepholes, as round as a ring, and behind them appeared a bright, friendly eye, one at each window – it was the little boy and the little girl who peeped out. His name was Kay and hers was Gerda.*

A Little Boy and A Little Girl – this is the heading given to the "Second Story" in "The Snow Queen". In the quotation the boy and girl are introduced as hero and heroine; only now are their names given, i.e. they become a pair – and this happens in connection with the peephole in the frost covering the windows. We know that an early variant of the first chapter of *Doctor Zhivago* was called "Boys and Girls". Commentators on the novel have noted a connection between this heading and Aleksandr Blok's poem "Boys and Girls..." ("Palm Saturday") and furthermore a connection with Book Ten in *The Brothers Karamazov* – "The Boys". To these links I shall add "The Snow Queen".

Readers of Pasternak's novel will recall the episode in which a peephole appears in the frost on a window – Lara's rendezvous with Pavel Antipov in his room. Pavel has placed a candle on the windowsill and lit it:

> (20) The flame choked on the stearine, shot crackling little stars in all directions, and sharpened into an arrow. The room filled with a soft light. *The ice on the windowpane at the level of the candle began to melt, forming a black eyehole.* (70)

---

we might recall that when Kay acquires the gift of imitation, he *puts on* the grandmother's *glasses* (cf. [1]). Finally, in this optical context it is hardly a matter of chance that Antipov's *false* death was observed through *field-glasses* – Galiullin "*supposedly* saw him die through his binoculars". (108)

Just then Iurii Zhivago and his future wife Tonia are passing by the house on their way to Christmas celebrations with the Sventitsky family.

> (21) They were driving down Kamergersky. *Yura turned his attention to a black hole melted in the icy coating of one window.* Through this hole shone the light of a candle, penetrating outside *almost with the consciousness of a gaze*, as if the flame were spying on the passersby and wating for someone. (72)

At the moment when the boy and the girl appear as a couple, this, as in Andersen, takes place under the sign of a little hole in the frost on a window. There, however, the peephole unites a couple of children, here an adult couple – since on this evening the boy and the girl cease to be children. In the novel two couples appear at the same time – not just Lara and Antipov, but also Iurii and Tonia, since they have just been "betrothed" (before leaving home) by Tonia's mother Anna Ivanovna. Thus, the Little Boy and the Little Girl of the fairy tale have been transformed into the novel's "Boys and Girls". Correspondingly, the sign of the peephole is repeated: it is observed twice – from the viewpoints of both couples.[14] However, this does not exhaust the meaning of the repeated observation of the peephole; it also corresponds to Antipov's general feature, which will be discussed below – his mirror-like doubleness.

The rowan
We have just seen that for one specific detail and its function in *Doctor Zhivago* there is a parallel in "The Snow Queen". This is also the case for another significant detail – the rowan:

> (22) At that time the partisans were halted in a new place.] ...] At the way out of the camp and the forest [...] there grew a solitary, beautiful, rusty-red-leafed rowan tree, the only one of all the trees to keep its foliage. (316-17)

Later it is emphasised that the rowan is considered to be "the camp's boundary marker" (325), and when the doctor leaves the camp for good, he makes his way to the tree:

> (23) It was half covered with snow, half with frozen leaves and berries, and it stretched out two snowy branches to meet him. He remembered Lara's big white arms, rounded, generous, and, taking hold of the branches, he

---

14 Pasternak, *Sobranie* sochinenii, 3, 652-53.

pulled the tree towards him. As if in a conscious answering movement, the rowan showered him with snow from head to foot. He was murmering, not realizing what he was saying, and unaware of himself: "I shall see you, my beauty, my princess, my dearest rowan tree, my own heart's blood." (336)

Again the rowan marks the border between the non-being of partisan imprisonment and life. In "The Snow Queen" there is a corresponding landmark in the form of a bush.[15] At Gerda's last stop in her search for Kay, her helper, the Finn woman, gives the reindeer instructions on how to get to the palace of the Snow Queen:

(24) The Snow Queen's garden lies about eight miles from here. You may carry the little girl there, and *put her down by the big bush covered with red berries* that grows on the snow. Then don't you stand there gossiping, but hurry to get back here. [...] but the reindeer did not dare to stop. He galloped on until they came to *the big bush that was covered with red berries*. Here he set Gerda down and kissed her on the mouth, while big shining tears ran down his face.

When Kay and Gerda leave the realm of the Snow Queen, the border between it and life is again marked by the bush with the red berries:

(25) Hand in hand, Kay and Gerda strolled out of that enormous palace. They talked about Grandmother, and about the roses on their roof. Wherever they went, the wind died down and the sun shone out. *When they came to the bush that was covered with red berries*, the reindeer was waiting to meet them.

The connection between Pasternak's rowan and this particular bush is confirmed by the motif of *feeding*; the passage quoted from the tale continues:

(26) He [the reindeer, P.A.J.] had brought along *a young reindeer mate who had warm milk for the children to drink*, and who kissed them on the mouth.

The rowan in the novel feeds the winter birds:

(27) Some living intimacy was established between the birds and the tree. As if the rowan saw it all, resisted for a long time, then surrendered, taking

---

15 In the novel the rowan is called a *tree* (cf. [22]); however, in linguistic tradition, Danish as well as English and Russian, the rowan is often considered *a shrub*.

pity on the little birds, yielded, *unbuttoned herself, and gave them the breast, like a nurse to an infant.* "Well, what can I do with you? Go on, eat, eat me. Feed yourselves." And she smiled. (317R)

(Here the words of the rowan and, even more so, its smiling, are very Andersenian.) We can see that the foster mother in the novel corresponds to the suckling reindeer in the tale. On closer consideration it turns out that feeding is likewise the feeding of *infants* there. Gerda saved Kay by singing a hymn – Kay "cried so freely that the little piece of glass in his eye was washed right out", and the bits of ice began to dance with happiness and then dropped into a pattern and formed the word "eternity". We recall the text of the hymn: "*Where roses bloom so sweetly in the vale / There shall you find the Christ Child, without fail.*" The hymn brings back to life the *child* in Kay so that he and Gerda leave the palace of the Snow Queen and go to the waiting reindeer precisely as little children. The feeding of the birds in the novel corresponds to the feeding of the children in the fairy tale.

3. Biographemes: Departure, Disappearance, Captivity, Death

Let us return to Antipov-Strelnikov and examine some parallels between important biographemes common to both Antipov and Kay, and along the way also the theme of cold and ice.

The moment of decision
We have already touched on "the moment of decision" when the hero decides to leave the heroine in order to become a disciple of the hobgoblin/the Snow Queen or to dedicate himself to utopian theory.[16] I shall have to revisit passages already quoted. Let us begin with Kay:

(28) Kay looked at her. She was so beautiful! [...] In his eyes she was perfect and he was not at all afraid. He told her how he could do mental arithmetic even with fractions, and that he knew the size and population of all the countries. She kept on smiling [...] and he began to be afraid that he did not know as much as he thought he did. He looked up at the great big space overhead, as she flew with him high up on the black clouds.

---

16 On the polemic of Pasternak's novel with classical utopias, see Smirnov, "Antiutopiia i teoditseia".

Kay's decisive moment consists of the following components: delight at the Snow Queen, exhibition of knowledge and awareness of its insufficiency, a look into infinite space, dark clouds, departure. Besides this the moment also contains cold and ice, the Snow Queen's sleigh and her demonic strength. Let us turn to Antipov's parallel moment; in Iuriatin, after an evening with "utter fools" (95), Antipov is unable to fall asleep and leaves the house:

> (29) It was a clear autumn night with frost. Fragile sheets of ice crunched loudly under Antipov's feet. The starry night, like a flame of burning alcohol, cast its wavering pale blue glow over the black earth with its clods of frozen mud. [...] Antipov sat down on the overturned boat and looked at the stars. [...] This can't go on any longer, he thought. [...] Why had she allowed him as a child to admire her so much? [...] Worst of all is that he loves her to this day as strongly as ever. She is maddeningly beautiful. But maybe what he feels is also not love, but a grateful bewilderment before her beauty and magnanimity? Pah, just try sorting it out! Here the devil himself would break a leg. What's to be done in that case? [...] He looked at the stars as if asking their advice. [...] Suddenly, eclipsing their glimmer, the courtyard with the house, the boat, and Antipov sitting on it were lit up by a sharp, darting light [...]. It was a military train, throwing puffs of yellow, flame-shot smoke into the sky, going through the crossing to the west [...]. Pavel Pavlovich smiled, got up from the boat, and went to bed. The desired way out had been found. (96-97)

With regard to its components and their sequence, this moment coincides at many points with Kay's moment of decision. Following the fragments of ice and the flickering Northern Lights – attributes of Kay's "game of ice-cold reason" (to be discussed in the following section), there come in turn: a boat, corresponding to the Snow Queen's sleigh, stupendous love, perplexity at inadequate knowledge, devilry, a look into infinitude, a sudden cloud (here of smoke), departure. It looks pretty much as if Antipov has decided to leave for the same destination as Kay.

"The game of ice-cold reason": on Kay and Antipov's goals
The reader learns about Kay's intention and goal only towards the end of the fairy tale when Gerda finds him in the hall of the Snow Queen (I have already referred to this remarkable description):

> (30) In the middle of the vast, empty hall of snow was a frozen lake. It was cracked into a thousand pieces, but each piece was shaped so exactly like the

others that it seemed a work of wonderful craftsmanship. The Snow Queen sat in the exact center of it when she was at home, and she spoke of this as sitting on her "Mirror of Reason"; [...] Little Kay was blue, yes, almost black, with the cold [...]. Kay was shifting some sharp, flat pieces of ice to and fro, trying to fit them into every possible pattern, for he wanted to make something with them. [...] Kay was cleverly arranging his pieces in the game of ice-cold reason. To him the patterns were highly remarkable and of the utmost importance, for the chip of glass in his eye made him see them that way. He arranged his pieces to spell out many words; but he could never find the way to make the one word he was so eager to form. The word was "Eternity". The Snow Queen had said to him, "If you can puzzle that out you shall be your own master, and I'll give you the whole world and a new pair of skates." But he could not puzzle it out.

On Antipov's goal the narrator writes:

(31) From an early age Strelnikov had striven for the highest and brightest. He considered life an enormous arena in which people, honorably observing the rules, compete in the attainment of perfection. (224)

This characterisation might be a translation of Kay's game on "the mirror of reason" into the language of chivalric tournaments. Lara describes the aspiration of her warrior husband in the following words:

(32) He needs to lay all these military laurels at our feet, so as not to come back empty-handed, but all in glory, a conqueror! To immortalize, *to bedazzle us! Like a child!* (271)[17]

In his confessional conversation with Zhivago Antipov-Strelnikov himself relates how he wished to combat the social denigration of man:

(33) Marxism appeared. It discovered what the root of the evil was and where the cure lay. It became the mighty force of the age. (411)

Marxism here corresponds to the hobgoblin's magic mirror, about which his pupils said that "for the very first time you could see how the world and its people really looked". Antipov went to war and joined the Revolution "so that there would be no return to the past", in order to achieve perfection:

17 The italicised words apply precisely to Kay as well and again link Antipov with *blinding*.

> (34) But I wanted first to carry my life's work to its conclusion. (412)
>
> Think, six years of separation, six years of inconceivable self-restraint. But it seemed to me that not all of freedom had been conquered yet. I would achieve that first, and then I would belong wholly to them, my hands would be unbound. (413)

Finish my life's work, years of separation, inconceivable self-restraint, freedom not yet conquered – all this is equally applicable to Kay almost black with cold at his "game of ice-cold reason". Antipov-Strelnikov played the very same game, and "Eternity" was similarly out of reach.

Disappearance and captivity. The heroine's search and the strength of her heart

In "The Snow Queen" Kay disappears, and he is thought to have perished: "Where could he be? Nobody knew. [...] People said that he was dead – that he must have been drowned in the river not far from town." In *Doctor Zhivago* Antipov disappears at the front and he is thought to be dead:

> (35) Larissa Fyodorovna began to worry and made enquiries. [...] *No one knew anything, no reply came from anywhere.* (98)
>
> False rumors went around about him. He was considered dead and buried under the earth in a shell crater. (100)
>
> Who was this man though? [...] had been held prisoner for a long time during the war, had been missing until recently and presumed dead [...]. (222)

Disappearance is a widespread motif and is not in itself sufficient to link Strelnikov with Kay. On closer inspection, however, we find that they both disappear *in the course of a game with other boys*: Kay and the other boys were tying their sled to the farmers' carts to be pulled along; and the war in which Antipov disappeared is a continuation of his game with other boys as observed by Lara in their childhood:

> (36) The boys were playing at the most dreadful and adult of games, at war [...]. There was a bloom of innocence on their dangerous amusements. They imparted the same stamp to everything else. To the *frosty evening, overgrown with such shaggy hoarfrost* that its thickness made it look not white but black. (45)[18]

---

18 This passage could also be related to the theme of cold and ice, which will be discussed in the following section.

In both works the heroine begins to seek for the hero, who has disappeared; Gerda runs down to the river, and, correspondingly, Pasternak's heroine takes off to search at "the scene of recent events" (98). Close to this place, in the hospital in Meliuzeevo, Doctor Zhivago interprets Lara's sadness in the spirit of a fairy tale:

> (37) And then amidst the joy that grips everyone, I meet your mysteriously mirthless gaze, wandering no one knows where, *in some far-off kingdom, in some far-off land.* (129)[19]

Like Kay, Antipov is also taken prisoner.[20] After this it is as if the ways of the two heroines part, at least in terms of plot; Gerda, convinced that Kay is alive, begins her long and distant searches, while Lara, uncertain about her husband's fate, returns to Iuriatin. However, verbally their paths meet again when Lara later declares her readiness to go to *the end of the world*; furthermore, the strength of both heroines, as opposed to the heroes, is defined as *strength of the heart*. Kay's rationality was set up against Gerda's heart (in both Danish and Russian the name *Gerda* rhymes with the word for heart: *hjerte*, serdtse), and in actual fact Kay not only was hit in the eye by the splinter from the magic mirror, but also hurt in his heart:

> (38) Kay and Gerda were looking at a picture book of birds and beasts one day, and it was then – just as the clock in the church tower was striking five – that Kay cried: "Oh! something hurt my heart. And now I've got something in my eye."

In *Doctor Zhivago* the narrator, analysing Antipov, explicates this opposition in very distinct terms:

> (39) And for doing good, he, a man of principle, *lacked the unprincipledness of the heart*, which knows no general cases, but only particular ones, and which is great in doing small things. (224)

What is spelled out here is *the strength of the heart* peculiar to Andersen's heroine; to the reindeer's question whether the Finn woman has something that could make Gerda all-powerful, the Finn woman answers:

---
19 The Russian original *v trideviatom tsarstve, v tridesiatom gosudarstve* is the traditional folk tale formula for very far away.
20 In the novel it is, of course, not only Antipov who disappears and is taken prisoner, but also Zhivago himself.

(40) – Don't you see how men and beasts are compelled to serve her, and how far she has come in the wide world since she started out in her naked feet? We mustn't tell her about this power. *Strength lies in her heart, because she is such a sweet, innocent child.*

In Pasternak's novel Lara herself tells Zhivago that in her relationship with Antipov she was governed by her heart:

(41) We were almost from the same courtyard. [...] I was his childhood passion. He swooned, he *went cold* when he saw me. [...] Right then I *chose him with my heart*. (360)

Making her fruitless attempt to gain an audience with Antipov-Strelnikov in Iuriatin, Lara was guided by "the voice of the heart" (270) and continuing the just cited conversation with Zhivago, Lara assures him of her love for Antipov with a promise that calls to mind Gerda's journey to the Far North:

(42) If somewhere far away, *at the edge of the world*, the window of our house miraculously lit up, with a lamp and books on Pasha's desk, I think *I would crawl there on my knees*. (361)

In his conversation with Antipov on the eve of the former's death Zhivago cites these very words as proof of Lara's love for her husband:

(43) I said, do you have any idea to what extent you were dear to her, dearer than anyone in the world? [...] She [...] said that if the vision of the home she once shared with you glimmered again on the far horizon, *she would crawl to its doorstep on her knees from anywhere at all, even the ends of the earth*. (412-13)

This twofold cliché regarding Lara's possible journey corresponds exactly with the little Robber Girl's remark on seeing Kay liberated:

(44) "You're a fine one for gadding about," she told little Kay. "I'd just like to know *whether you deserve to have someone running to the end of the earth for your sake!*"

The theme of cold and ice
A large part of *Doctor Zhivago* takes place in winter; unforgettable descriptions of winter figure on the pages of the novel, and it is therefore

not surprising that its characters often appear in a wintry setting. But snow, cold and ice acquire meaning in the novel and become part of its thematics. I am not able to consider this theme in depth here and shall limit myself to the question to what extent Antipov-Strelnikov as the bearer of this theme corresponds with "The Snow Queen" and with Kay. Snow and blizzards are connected with the Revolution,[21] and since Strelnikov is its main representative, he is, so to speak, born as the bearer of this theme; but is there also a link with Andersen's Kay here?

In a number of cases Antipov-Strelnikov's appearance on the scene of the novel is accompanied by the appearance of snow or ice, and the descriptions of it often contain recognizable elements from Kay's accessories.

Thus, his first steps in the novel – when as mentioned the boy was taken to a political demonstration – coincide with the first snow:

> (45) It was a dry frosty day in early November, with a still, leaden sky and *a few snowflakes*, so few that *you could almost count them*, swirling slowly and hesitantly before they fell to earth and then, in a fluffy gray dust, filled the potholes in the road. (31)

Here two of Kay's attributes are mingled – snowflakes and calculation.

Antipov's "moment of decision", discussed in (29) above, again coincides with the appearance of cold and ice: *frost, sheets of ice crunching* under Antipov's feet, a *wavering pale blue glow* in the sky, *frozen mud*. Here we meet two attributes of Kay's situation in the hall of the Snow Queen – besides the "cracked" ice slides also the illumination by "the flare of the Northern Lights".

What one might call Antipov's entrenchment in the theme of cold and ice is completed when Lara drops in on him on her way to the Christmas party at the Sventitskys'. Here we are given the first description of winter in the town; it contains a series of components of the theme, and they are concentrated on snow, ice and frost; in particular the icy encrustation on the windows is described, which presages the appearance of the peephole in the ice on one of them. This passage through the theme of ice and cold leads to Antipov:

---

21 On the evening when Zhivago learns the news about the Revolution in the street, a snowstorm is raging. (170) But the theme of snow and cold is far from exhausted by this; it is introduced in a blizzard on the night following the burial of Zhivago's mother on the first pages of the novel, to which I will return in "Blinded versus seeing" below.

(46) It was *freezing cold*. The streets were covered with *black ice*, thick as the *glass* bottoms of *broken* beer bottles. It was painful to breathe. The air was *choked with gray hoarfrost*, and it seemed to tickle and prickle with its shaggy stubble, just as *the icy fur* of Lara's collar chafed her and got into her mouth. With a pounding heart Lara walked along the empty streets. Smoke came from the doorways of tearooms and taverns along the way. The *frostbitten faces* of passersby, red as sausage, and the bearded muzzles of horses and dogs *hung with icicles* emerged from the mist. Covered with *a thick layer of ice and snow*, the windows of houses were as if painted over with chalk, and the colorful reflections of lighted Christmas trees and the shadows of merrymakers moved over their *opaque surface*, as if the people outside were being shown shadow pictures from inside on white sheets hung before a magic lantern.

In Kamergersky Lara stopped. "I can't do it anymore, I can't stand it" burst from her almost aloud. "I'll go up and *tell him everything*," she thought, regaining control of herself, opening the heavy door of the imposing entrance. (69)

In this frozen world the thick layer of opaque ice is mentioned twice – on the street and on the windows – and both times in connection with glass; we also note the presence of the adjective *glass* itself. In the centre of the icy landscape is Antipov. Soon the *peephole* will appear in the window ice and in immediate connection with it the theme of Iurii Zhivago's *sight*. In contrast to, as we see now, what is characteristic of the icy landscape hiding Antipov is opacity or blindness.[22]

One of the remarkable snow scenes in *Doctor Zhivago* is encountered en route for the Urals when snowdrifts stop the train, and the passengers get out to clear them. It turns out that along with the snowstorm, Antipov-Strelnikov too has been raging in the area. For this reason, while shovelling, Zhivago thinks of Antipov, and here the regularity of the cubes of snow leads his thoughts back to blocks of snow he played with in his childhood; this memory is, in turn, easily associated with Kay's game with the "regular and uniform" pieces of ice in the palace of the Snow Queen:

(47) The place where the Zhivagos went to dig was open, picturesque. [...] On a hill stood a solitary house [...]. Where were its former inhabitants, and what had happened to them? [...] Had Strelnikov spared them, if they stayed

---

22 When Lara bursts in on *him*, she finds him in front *the mirror*; in this way cold and opacity are connected with Antipov's *mirrorness* (see "Blinded versus seeing").

until recently, or had they been included in his summary justice along with the kulaks? [...] And the sun lit up the snowy smoothness with a *blinding white* brilliance. How *regular were the pieces* the shovel cut from it! What dry, diamond-like sparkles spilled from the cuts! How it reminded him of the far-off *days of childhood*, when [...] *little Yura* had cut *pyramids and cubes*, cream cakes, fortresses, and cave dwellings from the snow in the courtyard, which was just as *blinding*. Oh, how tasty it was to live in the world then, how everything around had been a *feast for the eyes* and for the stomach. (204R)

Below we shall see that the description of Antipov-Strelnikov's death is prepared by Zhivago's dreams "from his childhood". Antipov's presence in the passage above is a veiled introduction to childhood memories, childhood is the world of the fairy tale, and at once an image occurs that can be directly related with Kay. This is a characteristic example of the way in which the fairy tale functions as a kind of *figurative interpretant* through which Zhivago involuntarily apprehends his surroundings.[23] The first chain of associations: 'Antipov – the whiteness of the snow – *blinding* – clean cuts' is overlaid by a second: 'Iurii's childhood – blinding snow – pyramids and cubes – *feast for the eyes*'. In this way – i.e. through the figure of Kay as an interpretant including Antipov-Strelnikov – the figure of a little boy playing with cleancut pieces of snow or ice is superimposed with yet another opposition of the *types of sight* pertaining to Antipov and Zhivago: one was blinded, the other feasted his eyes.

Antipov's death
We have seen that in places Antipov-Strelnikov resembles a successor to Kay. Their kinship is suggested right away, in the presentation of the character, and from his very first steps Pavel Antipov acted like Kay. Now we shall see that also his death is depicted in a fairytale key.

Strelnikov commits suicide after nighttime conversations with Zhivago in the deserted house in Varykino. His apologetic confession contains a string of traits and details that can easily be associated with Kay's history and fate. Thus, for instance, his delight as a boy in Lara is reminiscent of Kay's thrilled admiration for the Snow Queen;[24] Pavel and Lara had been children from the same court, although they had not lived as close

---

23 By *figurative interpretant*, analogously to C. S. Peirce's concept of 'the interpretant', I understand an image that "governs" the perception of the given object.
24 We have seen examples of this parallel above in (29) "Why had she allowed him as a child to admire her so much?" and in (41) "I was his childhood passion. He swooned, he *went cold* when he saw me."

together as Kay and Gerda. These parallels, in themselves not too striking, prepare for the description of the night of Strelnikov's suicide, which can now be read almost as an epitaph bringing the figure of Antipov back into the world of the fairy tale.

This return begins at night when Zhivago, as mentioned above, has a dream from his childhood:

> (48) During the second half of the night, he began to have short, quickly changing *dreams from the time of his childhood, sensible and rich in detail, which it was easy to take for the truth.*
>
> Thus, for instance, his mother's watercolor of the Italian seacoast, which hung on the wall, suddenly tore off, fell on the floor, and the sound of *breaking glass* awakened Yuri Andreevich. He *opened his eyes.* No, it was something else. It must be Antipov, Lara's husband, Pavel Pavlovich, whose last name is Strelnikov, scarifying wolves in Shutma again, as Vakkh would say. Ah, no, what nonsense. Of course, it was the painting falling off the wall. There it is *in splinters* on the floor, he *verified,* as his dream returned and continued.
>
> He woke up with a headache from having slept too long. He could not figure out at first who or *where he was, in which world.* (414R)

Here we have a full identification form or a certificate of identity – *Antipov, Lara's husband, Pavel Pavlovich, whose last name is Strelnikov –* framed by the initial components of Kay's fate: *breaking glass – opened his eyes.* We also get the sequel *Strelnikov – in splinters – verified.* And this dual certification is in its turn introduced within a fairytale framework: *dreams from childhood / he could not figure out [...] in which world he was.*

The reader soon understands that in his sleep Zhivago heard the shot with which Antipov killed himself. The history of his life and the basic plot of the novel end as follows:

> (49) Yuri Andreevich started a fire in the stove, took the bucket and went to the well for water. A few steps from the porch, obliquely across the path, having fallen and *buried his head in a snowdrift,* lay Pavel Pavlovich. He had shot himself. *The snow under his left temple was bunched into a red lump,* soaked in a pool of spilled blood. The small drops of blood spattered around had rolled up with the snow into little red balls that *looked like frozen rowan berries.* (414)

In the night Zhivago had been unable to distinguish his dreams, "*sensible and rich in detail*", from "*the truth*". Now he sees *the truth* as it is. The description of it is also *sensible and rich in detail*, and, now that we have seen how Zhivago's dream is permeated by the fairy tale, we cannot help registering that his "truth" is likewise perceived in its key: Strelnikov has *buried his head in a snowdrift*, the snow gathered into *a red lump*, and his blood transformed into *little red balls*; we remember that when the Snow Queen wrapped Kay in her fur coat, "Kay felt as if he were sinking into a snowdrift", and her kiss turned his *heart* into an i*cy lump* (cf. also [30]). Thus Antipov has remained in the power of the Snow Queen and has perished in the realm of snow and ice; "the game of ice-cold reason" did not succeed for him, for, as was the case for Kay, "eternity" did not come out. In contrast to Kay, the love of his life did not reach Antipov; he has not let his Gerda come to him, and on his own he does not reach the boundary bush with the red berries. Shooting himself, Strelnikov mingles his blood with the snow, imitating the rowanberries. The mixture of blood and snow becomes his last, posthumous imitation.[25]

4. Three Contrasts: Sight, Belief, and Time

Now we shall take a close look at three constrasting parallels between our heroes which co-determine their fate.

Blinded versus seeing
A characteristic feature of Pavel Antipov's set-up is his *doubleness* – in both genesis and meaning. Thus, his biography is doubled. The boy Pavel has two families and two homes (in the absence of his parents he lives with the Tiverzins); the adult Antipov has two educations, two specialities; it is also as if he has two genders – Galiullin describes him as a girl (cf. [9]), and he teaches in both the boys' and the girls' gymnasium (cf. [18]); Antipov duplicates his marriage with Lara – he leaves it in order to resume it once more. These duplications accumulate until he has become another person under a different surname. Finally he dies twice.

Setting out from the idea that Antipov's fate is determined by the splinter from a mirror in his eye, I am inclined to interpret his doubleness as an expression of his *mirrorness*.[26] Already as a boy, Antipov would

---

[25] We remember that, standing in front of the rowan in the wood, Zhivago calls it "my beauty, my princess, my dearest rowan tree, my own heart's blood" (cf. [32]).

[26] Kay's "mirrorness" is connected not only with the splinter of glass in his eye but also with his game with the pieces of ice on the lake which the Snow Queen called her "Mirror of Reason" (cf. [30]).

adjust his appearance as one does before a mirror (cf. [2]), and when later Lara bursts in on the adolescent Antipov – on the significant evening with the peephole in the ice – he is occupied in front of a mirror:

> (50) Red from the effort, his tongue stuck in his cheek, Pasha struggled before the mirror, putting on his collar and trying to stick the recalcitrant stud through the overstarched buttonhole of his shirt front. (69)

Meanings of forced confinement are stowed close here; not seeing further than the mirror, Pasha is buttoning himself up. Antipov is literally *defined* by the glass of the mirror; he himself behaves as if in front of a mirror or is actually standing there, and the window of his room has iced up so that nothing can be seen through it;[27] all the facts of his biography are mirrored, duplicated; we remember Galiullin's impression that in Antipov's eyes he saw *some second person "as in the depths of a window"* (cf. [9]).

The significance of the opacity of the window glass is also confirmed when on his wedding night with Lara Antipov is disturbed by the light coming into the room from outside:

> (51) Across the yard from Lara's window there was a lighted street lamp, and no matter how Lara arranged the curtains a strip of light, narrow as the edge of a board, came through the space between the two panels. *This bright strip bothered Pasha*, as if someone were spying on them. Pasha discovered with horror that he was more concerned with this street lamp than with himself, Lara, and his love for her. (86)

Antipov is troubled by light from outside; opaque glass is one of his attributes. Furthermore we have seen that, like Kay, he is especially interested in *magnifying glasses*.

Now we realize that Zhivago's dreams at the moment of Antipov's suicide not only, as mentioned above, infuse the description of it with Kay's fate, but also interpret this death! In his dream Zhivago experienced the shot that killed Antipov as the breaking of glass. The *truth*

---

[27] Towards the end of the novel the appearance of frost – and opacity – coincides with Antipov's approach to Zhivago and Lara's hideaway in Varykino; the ominous moment when after a happy stretch of work Zhivago hears the howling of wolves close to the house is described in this way: "He went into the unlit next room to look out the window from there. During the hours he had spent writing, the windowpanes had become thickly *frosted over*, and *he could see nothing through them.*" (391)

of the dream is confirmed once more; a man of glass was broken – a magic mirror had been shattered.

Finally, mirrorness links Antipov with the theme of *sight*. Antipov is hemmed in by glass and sees nothing; in the image of the boy playing with pieces of ice (cf. [46]), we discovered an opposition between bedazzlement and feasting one's eyes; correspondingly, Lara declares that Strelnikov wished to bedazzle her (cf. [32]). At the end of the novel it emerges that this opposition is organised around the window of Antipov's room. Next to Zhivago's coffin in this very same room (one of many strange coincidences in the novel) the mourning Lara recalls her meeting with Antipov, the candle on the windowsill and the circle in the icy crust on the windowpane; we are reminded by the narrator that Zhivago had noticed the candle from outside and "that from this *flame seen from the outside* [...] his destiny had come into his life". (444) Here the symmetry of the two protagonists on either side of the windowpane is restored: *then* Antipov was with Lara inside, while Iurii and Tonia were outside; *now* Zhivago has taken Antipov's place inside. The plot of the novel revolves around the windowpane and the peephole in the frost; this particular image first establishes the opposition between the protagonists, and now the opposition in their way of seeing is summed up: the flame and light *seen* from outside versus ice and an unseeing eye within.[28]

Demonic versus divine
Thus, Antipov-Strelnikov's "mirrorness" is not only a feature of the character, but also an important factor in the composition of the novel. With the help of a series of replays, motivated by the very mirrorness itself, this quality of Antipov's brings about and determines his path in life. By the same token, through contrasting contacts, it also in many ways determines Zhivago's. Antipov is not so much Zhivago's *antipode* as he is his *anti-path*. The role of "The Snow Queen" in *Doctor* Zhivago, then, cannot be confined to the polemic with Antipov's abstract thought and to traits in his character that give expression to it. The fairy tale plays a more general and fundamental role, in particular as a "formant" of the two protagonists' life paths.

In that case we might expect to find signs of this role at the beginning and at the end of the path; and if the path is not confined within Antipov-Strelnikov's fate, then we should be able to find signs of the

---

28 If we are looking for Antipov-Strelnikov's common denominator, this might be the concept of 'reflection', with its two meanings: a mirror effect and abstract thought.

presence of Andersen's tale at the beginning and end of the novel as a whole. Are they there?

Let's turn to the first snow, to the blizzard in the night following the funeral of Iurii's mother:

> (52) *During the night* Yura was awakened by a tapping at the window. [...] *In just his nightshirt, Yura ran to the window and pressed his face against the cold glass.* [...] A blizzard was raging outside; the air was smoky with snow. One might have thought *the storm noticed Yura and, knowing how frightening it was, reveled in the impression it made on him.* It whistled and howled and *tried in every way possible to attract Yura's attention.* From the sky endless skeins of *white cloth*, turn after turn, fell on the earth, covering it in a winding sheet. The blizzard was alone in the world; nothing rivaled it. (4)

This first vision of snow in the novel corresponds to the first appearance of the Snow Queen in the fairy tale:

> (53) *That evening* when little Kay was at home and *half ready* for bed, *he climbed on the chair by the window and looked out through the little peep-hole.* A few snowflakes were falling, and the largest flake of all alighted on the edge of one of the flower boxes. This flake grew bigger and bigger, until at last it turned into a woman, who was dressed in the finest *white gauze* which looked as if it had been made from millions of star-shaped flakes. She was beautiful and she was graceful, but she was ice-shining, glittering ice. She was alive, for all that, and her eyes sparkled like two bright stars, but in them there was neither rest nor peace. *She nodded toward the window and beckoned with her hand. The little boy was frightened*, and as he jumped down from the chair it seemed to him that a huge bird flew past the window.

Here, surely, the fairy tale enters the novel, with the first snow! The parallels seem sufficiently evident, but this only underscores the new meaning attached to the snowstorm in *Doctor Zhivago*: if the terrifying female power facing Kay is demonic, the power facing Iurii seems rather to be divine – thanks to the association with the robe of the Virgin Mary.[29] As we shall see below, this important substitution is confirmed at the end of the novel where we will also find a parallel between the epilogue and the happy ending of Andersen's tale.

---

29 Cf. Pasternak, *Sobranie sochinenii*, 3, 682.

Between time and eternity

Doctor Zhivago is a novel about an artist between time and eternity. The novel begins in time and ends in eternity. The first words of the novel, the heading of Chapter 1 *The Five O'Clock Express,* could not be more "temporal": two of them combine enumeration with a unit of time and the last one denotes speed of movement with reference to a train, a highly pregnant symbol of historical progress. And the last words of the novel are the words of the poet Zhivago about how time will come to eternity to be judged.

Actually the text of the novel begins with this very opposition. The first words "They walked and walked and sang "Memory Eternal"" oppose a historical process – the walking – to eternity, and the subsequent description of Maria Nikolaevna Zhivago's funeral combines segments of a temporal narrative with elements representing eternity:

> (54) The last minutes flashed by, numbered, irrevocable. "The earth is the Lord's and the fullness thereof; the world, and those who dwell therein." The priest, tracing a cross, threw a handful of earth onto Marya Nikolaevna. They sang "With the souls of the righteous." A terrible bustle began. The coffin was closed, nailed shut, lowered in. A rain of clods drummed down as four shovels hastily filled the grave. Over it a small mound rose. A ten-year-old boy climbed onto it.

Eternity and time are also opposed by the two deaths with which the novel begins; Iura's mother is buried in eternity, while his father, on the contrary, throws himself out of the five o'clock express and perishes in time. Correspondingly, Iurii Zhivago repeatedly remembers his mother and returns to her burial place, while his father vanished into history – there is not a word in the novel about his burial or grave.

Later, finally, Antipov-Strelnikov and Iurii Zhivago are contrasted as representing two different approaches to time and eternity; the former strives to transform the future into eternity with the help of a historical utopia, while the latter unveils eternity in the present with the help of art. Both time and eternity are for them very different: Strelnikov is the prisoner of time, while Zhivago frees himself from captivity by raising time up to eternity – or, rather, bringing eternity "down" into time.

A similar opposition of time and eternity also determines the structure of "The Snow Queen." Kay's fate changes, as we know (cf. [38]), at a precisely designated point in time – "just as the clock in the church tower was striking five" he cries, "Oh! something hurt my heart. And now I've got something in my eye." (Wouldn't it be from here that Pasternak got the time of *The Five O'Clock Express*?) Here begin Kay's departure in search of a false eternity and Gerda's subsequent wanderings in order to bring him back into time and to an actual eternity. The fairy tale ends by contrasting time and eternity. On Kay and Gerda's return from the realm of the Snow Queen –

> (55)... *church bells rang*, and they saw the high steeples of a big town. It was the one where they used to live. They walked straight to Grandmother's house, and up the stairs, and into the room, where everything was just as it was when they left it. And *the clock said tick-tock, and its hands were telling the time.* But the moment they came in the door they noticed one change. They were grown-up now. The roses on the roof looked in at *the open window*, and their two little stools were still out there. Kay and Gerda sat down on them, and held each other by the hand. Both of them had forgotten the icy, empty splendor of the Snow Queen's palace as completely as if it were some bad dream. Grandmother sat in God's good sunshine, reading to them from her Bible: "Except ye become as little children, ye shall not enter into the Kingdom of Heaven." Kay and Gerda looked into each other's eyes, and at last they understood the meaning of their old hymn: "*Where roses bloom so sweetly in the vale,/ There shall you find the Christ Child, without fail.*" And they sat there, grown-up, but children still – children at heart. And it was *summer*, warm, glorious summer.

If the first words of *Doctor Zhivago, The Five O'Clock Express*, are connected with Andersen's *was striking five*, and the tale enters the consciousness of author and hero with the first snow, we might, as just mentioned, expect a corresponding coincidence at the end of Zhivago's life.[30] Indeed, the final page of the "Epilogue" is in many ways similar

---

30 The end of Zhivago's path in life is his collapse on the street next to the tram. Just before this he has been reflecting on the different speeds at which the lives and fates of different people pass. Now Mme Fleury, who had occasioned these reflections, comes up to the dying man. A little earlier, as the tram passed her, she was described as "a gray-haired old lady, in a light straw hat with cloth daisies and cornflowers and in a tight-fitting old-fashioned lilac dress". (436) This description, as it were, motivates her surname *Fleury*; but it also reminds us of *the old lady with the flower-bed* in "The Snow Queen": "[...] an old, old woman came out of the house. She leaned on a crooked stick; she had on a big sun hat, and on it were painted the most glorious flowers." Isn't Mme Fleury perhaps a visitor from the tale? To this it may be added that Zhivago's actual death after the heart attack in the tram (repeating the death of Relikvimini, the main character of early fragments by Pasternak, cf. Sobr. sochinenii, 4, 725, 733) is reminiscent of an episode from Andersen's memoir, when on the way back to London after a visit to Mary Howitt the author suffered an attack on an omnibus: "But before we had really left Clapton my limbs gave way; I felt ill and weak just as I had done in Naples. I was in danger of fainting and the omnibus became fuller and warmer all the time. It was stopping all the time, and soon it was full on top too. Booted

to the ending of the fairy tale. It is heralded by reflections on *children*, and the actual ending of the novel is introduced as follows:

"Five or ten years went by, and one quiet *summer evening they were sitting again*, Gordon and Dudorov, somewhere *high up by an open window* over the boundless evening Moscow; they were leafing through the notebook of Yuri's writings [...]." (460)

The setting high above the home town is identical, Kay and Gerda have been replaced by Zhivago's close friends, and the texts of the Gospel and the hymn have been replaced by the "notebook of Yuri's writings", which, however, also explains the relation between time and eternity: only now, like Gerda and Kay, do Gordon and Dudorov understand the meaning of the text.

Conclusion: "All children's dreams"

The epigraph of this article, quoted from the preparatory materials for *Doctor Zhivago*, apparently refers to Dostoevsky's novels; but our analysis has shown that the continuity to which Pasternak found himself subject, may also be related to "The Snow Queen." However, it is difficult to take what we have examined as *forgotten* examples; rather, "The Snow Queen" consistently informs Pasternak's novel, and as part of the fairytale world as such its significance permeates the work as a whole.

The "fairytale quality" of *Doctor Zhivago* is not limited to its folkloric elements;[31] the novel has absorbed the world of the fairy tale in a broad sense, a world intimately linked to the theme of childhood. This covers much more than the descriptions of the childhoods of the main characters; childhood is central not only for Zhivago's writing but also in Lara's worldview, so close to his, and in that of other important characters. The theme of childhood passes through the entire novel right up to Zhivago's poetry; there we meet Christmas and together with Christmas Aleksandr Blok. I conjectured initially that the early title of the novel "Boys and Girls" goes back to Andersen along with Blok, and we have seen how the peephole in the ice appears together with Blok on the way to the Christmas tree. Finally, fairy tale, childhood, Christmas and Blok are united in the poem "The Star of the Nativity", dedicated

---

legs hung down outside the open windows. Several times I was on the point of saying to the conductor, "Take me to a house where I can stay a while, for I cannot stand this." Sweat streamed out of all my pores. It was dreadful. And all the time we moved slowly forwards; at last it seemed to me that everything around me was fluid. When, at last, I reached the Bank I got out and into a cab, and now that I was alone and there was more air I recovered and reached home, but a more terrible journey than the one from Clapton I have seldom experienced". (Andersen, *The Fairy Tale of My Life*, 270-71)

31 On folkloristic motifs in the novel, see Lönnqvist, "From Dewdrops to Poetry."

by the author to Blok as "the manifestation of Christmas." (71) Some lines can be related to the world of fairy tale:

> All pranks of fairies, all tricks of sorcerers,
> All the Christmas trees on earth, all children's dreams. [...]
> *The frosty night was like a fairy tale.*
> *And from the heaped-up snowdrifts, all the while,*
> *Someone invisibly slipped into their ranks.* (485-86)

"The Star of the Nativity" incorporates not only Blok but Andersen as well. And the one who invisibly entered from the snowdrifts is probably Christ, the child of she who at the novel's outset came in with the blizzard for the boy Jura – replacing Kay's Snow Queen. There the fairy tale was present hiddenly; here it has come to the surface – together with the substitution of Christ for demonic forces, which may be seen as a major goal of the entire novel.

"On the borderline of a fairy tale"
In December 1945, the month when Pasternak began writing *Doctor Zhivago*, he wrote a letter to the famous ballerina Galina Ulanova in order to express his gratitude for having seen her perform the title role in Sergei Prokofiev's ballet "Cinderella" the night before: "I am particularly happy that I saw you in a role which, together with many other characters in world fiction, expresses the wonderful and victorious power of the child's purity, submissive to circumstances and true to itself."[32]
One of the other characters in world fiction who expresses this purity is, as we know, Andersen's Gerda, and it looks almost as if Pasternak has just read "The Snow Queen" and is alluding to the Finn woman's remark about the strength of Gerda's pure heart (cf. [40]). The whole letter indicates that on the threshold to the novel Pasternak was not only greatly inspired by the world of fairy tales as opposed to the so-called real world, but also identified himself and his position with it. In that case Gerda's victorious loving heart as opposed to the icy reason of Kay may have been the decisive force behind his work. If we compare the emphasis on strength combined with "submissiveness" in the letter with the diagnosis of Strelnikov's lack of "unprincipledness of the heart" quoted earlier (in [39]), we may have Pasternak's formula for his own existential position – and thereby for the novel as his apologia.

---

32 Pasternak, *Sobranie sochinenii*, 5, 437.

Thus, "The Snow Queen" was part of a vital substratum of *Doctor Zhivago* – that from which it grew. Nine years later, in a letter from November 1954,[33] when he was striving to finish the novel, Pasternak wrote that in it he had placed reality "almost on the borderline of a fairy tale." In the light of what we have seen above, this statement acquires an unexpected meaning – on the borderline of the literal.

Works Cited

Andersen, H. C. *The Fairy Tale of My Life*. Translated by W. Glyn Jones. Copenhagen: Nyt Nordisk Forlag 1954.

Andersen, H. C. *The Snow Queen*. Translated by Jean Hersholt. Available electronically: http://www.andersen.sdu.dk/vaerk/hersholt/TheSnowQueene.html.

Goethe, Johann Wolfgang von. *Faust. Part I*. The Harvard Classics. http://www.bartleby.com/19/1/1.html.

Jensen, Peter Alberg. "Nil's Liune i Jurii Zhivago. Forma i preemstvennost'". In *Christianity and the Eastern Slavs. III. Russian Literature in Modern Times*, edited by B. Gasparov, R. P. Hughes, I. Paperno, O. Raevsky-Hughes, Berkeley: University of California Press 1995, 244-87.

—. "Strel'nikov i Kai: "Snezhnaia koroleva" v 'Doktore Zhivago'". *Scando-Slavica* 43 (1997): 68-107.

Lönnqvist, Barbara. "From Dewdrops to Poetry: The Presence of Egorij Chrabryj in *Doctor Zhivago*". *Russian Literature* 34, no. 2 (1993): 161-85.

Masing, Irene. *A. Blok's "The Snow Mask". An Interpretation*. Stockholm: Almqvist & Wiksell, 1970.

Pasternak, Boris. *Doctor Zhivago*. Translated by Richard Pevear and Larissa Volokhonsky. New York: Pantheon, 2010.

—. *Sobranie sochinenii v piati tomakh*. Moscow: Khudozhestvennaia literatura, 1989-1992.

Smirnov, Igor P. "Antiutopiia i teoditseia v *Doktore Zhivago*." *Wiener Slawistischer Almanach* 34 (1994): 143-82.

Witt, Susanna. *Creating Creation: Readings of Pasternak's Doktor Zhivago*. Stockholm: Almqvist & Wiksell, 2000.

---

33 Letter to T. M. Nekrasova of Nov. 9, 1954. Ibid., 3, 675.

C)
*Andersen's Transformational Legacy
in the Soviet Union*

Hans Christian Andersen and Russian Classical Music:

Igor Stravinsky and Sergei Prokofiev

Vladimir Orlov

Having gained remarkable popularity in Russia in the twentieth century, the works of Hans Christian Andersen were made into numerous adaptations in different fields of Russian and Soviet culture, primarily in live-action or animated films. In Russian classical music, Andersen's fairy tales had attracted far less attention—with the major exception of two well-known composers, Igor Stravinsky and Sergei Prokofiev. Having come of age in *fin-de-siècle* St. Petersburg, these two are often regarded as primary competitors by their biographers and musicologists generally. Indeed, they shared much in common, particularly their use of musical images of magic, and their frequent recourse to the genre of fairy tale.[1] Moreover, all three of the Andersen-based compositions to be discussed here—Stravinsky's opera *The Nightingale* (*Solovei*, 1914), his ballet *The Fairy's Kiss* (*Potselui fei*, 1928), and Prokofiev's "musical fairy tale" (song) "The Ugly Duckling" ("Gadkii utenok," 1914)—demonstrate another striking parallel between them: each of these compositions, as will be discussed, bears a distinct attachment to the inner world of their respective composers. It might seem, therefore, that Russian music had absorbed Hans Christian Andersen, making the famed Danish storyteller a part of the personal inheritance of the Russian composers discussed in this essay. In this vein, Stravinsky's Andersen-based compositions served as a symbolic declaration of his reverence for other Russian classical composers, namely, Nikolai Rimsky-Korsakov and Petr Tchaikovsky. In turn, Prokofiev's composition, probably the best-known among the works discussed here, constitutes a famous manifesto of his own self in music.

Prokofiev and Stravinsky produced two of the three Andersen-based

---

1 Examples include Prokofiev's famous "symphonic fairy tale for children" *Peter and the Wolf* (1936), and several of his later operas and ballets, including the ballet *The Tale of the Stone Flower* (*Skaz o kamennom tsvetke*, 1953) and the opera *Khan Buzai* (*Khan Buzai*, unfinished); and numerous Stravinsky compositions from his Russian period, such as the ballet *The Firebird* (*Zhar-ptitsa*, 1910), *Three Tales for Children* (*Tri istorii dlia detei*, 1917), *The Soldier's Tale* (*L'Histoire du soldat*, 1918), etc.

compositions just mentioned in the same period, completing them in the same year of 1914. (Stravinsky had begun working on *The Nightingale* in 1907 but had to put it aside a year later, taking it up again only in 1913.) Subsequently, Prokofiev—despite his special interest in making music for children (epitomized by the world-famous *Peter and the Wolf* [*Petia i volk*])—would never again turn to Andersen. By contrast, Stravinsky would go on, much later, to write the above-mentioned ballet *The Fairy's Kiss*, albeit, as critics and biographers tend to remark, without any obvious motivation, except as an expression of his will to do so. Let us begin with the most popular example.

Prokofiev as the Ugly Duckling

For Prokofiev, the fact of his literal association with the main character of Andersen's tale has become a legend, reiterated in numerous musicological studies and people's memoirs. He took this title of the "ugly duckling" for himself in his early years, while still a student at the St. Petersburg Conservatory (1904-14). Especially known for his *épatage*, his aspiration to challenge the audience[2]—and Prokofiev loved to use animalistic associations for his treatment of the public, referring to his behavior as "teasing the geese"[3] (cf. poking the bear)—he was immediately recognized as the main character of his song "The Ugly Duckling," as evidenced by several documented sources. For instance, even before the song was created, Prokofiev was nicknamed "Nina's ugly duckling" by certain friends of his and his girlfriend Nina Meshcherskaia,[4] the future dedicatee of the song.[5] According to the memoir of a friend of Meshcherskaia, Prokofiev asserted: "Just you wait, the time will come, and I, too, will grow into a swan."[6] Attending a performance of the

---

2 See, for instance, the following concert review: "On the platform appeared a lad with the face of a Peterschule student. It is Sergei Prokofiev. He takes his seat at the piano and appears to be either dusting the keys or trying out the notes with a sharp, dry touch. The audience does not know what to make of it. Some indignant murmurs are audible. One couple gets up and runs toward the exit: 'Such music is enough to drive you crazy!' is the general comment. The hall empties. The young artist ends his concerto with a relentlessly discordant combination of brasses. The audience is scandalized. The majority hisses. With a mocking bow Prokofiev resumes his seat and plays an encore. The audience flees, with exclamations of: 'To the devil with all this futurist music! We came here for enjoyment. The cats on our roof make better music than this!'" Cited from Nestyev, *Sergei Prokofiev*, 30-31.
3 On Prokofiev's usage of geese metaphors, see Akopian, *Dmitrii Shostakovich*, 164.
4 Nina Meshcherskaia (Krivosheina), (1895-1981)—Russian émigré, author of the memoir *Chetyre treti nashei zhizni*.
5 See, for instance, the evidence cited in Nest'ev, *Zhizn' Sergeia Prokof'eva*, 102.
6 Cited ibid.

composition in 1917, the well-known writer Maksim Gorky likewise openly declared: "Why, he has written that story about himself."[7] Prokofiev never contested this association during his lifetime; much later, in 1940, this nickname would reemerge in his correspondence with his wife, the singer Lina Prokofieva (Codina), who performed this song on a regular basis; and she often addressed her letters to Prokofiev using the sobriquet "Duckie" (in English).[8] Prokofiev's whole life emulates certain twists and turns of the fairy tale, which, as I will argue, probably played a bad trick on the composer.

Even the song's opening words—"it was so beautiful out in the country"—would seem to echo Prokofiev's own childhood in the village of Sontsovka in Ekaterinoslav province (now the Donetsk region). Just as the duckling flees his native territory, Prokofiev left Russia in 1918, a year after the October Revolution. As detailed in his memoirs, his path abroad led through many parts of the civil war-ravaged empire.[9] Though various competing armies seized parts of the Trans-Siberian railway from time to time, he reached the Russian Far East safely; he would go on to Japan and, in that same momentous year of 1918, to the United States. His subsequent career in the West would never see hardship quite on the order of that suffered by the duckling—who, in Andersen's tale, experiences near-starvation and cold during the winter. Indeed, Prokofiev came to America full of bright expectations of his future success.[10] In general, these did not come true, as he acknowledged in his diary.[11] Moreover, the scandalized reception of him and his music continued also in his emigration, as can be seen from various reviews and critical responses. Thus, critics called Prokofiev "a white Negro" and "Russia's naughty boy,"[12] and compared his music to the sound of "a herd of mammoths," fit to be performed by "a dinosaur's daughter."[13] Such attempts by critics to associate Prokofiev with exoticism and purported "wildness" were regularly heard in many countries and contexts, and continued even after he had returned to his homeland in 1936. His final period in the USSR until his death in 1953 is sometimes interpreted by

---

7 Cited from Nestyev, *Sergei Prokofiev*, 38.
8 See, for instance, Vishnevetskii, *Sergei Prokof'ev*, 479.
9 See Prokof'ev, *Dnevnik*, 1: 681.
10 Ibid.
11 "Looking back on the results of my four-month-long American activities, with their concerts, successes, and long critical notices, I suddenly realized that the outcome was a big, fat zero" (Prokof'ev, *Dnevnik*, 2: 13).
12 From the headline of an article on Prokofiev in the *Cleveland News*, 9 January 1930; cited from Varunts, *Prokof'ev o Prokof'eve*, 84.
13 Cited from Nestyev, *Sergei Prokofiev*, 78.

scholars as the fiasco of his life and career; a "Soviet Tragedy," to cite one telling title (by Victor Seroff).[14] In recent decades, research by Prokofiev scholars, myself included,[15] has shown that Prokofiev's life and reception in the USSR was far more nuanced than previously thought: a roller-coaster in which he was now successful, now on the brink of disaster, his life in jeopardy.[16]

There is one aspect of his work, however, on which most scholars agree: much of Prokofiev's legacy remains undeservedly forgotten, unperformed and unpublished; on these grounds, Valerii Gergiev, the main conductor of St. Petersburg's Mariinsky Theater, has frequently referred to Prokofiev as "the most underappreciated composer of the twentieth century," and called for a dramatic reconsideration of him; indeed, nowadays the task of rediscovering and reexamining the composer's legacy is an explicit part of that theater's agenda.[17] Thus, as with the briefly sketched, largely unknown future of Andersen's tale (the former ugly duckling joins the swans, which should imply the absolute end of misfortunes in his life), we are entering the speculative area of what Prokofiev actually wrought with his own biography when he attached his fate to the ugly duckling.

Notably, the same kind of speculation—what would happen if the ugly duckling, now recognized as a swan, were to return to the old farmyard, willing to forget all grievances—has already been provided by the late-Soviet-era writer Vladimir Voinovich.[18] According to his story, the ducks begin to refer to *themselves* as swans, enabling them to disregard the *actual* swan once more. This storyline agrees, in no small part, with the circumstances of Prokofiev's life in the USSR. There is much evidence to suggest that, after his return, Prokofiev had to suppress his artistic nature, and conform to a Soviet aesthetics not always beneficial to him.

The music of the song—I say "song," although this composition's genre, like that of Stravinsky's *The Nightingale*, is defined by its score as a "musical fairy tale" (*muzykal'naia skazka*)[19]—illustrates all the tale's vicissitudes, the sardonic images of the duckling himself, along with the multifarious gallery of birds represented in Andersen's text, which Prokofiev adapted himself with no mention as to which of the numerous translations printed in Russia before 1914 he used. In keeping with

---

14 Seroff, *Sergei Prokofiev: A Soviet Tragedy*.
15 See, for instance, Orlov, "Soviet Cantatas and Oratorios by Sergei Prokofiev in Their Social and Cultural Context."
16 Among such studies, see, for instance, Morrison, *The People's Artist: Prokofiev's Soviet Years*.
17 On Gergiev's policy regarding Prokofiev, see Abbasova, "Gergiev i Prokof'ev."
18 The story of the ugly duckling's return is a side episode in his *The Fur Hat* (*Shapka*, 1987).
19 See the title page of Prokof'ev, *Gadkii utenok*.

his constant desire to surprise and challenge the audience, the music is extravagant, with clumsy, unnatural melodies occasionally interspersed with plain, song-like narrations bearing romanticist traits. Likewise, the piano part features strange, sometimes dissonant chords; the tonality of the composition is quite unstable, matching a storyline abundant with peregrinations. The musical texture is full of theatrical elements—such as arpeggiated chords that illustrate the funny flying of the birds, or grace notes that visualize twittering. When it comes to the depiction of the sufferings of the duckling, however, Prokofiev's music quickly modifies sarcasm into a tragic feeling.[20]

According to numerous reviews, the premiere was a success, as already explored by Prokofiev's primary biographer Izrail Nestev. One enthusiastic critic, Boris Asafyev, called the composition "a tale about Prokofiev told by himself."[21] Another noted that "[t]he duckling... is not entirely 'ugly,' an eventfulness, a fantasy are seen here."[22] Still, some found the song's ending, particularly the episode of the duckling's transformation into a swan, unconvincing. As Asafyev suggested, the problem was that Prokofiev himself had yet to become such a swan.[23]

In response to such a consideration, I would argue that this work is emblematic of how, in Prokofiev, theoretically positive endings are always, in fact, ambiguous. Such was most likely his intent. Thus, his next engagement with bizarre animalistic imagery, in perhaps his best-known work—the above-mentioned *Peter and the Wolf*—likewise features a not-fully positive conclusion. Peter's success in capturing the wolf is greatly compromised by the sufferings of the duck that remains alive in the wolf's stomach. Numerous details suggest that, without the experience of "The Ugly Duckling"—particularly, the song's grotesque depictions of the clumsy, duckish creature, at once evoking irony and sympathy—Prokofiev's oeuvre would be of a different essence entirely.

Stravinsky as the Nightingale[24]

While Prokofiev's association with Andersen's duckling is well known, the same could not be said for Stravinsky and his *Nightingale*, which premiered in May 1914, shortly after his emigration from Russia, as

---

20 A detailed analysis of the composition is provided in Nest'ev, *Zhizn' Sergeia Prokof'eva*, 122-24.
21 Cited ibid., 123.
22 Cited ibid., 124.
23 Cited ibid.
24 The author would like to thank Richard Taruskin for his help with sources on Stravinsky.

staged by Sergei Diaghilev's Ballets Russes at Paris's Palais Garnier. Having begun his career in the West, Stravinsky eventually conquered the leading role above all other composers in Europe, who regarded him as a lawmaker in music, calling him "Tsar Igor" in homage to his 1927 opera *Oedipus Rex* (*Tsar Edip*). Having tried on different stylistic masks throughout his long career, he tended to distance himself from this or that trend, eschewing the alignment of his music to a particular aesthetics or philosophy. According to his famous aphorism, "music expresses itself" only.

As with Prokofiev, albeit to a lesser extent, Andersen's composition plays a symbolic role in Stravinsky's oeuvre. The very image of the nightingale—a miraculous creature of extraordinary sublimity, a "personification of the soul"[25]—demonstrates all the basic principles of Stravinsky's vision of art: its absolute autonomy, its Orpheus-like power over supernatural entities (such as a personified Death), its aspiration toward different, nonexistent worlds (such as Andersen's imaginary China). Thus, according to the fairy tale (made into a libretto by Stepan Mitusov[26] and Stravinsky himself), the nightingale demonstrates a constant desire for absolute freedom, rejecting any compromise, such as the luxuries offered by the Chinese emperor (epitomized by "the order of the golden slipper"); and in its freedom outshines the purely mechanistic excellence of the clockwork nightingale. As Natalia Braginskaya shows, moreover, for Stravinsky the magical world of Andersen's fairy tale was deeply associated with images of Oranienbaum and St. Petersburg, where he lived when composing *The Nightingale*—the seashore, the Russian winter, deer-chariots during Maslenitsa (Shrovetide), and its palace architecture in the style of chinoiserie.[27] Stravinsky would much later sum up his reminiscences of his Russian impressions thus: "They were part of a realistic fairy-tale world whose lost beauty I have tried to rediscover later in life, especially in Hans Christian Andersen (*The Nightingale, Le Baiser de la fée*)."[28]

Appearing at the crossroads of different cultural trends and tendencies, the opera responds to the current European fashion for everything exotic and "Oriental," at the same time paying homage to the pseudo-Chinese style (the above-mentioned chinoiserie) represented in the Russian em-

---

25 Stravinsky's description, in a letter (7 June 1909) to Stepan Mitusov; cited from Braginskaia, "Fantaziia v manere chinoiserie," 141.
26 The composer, choral conductor, and music teacher Stepan Mitusov (1878-1942) was friends with numerous composers, including Rimsky-Korsakov and Stravinsky.
27 Braginskaia, "Fantaziia v manere chinoiserie."
28 Stravinsky and Craft, *Expositions and Developments*, 33.

peror's palace and gardens in Peterhof near St. Petersburg. As in many well-known compositions of the early twentieth century—for instance, Claude Debussy's *Pagodes* (from his piano cycle *Estampes*, 1903), with its East Asian themes; or Giacomo Puccini's *Turandot* (1924)—Stravinsky conveys his Western vision of China by means of bizarre musical imagery, such as the grotesque *Marche Chinoise* (act 2), which represents sophisticated harmonies and rhythmic ostinato motifs in trumpet and other instruments, resembling something like a bobble-head Mandarin doll (see the score, rehearsal mark 90).[29] Just as in the example discussed previously, the score, including the vocal part, provides random imitations of bird sounds, quite frequently in act 2, or the magnificent modulations of the nightingale's songs (see, for instance, his opening aria "From the sky a star," act 2, rehearsal mark 19; or his presentation to the emperor, act 2, rehearsal mark 86). In contrast to the imaginary Chinese context, the figure of the fisherman and that of the nightingale himself are stripped of any irony, expressing feelings of wonder and supreme enchantment—just as in the exchange between the fisherman and the nightingale in act 1, including the just-mentioned opening aria of the nightingale. A more detailed explication of the chinoiserie style created by the joint efforts of all those involved in the opera's production, including Mitusov and the famous artist Aleksandr Benois,[30] who designed the sets and costumes, is provided in the above-cited essay by Braginskaya. A detailed analysis of the numerous influences seen in Stravinsky's score has also been made by Anthony Pople.[31]

To continue the analysis of the artistic construction of an analogy between the life of the composer himself and that of his musical creature, their fates look somewhat similar: like his nightingale, Stravinsky kept up a ceaseless transcontinental tour. (Nor did the peregrinations of his emigration keep him from Russia itself, as his Soviet tour in 1962 witnesses.) So acts the nightingale, leaving the emperor, but promising to "return and sing till daybreak" (act 3, r.m. 128). Unlike the original Andersen text, the opera ends with the episode of the song of the fisherman (to whom the nightingale often comes down to sing at night), which suddenly draws *The Nightingale* closer to the analogously water-based ending of *The Ugly Duckling*, Prokofiev's alleged response to Stravinsky.

Unlike Prokofiev's *The Ugly Duckling*—which was regarded as a fully modernist composition—Stravinsky's *The Nightingale* demonstrates a

---

29 Stravinsky, *Le Rossignol* (*The Nightingale*).
30 Aleksandr Benois (1870-1960) was a Russian artist, art critic, historian, and a founder of the art movement and magazine *World of Art* (*Mir iskusstva*).
31 Pople, "*Early Stravinsky*," 58-78.

large number of references to the Russian musical heritage; for instance, to the works of Nikolai Rimsky-Korsakov, Aleksandr Borodin, and other composers. There are numerous harmonic and melodic allusions to predecessors, such as the analogous image of the golden cockerel from the eponymous opera by Rimsky-Korsakov (1907), and the "wonders of the sea" widely represented in his opera *Sadko* (*Sakdo*, 1896); such compositions of Scriabin as *Le Divin Poème* (*Bozhestvennaia poema*, 1904) and *The Poem of Ecstasy* (*Poema ekstaza*, 1908); and to Mikhail Glinka's imagery of the practitioner of black magic Chernomor in his opera *Ruslan and Liudmila* (*Ruslan i Liudmila*, 1842). The predominant significance of Rimsky-Korsakov was fully acknowledged by Stravinsky himself, as attested in his memoir.[32]

Thus, the respective preoccupations with the past (Stravinsky) and the future, including the future of his own artistic work (Prokofiev), may be seen as the most glaring difference between the two composers' Andersen adaptations. Additionally, unlike Stravinsky, who is focused on portraying magical and ethereal creatures, Prokofiev engages in caricature, not sparing even the main character (a stand-in for himself) from his irony.[33] Notwithstanding all these differences, both compositions in no small part address the identity of their composers and the role they played, as they saw it, in the history of music.

To be sure, there is no direct evidence that Prokofiev actually had Stravinsky's *The Nightingale* in mind when he composed *The Ugly Duckling*, or that in this case he was filtering his creativity through his critical orientation toward his elder rival. At the same time, it is quite well known that over the whole course of his life, Prokofiev took an extraordinary interest in Stravinsky; his references to Stravinsky's works and the manifold traces of Stravinsky's influence on him can be found in a considerable number of Prokofiev compositions made in different years. Thus, if not in *The Ugly Duckling*, then later in his opera *The Love for Three Oranges* (*Liubov' k trem apel'sinam*, 1919), there will be other allusions to *The Nightingale*. Importantly, these allusions actually *are* caricaturish, as if viewed in a distorted mirror. The most palpable example, in my view, is the transposition of the female personage known as "the cook" from *The Nightingale* to the libretto of *The Love for Three Oranges*, which Prokofiev composed on the basis

---

[32] According to Stravinsky, *The Nightingale* "was greatly encouraged by my master, and to this day I remember with pleasure his approval of the preliminary sketches.... [I]t grieves me much that he was never to hear them in their finished form, for I think that he would have liked them" (*An Autobiography*, 23).

[33] See the scores: Stravinsky, *Le Rossignol* (*The Nightingale*); Prokof'ev, *Gadkii utenok*.

of the Russian translation of Carlo Gozzi's original comedy (1761) by Vsevolod Meyerhold, Vladimir Nikolaevich Solovyov, and Konstantin Vogak (1915). The character of the cook—which is not found anywhere in Gozzi's original—is obviously added to the plot by Prokofiev himself; and the sharp contrast between Stravinsky's and Prokofiev's characters is seen in every possible detail. In *The Nightingale*, the cook is a central character, and an absolutely positive one: kind and warm-hearted, given to a soprano in Stravinsky's score. The cook in Prokofiev's opera, on the other hand, is drawn in exaggeratedly sardonic colors as a repulsive monster, a homicidal and dimwitted giant that lives in the castle of a wicked sorcerer. Her voice, fully in contrast to Stravinsky's character, is very low and strong, and is given to a male singer, a basso. Having threatened to kill the main characters, however, this cook subsequently does evince some trace of her gentle prototype, falling under the charm of the magic ribbon, which thwarts her dreadful intentions and allows the heroes to escape. There are other, less transparent examples of Prokofiev's paraphrase from Stravinsky's works, including from that same *The Nightingale*.

Despite the dramatic differences in the conception and aesthetics of *The Nightingale* and *The Ugly Duckling*, these compositions are afforded a surprisingly similar place on the Russian opera stage. Thus, in 2016, both were included in a program of music for children at the Mariinsky Theater, and even performed in the daytime as children's matinees. Unafraid to present little listeners with Stravinsky's peculiar writing, which features alternating styles and a primarily avant-garde, at times atonal musical syntax, the musicians coped with the performance quite well, I would contend. All managed to combine but also distinguish the different styles—those of Tchaikovsky, Scriabin, and others—always inherent to Stravinsky's scores. Still, it is the costumes and decorations that have been the principal highlight of the modern Mariinsky Theater, with the spectacle in this case prompting children to stand on their seats during the performance.

Stravinsky and Tchaikovsky Meet Hans Christian Andersen

Stravinsky would return to Andersen's work some fourteen years later—and once again, as when composing *The Nightingale*, impelled by his specific desire to return to the historical past. Only this time, *the past* specifically meant the figure of Petr Tchaikovsky, the thirty-fifth anniversary of whose death was to be commemorated in 1928. The commission for a ballet on a subject of Stravinsky's choice was made by Ida

Rubinstein in 1927—still a legendary dancer, who had decided to start her own ballet company. Stravinsky had readily accepted the proposal: just like Rubinstein, he was longing to leave an enterprise of the famous entrepreneur Sergei Diaghilev, with whom Stravinsky's relationship had grown more and more contentious.[34]

Indeed, there could hardly be a more fitting illustration of Stravinsky's attempt to break with the modernism with which he was so famously associated than this radical U-turn back to the forgotten, ultra-sensitive, and romantic music of Tchaikovsky. The venture was hardly a success: in addition to Diaghilev's irritated comments on the ballet's premiere— "It was like a drawing room in which someone has suddenly made a bad smell," with everyone "pretend[ing] [not] to notice"[35]—Stravinsky's new ballet received mixed reviews; for that matter, the critical esteem in which it is held even today is remarkably low. A significant number of critics and Stravinsky biographers speak of the ballet's various drawbacks, for instance what one calls the "creative humility" of its music,[36] which another in turn finds "tenuous, weak, and vapid."[37] The scholar David Bruce cites many of these evaluations in his essay on *The Fairy's Kiss* and even notes that some Stravinsky scholars choose to pass over the work in silence.[38] Thus, this ballet could even today be regarded as perhaps the most extraordinary breakdown on the path of one of the most celebrated composers of the twentieth century. Neither of the hallmark works created before and after it—namely, the ballet *Apollo* (*Apollon musagète*, 1928) and the *Symphony of Psalms* (*Simfoniia psalmov*, 1930)—have repeated its fate.

Looking for a source for his homage to Tchaikovsky, Stravinsky had turned to Andersen's fairy tale "The Ice Maiden" (1861). Having based numerous of his compositions on fairy tales, Tchaikovsky had never used Andersen as a source, although they were quite close in aesthetics and the subjects taken for their works. Thus, as the scholar Eric Walter White points out, Stravinsky, upon examining Tchaikovsky's scores, "was able to continue quite fluently in the same vein where Tchaikovsky had left off."[39] As indicated in Stravinsky's correspondence with the artist Aleksandr Benois, who was again invited to design the decorations for

---

34 See, for instance, Degen and Stupnikov, "Stravinskii: Balet 'Potselui fei.'"
35 Cited from Acocella, "Stravinsky's *The Fairy's Kiss*."
36 Griffiths, *The Master Musicians: Stravinsky*, 98.
37 Cited from Bruce, "Source and Sorcery," 11.
38 Ibid.
39 Cited ibid., 12.

the ballet, as well as in Stravinsky's memoir, the choice of Andersen's tale was made entirely by the composer.[40]

As Stravinsky later wrote, his search for the ballet's subject and scenario led him to consider such works of nineteenth-century literature as would match the "characteristic trend of Tchaikovsky's music."

> With that aim, I turned to a great poet with a gentle, sensitive soul whose imaginative mind was wonderfully akin to that of the musician. I refer to Hans Christian Andersen, with whom in this respect Tchaikovsky had so much in common. To recall *La Belle au Bois Dormant*, *Casse Noisette*, *Le Lac des Cygnes*, *Pique Dame*, and many pieces of his symphonic work is enough to show the extent of his fondness for the fantastic.[41]

As Stravinsky further describes, "[i]n turning over the pages of Andersen with which I was familiar, I came across a story I had completely forgotten, which struck me as being the very thing for the idea that I wanted to express." In his view, the fairy tale in question best suited his purpose.

> It was [a] very beautiful story.... I chose that as my theme, and worked out the story on the following lines. A fairy imprints her magic kiss on a child at birth and parts it from its mother. Twenty years later, when the youth has attained the very zenith of his good fortune, she repeats the fatal kiss and carries him off to live in supreme happiness with her ever afterwards. As my object was to commemorate the work of Tchaikovsky, this subject seemed to me to be particularly appropriate as an allegory, the muse having similarly branded Tchaikovsky with her fatal kiss, and the magic imprint has made itself felt in all the musical creations of this great artist.[42]

The resulting work—the allegorical ballet *The Fairy's Kiss*—matches this overview entirely; it constitutes a four-part structure that encompasses the short history of a young man who has been given a magic kiss in his childhood. Like the tale on which it is based, the ballet includes an episode in which the infant first encounters the fairy and receives the "fatal kiss"; an episode featuring a folk festival ("Danses suisses," as Stravinsky titled it when he turned the ballet into a divertimento in 1934); an episode set at a mill, when the fairy appears before the main character, disguised as his bride in order to kiss him a second time; and a

---

40 See, for instance, Degen and Stupnikov, "Stravinskii: Balet 'Potselui fei.'"
41 Stravinsky, *An Autobiography*, 146.
42 Ibid., 146-47.

finale in which the fairy leads the young man off into a magical "land of eternity,"[43] ending up in a perfect Tchaikovskian *pas de deux*. The reception of this ballet, as already noted, would be analogous to this description—beautiful and tragic—in part, because of the flawed performance of Rubinstein's company and choreographers; but also because, as noted above, Stravinsky's affection for Tchaikovsky—joltingly unexpected to so many critics—could not have earned him anything but bewilderment and even scorn. As Bruce observes, Stravinsky in this composition was most likely just too out of step with the zeitgeist.[44]

As numerous scholars and critics have noted, Stravinsky's objective was to mix stylistic pastiches from Tchaikovsky and himself, such that listeners would lose track of which fragment belonged to whom. But unlike with other works in which Stravinsky turned to such various material as baroque music or jazz, on this occasion, pastiche was not a winning strategy.[45] In full accord with his aim, the ballet constitutes an actual showcase of Tchaikovsky's imagery, featuring a great number of quotations and rearrangements of his vocal, symphonic, or piano compositions. In contrast to his use of chinoiserie in *The Nightingale* as discussed above, Stravinsky in *The Fairy's Kiss* entirely ignores such significant aspects of romanticist composition as "national flavor" or folk melodies. The references to geographic location, so important to Andersen, as seen in the fairy tale's opening ("Let us visit Switzerland"), are in this composition almost completely abandoned in favor of Tchaikovsky's lyrical universe. The ballet's opening and closing quotation from Tchaikovsky's well-known "Lullaby in a Storm" ("Kolybel'naia pesn' v buriu"), with lyrics by Aleksei Pleshcheev[46] (1883), creates the structural framework of the composition.

Thus, to return to the question posed at the outset of this essay: it seems impossible to deny the existence of an "Andersen tradition" in Russian music. Observing again all three compositions discussed here, I would propose that both Russian composers, Stravinsky and Prokofiev, have appropriated, indeed privatized Andersen, turning him into a vehicle to express the most intimate sides of their own artistic personality, even when it did them more harm than good. To sum up: Prokofiev turned himself into one of Andersen's characters; Stravinsky,

---

43 Stravinsky, *The Fairy's Kiss*, 116.
44 Bruce, "Source and Sorcery," 11.
45 For a more detailed analysis of the score, see Hyde, "Stravinsky's Neoclassicism."
46 Aleksei Pleshcheev (1825-93) was a Russian poet, and the author of numerous translations primarily from English and French; his poetry was set to music by Petr Tchaikovsky and Sergei Rakhmaninov.

likewise, expressed his creative vision, his alter-ego, through an allegorical character, whose fate in turn invites associations with Stravinsky's life; and the last composition discussed constitutes an homage to one of Stravinsky's favorite composers. Thus, even as musical adaptations of Andersen are technically quite few in number, we would be hard-pressed to find another foreign writer whose works would become so personal for Russian music. The "Andersenizing" of Russian culture we are entitled to speak of, given the vast amount of cinematic and other cultural adaptations of the Danish storyteller, encompasses works by Stravinsky and Prokofiev as well.

Works Cited

Abbasova, Leila. "Gergiev i Prokof'ev: strategii prodvizheniia kompozitora v Mariinskom teatre v postsovetskuiu epokhu." MPhil diss., St. Petersburg State University, 2016.

Acocella, Joan. "Stravinsky's *The Fairy's Kiss*." *The New Yorker*, 30 January 2017. Available electronically: www.newyorker.com/magazine/2017/01/30/stravinskys-the-fairys-kiss

Akopian, Levon. *Dmitrii Shostakovich: opyt fenomenologii tvorchestva*. St. Petersburg: Gos. institut iskusstvoznaniia Ministerstva kul'tury Rossiiskoi Federatsii, 2004.

Braginskaia, Natal'ia. "Fantaziia v manere chinoiserie." *Muzykal'naia akademiia*, no. 4 (2002): 137-142.

Bruce, David. "Source and Sorcery: 'Tenuous, Weak and Vapid' or 'A Little Piece of Magic'? David Bruce Looks Sympathetically at *The Fairy's Kiss*." *The Musical Times* 147, no. 1842 (1996): 11-15.

Degen, Arsen, and Igor' Stupnikov. "Stravinskii: Balet 'Potselui fei.'" Available electronically: http://www.belcanto.ru/ballet_fee.html

Griffiths, Paul. *The Master Musicians: Stravinsky*. London: J. M. Dent & Sons Ltd., 1992.

Hyde, Martha. "Stravinsky's Neoclassicism." In *The Cambridge Companion to Stravinsky*, edited by Jonathan Cross, 98-136. Cambridge: Cambridge University Press, 2003.

Krivosheina, Nina. *Chetyre treti nashei zhizni*. Paris: YMCA-Press, 1984.

Morrison, Simon. *The People's Artist: Prokofiev's Soviet Years*. Oxford and New York: Oxford University Press, 2009.

—. ed. *Prokofiev and His World*. Princeton and Oxford: Princeton University Press, 2008.

Nestyev, Israel. *Sergei Prokofiev: His Musical Life*. Translated by Rose Prokofieva. New York: Alfred A. Knopf, 1946.

Nest'ev, Izrail'. *Zhizn' Sergeia Prokof'eva*. Moscow: Vsesoiuznoe Izdatel'stvo Sovetskii kompozitor, 1973.

Orlov, Vladimir. "Soviet Cantatas and Oratorios by Sergei Prokofiev in Their Social and Cultural Context." PhD diss., University of Cambridge, 2011.

Pople, Anthony. "*Early Stravinsky.*" In *The Cambridge Companion to Stravinsky*, edited by Jonathan Cross, 58-78. Cambridge: Cambridge University Press, 2003.

Prokof'ev, Sergei. *Dnevnik*. Paris: SPRKFV, 2002.

—. *Gadkii utenok*. St. Petersburg: Kompozitor, 2007.

Seroff, Victor. *Sergei Prokofiev: A Soviet Tragedy*. London: Leslie Frewin, 1969.

Stravinsky, Igor. *An Autobiography*. London, New York: Simon & Schuster, 1936.

—. *The Fairy's Kiss*. In *Ballet Music* by Igor Stravinsky, 116-262. London: Boosey & Hawkes, 1999.

—. *Le Rossignol* (*The Nightingale*). London: Boosey & Hawkes, 1962.

Stravinsky, Igor, and Robert Craft. *Expositions and Developments*. Berkeley and Los Angeles: University of California Press, 1981.

Varunts, Viktor, ed. *Prokof'ev o Prokof'eve: Stat'i, interv'iu*. Moscow: Sovetskii kompozitor, 1991.

Vishnevetskii, Igor'. *Sergei Prokof'ev*. Moscow: Molodaia gvardiia, 2009.

The Double and Its Theater:

Evgenii Schwartz's Andersen Plays

Boris Wolfson

The first time we see Kay and Gerda, the protagonists of *The Snow Queen* (*Snezhnaia koroleva*), they are huddled together in the little garret they share with their kindly guardian, the elderly grandmother, listening to the sound made by the old wooden stairs that lead up to their front door. The children are giddy with anticipation. The wooden stairs, says Gerda, are singing like violins, and so the person approaching must be someone worthy of such singing—most likely, Grandmother. Kay agrees: when a grouchy neighbor once came to complain about him, he recalls, the stairs howled like hungry dogs. But this sound is different, and so something wonderful must be about to happen. So powerful is the sense that some great joy is about to arrive in their room that the children don't make much of the knock at the door that follows. Grandmother wouldn't knock: she knows that their door is never locked; so why knock now? The kids, eager to see their expectations come true, decide that this must be a silly game; they will simply have to respond in kind by hiding from Grandmother and then surprising her when she walks in. But when the door opens, it is not Grandmother who enters but a man in a black overcoat and top hat. In a minute, he will introduce himself as a Councilor of Commerce. And in another minute, we—the audience—will realize that his knock on the door has announced the arrival of a genuine calamity: the Councilor, who serves the Snow Queen, will ensure that Gerda is separated from Kay for a very long time.[1]

There is, of course, no councilor of commerce in Hans Christian Andersen's 1844 tale. There are no creaking stairs singing like violins. And there is no such scene. All are inventions of Evgenii Schwartz (Evgenii Lvovich Shvarts, 1896-1958), the prominent Soviet playwright, screenwriter, and author of fairy tales in prose, whose appropriations and transformations of Andersen's texts in three plays—*The Naked King* (*Golyi korol'*, 1934-37; i.e., "The Emperor's New Clothes"), *The Snow Queen* (1938) and *The Shadow* (*Ten'*, 1940)—left a deep mark on

---

1 Shvarts, *Bessmyslennaia radost'*, 238-39.

twentieth-century Russian culture. From the point of view of a reader whose primary interest lies in the cultural afterlife of Andersen's tales, the most immediately striking feature of Schwartz's plays is the extent to which he departs from the originals. Some characters and plot lines are added, others omitted; details from different tales are combined; and the dénouements differ from Andersen's in substantive ways. What, then, *is* the relationship of Schwartz's works to Andersen's?

Students of Soviet drama have diligently catalogued Schwartz's many departures from Andersen.[2] Scholarly attempts to uncover the logic behind Schwartz's alterations of Andersen's originals have generally led to two kinds of arguments. The first approach is to read Schwartz's inventions as testimonies to the plays' palpable political charge, which is always historically specific: recognizably "Soviet" in some way, and, more often than not, subversive. This means that the connections between the plays and the works they ostensibly adapt are tenuous, even arbitrary, and so of little relevance for scholars of Andersen. Schwartz, in this reading, could have chosen any number of alternative "sources" through which to ventriloquize his political commentary. In the other approach, changes introduced by Schwartz constitute material for exploring the playwright's idiosyncratic conception of the art of literary invention, as well as for unfolding his personal existential position. These may occasionally echo Andersen's, but are more likely to be at tension with them. Again, the textual differences are used as evidence of Schwartz's originality. In both cases, their connection to Andersen is seen, at best, as an homage to the Danish master's narrative gifts, at worst as a convenient, cynical "cover" from accusations of ideological irresponsibility, a way for Schwartz to deflect criticism with the shield of borrowed Andersenian cultural authority.

In both of these interpretive approaches, Schwartz's plays are *read* in the most literal sense of the word: they are treated as texts, written to be printed and consumed as books. But what about the most radical change of all—the transformation from Andersen's prose to Schwartz's dramas? For those who encountered Schwartz's plays in performance, the written or published texts were scripts for spectacles that involved many "extrascriptural" components, created many additional and different kinds of meanings, and possessed a specific experiential aesthetic force. What is the relationship between that performative force, Schwartz's scripts, and the imaginary world of Andersen's works? And how can this relationship

---

2   See, for example, Corten, "Shvarts as Adapter"; and Metcalf frequently touches on this subject in *Shvarts and His Fairy-Tales*.

help us move the conversation about Schwartz and Andersen beyond invoking the familiar interpretive paradigms of political subversion, on the one hand, and, on the other, relying on the romantic notion of the author as the all-powerful creative genius? This essay turns to Schwartz's Andersen plays in order to bring out their largely unexamined theatrical rhetoric.[3] As the plays explore, to varying degrees, the fundamental predicaments of enactment and spectatorship, they posit a particular understanding of what theater can, and should, do for, and with, its audiences. Interpreting these texts as play scripts helps us rethink how the political, the aesthetic, and the existential come together on Schwartz's pages and stages—and what that intersection might illuminate for us in the larger story of Andersen's Russian afterlife.

The Snow Queen: Misrecognition, Experience, Anxiety

Schwartz turned to Andersen on three occasions over a six-year stretch, between 1934 and 1940: the highly successful *Snow Queen*, with which we began, was preceded by *The Naked King*, never staged or published in Schwartz's lifetime; and followed by *The Shadow*, produced soon after it was completed, but cancelled after a few dozen performances by the original cast.[4] The Schwartz-Andersen story, then, is relatively brief—but also intense and fruitful: despite the significant differences in the plays' theatrical trajectories (and those of the film versions that followed in the sixties and seventies[5]), all three continue to occupy a place of honor in the canon of twentieth-century Russian literature; they are reprinted and performed regularly. The generations that came of age in the late Soviet period in particular mined these plays, along with Schwartz's other works, for witticisms and adages that were integrated into the complex cultural code of allusions that served as the intelligentsia's

---

3   I focus here on two of the plays, *The Snow Queen* and *The Shadow*, in part because they were produced in Schwartz's lifetime, and in part because they represent distinct approaches to theatricalizing Andersen's tales: *The Snow Queen* was staged explicitly and exclusively as a work for children, by professional children's theaters; *The Shadow* was presented as a work for adults staged by adults.
4   Between 1940 and his death in 1958, Schwartz wrote several more important fairy tales for stage and screen, but these were either based on original stories, such as *The Dragon* (*Drakon*, 1943) and *An Ordinary Miracle* (*Obyknovennoe chudo*, 1954), or adapted the works of authors other than Andersen (such as the screenplay for the hit 1947 film version of *Cinderella* [*Zolushka*]).
5   Feature films based on *The Snow Queen* (1966, dir. Gennadii Kazansky) and *The Shadow* (1971, dir. Nadezhda Kosheverova) are discussed in Andrei Rogatchevski's contribution to this volume. *The Naked King* served as one of the sources for the 1945 screenplay of *Cain the Eighteenth* (*Kain XVIII*, 1963, dir. Nadezhda Kosheverova and Mikhail Shapiro), revised after Schwartz's death by Nikolai Erdman.

lingua franca.[6] Even for those who knew Andersen's originals well and were keenly aware of the differences between the Danish tales and the Soviet plays, Schwartz's dramatic versions possessed a cultural authority that rivaled, if not supplanted, the popularity of the Andersen texts. This was especially palpable in the case of *The Snow Queen*, which entered the homes of thousands of Soviet children on vinyl records after 1949, when a radio play based on the legendary original production at Moscow's Central Children's Theater, and featuring most of the original cast, was issued as a two-LP set.[7] This audio adaptation, widely available today in digital form, ensured that generations of children, in the Soviet era and beyond, committed to memory entire scenes from the play.

For these multiple and numerous audiences of Schwartz's play, the sinister, newly invented councilor of commerce remained a more prominent antagonist than the Snow Queen herself: her stage time is a fraction of her consigliere's. Andersen's text is a romantic quest in the form of a picaresque; Schwartz's play turns that sequence of loosely connected episodes into a tightly structured role-playing game, the object of which is to advance to the next level by overcoming the obstacles created by the councilor. Unlike the Snow Queen with her supernatural abilities and charisma, the councilor is human and openly dangerous. The queen's evil is abstract, Manichean; the councilor is evil personified, vulgar and blunt: he bears grudges, he knows all the right people, and he has a lot of money. In reframing the dynamics of Gerda's quest, Schwartz altered the emotional stakes of Andersen's tale. But Gerda's attempts to win the councilor's game—to perform better than he expects—point to a broader concern. From its opening moment, Schwartz's play asked what it might mean that characters who are so unambiguously aligned with the Greater Good are so bad at being spectators: at interpreting key warning signs.

On the other side of *The Snow Queen*'s four acts, just moments before the play ends, Schwartz asks his spectators to listen once more to the sound of the stairs. This time it is the play's narrator who draws our attention to the squeaking steps. This is the Storyteller, or rather, "the teller of fairy-tales": Schwartz's Russian word is *skazochnik*—the same term that Konstantin Paustovsky used as a title of one of his bio-fictions about Andersen, discussed by Marina Balina elsewhere in this volume. An "eternal student" of sorts, Schwartz's storyteller is Kay and Gerda's tutor and guardian angel—and so, of necessity, the councilor's foil whenever

---

6   Lev Loseff attests to the role of Schwartz's plays in the imagination and language of the intelligentsia in his analysis of the "Aesopian language" of *The Dragon* (*Beneficence of Censorship*, 127-42).
7   Pyzhova and Bibikov, *Snezhnaia koroleva*.

the man in black attempts to thwart Gerda's quest. In the play's final scene, as Kay and Gerda's chances of surviving their confrontation with the Snow Queen appear to dwindle, the storyteller decides to entertain the motley crew of characters who have assembled in Grandmother's tiny room with a story about the secret life of the very stairs that featured so prominently in the play's opening scene. It is clear to everyone that he is making it all up as he goes—that is, improvising: very much in the manner of Andersen, whose professional interest in fairy tales he, after all, shares, and whose portrayal of the *improvisatore* as the protagonist of his eponymous 1835 novel is patently autobiographical. The storyteller's improvisation segues into an exhortation. "Listen!" he urges his audience, repeating almost verbatim the images of the opening scene: "The stairs are singing like violins. They are overjoyed. Because when good people walk upon them, they sing, and when bad people do, they howl like dogs. It must be *them! They* are here!"[8] The implication is that Kay and Gerda are about to enter, back from their travels. Once again anticipation builds. Once again, the door swings open. And once again behind it stands the evil councilor, this time accompanied by his queen.

It is tempting to link the outsized role assigned to the detail of the creaking stairs and the characters' fascination with what they foretell to the social context in which the play appeared. In the first two prewar theater seasons during which *The Snow Queen* was originally performed (1938-39), it became the single most frequently staged work of Soviet children's theater. Hundreds of theater companies, both repertory and touring, chose to produce it.[9] Tens of thousands of Soviet spectators, children and adults, appeared in its audience. And many in that audience were intimately familiar with the practice of staying up night after night listening to the sound of footsteps on the stairs of their apartment buildings and trying to guess who was coming, and for whom. The late 1930s saw the height of a wide-ranging, fabricated government campaign to identify and exterminate the hidden enemies of the state—saboteurs, spies, hired assassins—as the Soviet Union mobilized to defend against allegedly imminent attack by a united front of capitalist powers. Hundreds of thousands of arrests were made during this period; many, in a famously sadistic twist, were carried out in the middle of the night. The years of *The Snow Queen*'s theatrical triumph, then, were the very years when many of Schwartz's spectators spent night after night, month after month, dreading the possibility that the footsteps on the

---

8 Shvarts, *Bessmyslennaia radost'*, 295-96.
9 Shpet, *Sovetskii teatr dlia detei*, 276-78.

stairs outside their apartment would result in a knock on their door, and it would be their turn to say goodbye to loved ones for a very long time, perhaps forever.

By comparison with *The Naked King* and *The Shadow*, which teem with vibrant, biting caricatures of incompetent rulers and corrupt government officials, *The Snow Queen*'s political rhetoric is relatively subdued. Schwartz's experience with *The Naked King*[10] showed that satirical statements directed against petty tyrants and obsequious bureaucrats could backfire despite being in line with the rhetoric of the day: instead of sowing contempt for monarchy, they could be seen as ridiculing Soviet domestic politics. *The Snow Queen* does pay homage to several topoi of socialist-realist poetics: as Anja Tippner has shown, the play duly decries capitalist greed, as represented by the councilor's insatiable desire for material possessions; and the protagonists—Kay, Gerda, the storyteller, and Grandmother—are bound by a kind of lower-class consciousness.[11] Absent in Andersen's text, this class-based component of Schwartz's theatrical "game" established *The Snow Queen*'s ideological bona fides for the purposes of meeting the requirements of the censorship board (which examined play scripts with special zeal). And yet its role in the play's theatrical dynamic was minimal. According to the rules of Schwartz's game, Gerda's class identity has nothing to do—unlike her embodiment of traditional goodness—with defeating the evil councilor.

By contrast, the performative charge carried by the set piece of the creaking steps, with its uncanny doubling, is more potent and broader. Completely superfluous from the point of view of plot development, it is downright disruptive with respect to the play's symbolic and ideological structure. Kay and Gerda do return to their little dwelling in the play's final moments, and the Snow Queen is rebuked far more explicitly than in the Andersen tale.[12] But Schwartz's most likeable protagonists—the enthusiastic storyteller and his kindhearted charges—prove to be utterly incompetent interpreters of the reality in which they live. Schwartz turns the storyteller into Gerda's primary weapon in overcoming the councilor's embodied evil: in every scene of the play, it is only when the storyteller, the putative narrator, enters the fictional world of his own creation that Gerda is able to advance to the next "level" of the game. At one point, in order to rescue Gerda from danger, the storyteller puts on a disguise, which serves to demonstrate both his skill as a performer

---

10 Shvarts, *Predchuvstvie shchast'ia*, 425-502.
11 Tippner, "Shvarts's Dramas," 314-17.
12 "What can our enemies do to us as long as our hearts are aglow? Nothing at all!" (Shvarts, *Bessmyslennaia radost'*, 298).

and his inability to stay within the rules of his own latest fiction; at a crucial moment he absent-mindedly forgets to adjust the disguise, and his ruse is discovered. It is the storyteller, of course, who has invented the councilor and the obstacles; the game is rigged: he should win every time. How is it, then, that in the end he is still unable to distinguish Good from Evil? Gerda has succeeded in melting Kay's frozen heart, but the storyteller—the wise and creative *improvisatore* of fairy tales—fails to make sense of the same performance that tripped Gerda and Kay in the opening scene: he misinterprets the role of the creaking stairs. A creator of symbolic meaning himself, he has apparently not learned to interpret the signs that populate the world around him. Schwartz enables an ironic "justification" for this failure of judgment: he has the storyteller cross the meta-theatrical border between the narrative and the frame (often by breaking the fourth wall) so frequently that distinguishing reality from fiction may no longer be possible. In this reading, just as the storyteller survives his failed attempt to disguise himself, it may be of little consequence to the dramatic logic of the play if the visitors coming up the creaking steps turn out to be evil. The fairy tale has so fully replaced reality, for Schwartz's characters, that the reality has no power over them.[13]

This interpretation has the virtue of helping to justify some of Schwartz's other changes to Andersen's lavish parable about the power of faith and its crucial role in resolving the eternal struggle between the divine and the demonic. There is no evil troll in Schwartz's play, no magic mirror, no singing of hymns, no invocations of Christmas or Easter.[14] The conceit of a fairy tale that subsumes reality along with its vulgar, embodied evil obviates magical thinking as a narrative device. But in Schwartz's play, the fairy tale that grows larger than the world it describes is also not simply a fable about poor, idealistic, and brave youngsters who defeat repulsive capitalists with the help of a resourceful and wise mentor, as was the case with so many Soviet plays for children in the thirties. The bookended scenes of misinterpreting the sound of the creaking stairs point to a different, specifically performative, motivation of Schwartz's approach to Andersen. First Kay and Gerda, then the storyteller enact for us the predicament of an audience that struggles to make sense of a performance: the buildup of a spectator's trust—and its violation; the creation of an affective compact—and its deflation. The

---

13 This point was developed as part of an exchange with Marina Balina, whose generous involvement in my thinking about Schwartz, and invaluable advice on several key points in my argument, I acknowledge with gratitude and admiration.
14 Tippner, "Shvarts's Dramas," 314-15.

scene's justification, and its power, lie in the way the phenomenology of a theatrical experience subsumes ideological content. To foreground the ambivalent experience of an audience member (as proxied by Kay, Gerda, and the storyteller) in this way is to expose the audience of Schwartz's play to the performative power of moments in which doubt and discomfort dominate over conventional meaning.[15] The invocation of other, extra-theatrical sources of anxiety may or may not be subversive in intent or execution; an allusion to mass arrests, of intense and immediate concern to many adults in the audience in 1938, may or may not undermine the happy ending of the play. Enacting this moment from the lexicon of Soviet terror goes beyond subverting official rhetoric or emboldening those awaiting arrest. Even as it observes some formulaic conventions of conventional ideology (e.g., with respect to the rhetoric of class), Schwartz's play makes possible for its audience an experience that is political in a much broader sense. As the fairy tale subsumes reality in *The Snow Queen*, it invests the process of experiencing the predicament of an audience with the power to shape affect and meaning in the world beyond the stage.

The Shadow: Authors and Actors

The unsettling effect of such powerfully ambivalent moments as the scenes that open and close *The Snow Queen* is all the more striking because Schwartz's reputation in twentieth-century Russian literature rests so firmly on his skill as a writer of comedies: his wit is famous for its casually irreverent brilliance. This tension is of a piece with some of the other contradictions characteristic of Schwartz's style: his fondness for eclectic literary and cultural allusions and keen sensitivity to the political messiness and absurdity of the world in which he wrote, noted in earlier studies of Schwartz's encounters with Andersen.[16] Yet the affective frictions that come into view when Schwartz foregrounds the performative force of his Andersen plays reach beyond stylistic experimentation: they are part of the theatrical rhetoric that links the two writers.

Andersen's interest in the theater from his early days is a prominent feature of his autobiographical accounts and the subsequent biographic

---

15 My argument follows the reading of affect and presence in the theater developed by Nicholas Ridout in *Stage Fright, Animals, and Other Theatrical Problems*.
16 White, "Shvarts's *The Shadow*"; Tippner, "Shvarts's Dramas"; Corten, "Shvarts as Adapter"; Pyman, "Centenary Thoughts."

renditions.[17] Like Andersen, Schwartz began his career in the theater, as an actor; like Andersen, he moved to the big city (Petrograd, in 1921) from the provinces; like Andersen, Schwartz soon stepped back from acting in conventional plays, but quickly established a reputation—in his case, among the Petrograd literary intelligentsia—as a brilliant improviser.[18] Andersen's theatrical affections and his own talent as a virtuoso performer of the texts he made up find a powerful echo in Schwartz's work. Schwartz makes the link between the profession of storyteller and the role of an actor explicit in *The Snow Queen*: in a brief prologue, the storyteller promises to tell his audience a tale whose ending he does not yet know himself. Throughout the play, he speculates about the outcome of certain events, but, as we saw, his predictions are not always right. For Schwartz (not unlike Konstantin Paustovsky), Andersen the author is a skilled, inspired performer for whom to improvise is to "do things with words," in J. L. Austin's famous formulation. Performance, figured and thematized as literary invention, is invested with the responsibility for sustaining the narrative and dramatic coherence of the play.

The implications of this performance-oriented vector in Schwartz's rethinking of Andersen are especially vivid in the last of his Andersen plays: *The Shadow*. It has been read as a synthesis of Schwartz's experiments in the two plays that preceded it, precisely because it revels in a tragicomic, grotesque mode of laughter driven by angst, and because its text so explicitly engages both the ideological and the metaphysical.[19] Like *The Naked King*, *The Shadow* does not shy away from explicitly political themes: its protagonist—called, as in Andersen's original, the Scholar—finds himself in a kingdom that is searching for a new king, with court intrigue afoot. Like *The Snow Queen*, *The Shadow* devotes significant stage time to existential concerns: in the play's opening scene, the scholar describes a utopian vision of love and happiness that echoes the more earnestly emotional dialogues about the nature of human attachment between *The Snow Queen*'s Gerda and the little robber girl.[20] *The Shadow*, as the critical consensus seems to hold, was Schwartz's most ambitious effort yet in integrating these elements. As refracted in *The Shadow*, the theatrical rhetoric of Schwartz's plays helps us see the disorienting misrecognition characteristic of his Andersen reimaginings as a key element of Soviet theater's performative power.

---

17 Wullschlager, *The Life of a Story Teller*, 27-41; Binding, *European Witness*, 21-34; Andersen, *A New Life*, 19-25.
18 Isaeva, *Dramaturgiia Evgeniia Shvartsa*, 10.
19 White, "Russian Subtexts," 636; Lipovetskii, *Poetika*, 95.
20 Shvarts, *Bessmyslennaia radost'*, 360-61; 280-84.

On some level, a text in which a shadow is incarnated and then compels its former owner to take its place is almost too transparently theatrical in its premise. It is clear that identity and agency are in play. For one thing, this is already a theme in Andersen's story. When the scholar's shadow disappears, his first reaction is embarrassment, because he has read a story about a man who lost his shadow—Adelbert von Chamisso's 1814 novella *Peter Schlemihl's Miraculous Story*—and has no desire to become another *schlemiel*, to use his shadow as collateral in a bargain with the devil.

Schwartz's play takes that meta-literary move, the fictional character's awareness of the fictional underpinning of his experience, even further. Schwartz's scholar introduces himself as a friend of Hans Christian Andersen.[21] The unnamed southern country in which Andersen's story begins turns into a land populated by characters from folk- and fairy tales, such as Sleeping Beauty and Tom Thumb, who now lead ordinary lives, which means among other things that a lowly pawnbroker might very well turn out to be a man-eating ogre. And the very person who informs the scholar of this fact—another invention of Schwartz's, the servant girl Annunziata (who, in another subtle homage, bears the name of a character from Andersen's *Improvisatore*)—specifically warns the scholar not to reenact the story about a man and his shadow, which, as the context of the play makes clear, is Andersen's, rather than Chamisso's.

At first the scholar laughs these suggestions off. But in another almost entirely self-contained, uncanny moment, he is visited, in his hotel room, by a vision of three characters in the story from which he will, in the end, not be able to extricate himself. This transformation of the meta-literary detail into a meta-theatrical device was not lost on the director of *The Shadow*'s original production at the Leningrad Comedy Theater, Nikolai Akimov (1901-68), a charismatic man of theater and gifted visual artist who also designed the production's scenery and poster. Akimov's set recycled elements from the theater's other productions that, in the director-designer's reading, had a meaningful connection with the scholar's quest for happiness and love; the actor rehearsing this role was put literally in the position of acting amid stories that preceded him.[22] The sense that the scholar is working against a text he intuits but cannot control is echoed and travestied in the actions of other characters, who, as Duffield White has observed, constantly look for ways to avoid playing the role they have been assigned, and are looking over their

---

21 Ibid., 347.
22 Posner, "Making the Strange Familiar."

shoulder to see whether those around them are doing the same.[23] This is in particular the case with two of the play's villains: an innkeeper (Annunziata's father) and a journalist; in a plot twist with transparent connections to the realities of Schwartz's society, when they receive promotions upon the shadow's ascent to the throne, they discover that their new jobs depend on their camouflaging themselves in order to spy on the kingdom's subjects.

Schwartz's playful invocation of meta-theatrical motifs is present in the other Andersen plays. In *The Naked King*, Schwartz turns Andersen's con-men weavers into masks to be taken up by the play's protagonists in the hope of winning the heart of the princess for one of them. In *The Snow Queen*, the storyteller not only narrates but takes part in the action, and in order to do so incognito, uses makeup and wigs to turn himself into a robber or a palace guard. In *The Shadow*, the prominence of the play's meta-performative layer, with all the grotesque situations to which the conceit gives rise, sets the parameters for the play's investigation of the uncomfortable ambiguity of enactment.

Central to that line of theatrical inquiry is yet another invented character: the singer-actress Julia Julie (Iuliia Dzhuli), who befriends the scholar but eventually betrays him and, in a singularly odd set piece, performs for the courtiers, as the scholar is about to be beheaded, her ditty "Let's Not All Lose Our Heads Now!" ("Ne nado golovu teriat'"). Julia Julie is, on the one hand, a caricature that brings together many specific embodiments of the "seductive Western singer" archetype in the Soviet theater and film of the 1930s. But some of her most ludicrous qualities point to some of the play's most intimate theatrical concerns. Her nonsensically doubled name, for instance, echoes the mirror-like inversion of the names given by Schwartz to the scholar, Christian-Theodor, and his shadow, Theodor-Christian: Julia Julie is simultaneously a character in her own right and that character's double.

The transparent religious connotations of the main character's two names are literalized when, in a significant departure from Andersen's text, the scholar is brought back to life with the help of a potion called *aqua vitae*—in another literalized pun, it is both an alcoholic spirit *and* a life-restoring liquid. In the play, the scholar's attempt to confront the shadow and debunk its claim to power fails, but the second his own head is chopped off, the shadow's head falls off as well—and, even as his courtiers joke about the shadow's failure to keep his head on his shoulders, they are compelled to acknowledge that their ruler is no true

---

23   White, "Shvarts's *The Shadow*."

Theodor (literally, "God's gift"), and that it is Christian, resurrected after his execution, who is the true enactor of his destiny.

As important as it is to the play's plot to keep the fundamentally good Scholar and the fundamentally evil Shadow apart, to posit a clear separation between the true Actor and the impostor claiming his role—hence also to establish a border between the performer and the role—the mirroring of the protagonist and antagonist, and the parallel to another mirroring (Julia Julie's two nearly identical names), suggest that the relationship between enactment and performance is far more complex.

Schwartz was not a fan of theatrical radicalism. And even though by the time *The Shadow* was completed, Antonin Artaud had already made public the manifestos that formed his book *The Theater and Its Double* (1938), Schwartz's texts are far too dependent on a refined culture of the word to be of much relevance to the kind of theater, and the kind of doubling, that Artaud calls forth. But a different view of the theatrical stage that emerged in Russian intellectual circles in the 1920s-30s helps us see the theatrical power of Schwartz's most puzzling inventions in the Andersen plays. This is the perspective provided by Gustav Shpet, on the one hand, and Sigizmund Krzhizhanovsky, on the other: a philosopher and a fiction-writer, both intimately involved with important Moscow theatrical companies (the Moscow Art Theater and Aleksandr Tairov's Chamber Theater), and both involved in working out one of the earliest accounts of a theatrical phenomenology. Their essays on the topic[24] were known to few, and the chances of Schwartz encountering them are remote. So I am not proposing these as deliberate subtexts, and, generally speaking, the question of authorial intention is not my concern here. I am using these Russian phenomenologists to outline a view of the theatrical experience that resonates in and clarifies both the uncanny power of moments in *The Snow Queen* that foreground the experience of an audience member, and the peculiar ways in which enactment and doubling come to the fore in *The Shadow*. Schwartz's reimagining of Andersen's tales as experiments in peculiarly theatrical ambivalence comes into focus only when viewed from a perspective that does not privilege the narrative—the perspective for which Shpet and Krzhizhanovsky, in different ways, lay the groundwork.

Each of these two argues for a key shift: away from the presumption that the central event of theater involves an actor interpreting—"reading"—the text prepared by an author, and toward the sense that the basic unit of theatrical reality is an actor's act. Plays, Krzhizhanovsky

---

24 Emerson, "Actor's Task," 228; Shpet, "Teatr kak iskusstvo"; Krzhizhanovskii, 4: 43-88.

suggests, are the medium *in* which and *through* which an actor lives ("plays serve beings who are manifested playwise," according to his remarkable pleonasm [*p'esy obsluzhivaiu[t] p'esesoobrazno proiavliai-ushcheesia sushchestvo*])—and it is this dynamic that accounts for the genesis of theatrical power, figured as a force: the actor who drives the theatrical event acts with words by turning *words* into *acts*: "The stage does not speak the words but acts with them, hits with them" (*ne govorit slova, a diestvuet imi, b'et*).[25]

As Caryl Emerson puts it, Russian phenomenologists of the theater "redefine the aesthetically performed act of [the actor's individual tactile] body as constitutive of a special, highly permeable sort of identity, achieved not by feeling whole from within ('at one with the role'), but by being looked at and finalized by another perspective from without."[26]

The actor's material is the actor's own self. The creation of a role—a kind of potential being—requires, in Shpet's formulation, not identity with one's inner self, but a mastery of "outer forms" embodied in the actor's physical movement. Krzhizhanovsky, who was especially interested in the various forms of doubling that take place on stage, both on the level of plot and in the process of creating a role, uses the term "dividuum" to describe the essence of the actor's being, in opposition to the notion of an "*in*dividuum." "When an actor enters a room," he writes, "it becomes peopled. An actor is always made out of many, he is a creature divided into roles: he does not merely exist—because he in fact exists many times at the same time."[27]

This phenomenological insight into the nature and significance of theatrical action helps us see the promise and the peril of the plays that not only change the plot of Andersen's texts but reconfigure the audience's understanding of the very possibilities the theater affords them. Schwartz's *The Shadow* features a striking example of what J. L. Austin would, a little over a decade later, still in Schwartz's lifetime, call "the performative."[28] The scholar discovers that there is a way to defeat the shadow, if only temporarily. "Shadow, know your place!" he orders. And the incarnated shadow begins to shrink and almost vanishes. Yet this is not an entirely felicitous *performative* in Austin's sense: after a short while, the words cease to have their power, and the shadow returns in the flesh.[29] The effect of the scene is to demonstrate the precise range

---

25 Krzhizhanovskii, *Sobranie sochinenii*, 4: 74, 78.
26 Emerson, "Actor's Task," 229.
27 Krzhizhanovskii, *Sobranie sochinenii*, 4: 72-73.
28 Austin, *How to Do Things*.
29 Shvarts, *Bessmyslennaia radost'*, 402, 405-7.

and limitations of the force that drives a theatrical event—its performative power.

Schwartz's Andersen plays, as witty and full of insight into psychological and social predicaments as they are, do not simply communicate words and ideas. They are shaped in a way that allows the actions of their characters to enact for the audience the far more disorienting sense of the ephemeral but overwhelming power of a performance that hits the mark. The two misfired interpretations of the squeaking stairs' performance in *The Snow Queen* and the scholar's inability to control the shadow, through reason or otherwise, until, and unless, he himself completely loses control over his own body—offer a fluid, and disturbing, sense of what can be done with words on stage, aside from "mere" communication.

The agency of a shadow—of an actor—is both absolute and utterly dependent for its efficacy on an outside validation. And that validation, a process of intimate engagement and interpretation, enacted by Schwartz's characters for his audiences—can easily misfire. In retrospect, it is not hard to see the power and the terror of this theatrical sensibility for the original audiences of Schwartz's texts, though few among them could have been expected to articulate the effect in such terms. Even when Schwartz's ending is ostensibly not as tragic as Andersen's, as for instance in the case of the resurrected scholar Christian-Theodor, his texts often act not by speaking, but by striking—by shaping a situation in which the power of performance comes to the fore, and then is allowed to fail.

Works Cited

Andersen, Hans Christian. *The Fairy Tale of My Life: An Autobiography.* New York: Cooper Square Press, 2000.

Andersen, Jens. *Hans Christian Andersen: A New Life.* London: Duckworth, 2006.

Austin, J. L. *How to Do Things with Words.* Cambridge, MA: Harvard University Press, 1962.

Binding, Paul. *Hans Christian Andersen: European Witness.* New Haven: Yale University Press, 2016.

Corten, Irina. "Evgenii Shvarts as an Adapter of Hans Christian Andersen and Charles Perrault." *The Russian Review* 37, no. 1 (1978): 51-67.

Emerson, Caryl. "The Actor's Task as a Philosophical Quest in the Russian 1920s: Two Test Cases." In *Russian Performances: Word, Object, Action*, edited by Julie Buckler, Julie Cassiday, and Boris Wolfson, 227-34. Madison: University of Wisconsin Press, 2018.

Isaeva, Elizaveta. *Dramaturgiia Evgeniia Shvartsa*. Moscow: Teatral'nyi institut imeni Borisa Shchukina, 2009.

Krzhizhanovskii, Sigizmund. *Sobranie sochinenii*. Edited by Vadim Perel'muter. 6 vols. Moscow-St. Petersburg: b.s.g. press / symposium, 2001-13.

Lipovetskii, Mark. *Poetika literaturnoi skazki (na materiale russkoi literatury 1920-1980-kh godov)*. Sverdlovsk: Izdatel'stvo Sverdlovskogo universiteta, 1992.

Loseff, Lev. *On the Beneficence of Censorship: Aesopian Language in Modern Russian Literature*. Munich: Otto Sagner, 1984.

Metcalf, Amanda. *Evgenii Shvarts and His Fairy-Tales for Adults*. Birmingham: University of Birmingham, 1979.

Posner, Dassia. "Making the Strange Familiar: Nikolai Akimov's Productions of Shvarts's *The Shadow* (1940) and *The Dragon* (1944) at the Leningrad Theatre of Comedy." Presentation at the national convention of the Association for Slavic, East European and Eurasian Studies, 16 November 2012.

Pyman, Avril. "Evgenii L'vovich Shvarts (1896-1958): Centenary Thoughts." *Slavonica* 4, no. 1 (1997): 64-78.

Pyzhova, Ol'ga, and Boris Bibikov, directors. *Snezhnaia koroleva. Montazh spektaklia Tsentral'nogo detskogo teatra, zapis' 1949 g*. Script by Evgenii Shvarts, music by Viktor Oranskii. Melodiia D-24325-8, 1969. 2 LPs.

Ridout, Nicholas. *Stage Fright, Animals, and Other Theatrical Problems*. Cambridge: Cambridge University Press, 2006.

Shpet, Gustav. "Teatr kak iskusstvo." *Voprosy filosofii* 11 (1988): 77-92.

Shpet, Leonora. *Sovetskii teatr dlia detei*. Moscow: Iskusstvo, 1971.

Shvarts, Evgenii. *Predchuvstvie shchast'ia: proizvedeniia 20-kh–30-kh godov, dnevniki, stikhi i pis'ma*. Moscow: Korona-print, 1999.

—. *Bessmyslennaia radost' bytiia: proizvedeniia 30-kh – 40-kh godov, dnevniki i pis'ma*. Moscow: Korona-print, 1999.

Tippner, Anja. "Evgenii Shvarts's Fairy Tale Dramas: Theater, Power, and the Naked Truth." In *Russian Children's Literature and Culture*, edited by Marina Balina and Larissa Rudova, 307-23. New York: Routledge, 2008.

White, Duffield. "Shvarts's *The Shadow*: The Andersen Story and the Russian Subtexts." *The Slavic and East European Journal* 38, no. 4 (1994): 636-54.

Wilson, Seth. "Fairy Tale or Subversion? Evgeny Shvarts's *The Dragon* as Anti-Stalinist Theatre for Youth." *Theatre Symposium* 23 (2015): 52-66.

Wullschlager, Jackie. *Hans Christian Andersen: The Life of a Story Teller*. Chicago: University of Chicago Press, 2002.

Konstantin Paustovsky and the Making of Hans Christian Andersen, Paragon of the Soviet Thaw

Marina Balina

Introduction: Challenges of the Thaw

When in 1948 Nikolai Zabolotsky, the Russian avant-garde poet and himself a victim of the Stalinist purges, wrote his poem "The Thaw" ("Ottepel'"), his line on a warming having finally arrived after a long, severe winter storm was perceived as a metaphorical prediction of change coming to the country. However, expectations of new beginnings were premature, and the final years of Stalin's rule saw harsh and anti-Semitic campaigns against "rootless cosmopolitans," culminating in an all-out assault on the Jewish intelligentsia in August 1952 and the infamous Doctor's Plot of 1953, and ending only with Stalin's death on 5 March 1953.[1]

The liberalization that commenced in Soviet Russia the year of Stalin's death is referred to as "the Thaw" in particular due to the novel of that title by Ilya Ehrenburg (1954), which espouses the artist's right to self-expression, criticizes events of immediate history (such as the Doctor's Plot), and expresses hope for change. Often recognized as a hero of the early Thaw is the writer and critic Vladimir Pomerantsev: in groundbreaking statements made in his article "On Sincerity in Literature" ("Ob iskrennosti v literature") published in *New World* (*Novyi mir*) (December 1954), Pomerantsev insisted on sincerity as *the* criterion of literary-artistic achievement. His claim that the writer should follow personal creative impulses rather than official party doctrine was truly innovative and brave. Written in an untraditional first-person narrative, this article, both in style and content, was quite daring for the stagnant literary scene of the early 1950s and elicited accolades from prominent writers, as well as harsh criticism from those still hewing to official viewpoints; but in any case the silence over the situation in literature and the arts had finally been broken.

Poets and writers now raised their voices to reinstate literary values, defending the individuality of the poetic voice (Olga Berggolts); and

---

1 For more on this subject, see Brent and Naumov, *Stalin's Last Crime*.

declaring loyalty to the truth more important than following the government's course (Ilya Ehrenburg). Even Konstantin Simonov, the celebrated Soviet "court" writer, went so far as to suggest that works banned in the 1920s–30s be republished (as would indeed be done with writings by Marina Tsvetaeva and Anna Akhmatova). He also decried the use of clichés in characters' depiction in Soviet literature of the time. This liberal platform was attacked by conservative literary functionaries of the Stalin era—Aleksandr Fadeev, Konstantin Fedin, Aleksei Surkov—in the official press, which rendered the Thaw's first wave short-lived and led to the dismissal of the prominent Soviet poet and liberalization-supporter Aleksandr Tvardovsky from his position as editor-in-chief of the leading literary journal *New World*.[2] But it was in this very brief period that the new liberal requirements of literature were formulated: sincerity in the depiction of reality, the value of individuality in the representation of characters, a rejection of monumentalism in favor of a deep interest in the emotional side of human experience, and the unleashing of the artistic power of imagination.

In an authoritarian society, which Soviet Russia continued to be even after Stalin's death, no changes in artistic life could commence without key political reforms. Signaling liberalization of this sort was Nikita Khrushchev's "secret speech" at the Twentieth Party Congress on 25 February 1956. Here the Soviet leader denounced Stalin's "cult of personality" and blamed him for the destruction of many innocent lives during the purges.[3] This speech became a turning point for the Soviet intelligentsia, enabling a reappraisal of all revolutionary history, a reevaluation of October 1917 and its heroes. The literature of the Thaw led to the destruction of myths of the revolution, and as such this period could not have lasted long.[4]

---

2   For more detail on this episode, see Krementsov, *Russkaia literatura XX veka. Tom 2: 1940-1990-e gody*.
3   For more on this subject, see Taubman, *Khrushchev*.
4   The early 1960s saw a further de-Stalinization: by resolution of the Twenty-Second Party Congress in October 1961, Stalin's body, which had lain next to Lenin's in the mausoleum in Red Square, was removed, albeit still granted the honor of burial in the Kremlin wall among heroes of the revolution and civil war. The confusedness of this gesture was quite symbolic, insofar as now a big chunk of immediate Soviet history had to be reevaluated and rewritten. The return of victims of the Stalinist purges from the Gulag that began already in the late 1950s contributed to these efforts by providing eyewitness accounts and giving rise to a new corpus of fictional texts, such as Aleksandr Solzhenitsyn's *One Day in the Life of Ivan Denisovich* (*Odin den' Ivana Denisovicha*), published in November 1962 in *New World*. For the first time, the very topic of life and survival in the forced-labor camps of the Gulag system—Stalinism's great engine of human destruction—could be broached.

This era of relative openness and freedom of expression, moreover, was itself constantly interrupted by sudden "freezes" triggered by political changes within the country and outside it. The Hungarian Uprising in 1956 and rebellious demonstrations against the communist regime in Poland had immediate consequences for liberal processes at home. Thus, the almanac *Literary Moscow* (*Literaturnaia Moskva*), which had been initiated in 1955-56 by a group of writers (Konstantin Paustovsky, Aleksandr Bek, Veniamin Kaverin, and Margarita Aliger), was discontinued after just two volumes. This almanac had featured poetry by authors who for ideological reasons had previously been silenced: Marina Tsevaeva, Anna Akhmatova, Nikolai Zabolotsky, and Boris Pasternak. The second volume included such controversial pieces as Aleksandr Iashin's story "Levers" ("Rychagi"), which depicted the Soviet political system's corrupting influence on ordinary people in the countryside. The same fate befell another undertaking by writers seeking a new creative path, even within the framework of a censorship still in operation during the Thaw: in 1961, on Paustovsky's initiative, a provincial publishing house in Kaluga brought out *Pages from Tarusa* (*Tarusskie stranitsy*), which featured authors hitherto marginalized by the Soviet literary establishment—David Samoilov, Boris Slutsky, and Bulat Okudzhava—as well as a selection of verse of Marina Tsvetaeva, who otherwise remained *persona non grata* in Soviet literature.[5]

One key "freeze" during the Thaw of 1956-61 was the scandal surrounding the foreign publication of Pasternak's novel *Doctor Zhivago* (*Doktor Zhivago*, 1957). The writer was forced to refuse the 1958 Nobel Prize in Literature and faced grave career consequences; but he was never arrested or imprisoned, as would have been the case just a decade earlier.[6] Despite the constant "outbursts" of the authorities, the process of society's liberalization had a profound effect on the country's cultural life.[7] Among significant events of the Thaw was the

---

5   On the history of this almanac's creation and its fate, see Mil'shtein, "Kaluzhskii intsident."
6   Nevertheless, two major court cases of the 1960s—the poet Iosif Brodsky's 1964 sentencing to five years of administrative exile for "parasitism," and Iulii Daniel and Andrei Siniavsky's indictment on charges of anti-Soviet activity for smuggling their (indeed, politically critical) works to be published abroad in 1966, and their subsequent internment in a hard labor camp—reincarnated Stalin's persecution of creative individuals. In the almost two decades that followed (till the death of Brezhnev in 1982), artistic production was once again subordinated to the party's political agenda.
7   Cultural historians tend to agree on when the Thaw began, but differ as to the endpoint of this liberalization of Soviet society. Some connect its demise with major failures on the international front, such as the Cuban missile crisis and concomitant "freeze" in Soviet-American relations in 1962. Others point to domestic political developments, for example, the infamous "Manezh affair" (December 1962)—Khrushchev's face-to-face tirade against

creation of new literary magazines, such as *Youth* (*Iunost'*) (1955), *Neva* (*Neva*) (1955), *Friendship of Peoples* (*Druzhba narodov*) (1955), *Foreign Literature* (*Inostrannaia literatura*) (1955), *Our Contemporary* (*Nash sovremennik*) (1956), and *Urals* (*Ural*) (1956). The period of the Thaw was marked by a great diversity of innovative approaches and stylistic and aesthetic experimentation in literature and the arts. From Evgenii Evtushenko's poem "Babi Yar" ("Babii Iar") (1961), in which the theme of the Holocaust, and Soviet anti-Semitism, was first publicly addressed in Soviet literature, to Ehrenburg's memoir *People, Years, Life* (*Liudi, gody, zhizn'*, 1961-66), which both excavated Russian literature of the complex, early postrevolutionary period (in particular, the forgotten names of Isaak Babel, Mikhail Bulgakov, Osip Mandelshtam, and Iurii Olesha), and introduced Ehrenburg's readers to the previously unknown world of European modernist culture—these works ignited the contemporary imagination with new themes and new artistic devices. New theater and cinema productions such as Iurii Liubimov's Taganka Theater, with its persistent thematization of civic responsibility and individual ethics; or Georgii Tovstonogov's Gorky Drama Theater in Leningrad, with its particular focus on reading contemporary social meaning into classic texts; or Grigorii Kozintsev's *Hamlet* (*Gamlet*, 1964), which featured a Shakespearean and altogether contemporary dramatization of the individual's struggle to protect his personal world from the predations of the powerful—all these innovations demonstrated the incredible artistic potential of Thaw culture. Thus do Natan Leiderman and Mark Lipovetsky write: "Everything new forged its path with great difficulty, and any artistic phenomenon out of the ordinary found itself saddled with an ideological label; but unlike the political [liberalization] process, which in the mid-1960s reversed course, artistic development could not be halted. The 'sip of freedom' turned out to be invigorating."[8] One of the most important artists to serve up such a "sip of freedom" was Konstantin Georgievich Paustovsky (1892-1968), a person of high moral character whose behavior served, for many contemporaries, as a model of honest dealing even at the most fraught moments of Soviet existence. It was he who turned to the

---

Moscow artists whose paintings did not conform to the socialist-realist tradition. Another landmark would be the March 1963 meeting between Khrushchev and representatives of "the creative intelligentsia" that signaled the party's reassertion of ideological control over the arts. Some scholars extend the line into the "stagnation" period under Brezhnev, connecting the abrupt end of the Thaw to the "Prague spring" of 1968, when the attempt to build "socialism with a human face" was crushed by Soviet tanks.

8 Leiderman and Lipovetskii, *Sovremennaia russkaia literatura*, 1: 63.

legacy of Hans Christian Andersen in Russian literature and extended it far beyond Andersen's popularity as a writer of fairy tales. For the first time, the Danish author was introduced to his Russian readers as an emblem of imaginative freedom. Initially, Paustovsky's task was to write an introductory biography of Andersen for the 1955 Goslitizdat (State Literature Publishing House) edition of *The Tales and Stories of Andersen* (*Skazki i istorii Andersena*). But under Paustovsky's pen, Andersen's life story soon took on a life of its own: the writer created a particular sort of biography for the famous storyteller, one that proved closely intertwined with his own life story. The biographical and autobiographical elements of his telling transform the story of Andersen into a narrative about issues of creativity, about an artist's right to an independent vision of the world.

Konstantin Paustovsky and His Legacy in Russian Literature

Paustovsky has occupied a special place among writers of the Soviet era, not only as the author of works that clearly range beyond the requirements of socialist realism,[9] but also as a person with his own particular civic position. As his former literary secretary Valerii Druzhbinsky recalls: "Amazingly, Paustovsky managed to live through the period of the insane glorification of Stalin without ever writing a single word about the 'leader of all times and peoples.' He managed to not join the party, nor sign a single letter or statement denouncing anyone. He made every effort to remain himself and therefore managed to do so."[10]

In the politicized life of Soviet literature, such a situation did not come to a writer easily. Both the undertakings mentioned above—*Literary Moscow*, and *Pages from Tarusa*—were severely criticized; but Paustovsky considered it his civic duty to stand up for persecuted literature and persecuted writers. For example, he managed to restore Aleksandr Grin, an undeservedly forgotten romantic writer of the 1920s, to the attention of contemporary readers. Paustovsky was, moreover, one of the twenty-five figures of culture and science who on 14 February 1966 submitted a letter to the party's General Secretary Leonid Brezhnev to the effect that any partial or indirect rehabilitation of Stalin (a process that would indeed take place in the "stagnant" Brezhnev years) would

---

9   See the analysis of the categories of socialist realism in Giunter and Dobrenko, *Sotsrealisticheskii kanon*, 281-434.
10 Druzhbinskii, "Konstantin Paustovskii, kakim ego pomniu."

be unacceptable. And Paustovsky was among the few Soviet writers to support Andrei Siniavsky and Iulii Daniel during their 1966 trial for having their works published abroad.[11] A year earlier, Paustovsky penned a letter in support of the persecuted Aleksandr Solzhenitsyn. Ilya Ehrenburg wrote of Paustovsky's extraordinary spiritual steadfastness: "This mild and gentle man knows how to be surprisingly strict with himself.... I am grateful to him for his skill, exactingness, inspiration, and rare purity."[12] It is thus fitting that the prose of the Thaw, in breaking free of the canonical socialist-realist framework, did so, as Leiderman and Lipovetsky remark, "under the shadow" of Paustovsky. This prose was not "dominated by social ideas," and, returning to the interrupted tradition of the 1920s and early 1930s, appealed to "the private life of Soviet people, to their ordinary concerns, to everyday life."[13] Modern criticism, following Aleksandr Goldshtein, has defined this tendency as Soviet neo-sentimentalism.[14] For his part, Ilya Kukulin sees Paustovsky, with his love for the details of everyday life, as exemplifying the tradition of the "Soviet Biedermeier."[15] But if we turn to the definition of Paustovsky's style he himself frequently offered, we see that the writer did not hesitate to place himself within the romantic tradition, despite—even during the Thaw—being derided for his "romantic prettiness" (*romanticheskaia krasivost'*) and "tendency to exoticism."[16] Indeed, the author's first novel, begun in the period of 1916-23, was called *The Romantics* (*Romantiki*),[17] and described the internal emotional state of his characters—people of his generation on the eve of the First World War. In the preface to his six-volume collected works published in 1957, Paustovsky writes:

> It seems to me that one of the characteristic features of my prose is its romantic mood. This, of course, is a feature of my character. It would be absurd to demand of anyone, especially a writer, that he give up this mood. Such a demand could only be explained by ignorance.
>
> There is no contradiction between the romantic attitude and a keen interest in the "rough" life and love thereof. With rare exceptions, the seeds of romance lie in every field of reality and human activity.

---

11 See Nepomnyashchy, *Abram Tertz and the Poetics of Crime*, 37.
12 Cited from Levitskii, *Vospominaniia o Konstantine Paustovskom*, 84.
13 Leiderman and Lipovetskii, *Sovremennaia russkaia literatura*, 1: 231.
14 This term was first proposed in Gol'dshtein, *Rasstavanie s Nartsissom*, 153-74.
15 See Ilya Kukulin's contribution to this volume.
16 See L'vov, *Konstantin Paustovskii*, 20, 59, 87.
17 Ibid., 10. The novel was published in 1935.

They may go unnoticed or be trampled on, or, to the contrary, given the opportunity to grow, may decorate and ennoble a person's inner world with their flowering.[18]

But Paustovsky's romanticism is entirely bereft of the sort of elation and sentimentality of which he was frequently accused. It consists, rather, in a focus on the life of the human soul, independent of the individual's social engagement. Indeed, the above quotation could very well have been written by Paustovsky's hero Hans Christian Andersen, who could be equally preoccupied by the feelings and experiences of an emperor of China and those of a darning needle. Thus, in undertaking a biography of the storyteller, Paustovsky saw him first and foremost as a fellow-thinker, one whose writerly credo he shared, despite the difference of centuries and geography.

Konstantin Paustovsky and Hans Christian Andersen: An Attempt at (Auto)biography

The writing of literary biography always entails the complex matter not just of selecting material but interpreting it. In two essays on this genre, "The New Biography" (1927) and "The Art of Biography" (1939), so famous a biographer as Virginia Woolf emphasizes the internal contradiction embedded in biography's very structure—the dichotomy, first and foremost, between the "granite" of fact and "the rainbow" of personality. Woolf views the "biographer as a craftsman, not an artist," and biography, especially literary biography, "not as art but 'something betwixt and between.'"[19] As the subject of a biographical narrative, the writer's life experience is often replaced by analysis of his or her works; and just as frequently, the behavioral model of these works' characters is ascribed to their author him- or herself. The Soviet 1920s saw theoretical debates on literary biography as a particular genre, but these boiled down to a somewhat different literary stratum of analysis: the complexity, in particular, of dealing with biographical material, and with a literary biography's moments of cultural significance. This debate reflected formalist polemics, questions surrounding the "literature of fact," and whether biography may be treated as historical document. In his 1923 article "Literature and Biography" ("Literatura i biografiia"), so sophisticated a literary scholar as Boris Tomashevsky proposes that

---

18 Paustovskii, *Sobranie sochinenii*, 1: 12.
19 Woolf, *Selected Essays*, 95, 116.

biographical material should be approached critically: the creative individual, he observes, is bound to introduce a certain stylization into his or her life, inasmuch as that life is inseparable from his or her creation; and describing the behavior of an author as a character in a biographical text sometimes involves intentionally overdrawing the features of his or her literary characters.[20] Polemicizing with Tomashevsky four years later, Grigorii Vinokur asserts in his study "Biography and Culture" ("Biografiia i kul'tura," 1927) that any behavior on the part of an author who is the subject of a biographical narrative—even the stylization surrounding him or her just mentioned—nevertheless remains a "biographical fact."[21] For Vinokur, the category of *writer* is essentially unique among biographical subjects; against Tomashevsky's assertion that "the biography of a poet differs from that of a general only in its material," he counters with the "fate of the poet," which is an "utterly peculiar fate, even in a case where it might entirely coincide, in terms of outward events, with the fate of a general."[22] Aside from facts—the external structure of a biography—Vinokur proposes to address its internal structure, the history of how the author's personality was formed; thus the biography is centered upon the "sphere of emotional life [*perezhivanie*]," the "sphere of spiritual experience," insofar as it is specifically in this sphere that historical fact acquires distinctive or unique significance in the life of the biography's hero.[23] The biography's author ceases to be a collector of factual material, since his or her narrative is based on conveying the "creative meaning" (*tvorcheskii smysl*) of its subject.[24]

Paustovsky constructs his "biographies" of Andersen specifically as a paradigm of *perezhivanie* ("emotional life," "experience"), a concept he understands quite broadly. Thus, for instance, in his first biographical essay on Andersen, the "experience" (*perezhivanie*) of the biography's hero (Andersen) is closely intertwined with the personal experience of his biographer (Paustovsky), thereby forming an interesting fusion of "biography-cum-autobiography," as Marilyn Yalom defines a narrative structure of this sort.[25] It is precisely such a union of the emotional experience of biographer and subject that turns the preface of the 1955 Goslitizdat edition of *The Tales and Stories of Andersen* into an independent text, one that may be seen as part of the series of literary portraits

---

20 Tomashevskii, "Literatura i biografiia," 10.
21 Vinokur, *Biografiia i kul'tura*, 82.
22 Ibid., 66, 70.
23 Ibid., 83.
24 Ibid., 65.
25 Yalom, "Biography as Autobiography," 53.

that Paustovsky was at the time devoting to other non-Russian subjects such as Oscar Wilde, Charles Dickens, Rudyard Kipling, and Friedrich Schiller. But each of these latter biographies was presented under their subjects' names, while Andersen appears under the modest heading of "The Storyteller" ("Skazochnik").

The genre of literary portrait itself requires a particular level of intimacy between the person writing it and his or her subject. Vladimir Barakhov proposes that the literary portrait should be seen as "a particular method of cognizing a person aesthetically"; in the critic's view, the literary portrait is entitled to "a particular poetic vision of a concrete, real person."[26] Apparently guided by this very conception of the genre, Paustovsky immediately injects a personal autobiographical element into his narrative. He introduces the reader to *his* Andersen, privatizing his main character and the facts of his biography. The reader comes not only to see Andersen through Paustovsky's eyes, but also to perceive the Danish storyteller through the author's "experience." Andersen's biography is so closely bound up with the fate of his biographer that the author of the text (the narrator) becomes an Andersen character. Carol Hanbery MacKay defines a similar type of biographical narrative as "biography as reflected autobiography."[27] Ira Bruce Nadel likewise puts particular emphasis on the intimate connection between a biographer and his or her subject: "Biographers are fixated on their heroes in a very peculiar manner. They frequently select the hero as the object of study because, for personal reasons of their emotional life, they had a special affection for him from the very outset."[28] I would propose precisely such a reading of Paustovsky's first text on Andersen: the emotional connection between these writers dictates a "particular poetic vision," which is demonstrated to the reader through a decidedly autobiographical episode.

Paustovsky first encountered Andersen, we are told, mere hours ahead of New Year's Day, 1900. "The cheery Danish storyteller greeted me on the threshold of the new century."[29] Engrossed in his reading, the seven-year-old boy had a waking dream of being visited by Andersen himself. "He looked me over for a long time, squinting one eye and chuckling, then took a snow-white, perfumed handkerchief from his pocket," from which he shook loose a "white rose"; a "slow chiming" was heard—the sound of the rose's petals "hitting the brick floor of the basement our

---

26 Barakhov, *Literaturnyi portret*, 9.
27 MacKay, "Biography as Reflected Autobiography," 53.
28 Nadel, *Biography*, 119.
29 Paustovskii, *Sobranie sochinenii*, 5: 600; further citations from "The Storyteller" in the text refer to this edition.

family was living in at the time" (600). Reading another of the author's texts in parallel—the autobiographical tale *Distant Years* (*Dalekie gody*, 1945)—makes clear the full significance this encounter held for the little boy: this was the time of his family's disintegration, the father having left; and of the onset of grave material need. Hence the mention of the brick floor of the basement in which the impoverished family had been forced to settle—the landing-place of an imagined white rose. This was, in other words, the beginning of a fairy tale, which helped little Kostia forget all the unchildlike offenses and worries he had to endure, because there on the pages of a book, "the walls of ice castles shone like sparklers; wild swans flew over a sea reflecting pink clouds; and tin soldiers stood one-legged on clocks, clutching their long rifles" (602).

Andersen immediately takes his place alongside young Kostia's idol Pushkin: "I decided that Andersen and Pushkin must have been boon companions, that when they got together they slapped each other on the shoulder and laughed for a long time" (602). This autobiographical intrusion violates the borders of the biography genre; it removes the barrier between biographer, the observer of another person's life, and autobiographer, who in a sense takes part in the "other person's" life which is one's own. Andersen ceases to be the subject of a narrative; he is now a living teacher of life: "Andersen (a likeable oddball and poet) taught me to have faith in the sun's victory over darkness, in the victory of the kindly human heart over evil" (602). It is here that the conflict between the "granite" of fact and the "rainbow" of personality discussed by Virginia Woolf comes to the fore. After such an introduction, the facts of a life lose their immutable value, insofar as personality (the genial, life-affirming Andersen) becomes more important than the factological material of his life, which is immediately relegated to the second tier. Herein lies, for Paustovsky, the particular meaning of the poet's life, the reason his biography is worth writing. This is what Vinokur, as mentioned, emphasized in his theoretical research on the subject: the uniqueness of the creative personality's life experience, and the influence of this experience on those around him/her.

The holiday of childhood is interrupted, however, by the voice of the grownup author, who remarks that at the time, "I did not understand the double meaning of Andersen's tales. I didn't know that in every children's fairy tale, there is another tale, one that only an adult can fully understand" (608). This is a boundary-marking statement; it visually separates the text of autobiography from biography. Now begins a description of Andersen's life, structured according to the canon of the "rough childhood"—the "Gorky model" so firmly entrenched in narratives of childhood in the postrevolutionary period. Elsewhere I have described how the Gorky model mandates a particular "etiquette of childhood," consisting of the privations and deprivations, the gloomy life of the non-noble child growing up before the revolution;[30] but Paustovsky himself violates this etiquette in his own reminiscences. Interestingly, Paustovsky draws Andersen's life in a somewhat syncopated style: he constantly intersperses the description of real details—the cathedral at Odense, the island of Funen itself—with qualifying statements, lending the narrative an uneven or "saltatory" binarity. Odense, for instance, represents both a "toy city carved from blackened oak" (603) and the backbreaking labor of woodcarvers, whose toil goes to please the rich and benefit the Church. Again and again appears a significant *but*, always bringing us back to what had seemingly been lost sight of—the politically correct framework of a socialist-realist narrative. The woodcarvers, that is, do not just make altars and figurines of saints; no, their carving also decorates ships bound for distant lands. So their labor does not only glorify religion, but also does something useful.

Paustovsky self-identifies as one of Soviet literature's last romantics; he remains long under the spell of the storytelling magician who dropped a white rose on a stone floor: the "fairy tale of [Andersen's] life" is created via the constant intersection of the real and the imaginative. Following his biographical subject, Paustovsky's "vision" is enhanced to an almost magical degree—he can see the shingle of a cobbler's shop, "a wooden sign depicting an eagle with two heads, to signal that cobblers only make shoes in pairs"; immediately qualifying this observation, to be sure, with another: that little Hans's father did not have enough money for such a sign, as he was no guild master; he was too poor. The author creates a peculiar palimpsest, describing Andersen's "rough childhood" (610-11) as overlaid with Andersen's "The Ugly Duckling": just as no barnyard insults or ill-treatment could keep the unrecognized and aggrieved duckling from turning into a beautiful swan, so too does Andersen's talent begin to shine, despite the humiliation and affronts inflicted on him by the powers that be.

Softening this rough childhood is the presence of the constant listener of little Hans's tales—the old cat Karl, who always falls asleep in the middle of the story. The facts of Andersen's life are clearly borrowed from prerevolutionary biographies of him based on his own *Fairy Tale*

---

30 On the various descriptive models of childhood in Soviet literature, see Balina, "Literaturnaia reprezentatsiia detstva v sovetskoi i postsovetskoi Rossii"; and "Crafting the Self."

of My Life,[31] but Paustovsky throws this material into a melting pot to produce a peculiar "bio-fiction" in which fact and invention are hardly at odds. This was most likely the only *modus operandi* available to him: the demand to present Andersen as a "man of the people" looms over the whole text, even as Paustovsky clearly wants to talk about something else entirely: little Hans's ability to "take joy in everything that is interesting and good, everything you come across on every path and at every step"; his rare talent for "noticing what escapes the attention of lazy human eyes" (605). Here Paustovsky-as-biographer gives way to Paustovsky as writer and *teacher* (he conducted seminars at the Gorky Literature Institute for many years): using Andersen as a role model, he discusses the subject of artistic inspiration, which may derive—so far from some party directive—from "dry moss sprinkling out its emerald pollen" (600), from "a mother-of-pearl fragment shimmering and shining endlessly with the same multitude of soft colors you see glowing in the morning sky over the Baltic" (605).

Paustovsky as Andersen-biographer is concerned first and foremost with the power of imagination wielded by the Danish storyteller. As Paustovsky will later write in *The Golden Rose* (*Zolotaia roza*), his primary book on the craft of writing, out of all the received opinions and prejudices about writing, "the most debased is the imagination. People who don't know any better almost always seem to imagine it in the form of the poet staring goggle-eyed at the sky in incomprehensible rapture; or like some gnawed quill."[32] In "The Storyteller," the biographer appreciates Andersen's free spirit of fantasy, which enabled him to "see, in the nighttime, the glow of the sweetbrier [*svechenie shipovnika*], like the shimmering of a white night, and... to hear the grumbling of an old stump in the forest" (611).

---

31 *The Fairy Tale of My Life* was never published in the Soviet period—not even in the 1983 *Literary Monuments* (*Literaturnye pamiatniki*) collection edited by Liudmila Braude and Irina Steblova and including "Tales Told to Children. New Tales"; nor by other publishing houses, even as these brought out numerous editions of the tales. For her part, Braude would quote Andersen's autobiography in some of the textbooks she authored, but this would be the extent of her familiarizing readers with her original source. In the Soviet period, Irina Muravyova's biography of Andersen was published (1959) as part of the *Lives of Remarkable People* (*Zhizn' zamechatel'nykh liudei*) series; but this work contains no quotations from the writer's autobiography. In 2013, the same series brought out an Andersen biography by Boris Erkhov, which relies heavily on and frequently cites from *The Fairy Tale of My Life*, and makes use of a variety of biographical material from Andersen's personal correspondence. The four-volume Andersen edition brought out by the publisher Terra in 2014 contains the Hansens' translation of *The Fairy Tale of My Life*. See also Inna Sergienko's contribution to this volume on the various biographical essays on Andersen's life and work.

32 Paustovskii, *Sobranie sochinenii*, 2: 522; further citations from *The Golden Rose* in the text refer to this edition.

Leaving aside the clichés required by the times—e.g., of Andersen as a "poet of the poor," gleaning inspiration "from the seeds of the people's poetry scattered on peasant lands" (612)—Andersen's whole biography may be perceived as a response to the important shifts taking place in Soviet political and cultural life after Stalin's death. Andersen's biography enables Paustovsky to address the aspect of the writerly craft uppermost in his own thinking: the freedom of the imagination, which is such an essential tool for a writer, and takes a real writer far beyond the bounds of political regimentation. Paustovsky emphasizes the freedom necessary for true creativity:

> Free imagination catches hundreds of particulars in the life around us and unites them in a harmonious and wise tale. There is nothing to which the storyteller would not pay heed, be it the neck of a beer bottle, a drop of dew on a feather, a stray oriole, or a rusty street lamp. Any thought, the mightiest and most magnificent, can be expressed with the friendly assistance of these modest items. (608)

Significant in this quotation is not Paustovsky's knowledge of Andersen's fairytale plots; here the writer addresses, rather, his own critics, who accused him of getting carried away by details, of *melkotem'e*, a "narrow focus on trivialities"—of being unable to write about the big and important topics of the socialist way of life, and failing to attend to the politics of the moment in favor, by contrast, of describing the minutest facets of nature.[33]

Paustovsky, it turns out, has given his biography a somewhat misleading title: its subject Andersen hardly seems to matter to him as a "storyteller," but rather as an improvisatore. Alluding to the "hurriedness" of his pen, Paustovsky means this not as a critique but to Andersen's great credit: "Improvisation is the poet's quick responsiveness to any thought someone else might have, to any *external* [emphasis mine—MB] impulse; the immediate transformation of this thought into a flow of imagery and harmonious pictures" (614). Andersen's biography becomes, for Paustovsky the writer and teacher, a lesson for the latter's pupils and fellow litterateurs, a means to restore a gift that has been lost under the pressure of political persecution and censorship. Thus for Paustovsky, his own personal "thaw" begins with the biography of the storyteller Hans Christian Andersen.

---

33 The critics' accusation of *melkotem'e* is mentioned in L'vov, *Konstantin Paustovskii*, 18.

On the Principles of the Writer's Craft: Hans Christian Andersen and the Art of Improvisation

Corroborating my hypothesis is another of Paustovsky's texts, this one appearing in *The Golden Rose* (1955), his book on the craft of writing. Part of this collection consists of lectures Paustovsky delivered over the course of a decade at the Gorky Literature Institute, where his students included such signal figures of Russian literature as Iurii Trifonov, Vladimir Tendriakov, Grigorii Baklanov, and Iurii Kazakov. As Leonid Krementsov has remarked, *The Golden Rose* was a book ahead of its time.[34] October 1955 was still too early to count on any "thaw," and the same sharp criticism that would soon be leveled at the almanacs *Literary Moscow* and *Pages from Tarusa*—which, as mentioned, Paustovsky would have an active role in publishing—now poured forth amid the icy rejection of his book. Krementsov remarks that the literary establishment could not yet "accept the level of internal freedom, the relaxed stance [Paustovsky] was permitting himself, nor see its true value."[35] One of the stories Paustovsky includes in *The Golden Rose* to illustrate his ideas on writing is devoted, once again, to Andersen. This text, "The Night Stagecoach" ("Nochnoi dilizhans"), begins with a brief foreword:

> I wanted to write a separate chapter on the power of imagination and its influence on our lives. But having given it some thought, I decided instead to write a story about the poet Andersen. I think it can take the place of such a chapter, and its portrayal of the imagination will be even clearer than a general discussion of the subject would have been. (637)

The plot concerns a visit by Andersen to Venice. And again we are struck by Paustovsky's knowledge of the writer's biography, of his movements around Europe, his acquaintance with masters of world literature such as Heine, Balzac, and Dickens. But of particular interest for our purposes is that in this piece, Paustovsky revives a vignette from his previous biography of Andersen wherein the Danish writer finds himself in a stagecoach with three Italian girls he has just met, and presents them with fairy tales in which a happy fate is foretold to each.[36] As this episode appears in two different Paustovsky texts, one would assume it is not invented; and indeed, it does derive from Andersen's autobiography. In

---

34 Krementsov, *K. G. Paustovskii*, 49.
35 Ibid., 169.
36 Paustovsky had briefly described this episode in "The Storyteller" (615). In *The Golden Rose*, it expands to the dimensions of an interpolated tale, and acquires a symbolic meaning quite significant for Paustovsky himself.

1833, Andersen left behind the attacks of hostile critics and newspapers to go abroad. The grant he received enabled him to travel first to Paris and then Italy. On the way to a boarding house in Switzerland, Andersen describes the adventure that became the basis for Paustovsky's chapter:

> We had left the flat plains of France and reached the Jura Mountains; here in a little village, late in the evening, the conductor helped two young farmer's daughters to get into the diligence, where I was the only passenger....
>
> They asked me whether I was young, and married, and how I looked. I kept quiet in a dark corner, and gave them as ideal a description as I could; they understood the sport, and when in turn I asked them of their appearance, they made themselves out to be real beauties.
>
> They urged me to show my face when we arrived at the next station; I would not yield to their wishes; and so they covered their faces with their handkerchiefs and alighted, and, laughing merrily, held out their hands to me. They were young and had very beautiful figures. Those two unknown, invisible, gay girls represented a laughing image of my travelling life.[37]

But whereas, in the retelling of this episode from his own life, we hear in Andersen's voice a note of (albeit kindly) irony (the girls are said to recall from their geography lessons that "Denmark was the same as Norway,"[38] clearly eliciting Andersen's mockery of their schooling), for his part, Paustovsky turns this moment from the life of the Danish writer into a kind of hymn to improvisation as a key writerly credo. As noted above, Paustovsky had taken up the theme of improvisation as a special quality of creativity—"the poet's quick responsiveness to any thought someone else might have"—in "The Storyteller," also remarking in that earlier work that this talent requires "a great reserve of observations and an excellent memory" (614).

But free improvisation also means creative independence and a fearlessness in the face of attempts to shackle the imagination—a quality for which a creative person comes to pay dearly, not just in the world of political pressure, but also in personal loss. Such loss, which goes beyond the limits of politicized Soviet existence, is the subject of the interpolated tale about Andersen in *The Golden Rose*.

The filthy hotel in Venice, the sly servant aiming to rob Andersen, the Venetian prostitutes constantly arguing under his window—these things do not anger Andersen, as they might have someone more narrow-

---

37 Andersen, *The Story of My Life*, 93.
38 Ibid.

minded, but cause him to be enraptured by the power of life. He "looked admiringly upon their tousled braids, their faces reddening with rage, their eyes burning with a thirst for vengeance"; saw the "wrathful tears ... rolling down their cheeks like drops of diamond" (639). But to everyone around him, Andersen is, for a poet, "strange." "His blood did not seem to seethe. He did not take up a guitar and sing heartrending barcarolles. Only once did he take a scarlet rose from his buttonhole to present to the homeliest scullery girl. She limped, moreover, like a duck" (639).

Central to this episode is what Paustovsky has already described in his biography-as-autobiography on the theme of Andersen's life: the ability to see the beautiful in the everyday. According to the *Golden Rose* narrative, in the carriage Andersen takes from Venice to Verona, his fellow passengers include an Austrian priest and a lady in a dark cloak. "To Andersen, she seemed now young, now elderly, now a beauty, now plain. This was the candle-end in the lantern playing tricks on him. It kept illuminating the lady in different ways—however might come into his head" (640). Soon the stagecoach has more passengers—three girls, whose futures, as mentioned, Andersen undertakes to foretell. Key here is the description of Andersen's status as improvisatore ("I am a fortune-teller. I can divine the future, and see it in the dark" [643]), and the total freedom he experiences as he creates these life-stories: "He said this, and felt his face go cold. A certain state came over him, the state he always experienced when thinking up his poems and tales; it combined a mild anxiety, a flow of words from out of nowhere, and the sudden sensation of the force of poetry, of his own power over the human heart" (644). His reward for this creativity comes in the form of kisses from the three girls, and the potential for happiness with Elena Guiccioli, the (it turns out, indeed beautiful) stranger in the cloak. But the poet is overcome by fear: "Who knows?—perhaps this love would fade; perhaps the motley swarm of his tales would go away, never to return. And then what would he be worth?" (648). So he renounces love, as he fears life and does not know it; after all, "it is only in the imagination that love may last forever, eternally surrounded by the shimmering halo of poetry." It occurs to Andersen that he is "much better at making things up about love than actually experiencing it" (649). According to Paustovsky, then, imagination is a great but treacherous gift, one that can take the place of the reality of life. When his Andersen, toward the end of his life, gives advice to a young writer, he exhorts him to learn to "wield imagination to make others happy, and oneself; not to cause sorrow" (650).

Paula R. Backscheider states in her study of the biography as a genre: "The best biographers know that they are inventing through their selection and arrangement of materials; they are establishing cause-effect and other relationships, and they are determining what was formative and important for someone else, someone they do not know. They must choose what to include, leave out, emphasize, and subordinate."[39] In his biography-cum-autobiography on Andersen and his creative experience, Paustovsky indeed selects the most important moments—most important not factologically, but existentially: treating the figure of Andersen and describing collisions of his life-journey enables the Soviet-era writer to metonymically express his view of the creative process, to justify the rejection of dogma and the discovery, instead, of one's own individuality; to assert, that is, the right to one's freedom of imagination. It is quite typical of Russian biographers of the Danish writer, pre- and postrevolutionary alike, to use "The Ugly Duckling" as a palimpsest of his life; but in Paustovsky this model, albeit initially present, gives way to an entirely different story about a writer unafraid to discard preconceived canons and to seek inspiration in the simplest, technically superficial things. Paustovsky the biographer is constantly changing places with Paustovsky the autobiographer, for whom Andersen becomes a reflection of personal life-experiences, as well as a conduit for the expression of important postulates of creativity in general. To be sure, in the turbulent literary life of Soviet Russia in the latter half of the 1950s, Andersen makes for a rather unexpected champion of such crucial concepts as freedom of the imagination or the art of improvisation as a necessary condition for realizing this freedom. In the brief final chapter of *The Golden Rose*, which Paustovsky titles "Parting Advice to Oneself" ("Naputstvie samomu sebe") he writes:

> Working on this book is reminiscent of a journey through a little-known country, where at every step, new vistas and roads open before you. Where they lead, you don't know, but they promise much that is unexpected, giving food for thought. It is thus tempting, and simply necessary, to figure out—in however (so to speak) "rough draft" a form—how these roads intertwine. (699)

It is striking that, in his difficult journey along the roads of creativity in the Soviet 1950s, Paustovsky chooses for himself, just as he had at the outset of this turbulent period (in 1900), the same conduit or conductor—"this poet and storyteller, this charming oddball, who remained, until his death, a sincere child, this inspired improvisatore and fisher of people's souls—both children's and adults'" ("The Storyteller,"

---

39 Backscheider, *Reflections on Biography*, 18.

617). Paustovsky managed to "liberate" the figure of Andersen from the compartment labeled "The Great Storyteller" so familiar to the Dane's readers and followers. For him, Andersen is the embodiment of the spirit of free creativity, when a writer's pen follows his imagination, and the source of his inspiration is not subject to administrative control. Thus, with the help of this "Thaw Andersen," Paustovsky resurrects for his contemporaries the forgotten sense of true creative freedom.

Works Cited

Andersen, Hans Christian. *The Story of My Life.* Translated by Mary Howitt. Edited and additional authorial material translated by Horace E. Scudder. Boston: Houghton, Mifflin, and Co., 1871.

Backscheider, Paula R. *Reflections on Biography.* Oxford New York: Oxford University Press, 2001.

Balina, Marina. "Crafting the Self: Narratives of Prerevolutionary Childhood in Soviet Literature." In *Russian Children's Literature and Culture*, edited by Marina Balina and Larissa Rudova, 91-113. London: Routledge, 2008.

—. "Literaturnaia reprezentatsiia detstva v sovetskoi i postsovetskoi Rossii." In *I sprosila krokha: Obraz rebenka i sem'i v pedagogike postsovetskoi Rossiii*, edited by B. Barannikova and V. G. Bezrogov, 20-38. Moscow: Nauchnaia kniga, 2010.

Barakhov, V. S. *Literaturnyi portret.* Leningrad: Nauka, 1985.

Brent, Jonathan, and Vladimir Naumov. *Stalin's Last Crime: The Plot against the Jewish Doctors, 1948-1953.* New York: Harper Collins, 2003.

Druzhbinskii, Valerii. "Konstantin Paustovskii, kakim ego pomniu." Available electronically:
http://paustovskiy-lit.ru/paustovskiy/mesta/druzhbinskij.htm

Giunter, Khans, and Evgenii Dobrenko, eds. *Sotsrealisticheskii kanon.* St. Petersburg: Akademicheskii proekt, 2000.

Gol'dshtein, Aleksandr. *Rasstavanie s Nartsissom. Opyt pominal'noi ritoriki.* Moscow: NLO, 1997.

Krementsov, Leonid. *K. G. Paustovskii. Zhizn' i tvorchestvo.* Moscow: Prosveshchenie, 1982.

—. ed. *Russkaia literatura XX veka. Tom 2: 1940-1990-e gody.* Moscow: Academia, 2005.

Leiderman, N. L., and M. N. Lipovetskii. *Sovremennaia russkaia literatura. Kniga 1: Literatura 'Ottepeli' (1953-1968).* Moscow: Editorial UPSS, 2001.

Levitskii, Lev, ed. *Vospominaniia o Konstantine Paustovskom.* Moscow: Sovetskii pisatel', 1983.

L'vov, Sergei. *Konstantin Paustovskii. Kritiko-biograficheskii ocherk.* Moscow: Detskaia literatura, 1956.

MacKay, Carol Hanbery. "Biography as Reflected Autobiography: The Self-Creation of Anne Thackeray Ritchie." In *Revealing Lives: Autobiography, Biography, and Gender*, edited by Susan Groag Bell and Marilyn Yalom, 65-79. New York: SUNY Press, 1990.

Mil'shtein, I. "Kaluzhskii intsident." *Ogonek*, no. 14 (1989): 22-25.

Nadel, Ira Bruce. *Biography: Fiction, Fact and Form*. New York: St. Martin Press. 1984.

Nepomnyashchy, Catherine T. *Abram Tertz and the Poetics of Crime*. New Haven: Yale University Press, 1995.

Paustovskii, Konstantin. *Sobranie sochinenii v 6 tomakh*. Moscow: Khudozhestvennaia literatura, 1957.

Pomerantsev, V. "Ob iskrennosti v literature." In *Ottepel'. 1953-56. Stranitsy sovetskoi literatury*, edited with a preface by S. I. Chuprynin, 48-60. Moscow: Moskovskii rabochii, 1989.

Taubman, William. *Khrushchev: The Man and his Era*. New York: W. W. Norton & Company, 1990.

Tomashevskii, Boris. "Literatura i biografiia." *Kniga i revoliutsiia*, no. 4 (28) (1923): 6-28.

Vinokur, Grigorii. *Biografiia i kul'tura*. Moscow: Gos. akademiia khouzhestvennykh nauk, 1927.

Woolf, Virginia. *Selected Essays*. Edited, with an introduction and notes, by David Bradshaw. Oxford: Oxford University Press, 2008.

Yalom, Marilyn. "Biography as Autobiography: Adele Hugo, Witness of Her Husband's Life." In *Revealing Lives: Autobiography, Biography, and Gender*, edited by Susan Groag Bell and Marilyn Yalom, 53-65. New York: SUNY Press, 1990.

Zabolotskii, N. *Stikhotvoreniia i poemy*. Rostov-na-Donu: Irbis, 1999.

Hans Christian Andersen and the Soviet Biedermeier[1]

Ilya Kukulin

1. Formulating the Problem: The Concept of Cultural Transfer

This article will discuss how the fairy tales of Hans Christian Andersen were received and reinterpreted in Soviet culture of the 1950s–70s. The study's methodological "frame" is the theory of cultural transfer, whose groundwork was laid in 1985-86 by Michel Espagne and Michael Werner, who established the "Transferts culturels franco-allemand" laboratory at the Centre National de la Recherche Scientifique in Paris. The theory was subsequently developed in Russia in works by Ekaterina Dmitrieva and several other authors.

According to the theory of cultural transfer, when a given cultural phenomenon is "transferred" to an "alien" milieu, it is not simply "translated" (whether literally or metaphorically) into another language, but is also substantively modified according to the particular features of this milieu; and in this new context, it may take on meanings entirely different from those it had in its original setting. As Espagne puts it:

> Semantic appropriation profoundly alters an object as it transitions from one system to another.... The interpretation of Kant by academic philosophers of the Third Republic is no less interesting, nor should it be seen as a distortion of the original, for having turned the German philosopher into a spokesman of secular republican morality; for interpreting him other than as his German contemporaries had.[2]

Dmitrieva develops this viewpoint:

> The discovery of Bergson in Russia proves to have been unexpectedly prepared (and adjusted) by the previous fascination with Nietzsche, who would

---

[1] This research was financed through the "5-100" program of government support of leading universities of the Russian Federation.
[2] Espagne, *Les transferts culturels franco-allemands*, 21.

seem to have nothing in common with Bergson, and who in turn, having been a great admirer of Dostoevsky, was originally read in Russia through the prism of Dostoevsky.... The Russian "romantic" Schiller is not tantamount to the historical (German) Schiller; but it is precisely as transformed by the early nineteenth-century Russian consciousness that he would go on to profoundly influence Russian literature, in particular, Dostoevsky.... It is essential that "cultural transfer" encompass, aside from the realm of the intellectual proper, also economic, demographic, and mental life.[3]

The main idea of this article is that Andersen was a key author for late-Soviet "overground" culture—that is, the sphere not of the underground, but of the mainstream and officially sanctioned—because this culture, influenced by certain sociopolitical conditions, had developed a trend that may be called the Soviet Biedermeier. The Danish author's works were associated with certain stylistic and psychological experiments in Soviet literature, sung poetry, and film; but by and large, the reception of Andersen reinforced the conservative stylizing and escapist tendencies of Soviet culture of the late 1960s and early 1970s, and lent these trends a cultural legitimacy. At the same time, in the course of this development, a new image of Andersen himself was formed, one that would prominently feature stoicism, grief, and an inability to adapt to life. I will attempt to analyze both the "liberating" and the "obscuring" functions of the adaptation of Andersen, and the variants of the image of him produced in Soviet culture of this period.

2. Hans Christian Andersen as Biedermeier Writer

Literary scholars have frequently noted that Andersen's fairy tales are close to the aesthetics of the German Biedermeier of the 1830s–40s. The Biedermeier period contributed to the development of children's literature (especially illustrated children's books), insofar as it was in this period that the cult of the emotionally close bourgeois family became entrenched in the German states.[4] Andersen grew up in poverty, but many of his tales take place in well-off middle-class homes in which a domestic servant is employed; we might recall, for instance, the episode with the fish and the cook in "The Steadfast Tin Soldier." His characters constantly come in the form of speaking versions of the sort of objects characteristic of everyday life in this same middle class: teapots,

---

3 Dmitrieva, "Teoriia kul'turnogo transfera."
4 Ewers, "Romantik," 122–24.

fine toys, porcelain figurines on the mantelpiece. Andersen's tales were doubly addressed;[5] not just adults, but also children—an important part of the audience—were to imagine all these items. Sentimentality, the poeticization of everyday life, various sorts of eccentricity, and light humor—all these constants of Andersenian poetics are likewise characteristic Biedermeier features. Key motifs of this style include the sentimental depiction of an innocent little girl—and we find similar imagery in Andersen in "The Little Match Girl" and "Thumbelina."

Heinrich Detering has suggested that the particular features of Andersen's tales are in part due to the fact that in the 1840s, the author was first and foremost oriented toward the German literary market—in which, in this period, the Biedermeier style was the most widely understood and recognized.[6] However, the elements described are preserved also in many later Andersen works of the 1850s–60s, when the author's need to find a market for his books was not so urgent, and when the Biedermeier's time had already passed (according to the most common periodization, it is considered to have come to an end in 1848): "The Farmyard Cock and the Weathercock" (1859), "In the Children's Room" (1865), or "The Windmill" (1865).

Nevertheless, as Jürg Glauser and Hans-Heino Ewers have shown, in his stories Andersen rarely comes across as anything like a "pure" representative of the Biedermeier. Glauser observes that in his prose, including the fairy tales, Andersen regularly violates the usual taboos of this style. For example, the descriptions of amatory feelings in "The Little Mermaid" (1837) or of the main character's inner dualism in "The Marsh King's Daughter" (1858) are unconventionally expressive compared with the Biedermeier reticence in these matters. The irony characteristic of Andersen's tales, moreover, is close in tone to the romantic irony of Heine.[7] Another important feature of these works that was untypical for the Biedermeier is the constant motif of how social status is invariably fluid: at any moment the "last" might become "first," should they be judged according to their inner character, and the "first," "last." This motif, which is characteristic of stories of magic, is in Andersen maximally spiritualized in the Protestant vein, quite notably in "The Ugly Duckling," "The Emperor's New Clothes," "The Little Mermaid," and in that same "Marsh King's Daughter."

---

5   Glauser, *Skandinavische Literaturgeschichte*, 172.
6   Detering, "H. C. Andersen's 'Schiller Fairy Tale.'"
7   Glauser, *Skandinavische Literaturgeschichte*, 182.

3. The Soviet Biedermeier

In 1984, the cultural historian and philosopher Virgil Nemoianu published the book *The Taming of Romanticism*, which proposed to extend the term "Biedermeier," familiar from the history of German culture, to various European literatures in 1815-48, from British to Russian. "Nemoianu sees literature [of this period] as a set of compromises aimed at ... taming the early or 'high' romanticism."[8] My own hypothesis is that an aesthetics analogous to the Biedermeier may, under conditions described by Nemoianu, be reproduced in other periods as well—wherever and whenever it becomes necessary to "tame" the radicalization undergone by art in the immediately preceding epoch; to counter political anxieties with domesticity, coziness, light humor, and sentimentality.[9]

A significant portion of "overground," officially sanctioned Soviet culture of the late 1960s / early 1980s—the time now referred to as the "long seventies"—was of precisely this nature. On both sides of the "iron curtain," societies were recovering from the shocks of the 1960s. But in Soviet culture, the "conciliatory" tendencies were particularly notable in comparison to Western societies.[10] A great deal of songwriters, movie directors, and writers sought to adapt and "tame" the unsettling revelations that had crashed upon society in the previous decade. Some of these discoveries consisted of information partially allowed into print about the historical catastrophes of the twentieth century: the Gulag and Great Terror, and the enormous number of Soviet casualties of the Second World War. In the 1960s, many people found out about all of this not just from official publications, but from an ever more voluminous range of samizdat. Also discovered were works of formerly "displaced" pre-revolutionary literature and twentieth-century Western cultures, which involved unfamiliar—specifically, modernist—conceptions of subjectivity.

One of the most important representatives of the Biedermeier style in nineteenth-century Russian culture, as Ilya Vinitsky has shown, was the poet Vasilii Zhukovsky. Analyzing Zhukovsky's later (1840s) works, Vinitsky comments: "The idyllic character of the Biedermeier is ... deceptive: it serves as a sort of defense against the chaotic and demonic forces

---

8   Vaiskopf, *Vliublennyi demiurg*, 9.
9   Kukulin, "Legalizovannoe zaklinanie v inter'ere sovetskogo bidermaiera."
10 A prominent example of a "conciliatory" work in the West would be George Lucas's *Star Wars*, which adapted, for mass culture, the fashion for Eastern occultism and the various nontraditional spiritual doctrines that had become a notable component of the 1960s counterculture. *Star Wars* lent these doctrines a comfy and cozy image: cf. the figure of the teacher Yoda, with his clearly foreign accent (a hint at the many Eastern gurus who became famous in the US in the 1960s), and the benediction "May the Force be with you," which vividly recalls the phrasing of Carlos Castaneda.

that always threatened the happy tranquility of the quiet conservative."[11] The same could be said of many Soviet works in the period under discussion: they did not just adapt the anthropological and aesthetic discoveries of the 1960s, but were also meant to create a sensation of sentimental warmth that would counter the growing crisis in Soviet ideology and the Soviet regime as a whole. Symptomatic of this crisis were the ongoing arrests of dissidents (which one could find out about from the broadcasts of Western radio stations); vapid meetings of party, labor union, and other organizations; the constant shortage of goods in stores; and the emigration of many of the brightest representatives of the creative intelligentsia.

The combination of two kinds of meaning—adaptive and defensive—enables us to speak metaphorically of the central trend of overground culture of the 1970s as a Soviet Biedermeier. This trend was internally consolidated not via a stylistic unity, but by a kinship in emotional tone: works characteristic of the Soviet Biedermeier featured a fusion of melancholy, irony, and sentimental tenderness. Also typical of this trend was the cult of childhood, the home, and private life—the latter two motifs having been definitive for the historical nineteenth-century Biedermeier as well. Works of various genres and art forms can be categorized under the rubric of the Soviet Biedermeier, for instance: the musical film *The Straw Hat* (*Solomennaia shliapka*; dir. Leonid Kvinikhidze, 1974); the film *The Irony of Fate, or, Have a Nice Steam!* (*Ironiia sud'by, ili S legkim parom*; dir. Eldar Riazanov, 1975); the TV films *Hello, I'm Your Aunt!* (*Zdravstvuite, ia vasha tetia!*; dir. Viktor Titov, 1975) and *An Ordinary Miracle* (*Obyknovennoe chudo*; dir. Mark Zakharov, 1978); the songs of the husband-and-wife team of Sergei and Tatyana Nikitin, especially those set to the poetry of Iunna Morits; and the TV show "The 'Thirteen Chairs' Tavern" ("Kabachok '13 Stul'ev'"). Certain stars—for instance, Andrei Mironov and Zinovii Gerdt—physically incarnated on stage and screen, in their plasticity, their particular manner of acting or performing songs, the values of the Soviet Biedermeier.

The Soviet Biedermeier's "work" toward taming earlier aesthetic discoveries is clearly seen in the film *The Irony of Fate, or, Have a Nice Steam!*[12] This is a sentimental melodrama about a woman named Nadia and a man named Zhenia who live in different cities (Leningrad and Moscow, respectively), but through a string of humorous accidents suddenly

---

11 Vinitskii, *Dom Tolkovatelia*, 240.
12 The film was adapted from Emil Braginsky and Eldar Riazanov's play *Have a Nice Steam! or, Once on New Year's Eve* (*S legkim parom! ili Odnazhdi v novogodniuiu noch'*), which was written in 1969 and had a successful run in several theaters.

become acquainted on New Year's eve. They develop strong feelings, and after long wavering and being apart for a time, they realize that they cannot live without one another. The film involves the "taming" of certain aesthetic discoveries of the previous decade: the soundtrack includes poetry (sung to a guitar accompaniment) of the early Evgenii Evtushenko and Marina Tsvetaeva that had become well known in the USSR precisely in the 1960s.

In the scene in which Nadia realizes that after their parting, she simply must see Zhenia again, there is a voiceover by actress Valentina Talyzina of Aleksandr Kochetkov's (1900-53) tragic poem "The Ballad of the Smoke-Filled Train Car" ("Ballada o prokurennom vagone"), which was written in 1932 but circulated for many years solely in handwritten copies—before the word "samizdat" came into use. It was published—and this date is quite characteristic—only in 1966, in the *Day of Poetry* (*Den' poezii*) almanac.[13] This poem, which presents romantic love as the primary opportunity to save one's soul, had previously seemed overly hopeless and idealistic; now it was an ideal fit for the new emotional context. In the movie, Talyzina provided the voice for the Polish actress Barbara Brylska (who barely spoke any Russian), and so Talyzina's "incorporeal" voiceover may be perceived either as a verbalization of Nadia's thoughts; or as the voice of a suprapersonal subject (e.g., fate personified), attesting to the feelings the characters dare not confess even to themselves. Several elements of the film's plot directly allude to the tradition of early nineteenth-century Western European romanticism, which Riazanov likewise "domesticates," just as representatives of the historical Biedermeier had done.[14]

The emotional program of the Soviet Biedermeier is most clearly expressed in the Nikitins' song based on this poem by Aleksandr Velichansky:

> And it was so clear to us all,
> so clear! so clear!
> ....
> that life was in vain,
> that life was beautiful,
> that we will all be happy
> at some point, God willing
> ....

---

13 Published by Lev Ozerov.
14 Lesskis, "Fil'm 'Ironiia sud'by ...'"

To the strains of violins,
to the blizzard's howl,
let us agree to love one another
with all our strength.

И всем нам стало ясно,
так ясно! так ясно!
....
что жизнь была напрасна,
что жизнь была прекрасна,
что все мы будем счастливы
когда-нибудь, Бог даст
....

под скрипок переливы
под вьюги завыванье
условимся друг друга
любить что было сил ...[15]

In the intelligentsia milieu, this program was perceived as nonconformist, since it defied the Soviet mobilizational ideology, and cultivated the values of private life. However, in reality, it was more escapist than oppositionist.[16]

The Soviet Biedermeier was formed from tonally suitable works, even if the rest of the oeuvre of the authors thereof did not correspond to its basic emotional patterns. Most of Velichansky's other poems, for instance, have nothing of the Biedermeier about them: they are gloomy, at times caustically bitter, and often complex in their language. They could not be printed in Soviet publications both because of their emotional tone and because of their aesthetics. The poem just cited—from the poet's only collection to be published in the USSR until the perestroika period—appeared in the journal *New World* (*Novyi mir*) in 1969; but the song based on it was phenomenally popular among the Soviet intelligentsia in the 1970s.

---

15 Velichanskii, *Pepel slov*, 1: 101-2. For the sake of simplicity, Nikitin altered the text slightly: in the first line quoted, he sings: *I stalo nam tak iasno* ("And it was so clear to us"), and in the third from last, *pod zavyvan'e v'iugi* ("to the blizzard's howl").
16 Kukulin, "Legalizovannoe zaklinanie v inter'ere sovetskogo bidermaiera."

4. The Andersen Boom: The "Long Seventies"

Andersen's tales were published in the USSR more or less on a regular basis, and it was rare that he would be called an "alien" writer, even in the period of the xenophobic "war on cosmopolitanism." But it was specifically during the "long seventies" that interest in Andersen truly exploded in the USSR. This is the period that would see the greatest number of live-action film and TV adaptations of works by the Danish author: *An Amazing Story, Like a Fairy Tale* (*Udivitel'naia istoriia, pokohzaia na skazku*; based on "The Ugly Duckling"; dir. Boris Dolin, 1966); *An Old, Old Tale* (*Staraia, staraia skazka*; dir. Nadezhda Kosheverova, 1968); *The Little Mermaid* (*Rusalochka*; dir. Vladimir Bychkov, 1976); *The Princess and the Pea* (*Printsessa na goroshine*; dir. Boris Rytsarev, 1976); *The Nightingale* (*Solovei*; dir. Nadezhda Kosheverova, 1979); *The Will-o'-the-Wisps* (*Bluzhdaiushchie ogon'ki*; dir. Gytis Lukšas, 1979); and *The Autumn Gift of the Fairies* (*Osennii podarok fei*; based on "The Galoshes of Fortune"; dir. Vladimir Bychkov, 1984). This list does not include Nikolai Aleksandrovich's musical film *The Secret of the Snow Queen* (*Taina Snezhnoi korolevy*, 1986), as it represents a considerable alteration of the plot of Andersen's tale—its main characters are the teen Kay and Gerda, who find out that a fairy tale has been written about them.[17]

This same period saw the Malysh publishing house's release of two books for children that explain how Andersen's works *should be understood*: Gennadii Tsyferov's *My Andersen* (*Moi Andersen*, 1969; the title clearly alludes to Marina Tsvetaeva's essay "My Pushkin" ["Moi Pushkin"]—first published in the USSR in the journal *Science and Life* [*Nauka i zhizn'*] in 1967 [no. 2] —thereby underscoring Andersen's lofty status in the canon); and *How I Illustrated the Tales of Andersen* (*Kak ia risoval skazki G. Kh. Andersena*, 1981) by Anatolii Kokorin, one of the USSR's most prolific and sought-after illustrators of the Danish writer; a new edition of this pamphlet came out in 1988, after the artist's death.[18] It was extremely rare for such critical texts aimed at children to be published in the USSR, and Andersen may have been the only author to be deemed worthy of two such compositions at once.

At the same time, it becomes increasingly difficult to distinguish, in the Soviet public sphere, between the interpretation of the authorial intentions and styles of Andersen and Evgenii Schwartz.[19] Plays by Schwartz—who frequently refashioned Andersen plots (*The Emperor's New Clothes*

---

17 See Andrei Rogatchevski's contribution to this volume.
18 Kokorin died in 1987.
19 See Boris Wolfson's contribution to this volume.

/ *The Naked King* [*Golyi korol'*], *The Shadow* [*Ten'*], and *The Snow Queen* [*Snezhnaia koroleva*])—were among the most in demand in theaters in the 1960s, and were adapted into films (for instance, *Cain the Eighteenth* [*Kain XVIII*] by Nadezhda Kosheverova). He was perceived in the USSR (as well as in other countries of Europe[20]) as a markedly political author, an anti-totalitarian, requiring a certain risk and daring on the part of his interpreters—and thus marking a contrast with the fairly "moderate" Andersen. In 1962, Nikolai Akimov's revival of Schwartz's play *The Dragon* (*Drakon*) at the Leningrad Comedy Theater was removed from the repertoire after just a single theatrical season—throughout which, moreover, newspaper articles had been published hinting that in the play Akimov was drawing too much of a parallel between Stalinism and Nazism.[21] That same year, a young Mark Zakharov staged this play at Moscow State University's Student Theater; here the actor playing the dragon came onstage wearing a blatantly recognizable "Stalinist" uniform jacket.[22] The show was banned after seventeen performances—immediately after Nikita Khrushchev railed against avant-garde artists at Moscow's Manezh exhibition hall. However, in the late 1960s, the situation changed. In this period, that of the Soviet Biedermeier, the cinematic image of Schwartz comes to resemble Andersen: an author, that is, of cozy, touching, and melancholic plays tinged with a subtle irony, and having nothing to do with political issues. Such is the impression of Schwartz, for instance, given by the same Zakharov's film *An Ordinary Miracle* (1978).

In order to pinpoint just why Andersen proved so important for the Soviet Biedermeier era, we should briefly outline the Danish writer's reputation, and the reception of his aesthetics, in the preceding period, from the mid-1950s to early 1960s.

5. The Prehistory: Andersen in the USSR between 1955 and 1965

Works by Andersen were published in the USSR, as has been mentioned, but interpretive articles about him were rare. The situation abruptly changed in 1955, when the 150th anniversary of the author's birth was

---

20 Thus for instance, the East German nonconformist dramatist Heiner Müller, an author of sharply political plays, in 1969 adapted *The Dragon* into a libretto titled *Drachenoper* (coauthored with his wife Ginka Tscholakova), for which Paul Dessau, formerly resident composer at Bertolt Brecht's Berliner Ensemble theater, composed the music. Dessau, Muller, and Tscholakova's work was performed that same year at East Berlin's State Opera.
21 Zabolotniaia, "Delo o 'Drakone.'"
22 Soifer, "Akademik i student."

marked in the USSR with some fanfare: suddenly there were quite a few journal articles and essays about him.[23] One of the most prominent in a series of jubilee events was the publication of the large Andersen collection *Tales and Stories* (*Skazki i istorii*), with an introduction by Konstantin Paustovsky titled "The Great Storyteller" ("Velikii skazochnik"); soon thereafter, in 1956, Paustovsky included another piece on Andersen in his book of essays *The Golden Rose: Notes on a Writer's Work* (*Zolotaia roza. Zametki o pisatel'skom trude*).

The 1955 preface featured a Biedermeieresque description of Andersen's hometown of Odense and the assertion, requisite for Soviet articles, that Andersen was close to the "people of labor." But this text also included three motifs that to all appearances were important to Paustovsky personally. The first was the constant highlighting, in Andersen's image, of features of the "self-made man." Paustovsky himself had been one such person—or more precisely, had been forced to begin everything anew after the revolution, which had "nullified" all the advantages of his having been born into a middle-class family. The second motif is the touching depiction of the everyday life of a prosperous family in 1899: as a child, Paustovsky received his first-ever Andersen book as a New Year's present in 1900. In Soviet literature, the private life of the prerevolutionary well-off was a subject, if not entirely forbidden, at least risky in 1955. The third motif, and the main one for Paustovsky, was the proclamation of the cult of fantasy, which transforms life and is described in the spirit of the romantics and symbolists. The workings of fantasy are depicted in this preface through a Freudian psychoanalytic conception, albeit one the author could only hint at:

> I cannot recall which writer has said that fairy tales are made of the same substance as dreams.
>
> In dreams, the particulars of our real life come together freely and whimsically in a great number of combinations, like the multicolored glass fragments of a kaleidoscope.
>
> The work carried out in dreams by our twilight consciousness is performed, in waking hours, by our boundless imagination. Hence, clearly, the idea of the resemblance between dreams and fairy tales.[24]

---

23 Braude, "Andersen v russkoi i sovetskoi kritike," 317.
24 Paustovskii, "Velikii skazochnik," 9-10.

For Paustovsky, Andersen is first and foremost a poet who, in exercising creative freedom, uses his unpredictable fantasy and improvisational gift to make the world a better, more humane place.[25] Andersen's crucial feature is his talent for being free.

Appearing at the same time were two more responses to the poetics of Andersen's tales, albeit less obvious than in Paustovsky's case.

That same year when the preface to *Tales and Stories* was published (1955), the young satirist Feliks Krivin (1928-2016), who lived in Ukraine and was making a successful career writing fables in Russian (this didactic genre was quite common in Soviet literature, flourishing especially in the late 1940s and early 1950s), suddenly decided to change his style and principles of work, and began producing verse and prose fairy tales and parables that became a sort of first draft of the Soviet literary Biedermeier.

Krivin's own recollection of his decision to make this change is suffused with a rather Andersenian spirit. In a recent memoiristic essay, his longtime friend Samuil Kur reproduces Krivin's oral account—clearly embellishing and supplementing, but probably preserving the factual basis:

> He took a trip to a district town in Transcarpathia. Hotel accommodations were arranged ahead of time and, having finished the business of his day, he entered the small, cozy room. After the frosty outdoors, pleasant were the semi-darkness and the still-warm tiled stove [*gollandka*], next to which stood an emergency bundle of firewood and a beat-up old whisk broom. Warming his hands on the stove's tiled sides, Feliks Krivin opened its cast-iron door and threw a little log onto the smoldering embers. In the process, he almost also threw in the whisk broom, which had gotten caught on the log. Taking a seat a little bit away, he started to watch as the sprightly tongues of flame came to life. The log flared—and at that very moment, the thought flashed in his brain: the whisk broom... it could have been leaping after its beloved... into the fire... it could have burnt up... This was a sudden epiphany. This was the birth of a fairy tale....
>
> Fables were getting too constricting for him. You have to follow strict rules, always bring everything around to the moral. You can't really let yourself go, and the reader has no room for the flight of the imagination— they're served up a readymade moral. But now everything would change, he'd write fairy tales! Like Andersen! No, not like Andersen. After all, in order to express even the most profound thought, it's hardly necessary to use a

---

25 For more on Paustovsky's preface, see Marina Balina's contribution to this volume.

lot of words. His tales would be brief. Like the flaring of a flame. And their main characters would be Everything that Exists in the Whole Wide World.[26]

It is entirely possible that Paustovsky's preface to the Andersen edition had been one of the impulses spurring Krivin to decide to alter his literary life. Krivin wrote a fairytale play, *The Paper Rose* (*Bumazhnaia roza*, 1960), whose title, and the name of the eponymous heroine, may be read as a "nod" to Paustovsky.

Krivin seized upon one of Andersen's key devices: he wrote fairytale parables in which "freedom of speech" was granted to inanimate objects. However, while Andersen's own wordplay in the original Danish does not come through in Russian translations of him (nor, for that matter, in English), in his works Krivin made constant use of wordplay. Strangely, in light of the abundance of material on Krivin and how well known he is, it is only quite recently that the linguistic features of his prose have begun to be studied.[27] His favorite device is the ambiguous use of a word or expression of longstanding metaphorical meaning such that this lexical unit or turn of phrase is simultaneously direct and metaphorical:

> Having completed his higher education in the forest, Oak, instead of going to a construction project, decided to lay down roots in the city. And since there were no other open spots, he got a position as a Lamppost in the municipal park, in the darkest corner—a regular conservation area for lovers.
>
> Lamppost did not take his work lightly;[28] so well did he illuminate this previously secluded spot that not a single lover remained there.
>
> "And these are the young people!" lamented Post. "Young people who, you'd think, ought to be drawn to the light! How benighted they are, how uncouth!"[29]
>
> "Lamppost" ("Fonarnyi stolb," before 1964)

Parables of this sort made Krivin quite popular in the 1960s; in a later interview he would single out this decade as the time of his greatest

---

26 Kur, "Nastoiashchii iumor vsegda grustnyi." Kur reproduces the same account, but without mention of Andersen, in another essay on Krivin, published in the journal *Slovo/Word* in 2015. In the same 2016 essay quoted in the text, Kur cites the author's widow to mention that Krivin's home library had been adorned with books by Hoffmann and Andersen (who had been influenced by the former).
27 Beregovskaia, "Realizatsiia stilisticheskikh potentsii khiazma v tvorchestve Feliksa Krivina."
28 An attempt to convey the wordplay of *vzialsia za delo s ogon'kom*, "undertook his business with gusto," lit., "with a spark" or "twinkle of light"—trans.
29 Krivin, *Poluskazki*, 108.

recognition.[30] On the whole, his wordplay had two quite clearly "readable" aims: to critique ideologized Soviet discourse (according to fairly rational and consistently applied rules) and undermine the enduring meanings of everyday language.

Both Krivin's story of how he came to write fairy tales and the whole milieu of his works of the late 1950s and 1960s attest to the fact that the most important social context of his oeuvre was the post-Stalin period's ideological rehabilitation of private life.[31] Manifestations of this rehabilitation included the mass construction of the *khrushchevki*, which enabled many to receive private apartments; and, for instance, the 1961 Moscow exhibition "Art in Everyday Life," from which Soviet citizens could learn about modern design in furniture and utensils.

> The very fact that an exhibition of *household items*, items intended for everyone, had been organized at the capital's 'main' exhibit hall—this constituted a revision, not so much of the approach to everyday life, as of the whole value system of the 'ordinary Soviet person.' After all—*volens nolens*—the ordinary person suddenly turned out to be a *subject*!... The need to aestheticize everydayness in stylistically concrete forms—namely, in the spirit of (for lack of a better word) functionalism—emerged as an integral sign of *change* in general.[32]

Krivin's fairytale parables allegorized the psychological collisions occurring in everyday (and, much more rarely, professional) human relations—roughly as Andersen does in "The Windmill."

> The curious, breezy[33] Little Window [*Fortochka*] looked out at the courtyard ("I wonder who Sheet is getting herself all tied up in knots for now?"[34]) and saw the following picture.
>
> Flying around the courtyard, breaking tree branches and knocking plaster off the walls, was big Soccer Ball. It was a real kick to look at him,[35] and she was lost in admiration. "What beauty," she thought, "what strength!"

---

30 Gavrosh, "Poslednee interv'iu Feliksa Krivina."
31 Among many works on this subject, see for instance Reid, "Destalinization and Taste"; Lebina, *Povsednevnost' epokhi kosmosa i kukuruzy.*
32 Frumkina, "Bez narkoza."
33 An attempt to convey the wordplay of *vetrianaia*, "flighty," lit. "windy"; the *fortochka* is the small window-within-a-window one opens to get some air—trans.
34 An attempt to convey the wordplay of *po kom eto sokhnet Prostynia*—"who Sheet is pining for," lit., "drying out for"—trans.
35 An attempt to convey the wordplay of *Miach byl v udare*, "Ball was in fine form," lit., "in a kick [or blow]"—trans.

Little Window really wanted to meet Ball, but he kept flying and flying around, apparently uninterested in making any acquaintances.[36]

"Little Window" ("Fortochka," before 1964)

Krivin's works resonate with the Biedermeier aesthetic in a number of characteristics. They can be both sentimental and melancholic—this especially applies to the play *The Paper Rose* and the "A Bit of Lyric" ("Chut'-chut' liriki") section of the 1964 collection *Semi-Fairy Tales* (*Poluskazki*). Another Biedermeier feature, and one that is far more pronounced in Krivin than in Andersen, is the yearning for a social order that would be grounded in common sense.[37] The constant target of Krivin's barbs were Stalinesque, dilettantish but zealous administrators, power-mad demagogues, or careless, shortsighted people—everyone who made the social order so hard to bear.

In the latter half of the 1950s, Krivin reworked the aesthetic of Andersen's tales so as to create an artistic language for the new epoch—for a time when private and domestic life stood rehabilitated. But however much they resonated with Andersen, Krivin's early works had certain quite substantive differences from the Biedermeier, first and foremost their overt social engagement. In these earlier pieces, Krivin is either demonstratively allegorical, hence rational (and rationalism was uncharacteristic of the Biedermeier, whether of the historical or Soviet variety); or he abstains from this style's characteristic sentimentalism in favor of an outright romanticism, as in the well-known story "I Was a Tarpan" ("Ia byl tarpanom," 1966). Moreover, when Krivin engages in social satire, he does so with a causticness untypical of the Biedermeier.

In the course of his evolution, the writer maintained his inclination for parables and wordplay; but, despite his youthful espousal (if the above-cited account is true) of brevity, his works came to include some that were fairly lengthy. From the 1970s–2000s, Krivin's fairy tales and verse came to seem less and less like Andersen vis-à-vis their primary device (the participation of inanimate objects), and more and more like the works of Eastern European modernist writers (for instance, the prose of Julian Tuwim or Stanisław Jerzy Lec). From the early 1970s on, Krivin periodically wrote stories that dealt directly, unallegorically, with totalitarianism. Such for instance was "Exhibit Item No. 212" ("Eksponat

---

36 Krivin, *Poluskazki*, 97.
37 The significance of the social-structure theme for Krivin was noted as early as 1966 in a review article by the young writer Sergei Dovlatov, who would go on to be one of the major figures in Russian literature of the latter half of the twentieth century. Dovlatov, review of F. Krivin, *Kaleidoskop*.

No. 212," c. 1971), the two main characters of which, an investigator and a suspect, are united by their shared experience of having been in the Gulag.[38] The book that included this story, *Imitation of the Theater* (*Podrazhanie teatru*), was published in 1971, only to be immediately banned, with much of its print run destroyed.

Another author who became well known in the latter half of the 1950s and who engaged in an aesthetic dialogue with Andersen was the poet and singer-songwriter Bulat Okudzhava (1924-97). Especially characteristic in this regard is "The Song of the Paper Soldier" ("Pesenka o bumazhnom soldatike," 1959), which alludes to the plot of "The Steadfast Tin Soldier":

Fire? I don't mind. Go on! You'll go?
And one day he went marching,
And then he died for nothing,
For he was a paper soldier.[39]

В огонь? Ну что ж, иди! Идешь?
И он шагнул однажды,
и там сгорел он ни за грош:
ведь был солдат бумажный.[40]

"The real exploit of a toy hero is a theme that harks to Andersen," as Dmitrii Bykov has observed.[41] Aside from that work by the Danish storyteller, another intertextual source of the song would be the much-anthologized Lermontov poem "The Sail" ("Parus"): the lines "And he would keep cursing his fate, / No quiet life he wanted, / And he kept asking: Fire, fire!"[42] allude to Lermontov's "And he, restless, asks for a storm, / As if there is peace in storms!"

On the whole, Okudzhava's song combines elements reminiscent of the Biedermeier—e.g., the emphasis on the soldier's "toyness"—with a psychological allegory entirely opposed to the Biedermeier spirit: the song tells of a character who is ready to go to his death in defiance of his settled, calm life. In the Soviet context, this allegory took on a political

---

38 The story's epigraph is from George Santayana—which in the 1960s would have been unthinkable for a Krivin work, both because his short didactic texts had no need of epigraphs, and because Santayana's name would have seemed odd in the "minimalist" everyday context of the early Krivin.
39 Trans. cited from Beumers, *Pop Culture Russia!*, 204.
40 Okudzhava, *Stikhotvoreniia*, 177.
41 Bykov, *Okudzhava*, 18.
42 Trans. cited from Beumers, *Pop Culture Russia!*, 204.

meaning, insofar as it stated—in the spirit of the existentialists—that a sacrifice made by a constitutionally self-sacrificing person is in vain; that the true value of sacrifice lies in one's ability (here, the paper soldier's) to take a risk and to challenge the world.

Here we might note the resonance between "The Paper Soldier" and Krivin's plot about a whisk broom and a firewood log: this aesthetic of doom was most likely influenced by the experience of a generation that had lived through war and postwar repression.

From the 1950s on, Okudzhava's works developed a consistent set of motifs and a corresponding subgenre that may be termed Andersenian: song-tales based on the fantastic transformation of everyday household items. In "The Paper Soldier" this is obvious, but a similar approach may be seen also in the earlier song "The Midnight Trolley" ("Polnochnyi trolleibus," 1957).

> Midnight trolley, open your door!
> I know how in the chilly midnight
> Your passengers, your sailors
> Come to my aid.
>
> With them more than once I've left my troubles behind,
> We've rubbed shoulders together…
> Just imagine, what kindness there is
> In silence,
> In silence.[43]

> Полночный троллейбус, мне дверь отвори!
> Я знаю, как в зябкую полночь
> твои пассажиры—матросы твои—
> приходят
> на помощь.
>
> Я с ними не раз уходил от беды,
> я к ним прикасался плечами …
> Как много, представьте себе, доброты
> в молчанье,
> в молчанье.[44]

---

43 Translator unknown; cited from *Transitions*, 2: nos. 2-3 (1997): 13.
44 Okudzhava, *Stikhotvoreniia*, 140.

Crucially, in this world of transformed items, human relations seem to be under a magnifying glass: in Okudzhava's "fairytale" poems, it is as if trust, love, breakups, and antipathy become individual characters. His poems are not just sentimental; sentimentality becomes the basis for a new social identity, or more precisely, a new norm. This is directly proclaimed in one of Okudzhava's most famous songs, "Let Us Exclaim" ("Davaite vosklitsat'," 1976).

The optics of "everyday magic" as it appears in "The Midnight Trolley" or, for instance, another of Okudzhava's songs, "Farewell to a New Year's Tree" ("Proshchanie s novogodnei elkoi"), had been previously worked out in Soviet poetry by Mikhail Svetlov, whom Bykov calls, quite justly in my view, one of Okudzhava's teachers.[45] However, Svetlov's poems lack this new view of sentimentality: half-joking and half-serious, his persona is ready to admit his "political incorrectness."

> Comrade! O hymner of attacks and cannons,
> Sculptor of fine human statues,
> Forgive me,–I take pity on little old ladies,
> But this is my only failing.
>
> (Mikhail Svetlov, "The Little Old Lady" ["Starushka"], 1927)

> Товарищ! Певец наступлений и пушек,
> Ваятель красных человеческих статуй,
> Простите меня,—я жалею старушек,
> Но это—единственный мой недостаток.[46]

When the fairytale plot features sentimentality as a new form, Okudzhava's poetics appears, paradoxically, closer to Andersen than to Svetlov. This is especially notable when the fairytale milieu "dislodges" metaphorical meanings and the possibility of a straightforward interpretation. Perhaps the most striking of the early Okudzhava's "autonomous" fairytale texts is "The Old King" ("Staryi korol'," 1961?) (which in concert Okudzhava sometimes referred to as "A Little Song about an Old, Sick, Tired King Who Set out to Conquer a Foreign Country, and about What Came of This" ["Pesenka o starom, bol'nom, ustalom korole, kotoryi otpravilsia zavoevyvat' chuzhuiu stranu, i o tom, chto iz etogo poluchilos'"]). Its "modern" form, and the image of the "troop" standing "in the middle of the courtyard"–"five sad soldiers, five cheerful soldiers

---

45 Bykov, *Okudzhava*, 320-37, 340.
46 Svetlov, *Stikhotvoreniia*, 116.

and a lance corporal [*efreitor*]"—allude to the experience of the war generation;[47] the Workers' and Peasants' Red Army restored the rank of lance-corporal in 1940 (per Soviet military regulations, this was an aide to the squad commander); and the commander was, apparently, the king himself, whose provisions consisted of "a pack of cheap tobacco [*makhorka*] and salt in a rag." But unlike "The Paper Soldier," "The Old King" is not an extended metaphor. Rather, the fairytale plot hatches a fictitious morality that in the 1960s, with this period's officially required optimism, bore a politically and ethically oppositionist meaning.

> Play, you orchestras; ring out, songs and laughter alike.
> Friends, it's not worth giving in to a moment's sorrow.
> After all, there's no point in sad soldiers surviving,
> And incidentally, there's never enough gingerbread for everyone.

> Играйте, оркестры, звучите, и песни, и смех.
> Минутной печали не стоит, друзья, предаваться.
> Ведь грустным солдатам нет смысла в живых оставаться,
> и пряников, кстати, всегда не хватает на всех.[48]

The deeper meaning of this fairytale song is the ethical vindication of the "sad soldiers" as opposed to the "cheerful" ones, like in the blatantly satirical and pacifist "Ditty of the Cheerful Soldier" ("Pesenka veselogo soldata," 1960-61)—which, however, has no fairytale qualities whatsoever; it consistently describes a specifically Soviet soldier, and in its antiwar radicalism it recalls the antiwar works of Kurt Vonnegut and the German Group 47.

Taken as a pair, "The Old King" and "The Ditty of the Cheerful Soldier" illustrate how two trends, two types of songs, gradually took shape in Okudzhava's oeuvre. The first type, the Biedermeieresque songs, were of a fairytale nature or, more often, were based on a combination of heightened metaphoricalness, irony, and sentimentality; while the second were "traumatic" songs, speaking openly of catastrophic memories of the war, or representing war as a catastrophe from which recovery is impossible: "Oh, You Lousy War, What Have You Done?" ("Akh, voina, chto ty sdelala, podlaia?," 1958), "The Happy Lot (After a little rain the skies are vast)" ("Schastlivyi zhrebii [Posle dozhdika nebesa prostorny]," 1985), "The Raven" ("The Omen") ("Voron [Primeta]," 1985), etc.; and

---

47 Cf. Rozenblium, "*...Ozhidan'e bol'shoi peremeny*," 334.
48 Okudzhava, *Stikhotvoreniia*, 223.

there are transitional variants as well ("The Sun Shines, the Music Plays" [Solnyshko siiaet, muzyka igraet], 1986). These two trends function like communicating vessels, with the Biedermeieresque songs helping to sublimate and "tame" the feeling of horror blurted out in the "traumatic" ones. We can hear Andersen in the Biedermeieresque songs, influencing their melancholic plots. It is characteristic that Okudzhava's second album, which came out in the USSR in 1980 (the first appeared in 1978), consists exclusively of Biedermeieresque songs: this was the Okudzhava, it seems, that the censorship and ideological-control authorities found largely acceptable.

6. Andersen as the "Heavenly Patron" of Soviet Biedermeier Children's Literature: Gennadii Tsyferov and Sergei Kozlov

In the latter half of the 1960s, writers who carried on the Andersenian tradition became far more sentimental in their works, which unlike Krivin's were aimed not just at adults, but children as well. In their fairy tales for children, Gennadii Tsyferov (1930-72) and Sergei Kozlov (1939-2010) established a fundamentally new aesthetic that might be called sentimental hermeticism. They were well acquainted with one another and in 1963 even coauthored a book. They may be considered representatives of a single literary movement.

Like Krivin's early texts, Kozlov and especially Tsyferov's fairy tales are short, at times very much so—just one or two paragraphs. But unlike Krivin's parables, which unfold amid Soviet-like social realities, these two authors' tales take place in conventional, self-contained worlds, in which the primary values are the characters' mutual love (without erotic overtones), friendship, and a transcendental state that arises from the experience of nature. Tsyferov and Kozlov's characters do not engage in any purposeful activity; they simply live, take part in dialogue with interlocutors animate and inanimate, and experience the transience of life.

> Once a little froggy sat by a river and watched the yellow sun floating in the blue water. Then came a wind and said: "Whew." And the river and the sun became wrinkly. Now the wind became angry and said once more: "Whew, whew, whew." Very strongly. It apparently wanted to smooth out the wrinkles, but now there were more of them.
>
> And now the little froggy became angry. He took a twig and said to the wind: "I am going to chase you away. Why are you wrinkling the water and my beloved sun?"....

Someone might have thought: "He's trying to scare the birds." But he wasn't trying to scare anyone or anything.

He was little. He was an oddball. He was just hopping through the hills and shepherding the wind.[49]

(Gennadii Tsyferov, "About an Oddball Froggy"
["Pro chudaka liagushonka"], 1966)

Importantly, Tsyferov and Kozlov's works were primarily aimed at children rather than adults. A significant portion of the two authors' tales were reminiscent of the idyll genre so beloved during the historical Biedermeier. In Tsyferov, the idyll plot most typically hinges on a sense of fragility, the possibility that any moment might bring destruction; whereas key for Kozlov is the acuteness of feelings and the characters' paradoxical thinking.

Little Hedgehog sat on a mound under a pine tree and gazed upon the moonlit valley submerged in fog.

It was so beautiful that from time to time he would give a start: was he dreaming all of this?

And the midges did not tire of playing their fiddles; the moonlit hares danced; and the dog howled.

"If I told anyone, they wouldn't believe me!" thought Little Hedgehog, and started to look still more closely, so as to record all the beauty to the last blade of grass.

"Look, a star fell," he noticed, "and the grass leaned to the left, and all that's left of the fir is its top, and now it floats along with a horse... I wonder," thought Little Hedgehog, "if the horse lies down to go to sleep, will it drown in the fog?"

And he started to go slowly downhill, so as to wind up in the fog himself, and see what it was like inside it.[50]

("Little Hedgehog in the Fog" ["Ezhik v tumane"], 1975)

Tsyferov and especially Kozlov may be said to consistently combine the emotional tone of the Biedermeier with existentialist and absurdist motifs, and at times, perhaps, even with the traditional Japanese aesthetic of understatement and innuendo (here one could mention such versions thereof as *yūgen* and *mono no aware* or the "pathos of things").[51]

---

49 Cited from Iakhnin and Zaitseva, *Antologiia detskoi literatury*, 140.
50 Kozlov, *Ezhik v tumane*, 10-11.
51 Kozlov's 1973 fairy tale "Such a Tree" ("Takoe derevo") is about a little bear that comes to a clearing and decides to become a tree. In the Japanese writer Kenzaburo Oe's novel of

As mentioned above, Tsyferov published the book *My Andersen* in 1969. His 1968 cycle "Tales of the Old City" ("Skazki starinnogo goroda") is set in a conventional Western European city—now modern, now of the sixteenth or seventeenth century; this cycle was published only in 1991. In 1971 he coauthored, with Genrikh Sapgir, a theatrical adaptation of Andersen's memoir *The Fairy Tale of My Life*. Critics also compared the works of Tsyferov himself with the tales of Andersen.[52]

Kozlov's fairy tales are regularly compared with those of Andersen. As the journalist and fantasy writer Maks Frai (the pseudonym used by Svetlana Martynchik) put it in 1999:

> I wouldn't say that Kozlov's stories about Little Hedgehog and Little Bear and their friends are like the tales of Andersen. They aren't. But these two are the only ones to have succeeded in suffusing children's tales with such endless sorrow—almost hopeless, but with the meek sigh of "even so…" every time the sorrow becomes unbearable. Both Kozlov and Andersen are endlessly sentimental, but their sentimentality has nothing of the sickeningly mawkish about it. Andersen was perhaps more inventive, but Sergei Kozlov is wiser.[53]

Both Tsyferov and Kozlov are significant writers who did not take their cues from the fashionable, semi-official aesthetic trends but used it to work out their own artistic and moral issues. This goes for their reception of Andersen as well as their interpretation of the Soviet Biedermeier. It is thus crucial to understand why Tsyferov wrote so much about Andersen, and Kozlov was so frequently compared with Andersen—even given the fact (one is inclined to agree with Frai here) that the tales of these Russian writers do not particularly resemble the works of their Danish predecessor.

7. Sentimentality Transformed

Whereas Krivin takes up one of Andersen's most important *devices*, Tsyferov and Kozlov are sensitive to his emotional *tone* and ethical *pathos*. By "tone" I mean the combination of melancholy and exaltation—this

---

that same year, *The Floodwaters Have Come unto My Soul*, the main character, Oki Isana, wishes he could be a tree.

52 Vachkov, "Gennadii Tsyferov."
53 Frai, "Kogda zhe pridet slon?" Before Frai, this comparison had been suggested—albeit not developed—by Bulat Okudzhava in an essay on Kozlov published posthumously, in 1999. The author of an unsigned Kozlov obituary published in *Gazeta.ru* ("Pochemu oslik ne boialsia") also drew a comparison with Andersen, for the same reason adduced by Maks Frai: Kozlov and Andersen, as this writer puts it, were able to make fairy tales sorrowful and lucid.

could apply to almost any fairy tale by Kozlov; and among Tsyferov's works, to his screenplay for the cartoon *The Little Steam Engine from Romashkovo* (*Parovozik iz Romashkovo*) that he coauthored in 1967 with Genrikh Sapgir. Ethical pathos may be defined as a quest for and experience of a genuine, non-phony spiritual state, which requires intense psychological effort; true, Andersen, working within the Protestant tradition, wrote more about the long road of trials and difficult decisions (as in "Thumbelina" or "The Ugly Duckling"), while the two Russian writers' theme was simply the importance of making an effort; but in his screenplay for Iurii Norshtein's cartoon *Little Hedgehog in the Fog* (1975), Kozlov shows the hedgehog's path precisely as a spiritual trial and a wandering among temptations.

Both these authors keenly detected the tension, ever present in Andersen, between the "cozy" Biedermeier and discomforting romanticism. The Danish storyteller elaborated upon this aesthetic discovery over the course of his entire literary life. Both Tsyferov and Kozlov depict characters that seek to break rules in the course of their quest for "genuine" existence; such a plot harks back to romanticism, but in the 1970s, the closest historical successor to romanticism was the literature of the American and Western European "youth revolution"—works that demonstrated transformations of consciousness. Some of these were published in the USSR, for instance, Kurt Vonnegut's *Slaughterhouse Five, or the Children's Crusade*, in the outstanding translation by Rita Rait-Kovaleva. The presence of this counterculture background undermines the integrity of the Biedermeier world that Tsyferov and Kozlov both create.

So as to understand how these two writers reinterpreted Andersen, we should first outline the general features of Soviet children's culture in the "long seventies."

First and foremost is the fact that this period saw a notable increase in the significance of children's culture within Soviet culture generally. This was due to a complex confluence of causes, many of which have been analyzed in studies by Kuznetsov and Maiofis,[54] on which my comments will be based.

A paradoxical social situation had taken shape in this period. On the one hand, the Soviet order seemed quite stable,[55] with party and KGB structures ruthlessly curbing any attempts to publicly manifest dissent. On the other hand, Soviet society had come to resemble a postindustrial

---

54 Kuznetsov, "Cheburashka i drugie"; Maiofis, "Milyi, milyi trikster."
55 As crystalized in Alexei Yurchak's apt title: *Everything Was Forever, Until It Was No More.*

one: insofar as, for many people, the activity they were engaged in at work was trivial and boring, and the economy languished in that famous "stagnation," the sphere of leisure took on enormous significance, and art that went beyond Soviet norms was perceived as an oasis of "real" life.[56]

For many, the impossibility of social fulfillment lent a hypertrophied importance to microsocial connections in small circles, intrafamily ties, individual psychological reflection, the cultivation of emotional sensitivity. The refinedness of reflection and the love of "lofty idleness" in literature of this period is well illustrated in an untitled poem of Aleksandr Kushner from 1977:

The arrangement of items
On the surface of the table,
And the refraction of rays,
And the blue ice of glass.
The flowers, a tulip and a poppy, go here,
The wineglass with wine goes there.
Tell me, are you happy?—No.—What about like this?
—Almost.—What about like this?—Oh, yes!

Расположение вещей
На плоскости стола,
И преломление лучей,
И синий лед стекла.
Сюда—цветы, тюльпан и мак,
Бокал с вином—туда.
Скажи, ты счастлив?—Нет.—А так?
Почти.—А так?—О да![57]

But in many works for children, and for adults, all of these aspects of private life—interest in psychological details and emotional states, attention to the nuances of personal relationships—were tinged with melancholy, irony, and self-irony.

Beginning in the mid-1960s, as if to make up for the entirely imitative feel of public life, unofficial Soviet art saw the development of a cult of authenticity.[58] One of the primary manifestations of authenticity was

---

56 Frumkina, "Bez narkoza."
57 *Druzhba narodov*, nos. 7-9 (1976): 276.
58 Contemporary studies of Soviet culture distinguish between "unofficial" and "uncensored" (*nepodtsenzurnyi*) art and literature. Works of "unofficial" art and literature were created in the hope of being permitted by Soviet censors and not reworked too much by editors,

thought to be childhood as a period of life, and the child as the bearer of a special kind of consciousness.[59] The appeal to childhood takes on the meaning of a psychological utopia: "don't forget your childhood," "don't betray your childhood"—in the language of the "long seventies," such injunctions meant "don't betray yourself" in the false world of "grownups," that is, the world of conformists and careerists who value pragmatism.

Art now took up the subject of childhood loneliness—in part for demographic reasons: the generation of the 1970s was

> the first generation of children whose parents were getting divorced right and left, and the first generation of children to grow up in private apartments. The main characters of stories by [Viktor] Dragunsky [written in the 1960s] could still hide under the bed of the neighbor-lady [in a communal apartment]; more and more, the children of the 1970s sat motionless by the window waiting for when their mother was supposed to come home from work.[60]

Also motivating the theme of childhood loneliness was the situation, of which adults were keenly aware, of ideological and social crisis: some of your friends were changing their former views, others emigrating, and still others had taken to hard drinking due to poor life prospects.

> No one will ever tear us apart,
> But when I embrace you,
> I do it so melancholically,
> As if someone were trying to take you away from me.
>
> ....
>
> When I hear the nasty tirades
> of a friend who has stumbled,
> I seek not the likeness, but the original;
> It is him, the real him, that I mourn.
>
> Нас с тобой никто не расколет.
> Но когда тебя обнимаю—

---

but did not match officially recognized ideological and aesthetic norms—the upshot was that such works would either be printed or banned. "Uncensored" literature and art refers to works that were on principle not meant for publication in the USSR; these may have circulated in samizdat or been known only to a narrow circle of friends.

59 Maiofis, "Milyi, milyi trikster."
60 Kuznetsov, "Cheburashka i drugie," 356.

обнимаю с такой тоскою,
будто кто-то тебя отнимает.

....

Когда слышу тирады подленькие
оступившегося товарища,
я ищу не подобья—подлинника,
по нему грущу, настоящему.[61]

(Andrei Voznesensky, "Nostalgia for the Present"
["Nostal'giia po nastoiashchemu"], 1976[62])

In the 1960s, many in the Soviet intelligentsia discovered existentialism; somewhat fewer saw the films of the Italian director Michelangelo Antonioni, which spoke of modern mankind's alienation and uncommunicativeness (the ungainly term *nekommunikabel'nost'* became one of the key "watchwords" of the Soviet intelligentsia in the latter half of that decade). Writers able to learn (whether first- or second-hand) of all of this understood that, when it came to expressing feelings of loneliness or the loss of the meaning of life, artistic languages could be said to have already been essentially worked out. Strangely enough, it was easiest of all to express these things in a work aimed at children age six to nine, or, as the official classification for libraries and bookstores put it, "for older preschool and younger elementary school-aged children." Works aimed at older age cohorts were supposed to be lifelike, and to convey useful knowledge (except for young-adult sci-fi and fantasy, which also started to develop specifically in the 1960s), whereas fairy tales for young children naturally entailed the fantastic violation of any norms of realism. The new ideology of "childhood as the zone of authenticity" and attentiveness to children's psychology enabled authors of such tales to refrain from the sort of didacticism associated with an ideology increasingly losing its legitimacy.[63]

---

61 Voznesenskii, *Stikhotvoreniia*, 112.
62 Andrei Voznesensky's position in society in this period was hardly above reproach; the sense of moral superiority expressed here may thus be surprising, if we take these lines as a source of information as to the author's psychological life (which would not be entirely fitting). However, as far as can be judged, Voznesensky in this poem sought to express the essential "formulae of feelings" of the loyal intelligentsia of that time.
63 Maiofis, "Milyi, milyi trikster."

Fairytale films and books for the very youngest most typically did not have any "hidden agenda" or use Aesopian language; nevertheless, in this period they functioned as a sort of "antidote" that enabled a consistent recoding of repressive Soviet ideologemes into the values of emotional frankness, freedom, and open communication…. Authors and readers/viewers alike perceived fairytale books and films as a space in which social meanings were "converted"…. The modality described here of creating fairy tales for the very youngest in the 1970s "set the tone" and implicitly defined the criteria of quality.[64]

Taken as a whole, these processes meant that the children's fairy tale of the 1970s was imbued with irony and melancholy, not unlike works for "grownups" in the same period.[65]

In a 1921 article, Viktor Shklovsky introduced the term "motivation" ("*motivirovka*") to signify all the possible explanations for the presence of a given device, plot twist, or emotional pattern in a literary work.[66] In the 1970s, references to Andersen or the Andersenian milieu became a key motivation by which to lend a work (especially a film) a combination of irony, melancholy, and criticism of the longstanding social order—a combination that was, clearly, in and of itself not entirely endorsed by censors and editors.

This was most keenly sensed by Gennadii Tsyferov. His essay "My Andersen" takes up one of the themes of Paustovsky's book *The Golden Rose*: explaining great works of literature with reference to how their author's sense of fantasy transformed the circumstances of their lives. But Tsyferov's main idea is different from that of Paustovsky. Inventing fictional histories of how Andersen's early tales were written, the Soviet author declares a writer's right to be sorrowful, because, as he believes, sorrow enables a writer to enter into dialogue even with hardened readers not inclined to empathy and also because sorrow always attests to the authenticity of experience. Melodramatic, sentimental, and tragic motifs in a work, according to Tsyferov, thus give the reader the opportunity to become better (in a moral sense).

> Do you know, for instance, how bells are cast? A drop of silver is invariably added to every bell. That's why it chimes…
>
> If you add a drop of pure sorrow to a funny tale, it will chime as well.

---

64 Ibid., 258.
65 Kuznetsov, "Cheburashka i drugie."
66 Shklovskii, *O teorii prozy*, 226-45; Khanzen-Leve, "Russkii formalism," 189-91.

> Whenever you finish a tale by Andersen, you seem to hear a chiming, long and tremulous. Later you may even forget what the tale was about, but this tremulous chime stays in your heart forever.
>
> And if, sometime later, kindly reminiscences touch your heart, it will chime once more, and you will again recall your Andersen.[67]

As far as can be judged, this text was important for Sergei Kozlov as well. His tales rarely contain direct reminiscences from Andersen, but we can find allusions to Tsyferov's essay (as well, incidentally, as his tales). The ending of Kozlov's most poignant tale, "Will We Really Live Forever?" ("Pravda, my budem vsegda?," 1987), describes the death of one of his regular characters, Little Bear, and this fragment suddenly resonates with Tsyferov's description of Andersen's death:

No, great poets and storytellers never die. They just find a soft patch of land where flowers might be planted.

(G. Tsyferov)

"Listen," said Little Donkey to Little Bear, "don't be afraid. You're going to sprout up again in the spring."
 "Like a sapling?"
 "Yes. I'm going to water you every day. And hoe the soil."

(S. Kozlov)

As compared with Andersen and Paustovsky, Tsyferov transfers semantic accents in his essay. Andersen's tales are sometimes sorrowful and melancholic, but none of his works contains an *apologia for the right to grieve*. To the contrary, in the tale "The Child in the Grave" (1859), the author insists: even after a terrible loss, a person should once again regain their will to live. For Tsyferov, and perhaps for Kozlov, the assertion of the "right to grieve" is necessary to solve a more common problem. Their characters may not be lonely (in Kozlov's world, Little Hedgehog has his friend Little Bear), but the psychic life of each is unique and spontaneous, breaking general rules—and thus precious. Kozlov follows in Tsyferov's footsteps thus: in many of his tales, he presents the view

---

67 Tsyferov, *Moi Andersen*, no pagination; in the book, this whole text is in italics.

that every human condition is transitory and ephemeral, hence worthy of being noted and recorded.[68]

Tsyferov and Kozlov fit within the Soviet Biedermeier's overall cult of emotionality, sentimentality, and melancholy; they did not, however, try to "domesticate" the discoveries of the 1960s, but rather created a new genre of fairy tale, one that would imbue sentimentality with an existential dimension. For them, Andersen was the author—if we take Tsyferov's essay on him as a manifesto—who enabled them to understand how a sentimental narrative may be psychologically and aesthetically radicalized.

8. Andersen and the Restoration of Russian Modernism: Nadezhda Kosheverova and Veniamin Kaverin

Turning to a different type of reception of Andersen's legacy, let us examine how, during the "long seventies," authors of the older generations used references to Andersen to at least partially restore, in the Soviet context, the early twentieth-century modernist aesthetic, which had been virtually banned in the USSR in 1936, after *Pravda* in quick succession ran the editorials "On Hack Artists" ("O khudozhnikakh-pachkunakh") and "Muddle Instead of Music" ("Sumbur vmesto muzyki")—declarations of the war then commencing on "formalism" and "naturalism" in art. Thaw-era literature saw numerous attempts to combine modernism with Soviet aesthetic principles; but it was, strangely enough, the development of the Andersenian tradition that gave at least two authors new opportunities to revive the modernist aesthetic, in a form as close to the original as possible. "Strangely enough," because in Soviet culture, in the postwar decades, Andersen was first and foremost associated with nineteenth-century romanticism, but not with modernism.

In 1968, the director Nadezhda Kosheverova (1902-89) made the children's film *An Old, Old Tale*, based on Andersen's "The Tinderbox," "The Swineherd," and "Clumsy Hans," supplemented with new scenes devised by the screenwriters Iulii Dunsky and Valerii Frid. Kosheverova had begun her career in the cinema already in the 1930s, but was especially noted for her fairytale films for children, beginning with the famous *Cinderella* (*Zolushka*, 1947; screenplay by Evgenii Schwartz). Her first husband (married 1923) was Nikolai Akimov, an artist and director of

---

68 It is especially this aesthetic axiology that makes Kozlov's tales resonate with the medieval Japanese prose genre of zuihitsu, diaristic writing that attests to the multiformity of life and the ephemerality of each moment; this echo is already notable in his early cycle of prose poems *Seasons* (*Vremena goda*, 1973). The resemblance may be a matter of convergence.

(for the period) radically modernist sensibilities. The two would collaborate even many years after their divorce, with Akimov designing sets for Kosheverova's movies.

The film *An Old, Old Tale* is based on a complex system of aesthetic "quotation marks" and the "play within a play" device. It begins with a puppeteer coming to an inn in a conventionally Western European country at some point during (to judge from the milieu) the nineteenth century. He falls in love with the innkeeper's daughter—a secret known only to her—but they cannot marry because he is very poor. In love, the two decide that they will flee together the next morning; they will marry and, in order to support the family, the puppeteer will give up his craft and take a job as a clerk. That night, the puppets, having heard that their master is about to get rid of them, asks him for permission to perform one last show for him; the puppeteer assents, and now the primary action begins, with the main roles played by the same actors as in the "frame" novella: Oleg Dal, Marina Neiolova, and Vladimir Etush. In this act, it is as if we are transferred to the stage of a puppet theater. When the show is over, it is morning. The innkeeper's daughter comes to her beloved and tells him that she cannot go with him; having thought it over all night, she has realized that she must remain with her father to support him. They say their farewells, and the puppeteer takes his puppets and his portable puppet-booth, and leaves to wander anew.

The style of *An Old, Old Tale* is unlike anything Kosheverova had done previously, even *Cinderella*. Motivated by the setting of the puppet-booth, the action and scenery are as conventional and grotesque as possible, recalling the theatrical practice of the 1920s; in 1923, Kosheverova had graduated from the courses of the modernist Free Comedy Theater in Petrograd, and for a time had performed there as an actress, and thus would have well remembered these traditions.

Like Tsyferov and Kozlov, Kosheverova creates an utterly conventional onscreen world, but in doing so she employs different methods from those of the storytellers of the younger generation. The device of laying bare theatrical conventionality had first been used in Soviet children's film by Rolan Bykov in *Ow-It-Hurts-66* (*Aibolit-66*, 1967); but Kosheverova's demonstrative theatricality is a stylized one: like Bykov's film, *An Old, Old Tale* contains sight gags on modern subjects (like the minister turning in empty bottles so as to replenish the barren royal treasury); but the aesthetic of Kosheverova's film is defined by the idea of a poetically tinged game as the supreme manifestation of life. It may even be that Kosheverova and the screenwriters Dunsky and Frid were taking their cue from Nikolai Evreinov's idea of total theatricality (Evreinov had been one of the directors at the Free Comedy Theater, which had staged his plays). But this game is melancholic in meaning; and the glorification of everyday theatricality does not promise to transform all social life, as it was supposed to according to Evreinov. The post-utopian nature of *An Old, Old Tale* renders it one of the first works of the Soviet Biedermeier.

Kosheverova and the screenwriters Dunsky and Frid found it necessary to allude to Andersen so as to accommodate, within the framework of a single film: the comic grotesque, sentimentality, a sense of miracle (the film even includes a magical scene in which summer is transformed into winter), and psychological reflection. The most prominent example of the latter is the episode in which the capricious princess (who recalls the heroine of Andersen's tale "The Swineherd") talks to a mirror, in which appears a girl with her face (played by the same Marina Neiolova) who lectures her for refusing to marry the soldier just out of spite. Formally speaking, the scene itself recalls not Andersen but the Soviet children's book *The Kingdom of Crooked Mirrors* (*Korolevstvo krivykh zerkal*) by Vitalii Gubarev (1951); but the princess's dialogue with her reflection is more psychologically sophisticated than Gubarev's ingenuous text: the reflection upbraids the princess for not allowing herself to do what she herself considers right; it speaks on behalf of her conscience, to which the real princess does not wish to listen.

What the filmmakers found most important in Andersen was the sense of social instability, the open-endedness of social status: for instance, when the princess flees the palace to be with the soldier, she ceases to be a princess; for his part, the soldier is elevated to the rank of marshal one minute and sentenced to death the next. To sum up one of the main thoughts of *An Old, Old Tale*: in the world depicted in the film, a talented or just psychologically nontrivial person cannot occupy a prestigious or even just a stable, societally approved position. But it is precisely thanks to this social eccentricity that the hero or heroine attains freedom and the opportunity to encounter a miracle. The film was able to express this complex of ideas, both significant for and characteristic of the late 1960s, specifically via the screenplay's references to Andersen. Paradoxical as it may seem, it is precisely the Andersenian milieu that turns the film into a parable that viewers were free to correlate with modernity.

At the end of the film, as mentioned, the innkeeper's daughter tells the puppeteer that she cannot leave her father; he would die, she says. Because of this explanation, the film's finale may be seen as alluding to Aleksandr Pushkin's story "The Stationmaster" ("Stantsionnyi smotritel'"), whose plot is here as if replayed anew: in Pushkin, the daughter of the postal stationmaster Samson Vyrin flees to the city and marries a hussar officer, upon which the stationmaster (who has no wife) falls into a depression and dies; in the analogous situation devised by Dunsky and Frid, the daughter stays with her father. Aleksandr Arkhangelsky has suggested that the melancholy afflicting Samson Vyrin after his daughter's flight is of literary origin: Vyrin sees the world through literary models and believes that a daughter who has fled her home must invariably be unhappy, even as "in life" she is entirely prosperous. Arkhangelsky calls this literary model, which for Vyrin is more real than reality, a "petty-bourgeois [*meshchanskii*] idyll (a Biedermeierian one)."[69] In Kosheverova's film, such an idyll triumphs—but the ending is nevertheless melancholic.

In 1979, Kosheverova produced another film adaptation of Andersen: *The Nightingale* (*Solovei*). This time the screenplay was by Mikhail Volpin; but once again, major changes were introduced to the plot so that the idea of the open-endedness of social status would be even more prominent than in the corresponding Andersen tale ("The Nightingale," 1843): whereas in the original tale, the main character is the lawful Chinese emperor, in the film it is the apprentice Evan, who has been turned into an emperor by a wizard; and his former beloved passes herself off as a princess in order to get into the palace to see him. The action takes place not in China (in 1979, Sino-Soviet relations were cool to say the least), but in a conventionally Western European country.[70]

Another author who apparently saw the Andersenian atmosphere as a means of injecting the modernist aesthetic back into Soviet literature was Veniamin Kaverin (1902-89). In the early 1920s, Kaverin had been a member of the modernist literary group "The Serapion Brothers." Kaverin wrote not only "realist" novels but also fairy tales his whole life, perhaps thus continuing the line of fantasy stories he wrote in his youth. His tales likewise prominently feature the open-endedness of social status;

---

69 Arkhangel'skii, *Geroi Pushkina*, 179. This interpretation develops the observations of Mikhail Gershenzon, who in the book *The Wisdom of Pushkin* (*Mudrost' Pushkina*, 1919) describes Vyrin precisely as in the thrall of "petty-bourgeois morality"—a conventional model of behavior incarnate in the "German pictures" hanging on his wall. The first to note the parallel between *An Old, Old Tale* and "The Stationmaster" was Mariia Maiofis.

70 In 1975, the director Viktor Beliakovich staged a play based on Andersen's "The Nightingale" (adapted by G. Knaut) at the Young Muscovites' Theater (the theatrical studio of the Palace of Pioneers and Schoolchildren, Lenin Hills, Moscow); to judge from a program that has survived, the action of this play, too, was transferred to Western Europe—e.g., two characters have the entirely non-Chinese names of Matilda and Amalia.

still more do they pay tribute to hidden moral qualities inconspicuous to the casual glance, qualities that only a perceptive person would notice. One can single out three periods in Kaverin's career when he wrote fairy tales with a particular intensity: the late 1930s, the early 1960s, and the turn of the 1960s–70s. Most of Kaverin's fairy tales take place in the fictional city of Nemukhin.

In 1979, after all three of these periods had passed, Kaverin wrote his last fairy tale, "The Glazier's Son" ("Syn stekol'shchika"), a fairly lengthy text, with numerous literary quotations and allusions. Its plot is as follows: there lives in Nemukhin the Zabotkin family: the famous artist Nikolai Andreevich, his wife Mariia Pavlovna, and their daughter Tania. However, someone else wants to be Zabotkin's wife—Ms. Olol, a witch-school dropout. She turns Mariia Pavlovna into a bronze statue and leaves her at a consignment shop, and she herself takes a job as a housekeeper at the Zabotkins', where she gradually begins to subject Nikolai Andreevich to her will. Tania saves her mother with the help of a newcomer to town—an invisible knight errant who calls himself the Glazier's Son.

Allusions to early twentieth-century art in Kaverin's tale are more veiled than in Kosheverova's film, but they are there. For example, the Glazier's Son reads Tania a poem by the major Russian avant-garde poet Velimir Khlebnikov (1885-1922),[71] who, if never banned, was always considered suspect by censors and party bureaucrats.

More so than Kaverin's previous works, "The Glazier's Son" is marked by a perception of things as living beings, and a combination of melancholy and irony—in other words, this is the most Andersenian of his fairy tales. Given all that has been said above, the fact that it was written specifically in 1979 would seem to be no accident.

> That was the moment, they say, when all the glass panes in Nemukhin jingled in farewell, such that some timorous people like Pavel Pavlovich imagined that it was an earthquake. But in reality it just meant that the tale of the Glazier's Son was over.

In 1981, Kaverin combined his Nemukhin tales into a longer work titled "The Night Watchman, or, Seven Exciting Stories Told in the City of Nemukhin in the Year Nineteen Hundred Something" ("Nochnoi storozh,

---

71 The character himself does not specify the poem's author, but Khlebnikov's name was indicated in a footnote by Kaverin when the tale was first published in the journal *Pioneer* (*Pioner*).

ili Sem' zanimatel'nykh istorii, rasskazannykh v gorode Nemukhine v tysiacha deviat'sot neizvestnom godu").[72] Added to it were episodes that linked the formerly unconnected works into a single narrative. The epilogue to "The Glazier's Son" in some places is stylistically quite reminiscent of Russian translations of Andersen that seek to reproduce the rhythm of oral speech and the unusual syntax characteristic of the Danish original:

> The Museum had a storeroom—that's what they call the room where objects are kept that just can't wait to be finally put on display.
>
> Well, you can just imagine the goings-on in this storeroom! The wheels on an old bicycle—the big one and the little one—started spinning when we came in. A three-legged chair was leaning forward as if about to slip out of the storeroom through the open door. As if on command, the bobble-head Mandarin dolls turned their little heads toward us. It's just a shame that they could not speak!

For Kosheverova and Kaverin, references to Andersen were not a bridge to Russian modernism—these artists already bore modernism within themselves—but rather a motivation enabling the public rehabilitation of the poetics of modernism within the situation of the "long seventies."

9. Andersen and the Unmasking of the Soviet Biedermeier: Liudmila Petrushevskaia

I would like to conclude this article with an example showing how Andersen may be read in Russian literature *not* in the style of the Soviet Biedermeier; how an interpretation is possible, moreover, that would deconstruct this aesthetic itself, and dissociate Andersen from it. Such a deconstruction is carried out in Liudmila Petrushevskaia's fairy tale "White Teapots" ("Belye chainiki"), which parodies the idea of the "modern reading of Andersen."

The postmodernist author Liudmila Petrushevskaia (b. 1938) is one of the key Russian dramatists and prose writers of the late twentieth and early twenty-first centuries; she has written numerous fairy tales, aimed rather at adults than children. In the 1970s she wrote stories and

---

72 Titles using "or" plus a subtitle were particularly beloved by writers of the 1920s, including Kaverin, who in 1981 had not used this kind of heading since that period; cf. his novel *The Scandalist, or, Evenings on Vasilyevsky Island* (*Skandalist, ili Vechera na Vasil'evskom ostrove* (1927). The title of "The Night Watchman" was thus another veiled allusion to modernism.

plays featuring what could be called an anti-Biedermeier stylistics: they depicted everyday Soviet reality without any sentimentality, and told precisely of the sort of conflicts that the Soviet Biedermeier had been summoned to mask: domestic violence, ubiquitous hypocrisy, cynicism, and the perception of morality as a form of repressive state ideology. Petrushevskaia's fairy tales are absurdist, but in an entirely different way than Kozlov's; they have sarcasm, but no melancholy, nor do they have any interest in the transience of time. The brief text "White Teapots" was first published in the journal *Youth* (*Iunost'*) (no. 4, 1976); Petrushevskaia republished it in her fairy tale collection *The Suitcase of Nonsense* (*Chemodan chepukhi*).

The fairy tale tells of how "a kindly sorceress decided to take up residence at a theater, and not because she wished to perform miracles there, but simply because she was tired of conjuring herself up a theater ticket every evening."[73] Since the sorceress has settled right on the stage, the theater director asks her to become invisible. "The sorceress was a kindly old lady and agreed to become invisible, and the only thing you could still see was her teapot, from which she would occasionally pour herself some tea. 'Otherwise,' she said, 'if I make the teapot invisible, the tea will be cold.'"[74]

When staging a play about Little Red Riding Hood, the director tries to make the most out of the fact that there is a teapot unaccountably hanging over the stage: he has other teapots hung on bushes, so that the actress playing Little Red Riding Hood can point to them and say: "What beautiful white birdies with long nosies!" (In Russian, *nosik*, lit. a "little nose," may also signify the spout of a teapot.)

> The next show the next evening was the fairy tale about the ugly duckling.... First the white teapots played the role of the white ducks that nip the poor ugly duckling, and in the end the same teapots portrayed the beautiful white swans. And even the part of the ugly duckling was played by a white teapot—in the beginning they just put some gray paint on it, and it was indeed an ugly teapot; and in the end, when the ugly duckling grows to become a beautiful white swan with a proudly curved neck, they washed off the teapot, and it indeed became a beautiful white teapot with a proudly curved nosie-spout.

---

73 Petrushevskaia, *Sobranie sochinenii v piati tomakh*, 4: 109.
74 Ibid., 110.

The show could not have gone better. The whole town could talk of nothing but the new "white teapot" theater.[75]

But it transpires that the sorceress herself is not a fan of the shows that include teapots, and she quits her residence at the theater.

This clever parody of avant-garde performances was most likely aimed not at the theatrical avant-garde per se (which could exist in the USSR only in the underground or semi-underground), but at entirely specific Soviet circumstances. Both the avant-gardeness and the conventionality of the "White Teapot Theater" are born of the fact that the sorceress, who does "not wish to speak with [the director]," cannot be evicted from the premises. Petrushevskaia's fairy tale may also be read as an allegory: new readings of "The Ugly Duckling" are invented because the existing social circumstances cannot be changed, and it is easier simply to mask them. Petrushevskaia's text is jocular and explicitly conventional, but in it the writer has taken up the same issues treated in her serious works of the seventies—from the play *Music Lessons* (*Uroki muzyki*, 1973) to the story "Our Crowd" ("Svoi krug," 1979): the collective hypocrisy of Soviet society and people's desire to conform to the imagined norm of a prosperous life. However, it should be noted that—whether this occurred to the author or not—her irony in the fairy tale "White Teapots" unexpectedly recalls the irony of Andersen in such works as "The Emperor's New Clothes." Andersen is subtly doubled in Petrushevskaia's fairy tale: the author makes fun of how he is trivialized to become convenient material for experimentation; but in her very description of how the director tries to mask the sorceress's teapot so that everything comes out "properly," Petrushevskaia is unexpectedly close to the artistic manner of Andersen himself.

During the "long seventies," Andersen was read as an author who helped one survive amid Soviet social pressures and collective hypocrisy—helped one to ignore these things when possible. This was, perhaps necessarily, a one-sided interpretation: Andersen was not a revolutionary, but neither was he an escapist. Even given the significance of the works discussed here, Petrushevskaia's fairy tale stands as a necessary corrective to such a reading.

---

75 Ibid., 112.

Works Cited

Arkhangel'skii, A. *Geroi Pushkina*. Moscow: Vysshaia shkola, 1999.

Beregovskaia, E. M. "Realizatsiia stilisticheskikh potentsii khiazma v tvorchestve Feliksa Krivina." *Russkii iazyk v nauchnom osveshchenii*, no. 2 (14), (2007): 133-46.

Beumers, Birgit. *Pop Culture Russia! Media, Arts, and Lifestyle*. Santa Barbara: ABC-CLIO, 2005.

Braude, L. Iu. "Andersen v russkoi i sovetskoi kritike." *Trudy Institut istorii AN SSSR. Vyp. 11. Istoricheskie sviazi Skandinavii i Rossii. IX–XX vv.* (1970): 313-22.

Bykov, D. *Okudzhava*. Moscow: Molodaia gvardiia, 2009.

Detering, Heinrich. "H. C. Andersen's 'Schiller Fairy Tale' and the Post-Romantic Religion of Art." *Romantik: Journal for the Study of Romanticisms* 1 (2012): 49-64.

Dmitrieva, E. "Teoriia kul'turnogo transfera i komparativnyi metod v gumanitarnykh issledovaniiakh: oppozitsiia ili preemstvennost'?" *Voprosy literatury*, no. 4 (2011), 302-13.

Dovlatov, S. Review of F. Krivin, *Kaleidoskop* (Uzhgorod: Karpaty, 1965). *Zvezda*, no. 3 (1966): 218-19.

Espagne, M. *Les transferts culturels franco-allemands*. Paris: Presses Universitaires de France, 1999.

Ewers, H.-H. "Romantik." In *Geschichte der deutschen Kinder- und Jugendliteratur*, edited by R. Wild et al., 96-130. Stuttgart: Springer-Verlag, 2008.

Frai, M. "Kogda zhe pridet slon?" *Gazeta.ru*, 2 August 1999. Available electronically: https://gazeta.lenta.ru/frei/02-08-1999_kozlov_Printed.htm.

Frumkina, R. "Bez narkoza." *Novoe literaturnoe obozrenie*, no. 100 (2009): 216-22. Available electronically: http://magazines.russ.ru/nlo/2009/100/fr17.html.

Gavrosh, A. "Poslednee interv'iu Feliksa Krivina pered ot"ezdom iz Ukrainy." *Zerkalo nedeli* (Kiev), no. 49 (2001): 373. Available electronically: http://marie-olshansky.ru/ct/fkrivin-bio.shtml.

Gershenzon, M. O. *Mudrost' Pushkina*. Moscow: Kn-vo pisatelei v Moskve, 1919.

Glauser, J. *Skandinavische Literaturgeschichte*. Stuttgart: Springer-Verlag, 2006.

Iakhnin, Leonid, and Elena Zaitseva, eds. *Antologiia detskoi literatury*. Moscow: Olma-Press, 2003.

Khanzen-Leve, O. A. "Russkii formalizm: Metodologicheskaia rekonstruktsiia razvitiia na osnove printsipa ostraneniia." Translated from the German by S. A. Romashko. Moscow: Iazyki russkoi kul'tury, 2001.

Kozlov, Sergei. *Ezhik v tumane*. Moscow: Oniks-Lit, 2011.

Krivin, Feliks. *Poluskazki*. L'vov: Karpaty, 1964.

Kukulin, I. "Legalizovannoe zaklinanie v inter'ere sovetskogo bidermaiera: o vozmozhnykh zhanrovykh, stilisticheskikh i sotsiokul'turnykh istokakh stikhotvoreniia K. Simonova 'Zhdi menia.'" Available electronically: http://urokiistorii.ru/node/52199.

Kur, S. "Nastoiashchii iumor vsegda grustnyi ... Mir Feliksa Krivina." *Internet-zhurnal "Kstati,"* 10 January 2016: Available electronically: http://kstati.net/nastoyashhij-yumor-vsegda-grustnyj/.

Kuznetsov, S. "Cheburashka i drugie: Zoo, ili Fil'my ne o liubvi." In *Veselye chelovechki: kul'turnye geroi sovetskogo detstva*, edited by I. Kukulin, M. Lipovetskii, and M. Maiofis, 354-59. Moscow: NLO, 2008.

Lebina, N. B. *Povsednevnost' epokhi kosmosa i kukuruzy. Destruktsiia bol'shogo stilia. Leningrad 1950-1960-e gg.* St. Petersburg: Pobeda, 2015.

Lesskis, N. "Fil'm 'Ironiia sud'by ...': ot ritualov solidarnosti k poetike izmenennogo soznaniia." *Novoe literaturnoe obozrenie*, no. 76 (2005): 314-27.

Maiofis, Mariia. "Milyi, milyi trikster: Karlson i sovetskaia utopiia o 'nastoiashchem detstve.'" In *Veselye chelovechki: Kul'turnye geroi sovetskogo detstva. Sbornik statei*, edited by I. Kukulin, M. Lipovetskii, and M. Maiofis, 241-75. Moscow: NLO, 2008.

Nemoianu, V. *The Taming of Romanticism: European Literature and the Age of Biedermeier*. Cambridge, MA: Harvard University Press, 1984.

Okudzhava, B. *Stikhotvoreniia*. Forewords by V. Sazhin and V. Dubshan. St. Petersburg: Akademicheskii proekt, 2001.

Paustovskii, K. "Velikii skazochnik." In *Skazki i istorii* by Kh. K. Andersen, translated by A. Ganzen, S. Fridliand et al., 9-16. Moscow: Gos. Izdatel'stvo khudozhestvennoi literatury, 1955.

Petrushevskaia, L. *Sobranie sochinenii v piati tomakh*. Moscow: Folio, 1996.

"Pochemu oslik ne boialsia. Umer Sergei Kozlov." *Gazeta.ru*, 11 January 2010. Available electronically: https://www.gazeta.ru/culture/2010/01/11/a_3310047.shtml.

Reid, S. "Destalinization and Taste, 1953-1963." *Journal of Design History* 10, no. 2 (1997): 177-201.

Rozenblium, O. *"...Ozhidan'e bol'shoi peremeny": Biografiia, stikhi i proza Bulata Okudzhavy*. Moscow: RGGU, 2013.

Shklovskii, V. *O teorii prozy*. Moscow: Federatsiia, 1929.

Soifer, V. "Akademik i student." *Kontinent*, no. 114 (2002). Available electronically: http://magazines.russ.ru/continent/2002/113/soi.html.

Svetlov, M. *Stikhotvoreniia*. Edited by Zinovii Papernyi. Leningrad: Sovetskii pisatel', 1968.

Tsyferov, G. *Moi Andersen*. Moscow: Malysh, 1969.

Vachkov, I. V. "Gennadii Tsyferov: romantik detstva." *Sovremennoe doshkol'noe obrazovanie*, no. 6 (2016): 58-61.

Vaiskopf, M. *Vliublennyi demiurg: Metafizika i erotika russkogo romantizma*. Moscow: NLO, 2012.

Velichanskii, A. *Pepel slov*: In 2 vols. Progress-Traditsiia, 2010.

Vinitskii, I. *Dom Tolkovatelia: Poeticheskaia semantika i istoricheskoe voobrazhenie V. A. Zhukovskogo*. Moscow: NLO, 2006.

Voznesenskii, Andrei. *Stikhotvoreniia*. Moscow: Molodaia gvardiia, 1991.

Yurchak, A. *Everything Was Forever, Until It Was No More: The Last Soviet Generation*. Princeton: Princeton University Press, 2005.

Zabolotniaia, M. "Delo o 'Drakone.'" *Voprosy teatra*, nos. 1-2 (2009): 302-29.

Part III

Visualizing Andersen in Russian Illustration, Film, and the Digital Sphere

The Danish Little Mermaid vs. the Russian *Rusalka:*

Screen Choices

Helena Goscilo

> Since love grows within you, so beauty grows. For love is the beauty of the soul.
>
> St. Augustine

> All of our reasoning ends in surrender to feeling.
>
> Blaise Pascal

Multiple cultural genres, including painting, graphic art, music, literature, and handicrafts, have explored the ubiquitous mythological and folkloric water spirit variously called the medieval Melusine, mermaid, water sprite, naiad, lorelei, undine or ondine, and, in Slavic lore, *rusalka*.[1] Part of the Slavic and particularly Russian *rusalka*'s abiding fascination indisputably stems from her paradoxical nature: endowed with a destructive—indeed, fatal—potential through a seductive, largely aural, power that allies her with European aquatic sirens, on land she symbolizes vernal revivification and fecundity. Yet she simultaneously incarnates female vulnerability, inasmuch as she is the damned "soul" of a maiden who committed suicide by drowning in despair over betrayal in love.[2]

Intimately linked to the Greek siren, and to Sirin and Alkonost of Slavic mythology, the image of the *rusalka* underwent fascinating permutations in Russian music (Catterino Cavos, Aleksandr Dargomyzhsky),[3] painting (Ivan Kramskoi, Mikhail Vrubel, Konstantin Makovsky), graphic

---

[1] For an analysis of the *rusalka*'s commonalities with the Greek sirens, see Goscilo, "Watery Maidens." Also see Hubbs, *Mother Russia*, 24-36; and Siniavsky, *Ivan the Fool*, 122-24. Zelenin notes the connection (*Izbrannye trudy*, 179, 209), but does not elaborate on it.

[2] I use "maiden" in the sense of an unmarried girl or woman, not in the word's meaning as a former Scottish beheading device resembling the guillotine or a horse that has never won a race. See Merriam Webster dictionary.

[3] One of the best-known musical compositions devoted to her is Antonin Dvořák's *Rusalka* (1900), with a famous aria for the soprano in act I titled "Song to the Moon."

art (Ivan Bilibin), and literature (Aleksandr Pushkin, Orest Somov, Mikhail Muravyov, Mikhail Lermontov, Nikolai Gogol, Valerii Briusov, Zinaida Gippius, Aleksei Tolstoy, Tatyana Tolstaya, and Svetlana Vasilenko).[4] Her widespread appeal notwithstanding, in many instances Russian culture bypassed its endemic folkloric traditions in favor of the Danish Hans Christian Andersen's renowned protagonist of "The Little Mermaid" (1837)—a literary fairy tale manifestly indebted to Friedrich de la Motte Fouqué's *Undine* (1811). Indeed, in some cases determining whether the hypotext is Fouqué's or Andersen's presents a considerable challenge.[5] The Danish writer borrowed from Fouqué's verbose romantic novella the *dominanta* of a pagan entity's desire to acquire a soul through the love of a mortal male, but cast his narrative in an appreciably more concise and beguiling form. As a result, the German text has sunk into Lethe, whereas Andersen's "Little Mermaid" stimulates ever new adaptations to this day.

Though early versions of the Russian *rusalka* in film, literature, and graphics offered vivid, imaginative scenarios, with time what repeatedly proved more alluring for *Kulturarbeiter* was the Scandinavian water spirit created in a work of fiction. What motivates the preference for Andersen's protagonist on the Russian screen and in other visual genres? A comparative analysis of the *rusalka* and the Danish sea sprite offers a potential explanation, though various directors' and artists' selection of one over the other cannot, and should not, be reduced to a single motivating factor.

The Celluloid *Rusalka*

Given Russia's embattled historical attempts at self-definition vis-à-vis the West, one might expect its screen versions of the water spirit to privilege its national folklore, especially during the Soviet period. Such, however, has not been the case, and the native *rusalka* held sway only during the early period of Russian cinema. Produced at the Khanzhonkov Studio in 1910, the first Russian film to be titled *Rusalka*, by Vasilii Goncharov (1863-1915), closely adheres to Russian folk beliefs and the chief elements of Pushkin's unfinished play *Rusalka*, which also inspired Dargomyzhsky's opera of the same name (1855, staged

---

4 See Goscilo, "Watery Maidens."
5 The term hypotext, introduced by Gérard Genette and popularized by Robert Stam in his publications on screen adaptations, references the source of a subsequent work of any cultural form (literature, film, graphic, art, etc.) that thoroughly draws upon it. See Genette, *Palimpsests*, 5.

Fig. 1. Vasilii Goncharov's resplendently decadent underwater kingdom. Khanzhonkov Studio.

1856).[6] As in Pushkin, so in Goncharov's nine minutes on screen, the plot traces in radically, even confusingly, condensed form a love affair between a miller's daughter and a prince, who severs their liaison to marry someone from his own class. His abandoned beloved throws herself (off-screen) into the Dnieper, transforms into a *rusalka*, and eight years later mysteriously (by an "inexplicable power" [*nevedomaia sila*]) entices her former, possibly conscience-stricken lover to leap into the water and drown. The final scene permits Goncharov to delight viewers with an ornate, luxurious underwater kingdom, in which languorous *rusalki* in diaphanous garb, with flowers entwined in their hair, glide gracefully in aimless fashion; the dead prince sprawls on a couch; and his erstwhile beloved, now a necrophilic *rusalka*, caresses and kisses him (fig. 1). Goncharov's contemporary Evgenii Bauer (1865-1917) must have felt envious watching this gem, which freely elaborates on native sources. These invariably dramatize faithless male desertion of the trusting female lover through marriage to another, the abandoned young woman's suicide, and the supernatural/demonic power she exercises to unite with him after his death—by and large, hallmarks of Bauer's cinematic plots, above all his *Posthumously* (*Posle smerti*, 1915), based on Ivan Turgenev's late story "Klara Milich" ("Klara Milich," 1883).[7]

More than a half-century later, director Aleksandr Petrov's excellent 1997 animated short returned to Russian roots. His wordless, visually imaginative *Rusalka* likewise relies specifically on Russian folklore, plus

---

6   The pregnancy of the miller's daughter in Pushkin's play, however, is omitted in all subsequent works borrowing from it.
7   See https://www.youtube.com/watch?v=Se5yz_afRts.

Fig. 2. The *rusalka*. Aleksandr Petrov.

Pushkin's poem of the same title of 1819 (published 1825).[8] Petrov links the *rusalka* with spring, a young novice monk, and his elder, who in the distant past betrayed a young woman, causing her to drown herself and transform into the vengeful female water spirit (fig. 2) now rescued by the young monk (fig. 3). At film's conclusion, both the *rusalka* and the elder perish (fig. 4) in a violent storm and are buried by the chastened (and presumably still chaste) young monk (fig. 5). The scenario allies itself with popular beliefs about the malevolent *rusalka*'s revenge and interpolates the monk, whom Pushkin's poem intriguingly introduces as a Christian presence serving the divine, into a narrative about a pagan natural force.[9] Both films, then, focus on vengeance by the undead, anchored in endemic folk belief and developed into poetic narratives by Pushkin.[10] Their brevity notwithstanding, they effectively convey the

---

8   Petrov's unusual technique entails painting on glass, with breathtaking results. Four years later Petrov would win the first Oscar for animation ever awarded to a Russian, for his cartoon of *The Old Man and the Sea* (*Starik i more*, 2000), again using oil on glass, this time in 70 mm format.
9   See https://www.youtube.com/watch?v=7MpAr3rcEg0.
10 The title of Vadim Arapov's four-part TV melodrama *Rusalka* (2012) is misleading, for it merely references a place in a banal love story about a couple with socially disparate backgrounds that ends happily.

Fig. 3. The inexperienced monk. Aleksandr Petrov.
Fig. 4. The repentant, formerly treacherous elder. Aleksandr Petrov.
Fig. 5. The solitary young monk, who survives the punitive turbulence of nature. Aleksandr Petrov.

lethal faculties of the unclean, the succubus identified with dread and death, not dream.

Yet the two major Russophone films to treat a female dweller of the underwater realm would transpose to the screen, not Russian folk traditions and their dramatic enrichment by the country's most revered poet, but a foreign literary text. An examination of the constitutive features of Andersen's fairy tale suggests several reasons for such a choice and, more broadly, the widespread enthusiasm among Russian *Kulturarbeiter* for Andersen's version of the female water spirit.

The Appeal of Andersen's Mermaid

Both the folkloric *rusalka* and Andersen's literary little mermaid, as well as Fouqué's female protagonist, are associated with love, soul, and interaction with men.[11] Apart from these commonalities, they contrast in multiple, fundamental ways. The *rusalka* belongs to the lower demonology within Russian folk belief and, in addition to possessing

---

11 Though the object of Fouqué's mermaid is a knight, as opposed to Andersen's prince, the two narratives coincide on the essential points.

sexual seductiveness, has damned her soul through suicide. Indeed, as an underworld entity condemned for violating the Christian interdiction against self-slaughter, she incarnates the flesh bereft of soul, hence has no compunction about killing innocent male passersby as punishment for her suffering. In contrast, though Andersen's mermaid never attains her love object, instead of wreaking revenge for amorous duplicity, she loves her prince unconditionally, endures excruciating pain, and gives up her family and native environment, as well as her power of speech and song (not to mention fish-tail!), to remain masochistically at his side. Childlike and romantic instead of sexual, she yearns for a soul, and ultimately elects to die instead of killing him—a voluntary self-immolation rewarded by her metamorphosis into a "daughter of the air," an air spirit who ascends heavenward.[12] Contemporary popular jargon would characterize the *rusalka* as "sad but bad"—a diminished modern version of such tragic heroines as Medea and Lady Macbeth—whereas the little mermaid, a "good girl" and "do-gooder," sooner resembles a regressive ideal of womanhood and the purity and charitable impulses of Mother Teresa.

During his later years, Andersen cleaved to a religious perspective on life, as evidenced in his fiction and his idiosyncratic autobiography, *The Fairy Tale of My Life* (Danish 1855; English trans. 1871). In the opening of that volume, Andersen asserts: "There is a loving God, who directs all things for the best," and thereafter he repeatedly apostrophizes God, expresses trust in and love of his world, and articulates profoundly Christian convictions: "There are moments of thankfulness in which... we feel a desire to press God to our hearts"; "many a night in the time of our uncertainty I prayed God in my heart."[13] As W. Glyn Jones observes: "That Andersen believed in God is beyond dispute,"[14] and many of his tales testify to his public advocacy of spirituality. Accordingly, the Church figures prominently in "The Little Mermaid," as (literally) a measure of depth and as a constant reminder of Christian virtue. "Far out in the ocean the water... is very deep.... [M]any, many steeples would have to be stacked one on top of another to reach from the bottom to the surface of the sea." (Significantly, moreover, the little mermaid's initial

---

12 The mermaid's ascent in Andersen's tale coincides with the popular Russian belief that after *Rusal'naia* Week (also known as Trinity Week, the seventh after Easter), the *rusalka* would leave the earth and rise to the clouds, where she would live (Shaparova, *Kratkaia entsiklopediia slavianskoi mifologii*, 458). There is a certain logic to this notion, given the *rusalka*'s association with all forms of water.
13 Andersen, *The Fairy Tale of My Life*, 1: 225, 434.
14 Jones, "Andersen and Those of Other Faiths," 259.

attraction to the surface is associated with her elder sister's recounting of the ringing of church bells.) James Massengale's strenuous efforts to determine whether the mermaid's craving for a soul and her general beliefs and behavior reflect Protestant or Catholic principles, however, strike me as somewhat misguided, for the tale's emphasis falls on the transition from pagan to Christian, just as the *rusalka*'s psychodrama traces the reverse—the shift from Christian to pagan. Massengale's indecision whether the Mermaid's transformation constitutes "a" or "the" miracle ignores the fact that miracle by definition interprets her experience from a Christian (and therefore *post facto*) perspective, and sooner a Catholic than a Protestant one, given Protestantism's skepticism about miracles and Catholicism's ready embrace of them.[15] In a genre that by definition relies on fantasy, to dwell on the author's adherence to or deviation from religious precepts of a particular belief system seems counterproductive. Andersen's overriding concern in the narrative could hardly be clearer.

At the fairy tale's close, the pedagogical moral of the narrative, with the centrality of the soul, is articulated directly by the air spirits shepherding the now ethereal-voiced protagonist through ether:

> Your suffering and your loyalty have raised you up into the realm of airy spirits, and now in the course of three hundred years you may earn by your good deeds a soul that will never die.... This is the way that we shall rise to the kingdom of God, after three hundred years have passed.... We may get there even sooner... Unseen, we fly into the homes of men, where there are children, and for every day on which we find a good child who pleases his parents and deserves their love, God shortens our days of trial. The child does not know when we float through his room, but when we smile at him in approval one year is taken from our three hundred. But if we see a naughty, mischievous child we must shed tears of sorrow, and each tear adds a day to the time of our trial.

---

15 After a lengthy debate with himself, Massengale concludes that when writing the tale, Andersen came under the influence of his 1833-34 trip to Catholic Italy and at the conclusion located the mermaid in the transitional space of purgatory ("The Miracle," 571). In my view, his reading of the fairy tale does not allow sufficiently for Andersen's imagination, which surely did not subscribe to religious dogma. Similarly, Massengale's equation of the realm in which air spirits dwell with purgatory ignores the fact that the *Catechism of the Catholic Church* defines purgatory as "a state of final purification after death and before entrance into heaven for those who died in God's friendship, but were only imperfectly purified; a final cleansing of human imperfection before one is able to enter the joy of heaven" (896). Perhaps the concept of limbo, not part of Catholic doctrine, but sooner a theological theory, would be more appropriate in the mermaid's case, for it applies to the unbaptized. See Burke, "Purgatory, Limbo Explained."

Here Andersen, with seemingly unshakable faith in a benevolent divinity along Leibnizian lines ("all is for the best in the best of all possible worlds"), emphasizes religious probity, a life of charitable deeds, female self-sacrifice, and children's obedience—a far cry from the sexual desire, betrayal, and lust for vengeance that mark the folkloric and Pushkinian *rusalka*.[16] Whereas the latter seduces and breeds unease, Andersen's mermaid wholeheartedly strives for the goal of Christian salvation. Lise Præstgaard Andersen assigns the little mermaid to the category of Andersen's "loving and self-sacrificing, but also active and brave women" ("The Feminine Element," 513)—which from one standpoint is accurate: the mermaid doggedly pursues her heart's desire and remains true to her convictions. In a sense, she is an ideal Russian heroine, inasmuch as the spiritual and physical torments she endures, both through unrequited love and the anticipated experience of three centuries as an air spirit, fit neatly into the venerable Russian tradition of strong women, kenosis, and glorification of suffering by writers such as Dostoevsky.

Secondly, whereas the context and the features of the *rusalka* teem with contradictions, Andersen's tale propounds consistency and harmony through aesthetics. His text abounds with lush descriptions of beautiful settings in the sea world and above ground. In a relatively brief narrative, the word "beautiful" and its synonyms, applied to human and natural phenomena, occur more than thirty times. As in countless moralistic works, including those of sentimentalism (e.g., Samuel Richardson's *Clarissa* [1748] and Nikolai Karamzin's *Poor Liza* [*Bednaia Liza*, 1792]), aesthetics and ethics (i.e., beauty and virtue) are indivisible—the apparently deathless cliché of "beautiful inside and out." For instance, the little mermaid is a paragon of both, and worships a marble statue of a beautiful young male, whom the prince embodies in live form; her attraction is aesthetic, not sensual. Moreover, the prince appears not as a seducer and faithless lover, but as a generous and affectionate friend to the mermaid, whom he indulgently, if myopically, perceives as a child. Completely (albeit unconvincingly) unaware of her romantic love for him, he can hardly be accused of "doing her wrong" by marrying a princess, who also seems flawless. The issue of class pivotal for Pushkin's play and Goncharov's film is irrelevant, and all the personae in the fairy tale could hardly be more positive, except the pragmatic witch with special powers, who demands the mermaid's peerless voice

---

16 For basic information about Andersen's life and works, see Grønbech, *Hans Christian Andersen*. More detailed treatments may be found in Bredsdorff, *Hans Christian Andersen*; and Wullschläger, *Hans Christian Andersen: The Life of a Storyteller*.

as payment for her service. Yet even she attempts to discourage the mermaid's irrational plan and later offers her a second chance at life.

Loss of voice may potentially link Andersen's mermaid to the interiority of a religious life, but above all it analogizes her with ancient sirens, Echo, and—as feminists repeatedly have argued—a host of women deprived of speech in both a literal and metaphorical sense.[17] A rich interiority, of course, does not require muteness—a fact brought home by those adaptations of the fairy tale that dispense with that fateful deprivation.[18] As a female who willingly exchanges her ability to speak and sing for the role of an uncomprehending male's companion, the little mermaid would find little sympathy among feminists owing to her masochistic eagerness for self-abnegation and readiness to abjure everything for love, evolving from obedient daughter to enamored, infantilized victim. But then, in privileging a form of kenosis or *imitatio Christi*, Andersen's perspective is decidedly spiritual rather than sociopolitical (and, in Jack Zipes's view, misogynist [*Enchanted Screen*, 256]). The immortal human soul dominates Andersen's narrative, which relegates romance to secondary status, for the mermaid's decision to sacrifice her own life instead of killing the prince signifies above all that she has passed the test for which throughout the ages Christ has served as the (persuasively articulate rather than mute) exemplar. In short, readers' perceptions of the mermaid depend upon the critical lens through which they read the tale.

Of all Russian screen adaptations, the little-known 1968 animated feature *The Little Mermaid* (*Rusalochka*), directed by Ivan Aksenchuk and scripted by Aleksandr Galich,[19] most compactly reproduces Andersen's text, opting for expressive minimalism. A double framing sequence prompted by Copenhagen's famous statue of the mermaid launches the story of her melancholy fate. Executed in the comic style of cartoons, a fast-paced black-and-white prelude shows tourists frenetically descending upon Copenhagen and listening open-mouthed to a soulful Russian guide intent on narrating the mermaid's readiness to immolate herself for love. Responding to his comments, a group of comically skeptical fish provide a corrective for the benefit of the tourists and especially viewers, observing that mermaids exist, whereas love does not (fig. 6).

---

17 See, for instance, Cixous and Clément, *La Jeune Née* (1975) and Moi, *Sexual/Textual Politics: Feminist Literary Theory* (1985).
18 Regarding the question of anti-feminism in the tale, the editors of this volume and I part ways.
19 A popular poet and bard forced to emigrate in 1974, Galich (1918-77) is better known for his subversive musical compositions than his work as a screenwriter.

Fig. 6. Ivan Aksenchuk's ironic fish introduce the mermaid's tale. Soyuzmultfilm.

Fig. 7. The aesthetics of the icon and modernism spiritualize Aksenchuk's prince and especially the mermaid. Soyuzmultfilm.

In other words, the two groups represent the competing views of "land" and "water." Banal and lacking vivid colors, these humorous personae could hardly contrast more to the melancholy tale of transcendent love that follows.

The impressive aesthetics of the animated figures in the story proper draws on classical art—both icons and Renaissance painting (flatness, expressive large eyes, angularity)—to convey the spiritual dimension of Andersen's tale (fig. 7), and the solemnity of the highly textured, original artwork is abetted by Aleksandr Lokshin's orchestral score and the lovely soprano whose plangent song musically characterizes the mermaid.[20] These sources compensate for the limitations in facial expressiveness inhering in the genre of animation, for which motion is primary. Indeed, the underwater sequences are remarkable for the fluid balletic movements of the mermaid and her sisters, in dramatic contrast to the accelerated, clumsy jerkiness of the mundane tourists. Such juxtapositions serve to wrest the mermaid's story from the commonplace—a device abetted by the camera's focus on a disproportionately huge sun (fig. 8) and on the endless expanse of the sky/heavens.

Visually the film adheres to the hypotext and adds nothing narratively significant to it other than the frame and the song that conveys to the viewers the incalculable price the mermaid pays by bartering her voice.[21] Indeed, the animated film set a precedent for the inclusion of songs in later screen versions of the narrative, the diegetic inclusion here of the

---

20 See Natalie Belton's astute commentary on the film's assets at http://the-animatorium.blogspot.com/2013/08/rusalochka-little-mermaid-review.html.
21 Instead of the knife intended to kill the prince and his bride, Aksenchuk has the sisters bring the luckless mermaid a container of a violent storm that would cause the ship to capsize, thereby drowning the couple.

Fig. 8. The size and positioning of the sun lend a mythological dimension to Aksenchuk's mermaid's fate. Soyuzmultfilm.

Fig. 9. Aksenchuk's distraught prince gazes skyward as he seeks the vanished mermaid. Soyuzmultfilm.

mermaid's song intended as an equivalent, not for the *rusalka*'s beguiling voice, but for the mermaid's iterated belief in the imperishability of beauty—a view determinately embedded in Andersen's tale.[22] No mention of a soul impinges on the narrative about the triumph of boundless love,[23] kindness, and bravery (qualities underscored by the tour guide's voiceover at the film's conclusion), though at one juncture church bells ring (as in Andersen's tale) and the prince's upward gaze in the finale intimates the celestial ascent of the mermaid, even if the visuals sooner indicate her transformation into sea foam (fig. 9). For an animated film under half an hour in length, Aksenchuk's ability to retain so many of Andersen's major elements is impressive.

Not so Vladimir Bychkov's feature film *The Little Mermaid* (*Rusalochka*, 1976), broadly popular with Soviet audiences as well as viewers blogging on IMDb. A Russian-Bulgarian co-produced musical that revels in color, song (with lyrics by Bella Akhmadulina), numerous crowd scenes, and splashy scenery, it focuses in a lachrymose-romantic register on the mermaid's readiness to forfeit everything to win her prince (played by Iurii Senkevich). Though the film explicitly claims Andersen's tale as its source, it departs from it in several major respects: Bychkov introduces a narrative frame that boasts a male character, Sulpitius (Valentin Nikulin)[24] as a stand-in for Andersen (fig. 10); allows the mermaid (Vika Novikova) to retain her thready voice; reduces the competitor-princess

---

22 The prince mistakes the identity not only of his savior, but also of the singer, attributing both his rescue and the song to the princess he marries.
23 The contemporary tour guide calls the narrative a "story of love that knows no obstacles."
24 Bychkov doubtless chose his name, Sulpicius in Latin, for the Sulpicia family of Rome, which included prominent advocates of reform. Indeed, Sulpitius is an enlightened Renaissance man trapped in a medieval milieu.

Fig. 10. Vladimir Bychkov's mermaid and Sulpitius, transformed and transported into a different era, encounter each other as they travel by coach. Gosfil'mofond.

Fig. 11. Rivals for the prince's love, the mermaid and the conniving princess. Gosfil'mofond.

(Galina Artemova) to a vain, dishonest manipulator (fig. 11); and at film's end merely makes the mermaid invisible to the prince as she roams the earth, bringing happiness to everyone whom she encounters (thus running ahead of Andersen's tale). No explicit soul-seeking, no death, no transcendence. What the mermaid receives from the witch-cum-tavernkeeper (Galina Volchek) (fig. 12) is two legs, blonde hair instead of her "natural" green tresses (fig. 13), which the witch appropriates for herself, and a heart capable of breaking—an organ intended to replace the soul, which would be out of place in the atheistic Soviet Union. In short, the crucial spiritual dimension of Andersen's tale is absent.

To compensate, no doubt, Bychkov makes productive use of the film's frame, which intimates a grasp of Andersen's preoccupations in everyday life. The Andersen lookalike in the carriage at the film's outset proves to be the poet Sulpitius, who narrates/creates the events of the film's plot, in which he serves as the mermaid's guardian angel. In a sense he is also her double, for he saves her life through sacrificing his own, duplicating the mermaid's and Christ's self-renunciation; and neither he nor the mermaid has any regrets, despite the loss of their loved ones. Quite apart from this parallelism, as idealists, the two stand out starkly against the masses that Bychkov portrays in a carnivalesque spirit recalling Bakhtin's concept of the public square. Coarse, rowdy, drunk, easily swayed and driven solely by physical appetite, the ignorant populace could hardly be more vulgar and uncivilized (fig. 14). And their reaction to the mermaid, like those of the prince's crew, evokes popular beliefs about the Russian folkloric *rusalka*: namely, her demonic nature and her habit of luring men to their doom and capsizing ships.

Fig. 12. The witch and tavern owner who effects the mermaid's metamorphosis at a great price. Gosfil'mofond.

Fig. 13. Green-haired and instantly enamored, the mermaid gazes at the prince she has saved. Gosfil'mofond.

The world of Bychkov's film offers two untenable options for the mermaid and Sulpitius: the ignorant animalism of the fatuous masses, on the one hand, and the stifling, sanctimonious falsity of the upper classes, epitomized by the princess whom the prince weds, on the other (fig. 15). Neither can accommodate the integrity of the two "outsiders." For Sulpitius, Bychkov drew on Konstantin Paustovsky's story "The Night Stagecoach" ("Nochnoi dilizhans," 1955), which dramatizes Andersen's journey in a coach with several young women in whom he detects a colorful charm.[25] The travel motif here reflects Andersen's own peripatetic life, in the course of which he enjoyed countless chance encounters.[26] As a stand-in for Andersen, Sulpitius presumably voices Paustovsky's sense of alienation from what Pushkin called "the herd" or the philistines, whose imperviousness to "higher things" plunges civilization into dark medievalism.

In an enthusiastic response to the film, Zipes hypothesizes: "If Sulpicius [sic] represents the power of art, then the film appears to argue that its function is to save integrity and truth [i.e., the mermaid—HG] during a time of social and political degeneration."[27] That time in the film is portrayed as the brutal Middle Ages (which Zipes presumably

---

25 See the contribution to this volume by Marina Balina, to whom I am grateful for alerting me to this Paustovsky text.
26 On the pertinence of travel to Andersen's life and works, see the article "Hans Christian Andersen—The Journey of His Life" by the Danish/British scholar Hans Christian Andersen (!).
27 Zipes, *The Enchanted Screen*, 260. Zipes's hyperbolic praise of the film partly results from his contrasting it to the Disney version of *The Little Mermaid* (1989), which predictably features a "happy ending" worthy of a story about a cheerleader. But that has been precisely the function of Disney films from the very start, as Zipes surely knows.

The Danish Little Mermaid vs. the Russian Rusalka: 331

Fig. 14. The uncomprehending rabble to whom both the mermaid and Sulpitius are alien beings. Gosfil'mofond.

Fig. 15. The wedding that seals the mermaid's fate. Gosfil'mofond.

equates with the Soviet era?[28]), and since Sulpitius is hopelessly in love with the mermaid, just as she is with the prince, his impetus to protect her springs from his attraction to her rather than from social or aesthetic considerations. Not art but heart drives him. As a disciple of the Frankfurt School, Zipes is perhaps overly eager to interpret the film along universal political lines. Certainly the role of the writer and his role in society obsessed Andersen, ever anxious about appreciation of his writings as well as remuneration for them. But he also experienced unrequited love, which is precisely what occupies center stage in Bychkov's film. Given the Soviet Union's official atheism, the omission of Andersen's religious dimension hardly surprises, while the retention of optimism (however illogical) accords with the state's accent on a radiant future and purported absence of uncontrollable sexual drives, violence, and suicide—evils attributed to the decadent West. *Pace* Zipes, when all is said and done, the film reduces Andersen's tale to a double-barreled love story in an inhospitable environment, and the return to the coach at film's end implies that "all ends well," even as the dispiriting scenario presumably undergoes endless repetition, for all the personae in the coach are played by the cast of the major story (fig. 16).

Bychkov and his scriptwriter emphasize Russians' traditional fear of *rusalki*, especially during the on-board celebration of the prince's

---

28 The belligerent and easily swayed crowds wish to burn the mermaid, which may hardly be interpreted as coding exile to the Gulag or execution under Stalinism. Perhaps Zipes has a universal notion of sociopolitical degeneration in mind.

Fig. 16. Modernized versions of the prince and the dishonest princess he married are travelling companions in the coach. Gosfil'mofond.

Fig. 17. As the mermaid recedes from his sight, the prince confronts his loss through the device of a mirror that intimates both inner division and self-recognition. Gosfil'mofond.

birthday, but otherwise extract selectively from Andersen's fairy tale to fashion the mermaid as an ideal of young womanhood: beautiful, self-abnegating, subservient to men, and, at narrative's end, eager to infuse the social collective with joy and optimism. The spirit of the film borders on the insistent values of socialist realism, as the female protagonist substitutes the satisfaction of bolstering the community for lack of personal fulfillment in romantic love. And the prince's loss at the film's conclusion (fig. 17), given his haughty blindness (not to mention Senkevich's [1937-2003] limited acting abilities), can hardly distress audiences. In other words, the scenario of Bychkov's film completely coincides with Soviet gender disposition and may account, at least in part, for its popularity in the USSR and with pre-feminist audiences in the West (as well as among fans of green hair). Yet at the same time, the ability to wring an optimistic note from gruesome and horrendous circumstances allies Soviet ideology with Andersen's viewpoint on life, evidenced in such similarly sadomasochistic tales as "The Little Match Girl" and the transparent allegory of "alienation redeemed" in "The Ugly Duckling."

Iurii Tynianov, Bakhtin, and numerous theorists rightly observe that once a paradigm exhausts itself, it paves the way for parody or some form of laughter-based narrative.[29] As much is attested by the Armenian-Russian director Anna Melikian's highly self-conscious post-Soviet *Rusalka* (2007; known in English as *Mermaid*), which strives for humor and enjoyed limited success at the Russian box office, but won several

---

29 See Tynianov, "O literaturnoi evoliutsii."

awards;[30] generated considerable commentary; became Russia's official submission to the 2009 Academy Awards in the foreign-language film category; and achieved sufficient popularity to emerge as an easily purchasable DVD with Anglophone subtitles in the West.

Melikian's protagonist, signally called Alisa (Mariia Shalaeva)—a name conjuring up the magical world of Lewis Carroll's *Alice in Wonderland* (1865)—resides *by* instead of *in* the sea. She possesses neither beauty nor benign impulses (fig. 18), and spends most of the film in Moscow as a maid to a postmodern prince, Sasha (Evgenii Tsyganov)—that is, not royalty, but today's equivalent: an apparently successful businessman. His latest (shameless) project entails selling residences on the moon, traditionally the symbolic locus or stimulant of imagination and fantasy (as for instance in *Eugene Onegin* [*Evgenii Onegin*] or *The Master and Margarita* [*Master i Margarita*]).

The sea plays a minor role in the film, but Melikian cleverly retains and modifies recognizable motifs from Andersen's tale, scattering them throughout her narrative: Alisa originally lives with her vulgar, fleshy mother (Mariia Sokova, fig. 19) and senile grandmother (Albina Evtushevskaia) in a shack right by the Black Sea; she has no need to barter a mermaid tail for legs, but she does abandon dreams of ballet, for which strong legs and feet are necessary; whereas she does not give up her voice in exchange for human form, she does stop speaking temporarily at the age of six; though her supernatural powers are limited, she can make apples fall from trees at will, raise a hurricane, demolish the family home by fire, and have prophetic dreams; in Moscow, she saves her neurotic pseudo-prince from drowning when he attempts suicide; as in Andersen's original, she bonds with her rival for his affection (Rita, played by Irina Skrinichenko), in this case through companionable smoking (fig. 20); and at tale's end she dies, but... from being hit by a speeding car. Whereas Andersen accentuates beauty, of both the underwater realm and his protagonists, neither Alisa nor Sasha boasts good looks (fig. 21), and in fact Melikian ironizes modern advertising, which peddles beauty, success, and happiness through such banal slogans as "Everything depends on you," "Follow your own star," and the like. These clichés are the very stuff of urban fairy tales in today's Moscow.

Melikian modernizes the fairytale protagonist, demoting her to an unskilled worker pacing the city streets dressed up as a mobile phone and cleaning Sasha's apartment. Moreover, her love interest is no high-

---

30 These included the Berlin International Film Festival (FIPRESCI) prize in 2008 and the award for directing (drama) at the Sundance Film Festival.

Fig. 18. Anna Melikian's unprepossessing contemporary mermaid, Alisa. Central Partnership Film Company.

Fig. 19. Alisa's mother. Central Partnership Film Company.

Fig. 20. Alisa and Rita enjoy a friendly smoke. Central Partnership Film Company.

Fig. 21. Sasha and Alisa, with the latter's ludicrous job as ambulatory telephone portrayed in the background—a fantasy shot. Central Partnership Film Company.

minded prince, but a boorish, depressed egotist intent on self-enrichment by dubious means. Not he, but his friend/partner realizes that Alisa's otherworldly air renders her ideal for advertising their company's lunar scheme via "Moon Girl" commercials, and whereas Andersen and Bychkov emphasize the mermaid's concern for people's happiness, Alisa is terminally self-involved. Her contribution to humanity consists of her posthumous role in the ad for Sasha's questionable business, which looms on a huge billboard in the city, greeting passersby on the street.

Remarkably, in light of the film's humor and self-consciousness, its gender politics could hardly be more retrograde: as the besotted female occupying lowly social positions, Alisa devotes her life to capturing a worthless male for whom she presumably is prepared to die. She harbors no interest in anything else in life. In the contemporary context, which Melikian underscores, this stark limitation renders her pathetic instead of *sym*pathetic. Early in the film we see the introverted Alisa spending time in a school for mentally handicapped children, and the film's plot unwittingly suggests that as an adult she has not advanced beyond that stage—indeed, Alisa remains completely static in character from childhood to early adulthood, evincing no development whatever. Neither charming nor intelligent, the unbeautiful protagonist represents precisely the kind of woman against whom most politically engaged representatives of feminism have railed.

The problem is that, absent the idea of acquiring a soul—which resides at the very nexus of Andersen's fairy tale—the plot is reduced to yet another platitudinous story of an unhappy female yearning for a male and romance. Whatever else Melikian may ironize, she leaves this enervated scenario intact. Since neither sexuality nor spirituality receives its due, we are left with what is essentially a soap opera, devoid of Andersen's moralism, but also of particular significance. Whereas fascinating dark forces operate in folklore, Pushkin's poem and play, and Goncharov's film; and mysterious powers related to the transcendent are invoked in Andersen's tale, here the pseudo-mermaid's death is merely a commonplace traffic accident.

In fact, this widely circulated recent cinematic *Rusalka* would have fared better had Melikian developed those sections of the film implicitly criticizing contemporary advertising and its unscrupulous means of selling dreams (as in Andrei Konchalovsky's 2007 *Gloss* [*Glianets*]) or if she had reversed the gender relations dramatized by the folkloric *rusalka*: for instance, had Sasha fallen in love with Alisa, been spurned, and departed for the moon. As it stands, the film, despite widespread recognition, suffers from a peculiar irresoluteness. Russian reviewers have called it a drama or a melodrama, while Natascha Drubek-Meyer in a long review for *Art Margins* calls it a "tragic comedy." She expresses annoyance with it, largely because "[t]he film does not quite cope with the challenge of its genre. As a remake of an old fairytale [sic] by Andersen, the film misses a great opportunity to rethink the gender stereotypes present in its 19th century precursor."[31] Though Drubek-Meyer's appraisal generally strikes me as reasonable, the film does not aspire to tragedy, and Melikian certainly did not envision or label it as such; moreover, its intermittent melodramatic aspects seem halfhearted at best. Melodrama—chiefly a women's genre in traditional cinema owing to its heightened emotions, according to Western critics[32]—by definition does not consort with comedy; whereas this film lacks the hyperbole inherent in melodrama, and its frivolous music abets its comic aspects. In short, by straddling drama and comedy, Melikian's *Rusalka* courts and succumbs to schizophrenia, resulting in a hybrid that dwindles Andersen's protagonist into a silly, smitten girl obsessed with a rotter and romance.

Film directors such as Bychkov and Melikian doubtless chose to adapt Andersen's fairy tale instead of turning to Russian folklore because the Danish source provides a readymade plot with considerable human appeal. Additionally, its affirmation at the end, however contentious, harmonizes with the positive orientation of Soviet traditions. Yet neither director tapped into the most profound and promising aspect of Andersen's "The Little Mermaid"—a pagan creature's desire to acquire a soul, which in Slavic folklore the *rusalka* embodies, though with a minus sign, for she is a soul relegated to the nether regions.[33] Given Russian culture's fabled exploration of spirituality, the two directors' preference is both unexpected and, more importantly, unproductive. By boldly mining native folkloric sources, Pushkin's play and poem, as well as Goncharov's film and Petrov's animated *Rusalka*, yield incomparably richer texts: they engage metaphysics, acknowledge sexuality as well as

---

31 Drubek-Meyer, "A Little Mermaid in the World of Russian Advertising."
32 See Singer, *Melodrama and Modernity*. For an incisive examination of melodrama in Soviet film and TV, see Prokhorov and Prokhorov, *Film and Television Genres of the Late Soviet Era*, chapter 4.
33 The centrality of the soul to Andersen's narrative (like its absence in aquatic beings) was understood by Oscar Wilde, who wrote "The Fisherman and His Soul" (1888; published 1891) in response to Andersen's tale. An apostle of love's power, Wilde has his titular young fisherman fall in desperate love with a mermaid and willingly surrender his soul so as to unite with her. For the full text of Wilde's tale, copious illustrations, background information, and a series of pedagogical exercises, see https://fernandamaterial2014.files.wordpress.com/2014/05/e380902e380917-the-fisherman-and-his-soul.pdf. For an analysis of "The Fisherman and His Soul," as well as Wilde's other fairy tales, see Quintus, "The Moral Prerogative in Oscar Wilde."

dark impulses, confront paradox head-on, and rescue the *rusalka* from the platitudes and triviality of stories concerned almost exclusively with unrequited love, which reduce Andersen's tale to banality.

One can only hope that the next screen *Rusalka*, unlike the lightweight 2012 version, will follow their example or at the very least realize the captivating philosophical potential of Andersen's tale. After all, Andersen's narrative could be transposed into a film about Russia's historical transition from paganism to Christianity. The passionate desire for a soul holds out no less promise than its counter-impulse—the loss of soul through suicide, which the folkloric Russian *rusalka* experiences. Andersen's hugely popular tale, which has seen hundreds of adoptions and adaptations, from Austrian composer Alexander von Zemlinsky's symphonic poem *Die Seejungfrau* (1905) to the blockbuster Disney musical (1989), in a sense constitutes the other bookend to longstanding beliefs associated with Russia's *rusalka*.

Conclusion

Rich in metaphysical and narrative potential, Andersen's tale has attracted legions of artists in multiple visual fields for whom a scenario addressing such profound issues as Christianity versus paganism, the significance of the soul, the nature of love, and the issues of aesthetics, self-sacrifice, incompatible spheres, and related questions understandably offers unparalleled opportunity for both self-expression and collaboration across genres with one of Europe's most famous cultural figures. As with so many tales by Andersen—"The Snow Queen," "The Ugly Duckling," "Thumbelina"—the singular protagonist whose life trajectory arouses a plenitude of emotional responses from readers also prompts filmmakers to adapt his classic works. Even more than his fellow Danish paragons—Søren Kierkegaard in philosophy, Isak Dinesen (pseud. for Karen Blixen) in literature, Carl Dreyer in film, and Sara Blaedel and Jussi Adler-Olsen in contemporary crime fiction—Andersen enjoys worldwide popularity as the literary folklorist who tapped into the depths of the human psyche in narratives that seduce readers of all ages and nationalities. His posthumous fate, as the title of his autobiography registered and predicted, illustrates the timeless fairy tale of his life, which cannot be separated from the imaginative fairy tales he authored, now a fundamental part of the contemporary international folklore canon. Of these, "The Little Mermaid" indisputably represents one of the most memorable.

Works Cited

Andersen, Hans Christian. *The Fairy Tale of My Life: An Autobiography.* Translated by Mary Howitt. New York: Cooper Square Press, 2000. (This is a photographic reproduction of the Horace E. Scudder [Boston: Houghton, Mifflin, and Co.] edition of 1871.)

Andersen, Hans Christian. "Hans Christian Andersen—the Journey of His Life." *Bulletin of the John Rylands University Library of Manchester* 76, no. 3 (1994). Available electronically: https://www.escholar.manchester.ac.uk/api/datastream?publicationPid=uk-ac-man-scw:1m2349&datastreamId=POST-PEER-REVIEW-PUBLISHERS-DOCUMENT.PDF

Andersen, Lise Præstgaard. "The Feminine Element—And a Little About the Masculine Element in H. C. Andersen's Fairy Tales." In *Hans Christian Andersen: A Poet in Time*, edited by Johan de Mylius, Aage Jørgensen, and Viggo Hjørnager Pedersen, 501-14. Odense: Odense University Press, 1999.

Bredsdorff, Elias. *Hans Christian Andersen.* New York: Scribner, 1975.

Burke, Jennifer. "Purgatory, Limbo Explained." *Catholic Courier*, 20 December 2009. Available electronically: http://www.catholiccourier.com/in-depth/previous-topics/purgatory-limbo-explained

Catechism of the Catholic Church. USCCB Publishing, 2000.

Cixous, Hélène, and Catherine Clément. *La Jeune Née.* Paris: Union générale d'éditions, 1975.

Drubek-Meyer, Natascha. "A Little Mermaid in the World of Russian Advertising." *Art Margins*, 5 February 2009. Available electronically: http://www.artmargins.com/index.php/natascha-drubek-meyer-a-little-mermaid-in-the-world-of-russian-advertising

Fouqué, Friedrich de la Motte. *Undine.* In *Romantic Fairy Tales*, translated and edited by Carol Tully, 53-125. London: Penguin Books, 2000.

Genette, Gérard. *Palimpsests: Literature in the Second Degree.* Lincoln NE: University of Nebraska Press, 1997.

Golden, Joanne M. *The Narrative Symbol in Childhood Literature: Explorations in the Construction of Text.* Berlin: Mouton de Gruyter, 1990.

Goscilo, Helena. "Watery Maidens: Rusalki as Sirens and Slippery Signs." In *Poetics. Self. Place: Essays in Honor of Anna Lisa Crone*, edited by Catherine O'Neil, Nicole Boudreau, and Sarah Krive, 50-70. Bloomington IN: Slavica 2007.

Grønbech, Bo. *Hans Christian Andersen.* Boston: Twayne Publishers, 1980.

Hubbs, Joanna. *Mother Russia: The Feminine Myth in Russian Culture.* Bloomington IN: Indiana UP, 1988.

Ivanits, Linda J. *Russian Folk Belief.* Armonk NY: M. E. Sharpe, Inc. 1992.

James, George. "In Person: The World of His Imagination." *The New York Times*,

7 December 1997. Available electronically: http://www.nytimes.com/1997/12/07/nyregion/in-person-the-world-of-his-imagination.html

Jones, W. Glyn. "Andersen and Those of Other Faiths." In *Hans Christian Andersen: A Poet in Time*, edited by Johan de Mylius, Aage Jørgensen, and Viggo Hjørnager Pedersen, 259-70. Odense: Odense University Press, 1999.

Massengale, James. "The Miracle and a Miracle in the Life of a Mermaid." In *Hans Christian Andersen: A Poet in Time*, edited by Johan de Mylius, Aage Jørgensen, and Viggo Hjørnager Pedersen, 555-76. Odense: Odense University Press, 1999.

Moi, Toril. *Sexual/Textual Politics: Feminist Literary Theory*. London: Methuen, 1985.

Prokhorov, Alexander and Elena Prokhorov. *Film and Television Genres of the Late Soviet Era*. New York: Bloomsbury Academic, 2017.

Quintus, John Allen. "The Moral Prerogative in Oscar Wilde: A Look at the Fairy Tales." *VQR* 53, no 4 (1977). Available electronically: http://www.vqronline.org/essay/moral-prerogative-oscar-wilde-look-fairy-tales

Shaparova, N. S. *Kratkaia entsiklopediia slavianskoi mifologii*. Moscow: Astrel', 2001.

Siniavsky, Andrei. *Ivan the Fool: Russian Folk Belief. A Cultural History*. Translated by Joanne Turnbull. Moscow: GLAS, 2007.

Singer, Ben. *Melodrama and Modernity: Early Sensational Cinema and Its Contexts*. New York: Columbia University Press, 2001.

Tynianov, Iurii. "O literaturnoi evoliutsii." In *Arkhaisty i novatory* by Iurii Tynianov, 30-47. Leningrad: Priboi, 1929.

Wullschläger, Jackie. *Hans Christian Andersen: The Life of a Storyteller*. New York: Knopf, 2001.

Zelenin, D. K. *Izbrannye trudy. Ocherki russkoi mifologii: Umershie neestestvennoi smert'iu i rusalki*. Moscow: Indrik, 1995.

Zipes, Jack. *The Enchanted Screen: The Unknown History of Fairy-Tale Films*. New York and London: Routledge, 2011.

Filmography

Aksenchuk, Ivan. *Rusalochka* [The Little Mermaid]. 1968. Available at https://www.youtube.com/watch?v=Zvyt2fdWJAQ.

Bychkov, Vladimir. *Rusalochka* [The Little Mermaid]. 1976.

Goncharov, Vasilii. *Rusalka* [The Mermaid]. 1910. Available at https://commons.wikimedia.org/wiki/File:The_Mermaid_(1910).webm.

Melikian, Anna. *Rusalka* [The Mermaid].

Petrov, Aleksandr. *Rusalka* [The Mermaid].1996/7. Available at https://www.youtube.com/watch?v=7MpAr3rcEg0.

Reid, Tim. *The Little Mermaid*. 1979. Available at https://www.youtube.com/watch?v=7--cjJTnTGY.

Sander, Peter. *The Little Mermaid*. 1975. Available at https://www.youtube.com/watch?v=3-UpkwxUTo4.

Tales and Holes:

Illustrating Andersen the Russian Way[1]

Yuri Leving

Introduction: Borrowing, Appropriating, Transforming

The search for authenticity once led a contemporary Russian artist working on illustrations for Hans Christian Andersen's fairy tales, Mikhail Magaril, to make a trip to Denmark:

> I was looking for details to include in the book and thought visiting some of the huge palaces might give me some inspiration. However, I was disappointed by the emptiness of the rooms. I searched antique bookstores, looking for editions of Andersen's books that were published during his lifetime, but I found their styles to be overly traditional.[2]

Magaril's search, paradoxically, turned out to be in vain. Many café patrons, he noticed, were reading; however, instead of the "expected" works of their fellow countryman, "person after person was engrossed in a book that graces every American child's nightstand: Harry Potter."[3] After such a disappointing encounter, the artist decided to call off his planned visit to Andersen's birthplace, Odense, altogether; by his own admission, he was "afraid to find an American Disneyland in its place."[4] Magaril returned to his tiny, ridiculously expensive Danish hotel room, only to be pleasantly awakened by a wonderful sound: the song of nightingales, the very subject of the illustrations he was working on.

Hans Christian Andersen holds the title of world's most-translated author,[5] but he is also one of the most prolifically illustrated. The story of Russians illustrating Andersen's works dates back at least a hundred and fifty years now. In what follows, I will not be offering a compre-

---

1 I would like to thank Marina Balina and Mads Sohl Jessen for their comments on the earlier version of this article as well as for their continuous inspiration, which has made pondering fairy tales such a rewarding experience for an adult.
2 Magaril, "Migratory Birds," 253.
3 Ibid.
4 Ibid.
5 Krogh Hansen and Lundholt, *When We Get to the End*, 15.

hensive survey of this phenomenon,[6] but will focus rather on a few narrower questions: how has Andersen's literary output sparked specific creative ideas among artists of Russian origin? Does the shared cultural background of Russian graphic artists make illustrating a foreign author any different from the challenges experienced by their Western counterparts? And, finally, what common patterns and interconnectivity of imagery does this visual metatext offer across various styles, genres, and art mediums, whether in etchings and watercolors, or screen adaptations and video games?

The anecdote from Magaril's trip to the writer's homeland just mentioned is indicative of the dual nature of the reception of Andersen's writings by Russian artists and by the Dane's readers generally in Russia before, during, and after the Soviet period. His tales allure and deceive, such that imagery developed for and associated with the Russianized Andersen has gradually acquired cultural autonomy and meaning largely independent of its Danish roots. During the last century and a half (the first translated Russian edition of Andersen's stories appeared in 1857), these fairy tales became part and parcel of a typical Russian child's education.

Print illustrations serve as an essential element of early literacy instruction, and most young readers experience books especially via graphic art. Russia's inaugural readers of Andersen in translation had to be content with reproductions of artwork produced by foreign artists; the first Russian *Complete Tales* (*Polnoe sobranie skazok*, 1863-64) published by Mariia Trubnikova and Nadezhda Stasova included woodcuts by Vilhelm Pedersen. (For that matter, in Denmark itself, Andersen's writings had been published without visuals prior to the lavish 1850 volume illustrated by Pedersen.[7]) Pedersen's artwork was reprinted in many subsequent Russian editions of Andersen. The first known original illustrator of Andersen in Russia was Baron Mikhail Klodt, for the edition *New Tales* (*Novye skazki*, 1868); Klodt's drawings prompted Andersen to write from Denmark to St. Petersburg to express his admiration, and

---

[6] Illustrating Andersen in Russia has been extensively studied by L. Zvonareva and L. Kudriavtseva in their two coauthored books *Kh. K. Andersen i russkie illiustratory* and *Khans Kristian Andersen i ego russkie illiustratory za poltora veka*. On the illustrating of Andersen in the West generally, see the Hamelin Associazione Culturale edition commemorating the two-hundredth anniversary of the author's birthday, *Illustrare Andersen = Illustrating Andersen*.

[7] Vilhelm Pedersen (1820-59) was the first major Danish illustrator of Hans Christian Andersen, and was in fact handpicked by Andersen himself for this task to produce illustrations for a German edition *Gesammelte Märchen. Mit 112 Illustrationen nach Originalzeichnungen von V. Pedersen* (Leipzig: Verlag von Carl B. Lorck, 1849). The illustrations for the Danish 1850 single volume edition are the same as in the German original.

Illustrations for "The Snow Queen."

Fig. 1. By H. Tegner. *Fairy Tales.* Copenhagen: Nyt Nordisk Forlag, 1900.

Fig. 2. By V. Konashevich. *Skazki Andersena.* Moscow: Detskaia literatura, 1968.

Fig. 3. By B. Diodorov. *Snezhnaia koroleva.* Moscow: Kron-Press, 1996.

to hail this cross-cultural dialogue itself.[8] Andersen himself was an able graphic artist, which makes the compliment even more valuable.[9]

Influential Western illustrators of Andersen whose pictures have been much reproduced in Russia include the Danish artist Hans Tegner (1853-1932).[10] His artwork was so instrumental in shaping how Russians imagined both the material and fictional worlds of Andersen that at times the line between "drawing on a source of inspiration" and "outright plagiarism" may appear somewhat blurred.

Over the course of the publication of hundreds of editions of Andersen's tales in Russia, the borrowed literary texts have acquired sets of clichés and consistent visual references of their own. In 1894-95, the four-volume *Collected Works* of Andersen came out in a new skillful translation by the husband and wife team of Peter and Anna Hansen;

---

8   For Andersen's letter to N. Stasova and M. Trubnikova (28 August 1868), see Zvonareva and Kudriavtseva, *Khans Kristian Andersen i ego russkie illiustratory za poltora veka*, 43-44.

9   Five examples of Andersen's "skill as a maker of paper-cuts which are widely acknowledged as being among his best, and which display the diverse effects that he was able to achieve" are found in the scrapbook Adolph Drewsen produced with the help of his old storyteller-friend (Andersen and Drewsen, *Christine's Picture Book*, 5).

10 Commissioned for the so-called "world edition" of Andersen's fairy tales that came out in 1900 in fourteen countries, including the US and Russia, Hans Tegner's illustrations gained international popularity (this publication also featured an introduction by the influential Danish critic Georg Brandes). Curiously, Peter Hansen's archive at the Royal Library in Copenhagen contains a letter addressed to him from Ilya Repin—Hansen had a Danish translation of the Russian original prepared—in which the legendary Russian painter writes favorably about Tegner's illustrations, which his correspondent must previously have sent him. (My thanks to Mads Sohl Jessen for bringing this important information to my attention.)

since then, and to this day, nearly every edition of Andersen in Russia invariably reproduces the same text, but features new illustrations. At the early stages of publishing Andersen in Russia, his writings had often appeared along with drawings furnished by Western artists (for example, Pedersen's woodcuts copied from the German or Danish editions), but within a mere decade of the appearance of the Hansen translation, local talents seized their opportunity. This graphic art varied in the degree of its originality and faithfulness to the source material; nonetheless, it undoubtedly stands as a genuine attempt to constantly refresh the existing arsenal of Russian pictorial Anderseniana. Notably, approaches to illustration evolved during this process, depending on the political climate and individual artistic sensibilities. The artist Magaril, a product of the Soviet period, reports that 1955's *Stories and Fairy Tales* (*Skazki i istorii*) was his favorite edition; he could look at the illustrations in that book for hours, and as a boy he even slept with it under his pillow. After some years passed and the future artist matured, he "started to understand that each of Hans Christian Andersen's fairy tales held second meanings that were intended for adults."[11]

Let us examine precisely this aspect of Andersen's complex legacy in Russia: how did Soviet artists—who were, naturally, adults—use Andersen's texts to convey meaning through methods of representation that allowed them to channel nontraditional stylistics, untethered to the letter and spirit of socialist-realist doctrine?

The Silver Age Surrogate: Sovietizing Andersen

In an epoch when communist authorities were obsessively suppressing immediate precursors in the realm of artistic life, Hans Christian Andersen was not considered an agent of "corrupting foreign influence," although his writings were occasionally criticized by the prerevolutionary left and in the 1920s, when the fairy tale as a genre became a subject of examination by Soviet pedagogues (as a consequence, editions of Andersen were brought out primarily by private publishing houses in the nascent years of the Soviet printing industry). Despite the merciless inculcation of socialist realism as a dominant aesthetic, tales for younger readers were more or less exempt from the harsh treatment of Bolshevik cultural zealots. Even in the mid-to-late 1930s, when children's literature was increasingly scrutinized and censored (Vvedensky, Kharms, Zabolotsky, and Marshak, and the artist Vladimir Lebedev,

---

11 Magaril, "Migratory Birds," 254.

were all eventually harassed for their allegedly formalist, ideologically nonconformist art), such artists as Ivan Bilibin were able to promulgate Russian national folk traditions worthy of the prerevolutionary Talashkino and Abramtsevo art colonies; while Vladimir Konashevich fashioned himself into a careful homage to the refined émigré aesthete Aleksandr Benois. Illustrating Andersen during the Siege of Leningrad instead of painting Red Army propaganda posters, Konashevich incarnated a sense of profound escapism.

The major difference between artists of the previous generation and their Soviet successors was that the former had enjoyed an artistic and civic freedom as well as social and ideological mobility. The *miriskusnik*[12] Benois had had a chance to experience the Andersen world firsthand, while for Soviet artists this would be largely uncharted territory. Benois recalls his visit to Denmark in a striking contrast to Magaril's later disenchantment: "If Stockholm could fascinate me so," says Benois, "then just as much did Copenhagen, a city even more beautiful and curious. Copenhagen has entirely retained its welcoming old-world charm, *the very atmosphere of Andersen's fairy tales.*"[13] To Benois, each house on the narrow winding streets and market squares seemed to conjure the dwellings so poetically described by his favorite writer: "Behind the dull gleaming of windows I imagined rooms with fireplaces adorned with the figurines of a porcelain shepherdess and a chimney sweep, next to a steadfast tin soldier longing for a ballerina."[14] Benois goes on to say that by the time of the actual visit, he had already been somewhat familiar with Copenhagen; he loved to leaf through Danish architecture books from his father's library, and these supplied him with plenty of impressions and prepared him to experience the city *de visu*. The primacy, not of ontological reality, but of a mental picture recreated in the artist's mind should not be overlooked here (Benois speaks of "imagined rooms" filled with fireplaces and figurines, and not about what he actually saw or did not see inside); this key distinction will be significant as we examine subtle differences in how Russian artists of different historical periods represent Andersen.

For notorious reasons, after the October Revolution, foreign albums and photographs would long remain the only credible source of knowledge about the northern kingdom. Of course, there were rare exceptions; a chosen few could travel abroad under the auspices of the Communist Party.

---

12 I.e., member of the Mir iskusstva (World of Art) movement.
13 Benua, *Moi vospominaniia*, 420; emphasis mine—YL.
14 Ibid.

Illustrations for "the Swineherd."

Fig. 4. By E. Nerman. *Svinopas*. Berlin: Izdatel'stvo I. P. Ladyzhnikova, 1924.

Fig. 5. By M. Dobuzhinsky. *Svinopas*. Petrograd-Berlin: Izdatel'stvo Z. I. Grzhebina, 1922.

Among these was the trusted Soviet poet Aleksei Surkov, who in 1948, following a sanctioned visit to Andersen's homeland, composed a carefully crafted and ideologically balanced poem titled "A Danish Fairy Tale" ("Datskaia skazka"). Starting off with a sentimental appreciation of Odense, the storyteller's birthplace, where Surkov now finds a charm to match nostalgic memories from his own Andersen-suffused childhood,[15] the poem leads to something more befitting its author's status as a consummately prudish Soviet tourist. In the concluding two stanzas, Surkov condemns the behavior of a local young bourgeois, who is tipsily littering the carefully romanticized space with an orange peel and chewing gum: "The end of the fairy tale. No more romanticism / In the kingdom of the emperor with no clothes."[16] Modern Denmark, according to Surkov, has neglected its cultivated Andersenian roots in favor of capitalist-encouraged swagger.

The strategies for engaging the alien aesthetics embodied in Andersen's tales in Soviet Russia were thus twofold: one could either appropriate its universal message while denouncing the bourgeois context (as in Surkov's case), or allude to it in a covert way (for instance, by way of "visual quotations," as will be described below). Consider, for instance, Mstislav Dobuzhinsky's illustrations for "The Swineherd." Produced for the Petrograd publishing house Parus in 1917, these would have to wait a full five years to appear in print, in an edition of the Zinovii Grzhebin publishing house, which operated simultaneously in Petrograd and Berlin. Dobuzhinsky's manner is slightly reminiscent of an earlier edition of the same Andersen tale by the publishing house of

---

15 "Drowsy pigeons sit on eaves. / A sleepy breeze caresses the grass. / The dark green spires of churches / Are neatly carved in the blue sky. // Sleepy coffee shops smell of fresh rolls. / A little cloud from seaward threatens rain. / Via alleys and small lanes / We are on our way to visit the storyteller" (Surkov, *Sobranie sochinenii v 4-kh tt*, 2: 37).

16 Ibid.

I. P. Ladyzhnikov that contained illustrations by Einar Nerman (Berlin, 1911). Dobuzhinsky was among the cohort of Russians who moved to Europe following the Bolshevik revolution (he emigrated for good in 1924), a fact that contributed to the imposition of a virtual taboo on the method associated with this artist and his circle. Benois-Nerman-Dobuzhinsky's pseudo-rococo aesthetics was subjected to mockery either due to a shift in perception,[17] or because of the constructivist demands of the early socialist book market. The latter eventually gave way to ideologically safe illustrations of Andersen's tales that foregrounded cute animals and birds against the backdrop of a neutral natural habitat. For example, when illustrating "The Ugly Duckling" in the late 1920s and 1930s, Soviet artists made every effort to remain as "realistic" as possible, avoiding anything potentially construable as associated with magic rituals, folk superstitions, or the foreign petty bourgeois world (in the context of the regime's cultural politics, this general suspicion toward the fairy tale as a concept had extended far beyond the particular case of Andersen).

The artist Viktor Golman even went so far as to audaciously "update" Andersen's fairy tales by populating his bygone world with children who looked and dressed like replicas of contemporary Soviet kids (*Skazki*. Kharkov: Kosmos, 1929). The publisher included a disclaimer that some stories had been redacted to reflect changes having occurred in modern Denmark, while other texts had been omitted due to their pedagogical and ideological incompatibility with socialism. El Lissitzky's illustrated edition of Andersen's tales translated into Yiddish (Kiev, 1919) constituted an exception to the rule (perhaps due to its appearance in a geographic periphery, and a mere two years after the Bolsheviks came to power): it was executed in a predictably avant-garde

Illustrations for "The Ugly Duckling."

Fig. 6. By V. Kaabak. *Gadkii utenok*. Moscow: Knigoizdatel'stvo G. F. Mirimanova, 1929.

Fig. 7. By K. Spassky. *Gadkii utenok*. Moscow: Glavlit, 1934?

---

17 In the mid-1930s, the talented illustrator Nikolai Tyrsa (1887-1942), one of the founders of the "Leningrad school" in graphic art, espoused the view that Mir iskusstva as a movement had been artificially literary and devoid of national roots, and that its artistic tradition was essentially "German" (see the memoir of his pupil and colleague Vsevolod Petrov, "Vstrechi s N. A. Tyrsoi," 210).

Fig. 8. By Hans Christian Andersen (1859). Donation Jorn, Silkeborg.

manner, in line with the experimental early-Soviet book printing that leaned toward laconic expressionism. Intriguingly, Andersen himself as an artist was not averse to bold aesthetic gestures: for an 1859 scrapbook for little Christine, he made a paper-cut dancer alluding to "The Steadfast Tin Soldier." The figurine featured six arms, eight legs, and three faces in one body.[18]

This playful multi-limbed creature owes its shape to the medium of folded paper dolls, but also weirdly prefigures the experiments of the French Dada and Russian Rayonist artists[19] and the many-faced portraits by Picasso that would enter the avant-garde scene some fifty years in the future; oddly enough, this daring Shiva-like portrayal of a ballerina by Andersen himself remains more innovative than most of the illustrations subsequently produced for the same fairy tale. (The image was first made public in 1961 and has since figured, along with other designs, as a bas-relief on the massive fence of the KDD International Telecommunications Center in Tokyo.[20])

Illustrating Andersen afforded some Soviet artists an opportunity to indirectly hark back to former compatriots who had left their virtual footprint in the epoch of Russian modernism known as the Silver Age. Dobuzhinsky's creative ally and fellow member of the World of Art (Mir iskusstva) circle Aleksandr Benois had painted the sets for Diaghilev's production of Stravinsky's Andersen-based opera *The Nightingale* (*Solovei*, 1914).[21] Vladimir Konashevich had belonged to World of Art during its final years (1922-24), and from the 1930s on he devoted himself primarily to the genre of children's book illustration. His grotesque and decorative manner using watercolors and ink

---

18 Reproduced as plate 59 in Andersen and Drewsen, *Christine's Picture Book*, this is decorated with the following expressive sextet (translated into English by the book's editor): "Backwards, crabwise, / Stop, start, stop / Her eight fine legs / Go hop, hop, hop. / Such a graceful thing to see / And look at her face: one, two, three."
19 For example, in Marcel Duchamp's canvas *Nude Descending a Staircase* (1912); or in Natalya Goncharova's *The Cyclist* (*Velosipedist*, 1913), in which the rider's multi-leggedness is meant to convey a sense of dynamism.
20 This was designed by the Danish artist Jan Buhl (b. 1919) and affixed to the wall alongside several other bas-reliefs based on Andersen's paper-cuts. I am grateful to Elena Baibikova for verifying the Japanese sources for me.
21 For an analysis of this work, see Vladimir Orlov's contribution to this volume.

Fig. 9. By V. Konashevich. *Skazki*. Moscow: Detgiz, 1954.

was influenced by his elders in the former movement. Konashevich worked on Andersen illustrations in 1943, as if oblivious to starvation and bombings, in Leningrad during the Siege. As tragic as these circumstances were, the time also proved liberating: his pictures in *Fairy Tales* serve as a subtle tribute to Benois's canonical *ABC in Pictures* (*Azbuka v kartinkakh*, 1904).

Konashevich constructed his graphic masquerade akin to a visual puzzle, which can be demonstrated using this draft illustration for Andersen's "The Princess and the Pea": (fig. 9). Breaking this image by Konashevich up into its constituent parts, we can trace the origin thereof in Benois's *ABC*. The window vignette in Konashevich's "Ж" (*zh*) clearly comes from the very first page of Benois's alphabet—his illustration for the letter "A" (standing for *Arap*, "Moor"), parodying the "Moorish" boy's very pose and shifting the subject from the "exotic" south to the equally "exotic" far north, but, as if to wink to the attentive reader, leaving the half-sun in a window that serves as a near-exact replica of Benois's curtains.

Konashevich's toy-like symmetrical castles evoke Benois's illustration for the letter "Д" ("d") featuring a stately dacha. Floral designs appearing in the left and right corners of his predecessor's picture have migrated to Konashevich's cover, and so on.

Some Soviet artists, notably Boris Dekhterev (1908-93; the mentor of Vladimir Panov) and Boris Kalaushin (1929-99), continued to cultivate the lineage associated with Russia's Silver Age traditions (fig. 14). In the 1980s, as the Soviet regime loosened its ideological grip, it became less

Fig. 10. By V. Konashevich. Detail.
Fig. 11. By A. Benua. *Azbuka v kartinkakh*. St. Petersburg: Izdanie ekspeditsii zagotovleniia Gosudarstvennykh bumag, 1904.

Fig. 12. By A. Benua. *Azbuka v kartinkakh*. St. Petersburg: Izdanie ekspeditsii zagotovleniia Gosudarstvennykh bumag, 1904.

Fig. 13. By V. Konashevich. *Skazki*. Moscow: Detgiz, 1954.

Fig. 14. By B. Dektherev. *Diuimovochka*. Moscow: Ripol-Klassik, 2011.

Illustrations to "The Princess and the Pea."

Fig. 15. V. Panov. *Diuimovochka i drugie skazki*. Moscow: Detskaia literatura, 1983.

Fig. 16. By M. Petrov. *Sobranie sochinenii v 4 tt*. Moscow: Terra, 1994.

Fig. 17. By A. Benua. *Azbuka v kartinkakh* 1904.

risky for artists to echo decadent or Symbolist visual stylistics. An illustration by the artist Vladimir Panov (1931-2007) from a 1983 Soviet edition, elegantly executed in watercolor and ink, recalls the elaborate ornamentation and regal attire depicted by Nerman and Dobuzhinsky. Panov's pictures were most likely seen as an innocent nostalgic touch rather than some attempt to rehabilitate an almost forgotten style, let alone subvert the already crumbling censorship system. Juxtaposed is Mikhail Petrov's illustration to "The Princess and the Pea" showing a voluptuous young princess. This frolicsome drawing bears the hallmarks of the liberalizing spirit of post-perestroika publishing: the heroine's suggestive pose emphasizes her legs under tight-fitting negligée as well as cleavage uncommonly deep for a children's book. Not yet an innovation, this did mark a clear departure from the puritanical codes of socialist conventions[22]—soon to be abandoned altogether in favor of eroticized imagery, often employed with little artistic justification.

What was once considered an ornate stylization of European decor had by the late 1990s become almost inseparable from the very idea of Andersen's universe in the Russian cultural imagination. Anton Lomaev (b. 1971) appeals to Benois's legacy in illustrations for "The Steadfast Tin Soldier": the two artists encapsulate their letters "Б" and "Г" respectively in a rectangular headpiece; Lomaev's pensive boy, akin to that of Benois, plays with an army of toy soldiers in the foreground, while a family framed by a window in the background similarly recalls the composition of his predecessor.[23] Benois, who once expressed admiration for the miniature world of "The Steadfast

---

22 For more on the concept of "Soviet puritanism," see Balina, "Vospitanie chuvstv *a la sovietique*"; and Balina, "Narrating Love in Soviet Adolescent Literature of the 1930s."

23 Lomaev's portfolio also includes daring graphic works for J. R. R. Tolkien's *The Lord of the Rings*, Isaak Babel's *Red Cavalry* (*Konarmiia*), and Melville's *Moby-Dick*. See the artist's personal website: http://www.lomaevart.com/.

Fig. 18. By A. Lomaev. *Stoikii oloviannyi soldatik*. Moscow: Azbuka, 2015.

Tin Soldier," might himself have meant to allude to Andersen's tale in this particular picture "City, General" ("Gorod, General").[24]

The Topography of Unfamiliar Dreams

The genre of topographical city views is a classic example of the transformation from a graphic medium to the genre of painting. Svetlana Alpers has compared Jan Vermeer's *View of Delft*, showing "a city spread out in profile against the sky," with map materials and topographical town views, arguing that these do not so much result from mutual influence as belong to a common pictorial tradition.[25] The Russianized Andersen illustrations have fulfilled a function similar to that of Vermeer's paintings almost three hundred years earlier. The visual narrative, incorporating architectural elements immediately recognizable by the target Russian-speaking audience as distinctly Northern European, has provided a peculiar sense of defamiliarization and exoticism. Alpers describes the stated purpose of city imagery in Dutch painting of the late sixteenth—early seventeenth centuries as "to offer the pleasure of travel to those at home. This was travel...

---

24 Suggested in Zvonareva and Kudriavtseva, *Khans Kristian Andersen i ego russkie illiustratory za poltora veka*, 51. Cf. Benois: "In 'Tin Soldier'... I especially cherished the wonders of that miniature toy world" (*Moi vospominaniia*, 420).
25 Alpers, *The Art of Describing*, 152.

Fig. 19. By V. Panov. *Snezhnaia koroleva*. Moscow: Detskaia literatura, 1989.

Fig. 20. By G.A.V. Traugot. *Printsessa na goroshine*. St. Petersburg: Tsarskoe selo, 2005.

without an interest in business or gain, but purely for the sake of knowledge."[26] Whereas the limitation on the wanderings of the average Dutch person of that time was mainly of a technical-logistical nature, Andersen's Soviet readers were relegated to armchair travel due to political restrictions. In fiction, especially in the fantasy genre, with its abstract geographical borders and universally accepted moral messages, readers could afford to let their imagination run wild. The same held true for Soviet artists. As mentioned above, Benois travelled to Denmark; and Dobuzhinsky even got to visit the Andersen House Museum in Odense in 1912; but for those born shortly before the revolution, and long after it, journeying abroad was just a daydream. As a result, generically "Danish" buildings look as if they belong on the streets of Soviet Tallinn or Riga.[27] Most Russian Andersen illustrations seem almost obligated to feature vaguely medieval, ostensibly Scandinavian vistas, a typical European town punctuated by gothic spires and vaulted arches—everything but the practical representation of any realistic objects associated with Andersen's material world.

The insertion of Gothic shapes in these skylines adds *couleur locale*, reminding young readers that the text in question is a cultural import. Ironically, these foreign cityscapes function no differently than the stylized Kremlin-like edifices or onion-domed Slavic churches in Ivan Bilibin's elegant sketches to

---

26 Ibid.
27 For instance, the prolific artist Valerii Alfeevsky (1906-89), who illustrated numerous Andersen tales for Soviet children's books from the mid-1950s on, admits that in the spring of 1954, he happened to be in Tallinn, right as he began working on sketches for "The Snow Queen"; he was stunned by the beauty of the old town, and the facades and interiors of the local houses and castles fed his creative imagination (*Po pamiati i s natury*, 136). There were exceptions too: Anatolii Kokorin, elected an associate member of the USSR Academy of Arts in 1973, had a chance to travel to Copenhagen; the trip resulted in a series of beautiful illustrations for publications of Andersen's tales throughout the 1970s.

Russian fairy tales. Idiosyncratically reminiscent as they are of the Art Nouveau and Arts and Crafts movements flourishing in continental Europe around the turn of the twentieth century, moreover, Bilibin's exquisite folk tributes could have graced the pages of any highbrow German, Swedish, or Dutch fin-de-siècle magazine.[28] In the framework of visual adaptations, Russianized Europe and Europeanized Russia become interchangeable entities.

Here it might be methodologically useful to briefly digress on Mariia Maiofis's approach in her study of the Soviet adaptation of Astrid Lindgren's story about Karlsson-on-the-Roof. Maiofis insightfully formulates the wildly successful method of adapting this work in the Russian animated film of 1968 *The Kid and Karlson* (*Malysh i Karlson*) as "minus Sweden, minus reproduction."[29] Aside from the task of transforming the original text and translating it to a different medium (screen), the creators of the Soviet version faced the challenges of "devising innovative imaginary and discursive means for adapting Lindgren's texts."[30] And yet this foreign story is *visually* familiar, thanks to what Maiofis calls a "process of stylistic domestication":[31] the Soviet animators, that is, muted the specifically Swedish characteristics of the original while emphasizing features more readily recognizable by Russian viewers. For instance, the young boy's parents are modeled after a typical Soviet couple of engineers belonging to the technical intelligentsia.

Certain "deviatory" choices made by illustrators of Andersen's translated texts evince a similarly hybridizing approach; some scenes or characters in his tales were presented to the Soviet readership with a form of ideological domestication in view. However, as time passed and the political regime weakened, Russian readers were granted their long-deserved social and geographic mobility, a factor that, in turn, afforded graphic artists an opportunity to reconstruct Andersen's realm with almost photographic accuracy. The "Danish landscape" in Russian illustrations has undergone a traceable evolution: architectural imagery

---

28 Bilibin was praised both for his humorous touch in illustrating Russian fairy tales as well as his convincing attention to detail, in which he combined national and folk elements with a recognizably modernist approach to artwork (Shanina, *Skazka v tvorchestve russkikh khudozhnikov*, 40-42).

29 Maiofis, "Milyi, milyi trikster," 241-86.

30 Ibid, 263. The animated film depicts the country in which the little protagonist resides as a "conventional abroad": double-deckers roll through Westernized streets, and the hero's father reads newspapers bearing unmistakably English script—a made-up Stockholm that could just as easily serve as the setting for a tale set in (a fictitious) London. Despite the lack of visibly Swedish toponyms, Karlsson's city, with its red brick roofs and tall towers, comes across as a decidedly European locus.

31 Ibid., 264.

in post-Soviet reproductions became more nuanced and, compared to earlier schematic drawings, decidedly more convincing. On the other hand, the abstract broodingness that had characterized the Soviet drawings mostly disappears by the late 1990s, along with the very notion of *zagranitsa*—what had been, for the populace behind the Iron Curtain, the notoriously tempting concept of a distant forbidden "abroad."

Tales or Holes?

Wolfgang Iser claims in *The Act of Reading* (1978) that literary texts work with textual strategies and direct the reader during the act of reading. Cecilia Alvstad has applied Iser's theoretical approach to the interpretation of illustrations to Andersen's works, suggesting that "in an illustrated tale ambiguity can be created both verbally and visually and through the interaction between these two media."[32] If the exotic Northern cityscape could be regarded as a variation on a familiar terrain, then the underground adventures of Thumbelina enabled Soviet graphic artists to denote depths previously reserved mainly for heroes entering Hell amid mythological, folkloric, or religious explorations of the afterlife. I will thus now shift from the semi-realistic space of Russianized Copenhagen to the purely imaginary one envisioned in an episode from Andersen's "Thumbelina" (1835), specifically, that taking place in the Mole's hole.

Early Western illustrators of Andersen avoided depicting Thumbelina's underground sojourn, a decision that elicited a certain amount of criticism. A British reviewer (1871) says of Eleanor Vere Boyle's pictures that, despite producing artwork that is "both beautiful and fanciful, as well as very rich and gorgeous," the illustrator "has hardly chosen the subjects which we should have thought most characteristic of Hans Christian Andersen."[33] The artist is alleged to have missed "the most Andersenian elements" in the tale, neglecting to illustrate the matchmaking Field-mouse who is so anxious to marry the little heroine to blind Mr. Mole; or

> to give us a picture of that very narrow-minded gentleman himself, with his handsome black-velvet pelisse, and short legs, and those very utilitarian principles which naturally impressed Mrs. Field-mouse so much by their

---

32 Alvstad, "Illustrations and Ambiguity," 90.
33 "E. V. B.'s Illustrations of Andersen" (anonymous review of Andersen, *Fairy Tales* [London: Sampson Low, 1872]), *Spectator*, 25 November 1871, 1432.

worldly wisdom. We confess we were a little disappointed that "E. V. B." did not choose the following humorous passage to illustrate with her delicate pencil and brush.[34]

Russian literature has no shortage of underground dreamscapes; suffice it to mention here Antonii Pogorelsky's *The Black Hen, or The Underground Dwellers* (*Chernaia kuritsa, ili Podzemnye zhiteli*). (For his part, in this episode Andersen himself may have been inspired by the satirical fantasy novel *Niels Klim's Underground Travels* [1741] by fellow Dane Ludvig Holberg, one of his favorite writers.) Decades later, Russian artists would rectify their Western counterparts' omission. Representations of the mole's tunnel in Russian illustrations oscillate between a cozy little household and an ominous place hiding a dying swallow.

Ritta Oittinen has proposed that illustrators always "take stories in new directions; for instance, they stress certain scenes or certain characteristics of the persons described by the author. They add and omit and make the readers of the book pay special attention to certain parts of the story."[35] It is precisely this perceived selectivity of an artist that led the *Spectator*'s critic to protest the absence of illustrations for episodes deemed so graphic in Andersen's original narrative; the reviewer rightly inferred that the omission of a picture could affect the final interpretation of a translated text. Oittinen believes that there are "similarities between translation (into words) and illustration (translation into pictures) as forms of interpretation."[36] Alvstad notes an important difference: illustrations are published side by side with verbal texts, whereas verbal translations are rarely published together with their originals: "This means that the possibilities of interaction between verbal texts and illustrations in a picture book or an illustrated book are radically different from the interaction between a translation and its source text."[37]

In Andersen's Russian illustrations, the visual narrative folds into a kind of semantic vortex, forming, quite literally, black holes that suck various

---

34 The criticism focuses on "a passage typical of Andersen, and surely it would make a very humorous picture; the beautiful swallow lying apparently dead, Mr. Mole kicking at it with his short legs, and discoursing, with his broad nose held high in the air, on the worthlessness of the gift of song; good-natured but conventional Mrs. Field-mouse looking up at him with a genuine hero-worship for his worldly wisdom, and Thumbkinetta sad and sympathetic, stroking the swallow" (ibid). On the other hand, the *Spectator*'s critic hails certain successes in this "Thumbelina" as well, especially the choice to render the swallow's white breast and meek shining eyes far more attractive than the pretty fairies who spring up out of the flowers to receive the bird's fair little rider.
35 Oittinen, *Translating for Children*, 103, 106.
36 Ibid., 106; see also Alvstad, "Illustrations and Ambiguity," 91.
37 Ibid., 91.

Illustrations for "Thumbelina."

Fig. 21. By V. Pivovarov. *Skazki. Istorii.* Moscow: Khudozhestvennaia literatura, 1973.

Fig. 22. By I. Gukova. *Diuimovochka.* Moscow: Raduga, 1990.

characters into their ontological reality—be it a soldier disappearing into the subterranean dwelling of the three dogs in "The Tinderbox" or the miniaturized female protagonist of "Thumbelina" in the mole's tunnel (Lewis Carroll would use a similarly Andersenian discursive ploy to plunge Alice into the rabbit's hole). Holes as empty spaces of imagination that Russian graphic artists had to fill with readymade fictional constructs (see, especially, in the illustrations to "The Tinderbox" made by Konashevich and Viktor Chizhikov) were justified by the very genre of fairy tale; the magic plot served as a protective buffer against ideological state-sponsored harassment or censorship.

In the case of a classic text, artists are called upon not so much to constantly reinvent the visual story as to keep it attractive to new generations of young readers. To resist the automatization of our perception, familiar images are continually refreshed (as in the case of the underground scene once deemed underrepresented in British editions, but recreated since in numerous variants). The "visual holes" serve as intrinsic components of loosely structured fairy tales and make it possible to reinterpret fantastic ambiguities (i.e., "semantic holes") in different directions—from the perspectives of Freudian psychoanalysis, feminist theory, sociohistorical allegory, repressed autobiography, religious treatise, etc.[38]—as well as in different media, which will be the subject of my concluding remarks. As formulated by one of Andersen's Russian illustrators, Viktor Pivovarov, "the artist is responsible for ensuring the work's cultural continuity: it is up to an illustrator to keep the timeless texts that form the foundation of world culture from turning into dusty folios—they should be read and kept alive."[39]

Illustrations for "The Tinderbox."

Fig. 23. By V. Konashevich. *Ognivo*. Moscow: Detgiz, 1948.

Fig. 24. By V. Chizhikov. *Ognivo*. Moscow: Malysh, 1972.

---

38 See for instance Rosenblatt, "Thumbelina and the Development of Female Sexuality."
39 Pivovarov, "Ob illustratsii," 94.

The Post-Soviet Andersen in Synthetic Worlds

In this last section I will examine the transformative ways in which Andersen's fairy tales have been visually adapted to postmodernity, and examine how his texts have coped with the challenges of new media and popular culture both in Russia and elsewhere. I will focus mainly on "The Snow Queen" as a case study. In the Russianized version of Andersen's books in general, his magic world has been turned into a "Soviet Disneyland" (I refer once more to the artist Mikhail Magaril's record of his trip to Denmark quoted in the beginning of this article), operating much like a Baudrillardian simulacrum. In the Russian translations that incorporated phantasmagoric pictures, the spacetime of Andersen's works substituted an ideological utopia masking itself as a bygone tale. In the absence of a material equivalent of Disneyland entertainment parks, the Soviet ecosphere of Andersen's tales produced visual narratives of nonexistent European towns, travelogues of fictitious itineraries with intermittent stops at, to quote Baudrillard on Los Angeles and Disneyland, "'imaginary stations' which feed reality, reality-energy, to a town whose mystery is precisely that it is nothing more than a network of endless, unreal circulation."[40]

The story of "The Snow Queen" supplies both the exotic space of an imaginary North and the sense of an obstacle-fraught journey. Here I would like to linger on the interactive nature of the illustration in general, which usually forces a young reader to pause and unfold its graphic contents in nonlinear fashion. Books are only one medium for telling and *experiencing* a tale. Another is represented by participatory games merged with quest narratives that have been a favorite pastime for children of whatever cultural orientation. Board games were commercially exploiting this phenomenon long before the rise of the digital economy. There was, for example, a Russian board game in the 1880s (copied from a German prototype) called "The Swedish Traveler Nordenskiöld's Passage to the Northeast" (*Prokhod shvedskogo puteshestvennika Nordenshol'da na Severo-Vostok*). This was based on the expedition of Adolf Erik Nordenskiöld, who in 1878 sailed around the north coast of Asia, returning home by way of the Bering Strait, the first to traverse the whole length of the Northeast passage. According to the game's itinerary, the discoverer leaves Stockholm on 30 June 1879, and while overcoming various obstacles, the players find themselves involved in entertaining, at times comic adventures that evoke the exploits of Robinson Crusoe

---

40 Baudrillard, "Simulacra and Simulations," 406.

or Jules Verne's explorers.[41] Russian board games built on the travel principle were often modeled after German and French "postal games" (with topographic locations altered accordingly), but it was Andersen's tales that in the twentieth century truly expanded the Russian child's literary-oriented imaginary geography.

Andersen's Snow Queen has consistently been represented in Russia as a ripe, beautiful woman—an antagonist, but a sexually attractive one. This tradition of the objectification of a mature feminine beauty began with the Soyuzmultfilm studio's 1957 feature *The Snow Queen* (*Snezhnaia koroleva*), directed by Lev Atamanov.[42] This was so successful that the Japanese director Hayao Miyazaki would later admit to being strongly indebted to this Russian source and its main female character's embodiment of a brutal force of nature. In devising the Snow Queen's palace of ice and futuristic attire, Atamanov was most likely inspired by the constructivist sets and sci-fi wardrobe of the Mars-set film *Aelita* (*Aelita*, 1924; dir. Iakov Protazanov) or the German masterpiece *Metropolis* (1927; dir. Fritz Lang). The sexualization of Andersen's enigmatic Snow Queen has culminated in a recent edition by the Moscow boutique press "Clever"; on its cover, by fashionable young book designer Dima Rebus, the Queen confronts two hipster-looking teenagers. Watercolors are executed in the style of glossy magazine illustrations, part of a trend deriving from sophisticated comics for adults.[43]

Fig. 25. By D. Rebus. *Snezhnaia koroleva*. Moscow: Clever, 2015.

Notably, Andersen's writings transcend not only geographical borders but also various mediums, moving across genres and epochs; they were transplanted from the text page to the realm of popular audio plays on the Soviet *gramplastinki* (Andersen's tales were popular as vinyl recordings issued by the Melodiia label throughout the 1980s) and *diafil'my* (visual slides projected on a screen). Having furnished material

---

41 Marina Kostiukhina describes this and other typical games of this period in her comprehensive and well-illustrated investigation *Detskii orakul*, 194-96.

42 On this and other Soviet *Snow Queen* film adaptations, see Andrei Rogatchevski's contribution to this volume.

43 On Dima Rebus's work, see, on the publisher's website: https://www.clever-media.ru/CleverProducts/Books/book_3720. On the nuanced differences between graphic artist, designer, and illustrator in the modern publishing world, see Natalie Ratkovski's useful and generously illustrated *Professiia-illiustrator*.

Tales and Holes: 361

for numerous international screen adaptations, Andersen's tales also found a niche in personal computing, and joined the 3D video game industry.[44] For example, in "The Ugly Prince Duckling," a 2007 game by the Norwegian developer GuppyWorks (http://kongo.dk/guppyworks/), the player encounters old fairytale favorites while visiting Golden Age Copenhagen. The gamer explores elaborate shops, secret tunnels, and a deserted windmill. The navigation allows controlling characters in full 3D, and the product promotes its players' total cultural immersion:

> The Ugly Prince Duckling takes you into a unique fantasy world inspired by the works of Hans Christian Andersen. Day after day, a lovely young princess gazes out the window at a world she can't experience. On her 15th birthday, she runs away from her privileged life in search of an adventure. On her journey, she meets young Hans Christian Andersen—a poor teenager struggling to make his way in life. Together they meet the Little Mermaid, the Ugly Duckling, and other characters made famous in Andersen's fairytales. You'll also be challenged to save the Princess and the kingdom![45]

Like any quest-game, "The Ugly Prince Duckling" is constructed as a set of missions and micro-adventures. Shortly after its release, fans posted a step-by-step guide for accomplishing various levels of the game.[46] Instructions provided under the rubric "Free the Princess," for instance, warn that after you hear the princess scream, you should run toward her and talk to the townspeople. One is further advised to buy three matches from the match girl, and that a young boy will inform the player that the princess was taken away by trolls. A match will soon come in handy for lighting the candles inside the dark mill. The trolls do not like the light and leave. The scream of the princess means that she is near. Eventually the player is encouraged to click on a lever to lift the cage containing the princess...

English-language reviews of this video game were mixed, but in the Russian gaming market it was a definite success.[47] The Andersenian

---

44 In fact, as early as 1985, Gremlin Graphics released a children's adventure game for the ZX Spectrum home computer titled "Tinderbox," based on Andersen's eponymous tale, with all profits going to Ethiopian famine relief through Soft Aid.
45 See on the seller's page: https://www.amazon.com/Hans-Christian-Anderson-Ugly-Prince-Duckling/dp/B000MRSAFI. The game's mechanics is explained and shown here: https://www.youtube.com/watch?v=N0qyQHT_yWE
46 Dated March 2007, available at: http://www.gameboomers.com/wtcheats/pcUu/UglyPrince-Ducklingwalkthrough.htm
47 As a Russian gaming journal summed up: "the animation is magnificent. One of the best of its kind (at least among computer games)." (Lenskii, "Byt' G. Kh. Andersenom.") This is corroborated by the Russian user Nastia in her review on the "Smallgames" forum: "This is

plot affords both an *emotional outlet* (experiencing/imagining scary, fantastic events in a controlled environment) and a deep *interaction* with the story-telling architecture (navigation through a narrative structure). Darkness and unexpectedly violent encounters with trolls or malignant animals are part of the Andersen-inspired gaming sphere. In a chapter of his study of online gaming he titles "Topographies of Terror," Edward Castronova maintains that while "unsanctioned violence within a community is crime [and] violence between communities is warfare," it turns out that synthetic worlds, "because they warp reality and enable real-time communications, provide some rather frightening opportunities for people of bad intent."[48] Viewing aggression on the cinematic screen fulfills the same purpose; it is thus not surprising that someone like Timur Bekmambetov, one of the few contemporary Russian directors actively working in Hollywood, and known especially for his briskly violent films *Night Watch* (*Nochnoi dozor*, 2004) and the American *Wanted* (2008), would be interested in adding Andersen to his filmography. As a producer of the Russian animated film *The Snow Queen* (*Snezhnaia koroleva*, 2012), he designed it like a blockbuster for kids: this expensive project features epic shots, unusual angles, and complex computer-generated imagery. The success of Bekmambetov's production prompted the release of a sequel in 2015, titled *The Snow Queen 2: The Snow King* (*Snezhnaia koroleva 2. Snezhnyi korol'*).

The image of a Snow Queen in Russia has become so pervasive in the twenty-first century that it has engendered a popular fashion. Many Russian women choose to dress in a certain way and apply special makeup to emulate their favorite heroine. Data pulled from the Internet validate this general trend. The Girl-as-Snow-Queen photographic portraiture shares a commanding, erotically charged outlook ("cold + beauty"), as attested by results from the Russian search engine Yandex.ru for the three keywords *fotosessia snezhnaia koroleva* ("Snow Queen photoshoot").[49] Furthermore, the common denominator in these portraits is the very appearance of the Snow Queen as shaped by the aesthetics of the 1957 Russian animated film and its subsequent reverberations in Soviet and post-Soviet book illustrations that utilize Atamanov's influential image. Thus, as Roman Jakobson famously asserted, the question

---

a fabulous adventure game based on Andersen's tales. The action will transport you into fairytale worlds created by the famous Danish writer. Along the way... you will experience dizzying adventures familiar from the books" (entry from 27 November 2008. http://forum.smallgames.ws/index.php?showtopic=5758).

48 Castronova, *Synthetic Worlds*, 227.
49 A sample search was run on 23 February 2017, yielding over 200,000 images.

of relations "between the word and the world concerns not only verbal art but actually all kinds of discourse," adding that "however ludicrous may appear the idea of the *Iliad* and *Odyssey* in comics, certain structural features of their plot are preserved despite the disappearance of their verbal shape."[50] Andersen's fairy tales may have morphed into visual patterns, blended with popular culture, and even moved to extratextual domains; but the laws of general poetics preserve them as unmistakably Andersenian, whether on page or canvas.

Works Cited

Alfeevskii, V. *Po pamiati i s natury*. Moscow: Kniga, 1991.

Alpers, Svetlana. *The Art of Describing: Dutch Art in the Seventeenth Century*. Chicago: Chicago University Press, 1983.

Alvstad, Cecilia. "Illustrations and Ambiguity in Eighteen Illustrated Translations of Hans Christian Andersen's 'The Steadfast Tin Soldier'." *Meta: journal des traducteurs / Meta: Translators' Journal* 53, no. 1 (2008): 90-103.

Andersen, Hans Christian. *Fairy Tales and Stories*. Translated by H. L. Braekstad. Illustrated by Hans Tegner. New York: Century Co., 1900.

Andersen, H. C., and Adolph Drewsen. *Christine's Picture Book*. Footnotes and postscript by Erik Dal. New York: Holt, Rinehart, and Winston, 1985.

Andersen, Kh. K. *Skazki i istorii*. Moscow: Gosudarstvennoe izdatel'stvo khudozhestvennoi literatury, 1955.

Balina, Marina. "Narrating Love in Soviet Adolescent Literature of the 1930s: Ruvim Fraerman's *The Wild Dog Dingo*; or, *A Tale about First Love*." *The Russian Review* 73 (2014): 354-70.

—. "Vospitanie chuvstv *a la sovietique*: povesti o pervoy lyubvi." *Neprikosnovennyi zapas: spetsial'nyi vypusk, posviashchennyi detskoi literature* 2 (58) (2008): 154-66.

Baudrillard, Jean. "Simulacra and Simulations." In *Modern Criticism and Theory: A Reader*. 2nd edition, edited by David Lodge, 404-12. Harlow: Longman, 2000.

Benua, Aleksandr. *Azbuka v kartinkakh*. St. Petersburg: Izdanie ekspeditsii zagotovleniia Gosudarstvennykh bumag, 1904.

—. *Moi vospominaniia v 5 knigakh. Knigi pervaia, vtoraia, tret'ia*. Moscow: Izdatel'stvo 'Nauka,' 1990.

Castronova, Edward. *Synthetic Worlds: The Business and Culture of Online Games*. Chicago: University of Chicago Press, 2005.

Hamelin associazione culturale. *Illustrare Andersen = Illustrating Andersen*. Bologna: Cooperative Libraria Universitaria Editrice Bologna (CLUEB), 2005.

Iser, Wolfgang. *The Act of Reading: A Theory of Aesthetic Response*. Baltimore: The Johns Hopkins University Press, 1978.

---

50 Jakobson, "Linguistics and Poetics," 31-32.

Jakobson, Roman. "Linguistics and Poetics." In *Modern Criticism and Theory: A Reader*, edited by David Lodge, 31-55. Harlow: Longman, 2000.

Kostiukhina, Marina. *Detskii orakul. Po stranitsam nastol'no-pechatnykh igr.* Moscow: NLO, 2013.

Krogh Hansen, Per, and M. Wolff Lundholt. *When We Get to the End... Towards a Narratology of the Fairy Tales of Hans Christian Andersen*. Odense: University Press of Southern Denmark, 2005.

Lenskii, Andrei. "Byt' G. Kh. Andersenom. Skazka o gadkom utenke." *Luchshie komp'iuternye igry*, no. 4 (65) (April 2007). Available electronically: http://www.lki.ru/text.php?id=2335.

Magaril, Mikhail. "Migratory Birds: Illustrating Andersen's 'Nightingale.'" *Marvels & Tales: Journal of Fairy-Tale Studies* 20, no. 2 (2006): 249-56.

Maiofis, Mariia. "Milyi, milyi trikster: Karlson i sovetskaia utopiia o 'nastoiashchem detstve.'" In *Veselye chelovechki: Kul'turnye geroi sovetskogo detstva. Sbornik statei*, edited by Il'ia Kukulin et al., 241-86. Moscow: NLO, 2008.

Oittinen, Ritta. *Translating for Children*. New York: Garland, 2000.

Petrov, Vsevolod. "Vstrechi s N. A. Tyrsoi." In *Turdeiskaia Manon Lesko. Istoriia odnoi liubvi: Povest'; Vospominaniia* by Vsevolod Petrov, 202-30. St. Petersburg: Izdatel'stvo Ivana Limbakha, 2016.

Pivovarov, Viktor. "Ob illiustratsii." In *Po dorogam skazki. Knizhnaia grafika E. Bulatova, O. Vassilieva, I. Kabakova, V. Pivovarova iz chastnykh kollektsii i sobraniia GMII imeni A. S. Pushkina*, 92-94. Moscow: Izdatel'skii dom 'Art Volkhonka,' 2015.

Ratkovski, Natalie. *Professiia-illiustrator. Uchimsia myslit' tvorcheski*. Moscow: Mann, Ivanov i Farber, 2014.

Rosenblatt, Sidney M. "Thumbelina and the Development of Female Sexuality." In *Psychoanalytic Perspectives on Women*, edited by Elaine V. Siegel, 121-29. New York: Brunner/Mazel, 1992.

Shanina, N. F. *Skazka v tvorchestve russkikh khudozhnikov*. Moscow: Iskusstvo, 1969.

Surkov, Aleksei. *Sobranie sochinenii v 4-kh tt*. Moscow: Khudozhestvennaia literatura, 1979.

Zvonareva, L., and L. Kudriavtseva, *Kh. K. Andersen i russkie illiustratory*. Moscow: Arbor, 2005.

—. *Khans Kristian Andersen i ego russkie illiustratory za poltora veka*. Moscow: Moskovskie uchebniki, 2012.

Hans Christian Andersen and Russian Film:

The Case of "The Snow Queen"

Andrei Rogatchevski

Introduction

Hans Christian Andersen film studies have only begun to develop, and (post-)Soviet film adaptations of the author's texts have not yet received the attention they deserve. Elisabeth Oxfeldt's 2009 book on Andersen and film, which focuses on "Thumbelina," "The Nightingale," "The Little Mermaid," "The Little Match Girl," and other works as incarnated in Danish, Finnish, Czech, American, and Australian movies, is a seminal study; but it does not even mention any of the Russian films based on the same tales (by, for example, Amalrik [1964]; Aksenchuk [1968]; Douksha and Buzinova [1991]; and Kodiukova [1996], all animated shorts). Jack Zipes's favorable analysis (*Misunderstood Storyteller*, 117-22) of two feature-length films, Vladimir Bychkov's *The Little Mermaid* (*Rusalochka*, 1976) and Boris Rytsarev's *The Princess and the Pea* (*Printsessa na goroshine*, also 1976), valuable in itself, does little to give the reader a sense of Andersen's Russian/(post-)Soviet filmography, which includes dozens of titles, many of them remakes.[1]

Among inspirers of such remakes, the undisputed champion is "The Snow Queen" (1844). Between 1957 and 2016, at least seven film versions of this tale were made in the Soviet and former Soviet Union. My article briefly compares these adaptations, attempting to account for "The Snow Queen's" extraordinary popularity among Russophone filmmakers and filmgoers for over half a century. To ascertain why so many moviemakers have been preoccupied with this tale (possible explanations are offered in my conclusion), I adopt two approaches, one narratological, the other chronological.

Examining the film adaptations' narratives (including plot segments, characters, and visuals) in light of their literary source and of one another seems the easiest and most straightforward way of determining

---

1 Zipes discusses two other Russian film adaptations of Andersen in *Enchanted Screen* (95-96).

what unites and distinguishes them. Generally speaking (and especially in the case of multiple adaptations of the same source), no filmmaker worth his/her salt would wish to be accused of imitating an immediate predecessor too closely;[2] and so I take a chronological approach, tracing the development of "The Snow Queen's" adaptation process, that is, how each new production has dealt with the legacy of the previous one(s). At times this can help us understand the adapter's choice of genre: more than half a century separates the first animated adaptation (Atamanov in 1957) and the most recent (Sveshnikov and Barbe in 2012), arguably because several adaptations in other formats were attempted by Russian filmmakers in between.[3]

To summarize some of the summaries of the extensive literature on the subject of film adaptation in Russia and elsewhere:[4] so far as narrative is concerned, any (film) adaptation of a literary source can be analyzed from four principal complementary angles: what is excised from the original, what remains, what is added to it, and what is altered. Once these issues are addressed, it becomes possible to speculate as to why a particular adaptation has been attempted in a particular way. Also, given that film (and television) as a medium differs quite substantially from literature, the adaptations' faithfulness to their literary originals is not necessarily a virtue, and is not considered as such in this article.

Following one of my predecessors in "Snow Queen" adaptation studies (Pilipovets, "Russkie ekranizatsii," 221-22), for my theoretical framework I employ the classification of adaptations offered by Peeter Torop in *Total Translation*,[5] perhaps the most comprehensive system yet proposed. Torop treats filmmaking as the process of translation from page to screen. He calls translations that focus primarily on adherence to the original "analytic"; while "synthetic" translations, by contrast, attend more to transforming the original in accordance with the demands of the recipient culture (thus the role of cultural shifts and fickle public taste is taken into consideration). Whenever the translation process operates on the basis of a distinction between style and content, the content becomes,

---

2   This is in keeping with Iurii Tynianov's observation (in "The Literary Fact" ["Literaturnyi fakt"], 1924) that "evolution is caused by the need for a ceaseless dynamics. Every dynamic system inevitably becomes automatized and an opposite constructive principle dialectically arises" (cited from Steiner, *Russian Formalism*, 107).

3   This is not to say that adapters invariably avoid conscious parallels with previous treatments of the same source; sometimes homage is paid to a predecessor by openly borrowing his/her selected motifs.

4   See, for example, McFarlane, *Novel to Film*; Aragay, "Reflection to Refraction"; Hutchings and Vernitski, "The *Ekranizatsiia* in Russian Culture"; Nemchenko, "Ekranizatsiia kak pole interpretatsii"; and Leitch, "Across the Russian Border."

5   Torop, *Total'nyi perevod*, 132-33, 182-89.

in Torop's parlance, "transposed," whereas the style becomes "recoded." He uses "dominant," meanwhile, to connote a heavier dependence on the literary source than more "autonomous" adaptations.

Using this terminology, Torop lists eight different adaptation types: 1) the *macro-stylistic* adaptation (or dominant analytic recoding) prioritizes the original source and its formal properties (this category would include traditional adaptations of national classics, which sometimes even manage to keep the narrator's point of view, e.g., Vladimir Bortko's *Heart of a Dog* [*Sobach'e serdtse*, 1988], based on the eponymous story by Mikhail Bulgakov); 2) the *precise* adaptation (or autonomous analytic recoding) focuses on the source's content and information (such films sometimes feature highly detailed source-related events and behind-the-scenes commentary—for example, Igor Talankin's *Father Sergius* [*Otets Sergii*, 1978], based on Lev Tolstoy's novella); 3) the *micro-stylistic* adaptation (or dominant synthetic recoding) focuses on a specific personage from the source, not necessarily its ostensible main character (e.g., Nastasya Filippovna in Ivan Pyryev's 1958 adaptation of Dostoevsky's *The Idiot* [*Idiot*]), while often transferring the action to a different time and place (e.g., Akira Kurosawa's *Throne of Blood* [1957], in which Shakespeare's *Macbeth* is planted firmly in feudal Japan); 4) the so-called *quotational* adaptation (or autonomous synthetic recoding) foregrounds particular (leit)motifs employed by an author rather than a specific work thereof (e.g., Nikita Mikhalkov's Chekhov-infused *Unfinished Piece for Mechanical Piano* [*Neokonchennaia p'esa dlia mekhanicheskogo pianino*, 1975]); 5) the *thematic* adaptation (or dominant analytic transposition) focuses on a source's theme, which consists of several motifs (see item 4 above); the action is frequently also transferred to a different time and place (e.g., Robert Bresson's *L'argent* [1983], based on Tolstoy's story "The Forged Coupon" ["Fal'shivyi kupon"]); 6) the so-called *descriptive* adaptation (or autonomous analytic transposition) focuses on the source's conflict, which is enhanced and generalized by all the available means of expression (e.g., Elem Klimov's *Farewell* [*Proshchanie*, 1981], based on Valentin Rasputin's *Farewell to Matera* [*Proshchanie s Materoi*]; 7) the *expressive* adaptation (or dominant synthetic transposition) focuses on genre, either updating a source or attempting to make it timeless (e.g., Georgii Iungvald-Khilkevich's 1978 Dumas-based musical *D'Artagnan and the Three Musketeers* [*D'Artan'ian i tri mushketera*]); and 8) the so-called *free* adaptation (or autonomous synthetic transposition), a decidedly individual interpretation of a source—which may paradoxically be closer to the spirit of the original than a more faithful adaptation (e.g., Andrei Tarkovsky's *Ivan's Childhood* [*Ivanovo detstvo*, 1961], based on Vladimir

Bogomolov's *Ivan*). It would be helpful to categorize Russian adaptations of "The Snow Queen" according to these types, to try to take in the broad range of the filmmakers' approaches from a unified perspective.

With all this in mind, I propose comparing the (post-)Soviet film and television adaptations of "The Snow Queen" in accordance with the following criteria: the competence of the creative team, their choice of genre, the target audience, plot components (including new and missing characters), the political context, and the film's message. To provide a wider background, non-Russian film adaptations of the tale are occasionally cited.

The Original "Snow Queen"

This volume's reader is likely familiar with the outline of Andersen's story, but it might nevertheless help to begin with a recap, paying special attention to the details that film adaptations will either alter or leave unchanged.

In the story, a devil's mirror, one that belittles beauty and magnifies evil, is smashed into tiny pieces, which fall into people's eyes and hearts and distort their perception of the world. Two of those affected are the neighboring children Kay and Gerda, who grow roses in a rooftop window box and sing "Where roses bloom so sweetly in the vale, / There shall you find the Christ Child, without fail"; one summer day, shards of the devil's mirror get into Kay and change his personality. The following winter, the Snow Queen, whom Kay had seen earlier as a snowflake and threatened to melt, abducts him in a sleigh and kisses him, causing him to forget Gerda.

Gerda goes on a search for Kay. First, she finds herself in a garden of eternal summer; this belongs to a sorceress who makes Gerda forget Kay, until the sight of a rose reminds her. Gerda flees the garden and meets two ravens, who tell her that Kay must be the husband of a recently married princess. Upon investigation, the husband turns out to be merely a lookalike. The princely couple gives Gerda warm clothes and a coach, and sends her further on her way.

Then Gerda is captured by robbers, whose gang includes a little girl. The girl's pet doves say that they saw Kay being whisked away in the direction of Finnmark,[6] and her pet reindeer takes Gerda there, against the glorious backdrop of the northern lights.

---

6   In the story, "Andersen made a division of Northern Scandinavia into a southern and a northern part, Lapland and Finnmark, because little Gerda came travelling from the South

En route to Finnmark, Gerda meets two women, a Lapp and a Finn, who are both literate (despite living in abject poverty) and are said to be able to handle a man's job if necessary. The Finn declares that Gerda, too, has proved herself resourceful—enough to upset the Snow Queen's plans without any additional help. And so Gerda does (while the Snow Queen is away), returning Kay to humanity with a little help from her tearfulness and the song about the Christ-child.

The story is told in an omniscient third-person narrative, with "the double child/adult readership ... intended from the start," and foregrounds such core themes as "dislike of a reliance on reason and of the arid, intellectual life.... Woman's redemption of man.... Love triumphs over death."[7]

The story is marked by strong Christian overtones[8] (including Gerda's reading of the Lord's Prayer before entering the Snow Queen's palace; and the grandmother's from Matthew 18 in the denouement). Also present, however, are Andersen's trademark ambivalences,[9] which prevent "The Snow Queen" from becoming a straightforward morality tale. Thus, the garden of eternal summer hardly benefits Gerda; snow and ice are associated with deadliness throughout—but the reindeer likes them;[10] the little robber girl's mother sports a beard; the mother-robber and daughter-robber behave violently toward one another out of sheer love; and the Snow Queen goes off to peer into Etna and Vesuvius.[11]

Finally, although the quest presented in "The Snow Queen" can be described as an "evolution from childhood to maturity" (Draga-Alexandru, "Contrastive Values," 441), Kay and Gerda's age in the story is largely indeterminable. Abiding in fairytale, "once upon a time" time, they make the transition from little to marriageable somewhat imperceptibly,[12] while

---

to meet the Snow Queen ... [who] 'stays in the country' during summertime, that is in Finnmark" (Kleivan, "Arctic Elements," 295).

7 Wullschläger, *Life of a Storyteller*, 147, 76, 245, 23. As for "woman's redemption of man," the story's strong and numerous female characters eclipse the submissive and susceptible male ones. It has been suggested that Andersen's arguably more successful and favorable descriptions of women (as opposed to men) in his tales in general are "root[ed] in an overwhelmingly feminine element in himself which made him very sensitive and understanding towards women but stopped him from identifying entirely with his own sex" (Præstgaard Andersen, "The Feminine Element," 514).

8 Despite the "the existential doubt [that] haunted Andersen, and [that] his efforts at religious belief could not lay to rest" (Wullschläger, *Life of a Storyteller*, 249).

9 As Draga-Alexandru observes, in Andersen's tales, "the poles of ... oppositions coexist and alchemically turn into each other" ("Contrastive Values," 437).

10 Andersen was apparently "not without a sense of the pleasures that winters might give" (Kleivan, "Arctic Elements," 290).

11 As Andersen himself put it during a visit to Christiania (Oslo) in August 1871, "the Viking likes to go southwards" (cited ibid., 293).

12 In theory, in mid-nineteenth-century Denmark, marriage could take place from the age of fifteen on. Yet in urban areas in 1845, under 1 percent of males in the fifteen-to-nineteen

retaining much of their childlike nature (as the author himself puts it in the conclusion, "grown-up, but children still—children at heart"). This has clearly presented a wide range of opportunities for filmmakers, who have to specify the lead actors' and target audience's age whenever it comes to a new adaptation of "The Snow Queen."

Lev Atamanov's *The Snow Queen* (*Snezhnaia koroleva*, 1957)

The ambivalence of the protagonists' age was the first casualty of the very first Soviet film version of "The Snow Queen,"[13] directed by Lev Atamanov, a prize-winning animator and a pupil of the doyen of Soviet cinema Lev Kuleshov. Atamanov clearly chose to target pre- and earlyelementary school viewers, as Gerda and Kay's on-screen appearance duly reflects.

In order to link scenes together and explain things not readily obvious to little children, a personified narrator is introduced, recruited from a different Andersen tale ("Ole Lukoie," 1841).[14] In keeping with obligatory Soviet atheism, the Ole Lukoie character is quick to deny affiliation with any god of dreams: "Do I look like a god? I am just a little man of magic." And while the main conflict of Andersen's "The Snow Queen" can be defined as "religious,"[15] this adaptation eliminates "all references to religion. Instead of the Lord assisting Gerda in finding Kay, it is Gerda's great valor and tenacity that enable her to liberate Kay from captivity."[16]

As if it were not enough to render Andersen godless (which was standard procedure for the Dane's Soviet translations), the tale's message is also desexualized[17] by the film's claim that Kay is "like a brother" (*nazvannyi brat*) to Gerda. The "eternity" puzzle that Kay has to put

---

age group were married, and just over one percent of females; the average age for the first marriage was in fact around thirty for both genders (see Floor Clausen and Marker, "Marriage Pattern(s) in Denmark").

13 This was not, however, the first-ever Soviet film adaptation of Hans Christian Andersen. That distinction belongs to Aleksandr Macheret's *Cine-novellas in Color* (*Tsvetnye kinonovelly*, 1941), an anthology film of which "The Swineherd" formed the first part. One of the early Soviet experiments with color, it consists of a sequence of highly stylized *tableaux vivants*. The future founder of Moscow's Taganka Theater, Iurii Liubimov, looking painfully handsome, excels in the dual role of the swineherd/prince.

14 Perhaps to indicate to the viewer that there is more where "The Snow Queen" came from.

15 Pilipovets, "Russkie ekranizatsii," 223.

16 Zipes, *Enchanted Screen*, 96.

17 As Greenhill observes, "The Snow Queen" is notable for "incorporating but not condemning taboos such as adult-child sex (sometimes characterized by the slippery term *pedophilia*), incest (between social if not biological siblings), and lesbian attraction (most obviously between the Little Robber Girl and Gerda)" ("Queer Coding," 111).

together at the Snow Queen's behest is excised altogether, probably because the concept of eternity was deemed too difficult to grasp for the target audience. As a result, despite the seeming fidelity to Andersen's plot, precious little survives in Atamanov's film of what Pauline Greenhill terms "a parable about religion and emotion versus science and knowledge" ("Team Snow Queen," 36). Such deviations from the original, accompanied by elements from Andersen's *oeuvre* beyond "The Snow Queen," qualify Atamanov's effort as "quotational" on the Torop scale.

The changes wrought by Atamanov have apparently been rather typical of fairy tale adaptations for younger audiences in Russia. As one film critic puts it: "Aiming exclusively at children could only impose limitations on the fairy tales' film versions. A constant dependence on children's perception, accompanied by a subconscious desire to make films simpler and more accessible, have inevitably narrowed the genre's possibilities and arrested its development."[18]

It is quite possible that fairy tale adaptations for little children have inherited their aesthetics, at least partially, from the first decades of Russian cinema, when one of the chief tasks of film adaptation in general was to "make the classics more accessible to the largely illiterate population."[19] Throughout the Soviet period, moreover, "in adapting literary works for the screen, especially those from the prerevolutionary past, directors were encouraged, indeed required, to add an ideological gloss to the finished cinematic product. Literature, even the classics, had to bear a clear political message."[20]

Atamanov's adaptation is no exception. It is hard to escape the feeling that his Snow Queen, who assumes the functions of Andersen's devil in breaking the mirror (not by accident, however, but on purpose, to make people commit evil deeds), has something in common with Stalin, whose personality cult was denounced in 1956 at the Twentieth Congress of the Communist Party of the Soviet Union. By the same token, "the thawing of the icy Snow Queen's realm and the thawing of Kai's heart, while not overtly stressed, are clear references to the need of a thaw in the Soviet Union if there is to be any hope for the young" (Zipes, *Enchanted Screen*, 96).

Yet Atamanov's film is much more than an oversimplified political allegory. Its spectacular and memorable animation—a medium undoubtedly chosen because it "allows the juxtaposition of the real and the

---

18 Fomin, *Pravda skazki*, 212.
19 Gillespie, *Russian Cinema*, 12.
20 Ibid.

Fig. 1. Atamanov's Snow Queen looking into Kay and Gerda's living room. Soyuzmultfilm.

Fig. 3. Kazansky's Snow Queen (Natalya Klimova) looking into Kay and Gerda's living room (Slava Tsiupa and Elena Proklova). Lenfilm/Gosfil'mofond

Fig. 2. Atamanov's Ole Lukoie and inkwell. Soyuzmultfilm.

Fig. 4. Kazansky's inkwell-woman (Vera Titova). Lenfilm/Gosfil'mofond.

magic in the same space, in the same frame" (Beumers, "Comforting Creatures," 153) and thus fits many Andersen tales like a glove[21]— felicitously lends an escapist form[22] to an instructive message that transcends purely political sensibilities by associating the Snow Queen with the absence of feelings and urging the viewer to be selfless and fearless, helpful to others and protective of one's love. Paradoxically, because it was treated as a lesser art form,[23] Soviet animation was, "by contrast with ... children's film, ... much less affected by ideological

---

21 Cf. Draga-Alexandru's observation that the "marvelous/realistic appears as the major opposition of values that conditions all the others, defining the dialectical nature of Andersen's world" ("Contrastive Values," 440).

22 As Beumers notes, "[t]he fairy tale world functioned as a means of escape from the unpleasant reality of Stalin's tyranny" ("Comforting Creatures," 160).

23 Quite irrespective of how much talent and effort went into animation. The 1957 *Snow Queen*, for example, was collaborated upon by the outstanding authors Nikolai Erdman (a co-scriptwriter), Nikolai Zabolotsky, and Mikhail Svetlov (penning poetry and song lyrics for the film), as well as the renowned jazz composer Artemii Aivazian.

constraints and thus was able to instill in children universal moral values of right and wrong and often to make subversive comments on contemporary society."[24]

Gennadii Kazansky's *The Snow Queen* (*Snezhnaia koroleva*, 1966)

The second Soviet Snow Queen appeared a decade after the first, soon after the ousting of Khrushchev, upon the onset of a neo-Stalinist revival. In a number of aspects, this motion picture is a hybrid of sorts, not only in its combination of live-action[25] and animation,[26] but also because it bears certain characteristics associated simultaneously with Khrushchev's Thaw and (neo-)Stalinism. While under Stalin "the nuclear family became irrelevant in the world of state-sponsored happiness," the de-Stalinization of Soviet society under Khrushchev reestablished "the family as narrative's prime unit of social organization" (Prokhorov, "Arresting Development," 134, 142). Traces of the latter tendency can be seen in the fact that Kazansky's Kay is adopted into Gerda's family (we are told that his parents died when he was barely a year old). In other words, by fighting for Kay, Gerda is fighting for her (foster) brother, thus reinforcing nuclear family ties.[27]

On the other hand, for his film script, Kazansky utilizes Evgenii Schwartz's 1938 play *The Snow Queen* (*Snezhnaia koroleva*), penned at the height of Stalinism.[28] It is not that Schwartz rewrote Andersen with a Stalinist message in mind. Granted, while "Andersen illustrated the Christian conception of the child soul as pure and innocent, as well as the belief that faith overcomes all difficulties, [Schwartz's] Soviet version ... appears to be a tale of a superior collective that triumphs over the forces of capitalism and materialism."[29] But at the same time, "it was the per-

---

24 Beumers, "Comforting Creatures," 154.
25 The special effects in Kazansky's *The Snow Queen* have not aged well, but he was undoubtedly a consummate professional, responsible for the biggest Soviet science fiction hit of the decade, *The Amphibian Man* (*Chelovek-amfibiia*, 1962). The versatile soundtrack for his *Snow Queen* was provided by the modern classical composer Nadezhda Simonian.
26 In an apparent nod to its predecessor, certain frames and objects-cum-characters introduced by Atamanov (such as the Snow Queen looking at Kay and Gerda in their living room, as well as the inkwell [woman]) are creatively reused in the 1966 version (cf. fig. 1-2 and fig. 3-4).
27 This departure from Andersen's original may also be seen as continuing the desexualization process begun in Atamanov's *The Snow Queen*.
28 See Boris Wolfson's contribution to this volume.
29 Tippner, "Evgenii Shvarts's Fairy Tale Dramas," 315.

ceived playfulness, the deep humanism and the anti-ideological stance ... that made the play special in these times of great ideological pressure."[30]

Still, what Kazansky foregrounds are the social contrasts (commoners vs. royals, prisoners vs. courtiers, kennel vs. palace) and the physical aspects of resisting an enemy, which is quite in harmony with the black-and-white nature of the militantly mythologized Stalinist reality, underpinned by the concept of class struggle.[31] Thus, the storyteller,[32] played by Valerii Nikitenko, does not merely take over from Atamanov's Ole Lukoie, but actively interferes with the plot, freeing Gerda from the robber girl and fencing with the councilor of commerce (one of several non-Andersen characters added in Schwartz's play and retained in Kazansky's film, where he is played by Nikolai Boiarsky; another is the treacherous king, played by Evgenii Leonov).[33] As for Gerda, she is irreverent toward the king and confronts both the Snow Queen (verbally) and her palace snow guards (physically).[34] A Stalinist-type dominant masculinization[35] can be seen not only in Gerda's aggressive behavior (aggressiveness being traditionally associated with the legacy of the biological evolution of the male species)[36] but also in the complete absence of the original tale's Lapp woman and Finn woman.[37] The "eternity" puzzle, however, is reinstated (Kazansky's film is clearly aimed at elementary and secondary school children, who are better equipped to deal with such abstract notions than those in preschool).[38]

---

30 Ibid., 307. Pilipovets even claims that much of "The Snow Queen's" reception in Russia "has been mediated via Schwartz's interpretation" ("Russkie ekranizatsii," 229).
31 Kazansky "subordinates both the Little Robber Girl's and Kai's love relationship with Gerda to the needs of a political argument about class exploitation and the need for working-class solidarity.... [After defrosting,] Kai's clothes turn red to mark the return to his original, true, Communist self" (Greenhill, "Queer Coding," 122-23).
32 Some scholars see him as a stand-in for Andersen himself (see ibid., 120; and Pilipovets, "Russkie ekranizatsii," 225).
33 The Snow Queen is the councilor's ice supplier, while the king, a great ice-cream lover, and needer of "cold" weapons, is his debtor and has to imprison Gerda at his request.
34 In Atamanov, when Gerda comes for Kay to the Snow Queen's palace, the Snow Queen is present but surrenders the boy without a word. Kazansky's intense focus on conflict qualifies his film as "descriptive" on the Torop scale.
35 Cf. "Masculinity is the potential goal of every Stalinist subject" (Kaganovsky, *How the Soviet Man Was Unmade*, 159). This manifested itself, for example, in the state sponsorship of women competing with men in traditionally male-dominated occupations. Female beauty, moreover, was expected to conform to the standards of the robust physique (see Bulgakova, "Sovetskie krasavitsy"). Sergei Livnev's drama *Hammer and Sickle* (*Serp i molot*, 1994) grotesquely illustrates the general tendency through a fictional female-to-male sex-change operation taking place in the 1930s.
36 See, for instance, Buss and Duntley, "The Evolution of Aggression."
37 In Atamanov, both women are present.
38 Kazansky's omissions also include the devil's mirror (Kay's heart in any case turns to ice after the Snow Queen's kiss); and additions, a brief mention of other Andersen tales, e.g., "The Snowman."

The Snow Queen's Secret, or, A Tale about a Tale (*Taina snezhnoi korolevy, ili Skazka pro skazku,* 1986), by Nikolai Aleksandrovich

Twenty years later, on the eve of perestroika, a new cinematic reinterpretation of Andersen's classic came out. Meant chiefly for teenagers, this TV movie symbolically draws a line under the Soviet period of stagnation, taking aim, first and foremost, against apathy. The Snow Queen's secret is that she runs an "ice school" at which students are taught to be indifferent to others. To gain admittance, no mirror shards are necessary: the moment Kay says "I don't care," he falls under the Snow Queen's spell and is taken away by hip-twisting "snowflake" ballerinas. An obvious (albeit mild) resexualization does not feel out of place, as Kay and Gerda are neighbors again and look significantly more mature than their predecessors in Atamanov and Kazansky.[39] Masculinization makes further strides—five male characters are added to the original "Snow Queen" plot—yet most of these are trying to undermine Gerda's quest not by force, as had the councilor and king in Kazansky, but by varying degrees of sexual appeal.[40]

Aleksandrovich is determined to emphasize the everlasting relevance of Andersen's tale (the film asserts that "there is a Kay in every boy and a Gerda in every girl"; and that "the Snow Queen has to be defeated again and again"). On the Torop scale, this qualifies the film as "expressive." However, as the film's subtitle suggests, the original "Snow Queen" is often mentioned only to stress that in Aleksandrovich's storyline things happen somewhat otherwise. The difference is achieved not only by blending in other Andersen tales such as "The Swineherd" and "The Little Match Girl" (the Snow Queen's realm disappears only when Gerda uses one of the girl's matches, struck by a narrator-figure called the Tale's Voice, played by Oleg Efremov, head of the Moscow Art Theater); such a device had been used before. It is rather the film's eclectic mix of music,[41] animation, ballet dancing, and ice skating that was genu-

---

39 Incidentally, the same year saw the release, in Finland, of Päivi Hartzell's feature film *The Snow Queen*, in which preteens playing the prince and princess share a marital bed and pronounce Epicurean toasts over drinks served by scantily clad, muscular male servants. Needless to say, such a scene (meant to provoke laughter, not outrage) would have been completely unimaginable in a Soviet film for audiences of any age.

40 By contrast, only one female character (Autumn, played by Vija Artmane) is added to the cast, while the Lapp woman and Finn woman are once again omitted. Autumn is vaguely reminiscent of the garden sorceress, but is a helper to Gerda, not a hinderer.

41 Not all songs are sufficiently integrated into the action; Aleksandrovich's *Secret* is less of a musical than a film with a large number of songs.

inely new, as far as Russian adaptations of Andersen are concerned.[42] The project's creative team[43] apparently saw Andersen's original as too familiar for comfort and ripe for some enlivening. Technical updating (the Snow Queen's magic mirror is in fact a CCTV) and even dark humor (the reindeer is said to have died of homesickness for the northern lights) were seen as effective ingredients of such a revitalization. Alas, Aleksandrovich's changes to Andersen's tale pale by comparison with the dramatic real-life transformations taking place in the USSR at the time, which would eventually lead to the country's disintegration.

Maksim Papernik's *The Snow Queen* (*Snezhnaia koroleva*, 2003)

It would be seventeen years before another adaptation of "The Snow Queen" appeared. When a Russian-Ukrainian coproduction by a prominent Ukrainian music video director premiered on the Rossiia TV channel on New Year's Eve 2003-4, the post-Soviet economic troubles seemed a thing of the past, Ukraine was an independent country, and Russian-language television, as well as popular music culture, looked more slick and less ideological than in 1986.

Papernik's *The Snow Queen* was conceived broadly in the style of New Year's musical television shows, packed with pop stars and comedians, and watched across much of the former Soviet Union. The aim of such productions is to entertain rather than teach some moral lesson, and it is scarcely surprising that Kay's last spoken line before the film's closing song is "the main thing is love"—hardly an edifying message. It is equally unsurprising that the roles of Kay and Gerda are played by the singers Nikolai Baskov and Kristina Orbakaite, respectively in their early thirties and late twenties at the time: at last the grownups had seized their chance to revel in the adult side of Andersen's tale and make "The Snow Queen" their own.

On the one hand, Papernik's storyline constitutes a return to Andersen's

---

[42] In late Soviet culture, musicals had become fashionable as a form of film and TV adaptation since at least the above-mentioned *D'Artagnan and the Three Musketeers* (1979), *The Magicians* (*Charodei*, dir. Konstantin Bromberg, 1982), and *The Splendor and Death of Joaquin Murrieta* (*Zvezda i smert' Khoakina Mur'ety*, dir. Vladimir Grammatikov, 1983).

[43] Aleksandrovich was a pioneer of the practice of dubbing foreign films into Russian (his voice can be heard, for example, on the Soviet release of Federico Fellini's *Prova d'orchestra*). The music was composed by Mark Minkov, responsible for numerous hit songs. The lyrics were written by Vadim Korostylev, who co-scripted the cult Soviet children's film *Ow-It-Hurts-66* (*Aibolit-66*; dir. Rolan Bykov, 1967). The Snow Queen was played by a dramatic actress of outstanding talent, Alisa Freindlikh (perhaps best known for her role as the Stalker's wife in Andrei Tarkovsky's eponymous film of 1979).

original (well, almost), which on the Torop scale qualifies this adaptation as (more or less) "precise." As the new target audience is old enough to determine what is going on without a mediator, there is no narrator-figure in the film (the well-known plot milestones serve mainly as links between song-and-dance routines).[44] The garden sorceress, missing from both the 1966 and 1986 versions, is reinstated. The ravens, excluded since after Kazansky, also make a comeback (they are played by the famous stand-up comedians Gennady Khazanov and Klara Novikova)—and perform a rap song. The Lapp woman and Finn woman are back as well, reincarnated as the twin sisters Ksenia the Shaman (played by the cross-dressing Andrei Danilko, AKA Verka Serdiuchka) and Ingrid the Astrologer (Taisia Povaliy).[45]

The Snow Queen (yet another pop star, Laima Vaikule, moving about in a white limo, to give Andersen a little upgrade) is meant to steal the show. She is a cross between an ice maiden and a she-Bluebeard (keeping semi-naked men in ice capsules). Papernik's eroticism is notably raunchier than Aleksandrovich's, with hits like "Northern Gals Are Hotter" ("Severnye devki goriachei," performed by Danilko) and "Only Once" ("Tol'ko raz," performed by Vaikule) abounding in sexual innuendo. Adult themes notwithstanding, Papernik's is a musical made to be forgotten, not to last. Compared to Aleksandrovich's attempt, Minkov is probably less derivative than Krutoi as a composer—but Krutoi is much more of a showman; in Aleksandrovich, moreover, good actors sing unprofessionally, while in Papernik, professional singers act a little. All in all, Papernik's film seems to fulfill, at least partially, a function similar to *Bram Stoker's Dracula* (1992, dir. Francis Ford Coppola) and *Mary Shelley's Frankenstein* (1994, dir. Kenneth Branagh), i.e., reminding a major franchise that has deviated a little too far from its origins (plot-wise) what these origins actually are.

Elena Raiskaia's *The Snow Queen* (*Snezhnaia koroleva*, 2006)

In our postmodern times, this back-to-basics strategy cannot last and is likely to incite both renewed interest in the classic text and its further reinterpretation. Exemplifying the latter would be the first Russian Snow

---

[44] The music is by yet another highly popular songwriter, Igor Krutoi, with some lyrics by Viktor Peleniagre, who has combined countercultural roots with a wide appeal.
[45] Other minor deviations from the master plot include Gerda's mother (Nadezhda Babkina), not grandmother, looking after Kay since his childhood (presumably to allow for a stock mother-in-law situation, which many adult viewers can relate to).

Queen film by a female director,[46] released only three years after Papernik's. Known primarily for TV films and serials, Raiskaia observes in her *Snow Queen* how the "old" (Andersen's original story, as performed by actors in a children's theater in late- and post-Soviet Russia) morphs into the "new," influencing the lives of the actors' own offspring. These children (of two actress friends), a boy and a girl, are named Kay and Greta, in partial tribute to the roles their mothers played in the theater production. Having grown up together, they are poised to become a romantic couple, when Kay (played by Stanislav Erdlei, in his early twenties at the time) meets a pop star named Alina (Agnese Zeltina, in her mid-thirties) and becomes her temporary companion and sex partner, while Greta (Raiskaia's own daughter Iana, in her late teens) tries to win him back.

Thus, Andersen's plot is transformed—not without a "melodramatic" touch (Pilipovets, "Russkie ekranizatsii," 222)—into an archetypal romantic triangle involving a young man and his two women (one older than him, the other slightly younger), with the Snow Queen's literal iciness manifesting itself through Alina's emotional coldness and conscious rejection of motherhood in favor of her music career.[47] Partial nudity—a further step up from Papernik's mostly verbal eroticism—and a subplot about drug smuggling from Russia to Lapland under the pretext of a VIP tour, are included, presumably to increase this TV film's ratings. Among other transformations: here the ravens are an old tourist couple; the reindeer, a gay actor (don't ask!); and the robbers become drug addicts. A Lapland tour leader (doubling as the leader of a gang of drug runners) is added to the standard Andersen cast. All in all, on the Torop scale, Raiskaia's adaptation can be classified as "thematic."

Maksim Sveshnikov and Vladlen Barbe's *The Snow Queen (Snezhnaia koroleva,* 2012)

Meanwhile, the Russian animation industry's recovery from post-Soviet turmoil was eventually sufficient to contemplate a new version of "The Snow Queen" in the same medium as it had originally been filmed in the USSR. Just as early Soviet animation had been tasked with creating a viable (communist) alternative to Disney,[48] the 2012 *Snow Queen* pro-

---

46 For interpretations of "The Snow Queen" by non-Russian female directors, see Greenhill, "Team Snow Queen."
47 The music to the film, including a song that became a hit (first performed in the film by Alina and her ex-partner Andrei, later by Kay and Greta), was composed by Alena Sviridova.
48 The trend apparently continued well after the Second World War: the most talented Soviet animators, Atamanov included, "while still following the main naturalistic style brought

ducer, Timur Bekmambetov (a Roger Corman trainee with many recent commercial and artistic successes to his name), opted to vie for audience share with major studios in the West, taking this competition onto the Western animators' own turf.[49] It is not coincidental that Sveshnikov and Barbe's *The Snow Queen* was made in 3D, "in tune with the expectations of a blockbuster-animated film today" (Mjolsness, "Review"), and features music by Emmy winner Mark Willott, English-language signage, and visual references to *Oliver!, Avatar, Ice Age, Lord of the Rings, Harry Potter, The Chronicles of Narnia, Pirates of the Caribbean* (as stand-ins for Andersen's robbers), etc.[50] A certain Disneyization is noticeable in the characters of the ferret Luta and troll Orm, inserted in their capacity as sidekicks.

Orm's voice also acts as narrator at the film's start and finish (we are back to children's territory, after all, hence the renewed need for mediation). Naturally, under the circumstances, Kay and Gerda are portrayed as siblings.[51] For the first time in the Russian tradition of "Snow Queen" adaptations, Kay and Gerda's parents are introduced, too. Their father Vegard, a master glassmaker and a good wizard, is frozen to death along with his wife on the orders of the Snow Queen, whose influence he had resisted.[52] Murderous as she is, the Snow Queen is provided a theoretically redeeming backstory (she is in fact a Lapp girl named Irma who, unloved as a child, had never learned how to love others).[53]

---

by 'Disney's revolution' and adopting Disney's style to such an extent that some of the characters and animals looked very similar, tried to infuse their work with the Russian spirit" (Pontieri, *Soviet Animation*, 45). In the process of promoting the non-Disney "moral values of meekness and self-sacrifice" and presenting "a subversive social order… which allowed class mobility, women's emancipation and empowerment, and the toppling of rulers," by the late 1960s Soviet animation finally discovered that it "could do better than Disney; it would focus on short films rather than features, and would develop auteur animation" (Balina and Beumers, "To Catch Up and Overtake Disney?", 131-32). However, the financial and professional insecurity wrought by the Soviet Union's collapse left post-Soviet animators susceptible once more to the temptation to imitate Disney.

49 Sveshnikov and Barbe's film was released in the US a year before *Frozen*, Disney's latest version of Andersen's "The Snow Queen."

50 As well as a "subliminal" advertisement for bobsledding and snowboarding ahead of the 2014 Winter Olympics in Sochi (in which expectations were particularly high for the Russian men, who indeed took two gold medals in the three bobsledding events, and two gold and one silver in the five snowboarding events).

51 Re-immersed in fairytale time, by the way: both "appear to be of the same age at the end of the film, despite the fact that the opening scene shows an infant Kay with Gerda as a young girl" (Mjolsness, "Review").

52 Interestingly, there are two competing mirrors in Sveshnikov and Barbe: Vegard's shows things as they are, while the Snow Queen's offers useful advice to its owner. This has roots in Andersen's tale, which, in addition to the devil's mirror, features a frozen lake the Snow Queen calls her beloved "Mirror of Reason."

53 A similar "excuse" for the Snow Queen's behavior is advanced in Natalya Bondarchuk's film *The Mystery of the Snow Queen* (*Taina snezhnoi korolevy*), which premiered in 2016

Irrespective of Sveshnikov and Barbe's obvious commercial intentions, their film unequivocally states that "material possessions are not as important as the love of family and freedom" (Mjolsness, "Review"). Moreover, free as it seems to be on the Torop scale, it still "demonstrates the power of children to be both good and evil, resonating with [Andersen's] original" (ibid.)–unlike most of the adaptations I have analyzed. A box office success, the film saw its budget of USD seven million recouped twice over in worldwide sales.[54] However, as Balina and Beumers rightly observe ("To Catch Up and Overtake Disney?," 137), the film could not "quite compete with Disney's *Frozen* (2013), and certainly not yet on an international market."

Conclusions

My brief survey of the metamorphosis of Andersen's "The Snow Queen" master plot in film and TV adaptations demonstrates that only four (groups of) characters are invariably present in Russian/(post-)Soviet versions of the tale, i.e. Kay, Gerda, the Snow Queen, and the robbers (or pirates, in Sveshnikov and Barbe)–presumably, because the first three are central to the story, while the robbers usefully combine colorful presence with an anticipation of action. The Lapp woman and Finn woman (or such later reincarnations thereof as Papernik's Ksenia the Shaman and Ingrid the Astrologer) are the least common in adaptations, while the prince and princess, the garden sorceress, and the ravens are somewhere in between (in a descending order of frequency). Among scenes and characters not originally part of Andersen's "The Snow Queen," adapters most favor showing Gerda directly confronting the eponymous sovereign and/or her minions, with the narrator-figure being the second likeliest addition (albeit usually excluded from versions for grownups).

Alterations of various orders of magnitude are hardly unique to Russophone adaptations of "The Snow Queen." The narrator-figure, for instance, can be found in Jørgen Lerdam's 2004 Danish version. Osamu Dezaki's thirty-nine-episode *Snow Queen* anime (2005-6) introduces, as Gerda's travelling companion, the mysterious minstrel Ragi, said to

---

in several locations in Russia. In this version, the Snow Queen is put under a magic spell, which can be undone should anyone manage to melt her icy heart.

54 The film's commercial success inspired a sequel, *The Snow Queen 2* (2014) by Aleksei Tsitsilin, also produced by Bekmambetov. This capitalizes on the irresistibility of the figure of Orm, who is afforded so much character development in the Sveshnikov and Barbe version that he manages to switch sides (from the Snow Queen's to Gerda's) and morph into a polar bear. Tsitsilin's film has very little in common with Hans Christian Andersen and is thus disregarded here (see, however, Rogatchevski, "Review").

be an "apposite alter ego" for Andersen himself.[55] Päivi Hartzell's 1986 Finnish version, in which Kay is entranced by the Snow Queen after drinking a magic potion, and Kerttu (Gerda) is controlled by the garden sorceress with the help of chocolate sweets, admixes a theme of world domination, which the Snow Queen hopes to achieve by procuring, with Kay's help, a certain emerald for her crown. Most radically, in Chris Buck and Jennifer Lee's *Frozen*, there is a Snow Queen called Elsa, who can freeze anything she touches, but the story revolves around her troubled relationship with her sister Anna, not at all around any Kay and Gerda.

Generally speaking, just like some non-Russian versions of "The Snow Queen," the (post-)Soviet adaptations of the story exhibit the following common, sometimes overlapping tendencies: simplification (i.e., aimed mostly at children, the films contain little if any complexity, with everything explained by the narrator/voiceover); over-dramatization (i.e., retaining, first and foremost, the gaudiest characters, such as robbers and royalty, and adding scenes of tension); trivialization (i.e., tending to the banal, especially if aimed at adults); and modernization ("updating" in technological terms; conforming to currently fashionable tastes). But at the same time, every (post-)Soviet adaptation I have examined appears to belong to a different category on the Torop scale, perhaps reflecting the necessity "for new adaptations to say something new" (Pilipovets, "Russkie ekranizatsii," 231).

In any case, judging by the film adaptation numbers known to me, Russians' avidity for the "The Snow Queen" seems greater than any other nation's. Why would this be? It may in part have something to do with Russia's geographical location. Fifty percent of the country's land mass lies above the latitude of sixty degrees north, and seventy percent of its territory (northern European Russia, Siberia, and the Far East) is categorizable as "the North."[56] Given the strong Russian tradition of female personification of the Motherland (see for example Hubbs, *Mother Russia*), could "The Snow Queen" be emblematic of Russia's self-identification with the North?

The Snow Queen as an image, moreover, combines the idea of northernness with that of power.[57] Her forcefulness, coldness, and cruelty should have seemed natural to the many Russians and ethnic non-Russians sent to "the North" by the authorities as a form of punishment; and to their descendants. Paradoxically, the long Russian history of

---

55 Cavallaro, *Anime and the Art of Adaptation*, 75.
56 Ukrainians sometimes refer to Russia as "our northern neighbor."
57 On the image of the Snow Queen in post-Soviet Russia, see Yuri Leving's contribution to this volume.

state-sponsored population abuse does not necessarily weaken Russian nationalist sentiments. In the words of one expert on the matter: "The most extreme Russian patriots are matriots at heart. By this I mean that their devotion to 'Mother Russia' is so intense that the underlying maternal fantasy basis of patriotism comes to the surface as maternal imagery.... At the same time there is a willingness to indulge in or act out masochistic fantasies with respect to the maternal image" (Rancour-Laferriere, *The Slave Soul*, 225). In this context, the Snow Queen seems quite a befitting "bad mother" figure (in Kleinian terms).

Unsurprisingly, there are concomitant and consistent attempts to justify (or at least mitigate) the Snow Queen's personality traits and behavior; reference is made to her background as that of a mistreated child (Sveshnikov and Barbe), an overzealous career woman (Raiskaia), someone sexually frigid (Papernik), and even under an evil spell (Bondarchuk). Such attempts can be seen as evidence of Russia's extremely deep and perhaps partly irrational attachment to "The Snow Queen." It is this attachment that appears to bear ultimate responsibility for the highly elaborate Russian narrative linked to the Andersen tale.

Curiously, practically every new (post-)Soviet film/TV adaptation of "The Snow Queen" harks back more to previous Russophone adaptations than to those of other countries (e.g., Aleksandrovich's Baron Who Didn't Exist is an ice-cream fan, like the treacherous king in Kazansky; the knight's empty suit of armor in the prince and princess's castle appears in Atamanov's, Kazansky's, and Papernik's versions; and the castle in Sveshnikov and Barbe is divided in two halves, between the king and his children, just like in Kazansky). This can be explained by the Soviet Union's isolationism (very few films made outside the Soviet bloc, children's included, were widely and readily available in the USSR); but only partly. Papernik's and Sveshnikov and Barbe's adaptations were produced quite a while after the USSR's demise yet still speak to the viewer via (partially) recycled old Soviet Snow Queen images. Is it because there is indeed something specifically Russian about the way "The Snow Queen" has been perceived and treated in Russia?[58] Whatever it is, one thing is certain: we can look forward to even more Russophone film adaptations of "The Snow Queen."

---

58 Cf. Erkhov's observation that "Andersen's is a case when we [Russians] add a new quality to something we appropriate [*prisvaivaem*] from another country" ("Russkie otrazheniia," 6).

Works Cited

Aragay, Mireia. "Reflection to Refraction: Adaptation Studies Then and Now." In *Books in Motion: Adaptations, Intertextuality, Authorship*, edited by Mireia Aragay, 11-34. Amsterdam and New York: Rodopi, 2005.

Balina, Marina, and Birgit Beumers. "'To Catch Up and Overtake Disney?': Soviet and Post-Soviet Fairy-Tale Films." In *Fairy-Tale Films Beyond Disney: International Perspectives*, edited by Jack Zipes, Pauline Greenhill, and Kendra Magnus-Johnston, 124-38. New York: Taylor & Francis, 2015.

Beumers, Birgit. "Comforting Creatures in Children's Cartoons." In *Russian Children's Literature and Culture*, edited by Marina Balina and Larissa Rudova, 153-71. New York and London: Routledge, 2008.

Bulgakova, Oksana. "Sovetskie krasavitsy v stalinskom kino." In *Sovetskoe bogatstvo: Stat'i o kul'ture, literature i kino*, edited by Marina Balina, Evgenii Dobrenko, and Iurii Murashov, 391-412. St. Petersburg: Akademicheskii proekt, 2002.

Buss, David M., and Joshua D. Duntley. "The Evolution of Aggression." In *Evolution and Social Psychology*, edited by Mark Schaller, Jeffry A. Simpson, and Douglas T. Kenrick, 263-85. New York: Psychology Press, 2006.

Cavallaro, Dani. *Anime and the Art of Adaptation: Eight Famous Works from Page to Screen*. Jefferson, NC: McFarland, 2010.

Draga-Alexandru, Maria-Sabina. "Contrastive Values in Hans Christian Andersen's Fantastic Stories." In *Hans Christian Andersen: A Poet in Time*, edited by Johan de Mylius, Aage Jørgensen, and Viggo Hjørnager Pedersen, 437-49. Odense: Odense University Press, 1999.

Erkhov, B. A. "Andersen: Russkie otrazheniia." In *Andersen v russkoi literature: Pisateli o pisatele*, edited by B. A. Erkhov, 6-9. Moscow: Rudomino, 1997.

Floor Clausen, Nanna, and Hans Jørgen Marker. "Marriage Pattern(s) in Denmark in the 19th Century." Paper delivered at the 2012 Conference of the Social Science History Association (Vancouver, Canada). Available electronically: http://ddd.dda.dk/Marriage%20pattern%20in%20Denmark%20in%2019th%20century%20(SSHA%202012).pdf

Fomin, V. I. *Pravda skazki: Kino i traditsiia fol'klora*. Moscow: Kanon+, 2012.

Gillespie, David. *Russian Cinema*. Harlow: Pearson Education Ltd., 2003.

Greenhill, Pauline. "*The Snow Queen*: Queer Coding in Male Directors' Films." In *Marvels and Tales* 29, no. 1 (2015): 110-34.

—. "Team Snow Queen: Feminist Cinematic 'Misinterpretations' of a Fairy Tale." In *Studies in European Cinema* 13, no. 1 (2016): 32-49.

Hubbs, Joanna. *Mother Russia: The Feminine Myth in Russian Culture*. Bloomington: Indiana University Press, 1988.

Hutchings, Stephen, and Anat Vernitski. "The *Ekranizatsiia* in Russian Culture." In *Russian and Soviet Film Adaptations of Literature, 1900-2001: Screening the Word*, edited by Stephen Hutchings and Anat Vernitski, xiv–xxxii. London and New York: Routledge, 2009.

Kaganovsky, Lilya. *How the Soviet Man Was Unmade: Cultural Fantasy and Male Subjectivity under Stalin*. Pittsburgh: University of Pittsburgh Press, 2008.

Kleivan, Inge. "Arctic Elements in the Writings of Hans Christian Andersen." In *Hans Christian Andersen: A Poet in Time*, edited by Johan de Mylius, Aage Jørgensen, and Viggo Hjørnager Pedersen, 289-300. Odense: Odense University Press, 1999.

Leitch, Thomas. "Across the Russian Border." In *Border Crossing: Russian Literature into Film*, edited by Alexander Burry and Frederick H. White, 17-39. Edinburgh: Edinburgh University Press, 2016.

McFarlane, Brian. *Novel to Film: An Introduction to the Theory of Adaptation*. Oxford: Clarendon Press, 1996.

Mjolsness, Laura. "[Review of] *The Snow Queen* by Maksim Sveshnikov and Vladlen Barbe (2012)." *Kinokultura* 41 (2013). Available electronically: http://www.kinokultura.com/2013/41r-snezhnaiakoroleva.shtml

Nemchenko, Liliia. "Ekranizatsiia kak pole interpretatsii." *Toronto Slavic Quarterly* 44 (2013): 166-75.

Oxfeldt, Elisabeth. *H.C. Andersens eventyr på film*. Odense: Syddansk Universitetsforlag, 2009.

Pilipovets, Tat'iana. "Russkie ekranizatsii skazki 'Snezhnaia koroleva': Dialog interpretatsii." In *Russkaia filologiia* 26 (2015): 221-31.

Pontieri, Laura. *Soviet Animation and the Thaw of the 1960s: Not Only for Children*. New Barnet: John Libbey Publishing, 2012.

Præstgaard Andersen, Lise. "The Feminine Element—and a Little about the Masculine Element in H. C. Andersen's Fairy Tales." In *Hans Christian Andersen: A Poet in Time*, edited by Johan de Mylius, Aage Jørgensen, and Viggo Hjørnager Pedersen, 501-14. Odense: Odense University Press, 1999.

Prokhorov, Alexander. "Arresting Development: A Brief History of Soviet Cinema for Children and Adolescents." In *Russian Children's Literature and Culture*, edited by Marina Balina and Larissa Rudova, 129-52. New York and London: Routledge, 2008.

Rancour-Laferriere, Daniel. *The Slave Soul of Russia: Moral Masochism and the Cult of Suffering*. New York: New York University Press, 1996.

Rogatchevski, Andrei. "[Review of] *The Snow Queen-2: Refreezing* by Aleksei Tsitsilin (2014)." In *Kinokultura* 51 (2016). Available electronically: http://www.kinokultura.com/2016/51r-snow-queen-2.shtml

Steiner, Peter. *Russian Formalism*. Ithaca: Cornell University Press, 1984.

Tippner, Anja. "Evgenii Shvarts's Fairy Tale Dramas: Theater, Power, and the Naked Truth." In *Russian Children's Literature and Culture*, edited by Marina Balina and Larissa Rudova, 307-23. New York and London: Routledge, 2008.

Torop, Peeter. *Total'nyi perevod*. Tartu: Tartu Ülikooli Kirjastus, 1995.

Wullschläger, Jackie. *Hans Christian Andersen: The Life of a Storyteller*. London: Allen Lane, 2000.

Zipes, Jack. *The Enchanted Screen: The Unknown History of Fairy-Tale Films*. New York and London: Routledge, 2011.

—. *Hans Christian Andersen: The Misunderstood Storyteller*. New York and London: Routledge, 2005.

Filmography

Aksenchuk, Ivan. *The Little Mermaid* (*Rusalochka*). USSR, Soyuzmultfilm, 1968. 29 mins. https://www.youtube.com/watch?v=G8dbxwGIo5Q

Aleksandrovich, Nikolai. *The Secret of the Snow Queen, or, A Tale about a Tale* (*Taina snezhnoi korolevy, ili Skazka pro skazku*). USSR, TO Ekran, 1986. 140 mins. https://www.youtube.com/watch?v=mN8_56egPuI

Amal'rik, Leonid. *Thumbelina* (*Diuimovochka*). USSR, Soyuzmultfilm, 1964. 30 mins. https://www.youtube.com/watch?v=BRYcfKx-6H4

Atamanov, Lev. *The Snow Queen* (*Snezhnaia koroleva*). USSR, Soyuzmultfilm, 1957. 64 mins. https://www.youtube.com/watch?v=P8jN0oOvYi0

Bondarchuk, Natal'ia. *The Mystery of the Snow Queen* (*Taina snezhnoi korolevy*). Russia, Zolotoi vek, 2016. 85 mins.

Bychkov, Vladimir. *The Little Mermaid* (*Rusalochka*). USSR/Bulgaria, Boyana and Gorky Studios, 1976. 84 mins. https://www.youtube.com/watch?v=986hxa6rgP0

Douksha, Iosif, and Maiia Buzinova. *The Nightingale* (*Solovei*). USSR, Soiuztelefil'm, 1991. 18 mins. https://www.youtube.com/watch?v=tfptQ2CS8eA

Kazansky, Gennadii. *The Snow Queen* (*Snezhnaia koroleva*). USSR, Lenfil'm, 1966. 80 mins. https://www.youtube.com/watch?v=QPj0VNyPtZU

Kodiukova, Irina. *The Little Match Girl* (*Devochka so spichkami*). Belarus, Belarusfil'm, 1996. 10 mins. https://www.youtube.com/watch?v=FSLGCQ--2fM

Macheret, Aleksandr. *Cine-novellas in Colour* (*Tsvetnye kinonovelly*). USSR, Mosfil'm, 1941. 47 mins. https://www.youtube.com/watch?v=HcM9Q3y-vWA

Papernik, Maksim. *The Snow Queen* (*Snezhnaia koroleva*). Ukraine/Russia, TV Channel Inter / TV Channel Rossiia, 2003. 98 mins. https://www.youtube.com/watch?v=XQhEKttEE0w

Raiskaia, Elena. *The Snow Queen* (*Snezhnaia koroleva*). Russia, Central Partnership, 2006. 100 mins. https://my.mail.ru/mail/ykoch2042/video/3803/5000.html

Rytsarev, Boris. *The Princess and the Pea* (*Printsessa na goroshine*). USSR, Gorky Studios, 1976. 89 mins. https://www.youtube.com/watch?v=4hmskGXhg3w

Sveshnikov, Maksim, and Vladlen Barbe. *The Snow Queen* (*Snezhnaia koroleva*). Russia, Inlay Film / Wizart Animation, 2012. 76 mins. http://www.myvi.ru/watch/1HqXO3vxakewLyKGF3bqnQ2

Yearning for a Soul:

"The Little Mermaid" in Graphics

Helena Goscilo

> A children's book illustrated completely in the spirit of children's drawings will bring joy, not to children, but to adult, overly satiated aesthetes.
>
> Ivan Bilibin[1]

> I believe that a children's book, in addition to its utilitarian function, is also a memorial to culture and time, like any work of art. The more richly and complexly it expresses the ideas of the time, the more perfect its plastic qualities, the more convincing and long-lasting it will be. Here I see no fundamental difference between a monumental painting/mural and a children's illustration.
>
> Viktor Pivovarov[2]

While Russian paintings of *rusalki* exist, albeit in modest numbers[3] (most famously those by Konstantin Makovsky [1879] and Ilya Repin [1876][4]), the Danish Mermaid has not inspired canvas art in Russia. Off-screen images of her are largely confined to book illustrations, which comprise an ever-expanding gallery of individual artists' visual interpretations, varying dramatically in conception, style, and quality.

The function of book illustrations, and those in publications targeting children *a fortiori*, is a highly polemical issue, though consensus exists to the extent that no commentator deems illustrations superfluous. Among numerous theorists, Joanne Golden posits five different types

---

1   Bilibin, *Stat'i. Pis'ma. Vospominaniia o khudozhnike*, 62.
2   Cited from Gankina, *Khudozhnik v sovremennoi detskoi knige*, 93.
3   Sharing the Russian *rusalka*'s traits, the analogous Polish water spirit inspired many more Polish painters, such as Henryk Siemiradzki (1863), Witold Pruszkowski (1877), Jacek Malczewski (1888), Wilhelm Kotarbiński, Jarosław Pstrak, etc.
4   Makovsky's *Rusalki* depicts in naturalistic mode a plethora of *rusalki* disporting in and above water during a moonlit night, whereas Repin's painting, titled *Sadko in the Underwater Kingdom* (*Sadko v podvodnom tsarstve*), shows Sadko beside a procession of *rusalki*, who eye him. Ivan Kramskoi's painting clothes the *rusalki* in what resemble floor-length nightgowns!

of verbal-visual relationships in picture storybooks: "text and picture are symmetrical; text depends on picture for clarification; illustration enhances, elaborates text; text carries primary narrative, illustration is selective; and illustration carries primary narrative, text is selective."[5] For Jane Doonan, the possible goals of visuals vis-à-vis the verbal text are to elaborate, amplify, extend, complement, contradict, and deviate.[6] In a kindred, albeit somewhat profligate vein, Joseph Schwarcz (*Ways of the Illustrator*) identifies congruency, elaboration, specification, amplification, extension, complementation, alternation, deviation, and counterpoint as the possible interactions between text and pictures. W. J. T. Mitchell, however, famously and programmatically eliminates the longstanding binarism in this multimodal representation to explore what he calls the "imagetext,"[7] and to some extent Lawrence Sipe follows his example by citing "synergy" as the key element uniting verbal text and image.[8] Yet illustrations in which text and image are inextricably bound rarely occur, the most radical instance being El Lissitzky's revolutionary *About Two Squares: A Suprematist Tale of Two Squares in Six Constructions* (*Pro dva kvadrata: suprematicheskii skaz v 6-ti postroikakh*, 1922), which dispenses with text altogether and stands out precisely by virtue of its imagetext/iconotext nature, facilitated by Lissitzky's dual role of author and illustrator.[9] Such a synthesis, especially given the abstraction of the image, failed to provide a model congenial for subsequent graphic artists. Even today most illustrations of children's books, especially of substantial length (Lissitzky's is one of the shortest on record), fall into two of Golden's categories: enhancement and selectivity.

Starting in the nineteenth century and gaining momentum in the twentieth and twenty-first, Russians have issued innumerable editions of Hans Christian Andersen in translation, most of them illustrated by a gamut of artists in sufficient numbers to have prompted a comprehensive scholarly study: *A Century and a Half of H. C. Andersen and His Russian Illustrators* (*Kh. K. Andersen i ego russkie illiustratory*

---

5 Golden, *The Narrative Symbol in Childhood Literature*, 104.
6 Doonan, *Looking at Pictures in Picture Books*, 18.
7 Mitchell, *Picture Theory*, 9.
8 Sipe, "How Picture Books Work," 98. Apparently obsessed with nomenclature, Maria Nikolajeva and Carole Scott prefer the term "picturebooks" for those publications that perfectly blend visual with verbal. See Nikolajeva and Scott, *How Picturebooks Work*.
9 For an excellent analysis of Lissitzky's booklet, see Oushakine, "Translating Communism for Children," especially 191-95. The postrevolutionary era in Russia encouraged such avant-garde illustrations as Lissitzky's and Vladimir Maiakovsky's. The latter's ideologically freighted *Soviet Alphabet* (*Sovetskaia azbuka*, 1919) similarly strives for the inextricability of words and images, both also supplied by Maiakovsky.

Fig. 1. By V. Pedersen. Wikimedia Commons.

za poltora veka).[10] The significance of Andersen for children's books and of visuals for the genre may be deduced from the biennial Hans Christian Andersen Awards for authors and illustrators of children's books—the highest international recognition for lasting contributions to children's literature, established in 1956 and 1966 respectively. With Czechs the most frequent laureates in the category of illustration and Tatyana Mavrina (1902-96) the sole Soviet/Russian recipient, the award is decided by the International Board on Books for Young People, whose purview spans the globe.[11] Illustrations of Andersen's "The Little Mermaid" date from the 1849 German collection of Andersen's tales[12] (by the Dane Vilhelm Pedersen [fig. 1]) and multiply each year, with numerous images devised by internationally renowned illustrators, from Arthur Rackham[13] and Edmund Dulac in England (fig. 2) and Kay Nielsen in Denmark to Sulamith Wulfing in Germany, Andrea Farina in

---

10 I am much indebted to this excellent study by Kudriavtseva and Zvonareva.
11 See "Hans Christian Andersen Awards," at http://ibby.org/. The prolific Igor Oleinikov (b. 1953), who also works in film animation, illustrates Russian and other fairy tales, provides visuals for many children's magazines, and contributed visuals for a Taiwan (Grimm Press) edition of Andersen's "The Nightingale," was a nominee in 2014.
12 *Gesammelte Märchen. Mit 112 Illustrationen nach Originalzeichnungen von V. Pedersen. Im Holz geschnitten von Ed. Kretzschmar.* Leipzig 1849. My thanks to Mads Sohl Jessen for this information.
13 For Rackham's illustrations, see http://www.surlalunefairytales.com/illustrations/littlemermaid/rackhammermaid.html; for Dulac's, see
http://www.surlalunefairytales.com/illustrations/littlemermaid/dulacmermaid.html.

Yearning for a Soul:

Fig. 2. By E. Dulac. Wikimedia Commons.

Italy, Josef Paleček in Czechoslovakia, and Chihiro Iwasaki and Takato Yamamoto in Japan, to name but a few.[14] Russians are no exception in this creative responsiveness to Andersen's tale.[15]

---

14 For a sampling of the book illustrations by artists around the world, see the compilation at https://www.youtube.com/watch?v=IJtEEmL3QSc.
15 For an overly short and intermittently cloying glance at Russian illustrators of Andersen's fairy tales, see Gankina, "Illustrations." The 1969 and 1973 Soviet editions of his tales,

Fig. 3. By N. Murashko. Owner's photograph.

Yet during the nineteenth century, despite frequent Russian editions of Andersen's tales, "The Little Mermaid" seemingly attracted graphic artists much less than did several of his other works, such as "The Snow Queen," "Thumbelina," and "The Nightingale." One can only speculate why such was the case, and artists' personal preferences doubtless played a role. Yet, in light of the Russian spiritual tradition, the dearth of images for a tale focused on the soul and salvation remains puzzling.

both titled *Skazki*, were illustrated by the enormously prolific Traugot brothers (Valerii and Aleksandr) and Anatolii Kokorin respectively.

Perhaps his father's profession of icon painter explains a notable exception: the Ukrainian Nikolai Murashko (1844-1909). A friend of Repin and a specialist in lithography, Murashko contributed to an 1873 collection titled *Andersen's Fairy Tales* (*Skazki Andersena*), published in Kiev.[16] In addition to a highly atmospheric visual for the poem "Angel," which depicts an angel above a nocturnal cityscape carrying a child to heaven, the volume contains a rendition of the dramatic meeting between the mermaid and the witch. Murashko conveys the latter's malevolence through her physical appearance and her environment. Resembling an elongated vampire, with a gaunt face and dark, piercing eyes, she is enveloped in white robes recalling a shroud or sheets. The accoutrements of her supernatural powers—a steaming cauldron, a sea-snake, and a huge toad in the foreground, as well as four suspended, spiderlike creatures—surround her and the mermaid. Symbolically located below the figure of the witch, the supplicating mermaid receives a flacon from her. Her small size (roughly double that of the toad), her placement and body posture (she would be kneeling if her fishtail were legs), and her encirclement by forces clearly associated with evil or death communicate the mermaid's vulnerability and presage her physical demise (fig. 3). Murashko's emotionally charged visual conjures the witch as unambiguously villainous, and its impact on the viewer prompts regret that his contemporaries apparently had little interest in translating equally dramatic or lyrical moments of the tale into pictures.

By contrast, the twentieth century witnessed a plethora of "Little Mermaid" illustrations. Fascinatingly, Ivan Bilibin, a passionate practitioner of Art Nouveau decorativeness associated with the World of Art (Mir iskusstva) community, and the era's supreme illustrator of Russian folklore and fairy tales, produced only a couple of isolated and rather sketchy black-and-white images of the Russian *rusalka*, yet supplied eight full-page visuals for the slim French translation of Andersen's tale, *La petite sirène*, issued by Flammarion in 1937 to mark the centenary of the tale's original publication in Danish.

Ivan Bilibin (1876-1942)

One of many volumes for which Bilibin designed covers and illustrations during and after his prolific eleven-year sojourn in Paris (1925-36), the twenty-two-page *La petite sirène* is unusual in its combination of

---

16 Kudriavtseva and Zvonareva, *Kh. K. Andersen i ego russkie illiustratory za poltora veka*, 22.

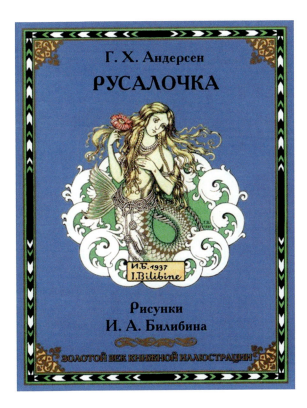

Fig. 4. By I. Bilibin. Wikimedia Commons.

four color and four black-and-white illustrations—a mélange that one commentator deemed disruptive to the unity of the ensemble,[17] yet was faithfully reproduced in subsequent translations of Andersen's tale into various languages.[18] In fact, Andersen's focus guided Bilibin's use of color, which he reserved for those episodes on which the narrative hinges, while, with one exception, relying on black and white for scenes of lesser consequence.

The volume's blue cover depicts the tale's protagonist as a blonde mermaid dreamily holding a flower, her body draped in her long, flowing hair and tasseled pearls, encircled by Bilibin's characteristic ornamental Art Nouveau patterning, here of green and white curlicues reminiscent of foaming waves (fig. 4). Whether by coincidence or not, her physical appearance would be near-duplicated in Vladimir Bychkov's screen mermaid (Viktoriia Novikova). Though the latter has

17 Verizhnikova, *Ivan Bilibin*, 60.
18 Bilibin's graphics now appear in English, German, and Italian publications of Andersen's tale.

a somewhat more childlike face,[19] the expressions of both project innocence and interiority—the traits fundamental to Andersen's vulnerable fifteen-year-old heroine.

The eight visuals interspersed within the text of *La petite sirène* capture what Bilibin evidently deemed key points in the tale's narrative, and the majority corroborate his sensitivity to Andersen's major concerns. Of the four color illustrations, the most elaborate comprise two highly-detailed images of the underwater kingdom (Andersen's "Elysium"—the pagan Greek paradise), rendered in flat colors with Bilibin's signature rigorous precision of line. Significantly, the first[20] includes the marble statue of the beautiful male holding a Pan pipe[21] (fig. 5), which, imprinted on the mermaid's imagination, predisposes her to love the prince at first sight—more accurately, at second sight, for in a transgendered Galatea scenario he incarnates the statue that she adores before encountering him in the flesh ("it seemed to her that he looked like that marble statue in her little garden"; "It was her one consolation to sit in her little garden and throw her arms about the beautiful marble statue that looked so much like the Prince"). Of all illustrators up to the late twentieth century, only Bilibin grasped the decisive importance of this highly psychological aspect of Andersen's tale. In fact, his third full-page visual in black and white (13), which situates the mermaid in the water gazing up at the pensive prince, seated on a stone balustrade and leaning against a column topped by the statue of a wild boar (presumably part of his ancestral coat of arms), in a sense iterates the aesthetic scenario of the initial color image (fig. 6). It also establishes animation and vision as central to a storyline exploring the differences between stasis and mobility, between invisible spirit and all too visible embodiment.

These two illustrations, their dissimilarities in style and palette notwithstanding, also install immediately and with impressive economy the mermaid's role of observer, of enamored wordless spectator enchanted by what she apprehends. Bilibin similarly resorts to this device in his

---

19 Bychkov's familiarity with the French translation of Andersen's tale seems unlikely, but the translation of the volume into Russian, published with Bilibin's illustrations, may have inspired his choice of Viktoriia Novikova for the titular role in his film.
20 Andersen, *La petite sirène* (1937), 5. Subsequent page numbers in the text refer to this edition.
21 By evoking the Greek rustic god Pan, the pipe alludes to the significance of music and sound in general within the tale. Adhering to Andersen's tale, while underwater the mermaid appears in her "natural," unadorned state, but in preparation for her contact with land, her grandmother decks her in a crown of white lilies and strands of pearls befitting her station as princess. Hereafter these baubles decorate her hair, neck, and arms. Pearls, of course, are associated with the goddess Venus/Aphrodite, born of the sea.

Fig. 5. By I. Bilibin. Wikimedia Commons.

color depiction of the mermaid's first glimpse of the prince's ship from afar, across a tranquil sea (9), placing her in the bottom right corner– precisely where she appears in the third black-and-white image. And the last color illustration (20) likewise features the ship, now in turbulent waters, from which a tiny mermaid (diminished in all but spiritual transcendence) throws overboard the knife intended to dispatch the prince, thereby voluntarily sealing her own doom.[22] These are all car-

---

22 Sold by the sea-witch to the mermaid's five sisters for their long hair, the knife plays a decisive part in the mermaid's existential decision whether to sacrifice herself or to eliminate the prince.

Yearning for a Soul: 397

Fig. 6. By I. Bilibin. Wikimedia Commons.

dinal junctures in the tale, and through rhythm—a judicious selection and disposition of elements—Bilibin links the color images with those in black and white, achieving a meaningful congruity that accords with the tale's ruling preoccupations. Defining the relationship of visuals to verbal text, Arthur Rackham asserted:

> For his illustrations to be worth anything, [the artist] must be regarded as a partner [to the author] not as a servant.... An illustration may legitimately give the artist's view of the author's ideas; or it may give his view, his independent view of the author's subject. But it must be the artist's view; any attempt to coerce him into a mere tool in the author's hands can only result in the most dismal failure.[23]

Whereas Rackham's own illustrations of "The Little Mermaid" sooner belong to the second, "independent" type, Bilibin opted for the first.

Attuned to Andersen's priorities, Bilibin's second variegated illustration of the underwater world (16) portrays the mermaid's fateful visit to the sea-witch, who uncannily combines aquatic and human traits. As in Andersen's text, snakes crawl over her body as she "let[s] a toad eat

---

23 Cited from Meyer, *A Treasury of the Great Children's Book Illustrators*, 57.

Fig. 7. By I. Bilibin. Wikimedia Commons.

out of her mouth." Sea creatures' eyes—evoking the mermaid's status as visually hypnotized onlooker—proliferate in this copiously particularized image, which marks a turning point in Andersen's tale (fig. 7). Here, as in the first color illustration, the abundance of hues, absent from Bilibin's graphic portrayal of scenes on land, conveys the resplendent bounties of the densely populated subaquatic realm as a pagan paradise. By contrast, the black and white of terrestrial life suggests its dearth of vitality and plenitude, distancing the viewer from the subjectivity of the mermaid's self-destructive perspective and desires.

Of the black-and-white illustrations, the second (11) shows the mermaid saving the unconscious prince amid the crashing waves of the tempestuous sea (the specifics unavoidably recalling Edmund Dulac's color rendition of the same scene [1911]),[24] while the first and fourth register episodes appreciably less critical to the plot. The first image depicts the mermaid's presumably introductory encounter with land, as a barking dog greets her (7)—a puzzling addition, insofar as, in the Andersen text, it is the eponymous little mermaid's third sister whom

---

24 Perhaps Bilibin chose not to render this critical scene in color because, as Dulac's visual confirms, it offers little for the artistic imagination. Indeed, until Gennadii Spirin's watercolor illustrations, most visuals of this scene seemed uniform, even perfunctory.

Yearning for a Soul: 399

Fig. 8. By I. Bilibin. Wikimedia Commons.

the dog terrifies (fig. 8). The fourth shows the companionship of the prince and the mermaid atop a plateau overlooking an isolated mountain range lashed by sea waves (18). From the standpoint of plot, both images border on the expendable, the seductive charm of their technical mastery notwithstanding.

In sum, Bilibin's distinctive illustrations testify to his World of Art allegiances and simultaneously to the imperative of preserving Andersen's emphases. Through graphic and painterly means they posit the underwater world (admiringly described at length in the opening passages of Andersen's tale) as a wonderland of magical, carefree, and resplendent beauty that trumps the mundane sphere of earthbound humanity. In that regard, Bilibin may be viewed not only as an aesthetics-based skeptic regarding the mermaid's priorities, but also as a forerunner of Jacques Cousteau and other pioneering discoverers of the sea's manifold natural treasures. And in light of subsequent graphic artists' choices, Bilibin's decision to restrict his images to eight nicely demonstrates that less can be more.

Viktor Pivovarov (b. 1937)

Like other artists during the Soviet era (e.g., Erik Bulatov, Ilya Kabakov,[25] Vladimir Sorokin), the Moscow conceptualist Pivovarov early in his career found professional refuge and a means of earning a livelihood by illustrating books, many of them for children. Graduating as a book designer and illustrator from the Moscow Polygraphic Institute (1962), he made his name by designing large-circulation children's magazines, notably the perdurable *Murzilka* (still going even now since its inception in 1924). His graphic contribution to a Soviet collection of Andersen's fairy tales edited by N. A. Terekhova (*Skazki* 1973, reissued in 1977) predated his emigration to Prague in 1982. Predictably, the concept and execution of his visuals for "The Little Mermaid" could hardly contrast more to Bilibin's, for the artistic philosophies of the World of Art and conceptualism have nothing in common.

The three full-page watercolors and twenty-five small images dispersed throughout the translated text suggest Pivovarov's debt to Vladimir Lebedev (1891-1967), the vastly talented, innovative graphic artist of the early-Soviet and Stalinist era. Like his predecessor, Pivovarov largely avoids linear outlines, relying instead on volume and gradations of color; the dearth of drawn outlines in his visuals projects a certain illusory casualness that departs fundamentally from Bilibin's meticulous attention even to minutiae. Scattered in the margins of the text, Pivovarov's mini-images of fish, shells, ship, seaweed, starfish, buildings, windmill, flowers, lantern, and knife, as well as both the mermaid and the prince, observe no particular sequence, instead supplying visual analogues for items of diverse importance in the tale: i.e., whereas the knife is crucial for the outcome of the plot, windmills are notably irrelevant. Collectively, the majority of these mini-visuals evoke the sea. While all three full-page illustrations definitively diverge from Bilibin's painstakingly intricate visual equivalent of Andersen's verbal account, Pivovarov's choice of subject for them corresponds to Bilibin's: the first depicts the mermaid's native sea realm; the second visualizes the prince's ship; and the third installs the sea-witch amid the elements of her "trade."

Just as film directors have relied on a blue filter to signal a *sui generis* alien domain, so Pivovarov limned an entirely blue underwater world.[26] At its center is a semi-transparent "open-door" castle, with a set of receding arches and halls, and a puzzling fountain on its tiled

---

25 Pivovarov rightly called Kabakov an active continuer of Vladimir Konashevich's tradition (Gankina, *Khudozhnik v sovremennoi detskoi knige*, 92).
26 While obviously associated with water, blue in film has served as a means of conjuring "another world," as in Werner Herzog's *Nosferatu* (1979) and James Cameron's *Terminator*

floor, which occupies the lower register of the image,[27] but in Andersen belongs (more sensibly) in the prince's palace. Four fish and the five mermaid sisters freely swim outside and within this mer-domain. As if not a denizen of this carefree environment, the motionless eponymous mermaid inside the castle pensively leans on a windowsill in contemplation, not of a beloved statue or the world above, as in Andersen, but of the seabed (9-10; fig. 9). By thus conveying a choice between freedom and physical confinement rather than pleasure in a harmonious setting of both artistic (statue) and natural beauty (aquatic Elysium), the image anticipates later developments in Andersen's tale, when the mermaid's yearning for the prince and land breeds a sense of frustrated constraint by her sea-environment. The image simultaneously suggests an artist's sense of oppressive strictures in the Soviet context.[28]

Yet the visual of the prince's ship (page facing 172) completely omits the mermaid's presence and perspective, instead focusing on the celebration of the prince's birthday, with brilliant fireworks projected against the darkness of the sky, musicians playing a trumpet, guitar, and bagpipes(!), and the prince and his cohort drinking at a table on deck—sooner a boozy birthday celebration in the fabled Soviet kitchen that recalls Bychkov's humorous sequence of the raucous festivities, but here with no mermaid as spectator. The final, also blue-dominated, illustration of the sea-witch, again with no mermaid, casts this powerful entity as a sexless, ominous figure with a huge hooked nose and enormous, prehensile hands (Dickens's Fagin!), surrounded by enigmatic trappings, including the cauldron over a blazing fire specified by Andersen. Its yellow and red contrast to all other (exclusively blue) elements in the witch's "laboratory," pointing to the dramatic significance of her magical brew and its role in all subsequent events (fig. 10).

Ella Gankina remarks that for Pivovarov, as he acknowledged, "the illustration of a children's book becomes... the materialization of the illusions of one's own childhood," and she goes on to point out that he credited children with the "subconscious ability to assimilate abstract concepts."[29] This insight elucidates the not unreasonable temptation to explain the complete absence of the mermaid from these two major il-

---

(1984) and *Terminator 2* (1991). The strategic incorporation of a blue filter references the identification of the color with the Virgin Mary in religious iconography.
27 Andersen, *Skazki*, 30. Subsequent page numbers in the text refer to this edition.
28 It is no accident that the window appears as a major motif in Pivovarov's other illustrations of children's books (in some cases also symbolizing a yearning for travel), as registered by Ella Gankina (*Khudozhnik v sovremennoi detskoi knige*, 71-74).
29 Ibid., 93. This perspective, reflected in Pivovarov's visuals, elicited criticism.

Fig 9. By V. Pivovarov. *Skazki*. Moscow: Detlit., 1977.

lustrations as part of the programmatic Soviet denigration of women. Anyone ignorant of Russian and unfamiliar with Andersen's text perusing the pages of this translation would be hard pressed to realize that Pivovarov's three small, literally marginal images of the mermaid reference the experiences of Andersen's chief literary persona. Her presence

Fig. 10. By V. Pivovarov. *Skazki*. Moscow: Detlit., 1977.

seems no more meaningful than a shell's; indeed, shells receive equal graphic attention. Whatever Pivovarov's resistance to Soviet ideology as a conceptualist, his choices here, however unwittingly, overlap with the gender politics of the Soviet state by sidelining the female protagonist at the very heart of Andersen's tale. Somewhat paradoxically, his illustrations in a Soviet children's book ultimately reflect the misogynistic inclinations of Moscow conceptualism in collusion with Soviet gender praxis.[30] Would children endowed with the insight he ascribes to them deduce as much from his illustrations?

Boris Diodorov (b. 1934)

Renowned less for his graphic contributions to works by Turgenev and Tolstoy than for his award-winning, remarkable illustrations of Andersen's "The Snow Queen" and above all for his now classic pen, ink, and watercolor drawings accompanying Boris Zakhoder's translation of A. A. Milne's *Winnie the Pooh* (*Vinni-Pukh i vse-vse-vse*, 1988; 1998), the vastly prolific Diodorov in 1998 followed in Bilibin's footsteps by supplying the visuals for *La petite sirène* (published by Albin Michel).[31] The French translation with Diodorov's images was reissued by Seuil Jeunesse in a 2005 collection of Andersen's tales titled *La petite Sirène*, which includes "Thumbelina" and "The Snow Queen."

Diodorov's illustrations for more than a hundred children's books display his versatility in elaborating an aesthetic individually geared to each work. Alert to the specifics of literary texts, his images for the Russian *Winnie the Pooh* brim with good-natured humor and the expressive lines often associated with satire. Those for "The Little Mermaid," however, evidence his debt to the fin-de-siècle aesthetics of Arthur Rackham and Edmund Dulac, showcasing a poetic concept of beauty and ornamental elements, though countered by other influences. The unusually high number of images—twelve in full page, plus sixteen smaller ones—militate against commentary on each of them, but several are worth analyzing.

A lyrical delicacy characterizes those visuals that nicely capture underwater depths as a bona fide discrete realm. The cover illustration, for instance, depicts three related registers along the vertical axis that reference aspects of the mermaid's fate: in the topmost register, dressed in a flouncy robe combining white with shades of pale blue, white flowers in her grassy-green hair, the mermaid reclines on a ship's deck, looking down at her five sisters, two of them partly above water, while three are fully submerged (fig. 11). Their long reddish-gold hair ripples behind them as their outstretched, upraised arms and gazes (all

---

30 Likewise reflecting Soviet praxis, incidentally, is this translation's omission of all references to the soul and the lengthy passage in which the daughters of the air explain the prerequisites for attaining heaven.
31 It is curious that for a French translation of a Danish text, the publishers would again seek a Russian illustrator instead of engaging a French graphic artist for the task.

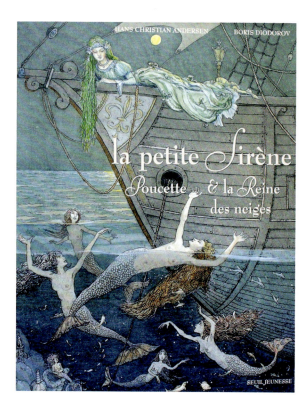

Fig. 11. By B. Diodorov. *La petite sirène*. Paris: Albin Michel, 1998.

fixed on her) suggest that they are appealing to her, as in Andersen's tale. This is the middle register, linking the incompatible realms of air and water/Christianity and paganism that the mermaid struggles to reconcile through a union with the prince that will vouchsafe her a soul. The lowermost third shows the seabed, where on a rock sits enthroned a figure that presumably is the sea-witch, her eyes likewise directed upward. Thus in a single image buttressed by a harmonizing color scheme Diodorov compactly links the three spatial categories of the mermaid's experience.

Inside the volume he likewise achieves both coherence and meaning by a considered use of color for an image of the five sisters swimming close to the surface of the water, with a figure that is possibly the eponymous little mermaid floating beneath them, but above, at a still deeper level, a small statue (her ideal). Diodorov's strategy again is to link yet differentiate several layers, primarily through chromaticism: the rich blue of the seabed, with its muted-colored buildings, gradually modulates to a greenish blue, with the water's surface almost completely grey-green, and the foam white against the waves tossing the prince's ship in the distance. Thus the mermaid, the sea, her sisters, and the land-dwelling prince are visually associated yet separated, as in Andersen's tale.[32] And the entire image of the mermaid's first encounter with land, in grey-blue tints, with light-pink shells and starfish scattered on the shore, is beautifully but selectively particularized, of a piece with the other images integrated and disciplined by a single color (12).

Elsewhere Diodorov is somewhat less successful: in establishing the underwater realm he retains the marble statue of the youth—a small figure to the left at the bottom of the sea—but places all six mermaids in a column to the right, without distinguishing *the* little mermaid from her sisters or establishing her infatuation with the statue (9). Moreover, for inexplicable reasons, one mermaid wears a turban, another a flimsy dress, while a third has water-snakes coiled around her—striking differences that counter their role of a "united front" in efforts to save their lovelorn sister. All are obtrusively colorful and projected against a set of equally colorful, "exotic" Eastern buildings, laden with fussy details. An ill-defined face peering out from an open window of one such building suggests Diodorov's homage to Pivovarov's illustration, but if the face belongs to the mermaid, why did Diodorov add another sister to the group frolicking in the water? And why is the mermaid staring at her sisters instead of contemplating her beloved statue?

In several instances Diodorov's illustrations, like Bychkov's film, betray the influence of Russian folklore and a departure from Andersen. An attractive visual orchestrated in ocher tones of the mermaid en route to the sea-witch depicts the bottom of the sea unaccountably littered with skulls as well as the requisite shells, fauna, bones, and mysterious entities (28). While extraneous to Andersen's narrative, the skulls clearly derive from the *rusalka*'s ascribed habit of seducing and drowning victims—a characteristic contrary to the mermaid's persona as conceived by Andersen. Skulls, as well as snakes and terrified-looking fish, likewise accompany the marvelously repellent sea-witch, with sagging breasts and a malevolent leer, in the next visual (28). Mounted on a steering wheel behind the witch, they suggest the intrusion of the fence surrounding Baba Yaga's hut on chicken legs in classic illustrations by Bilibin, Elena Polenova, and a host of other artists. Though they do not appear in Andersen's text, the skulls here, unlike in the preceding illustration, do not violate his overall concept of the sea-witch (fig. 12).

For the most part Diodorov's images are aesthetically enticing and often eloquent. Two related aspects of them, however, are disconcerting

---

32 Andersen, *La petite sirène, Poucette & la Reine des neiges*, 15. Subsequent page numbers in the text refer to this edition.

Fig. 12. By B. Diodorov. *La petite sirène*. Paris: Albin Michel, 1998.

and detract from their overall impact. Though not in all cases, Diodorov endows the mermaid's sisters with a knowing, "come-hither" look that subverts their collective image in the fairy tale. Above all, his enthusiasm for portraying naked breasts knows no bounds; even when the mermaid, fully clothed, dances at court, her breasts appear clearly visible through her conveniently transparent outfit (39). In such instances, Diodorov seems to have succumbed to the conventions of capitalist advertising, where women solicit viewers or readers by vamping them through exposed physical assets and a suggestive gaze or pose that will prompt them to buy the advertised product.[33] In short, the illustrations within the book only partially fulfill the promise of Diodorov's cover image, for they reveal a striking inconsistency in style and quality surprising in light of the stylistic integrity marking his imaginative contribution to Zakhoder's translation of *Winnie the Pooh*.[34]

---

33 On this phenomenon, see Berger, *Ways of Seeing*; and Williamson, "Woman Is an Island." On its role in post-Soviet culture, see Goscilo, "Style and S(t)imulation"; and "Negotiating Gendered Rhetoric."

34 Those pictures featuring the prince are particularly weak. A side panel (18) showing him flailing about in the water depicts two undifferentiated mermaids, while he resembles a bewhiskered old man; or is that one of the sailors? Elsewhere he resembles a contemporary

Gennadii Spirin (b. 1948)

Renowned for his stunning, award-winning watercolor illustrations of children's books even when he lived in the Soviet Union, Spirin moved to Germany in the 1980s, and in 1991 to Princeton, where he has resided and worked ever since.[35] With graphic contributions to Shakespeare's *The Tempest* and to an array of works by Gogol, Tolstoy, and Chekhov and to Christmas and Easter stories and fairy tales from around the world, Spirin has defined his priorities as an illustrator with uncommon precision: "You have to love with your whole heart that which you're illustrating…. You have to know a lot about the subject. And it has to be done with a passion. You have to know a lot about the costumes, the architecture, the life."[36] Of his graphics in children's books, Spirin has said: "Everything is in the realistic style because it is the most understood by children. Not photographic realism, but a fairy-tale realism"[37]—a philosophy of composition that allows ample room for imagination.

Even a cursory glance at Spirin's fairy tale illustrations confirms his painterly talent, for they are formidably precise and unified in concept, indistinguishable from fine art, particularly of the Renaissance, above all in their coloration. Indeed, their defining features prompted Andrew Solomon's observation that Spirin's works "recall the Northern Renaissance in clarity of light, abundance of detail and enamel-like precision of color."[38] His aesthetics lends credence to the report[39] that the foremost medieval Russian icon painter, Andrei Rublev, and the mid-sixteenth-century Flemish Pieter Brueghel, renowned for his narrative-focused landscapes and scenes of peasant life, are his idols. It is no exaggeration to say that, in his artistic allegiances and execution, Spirin has revised our concept of book illustrations.

Spirin's visuals accompanying Aaron Shepard's retelling of the Russian tale "Sadko," issued as *The Sea King's Daughter: A Russian Legend* (1997), received a half-dozen awards, not the least in recognition of Spirin's luminous renditions of the underwater kingdom, depicted in a wide range of modulated shades that harmonize with the sumptu-

---

rock star (20) or a tall transsexual (31). The profusion of images strangely undermines a unified aesthetic, one of the visuals even evoking a cloying Hallmark card (35).

35 After graduation from Moscow's Surikov School of Fine Art in 1967, Spirin received his advanced artistic education at the Moscow Stroganov Institute of Art (1972). In the US, Spirin's first name is spelled Gennady, and he publishes as Gennady Spirin. He has received repeated international recognition for his works.
36 James, "In Person: The World of His Imagination."
37 Ibid.
38 http://andrewsolomon.com/articles/those-sumptuous-russian-flavored-storybooks/
39 Kochetkova, "5 Leading Russian Children's Book Illustrators." Spirin confirmed as much in a conversation in Princeton on 29 September 2016, for which I thank him.

ously elaborate costumes of the subaquatic denizens. His subsequent spectacular visuals for "The Little Mermaid" appeared in an Anglophone volume titled *Little Mermaids and Ugly Ducklings* (2001), which Spirin dedicated to Andersen and which includes four tales in addition to the two plurally referenced in the title.[40]

Two major features set Spirin's illustrations for "The Little Mermaid" apart from all others: their painterly quality and their primacy in the design of the tale. Though to a lesser extent than in his *Frog Princess* (1994) and *The Tale of the Firebird* (2002), the visuals, bearing his unmistakable signature, occupy center stage, rendering the verbal text secondary. Aesthetically all of a piece, the images vary in size and format: the initial full-page visual[41] introduces the narrative as well as the underwater kingdom and is followed by three page-length marginal images (in form and dimension resembling bookmarks), three small, oval "cameos," two additional full-page images, and a double-page spread, as well as the concluding visual, which occupies a page and a half. All large illustrations feature the mermaid, including the highly original final one (58-59), which depicts the mournful newlyweds on deck, while the transfigured mermaid hovers as a spirit among the clouds overhead gazing down upon the prince's ship and the waters over which fly myriad birds (the traditional symbols of the soul). In short, Spirin's is a profound, reflective response to the conclusion of Andersen's tale.

If at first Spirin's introductory illustration seems to echo Diodorov's, that impression dissipates as soon as one examines both thoroughly. Unlike Diodorov (and other predecessors), Spirin bypasses both blue and green for his depiction of the sea, favoring instead a subtly nuanced palette of browns combined with beige, red, grey, white, and gold. Gradations of color serve to create a mysterious world with two castle-like structures that provide a backdrop for the five pale-bodied mermaid sisters and the eponymous little mermaid, swimming, significantly, above them (fig. 13). Spirin maintains this color strategy throughout, saving tones of blue for the sky in the two largest images, perhaps mindful of the color's association with the Madonna (as virginal Queen of Heaven) in Renaissance iconography.[42]

---

40 The others are "Thumbelina," "The Steadfast Tin Soldier," "The Nightingale," and "The Princess and the Pea."
41 Andersen, *Little Mermaids and Ugly Ducklings*, 38. Subsequent page numbers in the text refer to this edition.
42 Cf. paintings of the Virgin Mary by Fra Angelico, Botticelli, David, Perugino, Raphael, da Vinci and countless other artists of the period. For a survey of her image in art, see the volume by art historian and priest Timothy Verdon, *Mary in Western Art*.

Fig. 13. By G. Spirin. *Little Mermaids and Ugly Ducklings.* San Francisco: Chronicle Books, 2001.

Fig. 14. By G. Spirin. *Little Mermaids and Ugly Ducklings*. San Francisco: Chronicle Books, 2001.

Sensibly, the three elongated marginal images are reserved for representations of bodies: those of the subaquatic statue and the mermaid; of the barefoot, bejeweled mermaid, clad in a dull-red headdress, kimono, and skirt, dancing; and of the mermaid as she takes her fatal leap into the sea. In congruity with Andersen's tale, the first (40) positions the large marble statue of the young man above the mermaid; the visual symbolically conveys that he dominates her thoughts (and literally, the reader's perceptions). Moreover, this placement also implies his connection with land—notably with the prince, whom he prefigures. The second (56) and third (57) visuals contrast appreciably and meaningfully, for the third shows the mermaid, in a simple, frothy dress, jumping into the water—her natural element, for which she discards the preceding image's ornaments as if these solely befit the court on land. Unlike Pivovarov, Spirin visually preserves Andersen's focus on his female protagonist, undeviatingly documenting the stages of her chosen fate.

Whereas all three elegant ovals focus on setting (41, 48, 49), the second full-page visual captures the mermaid's rescue of the prince, with her childlike face and halo of flowers recalling Bilibin's illustrations, while the prince looks appropriately near death (46; fig. 14). An image of the mermaid not found in any earlier editions, the third, beautifully balanced full-page visual captures her, ethereal and vulnerably pale, dancing in what resembles a *pas de deux*, presumably with the prince (52), who, significantly, remains only half-seen, behind her (fig. 15). Here, before her complete assimilation into the prince's court, her diaphanous gown is white and off-white—the color also of her embellishments, in which pearls predominate, both hue and precious stone linking her to her sea-life. In other words, Spirin's intricate images inscribe a gradual process in tune with the sense of temporality in Andersen's tale.

Somewhat unexpected is Spirin's decision to devote a double-page spread to the birthday festivities on the prince's ship (44-45). Minutely detailed, the resplendent vessel dominates the illustration, with a slender mermaid (portrayed from the rear, with a garland of white flowers encircling her head) suspended on the crest of a wave that enables her to peer at the men and women celebrating the prince's birthday within the fantastically, profusely decorated craft.[43] Color here allies her with water

---

43 As a tribute to the author, Spirin places one of the two angels on the ship's bow atop a bunting with the name Hans Christian. The dramatic discrepancy between the size of the ship and the mermaid, as well as the former's resplendent riches and her simple naturalness, suggests the incompatibility of terra firma (prince) with the sea (mermaid). That incompatibility receives a satirical treatment in a story by Joanna Russ, "Russalka, or The Seacoast of Bohemia" (1978).

Fig. 15. By G. Spirin. *Little Mermaids and Ugly Ducklings*. San Francisco: Chronicle Books, 2001.

(both white) and the two angels (in pale blue) who oversee the ship's royal crest at its bow. In other words, the mermaid's first glimpse of the prince's vessel directs the viewer's gaze upward, toward her eventual self-immolation, coterminous with the tale's resolution.

Remarkably, unlike most illustrators of "The Little Mermaid," Spirin omits a depiction of the sea-witch, perhaps because of his principle of realism but also possibly not to repeat himself, having already painted an unusual, fanged Baba Yaga in *The Frog Princess*.[44] All other artists have tackled this scene in Andersen's tale as an opportunity to limn the repulsive and grotesque, that moment in the narrative when evil can generate a startling, melodramatic impact. By forgoing the representation of that moment, Spirin adheres to his concept of realism in a series of illustrations unparalleled for their exquisite beauty and vibrant wealth of detail.

Anton Lomaev (b. 1971)

Most post-Soviet illustrations of "The Little Mermaid" testify to Russian artists' eagerness to enter the lucrative international publishing market by borrowing from popular Western representational practices, usually with mixed results. Anton Lomaev is no exception. A resident of St. Petersburg born in Belorussia, Lomaev[45] has specialized in illustrating sundry Andersen tales, as well as those of the brothers Grimm and Charles Perrault, in addition to such "classics" as Catullus, Melville, Conan Doyle, Babel, Nabokov, Tolkien, and the series of *Wolfhound* (*Volkodav*) fantasy novels by Mariia Semenova.[46] His copious illustrations for Andersen's "The Little Mermaid" have appeared in several editions printed in Russia: in 2008, 2009, 2011, 2014, and 2015, with slight variations. My comments reference the 2015 publication.[47]

As an illustrator, Lomaev is above all a colorist, with an unbounded enthusiasm for vivid hues and a decorativeness that can spill over into disorienting immoderation, as attested by his profuse visuals for "The Little Mermaid." Of these, three occupy a full page; five overflow onto a second page; approximately a dozen populate half a page; and other,

---

44 Lewis, *The Frog Princess*, 25. A similar image of Baba Yaga appears in Spirin, *The Tale of the Firebird*, 15.
45 Like most contemporary artists in Russia and elsewhere, Lomaev has his own website: http://www.lomaevart.com/newsingl.html.
46 The original volume, *Volkodav* (1995), launched an entire series and inspired the film with the same title, directed by Nikolai Lebedev in 2006.
47 Andersen, *Rusalochka*. Page numbers in the text refer to this edition.

Fig. 16. By A. Lomaev. *Rusalochka*. Moscow: Azbuka, 2015.

smaller ones appear regularly on the top or bottom of a page or spread over two pages. In short, if Andersen's tale can be over-illustrated, this may be an instance of such supererogation in a text that, owing to the visuals, runs to forty-five pages.

Ebullience operates without restraint in Lomaev's images, which readers apparently appreciate.[48] Anyone familiar with the history of the tale's illustrated translations in Russia and with a comparative critical eye, however, will approach his visuals with reservations. Unlike Bilibin and Spirin, Lomaev ignores Andersen's emphases, eager instead to depict what makes for "pretty" or "dramatic" scenarios. Accordingly, his larger, insistently colorful visuals focus on the waterworld, the ship during revelries and the storm, the witch episode, and the prince with the mermaid (35)–the last in a tawdry image, striking in its similarity to chocolate box covers, that displays Lomaev's attachment to bright red for the prince's garish garb and to an incoherent plethora of mini-images: a dog, roses, shrubs and trees, musicians, a castle, sea and ships, birds,

---

48 The Internet abounds with praise for Lomaev, particularly for his images for Andersen's tale. This does not, of course, reflect the consensus of specialists in the field of illustration.

Fig. 17. By A. Lomaev. *Rusalochka*. Moscow: Azbuka, 2015.

statue, urns, and so forth (fig. 16). The mermaid, in a painfully ornate gown and headdress, wears a sad expression and no shoes. Even more chaotic details characterize the wedded couple on the prince's overly festooned ship (40-41), with a crowd on board and a populated Lohengrin swan-bark alongside, a jumble of birds, roses arbitrarily scattered over the crashing waves, other ships, and again a castle atop a hill—all rendered in bright red, aquamarine, and shades of the two.

Slightly less overburdened is the image of the waterworld (6), though the glut of sea creatures, algae, trees, lamps, castle, moon (?!), and various personae, including the sea-king, the mermaids' grandmother, and a female servant offering comestibles on a dish (!), make for a dizzying experience (fig. 17). The sea-king's headgear is equal to the length of his upper body, and the grandmother, who figures in several subsequent visuals, wears what resembles an inordinately tall eighteenth-century white wig interwoven with starfish and seahorses. Four of the five mermaid sisters display perky nipples and varicolored hair, while the green-haired eponymous little mermaid swims in front of them, presumably to indicate her "progressive" desires regarding land. Subsequently her hair undergoes several inexplicable color changes. The aesthetic here is that of commercials, with the mermaid resembling attractive young female stars in Hollywood or in video clips.

Possibly because it offers scant opportunity for embellishments, the mermaid's rescue of the prince (20) takes up less than half a page, though even here Lomaev manages to load the image with a bird, a sinking ship with a mast, a barrel, and part of a vessel disappearing under water. On the facing page (21) squawking birds (one with a fish in its beak!) above a castle and rock-lined waters contribute nothing whatever to the tale. The same may be said of several visuals of the mermaid and her sisters swimming underwater (12-13, 14-15, 22-23, 31, 37) once their presence there has been established (6-7). Yet the final image of the mermaid, now transformed into spirit and accompanied by her fellow sisters of the air, shows artistic insight, for Lomaev allies them with the white of the splashing waves and etherealizes them through delicate linear outlines contrasting with the aggressive gradations of red for the ship and the sky (44-45). They seem genuinely aerial, spiritualized.

Lomaev's witch differs from all others insofar as she is supremely masculinized—with crude features and beefy arms—dwelling in the dark depths, with a multitude of sea creatures and sporting a nasty sneer (29, 30). True to his aesthetic of "more is more," Lomaev portrays her twice, the second time with a splash of red at her side denoting blood. Whatever the drama of such an addition, blood seems inappropriate for a transubstantiation into spirituality, which is the mermaid's ultimate, voluntary fate.

As the repeated editions of the tale with his illustrations indicate, Lomaev's aesthetic accords with contemporary Russian readers' tastes, such as they are. Certainly the visuals pay scant attention to Andersen's values and focus, but they attract buyers through their all too obvious appeal, and in that regard they serve to popularize Andersen's text.

Vladimir Nenov (b. 1964) et al.

It would be difficult to imagine an artist further removed from Spirin and closer to Lomaev in his approach to illustrating children's books than Vladimir Nenov. His visuals for a 2012 Russian edition of "The Little Mermaid"[49] suggest his greater affinity for Pamela Anderson of

---

49 Andersen, *Rusalochka* (2012). The book was reprinted in 2015. The constant republication of Andersen's tale in Russian translation indexes its popularity in Russia.

Fig. 18. By V. Nenov. *Rusalochka*. Moscow: Rosmen, 2012.

Baywatch than for earnest Hans Christian Andersen.[50] Manifestly under the influence of Hollywood productions, Nenov depicts the prince as a juvenile "hunk" and the mermaid—aged fifteen in Andersen's tale—as a bleached blonde pinup, garbed in a low-cut, diaphanous peignoir (fig. 18). A visual showing her dancing barefoot at court actually includes a "cute" kitten among the appreciative audience. In short, the series attests to Nenov's intoxication with "prettiness" and the absence of an overall aesthetic concept. With the mermaid's changing outfits invariably bathed in tones of aquamarine and evoking a shampoo or even lingerie ad, the visuals add little that is noteworthy to the large gallery of the tale's illustrations.[51]

Mutatis mutandis, as much holds for the visuals of Anastasiia Arkhipova (b. 1955), an internationally recognized and extraordinarily active professional. Having worked for the Detskaia literatura (Children's

---

50 http://theartofanimation.tumblr.com/post/42295050725/vladimir-nenov
51 Nenov's final image, at odds with the preceding ones, suggests that he borrowed from Spirin's illustration of the mermaid's ascent to the spiritual realm.

Literature) publishing house early in her career, in 2003 she won first prize as Book of the Year's best illustrator in Russia, became head of the Moscow Association of Illustrators and Book Designers, and in 2008 inaugurated Image of the Book (*Obraz knigi*), an annual contest for book illustrators and designers. Her reputation led to her appointment as a member of the 2014 jury of the Hans Christian Andersen Award.[52] Perhaps best known for her illustrations of fairy tales by Andersen and the brothers Grimm, she supplied evocative visuals for Andersen's "The Snow Queen," but those for a 2011 Russian edition of "The Little Mermaid,"[53] in which her aesthetic approximates Nenov's, tend toward banality. Proficient and pleasing to the eye, they offer little that bears an individual stamp or stimulates the imagination.[54]

Natalya Akimova, who has illustrated *King Lear*, "Snow White," and several fairy tales by Andersen, including "Thumbelina" and "The Ugly Duckling," avoids the commonplace by a productive, *sui generis* addiction to black. Minimalist and elegant, her novel retro visuals for "The Little Mermaid" and other tales by Andersen favor the almost forgotten genre of the silhouette.[55] A form associated with earlier eras, notably the eighteenth century, when it was pioneered above all for portraits, the silhouette was revived subsequently in Rackham's *Cinderella* (1919), in Andersen's own cut-outs, such as that of the chimney sweep, and later in illustrations of *Eugene Onegin* (*Evgenii Onegin*) by Vasilii Gelmerson (1873-1937) and the work of microminiaturist Anatolii Konenko (b. 1954). In combination with beige, olive green, and a sparing use of red, her black silhouettes allow Akimova to create graceful images of striking clarity. As in Bilibin's illustrations, line is primary here, and Akimova controls it impressively in visuals that evoke the plasticity of ballet and the minimalism of Japanese calligraphy.

Highlighting the mermaid and the mer-kingdom, she avoids melodrama partly through the distanced nature of her images but also through the very nature of the silhouette, which eliminates facial expressions as visible symptoms of psychological states and reactions. Contours guide the eye in such winning images as the mermaid's lovely form underwater as she gazes upward in the completely empty, pale-olive

---

52 See https://ijbib.wordpress.com/tag/anastasia-arkhipova/
53 Andersen, *Rusalochka* (2011).
54 Arkhipova's illustrations of other Andersen tales, however, deserve greater attention, especially those accompanying "The Wild Swans," which share Spirin's painterly aesthetics.
55 Mariia Vasilyeva (b. 1982) also resorted to the silhouette for her illustrations (2004) to a Russian edition of Andersen's "The Swineherd" that, however, never appeared in print. See Kudriavtseva and Zvonareva, *Kh. K. Andersen i ego russkie illiustratory za poltora veka*, 312.

Fig. 19. By N. Akimova.

depths penetrated by the sun's rays, the shape of her body conjuring a seahorse; or her confrontation with the sea-witch, continuous with the red seaweeds from which the latter emerges (fig. 19).[56] The illustrations concisely render the little mermaid's solitariness and her aspirations beyond the sea. In her scrupulously restricted palette, Akimova reserves red for aquatic weeds, the witch, and land-related visuals—the skyline of the unnamed city and boats sailing in the sea, the fireworks on the prince's ship, and the wine in the glass held by the prince as he watches the mermaid dancing, now outfitted in a floor-length gown. Pared down and strictly disciplined, Akimova's simple yet stylish visuals resemble no previous illustrators' vision of Andersen's tale even as they offer a skeletal summary of its narrative.

No doubt countless other Russian graphic artists will undertake the task of visualizing Andersen's tale in the future. Svetlana Kim, Nikolai Ustinov, and many others have already done so, and their efforts,

---

56 See https://illustrators.ru/users/taschaka?page=5

however commendable, fall short of noteworthiness.[57] The three striking talents to have devised memorable *sui generis* illustrations of the tale are Bilibin, Spirin, and Akimova. What is problematic about other artists' contributions is their uneven, sometimes contradictory engagement with Andersen's values as articulated in "The Little Mermaid," and their failure to materialize a personalized graphic vision. Reconceiving the mermaid alternately as a young TV vamp and a tearful teen paired with a smiling Cupid, as does Nenov, hardly requires Andersen's tale as a collaborative text and, in fact, overturns it. With Bilibin long dead and Spirin an established, amply awarded artist who for decades has created exquisite artwork, the "discovered" illustrator whose visuals for "The Little Mermaid" impress by their independence of popular trends is Akimova, who, unlike the majority of her Russian contemporaries, seems inured to the lure of Western pop ads.

Handicrafts

As might be expected, in the category of handicrafts, the primary source of mermaid illustrations has been the venerable Palekh artistic community, renowned since the 1920s for its production of vibrant folkloric images that originally drew inspiration from Orthodox icons, above all in the form of lacquer boxes.[58] One of four major Russian handicraft centers—the others being Fedoskino (established 1796), Mstera (1931), and Kholui (1934), with the latter two Soviet-era factories organized specifically for the manufacture of souvenirs—Palekh originated in the sixteenth century as a site of icon production; when it transformed into a center for lacquer miniatures (tempera painting on varnished items of papier-mâché) intended to propagate national culture in a popular vein and exportable form, it retained the symbolism and symmetry inhering in icon conventions, but replaced religious content with folkloric and literary images. The best Palekh craftsmen, such as the immensely talented Ivan Golikov (1886/7-1937) and Ivan Vakurov (1885-1968), created stunningly vivid images from fairy tales and other folkloric genres. Much like the cheaper *matreshka* (nesting doll), specifically designed in the last decade of the nineteenth century as an emblem of Russia's fecundity, throughout the Soviet period a Palekh box (or tray, dish,

---

57 Obviously, personal taste plays a role in such judgments: in her positive review of the Kudriavtseva and Zvonareva volume, for instance, the Russian blogger "Iana" waxes enthusiastic about Pivovarov, Lomaev, and Arkhipova:
https://www.babyblog.ru/community/post/kids_books/1713229
58 For a thorough treatment of Palekh's fascinating history, see Jenks, *Russia in a Box*.

snuffbox, cigar case, jewelry, etc.) represented a relatively expensive version of "quintessential Russia" particularly enticing to tourists but also appealing to Soviet citizens, most of whom had at least one article executed by a Palekh artist in their homes.

The collapse of the lucrative state monopoly on Palekh art in 1989 forced Palekhians to confront a new market economy.[59] Following the dissolution of the Soviet Union, many broadened their subject matter in the interests of improving sales, simultaneously adopting pictorial conventions of Western popular culture (like Nenov and other Russian book illustrators) while continuing to preserve some of Palekh's instantly recognizable hallowed traditions.[60]

An artist clearly trained in those traditions yet just as clearly catering to foreign tastes is the prolific Vera Smirnova (b. 1966), perhaps best known for her illustrations of Aleksandr Pushkin's literary-folkloric narrative poem, *The Tale of Tsar Saltan* (*Skazka o tsare Saltane*), as well as "Sleeping Beauty," "Cinderella," and *Lord of the Rings*. The series of lacquer boxes picturing Andersen's "The Little Mermaid" that she designed in 2011 resemble her other works in their synthesis of Palekh style and generic decorative motifs that borders on kitsch.

The three boxes posted on the Internet capture three moments in the tale: the mermaid's rescue of the prince, her sisters' emergence from the water when she and the married couple stand on the ship's deck, and her decision regarding the knife as the murder weapon. All three demonstrate Smirnova's technical skill and her proclivity to indulge in an orgy of excess, particularly when detailing costume. The first illustration has an entirely green (!) mermaid wearing only a necklace around her neck and flowers in her hair as, hovering over the prince, she unaccountably looks out at the viewer instead of checking her beloved for signs of life. By contrast, the unconscious prince, despite almost having drowned and lying inert on a flamboyant red cloak, is garbed in immaculate aristocratic vestments that would not be out of place at a ball. An overcrowded background of castle, trees, and indeterminate shapes provides the generalized geographical context. Without knowledge of Andersen's tale, the scene would make little sense. Yet such knowledge renders the image risible, for the incoherent whole suggests, not An-

---

59 Ibid., 199.
60 It has also begun charging exorbitant prices for its artworks on the international market. Today lacquer boxes can sell on the Internet for more than $1,000. Part of their appeal is their spurious "Russianness," as also obtains for nesting dolls of Russian and American political leaders, sports stars, and anything for which there may be a demand. In that sense Russia has adopted the strategies of Western capitalism.

dersen's narrative, but a phosphorous creature suddenly inserted into a bucolic scene graced by a recumbent Endymion posing as a courtier.

How remote Smirnova's interests are from Andersen's narrative may be gauged by the second box, where once again ostentatious, busy clothing and a glut of objects dominate the tableau, as in some of Lomaev's visuals. While the newlyweds (both blonde in this instance) gaze lovingly at each other, the now normal-skinned mermaid looks down at her three green sisters, who have surfaced to rescue her from death. Whereas in Andersen's text all five of them have exchanged their hair for the salvific knife, here the trio possess opulent cascading tresses that vie for attention with everyone else's unfurled hair and the mermaid's long, fluttering blue cloak. Roses, greenery, small tables, candles, fruit, a flacon, drinking glasses, cushions, and all sorts of flouncy draperies transform this scene into an exemplar of New Russian bad taste.[61]

Like these two boxes, the third lacks Palekh's characteristic gold border and highlighting, as well as the black background that prominently displays to fine effect the vivid tempera hues traceable to icons. Here the scene on the lid comprises a mermaid clutching a knife, projected against an embracing couple once again decked in ornate, formal regalia appropriate for a royal ceremony. Additional elements include billowing ship's sails and two green, naked mermaids behind the trio, presumably as a shorthand of sorts for the tale's near-conclusion. Nothing distinguishes the mermaid's face, brown hair, or sumptuous apparel from her purported rival's (no longer blonde), and the riot of all possible colors and startling surfeit of embellishments (flowers, rosettes, jewels, ribbons) represent a decided departure from the structural and tonal precepts of typical Palekh design. The artist's attempt to prettify and cram too much into a limited space results in a sweeping incongruity at considerable variance with Andersen's straightforward narrative and aspects of its plot.

Just how globalization and the transition to a market economy have eroded the meticulous aesthetics and standards of Palekh artists may be deduced even more eloquently from Marisa Denisenko's "Little Mermaid" lacquer box. Her oval depiction of a feminized, dour-faced prince in

---

61 In fact, the New Russian Palekh items produced in the 1990s and sold at the Moscow store Mir novykh russkikh (New Russians' World) were executed in impeccable Palekh style, their content an ironic condensation of those features attributed to that decade's flashy entrepreneurs. The store owner, Grigorii Baltser, considered his emporium a museum housing material objects commemorating the historical phenomenon of the New Russians. On this topic, see the cluster of articles titled "The New Russians" in *The Russian Review* 62, no. 1 (January 2003): 1-90, especially 1-36.

the foreground, for some reason grasping a white lily, accompanied by a vaguely defined mermaid in a flimsy white gown and flowers in her hair, with a red ship in the background, all encircled by a busy floral frame (red roses, white lilies, plus greenery), is at an unbridgeable remove from the talented work of such Palekh masters as the above-mentioned Golikov and Vakurov. Here, gaudy and grandiloquent substitute for vivid and eloquent. In sum, judging by these products, one may conclude that Russia's post-Soviet handicraft industry, unlike its graphic illustrators, has not served Andersen's "The Little Mermaid" well. Of course, the new Palekh's clientele, ignorant of or indifferent to those desiderata that governed Palekh handicrafts for nearly a century, may well appreciate this immoderate potpourri of heterogeneous elements as an exciting or exotic novelty.

Conclusion

Perhaps one of the most striking features of Russian illustrations for "The Little Mermaid" is the extent to which they have increased, rather than diminished, with time. Illustrated Russian publications of the tale, whether published individually or in collections of the Danish writer's works, tend to undergo several editions (in some cases enhanced with "pop-up" or detachable parts), and always sell impressively well. The international popularity of Disney's *The Little Mermaid* (1989) on screen—despite the film's simplified, cosmetic revision of the complex original—has probably helped to advertise the tale and its vast promise in visual genres, but the readers' enduring love of Andersen's oeuvre surely accounts for the illustrators' desire to translate his narratives into images. As much is evident in a recent report by the Russian Book Chamber on the most popular children's books in Russia today. While Kornei Chukovsky remains the author most in demand, with seventy-six of his books printed in just the first half of 2016, and the children's poet Agnia Barto second, with forty-seven books, the third place belongs not to a Russian, but to Andersen, with twenty-four publications for the same period.[62] Children of all eras, in other words, respond wholeheartedly to his tales, and unquestionably will continue to do so, for he tapped into a world and an aesthetic that transcend historical time.

---

62 Obrazkova, "What Do Russians Read?"

Works Cited

Andersen, Hans Christian. *Little Mermaids and Ugly Ducklings: Favorite Fairy Tales by Hans Christian Andersen*. Illustrated by Gennady Spirin. San Francisco: Chronicle Books, 2001.

—. *La petite sirène*. Enluminé par I. Bilibine. Paris: Albums du Père Castor, Flammarion, 1937.

—. *La petite sirène*. Paris: Albin Michel, 1998.

—. *La petite sirène, Poucette & la Reine des neiges*. Paris: Seuil jeunesse, 2005.

Andersen, Kh. K. *Rusalochka*. Illustrated by Anton Lomaev. Moscow: Azbuka 2015.

—. *Rusalochka*. Illustrated by Anastasiia Arkhipova. Moscow: Ripol-Klassik, 2011.

—. *Rusalochka*. Illustrated by Vladimir Nenov. Moscow: Rosmen, 2012.

—. *Skazki*. Moscow: Detlit., 1977.

Berger, John. *Ways of Seeing*. London: Penguin, 1972.

Bilibin, I. Ia. *Stat'i. Pis'ma. Vospominaniia o khudozhnike*. Leningrad: Khudozhnik RSFSR, 1970.

Doonan, Jane. *Looking at Pictures in Picture Books*. Stroud, England: Thimble Press, 1993.

Gankina, E. Z. "Illustrations to the Tales of Hans Christian Andersen by Artists from the USSR." *Bookbird*, no. 2 (1972): 68-71.

—. *Khudozhnik v sovremennoi detskoi knige*. Moscow: Sovetskii khudozhnik, 1977.

Golden, Joanne M. *The Narrative Symbol in Childhood Literature: Explorations in the Construction of Text*. Berlin: Mouton de Gruyter, 1990.

Goscilo, Helena. "Negotiating Gendered Rhetoric: Between Scylla and Charybdis." In *Representing Gender in Cultures*, edited by E. Oleksy and J. Rydzewska, 19-37. Frankfurt/Berlin, Peter Lang, 2004.

—. "Style and S(t)imulation: Popular Magazines, or the Aesthetization of Post-Soviet Russia." *Studies in Twentieth-Century Literature* 24, no. 1 (2000): 15-50.

—. "Watery Maidens: Rusalki as Sirens and Slippery Signs." In *Poetics. Self. Place: Essays in Honor of Anna Lisa Crone*, eds. Catherine O'Neil, Nicole Boudreau, and Sarah Krive. Bloomington IN: Slavica 2007. 50-70.

James, George. "In Person: The World of His Imagination." *The New York Times*, 7 December 1997. Available electronically: http://www.nytimes.com/1997/12/07/nyregion/in-person-the-world-of-his-imagination.html

Jenks, Andrew L. *Russia in a Box: Art and Identity in an Age of Revolution*. DeKalb IL: Northern Illinois University Press, 2005.

Kochetkova, Natalya. "5 Leading Russian Children's Book Illustrators." *Russia Beyond the Headlines*, 10 June 2015. Available electronically: http://rbth.com/literature/2015/06/10/5_leading_russian_childrens_book_illustrators_46817.html

Kudriavtseva, Lidiia, and Lola Zvonareva. *Kh. K. Andersen i ego russkie illiustratory za poltora veka*. Moscow: Moskovskie uchebniki, 2012.

Lewis, J. Patrick. *The Frog Princess: A Russian Folktale*. Illustrations by Gennady Spirin. New York: Dial Books, 1994.

Meyer, Susan E. *A Treasury of the Great Children's Book Illustrators*. New York: Harry N. Abrams, 1997.

Mitchell, W. J. T. *Picture Theory: Essays on Verbal and Visual Representations*. Chicago: University of Chicago Press, 1994.

Nikolajeva, Maria, and Carole Scott. *How Picturebooks Work*. New York: Garland, 2001.

Obrazkova, Marina. "What Do Russians Read?" *Russia Beyond the Headlines*, 5 October 2016. Available electronically: http://rbth.com/arts/literature/2016/10/05/what-do-russians-read_636025

Oushakine, Serguei. "Translating Communism for Children: Fables and Posters of the Revolution." *Boundary 2* 43, no. 3 (2016): 159-219.

Schwarcz, Joseph H. *Ways of the Illustrator: Visual Communication in Children's Literature*. Chicago: American Library Association, 1982.

Shepard, Aaron, and Gennady Spirin. *The Sea King's Daughter: A Russian Legend*. New York: Simon & Schuster/Atheneum Books for Young Readers, 1997.

Sipe, Lawrence R. "How Picture Books Work: A Semiotically Framed Theory of Text-Picture Relationships." *Children's Literature in Education* 29, no. 1 (1998): 97-108.

Spirin, Gennady. *The Tale of the Firebird*. New York: Philomel Books, 2002.

Verdon, Timothy. *Mary in Western Art*. Manchester, VT: Hudson Hills Press, 2005.

Verizhnikova, Tat'iana. *Ivan Bilibin*. St. Petersburg: Avrora, 2001.

Williamson, Judith. "Woman Is an Island: Femininity and Colonization." In *Studies in Entertainment: Critical Approaches to Mass Culture*, edited by Tania Modleski, 99-118. Bloomington: Indiana University Press, 1986.

Hans Christian Andersen in Contemporary Russian Popular Culture

Elena Gurova, Elena Krasnova, and Boris Zharov

> He enters our homes even before we have learned to read—enters with a light, almost silent tread, like the wizard he made famous, the master of dreams and fairy tales, the little Ole Lukoie.
> Samuil Marshak, "A Festival of Fairy Tales" ("Prazdnik skazki")

There is no doubt that Hans Christian Andersen is an integral part of Russian culture; this has been frequently written about by researchers who have studied the reception of his texts and the various culturological and literary aspects connected with this reception.[1] Everyone living in Russia has known the great master of fairy tales since their earliest childhood. And although many of Andersen's works have been published in this country from the nineteenth century on, it was specifically the fairy tales that earned the genuine love of readers. Andersen's fairy tales have traditionally been categorized in Russia exclusively as children's reading.

Andersen works well known to the average Russian would number no more than fifteen fairy tales that have been published again and again in brightly colored children's editions. The Russian cultural fund also includes numerous stage productions and screen adaptations of the Danish fabulist's works; these often differ considerably from their original sources, such that "conceptions of Andersen's works, his plots and characters, are frequently based on one's acquaintance with their 'reflections.'"[2] Having left a luminous trail in Russian culture, and influencing a whole constellation of Russian writers, Andersen's tales did not remain exclusively within the domain of elite art, but also became part of the pop culture predominant in the modern information society.

There is no single opinion among researchers as to how to interpret the phenomenon of pop culture; in one study, John Storey cites six dif-

---

[1] Braude, "Khans Kristian Andersen v Rossii," 334-35; Erkhov, "Andersen. Russkie otrazheniia," 6; Zharov, "Dinamika vospriiatiia," 123 (Zharov, "Dynamism in Perception," 389); Sergeev, "Zhizn' v poeticheskom svete," 57; Chekanskii, "Kh. K. Andersen i sovremennost'," 257.

[2] Orlova, "Kh. K. Andersen. Vek XIX–vek XXI," 169.

ferent definitions.[3] The concept of pop culture is frequently identified with that of mass culture,[4] hence the synonymous use of these terms in this article. The primary distinctive features of mass culture are:

- an orientation toward the tastes and demands of the "average person";
- a singular degree of flexibility;
- its ability to transform artifacts created within the framework of other cultures, and turn these into objects of mass consumption;
- its commerciality;
- its use of clichés in creating artifacts;
- the distribution and consumption of its values primarily through mass-communication channels.[5]

Having passed through a period of assimilation in the late nineteenth and early twentieth century, Andersen's tales became part of the Russian cultural heritage, and now exist in the modern cultural space in the form of a whole range of artifacts: sculptures and architectural structures, commercial brands and works of online literature, school plays and live-action role-playing games. What is the secret of Hans Christian Andersen's popularity as a cultural phenomenon? Russian critics who have analyzed this writer's works, whether in the nineteenth century or the twenty-first, point to one and the same characteristics: subtle humor, tenderness, kindness of heart, and a firm boundary between good and evil.[6] The author's talent is absolutely undisputed. However, in our view, the very genre of fairy tale, with its accessibility and engagingness, conditions the tales' success as works of mass culture, the primary feature of which is the sort of simple ideas and imagery that persons of any age and social stratum can understand. It is no accident that, as Henrike Schmidt observes, "folklore genres are among the most popular literary forms practiced on the Runet [the Russian-language Internet]"[7]; while A. V. Fedorov notes that "in many popular media-texts, one hears, to some extent or other, echoes of biblical motifs, ancient Greek myths, and fairy tales about Cinderella, Little Red Riding Hood, Zmei Gorynich, Bluebeard, and Ali Baba and the forty thieves."[8]

---

3   Storey, *Cultural Theory and Popular Culture*, 6-12.
4   Strinati, *An Introduction to Theories of Popular Culture*, 1.
5   Kostina, *Massovaia kul'tura*, 345.
6   Orlova, "Kh. K. Andersen. Vek XIX–vek XXI," 169.
7   Schmidt, "Russian Literature on the Internet," 188.
8   Fedorov, "Mifologicheskaia osnova sovremennoi pop-kul'tury."

The images of characters from the most popular Hans Christian Andersen tales, and associations connected with them, are actively deployed when it comes to selecting trademarks and names for stores and other service enterprises. The spectrum of these goods and enterprises is rather broad, but they are mainly aimed at children and their parents, hence the fairly obvious motivation for choosing such a name: this is an image that one is well acquainted with, is memorable, and elicits positive fairytale associations:

"Andersen"	a children's bookstore[9]
"Andersen"	a children's clothing store[10]
"The Ugly Duckling"	a carwash[11] a tourism club for children and teenagers[12] a café-bar[13]
"Thumbelina"	a store for children's products[14] a line of children's furniture[15] a kindergarten[16] a brand of dress for little girls[17]
"Gerda"	a store for children's products[18]
"Kay and Gerda"	an online hat store[19]
"Ole Lukoie"	an online store for collectible dolls[20] a toy store[21] a musical group[22] a party-planning company[23]
"The Princess and the Pea"	a wedding hall[24] a garment factory[25] a bedding store[26]

9 http://andersen-kids.ru/about
10 https://vk.com/anderlavka
11 http://www.ivx.ru/infobase/infobase_592.html
12 http://www.g-utka.ru/club.php
13 http://nightout.ru/brnl/gadkiy-utenok
14 http://www.astrahan-catalog.ru/shop/magazin-detskih-tovarov-dyujmovochka/
15 http://f-mebeli.ru/djujmovochka_1
16 http://detsad-korolev.ru/ds6/, http://dujmovochka.uomur.org/
17 http://larisa-fashion.ru/detskaja-kollektsija/detskoe-platje-djujmovochka
18 http://www.gerdaru.com/about/
19 http://kai-i-gerda.ru/
20 http://ole-lukoe.com/kollektsionnye-kukly-talismany-elfos/geroi-mifov-skazok-i-legend
21 http://10644582.informerra.ru/
22 http://www.olelukkoye.ru/rus/discography/discography.htm
23 http://olelukoie.ru/
24 http://www.goroshina.spb.ru/
25 http://princessa-textil.ru/
26 http://www.princess-vl.ru/

"The Little Mermaid"	clothing and products for children[27] a store for fine women's underwear[28]
"The Snow Queen"	a fur shop[29] a hotel[30]
"The Steadfast Tin Soldier"	a military-historical performance and reenactment at Borodino Field[31]
"Snipp Snapp Snurr" (an incantation of the fairytale narrator in Evgenii Schwartz's *The Snow Queen* [*Snezhnaia koroleva*])	a brand of Christmas lights[32]

Particularly illustrative is the concept behind the brand "Andersen," in which the tales of Hans Christian Andersen serve to symbolize social success and refined taste:

> The "Andersen" stores recreate the atmosphere of a nineteenth-century children's room, in which children were read the tales of Hans Christian Andersen and acted out plays based on them. Here, children were dressed up to go out into society; their childhood was spent in expectation of meeting real knights and heroes, princes and princesses. They became worthy adults, with eyes aflame and hearts full of dreams. It was precisely they who made history, fashion, beauty, and art.
> The "Andersen" stores nurture taste and style from childhood on.
> Welcome to the fairytale world of "Andersen."[33]

The target group for most of the enterprises cited above is thus families with children, for whom mention of the tales of Andersen is meant to elicit exclusively positive associations. Only a few of the titles do not match this overall picture; however, in every instance a connection can be established between the name and an Andersenian image: the Snow Queen Hotel is located at a ski resort; the Ugly Duckling carwash conjures an association with the "duckling's" transformation into a beautiful white swan; and the Princess and the Pea bedding store obviously means to promise its customers a pleasant and deep sleep. In the case of the musical group calling itself Ole Lukoie, the meaning

---

27 http://www.rusalochka-shop.ru/about/
28 https://vk.com/club42757093
29 https://snowqueen.ru/
30 http://snezhnaya-koroleva-dombai.ru/
31 http://magput.ru/?id=10&viewprog=1205
32 http://www.utkonos.ru/item/1353230
33 http://andersen-kids.ru/about

of such a title is not clear on the surface, but the leader of the group, which performs psychedelic ethno-trance, explains it in an interview with a journalist thus:

- The group's name apparently also has particular meaning? Everyone thinks of Ole Lukoie first and foremost as the character in Andersen's tale, a kindly spirit, the master of dreams.
- Recall how the tale ends: Ole Lukoie tells about his brother, "the other Ole Lukoie," whom people see once in their life, and whose name is Death. This is precisely why we took this name. Although we also had dreams, travels, other realities in mind. You have to admit, calling a group "Death" wouldn't be too pleasant, if you don't, for instance, play death-metal. But this way you have an incentive to delve into the history of the question. One way or another, everyone is going to have to encounter this. [Our music] is geared toward delving into the self.[34]

The images of the characters of the Andersen tales most popular in Russia are also incarnated in sculpture and architecture. In Voronezh there is a Thumbelina fountain (refurbished in 2007), and Sochi's Riviera Park features a Thumbelina sculpture (2006).[35] In Mytishchi (near Moscow), next to the Tinderbox Puppet Theater, which is designed like a fairytale house, there is an Ole Lukoie sculpture.[36] The Wonder Island amusement park in St. Petersburg has a sculptural composition called Kingdom of the Snow Queen;[37] while the city of Sosnovyi Bor (97 km from St. Petersburg) has had a children's play center called Andersengrad (i.e., Andersen Town) since 1980, built in connection with the 175th anniversary of the writer's birth. The territory of Andersengrad has various structures connected one way or another with the tales of Hans Christian Andersen: there is a high-relief depiction of the writer; a Copenhagen-esque Town Hall tower reminiscent of "The Tinderbox", a Tin Soldier's tower, Ole Lukoie's house, a summer theater, ramparts, bridges, and an underground passage. A children's racetrack runs through the whole town. The town's artistic and architectural design employs mosaic paneling, stained glass, tapestries, and tiling stylized to resemble medieval Western European architecture. The town's overall area is two hectares. In 2008, a Little Mermaid statue was erected in the complex, and in 2010, a statue of the Steadfast Tin

---

34 http://insurgent.ru/ole-lukoye
35 http://www.park-riviera.ru/place/dyuimovochka
36 http://www.unmonument.ru/mon081.html
37 https://lori.ru/7067548

Soldier. Andersengrad annually holds over 300 different events; it features amusement rides in the summer and has a role-playing club and folk music festivals.[38]

Educational Resources

The tales of Hans Christian Andersen are actively used in various educational resources: on the one hand, printed (paper) textbooks and teaching materials and, on the other, electronic publications analogous to print versions, as well as numerous online resources that will be examined in greater detail below.

A child's first formal acquaintance with the tales of Andersen comes in kindergartens that operate according to special preschool curricula employing certain print editions of Andersen's tales or collections of preschool material that include, in particular, tales by Andersen. By this time, children already know many of the tales, insofar as their parents or grandparents have most likely read them to them at bedtime.

Interestingly, the older generation—the parents and grandparents of today's children—came to know Andersen in their own childhood not only through books, but perhaps even first and foremost through the children's radio programs that were popular in the latter half of the twentieth century both in major cities and provincial areas. Of course, radio no longer has the role it played back then, but insofar as more than one generation was raised on literary broadcasts, Andersen's popularity in Russia is owed, among other things, to the well-known radio shows based on his tales.

One of the successes of elementary-school education in contemporary Russia is the broad opportunity to use textbooks by various authors. For each subject there exists a variety of textbooks among which a particular school may choose the one it finds most suitable. One of the subjects in elementary school is called "Literary Reading." There are several textbook variants for this subject (currently, approximately fifteen) of equal status.

These textbooks typically feature several characters, whether from fairy tales or real life, that accompany pupils from first to fourth grade, comment on texts, and introduce the assignments to be performed. The texts are brief stories or excerpts from more substantial works, primarily by Russian authors, although also by foreign ones, with Andersen always among the most prominent of the latter.

---

38 https://ru.wikipedia.org/wiki/Андерсенград

For example, the set of "Literary Reading" textbooks that is part of the "School 2100" curriculum includes the tale "The Steadfast Tin Soldier," which is suggested for study in the third grade.[39] After reading the story, pupils are supposed to answer several questions, in particular: Why is the soldier called "steadfast"? What is the mood of this fairy tale?

The "Literary Reading" set included in the "Planet of Knowledge" curriculum suggests "Ole Lukoie" (in abridged form) and "The Nightingale" for reading and discussion.[40]

If the teacher finds that the course does not include enough Andersen tales, s/he may use materials of the "Supplementary Reading" subject and employ the numerous anthologies in which Andersen is featured quite prominently, particularly with the tales "The Princess and the Pea," "The Little Mermaid," and "The Ugly Duckling."[41] Discussion of the tale "The Little Mermaid" in third grade suggests answering these questions: Why did the little mermaid decide to bid farewell to the underwater life and become a person? Is it anyone's fault that her dreams did not come true? (Explain your point of view.) What is your opinion of the main character? And what is the author's opinion? Why? (Cite examples from the text. Write your own story about the little mermaid; tell what she was like.)

Beginning in fifth grade, tales by Andersen are included in the "Literature" curriculum, for which, likewise, several textbook variants have been issued. For example, textbooks by M. Cherkezova and V. Korovina include the tale "The Snow Queen," with a detailed analysis, materials on the author, and discussion assignments.[42] Russian schoolchildren, then, even as they are educated in Russian, read and study an average of three to five Andersen tales in the first five grades.

Russian elementary schools have a tradition of holding extracurricular thematic events, with quiz-contests and plays staged by pupils in connection with memorable dates in writers' lives; this is frequently done in conjunction with district and municipal libraries. For the youngest grades, such events are based on fairy tales by Russian or foreign authors, with tales by Andersen almost always included in the program. For Russian schoolchildren acquainted with the tales of Andersen since earliest childhood, the Danish storyteller has become so familiar that he has almost lost his national identity. During one quiz-contest, the children were asked: "What country is Andersen from?" One of the pupils

---

39 Buneev and Buneeva, *Literaturnoe chtenie. Dlia 3 klassa*, 24-29.
40 Kats, *Literaturnoe chtenie. Dlia 2 klassa*, 15-22; *Literaturnoe chtenie. Dlia 4 klassa*, 19-32.
41 Klimanova, *Literaturnoe chtenie. Dlia 2 klassa*, 167-93.
42 Cherkezova, *Literatura. Dlia 5 klassa*, 102-39; Korovina, *Literatura. Dlia 5 klassa*, 216-48.

answered: "He isn't from any particular country. First there was him, and then came the storytellers from different countries."[43]

Russian schools actively collaborate with children's libraries, and Andersen's birthday, which has become International Children's Book Day, is observed annually in every children's library in Russia. Taking the lead in St. Petersburg has been the A. S. Pushkin Central Municipal Children's Library, the biggest and most active of its kind.[44] Every children's library in the country, moreover, marked 2005, the two-hundredth anniversary of Andersen's birth, as the Year of Hans Christian Andersen.

Andersen's tales are so popular in Russian schools that in some places, English classes use adapted English translations of them (e.g., "The Snow Queen" and "The Marsh King's Daughter") for instructional purposes.[45]

Also promoting the incorporation of Hans Christian Andersen into the modern cultural space of Russia is undoubtedly the great breadth of current informational channels. In the digital age, there are ever more sources of information and of channels by which it is distributed, and the number of Internet users increases with each passing day: according to the latest data of the TNS Web Index project, as of January-March 2015 the Russian Internet numbered some eighty-two million people, i.e., 66 percent of the population of Russia aged twelve to sixty-four. Every day, 53 percent of the inhabitants of Russia age eighteen and older, or sixty-two million people, go online; and fifty million of the eighty-two million Internet users go online mainly using mobile devices.[46]

The number of sites on the Russian-language Internet that feature information on the works of Hans Christian Andersen is considerable. Most of these contain brief biographical sketches, as well as access to the texts of the most popular tales. An analysis of the sites shows that interest in Andersen's writings is not only not waning, it is experiencing a renaissance. Educational web-resources that provide information on the Danish writer's life and literary legacy come in the following groups:

1. Sites for children and their parents;
2. Sites of children's libraries;
3. Educational portals and information sites for teachers;
4. Audio and video collections;
5. Wiki-platforms;
6. Electronic libraries.

---

43 Maznjak and Zagorskaja, "Børn læser H. C. Andersen," 36.
44 On the considerable Andersen-based activities this library offers readers, see ibid., 31-36.
45 http://za4itaika.ru/Pages/English-books/English_club.php
46 http://www.bizhit.ru/index/users_count/0-151

Attesting in particular to the Russian readership's love of the Danish writer is the enormous number of sites (some interactive) aimed at children and their parents.

Of particular interest is the site with the Cyrillic domain-name *skazki-andersena.rf* (i.e., "tales-of-andersen.rf"),[47] which gives access to 160 of the writer's tales and audio-tales for online listening. Teachers can make use of the site's postings of the best school essays on Andersen's works and questions for quiz-contests on his tales, as well as a homeroom activity script titled "The Fairy Tale is the Homeland of Feelings" and a literary game called "Through the Pages of the Tales of Hans Christian Andersen."

Posted on the site deti-online.com (i.e., "children-online.com") are thirty-six tales and thirty-five audio-files for listening, arranged by the number of downloads. The five most popular are "The Snow Queen," "Thumbelina," "The Little Mermaid," "The Ugly Duckling," and "The Princess and the Pea." Attesting to the Danish writer's undying popularity are the following introductory comments:

> You've probably never met anyone who didn't know Andersen. After all, absolutely all schoolchildren have numerous lessons and competitions, put on plays, and watch cartoons and movies based on Hans Christian's stories. The characters in these audio-tales are not just famous, they have already entered our language, our life, and we often use them as bywords without even realizing it.[48]

Particularly noteworthy are the sites of city libraries that post various materials devoted to this writer's works. Among a whole slew of such resources, we could single out the website of the Hans Christian Andersen Children's Library of Novosibirsk,[49] as well as the project of the Riazan' Children's Library devoted to the translators of Scandinavian literature Anna and Peter Hansen.[50] The site of the children's library of the city of Bol'shoi Kamen' (Primorsky krai) features various interactive opportunities: you can take part in creating rebuses and riddles pertaining to Andersen's works, do crosswords, and make an online mosaic.[51] Notably, quite a few children's libraries are named for Andersen: aside from, as mentioned, that in Novosibirsk, also those in Moscow, Kaliningrad, and Tolyatti.

---

47 http://сказки-андерсена.рф
48 https://deti-online.com/audioskazki/skazki-andersena-mp3/
49 http://цбс-белинского.рф/filial_6/about_author.php/
50 http://rznodb.ru/ganzens/ganz_htm/home_ganz.htm
51 http://bk-detstvo.narod.ru/andersen.html

Especially popular on the Russian Internet are such educational portals as the federal Russian Education portal www.edu.ru, the Russian General Education portal www.litera.edu.ru, and the Combined Collection of Digital Educational Resources at http://school-collection.edu.ru/. As the Internet plays an ever more important role in educational activities, teachers and pupils use these resources more and more in preparing thematic lessons and projects. The number of presentations posted online that illustrate the creative career of Hans Christian Andersen gives a sense of the extent to which he is an integral part of the modern educational process.

But people become acquainted with this Danish author's works not just by reading his texts. A great number of cartoons and feature films have been made based on his works; these constitute a prism through which notions of Andersen plots and characters are formed, often differing greatly from the original source. The modern media-society is marked by its different use of visual information: a shift in modern methods of perception has been taking place, from the verbal to the visual and pictorial.[52] Mass culture, "whose primary form of existence is the screen form, materially transforms thinking, which is now marked by a superficiality, the ability to 'glide' along and perceive greater quantities of information without, however, comprehending it."[53] Online access to stage productions and film adaptations of Andersen's works helps to affix these Andersenian "reflections" in the Russian cultural consciousness.

Openly accessible on the video-hosting site YouTube are not only numerous screen adaptations of Andersen's works and professional performances of his tales, but also amateur plays by children's theater studios.[54] Of particular note is a project by Little Cinema, a foundation that supports and promotes moviemaking for children and young people; this is a web-portal called "Chitalkin" (a surname that sounds like *chitat'*, "to read") on which popular Russian actors as well as ordinary parents read classic and contemporary children's literature. Significantly, of the thirty-four fairy tales selected for video-recording, ten are by Andersen.[55]

On the site www.staroeradio.ru (i.e., "www.oldradio.ru"), you can listen to nearly eighty radio plays based on tales by Hans Christian Andersen that were produced during the Soviet period and feature some of the most famous actors of screen and stage.

Despite the stereotypical notion of Andersen as exclusively a children's

---

52 Drozdova, "Vizual'nost' kak fenomen sovremennogo mediaobshchestva."
53 Kostina, *Massovaia kul'tura*, 347.
54 https://www.youtube.com/results?search_query=андерсен спектакли
55 https://www.youtube.com/playlist?list=PL6ZF-9jmXX4NIA5oev1kPxj0c8MzOdqs-

writer, interest in his works among adults is experiencing a revival of its own. The literature-inspired travel project "Reality Clutch" (*pedal' stsepleniia s real'nost'iu*),[56] created by a group of travel and literature enthusiasts from St. Petersburg in 2010, and Nikolai Gorbunov's Andersen-based literary travel guide *The House on the Steam Locomotive's Caboose* (*Dom na khvoste parovoza. Putevoditel' po Evrope v skazkakh Andersena*), constitute vivid examples of how the addition of modern hypermedia, geoinformational, and navigational technologies is shifting reception of Andersen texts from the children's realm to that of adults. Among sites more oriented toward an adult audience, we might single out www.fairyroom.ru,[57] which posts, aside from the texts of Andersen tales and information on them, also book illustrations by Russian and foreign artists.

Electronic libraries have long since become an integral part of the Russian online space. Citing Eugene Gorny's PhD dissertation "A Creative History of the Russian Internet," Kåre Mjør observes that "[t]he proliferation of online libraries in Russia is a result of a specific attitude to property and especially intellectual property deeply rooted in Russian culture which tends to disregard private interests for the sake of a common cause."[58] Thanks to the availability of texts by Hans Christian Andersen on the sites of the major electronic libraries, readers of the younger and older generations have the opportunity to discover for themselves a new Andersen, one previously unknown to them. Thus for instance, the Runet's best-known library site, Maksim Moshkov's www.lib.ru, created in 1994, offers full access not just to the texts of most of Andersen's tales, but also to his novels, poetry, and travelogues, which are virtually unknown to the general reader; as well as a good deal of illustrations.[59] To the great credit of this library, moreover, it features the tales not just in the classic translations of Anna and Peter Hansen but also those of Aleksandr Fedorov-Davydov (early twentieth century). The other major e-library sites of the Runet give access only to Andersen's works in translations by the Hansens. Unfortunately, the latest translations of the Danish writer's works, undertaken by a collective of translators under the editorship of Anatolii Chekansky, Aleksandr Sergeev, and Oleg Rozhdestvensky and published by Vagrius in 2005,[60] is unavailable on the Runet.

The modern Internet would be unthinkable without the projects of the Wikimedia Foundation. When UNESCO awarded Jimmy Wales the Niels

---

56 https://vk.com/pedalnost
57 http://www.fairyroom.ru/?page_id=9226
58 Mjør, "Digitizing Everything? Online Libraries on the Runet," 216.
59 http://az.lib.ru/a/andersen_g_h/
60 Andersen, *Sobranie sochinenii v chetyrekh tomakh*.

Bohr Medal in 2013, with good reason did it call his creation Wikipedia "a symbol of the age of connectivity and participation that we live in. Wikipedia is not just a tool—it is the embodiment of a dream as old as humanity itself, as old as the Library of Alexandria."[61] Hans Christian Andersen could likewise be called a symbol of the age of interactivity, uniting people of different cultures; after all, his works have been translated into 159 languages, and the "Hans Christian Andersen" Wikipedia page at last check exists in 161 languages.[62] Open platforms such as Wikipedia, Wikisource, Wikiquote, and Wikimedia Commons give full access to, aside from the fairy tales, also prose and poetry texts and travelogues little known to the Russian reader, as well as photographs and famous quotations.

Social Networks

The extent of the younger generation's interest in Hans Christian Andersen may be judged by the existence of "lovers of Andersen" groups on various social networks. Consider, for instance, Russia's most popular social network VKontakte ("In Contact"), launched in October 2006, and originally positioning itself as a resource for students and graduates of Russia's colleges and universities, but later coming to call itself "a modern, fast, and aesthetically pleasing means of communicating online."[63]

According to TNS data (winter of 2015-16), VKontakte has a monthly usership of 46.6 million people, of whom 44 percent are men and 56 percent women. Thirty-three percent of the users indicate their age; of them (rounding to the nearest integer), 24 percent are eighteen and under; 32 percent are age eighteen to twenty-four; 32 percent are twenty-five to thirty-four; 7 percent are thirty-five to forty-four; 2 percent are forty-five to fifty-four; and 2 percent are fifty-five or older.[64]

According to Vitalii Leontiev, the advantages of VKontakte over analogous social networks are: 1) its broad audience; 2) its outstanding search system; 3) its enormous music- and movie-base, which makes this network the largest media aggregator in the world; and 4) its game applications.[65] An additional highlight of VKontakte is the variety of its communities. These are shared-interest groups that enable people to exchange opinions and information, get news, conduct business, or

---

61 http://es.unesco.org/node/182321
62 https://en.wikipedia.org/wiki/Hans_Christian_Andersen
63 https://vk.com/about
64 https://blog.br-analytics.ru/socialnye-seti-v-rossii-zima-2015-2016-cifry-trendy-prognozy/
65 Leont'ev, *Sotsial'nye seti*, 12-13.

simply have fun. According to Tine Roesen and Vera Zvereva, "online cultural consumption and the sharing of diverse media products are distinctive features of VKontakte."[66] It is no wonder, then, that specifically this social network should have groups devoted to lovers of the works of Andersen. The most numerous of these, titled "Fairy Tales of Hans Christian Andersen,"[67] at last check had 3,734 members. This group features access to the texts of works, well-known illustrations, audio-files of tales, and video-files of Andersen-based cartoons and movies. Analysis of the subjects dealt with by this community shows that discussion is most active regarding the members' favorite tales and characters, as well as particular books they are interested in locating.

The usership of LiveJournal, which is more oriented toward adults, is likewise not indifferent to the oeuvre of Andersen; blogs in this regard mainly feature postings of an informational nature, devoted to this or that cultural event connected with Andersen's works, as well as illustrations to his books.[68] Also noteworthy is the community for an Andersen-based role-playing game called "The Tales of Dear Denmark," which took place in 2010 near Moscow and used the plots of the writer's most famous fairy tales.[69]

The social network for booklovers www.livelib.ru not only offers the opportunity to buy or download Andersen books, but also gives access to readers' reviews of them, and narratives by readers themselves on the subject of Andersen's works. One of these, for instance, begins thus: "As a child I had my own Kay. Well, his name wasn't really Kay, but Kolia, but that's not important. Here's what happened" (user July-S).[70] The list of the five most popular and frequently downloaded Andersen tales does not fundamentally differ from ratings on deti-online.com, and illustrates the preferences of the adult readership:

Title	Number of readers	Reviews	Citations
"The Snow Queen"	3,021	44	31
"The Little Mermaid"	1,888	41	2
"Thumbelina"	1,656	9	2
"The Ugly Duckling"	1,110	36	7
"The Steadfast Tin Soldier"	1,078	9	1

66 Roesen and Zvereva, "Social Network Sites on the Runet," 78.
67 https://vk.com/club15462563
68 http://vsegda-tvoj.livejournal.com/17622868.html, http://kid-book-museum.livejournal.com/tag/*Андерсен
69 http://andersen-tales.livejournal.com/
70 https://www.livelib.ru/book/1000008221/stories-snezhnaya-koroleva-gans-hristian-andersen

Andersen's tales continue to inspire modern Russian writers as well as everyday Internet users. The Runet's most popular and visited fan fiction resource, www.ficbook.net, at last check featured fan fiction for fifteen Andersen tales, including crossovers, i.e., works of fan fiction that combine the plots of several works. Numeric data is given in the following table:[71]

No	Tale title	Number of works of fan fiction
1.	"The Snow Queen"	720
2.	"The Little Mermaid"	226
3.	"The Little Match Girl"	33
4.	"The Wild Swans"	36
5.	"Thumbelina"	38
6.	"Ole Lukoie"	21
7.	"The Steadfast Tin Soldier"	22
8.	"The Princess and the Pea"	20
9.	"The Ugly Duckling"	12
10.	"The Swineherd"	8
11.	"The Emperor's New Clothes"	5
12.	"The Tinderbox"	5
13.	"The Red Shoes"	5
14.	"The Shadow"	5
15.	"The Nightingale"	3

It is interesting that the tales "The Snow Queen" and "The Little Mermaid" should be in the lead position among fan fiction; these same tales lead the top-five most popular on deti-online.com and livelib.ru. In our view, this popularity is in no small part connected with the many screen adaptations of these works.[72] For many Russian children, moreover, as for many Americans as well,[73] the plot of "The Little Mermaid" is familiar first and foremost from the Disney cartoons bearing that name. This has led to the widespread dissemination of the specific (red-tressed, bikini-clad) image of "Ariel" on various toys, games, etc. On the one hand,

---

71 This information is available by entering "Андерсен" in the search field at https://ficbook.net/fanfiction/books.
72 See the contributions to this volume by Andrei Rogatchevski and Helena Goscilo.
73 Bom, "H. C. Andersen," 206.

then, the availability of Andersen texts in Russia's online space enables the Russian adult reader to discover lesser-known works by Andersen; on the other hand, the availability of video-files from stage productions and screen adaptations gives a distorted conception of this writer's works.

Widespread and varying interpretations of texts by Hans Christian Andersen have promoted the subsequent development of intertextual connections between modern literary, musical, and cinematic works on the one hand, and the fairy tales of Andersen on the other.

The concept of intertextuality that became popular in the late twentieth century—the idea that any text is constructed like a mosaic of quotations, absorbing and transforming some other text—is entirely applicable to a whole range of Russian literary works that make use of imagery from the tales of Hans Christian Andersen. Russian authors frequently employ hidden or explicit reference to Andersen's works to produce an ironic effect; this enables them to disengage from a specific (often complicated) situation. It would seem, however, that many modern Russian writers do not use imagery and situations from Andersen's tales solely to work out their own creative challenges (numerous examples of well-known allusions may be found in the 1997 anthology *Andersen in Russian Literature* [*Andersen v russkoi literature*] edited by Boris Erkhov); but often to engage Andersen in a cultural dialogue meant to solve eternal problems, enable the creation of new meanings, or simply propose a new interpretation of images that would already seem to be well known. A vivid example of this would be Liudmila Petrushevskaia's novella *Duska and the Ugly Duckling* (*Dus'ka i gadkii utenok*), which opens with the following words:

> Once upon a time there lived, on the municipal ponds, a middle-aged Ugly Duckling.
>
> Let us omit all the events of the foregoing years; let us not speak of his difficult childhood, when no one believed in him, but rather everyone plucked at him. Neither let us long belabor his current solitude, nor even mention the middle-aged Ugly Duckling's numerous kin, the kin that considered him a loser; no one in the whole world believed that from the middle-aged Ugly Duckling could ever emerge a Beautiful White Swan, whom beautiful Swans would take for one of their own, would admire, bow before, and hiss their words of welcome to.[74]

---

74 Petrushevskaia, *Dus'ka i gadkii utenok*.

The finale of Petrushevskaia's tale is nothing like that of Andersen's "The Ugly Duckling"; there is no magical transformation into a beautiful swan. It is an "open-ended" ending, one that invites the reader to collaborate and sets before her several important philosophical questions.

The well-known writer, literary critic, and public commentator Dmitrii Bykov, meanwhile, uses Andersen's tale "The Little Match Girl" to create a satirical work in the Christmas-story genre, one that also deals with current political subjects. His dialogue with Andersen in the story "The Little Match Girl Gives a Light" ("Devochka so spichkami daet prikurit'") begins thus:

> I won't frighten you with all the gory details that the sentimental sadist Andersen was so fond of, always subjecting his underage characters to unheard-of tribulations. Our little girl had neither cracked shoes on little legs red from the cold, nor torn sleeves on little arms blue from the cold, nor plaintive requests on lips white from the cold. She was not collecting money for her sick mother, did not ask for change to feed her little infant brother, and in general looked upon passersby with deep sympathy, as if it were not she but they who were in need of beneficent assistance.[75]

As Iuliia Danilenko aptly observes:

> The narrator comes to an agreement with the reader who grew up on the tales of Hans Christian Andersen that the former will tell a story like an Andersen one, but his own, a new one that will be addressed to the modern reader. For the modern author, the original source serves as an alphabet; it signifies that author and reader have a joint readerly experience and a shared cultural base.[76]

Liudmila Petrushevskaia and Dmitrii Bykov are writers well known to the reading public, but Andersenian imagery is actively used also by younger authors, as well as musicians, for whom the Internet has become a space in which to promote their works.

Characteristic of contemporary authors as opposed to those of previous generations is that intertextuality with Andersen ranges beyond the use of a single image in the context of a work; now uppermost is a free, postmodern interpretation of Andersen's texts involving the violation of genre models and a dialogue with the reader.

---

[75] Bykov, "Devochka so spichkami daet prikurit'."
[76] Danilenko, "Transformatsiia zhanra rozhdestvenskogo rasskaza," 590.

The image of Andersen's steadfast tin soldier receives an interesting treatment in Ilya Averbakh's film *The Monologue* (*Monolog*, 1972). The main character, Prof. Sretensky, is doomed by his eccentricity to solitude; he is a "steadfast tin soldier" trying to stand up to the vicissitudes of fate. Not once over the course of the whole film (which is accompanied by the remarkable music of Oleg Karavaichuk) is the title of Andersen's tale mentioned; but when the viewer sees the main character arranging toy soldiers from his collection on his desk, everything falls into place, and the viewer cannot help recalling Andersen's tale.

Further attesting to Andersen's inclusion in the cultural space of Russia is the use, in the Russian language, of a whole set of proverbial expressions from this writer's tales. While the average Russian reader is acquainted with no more than fifteen of the tales, the language most actively reproduces a mere six or seven images therefrom, but these come up fairly frequently in the media space.

Quite a few proverbial expressions from Hans Christian Andersen's tales have been included in Russian dictionaries, in particular, "ugly duckling," "the king is naked" (from the tale "The Emperor's New Clothes"—the Russian translation uses the word "king" [*korol'*] instead of emperor, and in the finale the boy cries out: "The king is naked!"), and a "thumbelina," "princess on a pea," and "steadfast tin soldier." It is interesting to note how certain entries are recorded in particular dictionaries; for instance, the phrase "a princess on a pea" appears in Ozhegov and Shvedova's *Dictionary of the Russian Language* (*Slovar' russkogo iazyka*),[77] in the *Dictionary of Proverbial Words and Expressions* (*Entsiklopedicheskii slovar' krylatykh slov i vyrazhenii*, ed. V. Serov), which gives the etymology and figurative meaning, with the note "ironic"; and in the *Dictionary of Russian Synonyms* (*Slovar' russkikh sinonimov*),[78] as a synonym of *nezhenka* (a "sissy" or "mollycoddle"); while the authors of the *Great Dictionary of Russian Sayings* (*Bol'shoi slovar' russkikh pogovorok*, ed. V. Mokienko and T. Nikitina) categorize this word combination as a Russian saying.

As further evidence of the resilience of many words and expressions from Andersen's tales in the Russian language, it could be noted that, for many of them, a subsequent transformation in meaning becomes possible, first and foremost, a metaphorization. Hence the transition of a character name into a byword: "The Ugly Duckling of the Russian

---

77 http://www.slovari.ru/default.aspx?p=244
78 http://www.classes.ru/all-russian/russian-dictionary-synonyms.htm

Aviation Industry"[79]—such is the headline of an article on problems in that industry. In certain cases a narrowing of meaning is also in effect, for instance, the expression "ugly duckling" may be used almost literally to refer simply to an unpleasant person, with the surrounding context not even presupposing any potential transformation into a beautiful swan. The word "thumbelina" can be used to refer to something small, for instance, a very small book, but in addition to such metaphorization is also the jocular-ironic usage, when it might refer to a large woman. Journalists frequently make puns based on images from Andersen. The active reinterpretation of Andersenian imagery is mainly characteristic of the media, but it occurs in oral speech as well.

Andersenian imagery plays a particular role in Russian headlines. It should be noted that it is considerably more characteristic of the Russian media than the Danish to make use—often, in reinterpreted form—of allusions, famous characters, quotations, and proverbial words and expressions in headlines. Famous quotations from Andersen are often used as a source to create a headline, with the media space's undoubted leader in this category being the image of the "emperor with no clothes" or literally the "naked king" (and the related word-combination "new clothes" or "new suit"), which is reproduced extensively in the most varied contexts. Also quite frequent in headlines in the Russian media are the images of the "princess on a pea," the "steadfast little soldier," and the "ugly duckling." So as to produce an ironic effect, or draw the reader's attention, authors of news items resort to a whole range of devices: 1) restoring components of these expressions to their literal meaning (e.g., "The Naked King Silvio Berlusconi" ["Golyi korol' Sil'vio Berluskoni"]);[80] 2) replacing or transposing these components, for instance, in the headline "The Clothed King and the Naked Writers" ("Odetyi korol' i golye pisateli"),[81] from an article about children's literature during the Stalin period; 3) using an image from Andersen as a cliché, without any direct reference to a work by that author, for instance in the headline "A Match Girl Causes an Explosion Near Moscow" ("Devochka so spichkami ustroila vzryv v Podmoskov'e"),[82] regarding an incident in which a nine-year-old girl had caused the explosion of a gas canister; 4) using oblique, synecdochic expressions that conjure an Andersenian image in the reader's memory (a "tin soldier" instead of a "steadfast tin soldier"); and 5) "contaminating" or conjoining an element from Andersen with

---

79 http://www.odnako.org/magazine/material/gadkiy-utenok-rossiyskogo-aviaproma/
80 https://news.rambler.ru/head/2977330-golyy-korol-silvio-berluskoni/
81 Krotkov, "Odetyi korol' i golye pisateli."
82 http://www.ntv.ru/novosti/395356/

some other proverbial expression or phraseology (e.g., *Gologo korolia vsegda igraet lzhivaia svita*,[83] roughly, "It's the conniving retinue that makes the king naked").

The fact that the Andersenian phrases used as precedents in such cases are so widely anthologized and known, and the possibility of reinterpreting them thus, attests to how firmly entrenched they are in Russian culture: they constitute an integral part of it—having long since gone beyond the framework of just "the tales of Andersen," they have become, broadly speaking, a fact of Russian culture. Some Andersen phrases become clichés of speech, a sort of readymade formula to facilitate the process of communication.

Virtually every child in Russia becomes acquainted with the tales of Hans Christian Andersen as a preschooler or in the earliest grades, and preserves a love for this writer their whole life. Factors determining this proclivity include the tales' engaging plots, vivid imagery, and their amazing richness of content—the "multi-layeredness" of these works that makes them interesting to persons of whatever age. The success of this writer's works, moreover, is conditioned by the very genre of fairy tale itself, contributing to their transposition into modern mass culture in the form of architectural and sculptural structures, commercial brands, film adaptations and theatrical productions, works of online literature, live-action role-playing games, school quiz-contests, and proverbial words and expressions. The enormous quantity of web-resources that provide information on this Danish writer's life and literary legacy make it possible for the Russian reader to discover "the unknown Andersen" for themselves. However, the online availability of video-files from stage productions and film adaptations causes many to form their conception of Andersen's tales based on their "reflections" rather than the works themselves.

Andersen's life-motto "to travel is to live" is widely known, and the writer continues to adhere to it even after his physical death. Having become a person of international provenance, a symbol of the interaction between cultures, he continues his traveling through time, remaining a modern person capable of reacting with sensitivity to every innovation of technology and culture. Andersen's uniqueness lies in the fact that he is comprehensible and inexhaustible in any period, and for people of any age.

---

83 http://veneteater.ee/?p=11777

Works Cited

Andersen, Khans Kristian. *Sobranie sochinenii v chetyrekh tomakh*. Moscow: Vagrius, 2005.

Bom, Anne Klara. "H. C. Andersen: Et kulturfænomen i teori og praksis." In *H. C. Andersen i det moderne samfund*, edited by A. K. Bom, J. Bøggild, and J. Nørregaard Frandsen, 185-206. Syddansk Universitetsforlag, 2014.

Braude, Liudmila. "Khans Kristian Andersen v Rossii." In *Skazki rasskazannye detiam. Novye skazki* by Kh. K. Andersen, 321-37. Moscow: Nauka, 1983.

Buneev, Rustem, and Ekaterina Buneeva. *Literaturnoe chtenie. Dlia 3 klassa.* Ch. 2. Moscow: Prosveshchenie, 2016.

Bykov, Dmitrii. "Devochka so spichkami daet prikurit'." *Ogonek*, no. 52 (31 December 2006): 44-47.

Chekanskii, Anatolii. "Kh. K. Andersen i sovremennost' (po materialam avtobiograficheskoi prozy pisatelia Kh. K. Andersena)." *Skandinavskaia filologiia / Scandinavica* IX (2007): 257-67.

Cherkezova, Medzhi. *Literatura. Dlia 5 klassa.* Ch. 1. Moscow: Drofa, 2015.

Danilenko, Iuliia. "Transformatsiia zhanra rozhdestvenskogo rasskaza v sovremennoi literature." In *Problemy istoricheskoi poetiki. Aktual'nye aspekty*, edited by V. N. Zakharov, 12: 587-98. Petrozavodsk: Petrozavodsk State University, 2014.

Drozdova, Alla. "Vizual'nost' kak fenomen sovremennogo mediaobshchestva." Available electronically: http://www.journal-discussion.ru/publication.php?id=1208.

Erkhov, Boris. "Andersen. Russkie otrazheniia." In *Andersen v russkoi literature. Pisateli o pisatele* by Boris Erkhov, 6-9. Moscow: Rudomino, 1997.

—. *Andersen v russkoi literature. Pisateli o pisatele.* Moscow: Rudomino, 1997.

Fedorov, Aleksandr. "Mifologicheskaia osnova sovremennoi pop-kul'tury i ee analiz na zaniatiakh v shkol'noi auditorii." Available electronically: http://psyfactor.org/lib/fedorov25.htm.

Gorbunov, Nikolai. *Dom na khvoste parovoza. Putevoditel' po Evrope v skazkakh Andersena.* Moscow: Livebook, 2016.

Kats, Ella. *Literaturnoe chtenie. Dlia 2 klassa.* Ch. 2. Moscow: AST-Astrel', 2015.

—. *Literaturnoe chtenie. Dlia 4 klassa.* Ch. 3. Moscow: AST-Astrel', 2016.

Klimanova, Liudmila. *Literaturnoe chtenie. Dlia 2 klassa.* Ch. 2. Moscow: Prosveshchenie, 2016.

Korovina, Vera. *Literatura. Dlia 5 klassa.* Ch. 2. Moscow: Prosveshchenie, 2015.

Kostina, Anna. *Massovaia kul'tura kak fenomen postindustrial'nogo obshchestva.* Moscow: Librokom, 2016.

Krotkov, Andrei. "Odetyi korol' i golye pisateli." *Nezavisimaia gazeta*, 30 June 2005. Available electronically: http://www.ng.ru/tendenc/2005-06-30/5_king.html

Leont'ev, Vitalii. *Sotsial'nye seti. VKontakte, Facebook, i drugie.* Moscow: OLMA, 2012.

Maznjak, Nina, and Jekaterina Zagorskaja. "Børn læser H. C. Andersen." In *H. C. Andersen i Rusland: Bidrag til et symposium på Skt. Petersborgs*

Universitet 17. maj 1996, edited by Aage Jørgensen, Boris S. Sjarov, and Michael Jacobsen, 31-36. Aarhus: CUK, 1997.

Mjør, Kåre Johan. "Digitizing Everything? Online Libraries on the Runet." In *Digital Russia: The Language, Culture and Politics of New Media Communication*, edited by Michael S. Gorham, Ingunn Lunde, and Martin Paulsen, 215-30. London; New York: Routledge, 2014.

Mokienko, Valerii, and Tat'iana Nikitina. *Bol'shoi slovar' russkikh pogovorok*. Moscow: OLMA, 2007.

Orlova, Gaiane. "Kh. K. Andersen. Vek XIX–vek XXI." In *Kh. K. Andersen i sovremennaia mirovaia kul'tura*, edited by A. N. Chekanskii, 162-70. Moscow: MGIMO-Universitet, 2008.

Ozhegov, Sergei, and Natal'ia Shvedova. *Tolkovyi slovar' russkogo iazyka*. Available electronically: http://www.slovari.ru/default.aspx?p=244.

Petrushevskaia, Liudmila. *Dus'ka i gadkii utenok*. Available electronically: http://books.rusf.ru/unzip/add-2003/xussr_mr/petrul70.htm?1/1.

Roesen, Tine, and Vera Zvereva. "Social Network Sites on the Runet: Exploring Social Communication." In *Digital Russia: The Language, Culture and Politics of New Media Communication*, edited by Michael S. Gorham, Ingunn Lunde, and Martin Paulsen, 72-87. London; New York: Routledge, 2014.

Schmidt, Henrike. "Russian Literature on the Internet: From Hypertext to Fairy Tale." In *Digital Russia: The Language, Culture and Politics of New Media Communication*, edited by Michael S. Gorham, Ingunn Lunde, and Martin Paulsen, 177-93. London; New York: Routledge, 2014.

Sergeev, Aleksandr. "'Zhizn' v poeticheskom svete.' Mir tvorchestva Khansa Kristiana Andersena." In *Sobranie sochinenii v chetyrekh tomakh* by Kh. K. Andersen, 1: 5-57. Moscow: Vagrius, 2005.

Serov, Vadim. *Entsiklopedicheskii slovar' krylatykh slov i vyrazhenii*. Moscow: Lokid-Press, 2005.

Storey, John. *Cultural Theory and Popular Culture: An Introduction*. Harlow: Prentice Hall, 2001.

Strinati, Dominic. *An Introduction to Theories of Popular Culture*. London; New York: Routledge, 2004.

Zharov, Boris. "Dinamika vospriiatiia Kh. K. Andersena v Santk-Peterburge, odnom iz samykh andersenovskikh gorodov mira." *Skandinavskaia filologiia / Scandinavica* VIII (2006): 111-24.

—. "Dynamism in Perception of Hans Christian Andersen in Saint Petersburg, One of the Most Andersenous Cities of the World." In *Hans Christian Andersen: Between Children's Literature and Adult Literature. Papers from IV International Hans Christian Andersen Conference 1 to 5 August 2005*, edited by Johan de Mylius, Aage Jørgensen, and Viggo Hjørnager Pedersen, 389-98. Odense: The Hans Christian Andersen Center, University of Southern Denmark, 2007.

Appendix

Anderseniana in Soviet and Post-Soviet Russia:

An Overview

Inna Sergienko

Despite fundamental changes in Russia's political, social, and cultural life, literary critics' and educators' interest in Andersen's work never disappeared, but would merely be interrupted for a time, only to reemerge with new vigor. To date, works on Andersen's life and oeuvre published in the Soviet and post-Soviet periods, from 1918 to 2017, number over 300; and the modern era of the Internet has turned Russian Anderseniana into a torrent of articles and pieces that defies calculation.

The materials listed in the bibliography to this article enable us to trace how the corpus of Russian critics' and educators' works on Andersen took shape, and what factors influenced its development.

To briefly describe the history of Russian Anderseniana over the last hundred years: the most meager period was from the 1920s to the latter half of the 1950s. In these years, some works on Andersen's oeuvre did appear in print, but they were published mainly to convey considerations as to whether Andersen's fairy tales were an appropriate ideological match for Soviet children's reading material (Stanchinskaia 1924; Gorbov 1927; Deich 1935; and Lopyreva 1937).

Critics differed on this score. Some saw Andersen's tales as hopelessly outdated and having no place on any Soviet children's reading list. "If we take the most beloved children's writer Andersen and recall his whole voluminous repertoire, it becomes clear how suffused his works are with love and devotion to kings. And this is such a common theme, running through most of his works, that it eclipses all their other, positive qualities," writes the educator Esfir Stanchinskaia (1924, 129). Others, such as the well-known literary critic Dmitrii Gorbov, believed that reading Andersen's books would do Soviet children, the future builders of communism, no harm, insofar as the dreams of social justice that Andersen expressed in his tales had already begun to be implemented in the young Soviet land.

In the 1930s, those who had fought for a radical purge of children's reading–to rid it of "old-regime literature," in particular, of the fairytale/fantasy genre as a whole[1]—were themselves condemned by official criticism, and Andersen became one of the classic children's authors to meet with the approval of the Soviet ideological censorship. "In the harsh period of the 'RAPPian frost,'[2] baleful critics subjected the fairy tale genre to a fearsome attack," wrote the well-known literary critic Aleksandr Deich in 1937;[3] "they tried to get Andersen's tales removed from children's reading.... But now that children's literature is successfully developing under the Stalinist slogan of socialist realism, we draw abundantly from the treasury of world literature all the best and noblest works that promote the victory of socialism" (Deich 1937, 13). In another article, developing Gorbov's idea of the Soviet system as embodying Andersen's aspirations, Deich says of Andersen's work: "[T]he Soviet Union brings this fairy tale to life every day.... The children of the Soviet land are accustomed to the fact that many members of the Soviet government, many pilots, engineers, scientists, and researchers, were once poor people, shepherds, farm laborers, and porters, and were able to achieve their aspirations thanks to the Great October Revolution" (Deich 1937, 14). From the 1930s through the first half of the 1950s, critics took note of Andersen's problematizing of social issues in his tales, and emphasized his democratic spirit, the "closeness in class terms" (*klassovo blizkoe*) of his background, etc. Still, as the prominent Soviet researcher Liudmila Braude observed (1970, 317), "until the Andersen jubilee, articles about him were a rather rare phenomenon." It thus seems appropriate to include several prefaces to editions of Andersen's fairy tales in this survey (Gorbov 1927; Lopyreva 1937; and Gorbatov 1947).

The World Peace Council[4] declared 1955 the Year of Andersen. In response, the Soviet press published a number of publications to mark the 150th anniversary of Andersen's birth and celebrate his oeuvre. The appendix includes seventeen works published in 1955; but in fact there were many more. These jubilee publications vary in form and content: some are short notes, limited to a brief account of the main facts of Andersen's biography, emphasizing the significance of his work for world

---

1 On the "war on fairy tales," see Olich, *Competing Ideologies and Children's Literature in Russia, 1918-1935*, 201-32.
2 RAPP (the Russian acronym for the Russian Association of Proletarian Writers) was a literary organization that existed in the USSR from 1925 to 1932. Its representatives were distinguished by their radical views on the literary heritage and took a firm stand against writers who were, in their view, "insufficiently Soviet."
3 In 1935, Deich oversaw the preparation of an edition of Andersen's tales for children as a supplement to the popular illustrated literary magazine *Spark* (*Ogonek*) (Andersen, *Skazki*).
4 The World Peace Council is an international NGO meant to unite supporters of peace in different countries. It was founded in 1950. During the Soviet period, the council was financed and directed primarily by the USSR.

literature (Narkevich 1955; Vertsman 1955; Chernevich 1955; Krymova 1955; Nikolich 1955; and Lukicheva 1955); while others constitute detailed essays describing Andersen's creative manner, discussing his influence on the genre of the literary fairy tale, and analyzing individual works (see the articles by well-known Soviet children's writers: Marshak 1955; Shvarts 1955; Paustovskii 1955; and Inber 1955; and the works by the literary critic Viktor Vazhdaev). In honor of the jubilee, the first Soviet book about Andersen was published—a brief monograph by the Soviet literary critic Aleksandr Pogodin titled *Hans Christian Andersen: A Classic of Danish Literature* (*Gans-Khristian Andersen: Klassik datskoi literatury*).

Every jubilee publication emphasizes, first and foremost, Andersen's democratic spirit, the people (*narod*)-oriented nature of his oeuvre, his confrontation with representatives of the bourgeois classes, and the denunciatory and satirical nature of his tales. "Having come up from the grassroots, the son of a simple craftsman, he learned from the people.... Andersen's life was the courageous struggle of a commoner.... With all his amazing talent, Andersen served his people; he hymned the working man, glorified his honesty, steadfastness, and diligence" (Vazhdaev 1955, 162, 168). "In Andersen's tales, it is usually the people from the cellars and garrets who come out on top" (Shvarts 1955, 168); "Andersen is the hymner of the simple working man" (Rozental' 1955, 11); "Andersen fought against the cult of violence and selfishness prevalent among the reactionary circles of noble-bourgeois society; Andersen's tales are suffused with a love for the working man" (Vertsman 1955, 17). It is characteristic that most of these works refer to Andersen as a "fighter for peace," a frame set by the ideological vector of a jubilee organized in the USSR, after all, on the initiative of the World Peace Council: "Andersen's fairytale world... has already joined the struggle for world peace. Thus are progressive people the world over so warmly celebrating the 150th anniversary of the great storyteller's birth" (Shvarts 1955, 168).

From this time on, articles and pieces on Andersen have regularly appeared in Russian literary and educational periodicals, with publications peaking in jubilee years: 1980 (the 175th anniversary of Andersen's birth), 1995 (the 190th anniversary), and 2005 (Andersen's bicentennial).

The latter half of the Soviet period, from the late 1950s to the late 1980s, saw a broadening in the thematic range of publications on Andersen: there were studies of the illustrations to his books (Zavarova 1969; Rakitin 1970; Tauber 1975), and of the history of the publication of Andersen's tales in tsarist Russia (Blium 1971), pieces on the writer's homes and haunts—Denmark, Copenhagen, Odense (Gankina

1972; Surova 1973), essays on Andersen aimed at child readers (Tsyferov 1968; Razgon 1972), etc. The first Soviet book-length biography of Andersen (Murav'eva 1959) came out in 1959 as part of the popular *Lives of Remarkable People* (*Zhizn' zamechatel'nykh liudei*) series, books of which were particularly beloved and trusted by the mass Soviet reader.

It was a commonplace in publications of this period to speak of Andersen as a recognized classic of children's literature. Aside from that, his oeuvre was evaluated and interpreted in accordance with the officially prescribed ideological vector, the current "social order" (*sotsialnyi zakaz*), and changing cultural orientations and public attitudes.

For example, the period of the Thaw[5] gave rise in the 1960s to a demand for lyricism, romanticism, and fable, and so critics began to emphasize this aspect of Andersen's works, drawing particular attention to the "poeticism" of his style: "Andersen was possessed of a rare poetic gift; a slight, at times unexpected push was enough to get him to unfold a fabulous narrative fabric.... The brilliant genius did not cotton to the gloomy world of religious fanaticism" (Zhernevskaia 1965, 79). Crucial to the formation of the Soviet "Andersen myth" was a slender book by the well-known children's author and screenwriter Gennadii Tsyferov titled *My Andersen* (*Moi Andersen*), first published in 1969 and based on a previously published essay of the same name. Aimed at young children, and representing a free interpretation of episodes from Andersen's life, the book taught the Soviet reader to see Andersen's oeuvre and personality as the quintessence of the fabulous and the magical. We might note that two broadly successful screen adaptations of Andersen's fairy tales—the films *The Snow Queen* (*Snezhnaia koroleva*, 1966) and *The Shadow* (*Ten'*, 1971)—likewise did their part to confer on Andersen, in Soviet mass culture, the status of Storyteller No. 1: a kind of wizard, and himself often like a character in his own tales.[6] The interpretation of Andersen's tales as a special key to the "world of wonder and

---

5 The Thaw is the unofficial designation of the period in Soviet history after the death of Stalin, lasting roughly ten years, from the mid-1950s to the mid-1960s. It was marked by condemnation of the "cult of personality" of Stalin and the repressions of the 1930s, a loosening of totalitarian power, the emergence of some measure of free speech, the relative liberalization of political and social life, openness to the Western world, and greater artistic freedom. On the subject of Andersen and Thaw culture, see Marina Balina's contribution to this volume.

6 For example, the film *The Snow Queen* features a character called "the storyteller," and the character known as "the scholar" in the film *The Shadow* is named Christian-Theodore and composes fairy tales. Both films are based on Evgenii Schwartz's eponymous plays of 1939 and 1940, in which the storyteller's and scholar's lines abound in quotations from Andersen's fairy tales, specifically, from the "authorial narrative" thereof. See Boris Wolfson's contribution to this volume.

magic" persists as a standing cliché in Soviet and post-Soviet literary and pedagogical criticism (see Grossman 1979; Borshchevskaia 1980; Belova 1980; Petukhov 1980; Sharov 1985; etc.).

At the same time, many Soviet publications about Andersen maintained an ideological engagement, offering interpretations tailored to this or that "social order." For example, amid the permanent Cold War and the need to propagandize against the bourgeois way of life, the critic Genadii Fish railed against the "Andersen cult in the mass culture of Western countries," where images of the writer and his characters can be seen "in an advertisement for a bank, on children's pajamas, a keychain, a silver spoon, a lamp, a handkerchief, and even in the name of a sandwich" (Fish 1967, 29). Exclaims the critic: "Andersen has been hijacked by hucksters!" A 1975 article by the prominent children's literature critic Sergei Sivokon, meanwhile, reminds us of the "war on philistinism" campaign launched at that time:

> We never tire of arguing about what philistinism is, and we forget to reread "Thumbelina" and "The Swineherd"; we snatch up and pore over all sorts of pamphlets on 'the subject of love' from bookstalls, and forget to reread "The Little Mermaid," in which, in a fairy tale (a third the length of such pamphlets!), the brilliant Dane expressed everything anyone could ever say about this feeling. (Sivokon' 1975, 49)

In the 1970s–80s, the ruling Communist Party issued various directives on the need to "educate a harmoniously developed person,"[7] and thus in a 1980 article on the 175th anniversary of Andersen's birth, Marianna Borshchevskaia remarks (1980, 94) that "in his modest, unpretentious manner, Andersen offered something important—a model of the harmonious personality."

The late 1980s and early 1990s, the period of the collapse of the Soviet Union and of pivotal political and socioeconomic transformations in the country, was naturally a time of scant publications on Andersen. It has thus far been possible to identify roughly ten publications for 1990-94, two of which are represented in the appendix. The situation regarding

---

7   In 1973, the USSR Supreme Council adopted certain "legislative fundamentals... on public education," enacted on 1 January 1974. This legislation designated one of the main tasks of Soviet schools as "ensuring the comprehensive, harmonious development of students" (*Vedomosti Verkhognogo soveta RSFSR*, no. 32 [1974], 850). This document was of a prescriptive nature, but at the same time contained quite vague formulations; amid widespread discussion of what the concept meant, a great number of "harmonious student development" programs emerged, as did rather demagogic course materials.

Andersen's books and works about him in this period was akin to the situation of 1918-20: Andersen's books for children continued to be published regularly, despite an extreme economic and social instability in some places bordering on devastation; but new studies of his oeuvre were temporarily reduced to nil. However, the 190th anniversary of Andersen's birth (which coincided with the beginnings of economic stabilization in Russia) would be marked by a number of publications, most interestingly, Samuil Lurie's article "Gilded Spheres of Justice" ("Zolochennye shary spravedlivosti"), in which the well-known literary critic seeks to revise the Soviet myth of the "kindly storyteller."

> Andersen's magnet is the human heart. Life is replayed anew. By an effort of faith, by modulating his voice, the storyteller tries to correct the disorderly course of events. This is why it is so easy to take him for a kindly wizard. And we see Andersen as the hero of a Schwartz play or a Paustovsky novella: a fearless, helpless, wise dreamer. (Lur'e 1995, 211)

Lurie is one of the first to write about Andersen's eccentricities and creative failures. He sees the tales' morals as amounting to "fortune cookie wisdom," and emphasizes the cruelty of the plot conflicts in "Thumbelina," "The Swineherd," and "The Red Shoes," the moralizing in the tales "The Cripple" and "The Porter's Son," and concludes: "I have come to understand that it is not Andersen that we love (and in any case, what author would be worth loving as a real character?)—and not even Andersen's fairy tales—but a fairy tale about his fairy tales" (ibid., 212).

With the dictates of communist ideology and censorship no longer shaping public opinion and media discourse, and "social orders" replaced by market demand, post-Soviet Anderseniana expanded its framework considerably: the late 1990s and early 2000s saw new topics, new interpretations, new forms and genres of publications about Andersen.

The corpus of post-Soviet works about Andersen is extensive and does not lend itself to exhaustive description, especially if one considers the numerous publications on the Internet. In the scope of this article, we can remark only on its primary trends. One of them is traditional literary and pedagogical criticism, often borrowing considerations, quotations, and formulations from Soviet articles and pieces (Sivokon' 2001; Sverdlov 2002; Gorbacheva 2004; Seliutina 2005; Rebrova 2005; Rusakova 2005; Medvedeva 2012; etc.). In these articles, Andersen's standing in the pantheon of classic children's literature is incontrovertible. In opposition to this trend are attempts by "grownup" literary scholars to dispel the Andersen myth, to look at his work with fresh eyes, wipe the canonical sheen from the figure of "the Great Storyteller." The most interesting in this latter category are Vail' 1997 and Skul'skaia 2011.

Andersen's eccentric personality, his life abounding in colorful conflicts, and, to a lesser extent, his oeuvre, are the subject of a variety of speculative publications by well-known authors (Pomerantsev 1995; Kuklin 2006), and by authors who write in a frankly sensational and tabloid style (Svechenovskaia 2006; Kazakevich 2007). Writers heatedly attribute to Andersen various pathological inclinations: necrophilia (Vail'), pedophilia (Pomerantsev), and misogyny (Kuklin); while the children's poet and representative of unofficial culture Zhenia Gliukk calls Andersen (2009) "a most remarkable freak" and inducts him into her gallery of "great oddballs." Some of the publications of this kind are included in the appendix; their abundance attests, among other things, to the firm place Andersen has in Russian culture.

One notable trend that could have emerged only in the post-Soviet period consists of works by authors who interpret Andersen's writings in the framework of the Christian paradigm. There are many such publications; in this appendix they are represented by articles and pieces published in the popular Orthodox magazine *Thomas* (*Foma*) (Gavrilova 2006; Bogatyreva 2012; Baglai 2017), and a pamphlet by Galina Sulzhenko. These works emphasize, first and foremost, the Christian component of Andersen's tales, and interpret his personal life as a Christian ministry, a kind of feat of faith. Andersen's monarchism and loyalism, which Soviet critics (to the extent they ever mentioned it) held against him, now become virtues. The authors of these works polemicize with Soviet interpretations: "Soviet publishers managed to create an image of Andersen as a kind of revolutionary and… fighter for the cause of the common people. His hatred for the rich, his love and devotion for the common folk became ideological clichés" (Sul'zhenko 2005, 4). On the one hand, viewing Andersen as a Christian writer revives the tradition of criticism of the late nineteenth and early twentieth century; but, on the other, contemporary Orthodox writers themselves engage in something quite different from literary criticism proper when they interpret Andersen's life and work in the spirit of religious radicalism. For example, in Sulzhenko's study, Andersen's life is described much like a hagiography: he fights tirelessly against demons, resists carnal temptations, engages in polemics with the enemies of the Church (in particular, Søren Kierkegaard), and trusts in the Lord throughout his life.

The Russian Anderseniana of recent years is rich and diverse. Perhaps most characteristic of the present moment is the quest for new forms of publications about Andersen and his work. In this regard we might note Valerii Ronshin's historical novel for children *Andersen* (*Andersen*, 2006); Lidiia Kudriavtseva and Lola Zvonareva's album *Hans Christian Andersen and His Russian Illustrators* (*Khans-Kristian Andersen i ego russkie illiustratory*, 2013); and Nikolai Gorbunov's Andersen-based European travel guide *The House on the Steam Locomotive's Caboose* (*Dom na khvoste parovoza*, 2016). It can be confidently predicted that Russian literary and pedagogical criticism will not lose interest in Andersen's life and works any time soon.

A few words about this index of publications on Andersen for the period from 1924 to 2017. This index includes 150 publications selected from the overall corpus: articles, essays, pieces, a few books, and three prefaces. The index does not include publications printed in newspapers, in editions still being tracked down, and in materials whose publication data cannot be determined. In connection with the subject of this study, also not included here are scholarly works or methodological materials intended for teachers and kindergarten personnel, reviews of adaptations of Andersen's works, or interviews with artists and publishers.

Works Cited

Andersen, G.-Kh. *Skazki*. Moscow: Izdatel'stvo i tipografiia Zhurnal'no-gazetnogo ob"edineniia, 1935.

Olich, J. *Competing Ideologies and Children's Literature in Russia, 1918-1935: How Powerful Actors Attempted to Establish Cultural Uniformity, How the Process was Contested, and How it Failed*. Saarbrücken: VDM Verlag Dr. Müller, 2009.

Ф.И.О. автора	название статьи	название журнала	год	номер	номера страниц
Станчинская Э.	Список книг для детей дошкольного возраста (от 4-8 л.): К III всероссийскому дошкольному съезду	На путях к новой школе	1924	9	129-134
Я. Т-н	Старый сказочник	Красная Нива	1925	49	1198
Горбов Д.	Предисловие	Г.-Х.Андерсен Сказки. Москва: издательство "Новая Москва", гос. типография имени Т.Зиновьева издательства "Ленинградская правда" в Ленинграде	1927		5-10
Дейч А.	Столетие сказки Андерсена	Огонек	1935	16	14
Дейч А.	Сказки Андресена	Детская литература	1937	12 (июнь)	13-14
Лопырева Е.	Андресен и его творчество	Х.-К.Андерсен Сказки и рассказы. Москва-Ленинград: Академия	1937		3-15
Горбатов Л.	Ганс-Христиан Андерсен	Андресен Г.-Х. Сказки. Сталинград: Типография Областного управления издательств и полиграфии	1947		3-4
Сурков А.	Датская сказка	Огонек	1950	3	
Верцман И.	Четыре юбилея (о творчестве Сервантеса, Шиллера, Мицкевича и Х.-К. Андерсена)	Начальная школа	1955	5	12-18
Лукичева Т.	Сказки Андресена: в помощь библиотекарю	Клуб	1955	2	28-29
Наркевич А.	Творец мудрой сказки	Сов. женщина	1955	4	38-39
Николич Д.	Андресен и его сказки: к 150 летию со дня рождения	Советский Казахстан	1955	4	99-100
Погодин А.С.	Ганс-Христиан Андерсен: классик датской литературы	Москва: "Знание"	1955		40
Познанская Л.	Ханс Кристиан Андерсен: к 150-ти летию	Наука и жизнь	1955	4	57-58
Розенталь Н.	Замечательный сказочник [к 150-ти летию]	Народное образование	1955	3	9-14

Ф.И.О. автора	название статьи	название журнала	год	номер	номера страниц
Важдаев В.	Сын датского народа: к 150-ти летию со дня рождения Х.-К.Андерсена	Знамя	1955	4	161-169
Важдаев В.	Ханс-Кристиан Андерсен 1805-1875	Новое время	1955	14	18-20
Инбер В.	Ганс-Христиан Андерсен	Вопросы детской литературы	1955		332-338
Маршак С.	Праздник сказки: к 150-летию со дня рождения Х.К.Андерсена	Вопросы детской литературы	1955		326-330
Крымова Н.	Великий сказочник: к 150-летию со дня рождения Х.К.Андерсена	Советский Союз	1955	4	24
Паустовский К.	Великий сказочник	Андерсен Г.Х Сказки и истории. Москва: Гослитиздат	1955		3-18
Шварц Е.	Три чуда	Нева	1955	2	167-168
Яхнина Ю.	Великий сказочник: к 150-летию со дня рождения Х.К.Андерсена	Смена	1955	6	14
Черневич М.	Любимый сказочник	Огонек	1955	13	12
Важдаев В.	Ганс-Христиан Андерсен: Очерк жизни и творчества	Москва: Детгиз	1957		117
Беленькая Л.	Сказки Андерсена в чтении детей и младших школьников	Сборник студенческих работ Московского Библиотечного университета	1959	вып.1	74-90
Муравьева И.	Андерсен	Москва: Издательство ЦК ВЛКСМ "Молодая гвардия" (серия "Жизнь замечательных людей")	1959		271
Жерневская И.	Сказка его жизни	Наука и религия	1965	4	77-79
Брауде Л.	Настоящая принцесса на горошине (заметки о сказках Андерсена)	Детская литература	1966	3	54-55
Фиш Г.	Вечный спутник: О популярности сказок Х.-К. Андерсена	Детская литература	1967	12	26-29
Цыферов Г.М.	Мой Андерсен	Семья и школа	1968	9	56-57

Ф.И.О. автора	название статьи	название журнала	год	номер	номера страниц
Брауде Л.	Сказки и истории Андерсена 1850-1870-х годов	О литературе для детей	1969	14	133-164
Заварова А.	Оле-Лукойе	Детская литература	1969	12	42-43
Сильман Т.	Сказки Андерсена	Х.-К.Андерсен Сказки и истории. Ленинград: Художественная литература	1969		5-26
Ракитин В.	Цельность восприятия	Детская литература	1970	10	50-57
Блюм А.	"Новое платье короля" и царская цензура	Детская литература	1971	2	60-62
Разгон Л.	Андерсен Ханс Кристиан	Мурзилка	1972	8	7
Ганкина Э.	Далекий и близкий Андерсен	Детская литература	1972	4	72-76
Неструх Я.	Ганс Христиан Андерсен	Начальная школа	1973	9	79-85
Овчинникова С.	Ганс-Христиан Андерсен	Дошкольное воспитание	1973	8	57-68
Сурова Е.	Там, где родился король сказочников	Дошкольное воспитание	1973	8	68-70
Сивоконь С.	Главный из сказочников	Семья и школа	1975	8	48-50
Брауде Л.Ю.	Традиции Андерсена в сказочной литературе	Детская литература	1975		144-157
Андерсен Х.	Из автобиографии	Детская литература	1975	4	36
Таубер В.	Зонтик Оле-Лукойе	Детская литература	1975	4	73-79
Брауде Л.	Литературная сказка Андерсена и фольклор	Детская литература	1978	10	55-61
Гроссман П.	Песни Андерсена	Детская литература	1979	10	55-56
Белова Н.	Лучшее в свете золото... К 175-летию	Огонек	1980	15	29
Краснов А.	Ханс Кристиан Андерсен: к 175 летию	Среднее специальное образование	1980	3	14-16
Петухов Ю.	Оле-Лукойе, сказочник	Семья и школа	1980	4	46-48
Светловская Н.	Сказка его жизни:к 175 летию	Начальная школа	1980	3	74-77
Борисов Б.	Андерсен: История и сказка	В мире книг	1980	4	80
Титова И.	Величайший мастер удивлять людей	Библиотекарь	1980	3	32-36

Ф.И.О. автора	название статьи	название журнала	год	номер	номера страниц
Степанова М.	Великий сказочник	Дошкольное воспитание	1980	3	49-52
Борщевская М.	Этот чувствительный Андерсен	Юность	1980	3	92-94
Смиренская И.	Сказочные юбилеи	Детская литература	1985	4	36-38
Степанова М.	Сказка его жизни	Дошкольное воспитание	1985	4	61-62
Шаров А.	Жизнь в сказке: Мигель де Сервантес; Ганс Христиан Андерсен	Волшебники приходят к людям. Москва: Детская литература	1985		309-317
Паустовский К.Г.	Ночной дилижанс	Золотая роза. Ленинград: детская литература	1987		148-159
Кокорин А.	В стране великого сказочника	Москва: Советский художник	1988		191 с.
Кленков А.	Миф на песке	В мире книг	1989	2	80
Толоконников Н.	Ханс Кристиан Андерсен: К 185летию со дня рождения	Начальная школа	1990	12	63
Ефимова Е.	Мертвое царство и его королевы	Литература в школе	1991	5	89-97
Трофимов А.	Здравствуй, сказочник прекрасный!	Слово	1995	11-12	65-67
Кудрявцева Л	Ах, мой милый Андерсен! (о русских иллюстраторах Андерсена)	Детская литература	1995	3	67-77
Лурье С.	Золоченые шары справедливости	Звезда	1995	7	210-212
Полякова Н.	Великий сказочник	Дошкольное воспитание	1995	4	86-89
Померанцев И.	Датский лепет	Новое время	1995	41	48
Фридкин В.	Зеркальце: [О последних днях жизни Андерсена]	Наука и жизнь	1995	12	94-97
Мурадян К.	"Дикая птица высокого полёта"	Витрина	1995	13-14	15
Вайль П.	Сказки народов севера: Копенгаген – Андерсен, Осло – Мунк	Иностранная литература	1997	12	215-229
Паустовский К.	Литературные портреты	Школьная роман-газета	1998	10	31-72
Трофимов А.	Сын башмачника	М.: Армада	1998		394 с.

Ф.И.О. автора	название статьи	название журнала	год	номер	номера страниц
Харитонова О.	Что есть красота и почему её обожествляют люди?	Литература в школе	1999	8	56
Анатольева М.	Золотая медаль Х.-К. Андерсена	Детская литература	1999	5-6	128-132
Корф О.	Сказке "Снежная королева" - 155 лет!	Детская литература	1999	5-6	112-113
Михайлова А.	Стойкий оловянный солдатик	Начальная школа: Приложение к газете "Первое сентября"	1999	19	15
Кривцов Н.	Живые предания старого замка: [Замок Кронборг и сказка Г.-Х. Андерсена "Хольгер датчанин"]	Всемирный следопыт	1999	8	12-18
Зюзюкин И.	Сказка его жизни	Смена	2000	9	24-251
Киреев Р.	"Дженни Линд не пригласила меня"	Наука и религия	2000	9	22-25
Овселян Н.	Волшебник и его тень	Новое время	2000	46	38-40
Никифорова С.	Снежная королева	Литература в школе	2000	1	107-110
Жуланова И.	Король сказки	Костер	2000	4	16-27
Сивоконь С.	Ханс Кристиан Андерсен:Сказка моей жизни	Детская литература	2001	4	38-39
Молдавская К.	Чтение в радость	Книжное обозрение	2002	52	22
Свердлов М.	Сказки и сказочники	Литература: Приложение к газете "Первое сентября"	2002	34	5-12
Шмелева В.	Знамя датского короля	Вокруг света	2002	4	30-38
Трофимов А.	"Не я выбрал сказку, а она меня …"	Детская литература	2002	4	9-13
Малая С.	Домашнее чтение: классические рождественские сказки и "всякая святочная всячина" - от Чарльза Диккенса до Аркадия Гайдара	Читаем, учимся, играем	2003	9	84-86
Рагозина К.	Кай, Кей и несчастная Герда	Книжное обозрение	2003	18	24

Ф.И.О. автора	название статьи	название журнала	год	номер	номера страниц
Горбачева А.	Торжество сказки: юбилей великого мастера	Библиотечное дело	2004	12	2-3
Жаров Б.	Переводчики Ганзены	Автобус	2004	2	6-8
Киреев Р.	Андерсен. Превращение гадкого утенка	Литература: Прил. к газ. "Первое сент."	2004	1	2-6
Симонова Н.	Сказки зарубежных авторов	Начальная школа: Приложение к газете "Первое сентября"	2004	23	25-27
	Сказка длиною в жизнь	Чиж и Ёж	2004	21-22	22-23
Сергеев А., Чеканский А.	Вступление: Ханс Кристиан Андерсен: Сказки и истории	Иностранная литература	2005	7	64-75
Квирикидзе Ир.	Мой Андерсен	Сеанс	2005	25-26	45-56
Багров П.	Свинарка и пастух: от Ганса Христиана к Христиану Гансу	Сеанс	2005	25-26	92-97
Трофимов А.	Флаг страны сказок	Начальная школа	2005	4	3-7
Селютина Е.	Новое платье Андерсена	Лицейское и гимназическое образование	2005	4	13-15
Александрова, Я.	В зачарованных далях: к 200-летию со дня рождения Ганса Христиана Андерсена	Культура и время	2005	3	209-211
Бегичева В.	Дикие лебеди	Наука и религия	2005	5	52-55
Кульбицкий Г.	Сказочник	Эхо планеты	2005	12	26-31
Августин (архмандрит Августин / Никитин)	В городе великого сказочника	Эхо планеты	2005	13	30-32
Каминская К.	Принцесса на Пречистенке	Эхо планеты	2005	15	18-20
Августин (архмандрит Августин / Никитин)	В Андерсеновском Копенгагене	Нева	2005	4	256-260
Зурабова К.	Песенка никогда не кончается: О Жизни и творчестве Ханса Кристиана Андерсена	Дошкольное воспитание	2005	7	97-105

Ф.И.О. автора	название статьи	название журнала	год	номер	номера страниц
Алексеев Н.	Сказка сказок: к 200-летию со жня рождения Г.-Х. Андерсена	Пионер	2005	4	10-12
	Однажды на острове Фюн	Костер	2005	4	12-13
Реброва А	Самый любимый сказочник: Ханс Кристиан Андерсен	Библиотека в школе: Приложение к газета "Первое сентября"	2005	5	46-47
Русакова Е.	К юбилею великого сказочника	Воспитание школьников	2005	7	63-64
Русакова Е.	Сказочный мир Андерсена	Детская роман-газета	2005	7	1-15
	С днем рождения, Сказочник!	А почему?	2005	5	32
Шеваров Д.	Даже самой большой стране хватит места на ладони сказочника	Начальная школа: Приложение к газете "Первое сентября"	2005	2	33
Казакова И.	На мои рисунки смотрит Андерсен	Костер	2005	4	4
Кудрявцева Л	Сказочник на все времена	Работница	2005	1	41-43
Платонова Н., Диодоров Б.	Уроки великого сказочника	Юный художник	2005	7	1-2
Романов О.	Карнавал в честь Андерсена	Книжное обозрение	2005	20	18
Онуфриенко Г.	Волшебник из датского королевства	Обсерватория культуры	2005	5	78-87
Сульженко Г.	Сказка его жизни: христианский путь Х.-К. Андерсена	Санкт-Петербург: Издательство "Шандал"	2005		96
Путилова Е.	Андерсен, прочитанный сегодня	Личность и культра	2005	2; 3	60-64; 54-58
Свеченовская И.	Андерсен. Плата за успех	Санкт-Петербург: Нева	2006		320
Гаврилова Е.	Божий мир в сказках и иллюстрациях Андерсена	Православный журнал "Фома"	2006	1 (33)	96-101
Куклин Л.	Жестокость добрых: Г.-Х.Андерсен и А.П. Чехов	Литература это интересно. Санкт-Петербруг: Издательство журнала "Нева"	2006		325-339
Роньшин В.	Андерсен	Москва: Белый город	2006		64

Ф.И.О. автора	название статьи	название журнала	год	номер	номера страниц
Щербаков В.	Снежная королева - кто она?	Наука и религия	2007	1	43-64
Киямова Н.	Вступительная статья к публикации фрагментов из книги Х.-К. Андерсена "Базар поэта"	Иностранная литература	2007	12	241-260
Казакевич А.	"Рабочие подкрались к нему сзади …"	Звезды как люди. Ростов-на-Дону: Феникс	2007		398-445
Веселова В.	История, увиденная в зеркалах	Вопросы литературы	2008	2	183-200
Гордиенко Е.	Великий сказочник	Смена	2008	2	140-145
Брауде Л.	По волшебным тропам Андерсена	Санкт-Петербург: Алетейя	2008		264
Дайс Е.	Алхимик Андерсен	Нева	2009	7	177-183
Онуфриенко Г.	Ах, мой милый Андерсен, Андерсен …	Мир библиографии	2009	6	45-53
Козьмина Л.	Михайловское и Копенгаген	Столицы и усадьбы	2009	6	59-62
Глюкк Ж.	Андерсен: Грустный сказочник веселого царства	Великие чудаки. Москва:Олимп, Астрель	2009		201-211
Скульская Е.	Буквальные истории	Знамя	2011	8	174-183
Бегичева В.	Огниво	Наука и религия	2012	1	47-50
Иванова Э.	Человек и его тень	Искусство в школе	2012	6	23-26
Богатырева Н.	Лучший иллюстратор Андерсена: О художнике Борисе Диодорове	Православный журнал "Фома"	2012	12 (116)	80-87
Авакова Ю.	"Сальная свеча" Х.-К. Андерсена "История одной сказки"	Театр. Живопись,Кино. Музыка	2012	4	171-183
Медведева И.	Мир добра и красоты великого сказочника	Практический журнал для учителя и администрации школы	2012	3	47-50
Пожидаева Е.	День рождения Сказочника	Начальная школа	2013	3	88-91
Ерхов Б.	Андерсен	Москва: Молодая гвардия (серия "Жизнь замечательных людей")	2013		252
Кудрявцева Л., Звонарева Л.	Ханс-Кристиан Андерсен и его русские иллюстраторы	Москва: Издательство Московские учебники и картолитография.	2013		352

Ф.И.О. автора	название статьи	название журнала	год	номер	номера страниц
Звонарева Л.	"Я стал заядлым рисовальщиком …"	Иностранная литература	2014	11	270-276
Сопин О.	Путешествие в страну Андерсена	Юный художник	2015	8	6-7
Стасевич В. А., Болурова-Кунавина П. В.	Христианские мотивы в сказках Г. Х. Андерсена "Снежная королева"	Юный ученый	2015	2	167-169
Горелик М.Я.	Хождение за возлюбленным	Новый мир	2016	7	166-176
Горбунов Н.	Дом на хвосте паровоза: Путешествие по Европе в сказках Андерсена	Москва: Livebook	2016		432
Баглай К.	Легендарные христианские книги: Х.-К. Андресен "Снежная королева"	Православный журнал "Фома"	2017	1 (165)	66-67

Contributors

MARINA BALINA

Marina Balina is Isaac Funk professor of Russian studies at Illinois Wesleyan University (Bloomington, IL). Her primary research interests are children's literature in Soviet Russia and its historical development, and the hybrid nature of life-writing in Soviet and post-Soviet Russia (autobiography, memoir, diary, and travelogue). She is the coeditor of *Politicizing Magic: An Anthology of Russian and Soviet Fairy Tales* (2005), *Russian Children's Literature and Culture* (2008), *Petrified Utopia: Happiness Soviet Style* (2009), *The Cambridge Companion to Twentieth-Century Russian Literature* (2011), *Killing Charskaia: Paradoxes of Soviet Children's Literature of the 1920s and 1930s* ("*Ubit' Charskuiu...": Paradoksy sovetskoi literatury dlia detei, 1920-e–1930-e gg.*, 2014), and *Pedagogy of Images: Depicting Communism for Children* (forthcoming).

JOHS. NØRREGAARD FRANDSEN

Johs. Nørregaard Frandsen is professor and director of the Hans Christian Andersen Center, University of Southern Denmark (Odense). He is Head of Danish Ministry of Culture's Board for Research and vice-chair of the National Hans Christian Andersen Foundation. Frandsen is the coeditor of *H. C. Andersen and Modern Society* (*H. C. Andersen i det moderne samfund*, 2014), *Hans Christian Andersen in China* (2014), *Hans Christian Andersen and José Rizal: From Denmark to the Philippines* (2018), and *Hans Christian Andersen and Community* (2019), and the author of numerous books and articles in the field of Danish literary and cultural history.

HELENA GOSCILO

Helena Goscilo is professor of Slavic at Ohio State University (Columbus OH). She has written on sundry aspects of Russian and Polish culture, ranging from folklore and literature to art and film. She is the coeditor of *Preserving Petersburg: History, Memory, Nostalgia* (2008), *Cinepaternity: Fathers and Sons in Soviet and Post-Soviet Film* (2010), *Celebrity and Glamour in Contemporary Russia: Shocking Chic* (2011), and *Russian Aviation, Space Flight, and Visual Culture* (2016); the editor of *Putin as Celebrity and Cultural Icon* (2012); and coauthor of *Fade from Red: Screening the Cold War Ex-Enemy 1990-2005* (2014). She is currently working on a monograph titled *Graphic Ideology: The Soviet Poster from Stalin to Yeltsin,* and a study (coauthored with Beth Holmgren) of contemporary Polish film.

KARIN GRELZ

Karin Grelz is a researcher and translator affiliated with Stockholm University, specializing in modern Russian literature in general and the authorship of Marina Tsvetaeva in particular. She is the author of *Beyond the Noise of Time: Readings of Marina Tsvetaeva's Memories of Childhood* (2004), as well as articles on Boris Pasternak, Anna Akhmatova, and Vladimir Nabokov, focusing on questions concerning art and ethics recurring among representatives of this generation of Russian writers. She has translated Lidiia Ginzburg's *Notes from the Blockade* (*Zapiski blokadnogo cheloveka*, 1985) and Petr Kropotkin's *Memoirs of a Revolutionist* (*Zapiski revoliutsionera*, 1894-95) into Swedish.

ELENA GUROVA

Elena Gurova is associate professor of Danish at St. Petersburg State University. She teaches Danish-Russian translation and Danish grammar, phonetics, and speaking etiquette. Her PhD dissertation (2008) analyzes the category of adjective-forming semi-affixes in modern Danish. Her primary research interests are Danish philology, stylistics, and cultural studies. She is the author of several articles on Danish word-formation, slang, and speaking etiquette. She has translated several Danish children's books, novels, and plays into Russian.

BEN HELLMAN

Ben Hellman is senior lecturer emeritus of Russian literature at the University of Helsinki. His fields of expertise include Russian children's literature and the history of the reception of Tolstoy in the Scandinavian literatures. Among his main publications are *Meetings and Clashes: Articles on Russian Literature* (*Vstrechi i stolknoveniia. Stat'i po russkoi literature*, 2009), *Fairy Tales and True Stories: The History of Russian Literature for Children and Young People* (2013, translated into Russian in 2016), *At Tolstoy's Place: Nordic Meetings in Life and Poetry* (*Hemma hos Tolstoj. Nordiska möten i liv och dikt*, 2017), and *Poets of Hope and Despair: The Russian Symbolists in War and Revolution* (1995, second ed. 2018).

PETER ALBERG JENSEN

Peter Alberg Jensen is professor emeritus of Russian literature at Stockholm University. His main field of interest is the development of modern Russian prose. He is the author of *Nature as Code: The Achievement of Boris Pilnjak 1914-1924* (1979) and of articles on, among other writers, Pilniak, Boris Pasternak and Anton Chekhov. Pasternak's life-long endeavor to write a great novel is a recurrent topic. Besides the analysis published in the present volume Jensen has also written about Andersen's "The Steadfast Tin Soldier" in Pasternak's story "Lyuvers' Childhood" and on Jens Peter Jacobsen's novel *Niels Lyhne* in *Doctor Zhivago*. He is co-editor of *Pasternak and His Time* (*Boris Pasternak och hans tid*, 1990). In general, his analyses deal with constituents of narrative, such as time and situation or (hi)story and lyricism. He has also written on intricacies in Mikhail Bakhtin's philosophy of dialogue.

MADS SOHL JESSEN

Mads Sohl Jessen is postdoctoral at the Hans Christian Andersen Center (Odense) specializing in nineteenth-century Danish literature. He has published in English and Danish on Andersen and the Grimm brothers, Søren Kierkegaard as a satirist (in the journal *Kierkegaard Studies Yearbook* and the volume *Between Vaudeville, Romantic Comedy and National Drama: The Heibergs and the Theater* [2012]), and Danish poets of the romantic and postromantic periods (Jens Baggesen, Adam Oehlenschläger, and Sophus Claussen). He is working on a monograph on Andersen's major tales as they relate to the European fairytale tradition from Straparola to the Grimms.

ELENA KRASNOVA

Elena Krasnova is associate professor of Danish at St. Petersburg State University, where she has taught Danish and a range of scholarly topics since 1981, and is currently chair of the Department of Scandinavian and Dutch Philology. She has served as a visiting lecturer at the University of Copenhagen and Aarhus University. Her research is focused on Danish lexicology, lexicography, translation theory, and cultural studies. She has published a Danish-Russian dictionary (2005), and translated about thirty Danish books into Russian.

ILYA KUKULIN

Ilya Kukulin is associate professor of cultural studies at the Higher School of Economics (HSE) (Moscow). He has published widely on Russian literature (especially poetry), the history of education in twentieth-century Eastern Europe, cultural practices of internal colonization in Russia, unofficial social thought in twentieth-century Russia, and the political discourses of Russian social media. In 2015, he was awarded the Andrei Bely Prize for his monograph *Machines of Noisy Time: How Soviet Montage Became an Aesthetic Method of Unofficial Culture* (*Mashiny zashumevshego vremeni. Kak sovetskii montazh stal metodom neofitsial'noi kul'tury*), and in 2017, the Bella Prize for the year's best article on contemporary poetry.

OLEG LEKMANOV

Oleg Lekmanov is professor of the humanities at the Higher School of Economics (HSE) (Moscow). The area of his scholarly interest encompasses Russian literature past and present, and film. Among his numerous books and articles are the monographs *Poets and Newspapers* (*Poety i gazety*, 2013), *Russian Poetry in 1913* (*Russkaya poeziya v 1913 godu*, 2014), *Here is the Cheering forward running… Football in Russian and Soviet Poetry* (*Likuyet forvard na begu… Futbol v russkoy i sovetskoy poezii*, 2016), and numerous other topics. His groundbreaking monograph on Osip Mandelstam was brought out in English in 2010 by Academic Studies Press.

YURI LEVING

Yuri Leving is University Research professor of Russian studies at Dalhousie University (Halifax). He is the author of six monographs and editor of six volumes of articles, most recently, *A Revolution of the Visible* (2018), *Marketing Literature and Posthumous Legacies* (2013), *Lolita: The Story of a Cover Girl – Vladimir Nabokov's Novel in Art and Design* (2013), and *Anatomy of a Short Story: Nabokov's Puzzles, Codes, "Signs and Symbols"* (2012). The 2017 recipient of AATSEEL's award for outstanding contribution to scholarship, he has published over a hundred articles on various aspects of Russian and comparative literature and cinema, and served as a commentator to the first authorized Russian edition of the collected works of Vladimir Nabokov.

VLADIMIR ORLOV

Vladimir Orlov is associate professor at St. Petersburg State University. His scholarly training is in both performance (piano and organ) and musicology. He received his PhD (for his dissertation on the Soviet cantatas and oratorios of Sergei Prokofiev) in 2011. He has been awarded several distinctions, including St. Petersburg State University's teaching award for 2017. He has published widely in English and Russian on Russian and Soviet music, music education, music and gender, and other subjects, and has spoken at conferences and delivered invited lectures in the United States, Europe, Japan, China, and Russia.

ANDREI ROGATCHEVSKI

Andrei Rogatchevski is professor of Russian literature and culture at UiT The Arctic University of Norway. Most recently he has co-edited *Punishment as a Crime? Perspectives on Prison Experience in Russian Culture* (2014) and *Russophone Periodicals in Israel: A Bibliography* (2016), as well as co-authored *A War of Songs: Popular Music and Recent Russia-Ukraine Relations* (2019).

INNA SERGIENKO

Inna Sergienko (Antipova) is a researcher at the Institute of Russian Literature (Pushkin House) of the Russian Academy of Sciences (St. Petersburg). Her primary interest is the history of children's literature and bibliography. She is the author of fifty publications on the history and theory of children's literature, and a member of the editorial board of the journal *Children's Reading* (*Detskie chteniia*).

BORIS WOLFSON

Boris Wolfson is associate professor of Russian studies at Amherst (MA) College and chair of its Department of Russian. He has published essays on nineteenth-, twentieth-, and twenty-first century Russian cultural history, and recently coedited *Russian Performances: Word, Object, Action* (2018), the first volume to bring the fields of performance studies and Russian studies into dialogue. He has also coedited *The Time of Catastrophe* (2015), a multidisciplinary examination of the catastrophic imagination, and a special issue of the journal *College Literature* on the future of the humanities. His study of theater, performance, and modes of self-understanding in the Soviet 1930s is forthcoming.

BORIS ZHAROV

Boris Zharov is professor emeritus of Scandinavian studies at St. Petersburg State University. He has published widely on topics in Scandinavian languages, literatures, and cultures. He contributed the English-language study "Dynamism in Perception of Hans Christian Andersen in Saint Petersburg, One of the Most Andersenous Cities of the World" to the volume *Hans Christian Andersen: Between Children's Literature and Adult Literature* (2007).

Index of Names

A
Adler-Olsen, Jussi 338
Akhmadulina, Bella 329
Akhmatova, Anna 14, 137-39, 143, 150-52, 155, 156, 188, 260, 261, 472
Akimov, Nikolai 252, 287, 306, 307
Akimova, Natalya 16, 420-22
Aksenchuk, Ivan 327-29, 367
Aleksandr Aleksandrovich 66, 67
Aleksandrov, Iakov 94-96, 98, 109
Aleksandrovich, Nikolai (film director) 286, 377-79, 384
Alexander I 27
Alexander II 47, 66, 67, 86, 88
Alexander III 13, 47, 52, 66, 67
Aliger, Margarita 261
Amalrik, Andrei 367
Anderson, Pamela 418
Annensky, Innokentii 139, 140, 142, 143, 180
Antokolsky, Pavel 190
Antonioni, Michelangelo 303
Arkhangelsky, Aleksandr 309
Arkhipova, Anastasiia 419
Arnim, Bettina von 180
Artaud, Antonin 254
Artemova, Galina 330
Asbjørnsen, Peter Christen 89
Atamanov, Lev 16, 361, 363, 368, 372-74, 376, 377, 384
Augustine 319
Austin, J. L. 251, 255
Averbakh, Ilya 445

B
Babel, Isaak 262, 352, 415
Bakhtin, Mikhail 130, 330, 333, 473
Bakhtin, Nikolai 97, 130, 131
Baklanov, Grigorii 272
Balmont, Konstantin 137, 138
Balzac, Honoré de 80, 272
Barbe, Vladen 368, 380-82, 384
Barto, Agnia 425
Baskov, Nikolai 378
Baudelaire, Charles 170, 173, 177
Baudrillard, Jean 360
Bauer, Evgenii 321
Bek, Aleksandr 261
Beketova, Mariia 105, 109

Bekmambetov, Timur 363, 381
Belinsky, Vissarion 80, 100
Bely, Andrei 138, 176, 196, 474
Benois, Aleksandr 235, 238, 345, 347, 348, 349, 352, 354
Béranger, Pierre-Jean de 28, 29, 39
Berggolts, Olga 259
Bergson Henri 279, 280
Berlusconi, Silvio 446
Bestuzhev, Aleksandr 44
Bilibin, Ivan 320, 345, 354, 355, 389, 394-401, 405, 407, 413, 416, 420, 422
Bjørnson, Bjørnstjerne 53, 54
Blaedel, Sara 338
Blixen, Karen 338
Blok, Aleksandr 138, 167, 173, 175-77, 180, 183, 185, 187-89, 192, 195, 204, 223, 224
Bogomolov, Vladimir 370
Boiarsky, Nikolai 376
Borodin, Aleksandr 236
Bortko, Vladimir 369
Boyle, Eleanor Vere 356
Branagh, Kenneth 379
Brandes, Georg 53-56, 89, 93, 94, 101, 104, 107, 109
Braude, Liudmila 12, 55, 454
Bresson, Robert 369
Brezhnev, Leonid 263
Briusov, Valerii 137, 138, 180, 320
Brueghel, Pieter 409
Brylska, Barbara 284
Buck, Chris 383
Bulatov, Erik 401
Bulgakov, Mikhail 262, 369
Buzinova, Maiia 367
Bychkov, Vladimir 286, 329-33, 336, 337, 367, 395, 402, 407
Bykov, Dmitrii 293, 295, 444
Bykov, Rolan 307
Byron, Lord 21, 31, 51

C
Carl Friedrich 27
Carroll, Lewis 334, 359
Catullus 415
Cavos, Catterino 319
Chamisso, Adelbert von 252
Chekhov, Anton 369, 409, 473
Chekhov, Nikolai 89

Chernyshevsky, Nikolai 80
Chizhikov, Viktor 359
Christian IX 66, 68
Chukovsky, Kornei 13, 425
Chulkov, Georgii 176
Collin, Jonas 23, 27, 94
Collin, Louise 44
Coppola, Francis Ford 379
Corman, Roger 381
Cousteau, Jacques 400

D
Dagmar 49, 57, 61, 65-71
Dal, Oleg 307
Dal, Vladimir 44
Daniel, Iulii 264
Danilko, Andrei 379
Dargomyzhsky, Aleksandr 319, 320
Debussy, Claude 235
Dekhterev, Boris 349
Delavigne, Casimir 28
Denisenko, Marisa 424
Desbordes-Valmore, Marceline 177
Dezaki, Osamu 382
Diaghilev, Sergei 234, 238, 348,
Dickens, Charles 64, 80, 117, 166, 267, 272, 402
Dinesen, Isak 228
Diodorov, Boris 343, 405-08, 410
Dobroliubov, Aleksandr 80, 82, 97, 100
Dobuzhinsky, Mstislav 144, 346-48, 352, 354
Dolin, Boris 286
Dostoevsky, Feodor 15, 115-19, 132, 223, 280, 326, 369
Douksha, Iosif 367
Doyle, Arthur Conan 415
Dragunsky, Viktor 302
Dreyer, Carl 338
Druzhbinsky, Valerii 263
Dulac, Edmund 391, 392, 399, 405
Dunsky, Iulii 306, 307, 308, 309

E
Efremov, Oleg 377
Efron, Elizaveta 166
Efron, Sergei 162, 164, 176, 177
Ehrenburg, Ilya 259, 260, 262, 264
Engelfeldt, Mariia Aleksandrovna 52
Erdlei, Stanislav 380
Ershov, Petr 126
Etush, Vladimir 307
Evreinov, Nikolai 308
Evtushenko, Evgenii 262, 284
Evtushevskaia, Albina 334

F
Fadeev, Aleksandr 260
Farina, Andrea 391
Fedin, Konstantin 260
Feoktistov, Ivan 90, 98, 102, 103, 104, 131
Flaubert, Gustave 80
Fouqué, Friedrich de la Motte 320, 323
Frai, Maks 299
Frid, Valerii 306, 307, 308, 309

G
Gaideburov, Pavel 94
Galich, Aleksandr 327
Gelmerson, Vasilii 420
Gelsted, Otto 43, 44
Gerdt, Zinovii 283
Gergiev, Valerii 232
Gippius, Zinaida 320
Glebova-Sudeikina, Olga 144
Glinka, Mikhail 236
Gogol, Nikolai 44, 131, 320, 409
Golikov, Ivan 422, 425
Golman, Viktor 347
Goncharov, Ivan 52
Goncharov, Vasilii 320, 321, 326, 336, 337
Gorky, Maksim 121, 231
Gorodetsky, Sergei 138
Gozzi, Carlo 237
Grimm, Jacob and Wilhelm 77, 84, 106, 126, 415, 420, 473
Grin, Aleksandr 263
Grundtvig, Svend 89
Gubarev, Vitalii 308
Guiccioli, Elena 274
Gumilev, Nikolai 138, 150-53, 155, 156
Günderrode, Karoline von 180

H
Hamsun, Knut 53
Hanck, Henriette 37
Hansen, Anna 51, 52, 58, 69, 70, 77, 107, 125, 141, 343, 437, 439
Hansen, Peter Emanuel 51-58, 69, 70, 77, 107, 125, 141, 343, 437, 439
Hartzell, Päivi 383
Hauff, Wilhelm 77, 106
Heiberg, Johan Ludvig 28
Heine, Heinrich 21, 29, 51, 272, 281
Herzen, Aleksandr 80
Hoffmann, E. T. A. 77, 126, 128, 131, 144, 161
Holberg, Ludvig 357
Howitt, Mary 34
Hugo, Victor 21, 28, 29, 51
Høedt, F. L. 51

Index of Names

477

I
Ianyshev, Ioann 66
Iashin, Aleksandr 261
Ibsen, Henrik 53, 54, 89
Ikskiul, Iuliia 81, 85, 100
Ingemann, B. S. 22
Iser, Wolfgang 356
Iungvald-Khilkevich, Georgii 369
Ivanov, Viacheslav 138
Iwasaki, Chihiro 392
Izmailov, Aleksandr 121

J
Jacobsen, Jens Peter 53, 473
Jakobson, Roman 363
Jensen, Johannes V. 53

K
Kabakov, Ilya 401
Kalaushin, Boris 349
Kant, Immanuel 279
Karamzin, Nikolai 44, 50, 326
Karavaichuk, Oleg 445
Kaverin, Veniamin 261, 306, 309-11
Kazakov, Iurii 272
Kazansky, Gennadii 374-77, 379, 384
Keilhau, Baltazar Mathias 37, 38
Kemnits, Evgenii 83, 84, 97
Kharms, Daniil 344
Khazanov, Gennady 379
Khlebnikov, Velimir 310
Khrushchev, Nikita 260, 287, 375
Kierkegaard, Søren 338, 459, 473
Kim, Svetlana 421
Kipling, Rudyard 267
Klimov, Elem 369
Klimova, Natalya 374
Klodt, Mikhail 49, 50, 342
Kobylinsky, Lev ("Ellis") 173, 175, 176
Kochetkov, Aleksandr 284
Kodiukova, Irina 367
Kokorin, Anatoli 286
Kommisarzhevskaia, Vera 183, 192
Konashevich, Vladimir 343, 345, 348-50, 359
Konchalovsky, Andrei 336
Konenko, Anatolii 420
Kosheverova, Nadezhda 286, 287, 306-11
Kozintsev, Grigorii 262
Kozlov, Sergei 297-300, 305-07, 312
Kramskoi, Ivan 319
Krivin, Feliks 289-92, 294, 297, 299
Kruglov, Aleksandr 98
Krutoi, Igor 379
Krzhizhanovsky, Sigizmund 254, 255

Kuleshov, Lev 372
Kur, Samuil 289
Kurosawa, Akira 369
Kushner, Aleksandr 301
Kuzmin, Mikhail 143, 144
Kvinikhidze, Leonid 283

L
Lagerlöf, Selma 53, 77
Lang, Fritz 361
Lebedev, Vladimir 344, 401
Lec, Stanislaw Jerzy 292
Lee, Jennifer 383
Lenin, Vladimir 123
Leonov, Evgenii 376
Lerdam, Jørgen 382
Lermontov, Mikhail 44, 293, 320
Lind, Agnethe 44-46
Lindgren, Astrid 355
Lissitzky, El 347, 390
Liubimov, Iurii 262
Lokshin, Aleksandr 328
Lomaev, Anton 352, 353, 415-18, 424
Lorck, Carl Berendt 23-26, 39
Louise 66, 68
Lugansky, Kazak 44
Luknitsky, Pavel 151
Lukšas, Gytis 286
Lundbye, Johan Thomas 119

M
Magaril, Mikhail 341, 342, 344, 345, 360
Mainov, Vladimir 95
Makovsky, Konstantin 319, 389
Makovsky, Sergei 94
Mandelshtam, Osip 138, 139, 143, 145-50, 152, 156, 183, 185, 188, 196, 262
Manderstjerna, Elisabeth von 48
Mariia Fedorovna 47, 52, 57, 61, 65, 67-71
Mariia Pavlovna 27
Marmier, Xavier 37
Marshak, Samuil 344, 429, 455
Martynchik, Svetlana 299
Mavrina, Tatyana 391
Melchior, Louise 69
Melikian, Anna 333-37
Melville, Herman 415
Meshcherskaia, Nina 230
Meyerhold, Vsevolod 237
Mickiewicz, Adam 35
Mikhalkov, Nikita 369
Milne, A. A. 405
Minkov, Mark 379
Mironov, Andrei 283
Mitchell, W. J. T. 390

Mitusov, Stepan 234, 235
Miyazaki, Hayao 361
Molbech, Christian 26
Morits, Iunna 283
Mother Teresa 324
Murashko, Nikolai 393, 394
Muravyov, Mikhail 320
Møller, Peder Ludvig 36, 43

N

Nabokov, Vladimir 415, 472, 474
Napoleon 22, 25-30, 33, 34, 39, 48, 124, 166
Narbut, Vladimir 138
Neiolova, Marina 307, 308
Nenov, Vladimir 418-20, 422, 423
Nerman, Einar 346, 347, 352
Nexø, Martin Andersen 43
Nicholas I 22, 35, 39, 47
Nielsen, Kay 391
Nietzsche, Friedrich 168, 191, 192, 279
Nikitenko, Valerii 376
Nikitin, Sergei 283
Nikitin, Tatyana 283
Nikolai Aleksandrovich 47, 49, 66
Nikulin, Valentin 329
Nordau, Max 89, 102
Nordenskiöld, Adolf Erik 360
Norshtein, Iurii 300
Novikova, Klara 379
Novikova, Viktoriia 329, 395

O

Oehlenschläger, Adam 22, 37, 473
Okudzhava, Bulat 261, 293-97
Olesha, Iurii 262
Orbakaite, Kristina 378

P

Paleček, Josef 392
Panov, Vladimir 349, 351, 352, 354
Papernik, Maksim 378-80, 382, 384
Parnok, Sofiia 180, 189
Pascal, Blaise 319
Pasternak, Boris 162, 188, 189, 195, 196, 198, 199, 204, 206, 211, 212, 221, 223-25, 261, 472, 473
Paul I 27
Paustovsky, Konstantin 246, 251, 259, 261-76, 288, 289, 290, 304, 305, 331, 458
Pavlova, Karolina 51
Pedersen, Vilhelm 342, 344, 391
Perrault, Charles 77, 415
Petrov, Aleksandr 321-23, 337
Petrov, Mikhail 351, 352
Petrushevskaia, Liudmilla 311-13, 443, 444
Pio, Jean 56

Pivovarov, Viktor 358, 359, 389, 401-04, 407, 413
Pleshcheev, Aleksei 240
Pogorelsky, Antonii 357
Pomerantsev, Vladimir 259, 459
Povaliy, Taisia 379
Proklova, Elena 374
Prokofiev, Sergei 224, 229-37, 240, 241, 474
Prokofieva, Lina 231
Protazanov, Iakov 361
Puccini, Giacomo 235
Pushkin, Aleksandr 31, 32, 35-37, 43, 44, 48-50, 120, 126, 131, 168, 268, 286, 309, 320-22, 326, 331, 336, 337, 423, 436, 475
Pyryev, Ivan 369

R

Rackham, Arthur 391, 398, 405, 420
Raiskaia, Elena 379, 380, 384
Rasputin, Valentin 369
Rebus, Dima 361, 437
Repin, Ilya 389, 394
Riazanov, Eldar 283, 284
Richardson, Samuel 326
Rimsky-Korsakov, Nikolai 229, 236
Rogova, Olga 88, 91, 92, 104, 105
Rublev, Andrei 409
Rue, Harald 43
Rückert, Friedrich 116-19
Rytsarev, Boris 286, 367

S

Samoilov, David 261
Sapgir, Genrikh 299, 300
Schiller, Friedrich 267, 280
Schwartz, Evgenii 243-56, 286, 287, 306, 375, 376, 432, 455, 458
Scott, Walter 31, 32
Scriabin, Aleksandr 236, 237
Scudder, Horace E. 68
Semenova, Mariia 415
Semyonov, Leonid 122
Senkevich, Iurii 329, 333
Serdiuchka, Verka 379
Shakespeare, William 262, 369, 409
Shalaeva, Mariia 334
Shcherbachev, Iurii 93, 105
Shepard, Aaron 409
Shklovsky, Victor 304
Simonov, Konstantin 260
Siniavsky, Andrei 264
Skrinichenko, Irina 334
Slutsky, Boris 261
Smirnova, Vera 423, 424
Sokova, Mariia 334

Solovyov, Vladimir 237
Solzhenitsyn, Aleksandr 264
Somov, Orest 320
Sorokin, Vladimir 401
Spirin, Gennadil 409-16, 418, 422
Stalin, Joseph 165, 259, 260, 263, 271, 291, 373, 375, 376, 446
Stasova, Nadezhda 49, 85, 105, 127, 342
Stendhal 80
Stravinsky, Igor 229, 230, 232-41, 348
Strindberg, August 53
Surkov, Aleksei 260, 346
Sveshnikov, Maksim 268, 380-82, 384
Svetlov, Mikhail 295
Sysoeva, Ekaterina 86, 103, 107

T
Talankin, Igor 369
Talyzina, Valentina 284
Tarkovsky, Andrei 369
Tchaikovsky, Petr 229, 237-40
Tegnér, Esaias 37
Tegner, Hans 108, 343
Tendriakov, Vladimir 272
Tesková, Anna 160
Thomsen, Vilhelm 56, 57, 70
Thorson, E. M. 43, 44, 50
Tietgen, Carl Frederik 61, 64, 65, 70, 72
Titov, Viktor 283
Titova, Vera 374
Tolkien, J. R. R. 415
Toll, Feliks 83, 97, 100, 101
Tolstaya, Tatyana 320
Tolstoy, Aleksei 51, 320
Tolstoy, Lev 52, 115, 119-25, 132, 369, 405, 409, 472
Tomashevsky, Boris 265, 266
Topelius, Zachris 89
Tovstonogov, Georgii 262
Treskin, Nikolai 87, 97, 102
Trifonov, Iurii 272
Trubnikova, Mariia 49, 85, 127, 342
Tsebrikova, Mariia 90, 97, 103
Tsiupa, Slava 374
Tsvetaeva, Marina 159-68, 170, 173, 175-81, 183-85, 187-92, 196, 260, 261, 284, 286, 472
Tsyferov, Gennadii 286, 297-300, 304-07, 456
Tsyganov, Evgenii 334
Turgenev, Ivan 50, 51, 321, 405
Tuwim, Julian 292
Tvardovsky, Aleksandr 260
Tverskoi, K. K. 144
Tynianov, Iurii 333

U
Ulanova, Galina 224
Undset, Sigrid 53
Ustinov, Nikolai 421

V
Vagner, Nikolai 102, 103, 115, 125-32
Vaikule, Laima 379
Vakhtangov, Evgenii 189
Vakurov, Ivan 422, 425
Vasilenko, Svetlana 320
Velichansky, Aleksandr 284, 285
Vermeer, Jan 353
Verne, Jules 361
Verner, Karl 69, 70
Vogak, Konstantin 237
Voinovich, Vladimir 232
Volchek, Galina 330
Volkonsky, Sergei 163
Voloshin, Maksimilian 160
Volpin, Mikhail 309
Vonnegut, Kurt 296, 300
Vrubel, Mikhail 319
Vvedensky, Aleksandr 344

W
Wales, Jimmy 439
Watt, James 63
Watt, Robert 47, 50
Wilde, Oscar 267
Willott, Mark 381
Woolf, Virginia 265, 268
Wulfing, Sulamith 391

Y
Yalom, Marilyn 266
Yamamoto, Takato 392

Z
Zabolotsky, Nikolai 259, 261, 344
Zagoskin, Mikhail 44
Zakharov, Mark 283, 287
Zakhoder, Boris 405, 408
Zeltina, Agnese 380
Zemlinsky, Alexander von 338
Zenkevich, Mikhail 138
Zhukovsky, Vasilii 131, 282

Ø
Ørsted, Hans Christian 63, 65